FAMILY VIOLENCE

Legal, Medical, and Social Perspectives

SECOND EDITION

Harvey Wallace
California State University, Fresno

Allyn and Bacon
Boston • London • Toronto • Sydney • Tokyo • Singapore

To my wife,
Randa F. Wallace

Editor-in-Chief, Social Sciences: Karen Hanson
Editorial Assistant: Heather Ahlstrom
Marketing Manager: Susan E. Ogar
Editorial–Production Administrator: Donna Simons
Editorial–Production Service: Shepherd, Inc.
Composition and Prepress Buyer: Linda Cox
Manufacturing Buyer: Megan Cochran
Cover Administrator: Jenny Hart
Electronic Composition: Shepherd, Inc.

A Viacom Company
160 Gould Street
Needham Heights, MA 02494

Internet: www.abacon.com

Library of Congress Cataloging-in-Publication Data

Wallace, Harvey.
Family violence : legal, medical, and social perspectives / Harvey Wallace.
p. cm.
2nd edition.
Includes bibliographical references and index.
ISBN 0-205-27696-2
1. Family violence—United States. 2. Family social work—United States. 3. Family violence—Law and legislation—United States. 4. Victims of family violence—Mental health—United States. 5. Victims of family violence—Health and hygiene—United States. 6. Victims of family violence—Legal status, laws, etc.—United States. I. Title.
HV6626.2.W35 1998
362.82'92—dc21 98-23706
CIP

Photo Credit: Chapter 2, Kempe Children's Foundation.

Printed in the United States of America
10 9 8 7 6 5 4 3 2 1 03 02 01 00 99 98

CONTENTS

PREFACE

The study of family violence is a complex, multifaceted experience. By its very nature, family violence involves physicians, nurses, psychiatrists, psychologists, family counselors, educators, social workers, attorneys, judges, and law enforcement officials. All these professionals have expertise in their own area of specialization. However, they may not understand or appreciate the difficulties experienced by others in their areas of interest. For example, a member of the medical profession may be able to diagnose physical injuries but not understand the complexities of the courtroom.

As a nation we are becoming more aware of the extent and nature of family violence. Nationally broadcast trials have brought family violence into our front rooms. The William Smith and Mike Tyson rape trials forced us to confront date rape. The Bobbitt trial raised the issue of spousal assault. The Menendez brothers caused everyone to discuss sexual child abuse. And who can forget O. J. Simpson and the 9-1-1 calls that to many symbolized the horror of stalking? The *au pair* murder trial caused controversy on both sides of the Atlantic as we argued over who really killed baby Matthew.

Many states require students in certain fields of study to take courses in specific areas of family violence as a condition of receiving a license to practice. Law enforcement agencies are not required by statutes in some jurisdictions to respond in certain ways to domestic abuse cases. Many times, members of the medical profession are the first to come in contact with victims of family violence. They must not only recognize the physical and emotional symptoms of the victims but also understand how their role relates to law enforcement and the legal system. Criminal justice professionals, including law enforcement personnel, are becoming more involved in cases of family violence. Mandatory arrest of spousal abusers, temporary restraining orders, vertical prosecution teams, and victim impact statements are all recent developments that have appeared in response to a recognized need to protect the victims of family violence. In our society, many forces continue to allow violence to occur in the home. As will be discussed, there is no single cause or factor that contributes to family violence. This, however, should not deter students and professionals from understanding the existing controversies in the field. These factors must be understood to appreciate fully the consequences of family violence.

Family violence courses are becoming more common at the junior and community college level. Many of these courses are offered in the areas of sociology, nursing, and law enforcement. They are providing students with a much-needed perspective on a topic that for too long has been left in the area of upper-division courses or graduate study. The study of family violence does not belong only in the rarified atmosphere of select university classes. Rather, it is a subject with which more people should become familiar.

A survey of law enforcement agencies indicated their desire for new recruits to receive formal training in family violence. Additionally, professionals are becoming more aware that they must adopt an interdisciplinary approach to this problem, and more and more seminars are being offered in the area of family violence. These developments are both a blessing and a curse. On one hand, as we learn more about family violence, we are better able to respond to it. At the same time, the more we learn, the more we must be aware that there is increasing data in this field and that we can be overwhelmed with studies and their results. We are rapidly approaching an overload of information based on this research and yet have failed to agree on something as simple as a definition for the term *family violence.*

The study of family violence has many excellent texts that completely cover specific areas of this topic. There are comprehensive treaties on spousal abuse, child abuse, treatment, intervention, and legal issues of family violence. Because this area is so fragmented and complex, it presents the problem of finding one source that provides an overview or introduction while supplying references that allow the reader to expand his or her knowledge in a specific area. This text is an attempt to examine the more commonly discussed topics of family violence from medical, social, and legal perspectives. It addresses specialized topics such as sexual harassment, stalking, and victim's rights that are normally not found within many family violence texts. The text is an introduction to this complex area, yet it provides the reader with sufficient knowledge to understand the various dynamics that are involved in family violence.

Since the publication of the first edition of this text in 1996, many aspects of family violence have changed. Numerous states have passed additional laws affording victims of family violence more protection. New textbooks and academic journals provide additional research into this complex area. However, the dilemmas faced by professionals in the field remain the same. New and important research is being conducted even as this text goes to print. I have attempted to add new information that affects professionals in the field. How we deal with victims of family violence who are different from you and me is something we must strive to understand. We must also understand the impact and consequences of family violence. To assist the reader in these areas, I have added two new chapters—

Chapter 12, Special Populations and Family Violence, and Chapter 15, Consequences of Family Violence—that I hope will provide professionals with a starting point in these newly emerging areas of family violence.

Over the long period of time it has taken to complete this project, I have become indebted to many people who provide advice, support, resources, and encouragement. First and foremost, I would like to thank my editor, Karen Hanson, Editor-in-Chief, Social Sciences, at Allyn and Bacon, who was always there whenever I needed her. Donna Simons, the production administrator, coordinated the many details of getting this text into print.

My students, at both the graduate and the undergraduate level at California State University, Fresno, as well as those attending the Victim Services Institute and the National Victim Assistance Academy, have provided me with insight into the teaching of family violence. I owe all of them a special debt of gratitude.

My colleagues at CSUF were especially helpful and supportive. Christine Edmonds, special consultant with the Office for Victims of Crimes, furnished me with material and data on a variety of topics. Several reviewers provided me with invaluable suggestions and corrections that helped improve this text: Barbara A. Carson, Mankato State University; M. Jenise Comer, Central Missouri University; Randy L. LaGrange, University of North Carolina at Wilmington; Barbara Manning, Troy State; Sharon McGee, Auburn University; and Eve Robinson, Fordham University. Finally and most important, I am indebted to my family and to my wife, Randa, for her loyalty, compassion, courage, and understanding in helping me put my thoughts on paper. All these people deserve the credit if any is given to this text. Any mistakes and inaccuracies, however, belong solely to me.

H. W.

1

CHARACTERISTICS OF FAMILY VIOLENCE

Chapter Outline

Learning Objectives

After reading this chapter, you should be able to discuss the following concepts:

- The various difficulties in defining family violence.
- The problems inherent in attempting to measure the extent of family violence.

- The National Family Violence Surveys and other methods of measuring family violence.
- The various theories of family violence.
- The Cycle of Violence and the Cycle Theory of Violence.
- How violence in the home may cause later aggression.

Introduction

The study of family violence is still in its infancy. In our society there are numerous myths and misconceptions that surround this problem. Many lay persons, students, and professionals still remain skeptical regarding the dynamics involved in family violence. It is not uncommon to hear, "Persons who molest children are mentally deranged" and "Women who stay with abusive partners must really like it." Otherwise knowledgeable individuals display an alarming lack of understanding regarding the various aspects of family violence.

During the 1990s, criminal trials brought the specter of family violence into our living rooms on a daily basis. The Menendez brothers shot and killed both their parents, alleging self-defense by claiming that the parents had physically and sexually abused them for years. The Bobbitt case involved a spouse who severed her sleeping husband's penis after he allegedly raped her. Mrs. Bobbitt testified that she was physically and sexually abused by her husband for years.

Numerous controversies in the area of family violence are discussed in this text. Because no definition for the term *family violence* is accepted by all scholars, researchers, and other professionals, its full extent and nature is still being debated. However, statistics gathered from independent research as well as projections from state and federal agencies clearly establish its widespread existence.

Definitional Issues

Simply defining the term *family violence* causes debate. Some argue that the use of the word *family* is too restrictive and should be replaced with the term *intimate,* since current research includes studies of couples that cohabitate but are not necessarily married. However, most professionals now accept the idea that a family unit may exist without any formal sanction such as a marriage ceremony. Therefore, the term *family* will be used to include situations in which individuals are living together regardless of whether they are legally married.

Violence implies physical acts that result in injuries to the victim. As will be discussed, some forms of family violence involve the withholding of physical or emotional support and can have devastating long-term consequences for the victim. Therefore, violence within this context includes physical or mental acts or omissions that result in injuries to the victim. Violence may also be directed at restricting or denying another person certain rights or liberties.

The concept of family violence includes several subtopics, such as child abuse, spousal abuse, and elder abuse. It is therefore a wide-ranging concept that must remain flexible to adaption as we learn more about its scope and impact. The definition of *family violence* for purposes of this text is: *any act or omission by persons who are cohabitating that results in serious injury to other members of the family.* This definition includes those who live together or are married. The term *serious injury* may involve physical or emotional harm or a violation of another family member's rights and freedom of choice. As will be seen, the great majority of victims of family violence are females or children. This is not to say that men are not battered.[1] However, they are in the minority, and the reasons for this disparity are discussed in detail in Chapter 8 that deals with spousal abuse. This definition is broader than Straus, Gelles, and Steinmetz's approach to family violence because their study did not include neglect.[2] It goes beyond Pagelow's definition in that it specifically applies to those who live with other persons.[3]

Family violence includes criminal offenses, behavioral acts, and medical problems. Each of these factors has its own proponents and advocates, and each defines family violence from its own perspective. Despite the need for an acceptable definition from which research and treatment can proceed, each of these interest groups claim their view or approach as the only true alternative. A quick review of the literature in the field highlights this disparate approach to family violence. Some texts deal with legal issues and child abuse, policing of spousal abuse, medical interventions for victims, and psychological treatment for survivors of abuse. While a few texts attempts to take a global approach to family violence, these are in the minority, and professionals continue to specialize within subgroupings of this form of aggression.

As the above discussion indicates, conflict exists among scholars, academics, and professionals regarding the definition of the term *family violence.* However, this should not hinder further study of this form of aggression. It simply means that we must remain flexible in evaluating all forms of aggression to determine if they fall within the realm of family violence. Defining the term *family violence* is only one of many controversies in this area.

Controversies in Family Violence

There are numerous other controversies in the study of family violence.[4] Specific controversies are addressed in chapters that deal with specific forms or types of family violence. However, an overview of issues that affect the study of family violence provides a basis for understanding that this form of aggression requires additional research before we can determine all its ramifications.

Family violence has several distinct subgroupings, such as child physical and sexual abuse, spousal abuse, and elder abuse. Many scholars have focused on these specific areas and ignored the broader view of family violence. Conversely, others have attempted to view family violence from a broad perspective by creating models of research that are so vague as to be difficult, if not impossible, to test or validate. How does one accurately study or research a phenomenon if a definition cannot be agreed on because the definition of any act both sets limits and focuses research within certain boundaries? The lack of agreement in defining *family violence* has led to confusion and disarray in attempts to determine factors that cause or contribute to family violence.

Just as there are numerous definitions for the term *family violence,* so are there myriad competing and conflicting theories on the causes. The psychological approach, the social–psychological approach, and the sociocultural approach are but a few of the more popular models or theories of family violence. While feminist theories may fall within one of these models, some authors argue that this is another valid method of classifying family violence. These approaches are discussed later in this chapter, but it must be remembered that no one approach or theory has yet to gain universal acceptance within the field of professionals who deal with this phenomenon.

Intervention strategies vary widely in dealing with family violence. There is a widespread agreement that in many instances a child should be removed from his or her home immediately to prevent further harm or injury. However, there are situations in which some experts argue that removal from the family is a very traumatic experience for the child and should be avoided at all costs. Intervention may also be challenged by defense attorneys who claim some therapists have brainwashed or planted the thought of abuse in the minds of impressionable children. This is a common technique that is being used by a number of defense attorneys today, although it is unknown how effective this strategy is in convincing juries.

Reporting and law enforcement's mandated response to child abuse, elder abuse, and spousal abuse is a current topic of controversy. Some authorities argue that mandatory reporting of child abuse and elder abuse should be expanded. Others believe that mandatory arrest of spousal abusers leads to increased risk to the victim. Still other professionals would expand some laws to require terms of incarceration for those who abuse their spouses.

If there is no agreement on the cause of family violence, how can the factors be addressed that are present in a violent relationship? Depending on the study one reads, different factors are found to exist in family violence. This chapter examines four of the more common factors that have been present in families where violence has occurred. This does not mean that these are the only factors that may exist in every form of abuse, only that these factors are the most common.

Does ritual abuse of children really occur? Probably no subject in family violence has generated as much controversy as the topic of ritual abuse of children. Some critics have suggested that the symptoms are therapist enhanced, whereas others claim ritual abuse clearly exists and is more widespread than believed.

As the above discussion indicates, many controversies exist in the field of family violence. Where appropriate, these subjects are examined in more detail in the chapters that deal with the specific form of abuse. These controversies should not create anxiety or apprehension, but they present a series of exciting and stimulating ideas that should cause healthy discussion and debate among all those interested in this topic.

FOCUS An Epidemic of Family Violence

Violence is not only as American as apple pie—it is often as homemade.

- Among the estimated 1.4 million hospital emergency department patients treated in 1994, of all persons treated for violence-related injuries:
  —7 percent had been injured by a spouse or ex-spouse.
  —10 percent had been injured by a current or former boyfriend or girlfriend.
  —8 percent had been injured by a parent, child, sibling, or other relative.
- The estimated number of persons treated in emergency departments for injuries inflicted by intimates was four times higher than estimates from the National Crime Victimization Survey.
- Many studies point out that domestic violence contributes to homelessness, particularly among families with children. For example, one study reported that 46 percent of cities surveyed by the U.S. Conference of Mayors identified domestic violence as the primary cause of homelessness.
- Half the murdered women in the United States are killed by a current or former partner. Women who are divorced, separated, or otherwise estranged from their partners are at highest risk of assault.
- A Texas survey found that 34 percent of domestic violence calls to police were repeat calls. A similar study in Kansas found that 85 percent of calls to police were repeat offenses. Fifty percent of the time it was the fifth or more offense.
- In one recent study, nearly 1 million children experienced demonstrable harm as a result of abuse or neglect. Some 1,100 died from abuse or neglect.
- Another 40,000 children were sexually abused with rape by a caretaker, and a higher number were sexually molested without rape.
- Children who are abused or witness domestic violence generally are stunted in social and emotional development.

Sources: Adapted from Mason, James O., Assistant Secretary for Health, "The Dimensions of an Epidemic of Violence," 108 *Public Health Report* pp. 1–3, (January/February 1993); "Domestic Violence and Homelessness," *NCH Factsheet #8, National Coalition for the Homeless* (March 1997) (*www.http://nch.ari.net/domestic.html*); and *Violence Related Injuries Treated in Elementary Departments,* Office of Justice Programs (U.S. Department of Justice, Washington, D.C., August 1997).

Nature and Scope of the Problem

The National Family Violence Surveys

Two of the most comprehensive studies of family violence were carried out by Murray Straus and Richard J. Gelles in 1975 and 1985.[5] Both surveys involved interviews with a nationally representative sample of 2,143 respondents in 1975 and 6,014 respondents in 1985. The results of these landmark surveys continue to provide information and data for the study of family violence. These surveys are continually cited as authority in numerous texts, articles, and research projects.

In both surveys, violence was defined as an act carried out with the intention or perceived intention of causing physical pain or injury to another person. Acts of violence that had a high probability of causing injury were included even if injury did not occur. Violence was measured by using the Conflict Tactics Scale (CTS). This tool was developed at the University of New Hampshire in 1971 and is still used today in many studies of family violence. The CTS measures three variables: use of rational discussion and agreement, use of verbal and nonverbal expressions of hostility, and use of physical force or violence. Respondents were asked how many times within the last year they used certain responses that fell within one of the three classifications when they had a disagreement or were angry with family members.

Both studies were judged to be reliable because of the sampling procedure, the large number of respondents, and the validity of the CTS as a measuring instrument. The studies surveyed families from all fifty states and assessed several different relationships: parent to child, child to parent, wife to husband, husband to wife, and sibling interactions. Interviews were conducted by trained investigators and lasted about one hour in the 1975 study and thirty minutes in the 1985 survey.

A comparison of the results of these studies indicated that physical child abuse declined from 1975 to 1985. Straus points out that there are several explanations for such a result. First is the increased awareness of child abuse from 1975 to 1985. During that ten-year period, child abuse became a common media topic. This knowledge, on the part of the respondents, may have lessened the likelihood of their reporting such acts of violence. Second, different data collection techniques were used in the two surveys: The 1975 data were obtained by telephone, and the 1985 results were collected through personal interviews. Finally, there may have actually been a decline in child abuse incidents from 1975 to 1985. Even if the last explanation is correct, as Straus points out, this still translates into one of every thirty-three children three to seven years old who are living with their parents being a victim of child abuse.

Other Sources of Data on Family Violence

Other social surveys have added to our knowledge of family violence. *Rape in America,* conducted by the National Victims Center, shed new light on this form of aggression, and a survey of Boston residents examined elder abuse. Both surveys are discussed in detail later.

Clinical studies are another source of information regarding family violence. These studies are carried out by practitioners in the field—medical professionals, psychiatrists, psychologists, and counselors—all of whom use samples gathered from actual cases of family violence. These researchers collect information from hospitals, clinics, and therapy sessions. Clinical studies normally have small sample sizes, and therefore caution must be used when drawing any conclusions. However, these studies provide valuable data on the nature of abuse and assist in evaluating the different types of interventions used in family violence as well as pointing out areas for further research.

Many different types of official reports are compiled by private or public agencies in the form of statistical data. These provide a much needed resource for further research into family violence. The most commonly relied on are reports by local law enforcement agencies, the American Humane Society, the Uniform Crime Reports, and the National Crime Victimization Surveys.

Since adoption of the mandatory reporting laws for child abuse, and in some states mandatory arrest of those accused of spousal abuse, local agencies have been able to provide researchers with a wealth of information regarding family violence. This information is usually limited to a specific geographic location and therefore does not reflect any national perspective. However, a national overview of child maltreatment is available to researchers from data collected by the American Humane Society. This organization collected data on all officially reported cases of child abuse and neglect from 1976 to 1987.

The Violence Against Women Act provides a fundamental change in the criminal justice system's gathering of information on violent crimes committed against women. A 1996 report of Congress indicated that both the federal government and most states are collecting data on family violence.[6] This report points out two continuing controversies: the need for uniform definitions and the need to include data from other parts of the criminal justice system.[7]

The Uniform Crime Reports (UCR) is this country's oldest form of criminal statistics. During the 1920s, the International Association of Chiefs of Police (IACP) formed the Commission on Uniform Crime Reports to develop a uniform system of reporting criminal statistics. The committee evaluated various crimes on the basis of their seriousness, frequency of occurrence, commonality across the nation, and likelihood of being reported to the police. In 1929, the committee finished its study and recommended a plan for crime reporting that became the foundation of the UCR program. Seven crimes were chosen to serve as an index for determining fluctuations in the overall rate of crime. These crimes became known as the "crime index" and included the following: murder, manslaughter, forcible rape, robbery, aggravated assault, burglary, larceny-theft, and motor vehicle theft. In 1979, Congress mandated that an eighth crime, arson, be added to the index. During the study phase of the project, it was recognized that differences in state criminal codes would cause the same act to be reported in various methods and categories. To avoid this problem, no distinction was made between felony and misdemeanor crimes and a standardized set of definitions was established to allow law enforcement agencies to submit data without regard for local statutes. In 1930, Congress enacted federal law that authorized the attorney general to gather crime information.[8] The attorney general designated the FBI as the national clearinghouse for all data, and since that time data based on this system has been obtained from the nation's law enforcement agencies.

The Uniform Crime Reports (UCR) program is a nationwide statistical computation involving over 1,600 cities, counties, and state law enforcement agencies that voluntarily report data on reported crimes. During 1996, law enforcement agencies in the UCR program represented over 245 million inhabitants, or about 95 percent of the total population of the United States. The program is administrated by the FBI, which issues assessments on the nature and type of crime. The program's primary objective is to generate a set of reliable criminal statistics for use in law enforcement administration, operation, and management.[9]

The FBI administers the UCR program and issues periodic reports addressing the nature and type of crime in the United States. While the UCR's primary objective is to issue reliable statistics for use by law enforcement agencies, it has also become an important social indicator of deviance in our society.

The UCR prepares an annual crime index composed of selected offenses used to gauge changes in the overall rate of crime reported to law enforcement agencies. The crime index is composed of the seven crimes discussed previously. Therefore, the index is a combination of violent and property crimes. In 1996, for example, 14 percent of the index offenses were violent crimes and 86 percent property crimes.

The UCR is an annual report that includes the number of crimes reported by citizens to local police departments and the number of arrests made by law enforcement agencies in a given year. This information is of somewhat limited value as the data are based on instances of violence classified as criminal and are reported to the local law enforcement agencies. Many serious acts of violence are not reported to the police and therefore do not become part of the UCR. The UCR does not provide detailed information needed to document the full extent of family violence–related events known to law enforcement agencies.

With the exception of the Hate Crime Statistics Act of 1990, the UCR remained virtually unchanged for fifty years. Eventually, various law enforcement agencies began to call for an evaluation and redesign of the program. Since the UCR lists only crimes that are reported to it, this presents a serious problem as not all police agencies report crimes to the FBI and the Department of Justice. Since the UCR relies on law enforcement agencies to report crimes voluntarily, there is the possibility of underreporting by some agencies based on the basis of political reasons.[10] The UCR generally provides only tabular summaries of crime and does not provide crime analysts with more meaningful information. Additionally, the method of counting crimes causes problems. For example, only the most serious crime is reported. If a person is robbed and his car stolen, police agencies are instructed to report only the robbery. Finally, some crimes, such as white-collar crime, are excluded from the UCR system. After several years of study, the FBI began to institute various modifications to the UCR program. These changes established a new, more effective crime-reporting system.

The newly redesigned UCR program is called the National Incident-Based Reporting System (NIBRS). In 1989, the FBI began accepting data, and nine states started supplying information in the new format. The NIBRS collects data on each single incident and arrest within twenty-two crime categories. Incident, victim, property, offender, and arrestee information is gathered for each offense known to the local agency. The NIBRS will provide much need detailed information regarding family violence–related offenses. While the NIBRS standard includes a major data collection system specifically related to the relationship between family violence and victim–offender, it does not measure other aspects of family violence.[11] The goal of the redesigned system is to modernize crime reporting information by collecting data presently maintained in law enforcement records. The enhanced UCR program is a byproduct of modern law enforcement records systems that have the capability to store and collate more information regarding criminal offenses.

The *National Crime Victimization Survey (NCVS)* attempts to correct the problems on nonreporting inherent in the UCR by *contacting a nationwide sample and interviewing citizens regarding victimization.* The report was originally called the National Crime Survey (NCS) but was renamed to reflect more clearly its emphasis on the measurement of victimizations experienced by citizens. Since 1972, the NCVS, has collected detailed information about certain criminal offenses, both attempted and completed, that concern the general public and law enforcement. These offenses include the frequency and nature of rape, robbery, assault, household burglary, personal and household theft, and motor vehicle theft.[12] The NCVS does not measure homicide or commercial crime.

A single crime may have more than one victim. For example, a bank robbery may involve several bank tellers. Therefore, a single incident may have more than one victimization. A victimization, the basic measure of the occurrence of crime, is a specific criminal act because it affects a specific victim. The number of victimizations, however, is determined by the number of victims of each specific criminal act.

The NCVS is an annual survey of citizens conducted by the U.S. Bureau of the Census in cooperation with the Bureau of Justice Statistics of the U.S. Department of Justice. Census Bureau personnel conduct interviews with all household members over the age of twelve. These households stay in the sample for three years and are interviewed every six months. The total sample size of this survey is about 66,000 households with 101,000 individuals.[13]

The NCVS provides data regarding the victims of crime, including age, sex, race, ethnicity, marital status, income, and educational level as well as information about the offender. Questions covering the victim's experience with the justice system, details regarding any self-protective measures used by the victims, and possible substance abuse by offenders are included in the survey. Periodic supplemental questionnaires address specific issues, such as school crime.

The NCVS has been recently modified by the Bureau of Justice Statistics as a result of a number of problems including the underreporting of family violence and sexual violence incidents.[14] The revised survey was fully implemented for the 1993 data set, and the first data from the survey became available in 1994. The first analysis of this information became available in 1996, and these figures need to be evaluated and compared with future data.

The NCVS continues to suffer from problems that mitigate its validity, such as respondents underreporting or overreporting crimes. The NCVS is based on an extensive scientific sample of American households. Therefore, every crime measure presented in the NCVS report is an estimate based on results of the sample. Since measures are only estimates, they will have a sampling variation or margin of error associated with each sample. Additionally, these estimates are only of criminal activity and do not mean that the crime actually occurred.

Each of the methods of collecting data on family violence presents a different perspective and has its own validity problems. What is certain is that family violence occurs on all social and economic levels in our nation. Its toll on victims is severe and long-lasting. No matter which statistic or sample is used, professionals agree that further research is necessary.

Factors That Contribute to Family Violence

Researchers have interviewed, tested, observed, and evaluated thousands of people in an attempt to discover the factors that contribute to family violence. Unfortunately, to date no one authority has discovered the single correct answer. However, it is incumbent on all professionals to have at least a cursory knowledge of the more commonly cited theories of family violence. These theories may be grouped into three main models or categories: the psychiatric classifications, the social–psychological models, and the sociocultural models.

The Psychiatric Model of Family Violence

The psychiatric model tries to understand family violence by analyzing the offender's personality traits and mental status. Some professionals also include individual characteristics of the victim in this approach. This model characterizes personality disorders, mental illness, and substance abuse as the primary causes of family violence.

The Psychopathology Theory

This theory is grounded on the concept that certain individuals suffer from mental illness, personality disorders, and other dysfunctions that cause them to engage in aggressive acts within the family. This mental disorder, or illness, causes the individual to react violently within the family.[15] It is not surprising that this theory was first proposed by those in the medical profession. Psychiatrists, clinicians, and psychologists were exposed to family violence because of their close association with the medical personnel who treated the victims. Although this is still a popular theory, researchers have failed to isolate any particular mental disorder common to those who abuse that distinguishes those who engage in violent behavior from the rest of the population. In addition, attempts to distinguish the personality traits of those who engage in family violence and to compare those characteristics with individuals who are not abusive have been inconsistent and difficult to apply in practice.[16] Furthermore, many individuals who suffer from various forms of mental illness do not engage in aggressive behavior.

The problem with the psychopathology model is its failure to explain which personality traits are associated with family violence. In addition, by focusing on mental illness as a cause of violence, it ignores the fact that many violent individuals are not considered mentally ill.

The Substance Abuse Theory

Many lay persons and nonprofessionals believe that alcohol or drugs cause family violence. *The substance abuse theory accepts the proposition that drugs or alcohol cause or contribute to family violence.* This theory is based on the concept that these substances impair judgment and lessen inhibitions and thereby allow violent acts to occur. Some authorities believe that these substances do not cause family violence. Rather, they are used as an excuse for violent acts.[17]

Numerous studies have linked alcohol or drugs to violent behavior, but no concrete evidence establishes that these substances directly cause family violence. In addition, this theory fails to explain why everyone who uses alcohol or drugs does not engage in violent acts.

The Social–Psychological Model of Family Violence

The social–psychological model analyzes external environmental factors that affect the family unit. Factors such as stress, family structure, the cycle of violence, and family interactions are all considered as primary causes of family violence. Because of the controversy surrounding the cycle of violence theory, it is discussed in more detail later in this chapter.

The Social Learning Theory

This theory assumes that the type of behavior that is most frequently reinforced by others is the one that is most often exhibited by the individual. *The social learning theory is an integration of differential associations with differential reinforcements so that the people with whom one interacts are the reinforcers of behavior that results in learning both deviant and nondeviant behavior.*[18]

The social learning process is accomplished by two important mechanisms: modeling and reinforcement. Modeling is an important tool in learning behavior. Children learn by watching and imitating others. This role model situation results in children adopting the behavior they observe in adults, including aggressive acts. Reinforcement occurs when certain behavior is rewarded and other behavior is punished. Studies have shown that behavior can be modified by praise more effectively than by punitive actions. Social learning continues as children mature and enter school and begin to interact with other children and adults. This process of interaction results in modification of behavior as the individual ages.

The social learning theory has been criticized as failing to explain certain kinds of spontaneous acts of aggression within the family, such as a frustrated parent who suddenly slaps a crying child.

The Exchange Theory

This theory is based on the premise that persons act according to a system of rewards or punishments.[19] *The exchange theory argues that family violence is based on a determination of costs and rewards.* Gelles accepted the basic premise of the exchange theory and modified it to apply to family violence situations. He entitled this approach *the exchange/social control theory.*[20] As Gelles has stated, "To put it simply, people hit family members because they can."[21] Interaction within the family is based on a pursuit of rewards and an avoidance of costs or punishments. Family members resort to violence to obtain goals as long as what they achieve is outweighed by the cost of aggression. The absence of social controls over family relations increases the likelihood that family members will engage in violence. The privacy of the family unit and the subsequent low risk of intervention decreases the cost of violence, thereby allowing it to occur.[22]

The Frustration–Aggression Theory

This concept is based on the premise that human beings display aggression toward objects that impede their achievement of certain goals.[23] *The frustration–aggression theory is based on the premise that individuals will react aggressively when some goal is blocked or frustrated.* In a family situation, there are many instances in which one or both parties attempt to obtain certain goals or objectives. Frustration may result when the attainment of those goals is blocked. Failure to attain desired goals can lead to aggression within the family by the frustrated party.

This theory does not explain the complexities of modern society. All of us at one time or another become frustrated. However, we do not automatically react with aggressive actions. The socialization process teaches people how to react to frustration. This process varies from culture to culture and group to group, so that what is accepted as appropriate behavior to frustration by one culture may not be condoned by another group.

The Ecological Theory

This theory is based on an analysis of the organism and the environment, the interacting systems in which family development occurs, and the environment in which the family resides.[24] Garbarino established two conditions that must be present under this theory for child abuse to occur: The environment in which the family lives must accept the use of force against children, and the family must be isolated from supporting community services or systems.[25] *The ecological theory assumes that family violence occurs when the parent, child, and family are mismatched with the neighborhood and community.* According to this theory, children who are disabled or otherwise below the expected norm in a society face the highest risk of abuse.[26] The interaction between spouses having to deal with the stress of parenting a disabled child increases the tension within the family. The final aspect of this theory views the total environment and suggests that if no agencies are available to support or assist the family, then the risk of abuse is greatly increased.

The Sociobiology or Evolutionary Theory

This theory is based on the concept that parents display aggressive acts toward children who are not their own or do not have the potential to reproduce. This concept postulates that individuals behave in certain ways so as to increase their chances of reproducing. One scholar theorizes that male aggression against females illustrates the effects of the male reproductive urges.[27] Male humans and primates use aggression as a form of intimidation against females so that they will

FOCUS Our Society and Violence

By the age of eighteen, according to one estimate, a youngster will have seen 200,000 acts of violence on television, including 40,000 murders. *TV Guide* looked at ten channels on one normal eighteen-hour day and found 1,846 individual acts of violence—and every hour of prime time carries six to eight acts of violence. Violence has become the norm, the Pied Piper to lure the vulnerable to a darker world.

Source: From Zuckerman, M. B. "The Victims of Violence." *U.S. News & World Report* 2, August 1993, p. 64.

not resist efforts to mate with them. *The sociobiology or evolutionary theory assumes that parents will not emotionally attach or invest themselves to children with low reproductive potential.*[28] Under this theory, stepchildren or children with low reproductive potential, such as children with disabilities, are at a higher risk of abuse than normal, healthy children. Thus, the risk of abuse is higher where there is a lack of bonding between the child and parent.

The Sociocultural Model of Family Violence

The sociocultural model of family violence focuses on the roles of men and women in our society as well as on the cultural attitudes toward women and the acceptance of violence as a cause of family violence. This is a macro level of analysis that focuses on the variables that cause violence.

The Culture of Violence Theory

Wolfgang and Ferracuti argue that certain subcultures within the United States accept values that justify the use of force.[29] *The culture of violence theory is based on the premise that violence is unevenly distributed within our society and that violence is more prevalent in the lower socioeconomic sectors of society.*[30] These subcultures use force as a response more often than the general population. This theory assumes that violence is a learned response and reflects a socialization or acceptance of violence as appropriate behavior.

One of the main limitations of this theory is that it does not explain how subcultural values originate or are modified. Furthermore, this theory limits the learning of violence to certain socioeconomic subcultures. However, violence in the media is received by all classes within our society.

As shocking as the television violence statistic is, it graphically illustrates how prevalent violence is within our society today. For the most part, our society glamorizes violence. This approval of violence and aggression is primarily a male perspective. Males believe it is macho to be strong, assertive, and aggressive.[31] As is discussed in later chapters, this view of violence and masculinity contributes to aggression toward women.

Violence is an everyday part of our existence. Sporting events, children's toys, cartoons, video games, movies, television, and the media's graphic depiction of

FOCUS The War against Women: It Crosses All Borders

Despite the toppling of military dictatorships in Latin America, the deregulation of India's economy, and the end of apartheid in South Africa, there has been no halt to what the United Nations has called a "global epidemic of violence against women."

Some authorities, such as Health and Human Services Secretary Donna Shalala, call this violence "terrorism in the home." Experts point out that women are raped in South Africa every 83 seconds. In Third World countries, famine still exists, and mothers are producing fewer children, but every year half a million women still die from pregnancy-related problems, including botched abortions.

Source: Adapted from MacFarquhar, E. "The War against Women." *U.S. News & World Report,* March 28, 1994, pp. 42–43.

violence all contribute to our desensitization to the effects of violence and contribute to an attitude that aggressive behavior is rewarded and condoned by society.[32]

Sporting events are often displays of violence. Professional wrestling is not so much a contest of strength and agility as it is entertainment featuring uncontrolled aggression, women clad in revealing bathing suits escorting the wrestlers, and frenzied crowds yelling for the champion to destroy the contender. Fights between players are a common occurrence in football, ice hockey, baseball, and basketball. Some international soccer matches end with hundreds of fans fighting each other on the field. Aggressive behavior and violence are rewarded by large signing bonuses, and those athletes who display it are accorded the status of celebrities.

Children's toys and the advertisements that promote them are a study in violence and marketing. Young children can buy toy soldiers, monsters that fire futuristic weapons, cars that crash into buildings, and all sorts of other violent playthings. As children mature, they "graduate" from toy soldiers to toy guns. The M-16 assault rifle made of plastic and painted in camouflage colors is a favorite for the preteen age-group. The real M-16 has been used in a number of shootings across the nation.

Cartoons animate violent behavior. The "Roadrunner" series is an excellent example of how violent acts are interwoven into cartoons. In other cartoons, make-believe characters fight evil by attacking with weapons, fists, hands, feet, and elbows. On any Saturday morning, the airwaves are filled with animated violence.

Video games and arcades promote and reward superior skills in violence. If players can destroy the enemy ships, persons, or planes, they are rewarded with an additional free game. Martial arts are used by the hero in his attempt to either rescue the lady or prevent the world from being destroyed.

Movies and television are a study in violence. The movie *Colors* brought gang violence into theaters across the nation. The movie focused on gang rivalry and the violence that accompanies it. Many violent movies are so popular that they have been developed into movie series. Jason of *Friday the Thirteenth* fame, Freddie Kruger from *Nightmare on Elm Street,* and Rambo are just a few characters that have made violence a successful enterprise for movie producers. Television continues to beam violent acts into our living rooms. Even on a mundane weekly series, cars cannot simply collide with each other—they must explode in a ball of flame and debris. Any hero worth prime-time rating must not simply shoot the villain once or twice, he must use an automatic weapon to riddle the body with bullet holes.

Media reporting of violence continues to show graphic scenes of mayhem and death that resulted from criminal acts. The Tonya Harding and Nancy Kerrigan incident became a daily subject on every evening newscast during the 1994 Winter Olympics. It is not uncommon to watch bloody victims being carried from the scene of a crime as we eat our evening meal. In the media's ever expanding quest for high ratings, it seems that anything goes, especially if it involves blood, victims, and violence. Who can forget the media feeding frenzy surrounding the O. J. Simpson trial?

Is it any wonder that we as a society accept violence as part of our culture? It is nearly impossible to avoid. We would have to live in the mountains, refuse to purchase our children certain toys, never read the local paper, and refrain from watching television to escape being inundated with our society's violent and aggressive acts.

The Patriarchy Theory

Dobash and Dobash have advanced this theory to explain violence toward women. *The patriarchy theory views society as dominated by males, with women in subordinate positions who are treated by men as possessions and things.*[33] According to the feminist perspective, social and economic norms directly and indirectly support a patriarchal structure within our society. The patriarchy theory holds that laws and customs combine to uphold this difference in power between men and women and legitimize their different status. This approach views male domination as explaining the historical pattern of violence toward women throughout the ages.

The General Systems Theory

This theory views the maintenance of violence as a result of the social system in which families live. *The general systems theory assumes that violence within the family is a result of a system rather than individual pathology of the family member.*[34] This family system operates to maintain, increase, or decrease levels of violence within the family. Straus proposes that a general system of family violence contain three elements: alternative courses of action, a method of feedback, and system goals.[35] Under Straus's approach, violence within the family has many causes. Whenever a family member engages in violence, there is or may be positive feedback because the violence produced the desired results. Finally, Straus points out that whenever violence occurs, family members who engage in these acts fulfill their own self-concept of being violent.

The Social Conflict Theory

This concept analyzes large-scale conflicts, marriages, and the communication process.[36] *The social conflict theory proposes that unacknowledged alienation and shame generate violence within the family.* A theory of escalation is central to this concept and holds that escalation of conflict or violence occurs when anger and shame within a relationship are not acknowledged.

The Resource Theory

This theory is based on the proposition that the one who controls resources, such as money, property, or prestige, is in the dominant position in a relationship.[37] *The resource theory holds that the use of violence within a relationship depends on the resources a family member controls.* The more resources one commands, the more force or power he can muster. Because men hold higher-paying jobs with more prestige, they will have more power in relationships than women. Some authorities argue that the more resources available to the male, the more force he can use. With this abundance of power, however, there is less likelihood of his employing force. Those males who have no resources such as high-paying jobs or status tend to resort to violence more often as a way of controlling the spouse.[38]

Common Features of Family Violence

As the above discussion illustrates, numerous theories exist on the causes of family violence. These theories approach family violence from a variety of perspectives. No one theory, however, is accepted by all scholars as the cause of this form of aggression. Other researchers have attempted to isolate certain factors that are common in all forms of family violence.[39] Each of these characteristics is discussed in more detail in the chapters that examine specific forms of family violence. However, to aid in understanding the dynamics of this form of aggression, the following discussion briefly examines some of the more common forces that are present in all forms of family violence.

Isolation

Family violence is the most private form of aggression. The concept of the privacy of the family, coupled with isolation, diminishes outside social control, lessens input from others, and increases the opportunity for violence. Whether it is a child who is physically or sexually abused or a spouse who is battered, the assault occurs in private and the victims are isolated from the normal support systems in our society. As the level of privacy in a family increases, the level of social control decreases. What one person may do in private is different from what that same person will do in public.

Isolation is a common characteristic of spousal abuse. The abuser will curtail the spouse's outside contacts and, eventually, she will believe that she is alone and helpless to prevent his assaults. Child abuse does not occur in a public environment. Children who are molested are told to keep the act secret or they will be punished. Elders suffer abuse in their own homes at the hands of their caretakers.

A support system within the community and among other family members may, for some persons, act as a regulator or inhibitor of family violence. If the victim receives input from others outside the immediate family, she may have the courage to leave the abuser. Social interaction may also provide a means to defuse potentially hostile situations by allowing the parties to talk with others whom they respect and love.

Power Differentials

The persons with the most power or resources have the ability to impose their will on other members of the family. This difference in power allows the spouse or parent to use force on the less powerful mate or child. This characteristic of power differentials is present in both spousal and child abuse. Finkelhor points out that abuse tends to gravitate toward relationships with the greatest power differential.[40]

Many professionals argue for reducing this power differential. As a result of a number of forces in society, the power differential in relationships is decreasing. More and more women are leaving the home to take positions in government and industry, and as a result they are slowly beginning to raise their power level to that of men. Children are taught they have the right (power) to say no to sexual advances. Child victims are now represented in some court hearings by attorneys who must look out for the children's best interests. Battered women's shelters have been established and laws passed in some states that mandate the arrest of any spouse who batters the other. These accomplishments have not diminished the difference in power between men and women to any great degree, but they represent a trend that society must continue to encourage.

Power/Powerlessness

This characteristic occurs when a person perceives that he or she has a lack of power or control in the work or social environment but has power in relationship to other persons in his family. The person has power over less powerful individuals. Power in this context is defined as the ability to control the behavior of others, with or without their consent.[41] Applying these concepts to a family environment, it is easy to see that within the family a man usually has the most power. Many men, however, work in jobs outside the home where they perceive or believe themselves to be powerless to control their environment. Therefore, after being powerless all day at work, a man can return home and dominate the family. This control and power may take the form of abuse. When a mother needlessly disciplines her child, she may be reacting to the fact that her spouse and others are controlling her. By disciplining the child, she can exert power or control over another person.

Substance Abuse

For every ten U.S. citizens, two are social users, five are drug or alcohol abusers, and one suffers from chemical dependence.[42] One scholar reported that there are 10 million adult alcoholics, 500,000 heroin addicts, and about 5 to 8 million regular cocaine users in the United States.[43] Those who engage in violent acts within the family also use and abuse these substances.

Drug and alcohol dependency was discussed briefly earlier in this chapter. It will be explored in more depth in relation to spousal abuse. Drug and alcohol abuse is a common characteristic of all forms of family violence. While substance abuse may be present in family violence situations, as indicated above, no causal link has been established to date. However, the concept that drugs and alcohol contribute to or cause family violence continues to be a popular and enduring belief among both victims and abusers.

The excuse of substance abuse is an attractive explanation for both the victim and the abuser. From the victim's point of view, the abuser is not really a bad person, but the drugs or alcohol cause him to commit the acts. The perpetrator can deny responsibility by claiming a lack of control caused by drugs or alcohol. This approach allows both parties to point to an external influence that "caused" the abuse. While it would be convenient to blame substance abuse as the cause of family violence, to do so would be to overlook all the interlocking dynamics that are involved in both substance abuse and family violence.

Effect on Victims

The full consequences of abuse are examined in more detail in later chapters. Family violence has a profound, long-lasting effect on its victims. All victims report a sense of loss of self-esteem. Battered spouses, maltreated children, and abused elders all feel shame and helplessness as a result of the abuse. Many victims of abuse blame themselves, feeling that if they had only pleased the abuser, he or she would not have had to resort to violence.

Low self-esteem is common for victims of physical and sexual child abuse. These children do not have the capacity to understand the dynamics of child maltreatment and therefore develop a negative view of themselves. Many victims of sexual abuse not only blame themselves but also develop a self-hatred that leads to increased vulnerability and problems in adjusting as they mature. Victims of spousal abuse are commonly degraded as unfit and unworthy by the abuser. Constant criticism and the abused person's inability to break the cycle of violence leads to a lack of confidence in themselves and a feeling of inferiority. The elderly are already disadvantaged because of the aging process, and abuse only increases their loss of self-confidence.

Victims of family violence have difficulty trusting others. There is perhaps no greater betrayal of trust than that experienced by children who are sexually abused by family members. Not only did a family member commit sexual acts with the child, but also other family members may have known of the abuse and failed to protect the child. Survivors of sexual abuse have trouble developing close relationships as they mature. Victims may believe that by not trusting others, they can avoid being betrayed or hurt again.[44] Many women who have suffered spousal abuse during a marriage are naturally hesitant to enter into another relationship.

ıological problems in adjusting even after the abuse has ended is a com- acteristic of victims of family violence. Emotional maladjustment and :y and character disorders have been reported among those who have ıbuse in the family environment.[45] Some abuse is so severe that victims dissociate from the trauma and develop alter personalities and are later ·d as suffering from multiple personality disorder.[46]

tion, power differentials, power/powerlessness, substance abuse, and ; on victims are common characteristics found in all forms of family vio- w these dynamics occur is explored in more detail later. At this stage it ınt to remember that victims of family violence are no different from se. They are human beings who, through no fault of their own, have ıpped in a nightmare of violence from which they believe there is no

·ce Theory

the Focus "The Cycle of Violence Theory Continues" is not from research conducted in the 1950s or 1960s. Rather, it comes from ·lars in a 1993 text on family violence. Because of its popularity and ·cycle of violence theory is discussed as a distinct and separate the- violence. Simply separating it from the other theories should not ; is the definite answer as to why people commit aggressive acts. ıgled out for examination because professionals and lay persons r to it as a scientifically accepted fact. As with other causes or the- violence, there is no way to prove or disprove the cycle of violence ·r, because there is widespread acceptance of this theory, it is nec- ·xplore both the premises it is founded on as well as the criticisms

·f violence concept has generated continuing controversy among several decades. Scholars have attempted to determine whether ·es can be inherited from the family of origin as a result of observ- ı victim of it. Other scholars have attempted to explain criminal ·rence to this cycle.[47]

/iolence Theory Continues

·hildren is perhaps · teaching violence, and eliminating it would be an important step in violence prevention."

Violence." R. L. Hampton et al., eds. *Family Violence: Prevention and Treatment.* 993, p. 20.

Definitions of the Cycle of Violence

The most commonly used term to describe the process involved in this concept is *cycle of violence.* This theory is also known as the *intergenerational transmission of violence theory.* Since many authors, researchers, and commentators use the former, that is the term that is used in this text. *The cycle of violence theory asserts that violent behavior is learned within the family and bequeathed from one generation to the next.* This theory holds that children who are victims of child abuse or who witness violent aggression by one spouse against the other will grow up and react to their children or spouses in the same manner. The childhood survivor of a violent family thus develops a predisposition toward violence in his or her own family. Therefore, so this theory holds, we have a never-ending chain of violence that is passed from one generation to the next. There have been numerous studies on the cycle of violence, and the results of these studies are discussed later in this section.

The Cycle of Violence and Family Violence

The sources for most studies of the cycle of violence theory are case studies, clinical interviews, self-reporting, and agency records. As discussed above, each of these approaches suffers from defects in methodology and definitions.

One of the most widely cited studies in support of the cycle of violence theory is Steele and Polick's research, which appeared in Helfer and Kempe's *The Battered Child Syndrome* in 1968.[48] Their study involved sixty parents who were referred to them as a result of their children being treated for child abuse. Steele and Polick gathered data by testing and interviewing the parents. The parents stated that as children they had experienced intense, pervasive, continuous demands from their own parents. Lost within the conclusions of the study was the fact that some parents were physically abused and others were not. While the researchers had cautioned against drawing too many inferences from their research, their study is constantly cited as evidence supporting the cycle of violence theory.

Strauss conducted an extensive study by interviewing 1,146 families with children.[49] The results of the study indicated an 18 percent rate of generational transmission of violence. This percentage may be low because the researchers limited the definition of abuse to physical acts that occurred during adolescence. As is discussed in Chapter 2, child abuse is more likely to occur at a younger age, with a gradual tapering off in incidents as the child reaches the teenage years.

During this same time period, Hunter and Kilstrom interviewed 282 parents of newborn infants.[50] These researchers followed the parents and determined that the intergenerational transmission of violence was 18 percent. However, 82 percent of the parents who were abused as children did not abuse their offspring. Those parents appeared to be able to break the cycle of violence because of social support, healthy children, and a more supportive relationship with one of their own parents. Hunter and Kilstrom's study is suspect because it examined only infants who had been admitted to an intensive care nursery. In addition, there was no extended follow-up of the families or their children.

In 1984, Egeland and Jacobvitz concluded a major study of 160 single-parent mothers.[51] Each mother had at least one child under the age of five years. The sample was divided into three groups: severe physical child abuse, including being struck by objects or burned; borderline child abuse, including weekly spankings; and those children who were being raised by another caretaker. The researchers found a 70 percent intergenerational transmission of violence for those mothers who had suffered severe abuse as a child.

In 1990, Cappell and Heiner analyzed 888 child-rearing families, measuring the incidence of aggression in each respondent's family.[52] The presence or absence of aggression was classified into family member relationships: husband to wife aggression, wife to husband aggression, and respondent to child aggression. These researchers found that women who witnessed or experienced violence as children were more likely to aggressively discipline their own children. Perhaps more important, these scholars suggested that children who are raised in a violent family learn or inherit vulnerability. Cappell and Heiner theorize that this intergenerational transmission of vulnerability causes men and women to provoke violence, accept violence as natural, and select aggressive partners. These scholars rightfully point out that this research is limited because the group was composed only of intact couples.

In 1997, Loos and Alexander examined 247 female and 155 male undergraduates at a large public mid-Atlantic university.[53] The focus of their study was to determine the long-term effects of parental physical abuse, verbal abuse, and emotional neglect on children. While the study did not directly address the cycle of violence, its conclusions add weight to this theory. These researchers found that physical abuse by parents is significantly related to anger and aggression by the survivors in adulthood. Perceived parental emotional neglect resulted in feelings of loneliness and social isolation in the survivors. These feelings of social isolation suggest that these survivors may have difficulty in establishing satisfying relationships with others. While there are potential problems with the study since it used retrospective self-reports, which are always subject to inaccuracy, it does support the cycle of violence theory by indicating that survivors of childhood abuse may feel anger and aggression as well as loneliness or isolation. These feelings may cause these survivors to enter into abusive relationships as adults.

The Cycle of Violence and Aggression

Dodge and his associates examined the effect of the cycle of violence on development of aggressive tendencies in children.[54] They studied a representative sample of 309 four-year-olds in kindergarten. This research was multisite in nature, and children were selected from Nashville and Knoxville, Tennessee, as well as Bloomington, Indiana. The researchers interviewed the mothers, evaluated the children, and received responses regarding the children's behavior from school personnel, peer ratings, and direct observation.

They found that children who had been physically abused were more aggressive toward other children than those who had not been harmed.[55] The teacher-rated aggression index for abused children was 93 percent higher than for nonabused children. The researchers also found that abused children were less able to process information and solve interpersonal problems. While the authors accurately point out several caveats to their study, it does demonstrate the harm inflicted on children by abuse.

This harm may translate into future acts of aggression that take the form of crimes against society. One of the most comprehensive studies in this area of child abuse and delinquency was undertaken by Widom in 1989.[56] She followed 1,575 individuals from childhood through young adulthood. The study compared arrest records of two groups:

- One group comprised 908 children with documented histories of abuse or neglect.
- The control group comprised 667 children with no reported incidents of child abuse.

These groups were tracked through official records over the next fifteen to twenty years. The children were eleven years or younger at the time of the abuse. Therefore, an inherent weakness in the Strauss research was avoided. The study classified abuse into three distinct areas: physical, sexual, and neglect cases. Court and probation records were the source of data for the initial acts of abuse, and subsequent arrest data was obtained from federal, state, and local law enforcement agencies.

The study found that children who had been abused were more likely to commit crimes as juveniles and adults than were those in the control group. Further, these children were arrested more often for violent crimes (11 percent versus 8 percent) of the nonabused children. Those children who were physically abused were more likely to be arrested for a violent crime. Interestingly, this study pointed out that the next biggest arrest rate for violent crimes comprised those children who had been neglected.

As the above discussion illustrates, the cycle of violence theory continues to dominate family violence literature. This and other theories of family violence will continue to be researched in an attempt to find the cause of family violence, predict its occurrence, and search for a cure.

Summary

Family violence is a multifaceted phenomenon. It includes abusive acts toward children, significant others in a cohabitating relationship, and the elderly. These acts may be sexual, physical, emotional or psychological, or involve neglect or a denial of rights to the other person. It has existed for centuries, but has only recently come to the consciousness of the public. Numerous studies have been done in an attempt to find answers to this form of aggression. We have yet, however, to agree on a definition that all professionals can accept.

Several different measuring techniques are used to determine the extent of family violence. Surveys, official reports, and clinical studies all offer professionals insight and information into the nature and extent of this form of aggression. Unfortunately, each of these measures has internal flaws that are acknowledged by those who use them.

Just as a number of significant controversies still exist in the study of family violence, so do a number of theories attempt to explain how or why one person would act aggressively toward another within the family environment. No one theory that identifies a single cause or multiple causes of family violence has yet gained total acceptance by all the professionals in this area.

It is clear that all professionals must have an understanding of various types of family violence and be able to respond to this form of aggression in a manner that protects the victims. In addition, society must examine its attitude toward women and strive to make them equal partners so as to avoid situations where males may take advantage of superior power and resources. Only by moving forward on a variety of fronts can we hope to diminish or stop this form of aggression that leaves its victims physically and mentally injured.

Key Terms

family violence—any act or omission by persons who are cohabitating that results in serious injury to other members of the family.

psychopathology theory—certain individuals suffer from mental illness, personality disorders, and other dysfunctions that cause them to engage in aggressive acts within the family.

substance abuse theory—accepts the proposition that drugs or alcohol cause or contribute to family violence.

social learning theory—an integration of differential associations with differential reinforcements so that people with whom one interacts are the reinforcers of behavior that results in learning of both deviant and nondeviant behavior.

sociobiology or evolutionary theory—assumes that parents will not emotionally attach to or invest themselves in children with low reproductive potential.

exchange theory—argues that family violence is based on a determination of costs and rewards.

frustration–aggression theory—based on the premise that individuals react aggressively when some goal is blocked or frustrated.

ecological theory—assumes that family violence occurs when the parent, child, and family are mismatched with the neighborhood and community.

patriarchy theory—views society as being dominated by males, with women and children in subordinate positions who are treated as possessions by men.

general systems theory—assumes that violence within the family is a function of a system rather than an individual pathology of the family member.

social conflict theory—proposes that unacknowledged alienation and shame generate violence within the family.

resource theory—holds that the use of violence within a relationship depends on the resources that a family member controls.

culture of violence theory—is based on the premise that violence is unevenly distributed within our society and that violence is more prevalent in the lower socioeconomic sectors of society.

cycle of violence theory—asserts that violent behavior is learned within the family and bequeathed from one generation to the next.

Discussion Questions

1. Based on your reading of this chapter, how would you define *family violence?* Draft a definition and justify your answer.
2. What is the most accurate method to measure the incidence of family violence? Why is this method more reliable than others?
3. Which of the theories discussed in this chapter appears to offer the most hope for understanding the cause of family violence? Why is that theory more complete or acceptable than the others?
4. Is the cycle of violence theory valid? Why? Why not?

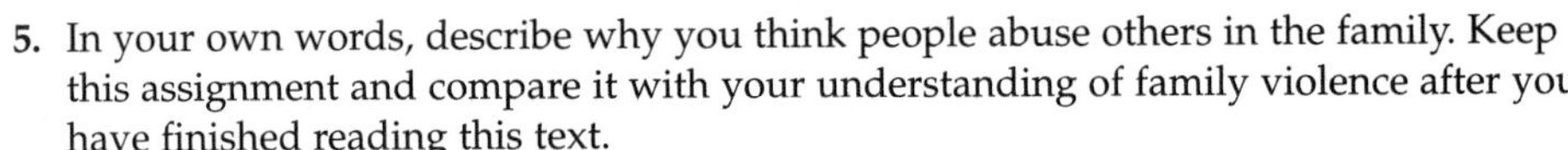

5. In your own words, describe why you think people abuse others in the family. Keep this assignment and compare it with your understanding of family violence after you have finished reading this text.

Suggested Readings

Akers, R. L. *Deviant Behavior.* (Wadsworth, Belmont, California) 1973.

Blau, P. M. *Exchange and Power in Social Life.* (Wiley, New York) 1964.

Coser, L. A. *Continuities in the Study of Social Conflict.* (Free Press, New York) 1967.

Dobash, R. E., and R. P. Dobash. *Violence against Wives.* (Free Press, New York) 1979.

Dollard, J., L. W. Doob, N. E. Miller, O. H. Mowrer, and R. R. Sears. *Frustration and Aggression.* (Yale University Press, New Haven, Connecticut) 1939.

Finkelhor, D., R. J. Gelles, G. T. Hotaling, and M. A. Straus, eds. *The Dark Side of Families: Current Family Violence Research.* (Sage, Beverly Hills, California) 1983.

Gelles, R. J. *The Violent Home.* (Sage, Beverly Hills, California) 1974.

———. *Family Violence.* 2d ed. (Sage, Newbury Park, California) 1987.

———. "Family Violence." In *Family Violence: Prevention and Treatment.* R. L. Hampton et al., eds. (Sage, Newbury Park, California) 1993.

———. *The Violent Home.* (Sage, Newbury Park, California) 1993.

Gelles, R. J., and D. R. Loseke, eds. *Current Controversies on Family Violence.* (Sage, Newbury Park, California) 1993.

Gil, E. M. *Outgrowing the Pain: A Book for and about Adults Abused as Children.* (Launch Press, San Francisco) 1983.

Giles-Sims, J. *Wife-Beating: A Systems Theory Approach.* (Guilford, New York) 1983.

Helfer, R., and C. H. Kempe, eds. *The Battered Child Syndrome.* 4th ed. (University of Chicago Press, Chicago) 1987.

Helfer, R. E., and R. S. Kempe, eds. *The Battered Child.* 4th ed. (University of Chicago Press, Chicago) 1987.

Ohlin, L., and M. Tonry, eds. *Family Violence.* (University of Chicago Press, Chicago) 1989.

Pagelow, M. D. *Family Violence.* (Praeger, New York) 1984.

Reiss, A. J. Jr., and J. A. Roth, eds. *Understanding and Preventing Violence.* (National Academy Press, Washington, D.C.) 1993.

Retzinger, S. M. *Violent Emotions: Shame and Rage in Marital Quarrels.* (Sage, Newbury Park, California) 1991.

Siegal, L. J. *Criminology.* 3d ed. (West, St. Paul, Minnesota) 1989.

Straus, M. A., R. J. Gelles, and S. K. Steinmetz. *Behind Closed Doors.* (Anchor, Garden City, New York) 1980.

Walker, L. E. *The Battered Women.* (Harper & Row, New York) 1979.

Weber, M. *The Theory of Social and Economic Organization.* Translated by A. M. Henderson and T. Parsons. (Free Press, New York) 1964.

Wolfgang, M. E., and F. Ferracuti. *The Subculture of Violence: Toward an Integrated Theory of Criminology.* (Sage, Beverly Hills, California) 1982.

Endnotes

1. Cook, P. W. *Abused Men: The Hidden Side of Domestic Violence.* (Praeger, Westport, Connecticut) 1977.
2. Straus, M. A., R. J. Gelles, and S. K. Steinmetz. *Behind Closed Doors.* (Anchor, Garden City, New York) 1980, p. 22.
3. Pagelow, M. D. *Family Violence.* (Praeger, New York) 1984, p. 21.
4. See for example, Gelles, R. J., and D. R. Loseke, eds. *Current Controversies on Family Violence.* (Sage, Newbury Park, California) 1993.
5. See Strauss, M. A., R. J. Gelles, and S. K. Steinmetz. *Behind Closed Doors: Violence in the American Family.* (Anchor/Doubleday, New York) 1980, for an in-depth discussion of the 1975 survey and M. A. Strauss's "Is Violence toward Children Increasing? A Comparison of the 1975 and 1985 National Survey Rates," In R. J. Gelles, ed. *Family Violence.* (Sage, Newbury Park, California) 1987, for an analysis of the 1985 survey.
6. *Domestic and Sexual Violence Data Collection: A Report to Congress under the Violence Against Women Act* (National Institute of Justice and the Bureau of Justice Statistics, Washington, D.C., July 1996).
7. Ibid, p. 1.
8. 28 USC 534 (1930).
9. "Crime in the United States, 1996," *Uniform Crime Reports* (Superintendent of Documents, Washington, D.C., 1997), p. 1.
10. Milakovich, M. E., and K. Weis, "Politics and the Measure of Success in the War on Crime." *Crime and Delinquency* 21 (January, 1975), pp. 1–10.
11. *Domestic and Sexual Violence Data Collection: A Report to Congress under the Violence Against Women Act,* (National Institute of Justice and the Bureau of Justice Statistics, Washington, D.C., July, 1996), pp. 26–28.
12. The UCR states that the NCVS started in 1973. See "Crime in the United States, 1996," *Uniform Crime Reports* (Superintendent of Documents, Washington, D.C., 1997).
13. The UCR presents a different estimate of households than the NCVS. See "Crime in the United States, 1996," *Uniform Crime Reports* (Superintendent of Documents, Washington, D.C., 1997).
14. *Domestic and Sexual Violence Data Collection: A Report to Congress under the Violence Against Women Act* (National Institute of Justice and the Bureau of Justice Statistics, Washington, D.C., July, 1996), p. 31.
15. Steele, B. "Psychodynamic Factors in Child Abuse." In R. E. Helfer, and R. S. Kempe, eds. *The Battered Child.* 4th ed. (University of Chicago Press, Chicago) 1987.
16. Caplin, D. J., J. Watters, G. White, R. Perry, and R. Bates. "Toronto Multiagency Child Abuse Research Project: The Abused and the Abuser." *Child Abuse and Neglect* 8(3), 1984, pp. 343–351.
17. Gelles, R. J. *The Violent Home.* (Sage, Beverly Hills, California) 1974.
18. Akers, R. L. *Deviant Behavior.* (Wadsworth, Belmont, California) 1973.
19. Blau, P. M. *Exchange and Power in Social Life.* (Wiley, New York) 1964.
20. Gelles, R. J. "An Exchange/Social Theory." In D. Finkelhor, R. J. Gelles, G. T. Hotaling, and M. A. Straus, eds. *The Dark Side of Families: Current Family Violence Research.* (Sage, Beverly Hills, California) 1983, pp. 151–165.
21. Gelles, R. J. *Family Violence.* 2d ed. (Sage, Newbury Park, California) 1987, p. 17.
22. Ibid., p. 158.
23. Dollard, J., L. W. Doob, N. E. Miller, O. H. Mowrer, and R. R. Sears. *Frustration and Aggression.* (Yale University Press, New Haven, Connecticut) 1939.

24. Garbarino, J. "The Human Ecology of Child Maltreatment." *Journal of Marriage and the Family,* 39 (November, 1977), pp. 721–735.
25. Ibid.
26. Porter, S., J. C. Yuille, and A. Bent, "A Comparison of the Eyewitness Accounts of Deaf and Hearing Children," *Child Abuse and Neglect,* 19(1)(January, 1995) pp. 51–62.
27. Smuts, B. "Male Aggression against Women: An Evolutionary Perspective." *Human Nature* 3(1) 1992.
28. Burgess, R. L., and P. Draper. "The Explanation of Family Violence: The Role of Biological Behavioral, and Cultural Selection." In L. Ohlin, and M. Tonry, eds. *Family Violence.* (University of Chicago Press, Chicago) 1989.
29. Wolfgang, M. E., and F. Ferracuti. *The Subculture of Violence: Toward an Integrated Theory of Criminology.* (Sage, Beverly Hills, California) 1982.
30. Coser, L. A. *Continuities in the Study of Social Conflict.* (New York Free Press, New York) 1967.
31. For an excellent analysis of Australian male violence, see K. Polk's "Male-to-Male Homicides: Scenarios of Masculine Violence," paper presented at the annual meeting of the American Society of Criminology, San Francisco, California, November 18–23, 1991.
32. See Pagelow, M. D. *Family Violence.* (Praeger, New York) 1984, pp. 127–138.
33. Dobash, R. E., and R. P. Dobash. *Violence against Wives.* (Free Press, New York) 1979.
34. Giles-Sims, J. *Wife-Beating: A Systems Theory Approach.* (Guilford, New York) 1983.
35. Straus, M. A. "A General Systems Theory Approach to a Theory of Violence between Family Members." *Social Science Information* 12, 1973, pp. 105–125.
36. Retzinger, S. M. *Violent Emotions: Shame and Rage in Marital Quarrels.* (Sage, Newbury Park, California) 1991.
37. Warner, R. L., G. R. Lee, and J. Lee. "Social Organization, Spousal Resources, and Marital Power: A Cross-Cultural Study." *Journal of Marriage and the Family* 48, 1986, pp. 121–128.
38. Gelles, R. *The Violent Home.* (Sage, Newbury Park, California) 1993.
39. See Finkelhor, D. "Common Features of Family Abuse." In D. Finkelhor, R. J. Gelles, G. T. Hotaling, and M. A. Straus, eds. *The Dark Side of Families.* (Sage, Beverly Hills, California) 1983, pp. 17–18, and Pagelow, M. D. *Family Violence.* (Praeger, New York) 1984.
40. Finkelhor, D. "Common Features of Family Abuse." In D. Finkelhor, R. J. Gelles, G. T. Hotaling, and M. A. Straus, eds. *The Dark Side of Families.* (Sage, Beverly Hills, California) 1983, pp. 17–18.
41. Weber, M. *The Theory of Social and Economic Organization.* Translated by A. M. Henderson, and T. Parsons. (Free Press, New York) 1964, p. 152.
42. Talbott, G. D. "Alcoholism and Other Drug Addictions: A Primary Disease Entity, 1991 Update." *Journal of the Medical Association of Georgia* (June, 1991), pp. 337–342.
43. Bays, J. "Substance Abuse and Child Abuse: Impact of Addiction on the Child." *Pediatric Clinics of North America* 37(4), 1990, pp. 881–904.
44. Gil, E. M. *Outgrowing the Pain: A Book for and about Adults Abused as Children.* (Launch Press, San Francisco) 1983.
45. Blumberg, M. L. "Character Disorders in Traumatized and Handicapped Children." *American Journal of Psychotherapy* 33(2), 1979, pp. 201–213.
46. Dunn, G. E. "Multiple Personality Disorder: A New Challenge for Psychology." *Professional Psychology: Research and Practice* 23(1), 1992, pp. 18–23.
47. Siegal, L. J. *Criminology.* 3d ed. (West, St. Paul, Minnesota) 1989, p. 188.
48. Steele, B., and V. Pollock. "A Psychiatric Study of Parents Who Abuse Infants and Small Children." In R. Helfer, and C. H. Kempe, eds. *The Battered Child Syndrome.* (University of Chicago Press, Chicago) 1968. It is interesting to note that later editions of this classic book on child abuse do not contain the article. For example, see the fourth edition, published in 1987.
49. Straus, M. "Family Patterns in a Nationally Representative Sample." *International Journal of Child Abuse and Neglect* 3(23), 1979.

50. Hunter, R. and N. Kilstrom. "Breaking the Cycle in Abusive Families." *American Journal of Psychiatry* 136 (1320) 1979.
51. Eneland, B., and D. Jacobvitz. "Intergenerational Continuity of Parental Abuse: Causes and Consequences." Paper presented at the Conference on Biosocial Perspectives in Abuse and Neglect. (York, Maine) 1984.
52. Cappell, C., and R. B. Heiner. "The Intergenerational Transmission of Family Aggression." *Journal of Family Violence* 5(2), 1990, p. 135.
53. Loos, E., and P. C. Alexander. "Differental Effects Associated with Self-reported Histories of Abuse and Neglect in a College Sample," 12(3) *Journal of Interpersonal Violence* (June, 1997), p. 340.
54. Dodge, K. A., J. E. Bates, and G. S. Pettit. "Mechanisms in the Cycle of Violence." *Science* 250, December, 1990, p. 1678.
55. Ibid., p. 1681.
56. Widom, C. S. "The Cycle of Violence." *Research in Brief, National Institute of Justice.* (U.S. Department of Justice, Washington, D.C.) October, 1992.

2

PHYSICAL CHILD ABUSE

Chapter Outline

Head and Internal Injuries
Head Injuries
Internal Injuries

Summary

Learning Objectives

After reading this chapter, you should be able to discuss the following concepts:

- The magnitude of physical child abuse.
- The abusers and the victims of physical child abuse.
- The indicators of physical child abuse.
- The dating of bruises by their color and shape.
- The different types of immersion burns and how they are caused.
- The various types of pattern burns.
- The medical terms for the various bones within the body.
- The types of fractures and why they indicate physical child abuse.
- The head and internal injuries children receive and how they are caused.

Introduction

Many would date the acceptance of the phenomena of child abuse from 1961 with Doctor C. H. Kempe's use of the term *battered child syndrome.* However, Kempe and his associates were not the first physicians to study child abuse. As early as 1860, Dr. Ambrose Tardieu, a forensic pathologist in France, documented thirty-two incidents of children who had died as a result of battering.[1] In 1946, Dr. John Caffey, a radiologist, reported that a study of six children with subdural hematomas also had other injuries including multiple long-bone fractures, bruising, and hemorrhages.[2] Caffey came to the conclusion that *in the absence of a skeletal disease, children who have both subdural hematomas and long-bone fractures are the victims of trauma.* Others in the medical profession accepted his premise, and this condition became known as *Caffey's syndrome.*

In 1961, when Doctor Kempe and his colleagues coined the term *battered child syndrome,* society began to accept the fact that parents, caretakers, and siblings do in fact engage in occasional or systematic battering of young children.[3] Dr Kempe and his associates wanted to use a catchy phrase to call attention to the serious medical problem they were studying. In 1961, at the meeting of the American Academy of Pediatrics in Denver, they used the term *battered child syndrome* to emphasize the problem of child abuse and point out that physical abuse was a significant cause of death and injury to children. Doctor Kempe's group stated, "The radiologic manifestations of trauma are specific and the metaphysical lesions in

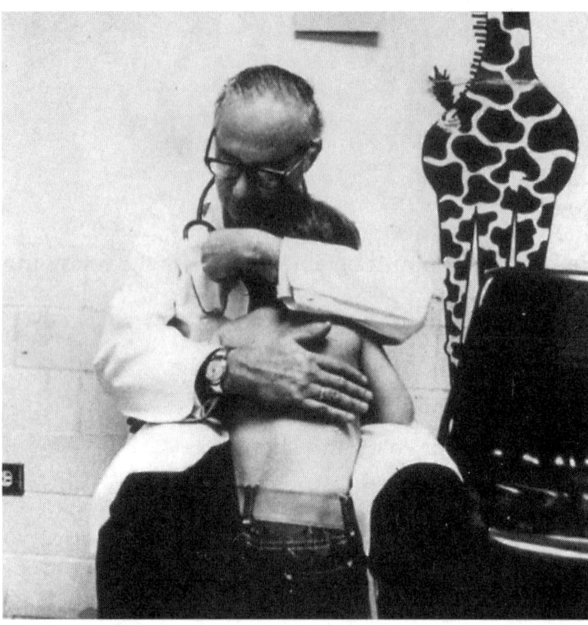

Doctor C. H. Kempe. Photograph provided courtesy of Kempe Children's Foundation, Denver, Colorado.

particular occur in no other disease of which we are aware."[4] *Battered child syndrome is a medicolegal term that describes the diagnosis of a medical expert based on scientific studies which indicate that when a child suffers certain types of continuing injuries, those injuries were not caused by accidental means.*[5]

Since the conference and the publication of Doctor Kempe's article, "The Battered Child Syndrome," in the *Journal of the American Medical Association* in 1962, professionals have made substantial progress in understanding and diagnosing physical child abuse. Kempe's article resulted in an outpouring of concern from the general public and was the impetus for drafting a federal model child abuse reporting statute. As we discuss later in the text, all fifty states now have child abuse reporting laws that mandate that caretakers report suspected cases of child abuse. This chapter discusses the various types of physical child abuse encountered by professional caretakers. As with other pictures and diagrams in this text, the pictures included in this chapter may not be pleasant to view but are considered essential in examining this topic.

What is child abuse? Child abuse deals with physical force and injury to a child. The amount of force or injury to a child is the characteristic that distinguishes child abuse from normal discipline. Most of us in our younger years pledged never to use corporal discipline on our children. However, many parents acknowledge slapping a child's hand to bring attention to or correct unwanted behavior. Is this child abuse? The Practicum "Discipline of Children—Is It Child

PRACTICUM Discipline of Children—Is It Child Abuse?

Assume none of the acts require the child to be hospitalized or treated by a physician. Which of the following acts are proper? Are any of them excessive? In your opinion, do any of them constitute child abuse?

Child, age one year:

The child is reaching for the side of a hot woodstove. Which of the following acts are proper and which are child abuse?

1. You allow the child to touch the stove to teach her a lesson.
2. You say "hot" and slap the child's hand.
3. You move the child to another part of the room without any infliction of punishment.

Child, age two years:

The child throws food off the table during dinner.

1. You go on with dinner and tell the child not to do that anymore.
2. You require the child to pick up the food and eat it.
3. You send the child to bed without allowing him to finish dinner.
4. You pick up the food and force the child to eat it by stuffing it in his mouth.

Child, age four years:

The child cusses at you.

1. You tell the child to stop and not do that again.
2. You wash the child's mouth out with strong soap.
3. You spank the child in a mild manner.
4. You slap the child across the face with your hand.
5. You use a belt on the child's legs and arms.

Abuse?" is designed to test values and judgments regarding corporal discipline before further discussing child abuse.

As the exercise demonstrates, there are many different views on disciplining children. Each of the acts described occurs in homes on a daily basis, and some result in children being treated at hospitals or walk-in clinics. If the injury is of sufficient magnitude, the medical practitioner may refer the matter to the authorities as a case of possible child abuse. The next section discusses the definition of child abuse and points out some of the problems encountered when attempting to define this concept.

Definition of Child Abuse

Is a parent considered unfit or abusive if, while bathing his one-year-old daughter, she slips from his grasp and hits her head against the faucet causing a cut over her eye that requires two stitches? Is this child abuse? While some might blame the father for not being alert to such dangers, most would not classify him as a child abuser. Accidents happen. They are a part of growing up, and, painful as they may be to the parent and the child, they are part of a normal, healthy sustained relationship. Thus, not all injuries children sustain can be classified as child abuse. If not all injuries are child abuse, and parents have a right to inflict corporal punishment on children as a form of discipline, how do we draw the line and define physical injuries to children?

Numerous authorities have defined child abuse. Part of the problem has been the continued debate on what the term *child abuse* means. Mildred Pagelow, Vincent B. Van Hasselt, Richard Gelles, and other scholars in the field have presented excellent discussions and definitions of this condition.[6] For purposes of this text and ease of understanding, one definition is used: *Physical child abuse may be defined as any act that results in a nonaccidental physical injury by a person who has care, custody, or control of a child.*

This definition contains two key aspects—the act is intentional or willful, and the act resulted in a physical injury. An accidental injury does not qualify as child abuse. In the example described above, an accidental slip in a bathtub does not qualify as child abuse even if the child received an injury that required several stitches. Child abuse as discussed in this chapter is manifested by physical injury that can be proved or documented. Simply yelling at the child is not child abuse within the meaning of this definition, nor is spanking the child on the hand, the face, or the buttocks if those acts did not result in a physical injury that can be documented. While it is true that any form of spanking causes injury in the form of pain and some trauma to the child, unless the force is sufficient to leave marks most medical and legal authorities do not classify these acts as child abuse. The lack of a clear definition is part of the problem of physical child abuse. The next section explores this issue and discusses the extent of child abuse in our society.

Magnitude of the Problem

The physical battering of children is not a new phenomenon. Children have suffered trauma at the hands of their parents and caretakers since the beginning of recorded history. In Egypt, at the birth of Moses, the pharaoh ordered the death of all male children. King Herod also ordered infanticide on a large scale when Jesus was born.

Early history records the practice of burying infants alive in foundations of buildings and bridges.[7] Excavations of Canaanite dwellings have uncovered jars of infant bones in the foundation of buildings.[8] Although officially outlawed, this practice continued in seventeenth-century Europe, and children were found buried in the foundations of London Bridge.

Plato (428–348 B.C.) and Aristotle (348–322 B.C.) both urged the killing of infants born with birth defects. Children with birth defects, female infants, and the children of poor families were killed as a matter of course several hundred years before the birth of Christ. In Rome, the law of the Twelve Tables prohibited raising a child with a defect or deformity. In Sparta, infants were examined by a local council of elders who had the power to throw children considered unfit into a canyon.[9]

Infanticide was not the only form of abuse practiced by early civilizations. During the Middle Ages, families often mutilated or severed limbs from children to make them more effective beggars. The histories of the European school systems are filled with records detailing beatings and abuse that teachers inflicted on their young charges.

The industrial revolution was characterized by repeated maltreatment of children. Young children were forced to work long hours under inhumane conditions in factories or other heavy industries. Many were beaten, shackled, or starved to force them to work harder at their tasks.

In 1874, an eight-year-old child named Mary Ellen Wilson was discovered by a social worker to have been beaten and starved by her adoptive parents. The social worker referred the case to the New York City Police Department, which refused to take any action because no laws addressed the abuse of children by their parents or caretakers. In an effort to save the child, the city filed charges against the caretakers using a statute that prevented cruelty to animals. The adoptive mother was sentenced to one year in jail, and the resulting publicity surrounding Mary Ellen's plight led to the formation of the Society for the Prevention of Cruelty to Children in 1875.

Every state now has laws preventing the physical abuse of children. The phenomenon of child abuse has generated many studies. One of the most commonly cited of these studies was conducted by the American Association for Protecting Children. The information contained in this annual report indicates that in 1982 about 1 million children were abused and neglected.[10] Other studies report figures ranging from 200,000 to 4 million children. Some researchers take the position that there is no method of obtaining reliable data in this field.[11] Even the federal government has failed to establish standards for reporting child abuse. The FBI's Uniform Crime Reports (UCR) are the accepted method for reporting crimes on a nationwide basis. The UCR publishes crime statistics reported by 16,000 law enforcement agencies. However, it provides no specific information on crimes against children. With the exception of murder, the UCR does not list the victim's age. The National Center on Child Abuse and Neglect (NCCAN), a division within the U.S. Department of Health and Human Services, has commissioned studies to provide a national estimate of the incidence of child maltreatment.

In 1986, the National Committee to Prevent Child Abuse (NCPCA) began collecting data from all fifty states and the District of Columbia on child abuse incidents.[12] In April 1997, NCPCA released its annual report, which indicated that nationwide, the rate of children reported for child abuse or neglect increased 12 percent from 42 per 1,000 children in 1991 to 47 per 1,000 in 1996. In 1996, approximately 3,126,000 children were reported to Child Protective Services (CPS) agencies as suspected victims of child abuse. While the data suggests a slight decline in the total number of child abuse deaths, the high number of these cases is troubling. An estimated 1,215 children were killed in 1996 as a result of child abuse or neglect. An astonishing 46 percent of these children had current or previous contact with local CPS agencies. Despite increased awareness of this problem, no significant decrease in this fatal statistic has been observed over the last ten years.

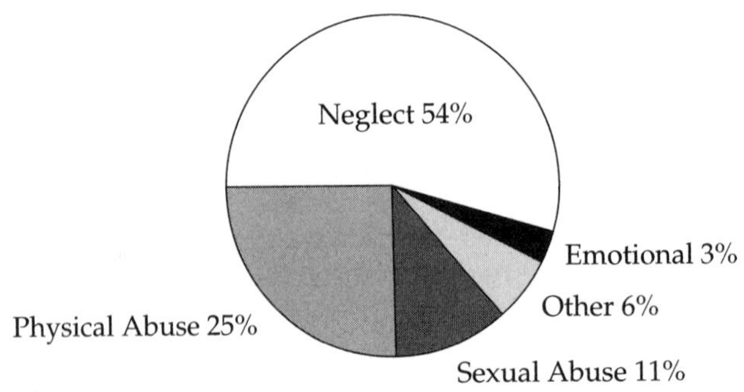

Fatalities by Abuse or Neglect

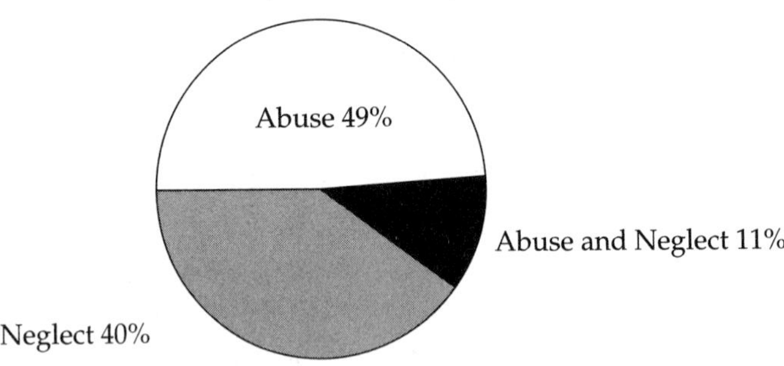

Age of Child at Time of Death

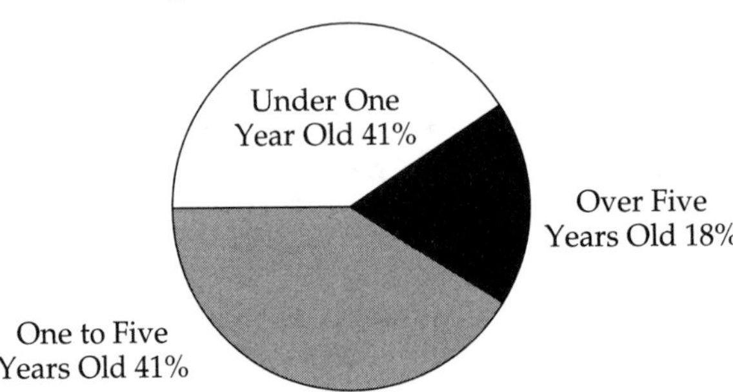

FIGURE 2.1 Substantiated Abuse and Neglect Cases, 1995

Source: Current Trends in Child Abuse Reporting and Fatalities: The Results of the 1996 Annual Fifty State Survey. National Committee to Prevent Child Abuse (Chicago, Illinois, April 1997) pp. 7–8.

As indicated in Figure 2.1, neglect represents the most common form of reported abuse and the most common form of substantiated maltreatment. 1n 1996, reported the following breakdown for reported cases: 62 percent involved neglect, 25 percent physical abuse, 7 percent sexual abuse, 3 percent emotional abuse, and 4 percent other forms of abuse. For substantiated cases, the following breakdowns were reported: 60 percent neglect, 23 percent physical abuse, 9 percent sexual abuse, 4 percent emotional abuse, and 5 percent other forms of abuse.

NCPCA indicates that in reviewing the past five years of information, only one state (Alabama) experienced a consistent decline each year while five states (California, Connecticut, Maryland, Oklahoma, and Washington) experienced consistent annual increases. These patterns do not necessarily indicate that child abuse is rising in these five states; rather, it points out the variability in reporting statistics over time and the sensitivity of the reporting system to changes in social, political, and administrative policies or practices.

Many authorities believe that the number of reported cases of child abuse is only the tip of the iceberg. This is particularly true for those children between the ages of twelve and nineteen. This age-group is far less likely than younger victims to report crimes, especially when the offender is not a stranger.[13] Part of the problem with determining the magnitude of physical child abuse may have something to do with the definition itself.

By defining the characteristics or hallmarks of physical child abuse differently, the research data itself can differ significantly. Researchers select their sample populations based on criteria that differ from scholar to scholar and from study to study. Some social scientists view physical child abuse in the context of determining whether the child is "at risk," whereas those working in the criminal justice field emphasize physical evidence. This multifaceted approach to understanding physical child abuse presents both problems and opportunities for growth. As mentioned earlier, the problem is how to reach consensus on the definition of physical child abuse and how we respond to it. The opportunities for growth are based on the premise that professionals can and should learn from each other. The social worker may learn of the difficulties in proving certain types of abuse while teaching the prosecuting attorney to accept the seriousness of a situation that might not otherwise be apparent from a legal perspective.

The Abusers and the Abused

Both the magnitude and the definition of child abuse have caused problems in the area of family violence. Although the previous discussion defines physical child abuse, it does not establish who the perpetrators and the victims are. This section briefly examines the parties to child abuse and how they relate to each other.

Who Are the Abusers?

As the next Practicum concerning Billy's abuse indicates, who the abuser is may vary depending on the facts. Some would argue that Julie is responsible, while others would lay the blame entirely on Howard. The fact that people who physically abuse children do not fit any stereotyped description further complicates the issue of physical child abuse. Abuse occurs in exclusive neighborhoods, middle-class suburbs, and inner-city slums, and it comes in all sizes, shapes, colors, and

PRACTICUM

Julie M. is the twenty-year-old mother of Billy, age two years. She is unmarried but has been living with Howard for the last year. Both Julie and Howard drink heavily and use cocaine. Six months ago, Julie returned from work and found a series of marks on Billy's legs. Howard stated that Billy would not quit crying, so he disciplined him with a belt. Howard believed this type of discipline was fine because his father used to beat him and he turned out all right. While Julie wasn't happy with Howard's actions, she did not want to confront him because she was hoping they would eventually marry. Three months later, Julie and Billy were playing when Billy knocked over Howard's glass of whiskey. Howard hit Billy with the back of his hand, causing a small cut and swelling of the lip. Julie and Howard had an argument over this, but Julie took no further action, nor did she extract a promise from Howard that he would not commit similar acts in the future.

Last week, Julie was called by the emergency room at the local hospital. Billy had been brought in by Howard and was comatose. Howard did not have an adequate explanation for the injury, stating only that when he went to wake Billy up there was a bruise on his head. The nurse stated that it appeared Billy had suffered some trauma to the head.

Assuming there is a diagnosis of nonaccidental injury to Billy, who should be help responsible? Should Howard be liable? Should the fact that Howard drinks and uses narcotics enter into the picture? Is it a consideration that Howard may have been abused as a child? What about Julie? Should she have taken some action to protect Billy? If you had to proportion the blame or responsibility, how much would each party receive?

sexes. Many studies, theories, and models have been constructed in an attempt to categorize abusers but without success. One thing scholars can agree on, however, is that there is no single way of determining who a child abuser is.[14]

Rather than attempt to describe all acceptable theories of the causes of child abuse, this section sets forth one model that encompasses several different theories. Cynthia Crosson Tower grouped several theories into three distinct models: the psychopathological model, the interactional model, and the environmental–sociological–cultural model.[15]

The psychopathological model stresses the characteristics of the abuser as the primary cause of abuse. The abuser's personality predisposes the abuser to injure the child. This model includes three separate approaches to child abuse: the psychodynamic model, the mental illness model, and the character-trait model.

The psychodynamic model is based on the work of C. Henry Kempe and Ray Helfer. This model theorizes that a lack of bonding between the parent and child is an important factor in child abuse. This theory assumes that the abuser was part of a cycle of parental inadequacy. These individuals are unable to bond with children, and, when a crisis occurs, they respond with abusive acts. This model also assumes the abuser will engage in role reversal. In other words, the parents expect the child to nurture them instead of vice versa.

The mental illness model sets forth the proposition that a parent's mental illness is the primary cause of child abuse. This is a readily accepted theory because it is easy to believe that anyone who would repeatedly beat or torture a child must be crazy. Justice and Justice suggested this model as a viable category.[16] While some scholars have found abusive parents to be mentally disturbed, many others argue that abusive parents do not fit any existing psychiatric classification. For example, Kempe found that less than 5 percent were psychotic.

The character-trait model focuses on specific traits of abusers without regard for how they acquired these traits. Scholars such as Merrill and Delsordo have categorized abusive parents by specific traits that cause child abuse.[17] Merrill's study included such traits as hostility, rigidity, passivity, dependence, and competitiveness. Delsordo's categorization of abusive parents' traits included mental illness, frustration, irresponsibility, severe discipline, and misplaced abuse.

The interactional model views child abuse as a result of a dysfunctional system. This category of abuse focuses on the following factors in child abuse: the role of the child, chance events, and the family structure.

The role of the child and the perceptions of the parent toward that child are viewed as causes of child abuse by some scholars. Martin suggests not only that abuse requires a certain type of adult but also that certain acts of the child trigger the abuse. If the parent has certain expectations that the child does not meet, abuse may occur.[18]

"Chance events" is the somewhat inaccurate name given to events that prevent the parent from bonding with the child. This lack of attachment is viewed as a predisposition toward child abuse. Lynch suggests that difficulties in pregnancy, labor, or delivery can have a bearing on the attachment of the mother to the child.[19]

The family-structure model theorizes that child abuse is a result of a dysfunctional family. The adult members of the family blame the child for their own shortcomings, and this leads to abuse.

The environmental–sociological–cultural model views child abuse as a result of stresses in society that are the primary causes of abuse. This category includes the following causes of child abuse: the environmental stress model, the social-learning model, the social–psychological model, and the psychosocial systems model.

The environmental stress model accepts the proposition that factors such as a lack of education, poverty, unemployment, or occupational stress result in child abuse. As these outside forces build, the parent or caretaker is unable to cope and reacts by hitting or injuring the child.

The social-learning model emphasizes the inadequacy of the parenting skills of abusive parents. These parents never learned appropriate responses to child rearing, and therefore their lack of skill leads to frustration. This frustration in turn causes abusive behavior.

The social–psychological model assumes that stress results from a number of social and psychological factors, including marital disputes, unemployment, and too many or unwanted children. These factors induce stress that causes the individual to react to the child in an abusive manner.

The psychosocial systems model stresses that abuse results from interactions within the family. The family as a system is out of balance and incapable of caring for the child. The child becomes the target for family members' frustration, and abuse is the result.

As the preceding discussion indicates, several theories attempt to explain who abusers are and why they abuse children. While no authority can point to one cause of child abuse, it is clear that it continues to occur. The causes of child physical abuse are multifaceted. Therefore, it is necessary to examine who the victims or recipients of this violence are to attempt to more fully understand this phenomenon.

The Victims

Children of all ages, all races, both sexes, and all socioeconomic backgrounds have been victims of physical abuse. Several studies have examined whether certain children are more at risk of being abused than others.[20] Ammerman points out that children who are abused have a higher percentage of prematurity, low birthweight, mental retardation, and physical or sensory handicaps. In general, children who are difficult to manage or control may be at a higher risk of abuse then other children.[21]

The American Association for Protecting Children (AAPC) publishes an annual report on child maltreatment. While the use of reported incidents of child abuse has inherent problems, it does provide an overview of this phenomenon in the United States.[22] The average age of the victim is eight years. Twenty-seven percent of all child maltreatment cases involve physical abuse. Three percent of these cases involve life-threatening injuries such as poisoning, fractures, or brain damage. Fourteen percent involve minor injuries, including bruises, cuts, or shaking. The remaining 11 percent are unspecified injuries.[23]

The National Incidence Surveys are another source for examining who the victims of physical child abuse are.[24] As with the AAPC report, there are problems in reporting and defining child abuse. Similar to the AAPC report, though, the National Incidence Surveys do provide insight into the nature and type of abuse and the most likely victims. In 1981 and 1988, two national surveys of professionals and their reporting practices provided information about the types of children who were abused or likely to be abused.

The National Incidence Surveys have clarified issues raised in earlier reports regarding duplicate reporting. This in turn has led to the elimination of the counting of duplicate reports in the NCCAN reports. These surveys, while subject to

Summary of Findings of the National Incidence Surveys

- Children from poor families—those earning less than $15,000 a year—were five times as likely to be abused and more than seven times as likely to suffer serious injury or impairment.
- Family size is associated with abuse—more children increased the chance or probability of abuse.
- Race, ethnicity, and where the children live have no relationship to abuse.
- The incidence of child abuse increased with the child's age.

criticism, have sparked intense research efforts by professionals in the field to understand the incidence and types of physical child abuse.

A third method of determining who the victims of physical abuse are involves surveys of the general public. Some of the earliest studies of physical child abuse were conducted by surveying nationally representative samples. In 1965, D. G. Gill surveyed 1,520 adults regarding whether they had personal knowledge of a child who was injured in a nonaccidental manner.[25] Straus, Gelles, and associates conducted two surveys in 1975 and 1985 regarding physical abuse. Their survey found a decrease in the rate in which parents engage in violent acts toward their children. One explanation of the decrease may be structural changes in the families, improved living conditions, and the availability of treatment programs.[26]

This section has explored the various methods used to determine the extent and nature of physical child abuse. Different surveys and studies have attempted to provide a profile of the abused child, but to date there is no accepted method of predicting who will be the next victim. However, certain factors indicate that a child may be currently suffering from physical abuse. The next section examines those indications.

Indications of Physical Child Abuse

All professionals should be aware of the indications of physical child abuse. Many times, less serious injuries precede more life-threatening injuries. As discussed later in this chapter, certain specific types of physical injuries are strongly associated with physical abuse. This section reviews the more commonplace indicators of physical child abuse that may be observed by a caretaker, teacher, or other professional.

Location and Types of Injuries

The location and types of physical injuries a child suffers may suggest physical child abuse. Many times the child, parent, or person responsible for caring for the child will deny any wrongdoing or that the child is even suffering from any physical injury.[27] While care should always be exercised when dealing with any checklist, the following facts should at the very least alert any professional to inquire further into the situation at home.

Psychological/Behavioral Symptoms

Unfortunately, many physically abused children are overlooked because the telltale marks of injuries are covered by clothing. Therefore, in addition to the physical indicators, caretakers and professionals must be aware of certain psychological or behavioral actions on the part of the child. These actions should be viewed with caution because nonabused children may exhibit some or all of the symptoms. It should raise a suspicion on the part of caretakers or professionals, however, and alert them to the possibility that the child may be a victim of physical child abuse.

Physical Indicators	
Unexplained bruises or welts that may be in various stages of healing, in clusters of unusual patterns, or on several different areas.	Unexplained skeletal injuries, stiff swollen joints, or multiple or spiral fractures.
Unexplained burns in the shape of a cigarette, rope, or iron or caused by immersion, which may appear sock- or glove-like.	Missing or loosened teeth.
Unexplained lacerations to mouth, lips, arms, legs, or torso.	Human bite marks.
	Bald spots.
	Unexplained abrasions.
	Appearance of injuries after school absence, weekend, or vacation.
Behavioral Indicators	
Easily frightened or fearful of adults and parents, physical contact, or when other children cry.	Runaway or delinquent behavior.
Destructive to self and/or others.	Reporting unbelievable reasons for injuries.
Extremes of behavior: aggressive or withdrawn.	Complains of soreness or moves awkwardly.
Poor social relations.	Accident prone.
Learning problems, poor academic performance, short attention span, delayed language development.	Wears clothing that is clearly meant to cover the body when not appropriate.
	Seems afraid to go home.

Source: Adapted from Layman, Richard. *Current Issues—Volume 1: Child Abuse.* (Omnigraphics, Inc., Detroit) 1990, p. 34. Originally circulated by the Children's Safety Project in Manhattan.

Explanation of Injuries

Many times, certain physical injuries are as consistent with child abuse as they are with normal, healthy childhood development. Every practitioner must be aware of the possibility of abuse and pay particular attention to the caretaker's explanation of the child's injury. The explanation and the injury may be inconsistent and therefore suggest child abuse. Following are some of the more common explanations that should be carefully evaluated by any professional in the field.

Unexplained Injury

When the caretaker claims to have no knowledge of the injury or denies any knowledge of how the injury occurred, a very strong likelihood of physical abuse exists.[28] Most nonabusive parents can explain how and why their child was injured. They will readily discuss the accident and injury with medical or professional staff.

Impossible Explanation

One of the strongest indicators of physical child abuse is a caretaker's statement that is implausible and inconsistent with common sense and medical judgment. Some caretakers will describe a minor accident that resulted in major or life-threatening injuries. In one case, a father stated his six-month-old daughter must have injured herself when she fell off the couch. The daughter died as a result of multiple injuries that were inconsistent with a simple fall from a couch.[29]

Different Versions of the Incident

When both caretakers are present, they should be questioned separately. Many times, they will have different versions of how the accident occurred. This is a strong indication of abuse. If the child is old enough, they should be asked to tell what happened. If the child's version is significantly different from the caretaker's story, the injury should be carefully evaluated for signs of abuse.

Different Explanations

An abusive caretaker may have difficulty keeping their story straight when it must be repeated to different persons. One story may be told to the emergency room doctor, a slightly different version to the Child Protective Services (CPS) worker, and still a third scenario described to the investigator. Different stories should immediately alert any professional to the possibility of physical child abuse.[30]

Delay in Seeking Medical Attention

Concerned parents usually bring their child for medical care as soon as possible after an accident. They have nothing to hide and are seeking care for their child. Delay in seeking medical care, especially for life-threatening injuries, is an indicator of possible child abuse.

Discovery of the location, nature, and extent of injuries in a child physical abuse case is only the first step in the process. The injury must be examined, documented, and treated. The nature or type of injury often will be suggestive of certain types of abuse. The next four sections review injuries normally associated with physical child abuse.

Bruises

Bruises come in all sizes, shapes, colors, and locations. Children are full of energy and attempt feats that they donot have the physical capability of achieving at their age. They fall when walking, trip on rugs and cut their lips, or try to climb stairs and topple down. This is part of growing up, but in some cases certain types of bruises, because of shape and location, will suggest a darker or more sinister cause. This section examined these types of bruises.

The first two situations in the next Practicum describing the injured eighteen-month-old child are consistent with normal, healthy child rearing. However, the last situation adds facts that should alert any practitioner to potential physical abuse. There is a description of multiple injuries: a cut lip, bruises on the forearm and back of the legs, and, most important, the mother's dating of the last accident is inconsistent with the typical aging of bruises.

Bruises should be examined from several aspects: time of injury, location, and pattern. Each of these factors alone may indicate nonaccidental injury. On the other hand, there may be an acceptable explanation for some of the injuries.

Timing of the Injury

Bruises can be a physical clock that can provide a date or time of the initial injury because as a bruise ages it changes color. Depending on the intensity of the injury, contusion resolution varies. However, typical bruises age in the following manner.

0–5 days	red/purple/blue
5–7 days	green
7–10 days	yellow
10–14 days	brown
2–4 weeks	clear

Location of the Bruise

As indicated previously, normal, healthy, well-cared-for children will injure themselves. Many times an injury manifests itself as a bruise. Bruises on the front portion of the arms, legs, and face may be consistent with normal childhood activities. Normal bruises occur over bony prominences such as the knees, anterior tibia (that portion of the bone that extends from the knee to the ankle on the front of the leg, sometimes called the shinbone), and forehead.[31] Bruises from falling onto objects are usually circular or oval with nondescript edges.[32] However, bruises on the back of the arms or legs or on the back, abdomen, genitals, buttocks, and other soft-tissue areas should be viewed with suspicion.[33] Careful attention should be given to any explanation offered by the parent or custodian of the child. The location of the bruise is an important indicator of nonaccidental injury. Also, the pattern or shape of the bruise may confirm this diagnosis.

Bruise Patterns

Normal bruising takes different shapes and sizes (see Figure 2.2 on page 44). However, some bruise patterns are strong indicators of abuse. These patterns are inflicted by objects or excessive force applied to a portion of a child's body. Schmitt described the traditional bruises left by belts, switches, cords, or ropes:

PRACTICUM

Situation 1. An eighteen-month-old child was brought to a walk-in clinic with a cut lip. He was accompanied by his mother, who stated that he had fallen against the edge of the living room table while playing. The doctor who examined the child determined it would take three stitches to close the cut. Does this fact pattern alert you to child abuse? Assume there are no more facts at this time. Justify your answer.

Situation 2. While conducting a preliminary examination of the child described above, the doctor observed pale green circular bruises on the front of the child's forearms. On questioning the mother, she replied that he had fallen approximately seven days earlier while playing on the cement patio at their apartment. Do the additional facts supplied in Situation 2 change your opinion? Why? Why not? Justify your answer.

Situation 3. In addition to the pale yellow bruises on the front of the child's forearms, the doctor observed two large round blackish-purple colored bruises on the back of the child's legs. The mother responded that the child was very active and two weeks ago had fallen against the back of a swing set, hitting the back of his legs. Do the additional facts have any bearing on your opinion?

> *Strap marks are sharp-bordered, one- to two-inch wide rectangular bruises of various lengths, sometimes covering a curved body surface. These are almost always caused by a belt. Sometimes, the eyelets or buckle of the belt can be discerned. Lash marks are narrow, straight-edged bruises or scratches caused by thrashing with a tree branch or switch. Loop marks are secondary to being struck with a doubled-over lamp cord, rope, or belt. The distal end of the loop strikes with the most force, commonly breaks the skin, and may leave loop-shaped scars.*[34]

These are not the only types of suspicious bruising patterns. Other typical patterns of nonaccidental bruises include the following:

Eyes	bilateral black eyes
Ear lobe	pinch and pull marks
Cheek	slap marks, squeeze marks, or gag marks
Upper lip	bruises
Scalp	bare head and broken hair, bruises
Neck	choke marks
Upper arms	grab marks
Chest	fingertip encirclement marks
Inner thighs	pressure marks and fingertip marks
Genitals	pinch marks and wrapping of penis
Ankles/wrists	tethering or friction burn marks
Feet	pen or razor tattoo marks

Simply because a child is bruised does not mean that he or she is abused. Medical personnel should be requested to conduct a blood coagulation study to

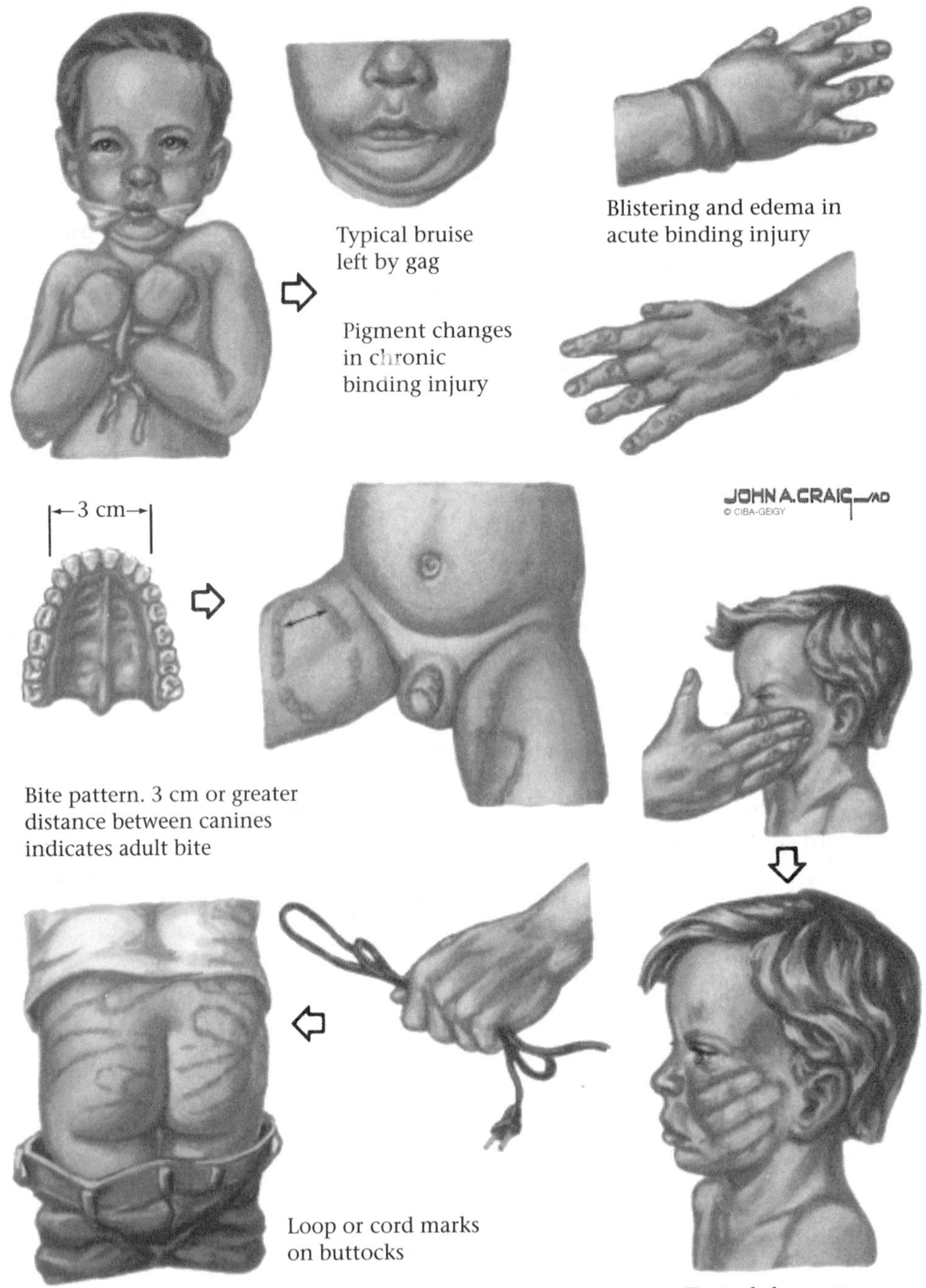

FIGURE 2.2 Injury Patterns

Source: Plate 3 from Kessler, D.B., and Hyden. "Physical, Sexual, and Emotional Abuse of Children." *Clinical Symposia* 43, no. 1 (1991): 9. © 1991 by Pharmaceuticals Division, CIBA-GEIGY Corporation. Reprinted with permission.

determine if the child bruises easily. Blood coagulation studies determine if a child's blood composition causes him or her to bruise more easily than other children.[35] In addition, care must be given to distinguishing between Mongolian spots or allergic shiners, which are accepted physical conditions that do not indicate physical abuse. Mongolian spots are irregular areas of deep blue pigmentation, usually in the sacral (lower back) or gluteal (buttocks) regions, seen predominantly in newborns of African, Asian, or Latin descent.[36] Allergic shiners, also known as acute contact dermatitis, are simply an allergic reaction on the skin. If these factors are considered and ruled out, the care provider should seriously consider physical abuse as the cause of the injury.

As the previous discussion indicates, normal bruising occurs in all sizes and shapes. However, there are certain bruises that, because of the timing, location, or pattern, should raise suspicion in any professional. As bad as bruises may seem, in the scheme of things they are probably the least serious form of physical child abuse. The next section examines a more deliberate and cruel form of abuse—intentionally burning a child.

Burns

Burns are a common form of child abuse and are often inflicted as a form of punishment (see Figure 2.3). The victim is normally an infant or child under the age of three.[37] As in the case of bruises, distinctive types of burns are highly indicative of physical child abuse.

Burns are referred to as either "partial" or "full thickness." The medical classification of burns include *first-degree burns,* which are partial thickness burns. These burns are characterized by localized redness, appear sunburnlike, and usually heal by themselves. They are not included when calculating burn size. *Second-degree burns* are also partial thickness burns. They are characterized by partial skin damage, blisters containing clear fluid, and pink underlying tissue. They often heal by themselves. *Third-degree burns* are full thickness burns. These burns exhibit full destruction of the skin, deep red tissue underlying the blister, the presence of

FOCUS The Oatmeal Case

Travis was a seventeen-month-old child who received a round burn on his face. The parents claimed innocence and stated that the burn was caused when Travis had an accident with a bowl of oatmeal. Medical experts at the trial testified that Travis's facial burn was circumscribed, or perfectly round, which indicated the child's face had been forced into the bowl of oatmeal and held there. The experts opined that if the burning were accidental, the burn mark would be irregular because the victim would be moving around, splashing, running, or dripping or involved in some avoidance act such as turning away from or wiping off the oatmeal (see *State v Church,* 99 N.C. App. 647, 394 S.E. 2d 468, 470 [1990]).

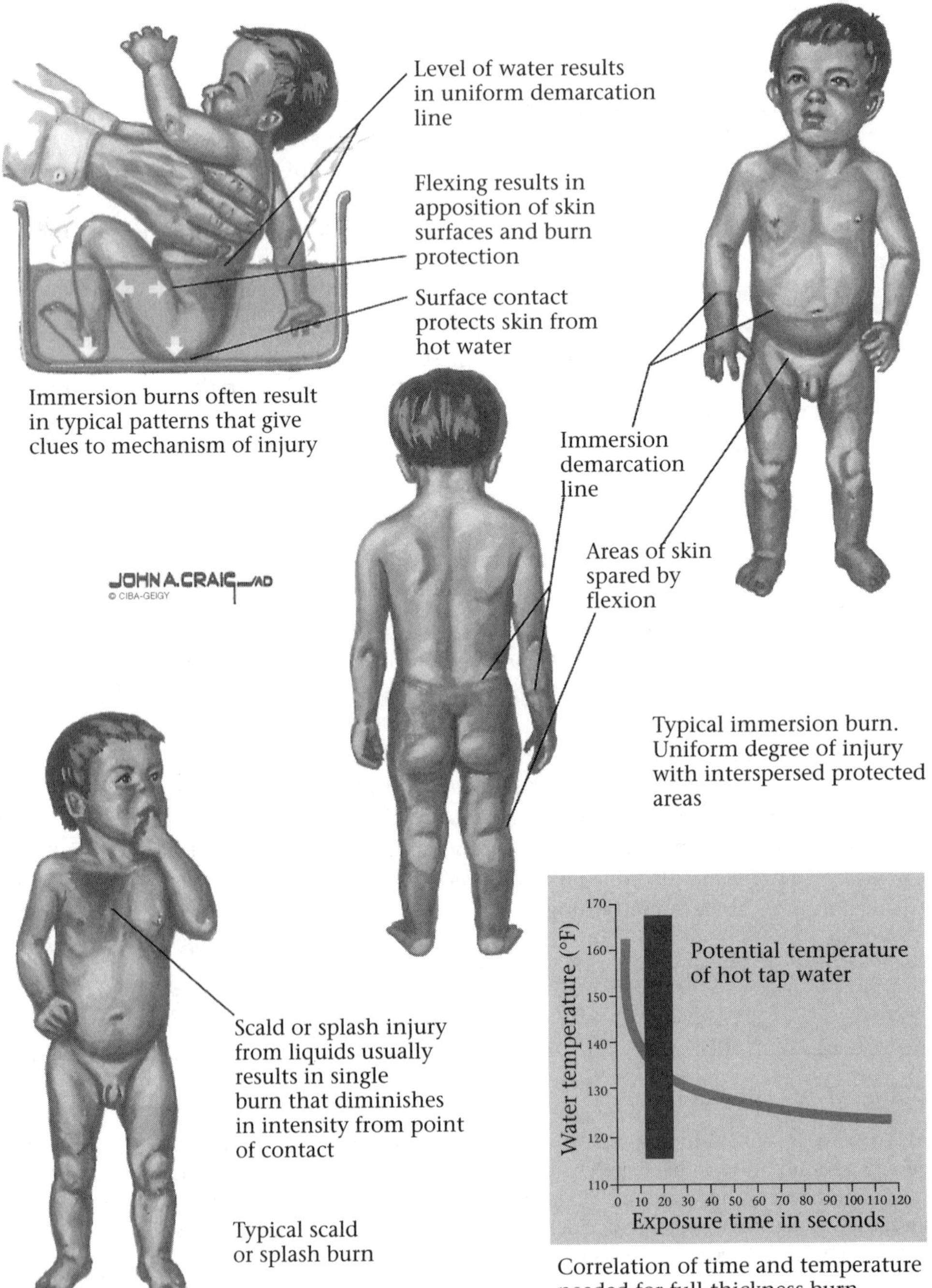

FIGURE 2.3 Immersion and Scald Injuries

Source: Plate 4 from Kessler, D.B., and Hyden. "Physical, Sexual, and Emotional Abuse of Children." *Clinical Symposia* 43, no. 1 (1991): 11. © 1991 by Pharmaceuticals Division, CIBA-GEIGY Corporation. Reprinted with permission.

bloody blister fluid, and sometimes muscle and bone damage. Third-degree burns require professional treatment. *Fourth-degree burns* are also full thickness burns and are considered the most serious type of burn. They are characterized by penetration of deep tissue to fat, muscle, and bone and require immediate professional treatment.[38]

Water or Immersion Burns

Water or immersion burns are a common form of physical child abuse. *These burns are caused by a caretaker holding the child in hot water.* Many times these burns result from the parents' frustration over bed-wetting or potty training.[39] The child may be forcibly restrained in scalding hot (130 degree) water. If the child is held down in a tub, many times the burn resembles a donut shape on the buttocks area. Glovelike or stocking-shaped burns indicate that the hand or foot of the child was immersed in hot liquid. An unrestrained child in hot water may not be able to get out but would thrash around and create splash burns and a blurring of the outline of the burn. When a child is held down in hot water, splash burns are minimized and the outline of the burn is clear.[40]

Pattern Burns

A second form of burn is known as the *pattern burn. These burns are caused by holding or pressing a portion of the child's body against a hot object.* The majority of these burns involve irons, stove burners, heater grates, or woodstoves. An accidental burn of this nature usually involves a brief, glancing contact with a small portion of the hot surface. Accidental burns are usually deeper and more intense on one edge of the burn. Intentional burns are characterized by symmetrical, deep imprints with clear margins of the entire burned surface.[41] Many times the actual outline of the grate or stove burner is imprinted on the child's body.

Cigarettes form another type of pattern burn. While it is possible for a small child to be accidentally burned by a lit cigarette, burns on the genitals, abdomen, and bottom of the feet are normally caused intentionally by a caretaker.[42] These burns are deep and circular and often are grouped together. Abuse is very likely if the burns are located on parts of the body that are normally covered with clothing.[43]

Some skin conditions may simulate intentional burns. Professionals should be aware that it is sometimes difficult to distinguish between burns inflicted as a form of child abuse and certain diseases and medical conditions. The following are two of the more common medical conditions that may be interpreted as intentional burns:

Cutaneous (skin) infections. Some infections may have patterns that resemble deliberate burn injuries. Impetigo or severe diaper rash sometimes resemble a scald injury. A careful medical history, microbiological tests, and observation of the lesion over a two- to three-week period will usually provide sufficient information to determine whether these conditions are child abuse burns or just infections.

Hypersensitivity. A substance in citrus fruits such as limes, when in contact with the skin and exposed to sunlight, may produce a pattern on the skin that resembles a splash burn. An allergic reaction may cause a severe local skin irritation that also may be mistaken for a burn. Finally, certain skin preparations such as topical antiseptics can cause a similar burn appearance. A complete medical history will allow professionals to distinguish between these conditions and child abuse.[44]

While burns are certainly serious and may be life threatening, they are not the most serious form of physical child abuse. Bone fractures constitute another type of child abuse and are discussed below.

Munchausen Syndrome by Proxy

Munchausen syndrome by proxy has recently become a widely discussed type of child abuse.[45] It may be defined as a psychiatric disorder whereby individuals intentionally produce physical symptoms of illness in their children.[46] The DSM-IV now classifies this condition as "Fictitious Disorder by Proxy" and states that the essential feature of this disorder is the deliberate production of feigning of physical or psychological signs or symptoms in another person who is under the individual's care.[47] It is still being researched but has surfaced as a diagnosis in a number of cases.[48]

Introduction

The term *Munchausen syndrome* was coined by Richard Asher in 1951 to describe patients who fabricated histories of illness. These individuals described complex medical histories and often displayed symptoms of the alleged disease. These fabrications invariably led to complex medical interventions and hospitalizations. Asher named this disorder after Baron von Munchausen, born Hieronymous Karl Fredrich von Munchausen, an eighteenth-century German baron and mercenary officer in the Russian cavalry. The baron was famous for dramatizing his "amazing" adventures. Some might describe him as a world-class teller of tall tales. Adult Munchausen is characterized by a person who seeks care from doctors for symptoms that are false or self-induced. These individuals are demanding and often display rage toward the medical caretakers. One authority has characterized their rage as directed toward their parents, whom they perceive abandoned them. The medical caretakers have taken the place of the parents and now receive the brunt of the person's rage and anger.[49]

There is some debate as to who first used the term "Munchausen syndrome by proxy." Money used it in 1976 to describe four children who were so severely abused that they were dwarfed.[50] However, in 1977 Meadow also used the term to describe the more commonly accepted definition of this form of abuse. Meadow examined two children who were being poisoned by a parent. The parent knew what was happening, but encouraged the medical professionals to

FOCUS People v Philips

Many believed that Priscilla Philips was a kind, loving person, a dutiful wife, and a devoted mother to their two sons. She was very intelligent, held a masters degree in social work, and was employed in the Marion County Health and Human Services Department. After the birth of their second son in 1973, Philips became ill and had a hysterectomy in 1975. She became deeply upset that she could not have another child, especially a daughter. She and her husband adopted Tia, who was a Korean infant found on the streets of Seoul.

Tia arrived at the Philips's home in November 1975. Philips promptly took Tia to a pediatrician in San Rafael for examination. Except for a diaper rash and an ear infection, Tia was in good health. Starting in January 1975 and continuing until February 2, 1977, Philips continued to seek medical treatment for her adopted daughter. Tia was admitted to a number of hospitals during this period. She displayed a variety of symptoms, including vomiting, diarrhea, severe dehydration, lethargy and unresponsiveness to stimulation. Tests indicated she was suffering from an extreme level of sodium in her blood. During this time, the doctors performed a variety of diagnostic procedures, including x rays, a lumbar puncture, intravenous injections, a myringotomy (an operation removing fluid from the eardrums), an intestinal biopsy, and a laparotomy to explore for tumors. On February 2, Tia was admitted to a hospital for the last time. She was in critical condition and having generalized seizures. She was unable to eliminate carbon dioxide from her body and began demonstrating abnormal posturing, which indicated damage to her central nervous system. Tia died on February 3, 1977.

Several months after Tia's death, the family adopted another Korean infant, Mindy. On February 3, 1979, Philips took Mindy to the hospital. She was vomiting and suffering from diarrhea. The child was suffering from the same symptoms that affected Tia. At a pediatric staff meeting on February 22, all the doctors agreed it was important to consider the possibility that Mindy was being poisoned. On February 25, the pediatrician on duty took a sample of Mindy's formula and had it analyzed. It was found to contain a sodium content of 448 milliequivalents per liter. The sodium content should have been only 15 milliequivalents per liter. Philips was forbidden to feed Mindy or visit with her without the supervision of a nurse. Mindy was placed in intensive care and recovered quickly.

Priscilla Philips was charged with murdering one of her children and endangering the life of the other. At each of the hospitals the children were admitted to, parents were encouraged to participate in the care of their children by remaining overnight and feeding them. Because of Philips's apparent dedication, she won the admiration, sympathy, and respect of the hospital staff for her obvious intelligence, her frequent presence, and her willingness to help, including administering the formula through an intravenous tube. Friends, acquaintances, and hospital staff testified regarding her reputation for truthfulness and her deep care and concern for her children.

Several experts, including a psychiatrist, testified regarding Munchausen's syndrome by proxy. Dr. Matin Blender stated that the mother is the typical perpetrator and that this person would flourish on the hospital ward. She would seem to blossom in the medical drama of the hospital. The apparent concern, competence, and intelligence of these mothers makes it extremely difficult for doctors to suspect them as the cause of their child's illness.

The jury chose to believe the physicians and other experts and convicted Philips on all counts. The appellate court refused to overturn the conviction.

Source: Adapted from *People v Philips,* 122 Cal. App. 3d 69 (1981).

search for a diagnosis. This diagnostic process was painful and dangerous to the children.[51]

Symptoms

The warning signs of the disorder include repeated hospitalizations and medical evaluations without definitive diagnosis, inappropriate symptoms and/or medical signs that are inconsistent, signs and symptoms that disappear when away from the parent, a parent who welcomes medical tests of the child even if they are painful, increased parental uneasiness as the child recovers, and a parent who is less concerned with the child's health and more concerned about spending time with hospital staff.[52]

More reports continue to surface that reinforce the conclusion that Munchausen Syndrome by Proxy is of continuing concern.[53] Some authorities predict that 10 percent of these child victims will die at the hands of their parents.[54] Professionals in the field must recognize this form of child victimization and respond accordingly.[55]

Fractures

The human body is an incredible machine that is supported by a series of connecting bones. Bones grow at a fast rate in the young and are very flexible, but as we mature these same bones become more brittle. Many students of family violence have experienced a broken bone or know someone who has. Most of the time this is a painful and traumatic experience. Normally, a great deal of force is needed to fracture or break one of the major bones, and while accidents may happen to young children and infants, certain types of fractures are very strong evidence of physical child abuse.

Unfortunately, this type of scenario occurs on a daily basis in medical institutions throughout the United States. Children are brought to walk-in clinics, emergency rooms, and family doctors with serious nonaccidental bone fractures. Certain types of fractures are strongly indicative of child abuse (see the next Practicum).

Types of Fractures

Unlike bruises and burns, fractures are internal and veiled in mystery, in part because of the Latin names associated with the different parts of the body. Professionals must have a basic understanding of the major bones in the body to understand the dynamics of physical child abuse and fractures in particular. The most common fractures in child abuse cases in order of occurrence are:

1. Rib — The rib cage is that portion of the chest that protects the lungs and heart.
2. Humerus — The upper bone of the arm from the elbow to the shoulder.

PRACTICUM

You have been called to the local emergency room by a doctor who is concerned about an eleven-month-old girl. The doctor informs you that the girl's father brought the infant to the emergency room at approximately 7:00 P.M. this evening. The child was crying and her left upper thigh appeared swollen. X rays revealed a spiral fracture of the femur.

The doctor informs you that in her opinion this is a nonaccidental injury that was caused by someone who grasped the child's leg in their hands and twisted it. Based on this information, you approach the father in the waiting room, identify yourself as a representative from the county child protective services agency, and ask if you can talk about the child's injury.

The father informs you that he just returned from a trip, and on arriving at home found his live-in girlfriend very upset and crying. The girlfriend stated that his daughter had injured herself by catching her foot in the bars and falling down inside the crib. The father immediately brought the child to the emergency room. On further questioning, the father indicated that he has been dating the girlfriend, a registered nurse, for five months, and she has never displayed any anger toward the child or himself.

Using this information, what is your next course of action?

3. Femur	The thigh bone. It extends from the hip to the knee and is one of the strongest bones in the body.
4. Tibia	The shinbone. It is the inner and larger bone of the leg between the knee and the ankle.
5. Skull	The bony framework of the head.
6. Hand	That part of the body that is attached to the forearm at the wrist.
7. Ulna	The inner and largest bone of the forearm, located between the wrist and the elbow on the opposite side of the thumb.
8. Radius	The outer and shorter bone of the arm, located between the wrist and the elbow on the same side as the thumb.

Fractures in children may be inflicted by hitting, shaking, or squeezing. Many times a frustrated caretaker will suddenly strike out at a child, and an injury results. As indicated earlier, the abusive parent's explanations of the injury are often not consistent with the medical evidence. This is especially true in the case of fractures.

Anytime a professional suspects child abuse, consideration should be given to a complete x-ray series. Radiologists can detect multiple healed fractures by the presence of calcium deposits around them. Numerous fractures are a strong indication of physical abuse.

Because of certain distinctive characteristics, one particular type of fracture deserves special attention. Spiral fractures in children under the age of three almost always support a diagnosis of physical child abuse. The next section examines this serious form of physical abuse.

Spiral Fractures

Spiral fractures are usually a break in the humerus or femur resulting from a twisting motion. While any adult skier may have experienced a spiral fracture on the ski slopes, it is extremely rare as an accidental injury in children under three years of age. A spiral fracture may occur during skiing when the leg is held motionless and the body twists, causing the femur to break in a turning or twisting motion. Nonaccidental spiral fractures occur when the caretaker grasps the leg or arm at the top and bottom and gives it a powerful twist.

Many times, parents will claim the child's foot was stuck under something and the fall caused the injury. Most medical professionals will discount this explanation because there is insufficient force with that type of fall to cause a spiral fracture in children under three. Also, young children have very limber bones that bend before they break. Other explanations may include jumping off the couch, falling while playing, slipping in the bathtub, and so on. None of these acts are capable of producing the force necessary to twist and break a bone (see Figure 2.4).

It is hard to believe that any adult would intentionally injure a child by striking, squeezing, or twisting the child's body or limbs to the point of causing these types of

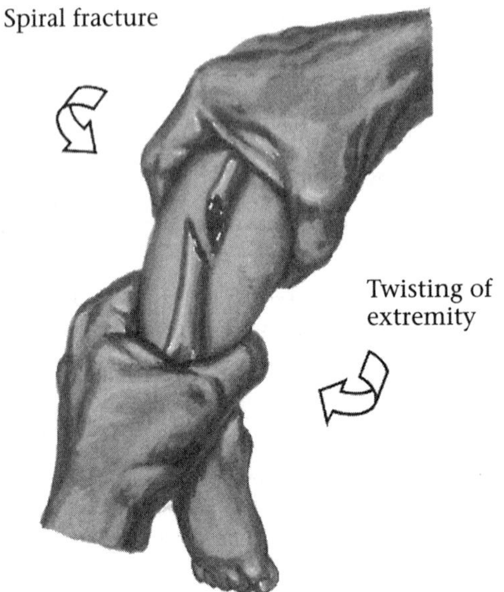

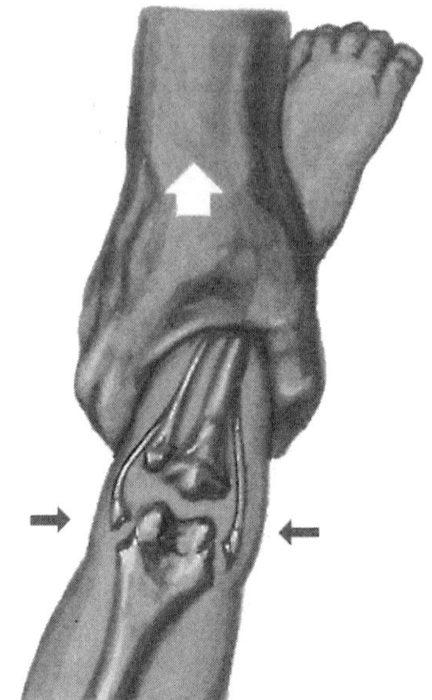

FIGURE 2.4 Skeletal Injury

Source: Plate 10 from Kessler, D.B., and Hyden. "Physical, Sexual, and Emotional Abuse of Children." *Clinical Symposia* 43, no. 1 (1991): 21. © 1991 by Pharmaceuticals Division, CIBA-GEIGY Corporation. Reprinted with permission.

The More Common Types of Physical Child Abuse Fractures

Avulsion of the metaphyseal tips (chip and bucket handle): traction force, jerking, and twisting—most commonly observed on the humerus, radius, and femur.

Rib fractures: blunt force trauma—the child has been hit, punched, thrown, tossed, swung, or pummelled, resulting in compression trauma—the child has received pressure pushing inward on the rib cage or has been squeezed.

Sternum and scapula fractures: direct blows to the body.

Skull fractures: may indicate increased inter-cranial pressure—the child has received blunt-force trauma of some sort to the head.

Clavicle fractures: not necessarily related to physical abuse but should be viewed with suspicion with other findings that may indicate abuse, such as multiple injuries or inconsistent stories by the caretaker.

injuries. However, fractures in young children are a common form of physical abuse. The final type of physical injuries may be the most dangerous form of child abuse.

Head and Internal Injuries

These last two forms of physical child abuse are among the most dangerous and life threatening. Frustrated caretakers often shake, punch, or kick a child with resulting head or internal injuries. Additionally, many times these caretakers postpone seeking medical treatment, which increases the life-threatening nature of the injury.

Head Injuries

Head injuries are the most common cause of morbidity and mortality in abused children.[56] Injuries to the brain are often caused by a direct blow with a blunt instrument such as a fist, stick, or other object. Other children suffer brain injuries as a result of being thrown against the wall or onto the floor (see Figure 2.5).

The whiplash shaken baby syndrome is neurological damage caused by shaking the child violently back and forth. As the child's head is whipped from one direction to another, the brain moves inside the skull and causes the blood vessels inside the skull to stretch and tear. This form of abuse is an accepted medical diagnosis. Shaking a child in this manner can cause permanent brain damage or death.

The brain is covered with three thin membranes (meninges). The membrane next to the brain is the *pia mater.* The next membrane is the *arachnoid.* The outer membrane is called the *dura mater.* The space between the pia mater and the arachnoid contains spinal fluid. Blood veins traverse the subarachnoid area. Violent shaking can cause bleeding in this space. The accumulation of blood in this area is called a *subdural hematoma.*[57] *Subdural hematomas (SDH) occur over the surface of*

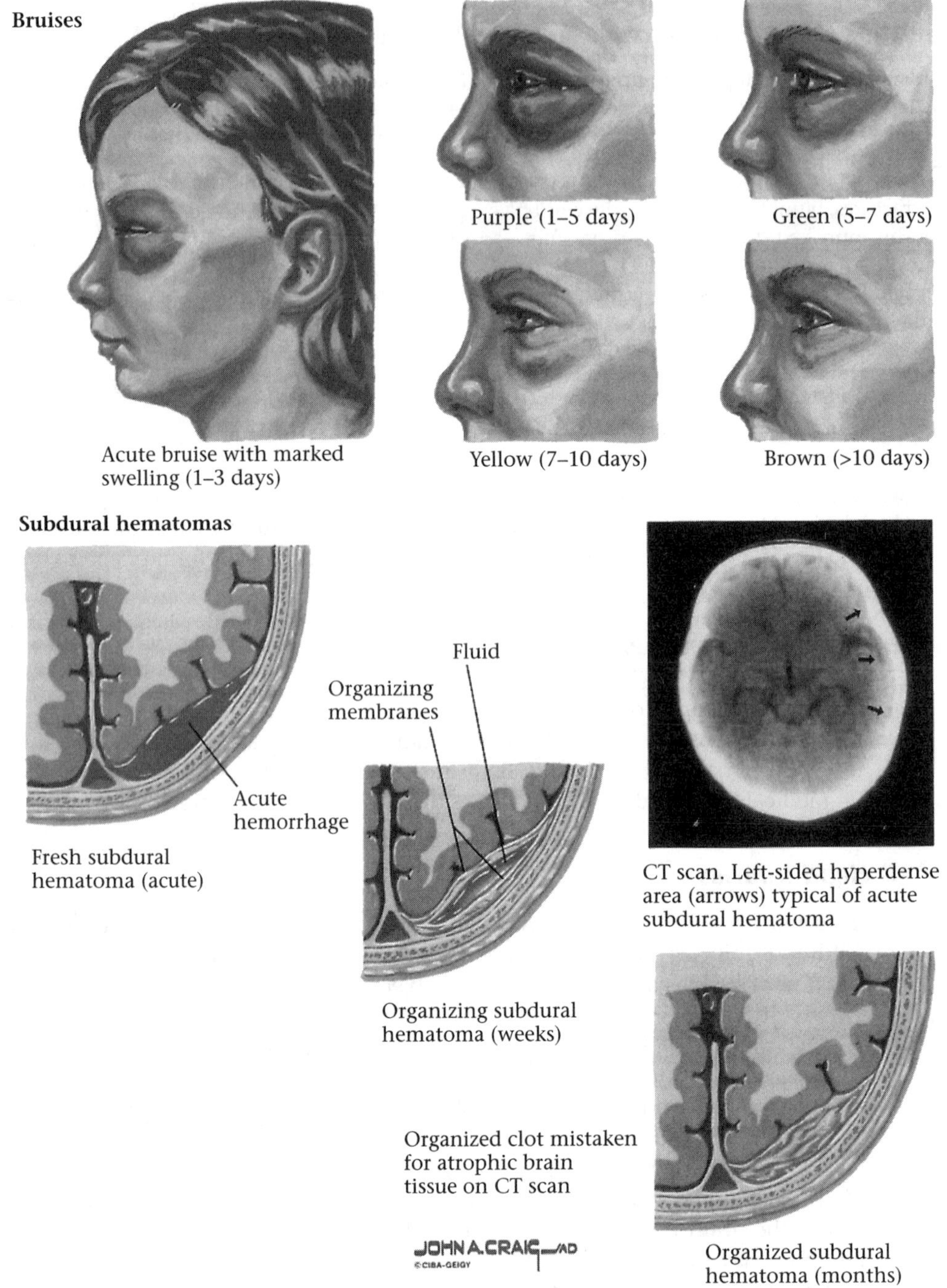

FIGURE 2.5 Staging of Injuries

Source: Plate 1 from Kessler, D.B. and Hyden. "Physical, Sexual, and Emotional Abuse of Children." *Clinical Symposia* 43, no. 1 (1991): 6. © 1991 by Pharmaceuticals Division, CIBA-GEIGY Corporation. Reprinted with permission.

FOCUS The Au Pair Trial

A recent controversial child abuse case points out the conflicting views that sometimes surface in this area of family violence. An au pair is a nanny who cares for children in exchange for living expenses. A teenage British girl, Louise Woodward, became the center of an international media feeding frenzy when she was accused of killing eight-month-old Matthew Eappen.

On February 4, 1997, Louise Woodward called the police and stated that Matthew Eappen was having difficulty breathing. Woodward was an au pair who had been hired by the family to babysit their youngest child. When the paramedics arrived they diagnosed Matthew as suffering from a two-and-a-half-inch skull fracture. The baby spent four days in the intensive care unit of the hospital before he died. In addition to the skull fracture, Matthew also had a month-old wrist fracture.

Woodward was charged with first-degree murder for allegedly shaking Matthew to death. The prosecutors stated that she admitted to shaking the baby and to dropping him on the floor and tossing him on a bed. The prosecutors also asserted that Matthew hit the floor with the force equivalent to being thrown from a second-story window. They concluded by stating that the injuries from the fall and the shaking caused Matthew's death and in Massachusetts that conduct constitutes murder.

The lead defense attorney was Andrew Good who was assisted by Barry Scheck, the forensics expert who helped the O. J. Simpson defense team. They argued two theories: (1) a preexisting medical condition caused the death and (2) Matthew's two-year-old brother inflicted the injuries.

On October 7, 1997, the first day of the trial, the prosecution began to present the evidence against Woodward. This evidence included testimony by the officers who responded to her 911 call and a series of medical experts who testified on direct examination that Matthew died as a result of severe head trauma normally associated with shaken baby syndrome. However, the defense was able to cross-examine the experts in such a manner as to weaken the effect of their testimony. The defense presented a number of character witnesses regarding Woodward's honesty and affection for children. Expert testimony by the defense raised the specter that William died from an earlier injury. Finally, Louise Woodward testified and denied ever shaking Matthew.

Outside the presence of the jury, the prosecution asked for jury instructions that would allow the jury to consider verdicts of murder or voluntary or involuntary manslaughter. The defense objected to these instructions and asked the judge to tell the jury that their options were first- or second-degree-murder or acquittal. The defense motion was based on the assumption that Woodward would stand a greater chance of being convicted if the jury had several options to choose from. Judge Hiller Zobel agreed with the defense's request.

The jury deliberated approximately thirty hours before returning with a second-degree-murder verdict against Louise Woodward. During sentencing, Woodward maintained her innocence, claiming not to know what happened to Matthew. The nineteen-year-old au pair was sentenced to a mandatory life imprisonment with the possibility of parole after fifteen years. The trial and verdict caused an uproar on both sides of the Atlantic as Britishers formed committees to raise funds to help Woodward.

The defense then filed a motion to set aside the verdict or to reduce the charges to manslaughter. On November 10, the judge issued his ruling and reduced Woodward's charge to manslaughter, releasing her with credit for time served.

- Do you agree with the judge's ruling? Why? Why not?
- Much of this case hinged on a battle of expert witnesses. Can you think of any other way to handle this type of child abuse?
- Who else could have injured Matthew? On the basis of your reading of the next section, who are the possible suspects? Matthew's two-year-old brother? His mother? His father?

the brain and are caused by the tearing of the bridging vessels between the brain and the dura. The acceleration–deceleration and rotational forces associated with trauma are the major causes for SDH development.[58] Bleeding may also occur within the other membranes surrounding the skull. Subarachnoid hematoma (SAH) is bleeding between the arachnoid and the pia mater. Epidural hematoma (EDH) is a collection of blood between the skull and the dura.[59]

Skull fractures result from sharp blows to the head or from throwing the child against a wall or onto the floor. In a depressed fracture, bone fragments are pressed into the skull cavity. Caretakers often claim that this type of severe head injury resulted from the child falling off the couch or bed. This type of story should be viewed with suspicion because medical research indicates that a life-threatening injury to the head requires at least a fifteen-foot fall.[60]

Two less serious forms of head injury to children are concussions and cerebral contusions. *A concussion is a mild form of diffuse brain injury associated with the acceleration–deceleration of shaking the child's head. A cerebral contusion is the bruising of the brain without puncture or tearing of the pia membrane.* Contusions are caused by the absorption of energy into the cerebral tissue from a blow to the head.

Internal Injuries

Chest and abdominal injuries are common physical child abuse injuries (see Figure 2.6). Rib fractures may be caused by grasping a child around the chest and shaking the child. Additionally, the caretaker may strike a child with his or her fist or a blunt object.

Abdominal injuries are caused by hitting a child in the stomach area. This striking may be a kick, punch, or blow from a blunt object. As with other forms of physical child abuse, these injuries usually result from a frustrated caretaker who lashes out at the child.

The previous discussion briefly examined head and internal injuries. Care should be taken that medical assistance is obtained as soon as possible whenever a child is suspected of being physically abused. Many of these injuries are not visible to the naked eye but, if left untreated, may become life threatening.

FOCUS How Much Force Is Necessary?

Internal injuries are not caused by simply spanking or slapping the child. A significant amount of force is necessary to rupture the liver or spleen, cause intestinal perforation, or inflict serious damage to the pancreas. Children who fall from their cribs do not sustain these types of injuries.

In one case involving internal injuries that resulted in a child's death, a medical expert testified that the force necessary to inflict the injuries was ". . . a concentrated force comparable to what . . . would result from a fifty or sixty mile per hour head-on collision." (See *State v Johnson,* 135 Wis. 2d 453, 400 N.W. 2d 502 [Ct. App. 1986] at 505.)

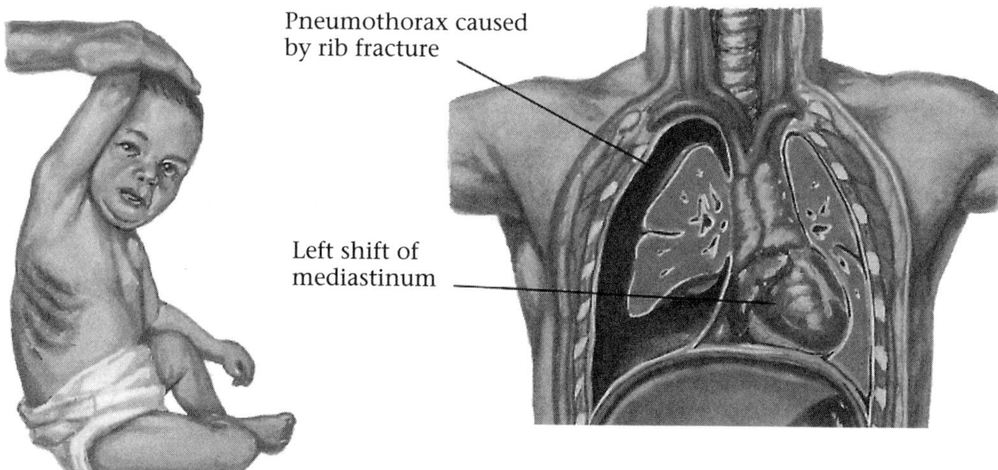

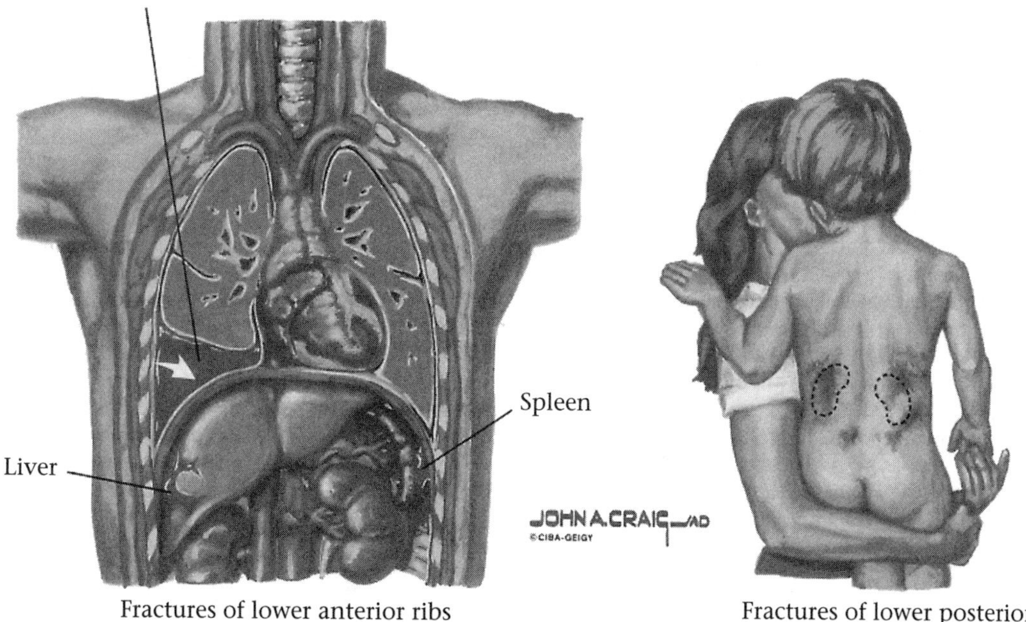

FIGURE 2.6 Chest and Abdominal Injuries

Source: Chest Injury, Plate 8 from Kessler, D.B., and Hyden. "Physical, Sexual, and Emotional Abuse of Children." *Clinical Symposia* 43, no. 1 (1991): 18. © 1991 by Pharmaceuticals Division, CIBA-GEIGY Corporation. Reprinted with permission.

Summary

This chapter discussed the various types of physical child abuse. We cannot prevent all forms of child abuse, so we must be alert to their existence and understand how and why they occur. Additionally, professionals need a basic understanding of the different types of physical abuse and how they are inflicted. We have won half the battle if we are aware that physical child abuse occurs in all segments of our society and stand ready to diagnose it when we observe it. On the other hand, we must be willing to accept reasonable explanations for injuries. Children are active human beings—they will trip, fall, and run into objects. Our goal is to be able to distinguish between a normal injury and a nonaccidental one. This ability may save a child's life.

Key Terms

Battered child syndrome—a medicolegal term that describes the diagnosis of a medical expert based on scientific studies that indicate that when a child suffers certain types of continuing injuries, those injuries were not caused by accidental means.

physical child abuse—any act that results in a nonaccidental physical injury by a person who has care, custody, or control of a child.

Caffey's syndrome—in the absence of a skeletal disease, children who have both subdural hematomas and long-bone fractures are the victims of trauma.

Psychopathological model—stresses the characteristics of the abuser as the primary cause of abuse. The abuser's personality predisposes the abuser to injure the child.

Interactional model—views child abuse as a result of a dysfunctional system.

Environmental–sociological–cultural model—views child abuse as a result of stresses in society.

immersion burns—burns caused by holding the child in hot water.

pattern burns—burns caused by holding or pressing a portion of the child's body against a hot object.

spiral fractures—usually a break in the humerus or femur resulting from a twisting motion.

Whiplash shaken baby syndrome—neurological damage caused by shaking the child violently back and forth.

subdural hematoma (SDH)—tearing of the bridging vessels between the brain and the dura occurring over the surface of the brain.

concussion—a mild form of diffuse brain injury associated with the acceleration–deceleration of shaking the child's head.

cerebral contusion—the bruising of the brain without puncture or tearing of the pia membrane.

Discussion Questions

1. If a child is injured and the physician is uncertain of whether the injury is physical child abuse, should he or she alert the police? Why? Why not? Would it make any difference if the physician knew the parents and had been to their home for a social event?
2. What is the most serious form of physical child abuse? Why?

3. If a child has been seriously injured by his mother, should that child ever be returned to the mother's care? Why?

4. If a mother has a criminal record of physically abusing her two young children, should a judge have the power to order her to take birth control measures so as to prevent the birth of another child? Why? Why not?

5. Should a convicted child abuser be required to inform all social partners of his crimes? What if he is dating someone who has small children and his date asks him to watch the children while she goes to work for the day?

Suggested Readings

DePanfilis, D., and M. K. Salus. *A Coordinated Response to Child Abuse and Neglect* U.S. Dept. of Health and Human Services (DHHS Pub. No. [ACF] 92-30362) Washington, D.C., 1992.

Gerber, G., C. Ross, and E. Zigler, eds. *Child Abuse: An Agenda for Action.* (Oxford University Press, New York) 1980.

Gil, D. G. *Violence Against Children: Physical Child Abuse in the United States.* (Harvard University Press, Cambridge, Massachusetts) 1973.

Van Hasselt, Vincent B., et al., eds. *Handbook of Family Violence.* (Plenum Press, New York) 1988.

Helfer, R., and C. H. Kempe, eds. *The Battered Child,* 2d ed. (University of Chicago Press, Chicago) 1974.

Justice, B., and R. Justice. *The Abusing Family.* (Human Services Press, New York) 1976.

Koster, K., ed. *Child Abuse: Opposing Viewpoints.* (Greenhaven Press, Inc., San Diego) 1994.

Martin, H. P., ed. *The Abused Child.* (Ballinger, Cambridge, Massachusetts) 1976.

Seidel, H., J. Ball, J. Dains, and G. Benedict, eds. *Mosby's Guide to Physical Examination.* 2d ed. (Mosby Year Book, New York) 1991.

Sorel, N. C. *Ever Since Eve: Personal Reflections on Childbirth.* (Oxford University Press, New York) 1984.

Tardieu, A. *Etude medico-legale sur les services et mauvais traitements exerces sur des enfants.* (Originally published in 1860.) S. M. Smith, ed. *The Battered Child Syndrome.* (Butterworths, London) 1975.

Thelan, L., J. Davie, and L. Urden. *Textbook of Critical Care Nursing.* (C. V. Mosby Company, St. Louis, Missouri) 1990.

Tower, C. C. *Understanding Child Abuse and Neglect.* 2d ed. (Allyn & Bacon, Needham Heights, Massachusetts) 1993.

Endnotes

1. Tardieu, A. *Etude medico-legale sur les services et mauvais traitements exerces sur des enfants,* (Originally published in 1860.) S. M. Smith, ed. *The Battered Child Syndrome.* (Butterworths, London) 1975.
2. Caffey, J. "Multiple Injuries in the Long Bones of Infants Suffering from Chronic Subdural Hematoma." *American Journal of Roentgenology* 56, 1946, pp. 163–173.
3. Kempe, C. H., F. N. Silverman, B. F. Steele, W. Droegemueller, and H. K. Silver. "The Battered Child Syndrome." *Journal of the American Medical Association* 118, 1962, pp. 105–112.
4. Ibid., p. 23.
5. See *State v Byrd,* 309 N.C. 132, 305 S.E. 2d 724, 729 (1983).
6. See, for example, Van Hasselt, Vincent B., et al., eds. *Handbook of Family Violence.* (Plenum Press, New York) 1988.
7. Radbill, S. "A History of Child Abuse and Infanticide." In R. Helfer, and C. H. Kempe,

eds. *The Battered Child.* 2d ed. (University of Chicago Press, Chicago) 1974.

8. Potter, C. F. "Infanticides." In M. Leach, ed. *Dictionary of Folklore, Mythology and Legend.* Volume 1. (Funk & Wagnalls, New York) 1949.
9. Sorel, N. C. *Ever Since Eve: Personal Reflections on Childbirth.* (Oxford University Press, New York) 1984.
10. American Association for Protecting Children, Inc. *Highlights of Official Child Neglect and Abuse Reporting, 1983.* American Humane Association.
11. Uviler, R. "Save Them from Their Saviors: The Constitutional Rights in the Family." In G. Gerber, C. Ross, and E. Zigler eds. *Child Abuse: An Agenda for Action.* (Oxford University Press, New York) 1980, pp. 147–155.
12. This material is adapted from *Current Trends in Child Abuse Reporting and Fatalities: The Results of the 1996 Annual Fifty State Survey* (National Committee to Prevent Child Abuse, (Chicago, Illinois, April, 1997.) Reprinted with permission.
13. U.S. Department of Justice, Bureau of Justice Statistics. *Criminal Victimization in the United States, 1987.* (Government Printing Office, Washington, D.C., 1989). See table 4.
14. Rondell, P., and J. Parker, "Factitious Disorder by Proxy and the Abuse of a Child with Autism." *Educational Psychology in Practice* 13(1), April 1997, p. 39.
15. Tower, C. C. *Understanding Child Abuse and Neglect.* 2d ed. (Allyn & Bacon, Boston) 1993.
16. Justice, B., and R. Justice. *The Abusing Family.* (Human Services Press, New York) 1976, p. 37.
17. See Delsordo, J. D. "Protective Casework for Abused Children." *Children* 10, 1963, pp. 213–218.
18. Martin, H. P., ed. *The Abused Child,* (Ballinger, Cambridge, Massachusetts) 1976.
19. Lynch, M. "Risk Factors in the Child: A Study of Abused Children and Their Siblings." In H. P. Martin, ed. *The Abused Child* (Ballinger, Cambridge, Massachusetts) 1976, pp. 43–56.
20. See Ammerman, R. T., V. B. Van Hasselt, and M. Hersen. "Maltreatment in Handicapped Children: A Critical Review." *Journal of Family Violence.* (3), 1988, pp. 53–72.
21. Loeber, R., D. K. Felton, and J. Reid. "A Social Learning Approach to the Reduction of Coercive Processes in Child Abuse Families: A Molecular Analysis." *Advances in Behavior Research and Therapy* 6, 1984, pp. 29–45.
22. Problems with reported cases of child abuse range from reporting bias—poor and minority families are more likely to be reported as maltreating to the position that reported cases are only a portion of the total incidents of child abuse. For a discussion of reporting bias, see R. L. Hampton, and E. H. Newberger, "Child Abuse Incidence and Reporting by Hospitals: Significance of Severity, Class, and Race." *American Journal of Public Health.* (75) 1885, pp. 56–60. For a review of the issue regarding underreporting, see National Center on Child Abuse and Neglect, *Study Findings: Study of National Incidence and Prevalence of Child Abuse and Neglect: 1988* (U.S. Department of Health and Human Services, Washington D.C.) 1988.
23. American Association for Protecting Children. *Highlights of Official Child Neglect and Abuse Reporting 1986.* (American Humane Society, Denver) 1988.
24. National Center on Child Abuse and Neglect. *Study Findings: National Study of the Incidence and Severity of Child Abuse and Neglect* DHHS Publication No. OHDS 81–30325. GPO (Washington D.C.) 1981, and National Center on Child Abuse and Neglect. *Study Findings: National Study of the Incidence and Severity of Child Abuse and Neglect: 1988.* (U.S. Department of Health and Human Services Washington, D.C.) 1988.
25. Gil, D. G. *Violence against Children: Physical Child Abuse in the United States.* (Harvard University Press, Cambridge, Massachusetts) 1973.
26. Gelles, R. J., and M. A. Straus. "Is Violence toward Children Increasing? A Comparison of 1975 and 1985 National Survey Rates." *Journal of Interpersonal Violence* 2, 1987, pp. 212–222.
27. Finkel, M. A., and L. R. Ricci. "Documentation and Preservation of Visual Evidence in Child Abuse." *Child Maltreatment* 2(4), 322 (Nov. 1977).
28. *State v Jones,* 59 Wash. App. 744, 801 P. 2d 263 (1990).
29. See *Estelle v McGuire,* 112 S. Ct. 475 (1991).

30. In *People v Turner,* 193 Ill. App. 152, 549 N.E. 2d 1309, 1313 (1990), the defendant first stated to the paramedics that the child was not breathing as a result of a fall. She later changed her story to indicate she had put the child to bed and upon checking her found that she was not breathing.
31. Schmitt. "The Child with Nonaccidental Trauma." In R. Kempe, and R. Helfer, eds. *The Battered Child* 4th ed. (University of Chicago Press, Chicago) 1987, p. 178.
32. Supra, p. 186.
33. *State v Jones,* 59 Wash. App. 744, 801 P.2d 263 (1990), and Schmitt, p. 180.
34. Schmitt, p. 186.
35. Coagulation is the process of clotting. Coagulation of the blood depends on the presence of several substances. For further information, see C. L. Thomas, ed. *Taber's Cyclopedic Medical Dictionary* 14th ed. (F. A. Davis Company, Philadelphia) 1981, pp. 302–303.
36. Seiden, H., J. Ball, J. Dains, and G. Benedict, eds. *Mosby's Guide to Physical Examination.* 2d ed. (Mosby-Year Book, New York) 1991, p. 115.
37. Showers and Garsion. "Burn Abuse: A Four-Year Study." *Journal of Trauma* 28 (1581), 1988.
38. Adapted from Bilchik, S. *Burn Injuries in Child Abuse* (U.S. Department of Justice, Washington D.C. May, 1997)
39. Kessler and Hyden. "Physical, Sexual, and Emotional Abuse of Children." *Clinical Symposia* 43 (1), 10:1991.
40. *State v Church.* 99 N.C. App. 647, 394 S.E. 2d 468, 470 (1990).
41. Feldman. "Child Abuse by Burning." In R. Helfer, and R. Kemp, eds., *The Battered Child,* 4th ed. (University of Chicago Press, Chicago) 1987.
42. See *State v Williams,* 541 N.W. 2d 886, 888 (Minn. Ct. App. 1990) for a case dealing with cigarette burns to a child.
43. Feldman. "Child Abuse by Burning." In R. Helfer, and R. Kempe, eds. *The Battered Child.* 4th ed. (University of Chicago Press, Chicago) 1987, pp. 205–206.
44. Adapted from Bilchik, S. *Burn Injuries in Child Abuse* (U.S. Department of Justice, Washington D.C., May, 1997).
45. See, e.g., Jones, D. P. "The Syndrome of Munchausen by Proxy," 18 *Child Abuse and Neglect* 769 (1994).
46. See Randall, P. and J. Parker. "Factitious Disorder by Proxy and the Abuse of a Child with Autism." *Educational Psychology in Practice* 13(1) (April, 1997).
47. See *Diagnostic Statistical Manual, Volume IV* (American Psychological Association, Washington D.C., 1994), p. 725.
48. Kudsk, E. J., and J. A. Nolan. "Munchausen Syndrome by Proxy: The Case for Adult Victims," paper presented at the Annual Meeting of Academy of Criminal Justice Sciences, Boston, Massachusetts (March, 1995).
49. Schreier, H. A. "The Perversion of Mothering: Munchausen Syndrome by Proxy," *Bulletin of the Menninger Clinic* 56(4), 1992, pp. 421–437.
50. Money, J. "Munchausen's Syndrome by Proxy: Update," *Journal of Pediatric Psychology,* November 1986, p. 583, discussing an earlier article that appeared in the *Bulletin of the American Academy of Psychiatry and the Law* in 1976.
51. Meadow, R. "Munchausen Syndrome by Proxy: The Hinterland of Child Abuse," *The Lancet* (1977) p. 351.
52. Boros, S. J., and L. C. Brubaker. "Munchausen Syndrome by Proxy,' *FBI Law Enforcement Bulletin* (June, 1992) p. 16.
53. See Bilchik, S. *Child Neglect and Munchausen Syndrome by Proxy,* (U.S. Department of Justice, Washington, D.C. September, 1996).
54. Ibid., p. 20.
55. For an excellent discussion of this form of abuse, see Parnell, T. F., and D. O. Day, eds., *Munchausen by Proxy Syndrome,* (Sage Publications, Thousand Oaks, California) 1988.
56. Kessler and Hyden. "Physical, Sexual, and Emotional Abuse of Children." *Clinical Symposia* 43 (1), 1991.
57. For an excellent discussion of this type of injury, see Thelan, L., J. Davie, and L. Urden. *Textbook of Critical Care Nursing.* (C. V. Mosby Company, St. Louis) 1990, pp. 543–549.
58. Ibid., p. 546.
59. Ibid., p. 545.
60. Chadwick, Chin, Salerno, Landsver, and Kitchen. "Deaths from Falls in Children: How Far Is Fatal?" *Journal of Trauma* 31 (1353) 1991.

3

CHILD SEXUAL ABUSE

Chapter Outline

Learning Objectives

After reading this chapter, you should be able to discuss the following concepts:

- The definition of child sexual abuse and the various types of activities that are included within the definition.
- The characteristics of both the abuser and the abused.
- Behavioral, physical, and medical indicators of child sexual abuse.

- The taboo of incest.
- The various consequences of child sexual abuse.

Introduction

Child sexual abuse is one of the most emotional topics in the field of family violence. Repeated media stories report accounts of both long-term and situational incidents of children being sexually abused by family members, caretakers, or strangers. Unlike the definition for child physical abuse or neglect, the definition of child sexual abuse is relatively easy to understand. What is hard to accept is why a middle-aged adult would want to engage in sexual activities with a prepubescent child.

This chapter examines several major aspects of child sexual abuse. As with the other forms of child abuse, this is not a pleasant topic. However, child sexual abuse is a harsh reality, and professionals must understand what it is, know the factors—both physical and behavioral—that may indicate its existence, and be familiar with the procedures utilized to prove it occurred.

The U.S. population has a widespread interest in child abuse. However, the true magnitude of this problem is difficult to establish.[1] The general agreement among both scholars and professionals in the field is that the incidence of child abuse reporting is understated.[2] Estimates on the number of child sexual abuse cases vary from source to source. Finkelhor's 1979 study of 796 college students indicated that 19 percent of females and 9 percent of males had been subjected to sexual abuse as children.[3] A later study by Finkelhor of 521 Boston parents indicated that 15 percent of females and 6 percent of males had been sexually abused by the age of sixteen.[4] Russell's survey of 930 San Francisco women found that 28 percent had been victims of child sexual abuse before the age of fourteen.[5] In 1985, the *Los Angeles Times* conducted a random survey of 2,627 adults across the United States. The survey revealed that 27 percent of women and 16 percent of survey participants had been molested as children. The total percentage (combining men and women) for those who suffered child sexual abuse was 22 percent.[6] In 1991, researchers came to the conclusion that as many as 10 to 15 percent of all boys and 20 to 25 percent of all girls had experiences of at least one instance of sexual abuse prior to the age of eighteen.[7]

Rape in America, which was published by the National Victim Center, indicates that sexual violence occurs at a much higher rate than previously expected.[8] This study will be discussed in more detail in Chapter 12 dealing with women and sexual violence, but it illustrates that sexual violence is still a major problem in the United States. On the basis of this study, the National Victim Center estimates there are at least 12.1 million women in the United States who have been subjected to sexual violence as a child or an adult.

Using some of these statistics we can project the possible prevalence of child sexual abuse in the United States today.[9] The most conservative estimate indicates 10 percent of all women and 2 percent of all males have been molested. The most recent census indicates a population of 60 million minors within the United States. Using these figures, a projection can be made that there are 210,000 incidents of child sexual abuse that occur every year. Comparing this number with the 44,700 cases reported to professionals clearly indicates a lack of reporting of this type of abuse.[10]

Although the figures may vary from study to study regarding the types and incidences of child sexual abuse, there is some agreement among researchers that the following classification of offenders is a valid estimate.

Strangers as the offender	approximately 8–10 percent
Family members as the offender	approximately 47 percent
Acquaintances as the offender	approximately 40 percent[11]

Child sexual abuse is an unfortunate fact of life. One of the best ways to deal with it is to understand what it is and who the perpetrators and victims are of this form of child maltreatment. The following sections will examine these issues.

Definitions

Child sexual abuse is sexual exploitation or sexual activities with a child under circumstances which indicate that the child's health or welfare is harmed or threatened.[12] This definition includes inappropriate sexual activities between children and adults. The inappropriate behavior may be between family members or between a stranger and the victim. *Intrafamilial sexual abuse includes incest and refers to any type of exploitative sexual contact occurring between relatives. Extrafamilial sexual abuse refers to exploitative sexual contact with perpetrators who may be known to the child (neighbors, babysitters, live-in partners) or unknown to the child.*[13]

One of the major problems with this definition is the requirement that the child be harmed. From a legal perspective, harm to the victim is not an element of the crime of child sexual abuse. If certain physical acts occur, the crime is complete. In criminal proceedings it is not necessary to prove that the perpetrator intended to harm or actually harmed the child. However, this definition is useful for exploring the consequences of child sexual abuse, and retaining the requirement of an injury to the child will allow for such a discussion.

The following acts are examples of child sexual abuse: exposing one's sexual organs to the child, voyeurism, touching the sex organs of the child, mutual or self-masturbation with the child, oral sex, intercourse, and anal sex. In addition, allowing the child to view or participate in pornographic or obscene movies is considered child abuse.

Child sexual abuse may be distinguished from rape in that the perpetrator may use a variety of different "techniques" to achieve the objective of sexual gratification. Rape normally involves sexual acts as the result of force or fear. Child abuse offenders may also use force or fear. However, they also employ other pressures or influences to accomplish their goal. These actions include manipulation of the child (psychologically isolating the child from other loved ones), coercion (using adult authority or power on the child), force (restraining the child), and threats or fear (informing the child that if he tells, no one will love him).[14]

The Abuser and the Abused

This section deals with who the abusers are rather than why they abuse. Scholars agree that at this stage in our research and understanding of child sexual abuse, the latter question cannot be answered. However, studying the abusers may lead to an understanding of why these acts occur.

Numerous studies indicate that child abusers do not fit any stereotype.[15] The common perception that all abusers are ugly old men who prey on children is simply not true. Nevertheless, researchers have attempted to find a common thread or factor that connects all child abusers. They have examined the degree of violence, the age of the victim, the age and education of the offender, preoffense social and occupational adjustment, alcohol abuse, physiological responses of offenders, and aggression. Conte reviewed the literature in this area and described the following factors that were considered important when evaluating the characteristics of abusers.[16]

1. Measurement of sexual arousal is essential to discriminate between various categories of sexual offenders.
2. The role of sexual fantasies with children is important because of its connection to deviant sexuality. Fantasies about children coupled with masturbation during these fantasies serves as a form of rehearsal for contact with the victims.
3. The types of rationalizations used by adult offenders who have sexual relations with children is a crucial point. These rationalizations commonly take the form of statements or thoughts to the effect that "A child who does not resist really wants to have sex" or "Having sex with a child is the best way to teach her about sex" or "You become closer to the child when you share sex with him."

In addition to the various forms of psychopathology present in child abuse, Finkelhor established four factors involved in sexual abuse.[17] He called this theory the *Four Preconditions Model of Sexual Abuse. This model establishes preconditions that create a personal and social context for expressing sexually abusive behaviors.* These preconditions include the motivation to sexually abuse, overcoming internal inhibitors, factors predisposing to overcome external inhibitors, and factors predisposing to overcome the child's resistance.

Precondition I: Motivation to Sexually Abuse

The motivation to sexually abuse a child includes emotional congruence, sexual arousal, and blockage. Emotional congruence involves satisfying an emotional need by relating to the child in a sexual manner. Sexual arousal occurs when the child becomes the source of sexual gratification. Blockage occurs when other alternative forms of sexual satisfaction are not present, not available, or less satisfying. The motivation to abuse a child is based upon individual as well as sociological grounds. Individual explanations include the need for power and control, unconscious reenactment of a childhood trauma, and biological abnormality. Sociological reasons include the male-oriented society that demands male dominance, child pornography, and erotic portrayal of children in the media.

Precondition II: Overcoming Internal Inhibitors

The perpetrator must overcome internal controls that would prevent him from sexually abusing the child. Some of these controls are overcome by the use of alcohol or drugs, an existing psychosis, the inability of the offender to identify with the needs of the victim, weak criminal sanctions against offenders, and child pornography.

Precondition III: Factors Predisposing to Overcome External Inhibitors

These conditions are outside the control of the perpetrator. These factors include social situations such as the type and amount of supervision a child receives, the lack of a parental figure close to or protective of the victim, and unusual sleeping or living arrangements. Additionally, the lack of social support for mothers, barriers to equality, and erosion of the family's social networks contribute to the ability of the offender to overcome external inhibitors.

Precondition IV: Factors Predisposing to Overcome Child's Resistance

These factors concern the victim's ability to resist the sexual advances. The child may be emotionally insecure, deprived, or lacking in sexual experience or knowledge. The victim may feel powerless or a situation of trust may exist between the offender and the victim.

There is no distinct or clear answer as to why adults sexually abuse children. The offender may commit these acts for a variety of reasons. Both psychological forces and the social structure enter into this complex mesh that allows individuals to engage in sexual activities with young children.

Traditionally, the abuser is thought of as a male and the victim as a young female. However, studies indicate that boys may be the victims of sexual abuse at a higher rate than previously thought. One study in San Jose, California, indicates a rise in the reported incidents of sexual abuse of boys.[18] Between 1970 and 1975, only 5 percent of the reported victims of sex abuse were boys. However, this figure rose to over 22 percent by 1986.[19]

Boys who are victims of abuse may not report the acts or incidents for several reasons. First, boys may not want to be viewed as victims or sissies or perceived as weak. Second, boys normally do not have to account for their movements and are given greater degrees of freedom and less protection through supervision, and parents, therefore, may not notice any unusual behavior that may indicate sexual abuse. And third, our stereotypes lead us to look for abuse with girls, not with boys.[20]

The high-risk years for child sexual abuse range between four and nine years old.[21] At the former age, children are naive and sexually curious, and by the time they reach nine, their loyalty, desire to please, and trust of adults are traits manipulated by offenders to accomplish their goal of molestation. Generally, sexual abuse is terminated by the time the child reaches fourteen. This termination occurs because the victim may threaten the offender with disclosure or engage in activities such as running away that would lead authorities to suspect abuse.[22]

Contrary to popular belief, the actual physical attractiveness of the female child has little if anything to do with whether the child becomes a victim of molestation. Additionally, the seductiveness of the female child is now discounted as a contributing factor in sexual abuse situations. While dispelling certain stereotypes about female victims, there needs to be more research on the issue of male victims. Two scholars have isolated at least one factor that may clarify why certain male children are molested. Finkelhor and Porter suggest that less assertive boys are more likely to be victims of sexual abuse.[23]

Children are at a higher risk of sexual abuse if they are socially isolated, left alone, and unsupervised. If the mother is absent from the home for long periods, either because of work or other commitments, the child is more likely to be abused. Some authorities theorize that the presence of a stepfather in the home adds to the risk of sexual abuse.[24] These factors establish situations that make the child vulnerable to the perpetrator.

Professionals are still researching and learning about the characteristics of those who abuse and who or why certain children are chosen for abuse over others. Misconceptions and stereotypes have contributed to the confusion in this very important area. Although researchers do not have all the answers to why children are abused and who commits child sexual abuse, they have developed a fairly comprehensive list of factors that may indicate whether a child is the victim of sexual abuse.

Indications of Sexual Abuse

Victims of child sexual abuse may disclose the fact that they have been sexually abused at different times during their lives, and this disclosure may take many forms. Early warnings of sexual abuse may take the form of indirect statements made by the child or acted out in play. These signals can be subtle such as a child describing a sexual event without identifying himself as the victim or naming the offender.[25]

Children may also make direct statements to their friends or to adults about being molested. Children sometimes say odd things in order to observe the adult's reaction before proceeding any further. These odd or partial statements are designed to test the water before saying anything else. Many times the victim is told by the perpetrator that bad things will happen if the abuse is ever discussed. If the adult fails to pick up on the signals or reacts negatively to the statements, the child may not proceed any further. Refer to the next section for a list of behavioral changes or patterns that are most commonly associated with child sexual abuse.

Behavioral Indicators

Although not all behavioral patterns will be present in every sexual abuse case, any professional who observes these symptoms should be alert to the possibility of child sexual abuse. Once alerted to this situation, the professional should begin a careful inquiry into the facts.

Physical Indicators

Physical characteristics may suggest that a child has been, or currently is, a victim of sexual abuse. However, lack of any physical findings only means that the acts did not leave any physical evidence. A child, depending on his or her age, may be the victim of an ongoing series of sexual acts and not exhibit any physical signs. The following is a list of physical signs of sexual abuse:

Difficulty in walking or sitting
Torn, stained, or bloody underwear
Genital/anal itching, pain, swelling, or burning
Genital/anal bruises or bleeding
Frequent urinary tract or yeast infections
Pain on urination
Poor sphincter control
Venereal disease
Pregnancy
Chronic unexplained sore throats
Frequent psychosomatic illnesses
Loss of appetite[26]

Knowledge of physical indicators of possible child sexual abuse is especially important for those professionals who come into contact with the child on a daily basis. School personnel, including nurses and teachers, should always be alert to the message these symptoms send.

Medical Indicators

Although medical evidence may not be present in all cases, when such facts are present they provide strong evidence of abuse. As indicated, simply because there is no physical evidence or injuries, sexual abuse cannot automatically be ruled out. Testimony from physicians can assist the jury in understanding this fact.

Behavioral Indicators of Child Sexual Abuse

Fear: The most common initial reaction. For that reason, the child who expresses extreme fear (and/or anxiety) for no apparent reason should be viewed with caution.

Inability to trust: Because of the betrayal that the child has suffered at the hands of an adult and because the child has been made to feel helpless by the adult, the child becomes severely limited in his ability to trust. This deficit of trust may impair his future relationships in many ways.

Anger and hostility: Children are rarely able to express their anger toward an assailant, and as a result it is often displaced onto others. However, in some cases (usually those that involve extrafamilial abuse) the child does find an opportunity to release her anger toward the abuser.

Inappropriate sexual behavior: Sexually abused children may attempt to show or tell others what happened by doing or acting out what was done to them. A child may also attempt to gain a sense of mastery over the trauma by repetition of the events in a symbolic form. For example, child victims of sexual assault (especially male victims) may attempt to undo their feelings of helplessness by doing to other children what was done to them—a manifestation of "identification with the aggressor."

Depression: Because of not being able to express their feelings of helpless rage for what was done to them, abused children may become clinically depressed, showing signs of emotional constriction, flat or bland affect, and so forth.

Guilt or shame: Since young children are by nature egocentric, they may mistakenly accept responsibility for other people's actions toward them; this tendency, when added to the molester's attempts to shift blame onto the victim, often results in the child's experiencing intense feelings of guilt for what has happened.

Problems in school: A sudden drop in school performance may be a symptom of sexual abuse; even so, in some cases performance does not falter because the child may find security in the structure of the school environment.

Somatic complaints: Many sexually abused children internalize their trauma and may demonstrate varied somatic disorders such as headaches or stomach aches that have no organic cause.

Sleep disturbances: Frequently, sexually abused children experience difficulty in sleeping, fear of sleeping alone, nightmares, or even night terrors.

Eating disorders: Some victims of sexual abuse exhibit eating disorders as evidenced by a sudden marked increase or decrease in appetite or the hoarding of food. A clinician should be especially observant when treating anorexia or bulimia in adolescents because those symptoms may mask trauma caused by sexual assault.

Phobic or avoidant behavior: Child victims may display a wide range of avoidant behaviors from agoraphobia to school phobia to the fear of someone who even slightly resembles the molester in appearance.

Regressive behavior: Children may become regressive as a result of sexual trauma. Hence, cases of regression that are not readily explained should be checked carefully for possible evidence of abuse.

Self-destructive behavior or accident proneness: These may become outlets for the child's feelings of guilt and shame. Many molested children feel damaged or worthless, and their acting out takes this form.

Running away: Older children and adolescents may attempt to cope with sexual abuse by running away from home.

Source: Adapted from Everstine, D., and L. Everstine. *Sexual Trauma in Children and Adolescents* (Brunner/Mazel, New York) pp. 17–18. Reprinted with permission from Brunner/Mazel, Inc.

Most authorities agree that medical evidence of sexual abuse is found in only 10 to 50 percent of all cases.[27] In one study, 382 children were evaluated for sexual abuse. Seventy-one percent did not display any medical signs or symptoms of abuse. This 71 percent figure included 48 percent who had a history of sexual penetration.[28]

Some medical scholars now believe that child sexual abuse is a recognized medical diagnosis.[29] For a physician to come to this conclusion, a complete medical evaluation is recommended. This evaluation should include a medical history, physical examination, and laboratory tests.

A medical history includes the chief complaint, history of the present illness, past medical history, family history, psychosocial history, and review of the body systems. For children, this information is many times obtained from adults. The medical history allows the physician to exclude or confirm a diagnosis. The history may also indicate if the offender still has access to the child, thus indicating whether the child is still at risk. The history assists the physician in determining what laboratory tests to order.

The physical examination should cover the entire body of the victim. The genitals and anal opening must be examined with care and in detail. As mentioned previously, sexual abuse often occurs without leaving any physical evidence. Contrary to popular belief, sexual intercourse may occur without damage to the hymen.[30] Many laypersons do not understand how a small hymenal opening could accept an object as large as an erect penis. The adult penis averages 3.5 cm at the glans penis, while the normal size of the vaginal opening at puberty is 0.7 to 1.0 cm. The vaginal opening and hymen are flexible and able to distend. Thus, penetration may occur without damage to the hymen. Additionally, certain types of child abuse involve neither anal nor vaginal intercourse. These acts include fondling, kissing, fellatio, cunnilingus, or mutual masturbation.

Laboratory tests may provide confirmation of sexual abuse. If the sexual abuse is recent, tests may indicate the presence of ejaculate or phosphatase. Acid phosphatase is a chemical found in ejaculate even in the absence of sperm. Additionally, laboratory tests may confirm the presence of certain venereal diseases. The presence of specific types of venereal diseases is almost a presumptive sign of abuse. Gonococcal or syphilitic infections can only be contracted through sexual activity. Other infections such as the herpes virus or lymphogranuloma (venereal warts) may be transmitted other than sexually, and therefore further inquiry is necessary.

Unlike rape, few children are brought into an emergency room right after a sexual assault. A child may exhibit either behavioral, physical, and/or medical symptoms of abuse, and professionals must be aware of these characteristics. Only by recognizing these indicators of sexual abuse can it be prevented.

Sexual Abuse

No clearly defined pattern or course of conduct leads to sexual child abuse. When a father bathes his two-year-old daughter, this does not necessarily lead to sexual urges or acts. Nor are there specific relationships that cause a molestation. Sexual acts may be committed by fathers, mothers, stepparents, uncles, siblings, babysitters, and, of course, strangers. The consequences of sexual abuse to children are still being researched. However, professionals know that the effects of sexual acts last far beyond the time of the molestation. This section will examine the dynamics of child sexual abuse including the various types of sexual relationships and the consequences of sexual abuse on the development and growth of the child.

Forms of Sexual Abuse

Pedophilia is a term used to describe a person who has a sexual fixation on young children. This fixation is usually translated into sexual acts with the victim. The psychiatric definition of a pedophile requires the following three conditions: over a period of at least six months, the person has recurrent intense sexual urges and sexually arousing fantasies involving sexual activity with a prepubescent child (generally age thirteen or younger), the person has acted on these urges or is markedly distressed by them, and the person is at least sixteen years old and at least five years older than the child.[31]

Numerous studies have been conducted about why certain individuals molest children. Groth's research concentrated on convicted sex molesters. He concluded that there were two types of perpetrators: the fixated offender and the regressed offender.[32] The *fixated offender* is usually attracted to male children, and he is unable to form a heterosexual relationship with someone his own age. His compulsive premeditated acts are based on the need to repeat his own victimization. The *regressed offender* primarily chooses young females as his victims. He is able to maintain the appearance of a heterosexual relationship with someone his own age.

Although it would be convenient to accept a classification such as Groth's clinicians have found that such stereotyping does not fit everyday experiences.[33] Many molesters have combined characteristics from both categories. Other researchers continue to classify offenders on the basis of distinct differences. Some scholars argue that whereas an incestuous father may establish a long-term sexual relationship with his victim, the pedophile loses interest in the child once the victim passes into puberty.[34] Additionally, it was once thought that an offender who molested in the home or family circle did not actively engage in sex outside the home. However, there is some authority to believe that incestuous fathers may also molest victims outside the family.[35]

The conflict regarding pedophiles and their sexual habits continues to be debated in professional circles.[36] What is certain is that there are males who have an obsession for young children—male or female—and that they prey on them sexually. This molestation can be perpetrated by a stranger who kidnaps a young child or by a family member who sexually molests a blood relative. The latter form of sexual abuse is known as incest.

Incest has a long and varied history in our society. It has various definition,s however. One of the more accepted definitions states that *incest is sexual relations between blood relatives.* It is prohibited in many cultures and accepted as normal in others. The prohibition against incest may be classified into five major categories:

psychological, biological, familial, feminist, and multidimensional. Each of these theories offers a rationale for the prohibition against sexual relations with family members.

The psychological theory holds that the taboo against incest is a method of preventing family members from engaging in unconscious sexual desires with other family members. Sigmund Freud accepted this justification of the prohibition against incest because he believed male family members had deep-seated unconscious desires to have sex with their mothers and daughters. Freud wrote an article entitled "The Etiology of Hysteria," which discussed the effects of family molestation on patients he treated. He theorized that the hysteria suffered by the patients was the result of sexual abuse by family members.[37] However, Freud later changed his position and repudiated his theory, stating the patient's memories were fantasies.

The biological theory prohibits sexual relations between family members as a method of ensuring survival of the race. This theory holds that such activity causes recessive or defective genes to multiply, resulting in deformity in the human race. This prohibition stresses the harmful effects of inbreeding.[38] One of the leading proponents of this theory is L. H. Morgan.[39] He based his assumptions on the experiences of animal breeders who discovered that inbreeding caused physical and mental deformities and disabilities. There were several flaws in Morgan's approach, and it has generally been discredited. Today, however, modern science now accepts that although inbreeding may produce physical and mental disabilities, it may also be capable of producing a superior species.[40]

The familial theory against incest holds that the taboo creates order, unity, and cooperation among family members. The taboo establishes roles within the family that would otherwise be blurred by sexual involvement of its members. Without such a taboo, there would be disorder, disruption, and confusion within the family system.[41]

The feminist theory regarding incest holds that this taboo establishes the father as the authority figure in the family and preconditions women to accept this domination in society.[42] The authority granted the father establishes a patriarchal social system that discriminates against women. Under the feminist theory of taboo, males have the ability to restrict access to certain women, thereby increasing their own authority, power, and domain.

The multidimensional approach combined a number of the preceding theories to explain the incest taboo. Several authorities have argued that the incest taboo was and is important to the family structure and the child's development. Talcott Parsons believed that the taboo forced the child to develop autonomy and social roles necessary to leave the family. Carl Jung theorized that the incest prohibition was a necessary part of the child's development as a distinct individual.

Each of these theories has its proponents and opponents. Although they are helpful in understanding differing views as to why incest is considered bad or harmful, evidence to support their conclusions is lacking. As a result, none of them have been accepted by all scholars in the field.

As mentioned above, not all cultures accept incest as an immoral or illegal act. Some societies accept sexual activity between family members, including father–daughter liaisons, as natural, healthy, and proper.[43] Even in the United States there are groups referred to as the Pro-Incest Lobby that believe that sexual activity with young girls is an acceptable lifestyle.[44] One organization, the Rene Guyon Society, has a slogan: "Sex before eight, or else it's too late."[45] This organization lobbies legislatures for the abolition of incest laws. The society claims to have in excess of five thousand members, each of whom has filed an affidavit with the organization stating that the individual himself has deflowered a male or female child under the age of eight.[46] The group argues that the laws prohibiting incest are unenforceable because it is so prevalent, that the intervention by law enforcement agencies causes more harm than the "consensual" sexual act, and that the prohibition is old-fashioned and not in tune with the new sexual freedom in our society.

Child pornography is another form of child sexual abuse that is alive and flourishing in the United States. In New York City, one shelter that cares for runaway children discovered that out of five thousand runaways in one year, two thousand of them had been involved in child pornography.[47]

Children who run away from home are prime targets for child pornography rings. The adults who control these rings recruit and maintain these children using a variety of techniques including material and psychological rewards. Ann Burgess studied various child pornography rings and found that different structures exist in these rings depending on their purpose. Solo rings are typified by an individual who keeps the sexual activity and pornographic material secret and does not inform or involve other adults. Transition rings are impromptu gatherings that come together for the purpose of selling photos and trading sex, and victims may be traded among members at this time. Syndicated rings are well-organized businesses that recruit and peddle children to customers who desire certain types of sexual activity. Syndicated rings are very structured and engage in child pornography, prostitution, and other sexual activities.[48] Also, the commercial exploitation of children in sex movies continues to be a highly emotional and legal problem. The stakes are high, and enormous profits are made from the publishing of these types of movies and videos. Child pornography has developed into a highly organized, multi-million-dollar industry that operates on a nationwide scale.[49]

Child pornography is really an inaccurate term. Pornography is any form of expression that deals with explicit sexual activity that is not considered obscene. The First Amendment to the Constitution protects our freedom of expression. This includes the right to make, sell, and view sexually explicit material so long as it does not cross over the line and become obscene. Although the First Amendment protects freedom of speech and expression, not all such activity is protected. United States courts have determined that certain speech-related activity does not warrant First Amendment protection. This means that the states are free to regulate and make it a crime. This is the case with obscenity. The U.S. Supreme Court has defined *obscenity as requiring a finding of all three of the following elements:*

1. An average person, by applying contemporary community standards, would find that the work, taken as a whole, appeals to mainly prurient interest in sex;

2. The work depicts or describes sexual conduct in a patently offensive way;
3. The work, taken as a whole, lacks serious literary, artistic, political, or scientific value.[50]

Thus, the Supreme Court has established the principle that regulates obscene movies. Clearly, a movie that depicts a minor involved in sex acts with another person falls within this category. Therefore, such activity is not protected under the First Amendment. As a result, state and federal statutes can and have made it a crime to involve a minor in a sexually explicit movie. The U.S. Congress enacted a federal statute in 1978 (and amended it in 1984) prohibiting the use of minors in sexually explicit films. This statute is known as the Child Protection Act of 1984. It prohibits any person from enticing a minor to engage in any sexually explicit conduct for the purpose of producing any visual depiction of that conduct. The act imposes liability on parents, guardians, producers, and distributors of child pornography. The statute has been upheld by the courts as a valid exercise of the police power of the state.[51]

There are numerous forms of child sexual abuse. It may occur within or outside of the family. No matter what form child sexual abuse takes, the consequences to the victim are long-lasting and severe. The next section examines some of these consequences.

Consequences of Sexual Abuse

The impact of sexual molestation on children has been studied and researched by numerous authorities. Conte set forth the following reasons for the wide range of interpretations and differing results from the various studies of child sexual abuse.[52] These differences can be attributed to several factors:

1. *Differential Impact:* Some victims of sexual abuse are affected more than others, and this issue has caused trouble for researchers. However, a wide range of factors contribute to this problem; age of the victim, use of force, duration of the molestation, and other variables all contribute to methodological problems.
2. *Substantive Implications:* Some of the substantive implications of sexual abuse focus on the behavioral and psychological effects on the victim. The presence of force, duration, and age of the victim at the time of the last incident are all associated with negative effects.
3. *Political Contexts:* The continuing debate over the effects or lack of them add to the confusion in this area. As discussed above, some groups advocate sex with children versus the vast majority of U.S. citizens, who argue such acts cause harm to the children.
4. *Methodological Issues:* Studies of the consequences of child sexual abuse have been criticized as drawing samples from special populations such as prostitutes, college students, prison inmates, and other nonrepresentative populations.

Although scholars differ on mythology and variables, certain consequences to the victim should be examined. This section does not discuss intervention or treatment as this aspect of family violence is covered in detail in Chapter 12. However, because of the special impact of sexual molestation on victims, all should be aware of some of the major consequences of sexual abuse on children and their development.

These consequences may be classified into different aspects or reactions. Any set or classification of traits may be used to judge the impact of sexual abuse on the victim. One of the most common consequences of child sexual abuse is the exhibition of stress. Stress may be classified as acute, secondary, or tertiary.

Acute symptoms of stress may appear at the onset of the abuse or when the acts are disclosed to others. Physical or emotional actions by the victim could be symptoms of acute stress. The child may exhibit any of the symptoms listed in the section discussing indications of sexual abuse.

Secondary stress may occur if abuse has continued for a long period of time. The victim has adapted to the situation and is able to function normally, at least on the surface. Some scholars argue that shame, guilt, and low self-esteem are secondary stress symptoms found in sexually abused children. However, these conclusions are subject to criticism by other authorities who argue that these findings do not always hold up. Suicide attempts and self-mutilating behavior appear to be higher with these victims than with the general population.[53] Fear, anxiety, a feeling of isolation, and stigma have been found to be present in some follow-up studies of victims of child sexual abuse.[54] Other secondary stress symptoms include difficulty with interpersonal relations and sexual maladjustment.

Tertiary stress symptoms include situations where the victim identifies with the offender. Many times there will be no outward symptoms of tertiary stress.

Tower set forth various factors affecting the degree of stress or trauma a child victim experiences:

1. *The Type of Abuse:* Some victims of incest appear to be more affected by the acts than victims of stranger molestation. However, if the nonfamily member engaged in sadistic or violent acts, this can have profound effects on the victim.
2. *The Identity of the Offender:* When the molester is known and close to the victim, the trauma appears to be greater than that from sexual molestation by a stranger. This trauma is based on feelings of a betrayal of trust by the known abuser.
3. *The Duration of the Abuse:* Most incestuous relationships last from one to three years. Long-term abuse of this nature seems to cause more stress than a one-time event. The exception to this rule is the one-time event that involves violence.
4. *The Extent of the Abuse:* The more intrusive or progressive the abuse, the more trauma. Intercourse, sodomy, and oral copulation cause more trauma than fondling or masturbation.
5. *The Age the Abuse Started:* Children develop incrementally. When the abuse began will cause different types of problems, depending on the age of the child.

6. *The Reactions of Others to Disclosure of the Abuse:* When the child tells other adults of the abuse, their reaction may affect how the child perceives themselves. If the adult discounts the abuse or blames the child, they may not discuss the incidents until adulthood. Keeping the abuse secret does in fact add to the trauma suffered by the victim.
7. *The Personality of the Child:* We are each a distinct individual. Each victim will react in a different way to the abuse and suffer different types and forms of trauma.[55]

Hartman and Burgess have developed a conceptual framework for understanding the linkage between sexual abuse and the victim's level of adjustment.[56] This process has two aspects: the phases of sexual abuse and recovery and concepts for processing traumatic life events. The first phase discusses the experiencing, disclosing, and recovering from child sexual abuse. The second phase addresses how the child views the event and adjusts to the fact of abuse.

The first aspect of this conceptual framework is composed of four distinct phases: pre-abuse conditions, processing the event, revealing the event, and patterned responses to the event.

Phase 1: Pretrauma—Pre-Abuse Conditions

As the title implies, this is the period before the sexual activity. The total sum of the victim's experiences and emotional makeup give an indication of the child's vulnerabilities and risk factors for maladjustment. These experiences include the quality of relationships with siblings and adults, early socialization experiences, and other resources. Preexisting beliefs and values are critical to coping with the abuse.

Phase 2: Trauma Encapsulation—Processing the Event

This phase encompasses the actual sexual activity and disclosure of the abuse. the activity may be a one-time event or a series of acts. Factors such as the relationship of the molester to the victim, the degree of violence of force used during the assault, the type of defensive mechanisms used by the victim during the abuse, and the child's age all contribute to the level of stress encountered during this phase.

Phase 3: Disclosure—The Process of Revealing the Event

The disclosure phase deals with stress factors associated with external forces outside the child's control. How the system responds to the victim's disclosure will affect the amount of stress imposed on the child. Physical examinations, interviews with adults in the criminal justice system, and family members all exert pressure and stress on the child. Different forms of stress will occur, depending on whether the assailant is a family member or a stranger. If the molester is a family member, how others react to the disclosure will affect the child. If the molester is a stranger, whether the stranger is in custody or free will determine the child's stress level.

Phase 4: Post-Trauma Outcome—Patterned Responses to the Event

This phase extends at least two years after the criminal action and/or therapy. How is the child adjusting to the situation? Is the child and family discussing the abuse and responding to the child's reactions to it? How the immediate family handles this time period will affect the stress the child feels.

The second phase of processing the sexual molestation involves examining the victim's post-abuse reactions. The details of the abuse are retained in active memory until the victim can transfer it to distant memory. Therapy assists in processing this event. This processing of information and storage of unpleasant memories allows the child to function in society. the ability of the child to adjust to sexual molestation is dependent on a number of factors. Professionals are still learning how children cope with abuse and how they adjust to the trauma of sexual molestation.

Parricide

Parricide is a form of family violence that has received little if any research and discussion. Since 1976, when the FBI began reporting homicides according to victim-offender relationship, parricide is listed in three to four hundred cases. This amounts to 1.5 to 2.5 percent of all homicides committed in the United States each year. Mones points out that except for brothers killing their sisters, parricide is the rarest form of interfamily homicide.[57]

The most common parricide offender may be a chronically abused child who as an adolescent kills the abusing parent.

Four distinct issues are raised whenever parricide is discussed:

1. The debate regarding the definition of parricide. Generally speaking, *parricide refers to the killing of one's parents.* Parricide may take three forms: (1) patricide, or killing one's father; (2) matricide, or killing one's mother; and (3) double parricide, or killing both parents.
2. Most parricide cases involve the existence of long-term and debilitating child abuse. Lawyers who represent parricide offenders claim that over 90 percent of all their clients have been abused.[58]
3. Sons are more likely than daughters to strike back at their parents.
4. Abuse sometimes increases during adolescence as the child experiences independence and personality changes. These changes cause some parents to feel a loss of control and power which they compensate for by increasing abuse. One authority indicates that because the teen years are a very emotional time, parricide commonly occurs during this period.[59]

Heide points out that parricide is typically committed by youths who fit in one or more of the following classifications: (1) the severely abuse child pushed beyond his or her limits, (2) the severely mentally ill child, or (3) the dangerously antisocial child.[60] The severely abused child may have suffered physical, sexual, or emotional abuse. The mentally ill child may be suffering from a mental disorder so severe that he or she may be unable to cooperate with the defense attorney and therefore unable to stand trial. The dangerously antisocial child may be the psychopath or sociopath who is suffering from mental disorder and yet is aware of the nature and type of his or her actions. Heide correctly concluded that some parricide offenders may represent a blend of this typology. We are still researching this form of family violence. It is controversial and steeped in misinformation and emotion. What is known about this type of homicide is sketchy and subject to debate. The next sections briefly examine parricide as it relates to child abuse.

History

Parricide is discussed in early Greek mythology. Oepidus's killing his father and married his mother is an example of an early parricide. Alcmaeon murdered his mother, Eriphyle, to punish her for sending his father to his death, and Orestes murdered his other mother, Clytemnestra, to avenge her killing of his father.[61]

Parricide is also documented in early Rome. In A.D. 59, Nero was crowned emperor of Rome. His mother, Agrippina, had plotted and maneuvered for years to secure the crown for her son. She also psychologically abused Nero during his childhood. Even after being crowned emperor, Nero was frightened and controlled by his mother. When Nero finally confronted his mother, she threatened him publicly. Aware of his mother's power over him and fearing that she would kill him, Nero ordered her death.[62]

One of the earliest recorded parricides in the United States occurred in 1867, when a seventeen-year-old girl murdered her stepfather. Prior to the killing, she disclosed to others that he had been abusing her since she was thirteen. No one reacted to her pleas for help, and when her stepfather learned of her actions, he ordered her to be silent or he would send her to a reform school. Feeling trapped and with no one to turn to, she poisoned her stepfather. She was found guilty and sentenced to an insane asylum.[63]

One of the most famous parricides involved Lizzie Borden, who, in 1892, is alleged to have murdered her mother and father with an ax. She and her sister were heirs to a sizable inheritance. The theory behind the prosecution case was that Lizzie killed her parents on the basis of greed and a desire to obtain their estate. The jury acquitted her on the basis of the fact that she was a nice Christian lady who was simply incapable of committing such a violent crime. One author suggests that in retrospect evidence suggests that Lizzie Borden may have been a victim of sexual abuse by her father and killed her parents as a result of this long-term relationship.[64]

The relationship between child abuse and parricide was first acknowledged in the Richard Jahnke case. In 1982, after years of physical abuse, sixteen year old Jahnke shot and killed his father. He was convicted of voluntary manslaughter and sentenced to five to fifteen years in state prison. This case captured the nation's attention and was the first case in which a parricide offender raised the issue of self-defense. The defense also used expert witnesses to support their theory of self-defense, and this may account for the jury's verdict of voluntary manslaughter instead of murder.[65]

The next widely publicized parricide case occurred in 1986, when Cheryl Pierson had her father killed. Cheryl was a sixteen-year-old high school cheerleader who was found guilty of manslaughter for hiring a classmate to murder her father. Cheryl claimed that when her mother became ill when she was twelve, her father began sexually molesting her. When her mother died, the sexual attacks intensified, and he also started to physically abuse her. As her younger sister was about to turn twelve, Cheryl was afraid she would be her father's next victim, so she hired a classmate to kill her father. Her story seemed to sway the judge who imposed a light sentence for such a crime of only six months in jail with five additional years on probation.[66]

In August 1989, brothers Lyle and Erik Menendez allegedly left their bedrooms, armed with shotguns, and entered the family room of their wealthy Beverly Hill estate, where they shot and killed both their parents as they were eating ice cream. The slaying of their parents and their subsequent trials resulted in widespread publicity regarding this form of violence. In 1993, their first trial resulted in hung juries (the brothers were tried together, but each had a separate jury). Two years later, the second trial resulted in their conviction of murder despite their claims of years of sexual abuse. The brothers claimed they had endured years of psychological and physical abuse from both parents and that their father sexually molested them. They claimed that they killed their parents out of fear for their own lives because they believed that their parents were about to kill them for threatening to expose the abuse to the authorities. The prosecution alleged that the brothers were pathological liars who shot their parents in cold blood for the millions of dollars they would inherent.[67]

Who Are the Killers?

Most juveniles who commit homicide kill either strangers or acquaintances. Adolescent parricide offenders are more likely than other juvenile homicide offenders to have been victims of child abuse.[68] Another study indicates that adolescent parricide offenders are mainly submissive and nonviolent with a few incidents of poor impulse control, whereas adolescents who kill strangers or acquaintances have a history of violence.[69] Simply put, most parricide offenders do not have a history of lawbreaking.

Society's reaction to parricide is still steeped in the traditional view that children should love and obey their parents. When a child kills his or her parents, we attempt to attribute this to the "bad seed" theory or argue that the child somehow is at fault. Many times, the claim of abuse is seen as an excuse for murder. However, as pointed out in other sections in this text, children rarely lie about abuse. We simply do not have the answers to a number of questions in this area. A great deal still needs to be done in the area of researching the dynamics and causes of parricide.

Expert Witnesses and Child Sexual Abuse

Sexual abuse of children is a multifaceted phenomenon. There may be a progression of activities that lead up to the molestation. It can take many forms and can involve family members or strangers. The consequences of these activities leave a scar on the victim that may not heal for years. By its very nature, child sexual abuse occurs in secret with no witnesses. Many times, the child will not be a credible witness. In these situations, it is necessary to utilize various expert witnesses to present evidence of sexual abuse.

Earlier in this chapter, the medical aspects of child abuse were reviewed. Medical evidence by its very nature involves the use of expert witnesses.[70] This section examines the use of these expert witnesses in child abuse cases. Most people are familiar with the university professor with multiple degrees who can testify as an expert regarding a specific subject. However, a person with specialized experience and little if any formal education beyond a bachelors degree may also qualify as an expert witness in certain situations. The following sections discuss the use of expert opinions in child sexual abuse cases.

Admission of Expert Witness Opinions

In order for a person to testify as an expert, the court must determine whether he or she is qualified to render an expert opinion. Federal Rules of Evidence Rule 702 is a representative statute that sets forth the requirements of admission of expert opinion in court:

> *If scientific, technical, or other specialized knowledge will assist the trier to understand the evidence or to determine a fact in issue, a witness qualified as an expert by knowledge, skill, experience, training, or education may testify thereto in the form of an opinion or otherwise.*

When the court is determining the admissibility of certain expert opinions, it looks at whether the testimony will assist the jury.[71] It should be emphasized that expert opinion is admitted not only in highly technical cases but also in any case where the testimony can assist the jury in understanding the evidence or determining a fact that is in issue.[72] Before a court will admit expert testimony, it must establish that the person offering the testimony has "knowledge, skill, experience, training, or education" to qualify as an expert on the matter before the jury.[73] The party utilizing experts calls them to the stand, has them sworn in, and asks a series of questions regarding their education, training, and experience that would qualify them in the area of child sexual abuse.

Once qualified as experts, the party calling them to the stand proceeds to question them regarding their opinion. This opinion may take various forms and carry either a great deal or little weight with the trier of fact. The next section examines the bases and forms of expert opinions in child sexual abuse cases.

FOCUS Qualifying a Witness as an Expert in Child Sexual Abuse Cases

State your full name and spell it for the record.

What is your present occupation?

What is your education that qualifies you for this position?

Are you licensed by this or any other state to practice (medicine, etc.)?

Do you have any specialized training in the area of child sexual abuse? Please list that training.

Explain your experience in treating (etc.) sexually abused children.

Are you familiar with the current literature in the area of child abuse? Specifically, are you familiar with the literature in the area of child sexual abuse?

Are you a member of any professional organizations that focus on sexual abuse of children?

Please list those organizations and your activities in them.

Have you presented any papers at any professional conferences that deal with sexual child abuse? Please list them and the dates.

Have you published any articles in professional journals regarding sexual child abuse? Please describe those articles.

Have you qualified in court on previous occasions as an expert witness in child sexual abuse? How many times?

Types of Expert Opinions

The facts an expert relies on in forming her opinion may come from many different sources. Sometimes the expert may have personal knowledge about the abuse from treating or interviewing the child. On other occasions, the expert may rely on reports from other professionals as the basis for the opinion. The expert need not have personal knowledge in order to form an opinion. Federal Rules of Evidence Rule 703 states,

> *The facts or data in the particular case upon which an expert bases an opinion or inference may be those perceived by or made known to the expert at or before the hearing. If of a type reasonably relied upon by experts in the particular field in forming opinions or inferences upon the subject, the facts or data need not be admissible in evidence.*

The latter section of the federal rule allows an expert to base the opinion on evidence that would normally not be admissible in court. These facts or data may be written and/or verbal hearsay. Writings include medical records, police reports, and psychological reports. Verbal statements by the child or caretaker are often critical in proving sexual abuse.

Expert testimony may take three distinct forms in child sexual abuse: opinion, dissertation, and answers to hypothetical questions. Each of these forms of expert testimony serves a distinct purpose.

The most common form of expert testimony in child sexual abuse cases is the rendering of an opinion. An expert might testify that certain behavioral symptoms displayed by the child are consistent with incest. Although there is no requirement that an expert state the facts on which an opinion is based, the better practice is to ask the expert to state those facts that caused them to form the opinion. This technique assists the trier of fact in understanding the basis of the opinion. Experts do not have to establish any level of proof for their opinions. In other words, they do not have to testify, "I am certain beyond a reasonable doubt and to a moral certainty that the child was sexually molested." The jury must determine how much weight to give an expert opinion, and in many jurisdictions the court instructs the jury that it may give the expert's testimony whatever weight it desires or that it may completely disregard the opinion. Normally, experts will be asked questions that allow them to testify from the point of view of their professions. For example, a medical doctor might be asked, "Do you have an opinion based upon reasonable medical grounds that the child is a victim of sexual abuse?" This allows the opinion to be based on medical reasons and not legal grounds.

A dissertation is expert testimony that does not include an opinion but sets forth scientific facts or other principles relevant to the case that allows the triers of fact to draw their own conclusion. In this situation, the expert might not testify that the victim has been molested but would testify to certain medical or psychological indicators of abuse. The jury would then apply these principles to the actions of the child and determine whether it should give the expert's opinion any weight.

A hypothetical question sets forth certain facts and asks the expert to give an opinion on the basis of these facts. The facts may not have been admitted into evidence at the time the expert testifies. Many authorities argue that hypothetical questions confuse the lawyers, the court, and the jury.[74]

Various forms of expert testimony exist in child sexual abuse cases. The most traditional expert opinions are either medical or psychological. Medical opinions are provided by doctors, nurses, and other qualified personnel. Psychological opinions are rendered by psychiatrists, psychologists, and in some instances social workers. Medical opinions may be based on physical examinations, laboratory results, and a medical history. For example, if a child has a certain type of venereal disease, child sexual abuse is the only rational explanation. Psychological opinions are based on certain tests, interviews, and observations. One of the most controversial areas in the field of psychological opinions deals with the delayed discovery of abuse. Some victims have suppressed the acts, and once they are free of the abuser and out of the situation that allowed the abuse to occur, they may remember the acts. There are cases where the victim suddenly remembered acts of abuse ten or twenty years ago. This topic is discussed in more detail in Chapter 6, which examines ritualistic child abuse.

Experts serve a valuable purpose in child sexual abuse cases. They assist the trier of fact in understanding this often complex and emotional area of family violence. A good expert opinion can shed light on what would otherwise be a confusing and difficult area.

Summary

Child sexual abuse is one of the most emotional areas of family violence. It is a crime that occurs in secret and may last only moments or for years. Even the definition of child sexual abuse is shrouded in controversy. Although professionals cannot explain why it occurs, some scholars have established certain profiles or characteristics of both the abuser and the abused.

Unlike other forms of child abuse, sexual molestation may not leave scars that are visible to other persons. However, certain symptoms should raise the suspicion of any professional. Physical, behavioral, and medical indicators may lead a professional to uncover incidents of sexual abuse. As with all indicators, these must be viewed with caution. Concerning medical indicators, the general public must be made aware that certain commonly held beliefs may be misleading. For example, it is possible to have a completed act of intercourse and still retain an intact hymen in young girls.

Child sexual abuse takes many forms. Incest is an act of sexual activity with blood relatives. In some countries, this is accepted as normal. In the United States, however, it is both a crime and a moral wrong.

Child pornography is alive and well in the United States. It is a multi-million-dollar business that preys on unsuspecting children. The U.S. Supreme Court has established a definition of obscenity, and films depicting children engaged in sexual activity clearly fall within this definition. However, child pornography continues as a profitable business despite severe criminal sanctions and public condemnation.

The consequences of child sexual abuse are traumatic and long lasting, and various scholars have attempted to study the ramifications of this type of child maltreatment. Although there is disagreement among these authorities, all agree that it is a serious problem that must be studied. Hopefully, a solution can be found to ease the pain of the survivors of sexual abuse.

Key Terms

child sexual abuse—sexual exploitation or sexual activities with a child under circumstances that indicate that the child's health or welfare is harmed or threatened.

intrafamilial sexual abuse—includes incest and refers to any type of exploitative sexual contact occurring between relatives.

extrafamilial sexual abuse—exploitative sexual contact with perpetrators who may be either known or unknown to the child.

Four Preconditions Model of Sexual Abuse—establishes preconditions that create a personal and social context for expressing sexually abusive behaviors.

pedophilia—a term used to describe a person who has a sexual fixation on young children. This fixation is usually translated into sexual acts.

incest—sexual relations between blood relatives.

obscenity—material that an average person, by applying contemporary community standards, would find that taken as a whole, appeals to mainly prurient interest in sex; depicts or describes sexual conduct in a patently offensive way; and taken as a whole, lacks serious literary, artistic, political, or scientific value.

parricide—the killing of one's parents.

dissertation—expert testimony that does not include an opinion but sets forth scientific facts or other principles relevant to the case that allows the triers of fact to draw their own conclusion.

hypothetical question—sets forth certain facts and asks an expert to give an opinion on the basis of these facts.

Discussion Questions

1. On the basis of your reading of this chapter, can you provide a more comprehensive definition of child sexual abuse? What about a more specific definition?
2. Can you list at least two reasons why offenders sexually abuse children? Justify your answer.
3. What in your opinion are the strongest physical, behavioral, and medical indicators of child abuse? Why?
4. If you were a professional working in an environment that includes young children and you observed a child exhibiting symptoms that led you to suspect child sexual abuse, what would you do?
5. Which should be punished more strongly—incest or stranger sexual abuse? Why?
6. Should we punish or treat child molesters? Some argue that you can never cure a pedophile. Does this mean they should be locked up for life?
7. Should experts be used in child abuse cases? Is the use of paid professionals subject to abuse by the highest bidder?

Suggested Readings

Ammerman, R. T., and M. Hersen, eds. *Treatment of Family Violence.* (John Wiley, New York) 1990.

Burgess, A. W. *Child Pornography and Sex Rings.* (Lexington Books, Lexington, Massachusetts) 1984.

Cicchetti, D., and V. Carlson, eds. *Child Maltreatment.* (Cambridge University Press, Cambridge, Massachusetts) 1989.

Finkelhor, D. *Sexually Victimized Children.* (Free Press, New York) 1979.

Finkelhor, D. *Child Sexual Abuse: New Theories and Research* (Free Press, New York) 1984.

Fox, R. *The Red Lamp of Incest.* (E. P. Dutton, New York) 1980.

Groth, A. N. *Men Who Rape.* (Plenum Press, New York) 1979.

Van Hasselt, V. B., R. L. Morrison, A. S. Bellack, and M. Hersen, eds. *Handbook of Family Violence.* (Plenum Press, New York) 1988.

Herman, J. *Father–Daughter Incest.* (Harvard University Press, Cambridge, Massachusetts) 1981.

Justice, F., and R. Justice. *The Broken Taboo: Sex in the Family.* (Human Services Press, New York) 1979.

Lederer, L., ed. *Take Back the Night.* (William Morrow, New York) 1980.

Pence, D., and C. Wilson, *Team Investigation of Child Sexual Abuse.* (Sage, Thousand Oaks, California) 1994.

Porter, E. *Treating the Young Male Victims of Sexual Assault.* (Safer Society Press, Syracuse, New York) 1986.

Russell, D. *Rape in Marriage.* (Macmillan, New York) 1982.

Endnotes

1. Luster, T., and S. Small. "Sexual Abuse History and Problems in Adolescence: Exploring the Effects of Moderating Variables," *Journal of Marriage and the Family* 59(1) February, 1997, p. 131.
2. Hartman, C. R., and A. W. Burgess. "Sexual Abuse in Children: Causes and Consequences." In D. Cicchetti, and V. Carlson, eds. *Child Maltreatment.* (Cambridge University Press, Cambridge, United Kingdom) 1989, p. 98.
3. Finkelhor, D. *Sexually Victimized Children.* (Free Press, New York) 1979.
4. Finkelhor, D. *Child Sexual Abuse: New Theories and Research.* (Free Press, New York) 1984.
5. Russell, D. *Rape in Marriage.* (Macmillan, New York) 1982.
6. Timnick, L. "22% in Survey Were Child Abuse Victims." *Los Angeles Times,* p. 1 (25 August 1985).
7. Friedrich, Grambsch, Broughton, Kuiper, and Beilke. "Normative Sexual Behavior in Children." *Pediatrics* 88, 1991, p. 456.
8. Kilpatrick, D. G., C. N. Edmonds, and A. K. Seymour. *Rape in America: A Report to the Nation.* (National Victim Center, Arlington, Virginia) 1992.
9. Finkelhor, D. *Child Sexual Abuse: New Theories and Research.* (Free Press, New York) 1984.
10. The figure of 44,700 comes from the National Incidence Survey of 1981. See *National Study of the Incidence and Severity of Child Abuse and Neglect: Technical Report Number 1.* K. Bergdorf, and J. Edmonds, eds. (Washington D.C. DHHS Publication No. (OHDS) 81-30326) 1981.
11. Hartman, C. R., and A. W. Burgess. "Sexual Abuse of Children." pp. 98–99.
12. This is a shortened version of the definition contained in the Child Abuse Prevention and Treatment Act of 1974, which is one of the most widely adopted statutes defining child sexual abuse.
13. Wolfe, D. A., V. V. Wolfe, and C. L. Best. "Child Victims of Sexual Assault." In V. B. Van Hasselt, R. L. Morrison, A. S. Bellack, and M. Hersen, eds. *Handbook of Family Violence.* (Plenum Press, New York) 1988.
14. Conte, J. R. "Victims of Child Sexual Abuse." In *Treatment of Family Violence.* R. T. Ammerman, and M. Hersen, eds. (John Wiley, New York) 1990, pp. 64–65.
15. Mcilwaine, S. D. Interrogating Child Molesters." *FBI Law Enforcement Bulletin,* June, 1994, pp. 1–4.
16. See Conti, J. "The Effects of Sexual Abuse on Children: A Critique and Suggestions for Future Research." *Victimology: An International Journal,* 10, pp. 110–30, 1985; and Conti, J., I. Berliner, and J. Schurman, "The Impact of Sexual Abuse on Children: Final Report." Available from the authors at the University of Chicago, 969 E. 60th Street, Chicago, Illinois, 60637.
17. Finkelhor, D. *Child Sexual Abuse: New Theories and Research.* (Free Press, New York) 1984.
18. Porter, E. *Treating the Young Male Victims of Sexual Assault.* (Safer Society Press, Syracuse, New York) 1986.
19. Ibid.
20. Groth, A. N. *Men Who Rape.* (Plenum Press, New York) 1979.
21. Gelinas, D. J. "The Persisting Negative Effects of Incest." *Psychiatry* 46, 1983, pp. 312–322.
22. Courtios, C. A. "Studying and Counseling Women with Past Incest Experience." *Victimology: An International Journal* 5, 1980, pp. 322–334.
23. Finkelhor, D. *Child Sexual Abuse;* and E. Porter. *Treating the Young Male Victim of Sexual Assault.*
24. Finkelhor, D. *Child Sexual Abuse.* (Free Press, New York) 1984.

25. Petronio, S. "Disclosure of Sexual Abuse by Children and Adolescents," *Journal of Applied Communication Research* 24(3) August, 1996, p. 181.
26. Adapted from Laymen, R. *Current Issues, Volume I: Child Abuse.* (Omnigraphics, Inc., Detroit) 1990, p. 36. Originally circulated by the Children's Safety Project in Manhattan.
27. De Jong and Rose. "Frequency and Significance of Physical Evidence in Legally Proven Cases of Child Sexual Abuse." *Pediatrics* 84:1022, 1989.
28. Marshall, Puls, and Davidson. "New Sexual Abuse Spectrum in an Era of Increased Awareness." *American Journal of Diseases of Children* 142:664, 1988.
29. Dubowitz, Black, and Harrington. "The Diagnosis of Child Sexual Abuse." *American Journal of Children* 146:688, 1992.
30. Enos, Conrath, and Byer. "Forensic Evaluation of the Sexually Abused Child." *Pediatrics* 78:385, 395, 1986.
31. See Classification 302.2. *Diagnostic Criteria,* DSM-IV. (American Psychiatric Association, Washington, D.C.) 1994, pp. 527–528.
32. Groth, A. N. *Men Who Rape.* (Plenum Press, New York) 1979.
33. Conti, J. "The Effects of Sexual Abuse on Children: A Critique and Suggestions for Further Research." *Victimology: An International Journal* 10, 1985, pp. 110–130.
34. Justice, B., and R. Justice. *The Broken Taboo: Sex in the Family.* (Human Services Press, New York) 1979.
35. Conti, J. "The Effects of Sexual Abuse on Children: A Critique and Suggestions for Further Research." *Victimology: An International Journal* 10, 1985, pp. 110–130.
36. Johnston, F. A., and S. A. Johnson, "A Cognitive Approach to Validation of the Fixated—Regressed Typology of Child Molesters," *Journal of Clinical Psychology,* 53(4), June, 1997, p. 361.
37. Freud, S. "The Etiology of Hysteria." In *The Complete Psychological Works of Sigmund Freud.* Translated by James Strachy. Standard Edition. (Hogarth Press, London) 1896.
38. Lindsey, G. "Some Remarks Concerning Incest, the Incest Taboo and Psychoanalytic Theory." 22 *American Psychologist* 22, 1967, pp. 1051–1059.
39. Morgan, L. H. *Ancient Society.* (Kerr, Chicago) 1877.
40. Meiselman, K. *Incest.* (Jossey-Bass, San Francisco) 1978.
41. Malinowski, B. *Sex and Repression in Savage Society.* (Routledge and Kegan Paul, London) 1927.
42. Herman, J. *Father–Daughter Incest.* (Harvard University Press, Cambridge, Massachusetts) 1981.
43. Fox, R. *The Red Lamp of Incest.* (E. P. Dutton, New York) 1980.
44. Demott, B. "The Pro-Incest Lobby." *Psychology Today.* March 1980, p. 12.
45. Summit, R. and J. Kryso. "Sexual Abuse of Children: A Clinical Spectrum." *American Journal of Orthopsychiatry* 48(2), p. 242.
46. Densen-Gerber, J. "Child Prostitution and Child Pornography: Medical, Legal, Societal Aspects of the Commercial Exploitation of Children." In K. MacFarlane, B. B. Jones, and L. L. Jenstrom, eds. *Sexual Abuse of Children: Selected Readings.* pp. 77–81. (Department of Health, Education and Welfare, GPO Pub. No. 78-30161, Washington, D.C.) 1980.
47. Lederer, L. ed. *Take Back the Night.* (William Morrow, New York) 1980, pp. 77–78.
48. Burgess, A. W. *Child Pornography and Sex Rings.* (Lexington Books, Lexington, Massachusetts) 1984.
49. S. R. Rep. No. 438, 95th Cong., 2d Session, 1978.
50. *Miller v California.* 413 U.S. 881, 1973.
51. *United States v Reedy.* 632 F. Supp. 1415 (W. D. Okl. 1986), affirmed 845 F.2d 239 (10th Cir. 1988).
52. Conte, J. R. "Progress in Treating the Sexual Abuse of Children." *Social Work,* 1984 pp. 258–263.
53. Briere, J. "The Effects of Childhood Sexual Abuse on Later Psychological Functioning: Defining a *Post-Sexual-Abuse Syndrome.* Paper presented at the Third National Conference on Sexual Victimization of Children, Washington, D.C., 1984.
54. Herman, J. A. *Father–Daughter Incest.* (Harvard University Press, Cambridge, Massachussetts) 1981.

55. Tower, C. C. *Understanding Child Abuse and Neglect.* 2d ed. (Allyn & Bacon, Boston) 1993, pp. 146–147.
56. Hartman, C. R., and A. W. Burgess. "Sexual Abuse of Children: Causes and Consequences." In *Child Maltreatment.* D. Cicchetti, and V. Carlson, eds. (Cambridge University Press, New York) 1989, pp. 114–122.
57. Mones, P. "Parricide: Opening a Window through the Defense of Teens Who Kill," 7 *Stanford Law & Policy Review* 61 (Winter, 1995–1996).
58. Mones, P. *When a Child Kills: Abused Children Who Kill Their Parents* (Simon & Schuster, New York) 1991.
59. Post, S. "Adolescent Parricide in Abusive Families," 61(7) *Child Welfare* 445 (1982).
60. Heide, K. M. *Why Kids Kill Their Parents,* 2d ed. (Sage, Thousand Oaks, California) 1995, p. 6.
61. Weigall, A. *Nero: The Singing Emperor of Rome* (Garden City Publishing, Garden City, New York) 1939.
62. Ibid.
63. Carlisle, M. R. "What Made Lizzie Borden Kill?" *American Heritage* 66 (1992).
64. Ibid.
65. Mones, P. *When a Child Kills: Abused Children Who Kill Their Parents* (Simon & Schuster, New York) 1991.
66. Heide, K. M. *Why Kids Kill Their Parents,* 2d ed. (Sage, Thousand Oaks, California) 1995.
67. Inman, R. *The Case of the People vs. Lyle and Erik Menendez,* www.cyberspace.com/sidebar2.html (September 17, 1996).
68. Corder, B. F., et. al., "Adolescent Parricide: A Comparison with Other Adolescent Murder," 133 (8) *American Journal of Psychiatry.* 1976, pp. 957–961.
69. Mones, P. *When a Child Kills: Abused Children Who Kill Their Parents* (Simon & Schuster, New York) 1991.
70. For an excellent discussion of controversies surrounding the use of experts, see Chadwick, D. L., and H. F. Kraus. "Irresponsible Testimony by Medical Experts in Cases Involving Abuse and Neglect of Children." *Child Maltreatment* 2(4) November, 1977.
71. See *State v Lindsey.* 149 Ariz. 472, 273, 720 P.2d 73, 74 (1986) regarding the admission of expert testimony describing the behavior of incest victims.
72. *State v Moran.* 151 Ariz. 378, 380, 728 P.2d 248, 250 (1986).
73. *State v. Higgins.* 61 Ohio App. 3d 414, 572 N.E. 2d 834, 837 (1990).
74. *Ingram v. McQuiston.* 261 N.C. 392, 134 S.E. 2d 705 (1964), which sets forth an example of misuse of hypothetical questions.

4

CHILD NEGLECT

Chapter Outline

Learning Objectives

After reading this chapter, you should be able to discuss the following concepts:

- The distinction between child neglect and physical child abuse.
- The various physical and emotional indicators of child neglect.
- Failure to thrive as a form of neglect.
- The difference between physical neglect and emotional neglect.

- The various types of acts or omissions that constitute emotional neglect.
- Other types of neglect that threaten the welfare of children.

Introduction

Some scholars have stated that child neglect is the most common form of maltreatment. According to Arthur Green, in New York the reported cases of neglect outnumbered those of physical abuse by eleven to one in 1987.[1] Other studies indicate that physical abuse is more prevalent than neglect. No matter who is right, child neglect is an important topic that all professionals should understand. Neglect is less obvious than physical or sexual abuse, and it may continue for years without any outsiders ever being aware that the child they see daily is a victim. It has many faces, forms, and appearances. There are serious cases in which a child's life is threatened and more mundane acts where the child is simply neglected on a daily basis. This chapter explores some of the more common forms of child neglect.

In the past twenty years, numerous texts, articles, and studies have been published that deal with neglect. The literature runs the gamut, from examining assessment techniques of neglect[2] to listing all the different forms of this abuse.[3] Except for rare instances, such as the *Home Alone* case discussed in the next Focus, child neglect does not receive the public attention that child sexual and physical abuse generates.[4] Part of the reason for this lack of emphasis may lie in the definition and nature of child neglect.

FOCUS *Home Alone:* The Movie or Real Life

The movie *Home Alone* was a surprise comedy hit during 1991. Then life imitated art. In Geneve, Illinois, the world read of a married couple who left their two young daughters home alone while they vacationed in Mexico. David and Sharon Schoo were arraigned on sixty-four criminal counts for leaving their daughters, age four and nine, alone for nine days. These counts included allegations that the parents had beaten the children with a belt and pulled their hair. additionally, the criminal complaint alleged that the Schoos locked one daughter in a crawl space for seven hours.

The authorities discovered that the children were alone after they ran to a neighbor's house when a smoke alarm in their home accidentally went off. The police placed the children in foster care and arrested the parents when they arrived at O'Hare International Airport as they returned from their vacation in Acapulco, Mexico.

The parents pled guilty to contributing to the neglect of a child and received two years probation. The couple's defense attorney stated that the children could be returned to the custody of the Schoos in a couple of months. The Schoos will participate in counseling and be electronically monitored while on probation.

Definition

Child neglect is the negligent treatment or maltreatment of a child by a parent or caretaker under circumstances indicating harm or threatened harm to the child's health or welfare. Although this appears at first glance to be a simple and straightforward statement, it covers a wide range of activities or omissions that impact on the physical and emotional well-being of a child.

At what point does mere inattention or lack of knowledge translate itself into child neglect? The definition given earlier would require an act or omission that results in harm or threatens to cause harm to a child's health or welfare. This act or omission may be physical or psychological. A strict interpretation of this definition would require that parents or caretakers guard their children like prisoners. However, this is unrealistic because children are mobile. They get into drawers, cabinets, and every corner in the house and yard. Therefore, there is a continuum that stretches from momentary inattention to gross inaction (see Figure 4.1).

Somewhere along this line acceptable parenting ends and child neglect begins. The following sections define the circumstances that professionals and courts have agreed on as clear cases of child neglect.

Causes of Neglect

Are poor children neglected and rich children well cared for? Unfortunately, a substantial number of people in society equate poverty with neglect, but simply being poor does not make a neglectful parent. There are children who live at the edge of poverty or below the poverty level and are loved and nurtured. On the other hand, there are children who live in million-dollar homes but are neglected or psychologically abused on a daily basis. The causes of neglect are varied and wide ranging.

Polansky and his colleagues in their classic text *Damaged Parents: An Anatomy of Child Neglect* established three major causes of neglect: economic causes, ecological causes, and personalistic causes.[5] *The economic theory suggests that neglect is caused by stress as a result of living in poverty. The ecological theory views family behavior and neglect as a result of social causes. The personalistic theory attributes child neglect to individual personality characteristics of the caretakers.*

Numerous studies have indicated that poverty is an important factor in the parents' ability to care for their children, and the question must be asked whether poverty causes neglect or whether poverty is the result of the parents' inability to function.[6]

FIGURE 4.1 Continuum of Neglect

PRACTICUM

Situation 1:

Howard is babysitting his eight-month-old daughter while his wife works nights. Howard is a smoker and has run out of cigarettes. He checks the baby, sees that she is sleeping, walks over the neighborhood store, and buys a pack of cigarettes. Has Howard committed child neglect?

Situation 2:

Jane has had to battle a weight problem all her life. She is determined that her two-month-old baby will not have the same problem. Therefore, Jane only feeds the baby six bottles of nonfat milk a day. (A traditional feeding of a two-month-old baby is approximately thirty-two ounces of formula a day.) The baby is losing weight and is constantly crying. Has Jane committed child neglect?

Situation 3:

Karen is a housewife who lives in an expensive four-thousand-square-foot home. While talking to a friend on the phone, Karen's two-year-old son went into the backyard and climbed over the fence surrounding the swimming pool. He fell into the pool and would have drowned except that their dog jumped in and pulled him out. Has Karen committed child neglect.

Situation 4:

Bill was watching television when his eighteen-month-old child walked into the kitchen and fell on the tile floor. She cut her lip and required three stitches. Has Bill committed child neglect?

Some scholars have indicated that families who neglect their children live in an environment that is unfriendly and characterized by low morale and hopelessness.[7] As indicated earlier, the issue is whether the environment causes neglect or is the environment a characteristic of the parents' inability to function.

A more reasoned approach seems to be that of the personalistic theories. In this approach, neglect is viewed as being caused by complex maladaptive interactions and/or lack of essential caretaking behaviors that are influenced by the level of parental skill, knowledge deficits, and other stress factors.[8]

Characteristics of Parents or Caretakers Who Neglect Their Children

Inability to plan: These parents lack the ability to establish goals, objectives, and direction. These parents may have low frustration levels and little ability to delay gratification.

Lack of knowledge: Parents have little or no knowledge about children's needs, housekeeping skills, cooking, and so on.

Lack of judgment: Parents may leave a young child alone and unsupervised.

Lack of motivation: Parents lack energy, have little desire to learn, and no other standard of comparison. These parents are apathetic–futile in that they are withdrawn and feel that nothing is worth doing.

Source: Adapted from Contwell, H. B. "Child Neglect." In C. H. Kempe, and R. E. Helfer, eds. *The Battered Child.* (University of Chicago Press, Chicago) 1980, pp. 183–197.

There are other models that profile personalities of neglectful parents or caretakers, and no study or theory has gained universal acceptance. However, certain factors have been established that indicate when a child is or may be neglected.[9] The following section examines those factors.

Indications of Child Neglect

No single set of factors establishes a clearly defined line dividing neglect and poor parenting. Any list must be viewed with caution. However, any professional who observes certain characteristics in young children should be suspicious. At the very least, professionals need to reassure themselves of the welfare of the child. Initial suspicion may lead to verification of child neglect. On the other hand, further checking may indicate a situational fact pattern that can or will cure itself without the intervention of public agencies.

Physical Indicators

Poor growth pattern.

Constant hunger, malnutrition.

Poor hygiene, body odor, and lice; inappropriate clothing.

Constant fatigue; listlessness; falls asleep in class.

Consistent lack of supervision, especially for long periods or in dangerous conditions.

Unexplained bruises or injuries as a result of poor supervision.

Unattended physical problems or medical needs such as lack of proper immunizations, gross dental problems, needs glasses/hearing aids.

Behavioral Indicators

Developmental lags.

Begs or steals food, forages through garbage; always hungry.

Destructive to self and/or others; extremes in behavior—aggressive and withdrawn; hyperactive.

Assumes adult responsibilities or acts in pseudo-mature fashion; exhibits infantile behavior; delinquent behavior.

Depressed/apathetic; states "no one cares."

Frequent school absences or chronic tardiness; seeks attention and/or affection.

Hypochondria.

Source: Adapted from Layman, R. *Current Issues—Volume 1: Child Abuse.* (Omnigraphics, Inc., Detroit) 1990, p. 37. Originally circulated by the Children's Safety Project in Manhattan.

Certain physical acts by children should alert teachers, nurses, social workers, and others to look for the reasons for these actions. Individual acts may appear and, in many instances, are simply normal childhood activities. However, if more than one of these acts continue, the professional should begin to look for a possible pattern of neglect.

Professionals should not only be alert to physical indications of neglect but watch for emotional or psychological indications that may signal child neglect or maltreatment. These factors may be normal stages of childhood development or may indicate a darker secret that should be examined.

Physical or emotional indicators may assist in determining whether a child is suffering from neglect. One form of child neglect occurs prior to the preschool years and can be life threatening. The next section discusses this serious form of child neglect.

Failure-to-Thrive Syndrome

Failure to thrive is a term that has generated controversy among scholars and medical professionals. The term has come to mean different things to different groups. One perspective states that failure to thrive is a result of the parents' failure to meet the nutritional needs of their children. The child exhibits a low height and weight and small head circumference when compared with other children.[10] Ruth Kempe and Richard Goldbloom argue that the term *failure to thrive* is misleading. They have used the term *malnutrition and growth retardation* or *growth failure without other disease* to describe the same or similar symptoms.[11] Kempe and her colleagues believe that the term *failure to thrive* is misleading in that the condition may be caused either by a disease or by a nonorganic cause. Many authorities believe that these distinctions are mutually exclusive. Kempe argues that clinical evidence supports her position. However, numerous scholars and medical professionals continue to identify the symptoms of malnutrition and growth retardation as *failure to thrive.* by whatever name this form of neglect is called, it can have devastating consequences for the infant.

Definition

Failure to thrive is an identifiable medical diagnosis. This designation classifies children whose development is deficient in relation to the established norms and whose physical condition is incompatible with viability and growth.[12] What is not so clear is the cause of this condition. It may be disease based or organically caused or may be attributed to nonorganic or family causes.

Nonorganic failure to thrive (NFTT) has been defined as a condition found in infants and diagnosed by the presence of two factors: the infant is under the fifth percentile in both height and weight, and the infant at one time weighed and was of a height within the

FOCUS Failure to Thrive—A Medical Response

The following is an example of a medical protocol for emergency room physicians.
EMERGENCY DEPARTMENT ASSESSMENT OF FAILURE TO THRIVE

1. *Failure to thrive (FTT) can be defined as an underweight (malnourished) condition in a young child.* The causes of FTT are 50 percent due to neglectful underfeeding, 30 percent organic, and 20 percent accidental underfeeding.

   Assessment of FTT in an emergency department is difficult because diagnosis requires historical documentation of prenatal and birth, past medical, family, nutritional, social, and developmental histories. Diagnosis is confirmed only when a child who has not been able to gain weight at home easily gains weight in a hospital.
2. *When should a child (eighteen months and younger) seen in an emergency department who is under the 5 percent-in-weight category be reported to the child abuse registry as suspected FTT?*

   When *any* of the following risk factors are present, call CAR immediately:
   a. Child displays a ravenous appetite, deprivational behaviors, or wrinkled skin from severe malnutrition.
   b. Family does not have a regular source of medical care for the child (should be able to provide name/address of physician or clinic).
   c. Child has not seen a doctor in the past six months for well-child care.
   d. Child has not had immunizations.
   e. Caretaker is vague about child's nutritional intake.
   f. Caretaker is oblivious or disinterested in child's condition.
   g. Caretaker appears to be under the influence of alcohol or drugs or is emotionally unstable.
   h. Family is residing in a temporary (i.e., in friends' or relatives' home) or transient (i.e., car/park/motel) residence.
3. Special Considerations
   a. Organic causes include chromosomal, gastrointestinal, renal, cardiac, and endocrine disorders, as well as prenatal, CNS abnormalities, chronic infections, cystic fibrosis, and idiopathic short stature.
   b. Ten percent of nonorganic FTT have fractures from physical abuse.
   c. Mixed etiology of FTT occurs frequently.
   d. Hospitalization is frequently the only realistic means to provide the child with protection while assessment for FTT occurs.
   e. CBC may be helpful in assessing for nutritional anemia.

Source: Adapted from Dr. James Williams' (Children's Hospital, Oakland) presentation entitled "Medical Evidence." *Physical Child Abuse Prosecution.* (California District Attorneys Association, Sacramento, California) 1992, p. 30.

expected norm.[13] Failure to treat this condition can result in the death of the infant. The child simply wastes away and dies.

Characteristics

Children suffering from NFTT exhibit emaciation, paleness, weakness with little subcutaneous fat, and decreased muscle mass. Most of the children appear listless, apathetic, and motionless.[14] The responding professional must be careful not to confuse NFTT with other physical ailments. Diseases such as chronic renal disease, food allergies, or congenital heart disease may cause a child to fail to grow and gain weight. Nonorganic failure to thrive is a complex medical condition that requires even physicians to carefully examine the child.

Although the main cause for this condition is lack of adequate calories, the roots of NFTT can normally be associated with the lack of parent–child relationship. The inability of the parents to respond to the physical needs of the child is a symptom of their lack of parenting skills that may manifest itself in other ways. The lack of parenting skills may prevent the parents from recognizing and responding to the child's emotional and developmental needs. Simply providing the infant with the necessary nutritional supplements does not solve the problem of NFTT. Professionals should work with family members to improve their ability to interact with each other and the child. This approach does not work overnight. It is a time-consuming and prolonged treatment program that must be carefully monitored.

The consequences of NFTT on the child are substantial. Even if the child is initially treated and the original symptoms disappear, the long-term effects of NFTT are not easily remedied. Several follow-up studies have been conducted on children who were initially hospitalized for NFTT. These studies indicated continued growth problems, school failure, and psychological problems including retardation.[15] Failure to thrive is a physical condition that results from the inability of the parents to physically care for the child. The next section discusses emotional neglect and explores the parents' inability to respond to the child emotionally.

Emotional Neglect

Emotional neglect is used as a definition to distinguish this type of abuse from *physical maltreatment*. Some scholars use the latter term to include all forms of neglect. However, emotional neglect is a specific form of abuse that should be examined independently. Unlike child abuse or certain types of child neglect, there may not be any physical scars on a child who is suffering from emotional abuse. The bruises or scars are implanted on the child's mind as a result of the caretaker's actions or inactions. Many jurisdictions require proof that the psychological injury to the child is a direct result of emotional abuse. Consequently, this is one of the most difficult forms of child neglect to prove. Whereas emotional abuse may cause adverse physical reactions in the child, these responses are caused by acts of the caretakers that affect the child's psyche.

Definition

Emotional neglect consists of acts or omissions which are judged by community standards and professional expertise to be psychologically damaging to the child. These acts are traditionally committed by caretakers who are in a position of power over the child. This power differential may be based upon any number of characteristics including age, status, position, or relationship. These acts affect the child's psychological stability. This in turn may cause behavioral, cognitive, or physical problems in the child.[16]

As indicated previously, a child suffering from emotional abuse will not have a visible bruise, scar, burn, or broken bone. However, the child's mind may suffer a more terrible and long-lasting injury. Children who are emotionally abused may suffer from feelings of inadequacy, isolation, or being unwanted or unloved. They may have low self-esteem and consider themselves unworthy.[17]

Emotional neglect is hard to detect because there are no physical scars. However, the internal injuries may be manifested by numerous acts or actions. While the definition of emotional neglect may appear simple, describing the characteristics or acts of the caretaker that comprise this form of neglect is more difficult. the following section briefly examines some of the more common forms of this type of child neglect.

Characteristics

Which if any of the situations in the next Practicum are examples of emotional neglect or simply inexperienced or bad parenting? Clearly, situations 1 and 3 would fall within the definition set forth earlier. Situation 2 may well be acceptable depending on the activities engaged in by the father and mother, or it might fall into the classification of sexual abuse discussed in the previous chapter.

Hart and Brassard in their seminal study identified specific categories of emotional neglect.[18] These acts form a pattern of behavior that includes the following:

> *Spurning or rejecting the child:* The caretaker refuses to acknowledge the child's worth or emotional needs. Examples of spurning include treating the child differently than his or her siblings or calling the child stupid, weak, or worthless.
>
> *Isolating the child:* The caretaker refuses to allow the child to interact with others. Examples of isolation include locking the child in a room, closet, or other

PRACTICUM Emotional Neglect or Bad Parenting?

Situation 1:

Both Sally and Bob work nights. Sally's mother watches Billy, age two years, at night. After they pick up the baby, they are in need of sleep, so they put Billy in his room and tie the door shut so they can sleep for six to eight hours.

Situation 2:

Jill and Howard believe in nudity within the home. They also undress their three-year-old daughter. They eat, watch television, and to housework undressed.

Situation 3:

Liz and Jeff do not believe in corporal punishment. Instead of spanking their four-year-old son, they tell him that, unless he is good, they will leave him and the night monsters will eat his legs.

confined space for an extended period of time and denying the child complete access to other adults or children.

Terrorizing the child: The caretaker establishes a state of extreme fear, fright, or dread in the child. Examples of terrorizing include threatening to hurt, mutilate, or abandon the child or placing the child in a frightening environment.

Corrupting the child: The caretaker engages in antisocial behavior with the child. Examples of corrupting the child include requiring him to stay home and act as a servant instead of attending school, involving the child in sexual acts with adults or siblings, and exploiting the child by using him in pornographic movies.

Denying the child emotional responses: The caretaker fails to provide emotional responses necessary for the healthy psychological development by the child. Examples of this form of emotional neglect include mechanical responses to the child, lack of touching and caring, and no eye contact with the child.

Although one act in the above categories may not establish emotional neglect, when engaged in for prolonged periods of time, emotional injury to the child is almost inevitable. Other scholars have established comparable types of categories for emotional neglect.[19] The National Center on Child Abuse and Neglect (NCCAN) established a similar set of categories for its National Incidence Studies in 1980 and 1986. Emotional abuse is also referred to as psychological abuse or maltreatment. It is receiving more and more attention as scholars and researchers continue to study this form of violence. Max Lesnik-Oberstein and his associates in The Netherlands have conducted research on psychologically abusive mothers and concluded that mothers who have high levels of hostility are more likely than other parents to commit psychological abuse.[20] Other scholars, such as Davis, are examining whether the threat of physical punishment (spanking) is a form of emotional abuse.[21] Still other researchers are attempting to validate a method of measuring emotional abuse. Two examples of such tools are the *Psychological Maltreatment Inventory* and the *Child Abuse and Trauma Scale.*[22]

Characteristics of Children Who Have Been Emotionally Neglected

Clingy and indiscriminate attachment.

Fearfulness—exaggerated.

Depressed, withdrawn, apathetic.

Sleep, speech, or eating disorders.

Substance abuse.

Antisocial, destructive behavior.

Enuresis and encopresis.

Habit disorders (biting, rocking, whining, picking at scabs).

Source: Adapted from Dr. James Williams' (Children's Hospital, Oakland) presentation entitled "Medical Evidence." *Physical Child Abuse Prosecution.* (California District Attorneys Association, Sacramento, California) 1992, p. 10.

Whether a caretaker is engaging in emotional neglect may vary according to the culture of the family. For example, in some Asian cultures shame is an accepted technique to reinforce family behavior within and outside of the family.[23] Other cultures have their own methods of raising children that are not viewed as abusive by either the parents or the child and therefore do not psychologically damage the child. In our own cultures, many of us have experienced the use of guilt by parents, siblings, loved ones, and others to induce us to respond in certain ways.

The distinction between the use of normal child-rearing techniques and emotional neglect is the psychological damage that is inflicted on the child. If the child suffers as a result of the caretaker's acts or omissions and if that suffering is beyond the accepted norm in society, those actions may be labeled as emotional neglect.

Other Types of Child Neglect

The preceding sections briefly discussed some of the more common forms of child neglect. Unfortunately, those types of neglect are not the only types of acts or omissions that result in child neglect. This section examines other types of neglect that threaten the welfare of the child.

Dirty Homes

Dirty homes are those living situations that expose the child to injury or life-threatening illness.[24] The term *dirty home* is used in lieu of *unsafe home environment* to identify a specific form of neglect. Examples of dirty homes include those living arrangements that have exposed wiring, shattered or broken glass, animal feces, lice or rodents, and other situations where children might injure themselves. The Home Accident Prevention Inventory was developed to measure the safety of the home environment. It evaluates fire and electrical hazards, suffocation risks, and the presence of firearms and poisons.[25]

Simply having a sink full of dirty dishes and soapwater for several days does not raise a household to the level of this form of neglect. A home may be unclean and chock-full of dirty clothes and unwashed dishes and still provide a loving environment for children. Some parents do not have money to do the laundry or wash dishes on a daily basis.

The discovery of dirty homes may be made by police officers, welfare workers, social workers, nurses, or teachers paying a home visit. Once these professionals are aware of the situation, they should alert the proper agency to evaluate whether the child should be removed from the home or the parents given assistance in learning how to maintain a safe and healthy living situation for the child. Sometimes the dirty home is a result of extreme poverty and the resulting hopelessness that accompanies it. On other occasions, the landlord simply is not responding to requests from low-income tenants. In these situations, intervention by social service agencies may be sufficient to remedy the problem. a dirty home is often a

FOCUS When Should a Child Be Removed from the Home?

Jeannette S., age five, lived with her mother, Margery, in Merced, California, until she was removed from the home by child protective services (CPS) workers. The mother's psychological profile indicated that she was of above-average intelligence, suffered from chronic anxiety, and had a somewhat schizoid personality. Margery's relationship with her daughter was characterized as a close and loving one.

Margery had a limited income and had been active in seeking assistance from local county social service agencies. She had requested and received visits from a public health nurse who had instructed her on child care techniques for Jeannette. She had also received one visit from a homemaker service. The CPS representatives visited her home and found it dirty and cluttered with debris. There were extensive dog feces on the kitchen floor and cat feces in the bathroom. Additionally, the house smelled of urine, and spoiled food was on the stove. Jeannette had been sleeping on the couch in the living room because her bedroom was a mess.

School authorities testified that Jeannette sometimes appeared at school in dirty clothes that were soiled with urine. They stated that this caused Jeannette to be teased by the other children. However, they also stated that her academic progress is good and she is considered a bright child who gets along well with other children.

The juvenile dependency court found sufficient evidence to support a finding of dependency and ordered Jeannette removed from the care and control of her mother. The court stated that filthy homes are difficult cases to evaluate and that care must be taken when considering removing the child from the mother, especially when the mother is a loving parent even if inept at homemaking. The appellate court, while agreeing to the determination of dependency, reversed the removal of Jeannette from the home, stating that there were other less severe alternatives available, such as ordering CPS and other social service agencies to work with the mother.

Source: In re Jeannette S., 94 Cal. App. 3d 52 (1979).

symptom of more serious underlying family problems such as incest and sexual abuse. Occasionally, authorities will discover a dirty home that results from the parents' inability to cope with everyday life. In these situations, long-term counseling may be required. In the event that the decision is made to remove the child from the home, a critical aspect of the court case will be a description of the home environment. this may come in the form of a narrative, diagrams, or photographs.

Dirty-home cases normally require an expert witness to testify to specifics in the home that place the child at risk. Doctors, public health nurses, and in some instances building code inspectors may provide the necessary testimony to establish that the living environment is injurious to the well-being of the child.

Drugs and Alcohol

Caretakers who use drugs or alcohol in excess are emotionally unavailable to parent and may not be able to properly supervise their children. Additionally, the child may find some portion of a narcotic, ingest it, and suffer serious injury or death. Studies have indicated that substance-abusing parents are highly resistant to changing their behavior.[26] This type of neglect requires long-term intervention by social service agencies.

Another aspect of drug and alcohol neglect concerns mothers who use drugs while pregnant or during nursing. Infants may be born addicted and suffer withdrawal immediately after birth if the mother ingested drugs during her pregnancy. In either situation, the infant is at risk.

If the mother uses drugs during pregnancy, they will readily cross the placenta into the fetus's body. Some parents expose children to drugs in other manners. Prenatal abuse of drugs can cause a wide variety of serious medical complications to the child, including neurological and physical defects, growth retardation, premature delivery, and long-term developmental abnormalities.[27] One source states that one in every ten newborns in the United States has been prenatally exposed to drugs.[28] Another authority estimates that 20 percent of all newborns in California have been prenatally exposed to drugs.[29] Cocaine has been used as a topical anesthetic on sore nipples, bottles and pacifiers have accidentally been contaminated with drugs, and some parents use drugs as an intentional method to soothe an irritable infant.

Cocaine may cause a variety of problems during and after pregnancy.[30] It may lead to spontaneous abortions and increase the chances of premature labor. Neonates exposed in utero suffer a variety of problems, including cardiac and central nervous system abnormalities, hyperactivity, and persistent irritability. These problems may appear at birth or later, during the infant's childhood.

Mothers who smoke marijuana more than once a month have an increased risk of delivering a preterm, low-weight infant. It has been reported that the use of marijuana has a stronger effect on newborns than smoking twenty cigarettes each day during pregnancy.[31] However, other scholars reported no long-term effects from the use of marijuana during pregnancy.

There continues to be controversies regarding the effects of drugs and/or alcohol on the fetus. Despite these limitations and the lack of clearly accepted research, states have enacted a number of laws mandating the reporting of newborns that have been exposed to drugs.[32] For example, Wiese and Daro report that by 1994 twenty-seven states mandate reporting of newborns who have been exposed to drugs.[33]

Alcohol is one of the most commonly abused substances in the United States. It may be one of the leading causes of mental retardation in children. Mothers who are alcoholic or drink excessively during pregnancy may have their babies suffer from fetal alcohol syndrome (FAS). This is a condition in which the alcohol ingested by the mother crosses the placenta, causing the fetus to have the same blood-alcohol level as the mother. The infant will exhibit alcohol withdrawal within the first few days of birth. These signs may include hyperactivity, tremors, seizures, and difficulty in feeding and sleeping. Children who have been exposed to alcohol in utero and who as a result suffer from FAS have an average IQ of 63.[34] Growth failure and abnormalities in the heart, kidneys, ears, and skeletal system

PRACTICUM How Many Drinks Is Too Much?

Stephanie and Bob are married. Stephanie is seventeen, Bob is twenty-one. Stephanie just found out that she is two months pregnant and is very excited about it. Bob has explained that it's okay as long as the pregnancy or the child doesn't interfere with their social activities. Both Bob and Stephanie drink hard liquor, wine, beer, coffee, and soft drinks. They both smoke cigarettes, and Stephanie loves to eat chocolate candy bars.

1. At each football tailgate party, Stephanie has four or five shots of tequila and several beer chasers.
2. In the evening, Bob likes to smoke a joint of marijuana before bed, claiming that it relaxes him. Stephanie stays in the room while he smokes the joint because she likes the smell of marijuana.
3. While Bob smokes his joint, Stephanie has one or two glasses of red wine because she has read somewhere that drinking wine is good for your heart.

Which, if any, of the above acts are proper parenting? Even if they are not model parenting practices, can they be classified as neglectful? Should the state intervene? Why or why not? If the state is to act, what should it do?

have also been reported. It should be noted that not all mothers who have an occasional drink give birth to children suffering from FAS, of which we are just beginning to study the extent and dynamics. Scholars estimate that between 1 and 3 infants out of 1,000 newborns suffer from FAS.[35]

Clear legal authority exists for courts to remove the child from the custody of the mother immediately after birth in these situations. In the *Matter of Baby X,* the Michigan Court of Appeals stated,

> *Prenatal treatment can be considered probative of a child's neglect. . . . We hold that a newborn suffering narcotics withdrawal symptoms as a consequence of prenatal maternal drug addiction may properly be considered a neglected child within the jurisdiction of the . . . court.*[36]

Drug and alcohol neglect is a serious form of child maltreatment. The child may be exposed to these substances during or after pregnancy. Normally, these situations involve action or omissions on the part of the caretakers. Just as there is a controversy surrounding the effect of drugs and/or alcohol on newborns, so is there a raging debate regarding the appropriate remedy or action once this condition is discovered. Some authorities urge removal the child from the custody of the mother to ensure the child is properly cared for. Others claim that such activities infringe on the mother's constitutional right of privacy.[37] Still others argue for treatment of the pregnant mother in hopes of rehabilitating the mother and keeping the mother and child together.[38] The next section explores medical neglect, which is a type of neglect that occurs when the parents refuse to act.

Medical Neglect

Medical neglect is the refusal of a parent or caretaker to obtain acceptable medical services for the child. This chapter has indicated that parents and caretakers must provide their children with food, clothing, and shelter. Failure to do so may be classified as neglect. It is equally clear that failure to obtain necessary lifesaving medical care if also neglect.

In *Heinemann's Appeal* in 1880, the courts established the principle that when parents fail to provide medical care for their children, the state may intervene to do so.[39] In that case, the father refused to seek medical care for his wife and three of his children who were all suffering from diphtheria. All four of them died as a result of his failure to act. The maternal grandmother sought guardianship of the two remaining children, alleging that she was afraid the same fate would befall them. The Pennsylvania Supreme Court upheld the lower court's granting of the guardianship, stating that the deceased children had been shamefully neglected in regard to their medical treatment.[40] The authority for the state to intervene in neglect cases is based on the state's inherent *parens patriae* authority to protect children.[41]

One of the most emotional and hard-fought battles dealing with medical neglect concerns the conflict between parents' religious beliefs that may prevent them from seeking and accepting medical care and the state's interest in protecting children. When care is necessary to protect the child's life, the state's interest in the welfare of the child will normally prevail. This is based on the constitutional distinction between the right to believe in a religion and the freedom to act in accordance with that belief.

In *Prince v Massachusetts,* the U.S. Supreme Court set forth a well-reasoned opinion laying out the distinction between the right of belief and the liberty to act on that belief:

> *Acting to guard the general interest in youth's well being, the state as* parens patriae *may restrict the parent's control by requiring school attendance, regulating or prohibiting child labor, and in many other ways. Its authority is not nullified merely because the parent grounds his claim to control the child's course of conduct on religion or conscience. Thus, he cannot claim freedom from compulsory vaccination for the child more than for himself on religious grounds. The right to practice religion freely does not include liberty to expose the community or the child to communicable disease or the latter to ill health or death. . . .*
>
> *Parents may be free to become martyrs themselves. But it does not follow they are free, in identical circumstances, to make martyrs of their children before they have reached the age of full and legal discretion when they can make that decision for themselves.*[42]

Since 1944, when this decision was rendered, its reasoning has been consistently followed by both the Supreme Court and state courts. There are numerous court decisions upholding the state's right to intervene and order medical treatment over the parent's objections when the alternative might be a life-threatening illness or injury to the child.

When parents refuse medical care that might be advisable but is not essential to the life of the child, courts are divided on whether the state has the same authority to intervene. The greater the threat of harm to the child, the more likely courts will authorize medical treatment. In addition to evaluating the degree of harm or threat to the child, courts will examine whether the medical condition is progressive or stable. If the medical condition is stable, some courts will not allow the state to intervene. Some courts will also consider the child's preferences if they are old enough to express a knowing and intelligent answer.

The failure of a parent to obtain medical treatment for a child is clearly a form of child neglect. The state has a right and obligation to protect its citizens and, especially, children, who cannot make informed decisions for themselves. The controversy of medical neglect due to failure to treat based on religious grounds is an emotional and sometimes heartbreaking process for both professionals in the field and the parents.

Abandonment

Abandonment is parental conduct that indicates a conscious rejection of the obligations of parenthood. Abandonment may take many forms and is usually established by presenting evidence of the parents leaving the child without proper care or custody. Almost everyone has read in newspapers or seen on television cases of newborn babies found in trash containers or on doorsteps of social service agencies. The identity of the mother or father is almost always unknown. These are clear-cut cases of abandonment.

The sanction for abandonment of a child may be a termination of the parental rights. This is accomplished by either the state or the party with whom the child placed filing a petition requesting that the parents' rights and obligations to the child be terminated. In the trash container type of case mentioned above, courts will hesitate to grant such a petition.

In other situations, the issue of abandonment is not so clear. What if a parent leaves the child with caretakers and does not communicate with them or the child for a two-year period? The caretakers may file a petition to terminate parental rights. At the hearing, the parent shows up and states that he or she would like custody of the child. A parent may abandon a child and then evidence intent to reestablish the parent–child relationship. The question to be asked in the factual situation presented above is whether the parent indicated a conscious rejection of the obligations of parenthood. Some courts will examine all the facts before finding that the child has been abandoned and terminating the parents' rights. Factors such as why the parent left the child, the parent's expressed intentions to now care for the child, and whether the parent attempted to communicate with the child while separated from him are all important considerations in determining whether the parent abandoned the child. Abandonment of a child is a form of child neglect, and the state will intervene to protect the child. This intervention may take the form of the termination of parental rights.

Summary

This chapter has examined the various types of child neglect. In many instances, no clear line exists between poor parenting and neglect. Each situation must be evaluated on its own merits, and professionals must look at the totality of the circumstances to determine whether the child is a victim of neglect.

The causes of neglect are varied and do not simply rest on the assumption that poverty is the cause. The rich and famous can and do subject their children to acts that are clearly child neglect. Although there is no complete or all-inclusive list of physical or behavioral actions that signal that a child is a victim of neglect, there are indicators that should raise suspicion in any professional. Caution must be exercised and care taken not to react to a situation that may not be neglect.

Failure to thrive is one of the more serious forms of child neglect. However, there are other valid medical reasons for a child to be under the 5 percent category in height or weight. Medical personnel must carefully evaluate any child who is suspected of suffering from failure to thrive to ensure that they do not misdiagnose the cause.

Emotional neglect is one of the hardest forms of child neglect to define and evaluate. Many parents yell at their children. Has anyone not experienced or heard of a parent raising his or her voice to a young child? The key to emotional neglect is the degree of injury the child suffers from the caretaker's actions. Normal parenting may require a caretaker to raise his voice to a child. When this act becomes the norm and the child is terrorized, threatened, or worse, the situation clearly becomes one of emotional neglect.

There are numerous other forms of child neglect. Some of the more common types include dirty homes, drug abuse, medical neglect, and abandonment.

Key Terms

child neglect—the negligent treatment or maltreatment of a child by a parent or caretaker under circumstances indicating harm or threatened harm to the child's health or welfare.

Economic theory of child neglect—suggests that neglect is caused by stress as a result of living in poverty.

Ecological theory of child neglect—views the family behavior and neglect as a result of social causes.

Personalistic theory of child neglect—attributes child neglect to individual personality characteristics of the caretakers.

Nonorganic failure to thrive (NFTT)—a condition found in infants and diagnosed by the presence of two factors: the infant is under the fifth percentile in both height and weight, and the infant at one time weighed and was of a height within the expected norm.

emotional neglect—acts or omissions that are judged by community standards and professional expertise to be psychologically damaging to the child.

dirty home—those living situations that expose the child to injury or life-threatening illness.

medical neglect—the refusal of a parent or caretaker to obtain acceptable medical services for the child.

abandonment—parental conduct that indicates a conscious rejection of the obligations of parenthood.

Discussion Questions

1. Based on your reading, what is the single most important cause of neglect? Why?
2. Should professionals rely on charts that list possible indicators of neglect? What are the dangers inherent in these lists?
3. How can physicians and nurses protect themselves from charges that they misdiagnosed a child as a failure to thrive? If they are unsure of the medical condition, should they allow the child to return home with the parents? What are the advantages and disadvantages of this approach?
4. Emotional neglect is a gray area in family violence. Can you list absolute factors that in your mind establish a fact pattern for emotional neglect?
5. If a mother is found to be addicted to and using drugs during her pregnancy, should the court order the child removed from her custody before it is born? Why? Why not?

Suggested Readings

Ammerman, R., and M. Hersen, eds. *Case Studies in Family Violence.* (Plenum Press, New York) 1991.

Ammerman, R. T., and M. Hersen, eds. *Assessment of Family Violence.* (John Wiley, New York) 1992.

Garbarino, J., E. Guttmann, and J. W. Seeley. *The Psychologically Battered Child.* (Jossey-Bass, San Francisco) 1986.

Katz, S. N. *When Parents Fail.* (Beacon Press, Boston) 1971.

Kempe, C. H., and R. E. Helfer, eds. *The Battered Child.* (University of Chicago Press, Chicago) 1980.

Myers, J. *Evidence in Child Abuse and Neglect.* 2d ed. (John Wiley, New York) 1992.

Polansky, N., M. Chambers, E. Buttenwieser, and D. Williams, eds. *Damaged Parents: An Anatomy of Child Neglect.* (University of Chicago Press, Chicago) 1981.

Weisz, V. G. *Children and Adolescents in Need.* (Sage, Thousand Oaks, California) 1995.

Young, L. *Wednesday's Children.* (McGraw-Hill, New York) 1964.

Endnotes

1. Green, A. H. "Child Neglect." In R. Ammerman and M. Hersen, eds., *Case Studies in Family Violence,* (Plenum Press, New York) 1991, p. 135.
2. Ammerman, R. T., and M. Hersen. *Assessment of Family Violence.* (John Wiley, New York) 1992.
3. Myers, J. *Evidence in Child Abuse and Neglect.* 2d ed. (John Wiley, New York) 1992.
4. Dubowitz, H., and L. Berliner. "Neglecting the Neglect of Neglect," *Journal of Interpersonal Violence.* (4/9) December 1994, pp. 556–561.

5. Polansky, N., M. Chambers, E. Buttenwieser, and D. Williams. *Damaged Parents: An Anatomy of Child Neglect.* (University of Chicago Press, Chicago) 1981, p. 21.
6. See L. Young's *Wednesday's Children.* (McGraw-Hill, New York) 1964, and S. N. Katz's *When Parents Fail.* (Beacon Press, Boston) 1971.
7. Wolock, I., and B. Horowitz. "Child Maltreatment and Maternal Deprivation among AFDC Families." *Social Service Review* (53) 1979, pp. 175–184.
8. Hansen, D. J., and V. M. MacMilian. "Behavioral Assessment of Child Abuse and Neglectful Families: Recent Development and Current Issues." *Behavior Modification* (14) 1990, pp. 225–278.
9. Compare Polansky, N. A., N. D. Borgman, and C. DeSaix's *Roots of Futility.* (Jossey-Bass, San Francisco) 1972, and Hally, C., N. F. Polansky, and N. A. Polansky's *Child Neglect: Mobilizing Services.* (National Center on Child Abuse and Neglect, U.S. Dept. of Health and Human Services, Washington D.C.) 1980.
10. *Child Abuse Prevention Handbook.* (Office of the Attorney General, Crime Prevention Center, Sacramento, California) 1982, p. 9.
11. Kempe, R. S., and R. B. Goldbloom. "Malnutrition and Growth Retardation (Failure to Thrive) in the Context of Child Abuse and Neglect." In *The Battered Child.* 4th ed. R. E. Helfer, and R. S. Kempe, eds. (University of Chicago Press, Chicago) 1987, pp. 312–332.
12. Giovannoni, J. "Definitional Issues in Child Maltreatment." In D. Cicchetti, and V. Carlson, eds. *Child Maltreatment.* (Cambridge University Press, United Kingdom) 1989, pp. 12–13.
13. See English, P. C. "Failure to Thrive with Organic Reason." *Pediatric Annuals* (7) 1978, pp. 774–780.
14. Kempe and Goldbloom. "Malnutrition and Growth Retardation." p. 318.
15. Hufton, I. W., and R. K. Oates. "Nonorganic Failure to Thrive: A Long Term Follow-up." *Pediatrics* 8, 1977, pp. 73–77; and Oates, R. K., A. Peacock, and D. Forrest. "Long Term Effects of Nonorganic Failure to Thrive." *Pediatrics* (75) 1985, pp. 36–40.
16. Rorty, M., J. Yager, and E. Rossotto, "Childhood Sexual, Physical, and Psychological Abuse and Their Relationship to Comorbid Psychopathology in Bulimia," *The International Journal of Eating Disorders.* (16/4) December 1994, pp. 317–335.
17. Krugman, R. D., and M. K. Krugman. "Emotional Abuse in the Classroom." *American Journal of Diseases of Children* (138) 1984, pp. 284–286.
18. Hart, S. N., and M. Brassard. "Developing and validating operationally defined measures of emotional maltreatment: A multimodal study of the relationships between caretaker behaviors and child characteristics across three developmental levels." (Grant No. DHHS 90CA1216–01). Washington D.C.: Department of Health and Human Services and the National Center on Child Abuse and Neglect, 1986.
19. See Garbarino, J., E. Guttmann, and J. W. Seeley, *The Psychologically Battered Child.* (Jossey-Bass, San Francisco) 1986.
20. Lesnik-Oberstein, M., A. J. Koers, and L. Cohen. "Parent Hostility and Its Sources in Psychologically Abusive Mothers: A Test of the Three-Factor Theory," 19/1 *Child Abuse & Neglect* 1995, p. 33.
21. Davis, P. W. "Threats of Corporal Punishment as Verbal Aggression: A Naturalistic Study," 20/4 *Child Abuse and Neglect* 1996, p. 289.
22. See Engels, M. L., and D. Moisan. "The Psychological Maltreatment Inventory: Development of a Measure of Psychological Maltreatment in Childhood for Use in Adult Clinical Settings," 74 *Psychological Reports* 595 (1994), and Sanders, B., and E. Becker-Lausen. "The Measurement of Psychological Maltreatment: Early Data on the Child Abuse and Trauma Scale," *Child Abuse and Neglect* 315 (1995).
23. Ho, M. K. "Social Work Practices with Asian Americans." In A. Morales, and B. W. Sheafor, eds. *Social Work: A Profession of Many Faces.* (Allyn & Bacon, Boston) 1989.
24. See Hansen, D. J., and J. E. Warner, "Child Physical Abuse and Neglect." In R. T. Ammerman, and M. Hersen, eds. *Assessment of Family Violence.* (John Wiley, New York) 1992.

25. Ibid., p. 134.
26. Famulara, Kinscherff, Bunshaft, Spivak, and Fenton. "Parent Compliance to Court-Ordered Treatment Interventions in Cases of Child Maltreatment," *Child Abuse and Neglect: A Guide for Intervention.* (U.S. Department of Health and Human Services, April 1993).
27. Petitti, D., and M. Coleman. "Cocaine and the Risk of Low Birth Rate," 80 (1) *American Journal of Public Health* 25 (1990), and D. R. Weston, et. al., "Drug-Exposed Babies: Research and Clinical Issues," 9(5) *National Center for Clinical Infant Programs Bulletin* 7 (1989).
28. Toufexis, A. "Innocent Victims," *Time,* May 13, 1991, p. 56.
29. Atkins, E. "Reporting Fetal Abuse through California's Child Abuse and Neglect Reporting Act," 21(1) *Southwestern University Law Review* 1992, pp. 105–123.
30. Ibid. p. 883.
31. Hatch, E. E. and M. B. Bracken. "Effect of Marijuana Use in Pregnancy on Fetal Growth," 124 *American Journal of Epidemiology* 986 (1986).
32. Wiese, D., and D. Daro. *Current Trends in Child Abuse Reporting and Fatalities: The Results of the 1994 Annual Fifty State Survey* (National Committee to Prevent Child Abuse, Chicago, 1995).
33. Ibid.
34. Bays, J. "Substance Abuse and Child Abuse," 37 (4) *Pediatric Clinics of North America,* p. 881 (August 1990).
35. Little, B. B., et al., "Failure to Recognize Fetal Alcohol Syndrome in Newborn Infants," 144 *American Journal of Diseases of Children* (1990), pp. 1142–1146.
36. 293 N. W. 2d 736 at 739 (1980). See also *In the Matter of Stefanel Tyesha C.,* 157 A.D. 2d 322, 298 N. Y. S. 2d 280 (1990) involving a mother who used drugs during her pregnancy where the court held it did not have to wait until the child suffered a broken bone or shattered psyche before it acted.
37. Garrity-Rokous, F. E. "Punitive Legal Approaches to the Problem of Prenatal Drug Exposure," 15 *Infant Mental Health Journal* 218 (1994).
38. Finnegan, A., et al., "Comprehensive Care of the Pregnant Addict and Its Effect on Material and Infant Outcome," 1 *Contemporary Drug Problems* 795 (1992).
39. 96 Pa. 112 (1880).
40. Ibid., p. 115.
41. See *Prince v Massachusetts,* 321 U.S. 158 (1944), where the U.S. Supreme Court stated that the state has a wide range of power for limiting parental freedom and authority in things affecting a welfare.
42. 98 U.S. at pp. 166–167, 170 (footnotes omitted).

5

SIBLING ABUSE

Chapter Outline

Learning Objectives

After reading this chapter, you should be able to discuss the following concepts:

- The nature and extent of sibling abuse.
- Why children abuse their siblings.
- Society's response to the abuse of a sibling by a parent.
- The rationale for removing a child from the home when a sibling has been abused.
- The arguments in favor of and in opposition to sterilization of abusing parents.

Introduction

Sibling abuse is probably the most common form of family violence in the United States. Gelles and Cornell stated this fact in another manner when they wrote that the most commonly victimized family members are siblings.[1] If sibling abuse is in fact the most common form of family violence, why is there such a reluctance on the part of society and professionals to discuss it? Very few texts are devoted exclusively to this topic. Most academic articles dealing with child abuse may include as an afterthought a discussion of sibling abuse. Two areas of sibling abuse that are being examined in some detail are incest and the abuse of a sibling by parents.

A variety of reasons exist for this lack of discussion regarding sibling abuse. Many people consider sibling aggression to be a normal part of growing up. Everyone has heard excuses for sibling aggression. They are common refrains in families with more than one child. Society tends to minimize sibling aggression. Yet, early studies in New York and Philadelphia indicated that 3 percent of all homicides committed in those cities were committed by siblings against siblings.[2] In another classic study of sibling abuse, Steinmetz found that parents did not consider their children's physical aggression toward siblings as abuse. They would even talk with friends, neighbors, and relatives about the aggression, viewing it as an inevitable part of growing up.[3] Whipple theorized that violent families often face multiple problems that include chaos and deprivation. She believes that sibling abuse may be more likely to occur in such overburdened families because parents who are overwhelmed with multiple stressors may selectively ignore what they perceive as normal sibling rivalry when in fact such acts are in reality sibling abuse.[4]

Extent of the Problem

No one has accurate figures on the nature, type, or extent of sibling abuse. However, most authorities agree that it is the most common form of family violence. The popular media first addressed this issue in 1979 with a report in *U.S. News &*

FOCUS Sibling Abuse and Excuses

How many of the following excuses have you heard used to justify one sibling's acts toward another?

- Don't worry about it; it's just normal sibling rivalry.
- They were just playing doctor.
- Kids will be kids.
- He really didn't mean to hurt his sister. He loves her.
- It's just normal childhood curiosity.
- Kids are always calling each other names.
- I told him not to hit her again.
- They will grow out of it.

World Report that stated that 138,000 children aged three to seventeen years had used a weapon on a sibling within the last year.[5] In a 1980 study, Straus, Gelles, and Steinmetz reported that 82 percent of parents of children surveyed considered sibling violence to be the most common form of intrafamily violence.[6] In another early study, Steinmetz (1981) found that a clear majority of children used physical violence to resolve conflicts with their siblings.[7]

In 1988, Pagelow presented the findings of her study of 1,025 college students at three university campuses in Southern California at the annual meeting of the Pacific Sociological Association. Pagelow's survey revealed that almost half the siblings living at home at the age of twelve were either aggressors or victims of violent acts, including kicking and punching. Ten percent said their siblings beat them up, and 4 percent stated that their siblings had threatened them with a gun or knife or used a gun or knife against them.

In 1992, Carson and Daane presented the results of their study of 3,357 students in an Indiana school district at the annual meeting of the American Sociological Association. Seventy-four percent of the students approved of hitting their sibling if they were reacting to being hit first. Forty-three percent approved of striking their sibling if he or she broke their stereo. Thirty-eight percent believed it was appropriate to hit their sibling if that sibling made fun of the student in front of friends. Almost one-quarter of all the students surveyed approved of hitting their sibling if there was an argument and the other sibling did not listen to reason.

These and other studies indicates that sibling abuse is a common form of family violence. Its existence can no longer be denied. However, researchers are still studying its nature, causation, and extent. As with many other forms of family violence, there is no single definition of sibling abuse.

Definition

Clearly, sibling abuse falls within the definition of family violence discussed in Chapter 1. In that chapter, *family violence* was defined as any act or omission by persons who are cohabitating that results in serious injury to other members of the family. The question then must be whether a separate definition of sibling abuse is needed or whether other definitions within this text cover most if not all the situations that arise in which children commit acts of violence toward their siblings.

In an earlier chapter, *physical child abuse* was defined as any act that results in a nonaccidental physical injury caused by a person who has care, custody, or control of a child. Many acts of sibling abuse occur when the older or more powerful sibling has care or control over the victim. However, some acts of sibling abuse occur within the home when parents are present but unaware of the acts of the abusing sibling. Therefore, the definition of physical child abuse does not cover all situations that might arise in sibling abuse. Although it is possible to draft a broad definition of child abuse that would cover acts of sibling abuse by defining it as a separate and distinct form of child abuse, its importance in any study of family violence is highlighted.

Sibling abuse is any form of physical, mental, or sexual abuse inflicted by one child in a family unit on another. This definition covers the various types of abuse that will be discussed later. Additionally, it does not require that the child be related by birth. There are situations where children from different marriages end up in the same household. Finally, the definition uses the term *child,* which requires further explanation. There are reported incidents of one sibling abusing the other after they have both reached the age of eighteen. However, it appears that most abuse occurs before the victim and/or the abuser reach adulthood. Therefore, child *is defined as a person under the age of legal majority, which is typically stated to be eighteen.* It should be clear that this definition does not include abuse of different children within the same family by an adult member of the household. That particular form of family violence is discussed later in this chapter.

Siblings as Perpetrators

Professionals within the service fields must understand that children, even at relatively young ages, can be violent toward their siblings. To automatically discount sibling abuse by a five- or six-year-old committed against his younger brother or sister is to ignore the realities and dynamics of family violence. This section examines more characteristics of sibling abuse.

Types of Abuse

As with other types of family violence, sibling abuse can be divided into three distinct forms of abuse: physical, emotional, and sexual. The dynamics involved in each type of abuse is similar if not the same as those interactions that occur with other forms of abuse. The critical difference in this type of family violence is that the perpetrator is a sibling.

Physical abuse of a sibling includes any of the acts or omissions discussed in Chapter 2. Striking, kicking, punching, and the use of instruments such as sticks, appliances, and other items as weapons are common in sibling abuse. Wiehe conducted an extensive study of physical, emotional, and sexual abuse of siblings.[8] His definition of physical abuse is similar to the one used in this text, with one significant distinction. Wiehe includes tickling as a form of physical abuse. He reports that tickling is used by siblings as a form of prolonged physical abuse. The stronger sibling restrains the smaller victim and engages in prolonged tickling.

Emotional abuse of siblings includes those acts or omissions discussed in Chapter 4. While Wiehe acknowledges the more accepted definition of emotional abuse discussed previously, he narrows its scope in his research to define emotional sibling abuse as name-calling, ridicule, degradation, exacerbating a fear, destroying personal possessions, and torture or destruction of a pet. Defining concepts is one of the existing controversies in family violence. Therefore, rather than establishing a series of distinct definitions for each separate form of violence, it may be more acceptable to use a single definition if it can be applied to the facts.

PRACTICUM Curiosity or Sexual Abuse?

Situation 1:	Both Curious	Both "Consent"*	Same Age—Under Four
Situation 2:	One Curious	Both Consent	Different Ages
Situation 3:	One Curious	One Consents	Same or Different Ages

*Consent in this context focuses on mutual agreement by the minors and does not deal with the legal issue of consent. Legally, as was pointed out in other chapters, persons under the age of majority cannot consent to sexual activities.

Because all these acts conform to the previously established definition of emotional abuse, there is no need to add an additional definition at this time.

The third type of sibling abuse is sexual abuse. Chapter 3 defined child sexual abuse *as sexual exploitation or sexual activities with a child under circumstances that indicate that the child's health or welfare is harmed or threatened.* Intrafamilial sexual abuse *was defined as incest and refers to any type of exploitative sexual contact occurring between relatives.* Clearly, sibling sexual abuse falls within these definitions. In some situations, however, certain activities may be considered simple curiosity; in others, it is sexual abuse.

Depending on what other facts are added to the Practicum "Curiosity or Sexual Abuse?" what appears to be simple curiosity may be sibling sexual abuse. Situation 1 may indicate normal curiosity that many children experience regarding body differences.[9] Situation 2 may be simple curiosity but is more likely to be sexual abuse, depending on the difference in age and the type of activities engaged in by the siblings. Clearly, situation 3 is sexual abuse.

Early thinking characterized sibling sexual abuse as relatively benign. Professionals have rejected this view, and most authorities now accept the proposition that sibling sexual abuse can be coercive and have serious long-term consequences for the victim.[10] Laredo established a continuum of motivations of perpetrators of sibling sexual abuse.[11] At one end is the relatively common childhood activities of exploration, and at the other is power and control.

Laredo explained that exploration often takes the form of play or games. Retribution is common in sibling sexual abuse and is used to get even with younger siblings for perceived or actual past slights or injuries to the abusing sibling. Third, power and control, common ingredients in family violence, also play a major role in sibling sexual abuse (see Figure 5.1).

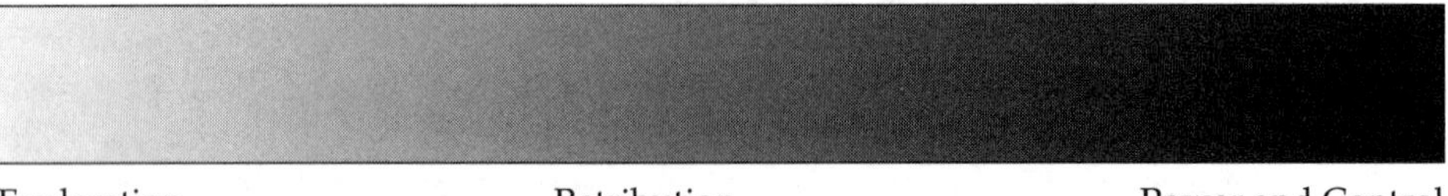

FIGURE 5.1 Continuum of Motivations

O'Brien studied various forms of adolescent sexual abuse, including sibling sexual abuse.[12] It was found that siblings committed more serious types of sexual abuse than other adolescent offenders. O'Brien theorized that this increased sexual activity was based on two factors: the easy and continuing access the sibling had to the victim and the secrecy that surrounds the activities of the family unit.

This section has examined the dynamics and types of sibling abuse. Many of the forces involved in family violence contribute to these dynamics. The next section discusses certain characteristics of sibling abuse.

Characteristics of Sibling Abuse

Even though sibling abuse has been studied for over thirty years, an absence of information regarding its characteristics remains. What is known has come from small samples and is subject to debate. The lack of adequate research should not reflect negatively on the researchers because the size of the sample is obviously limited to family units that have more than one child.

Hotaling and his associates used the two National Family Violence Surveys and a survey of university students to construct a profile of sibling abuse.[13] These respected researchers established the following characteristics of sibling abuse:

- Sibling abuse occurs at a higher rate among children in families in which both child abuse and spousal abuse are present.
- Sibling assaults are higher in families with child abuse than in those with spousal abuse.
- Although boys are more likely than girls to engage in sibling abuse, both sexes participate in this form of family violence.
- Sibling abuse crosses all racial and socioeconomic lines.
- Sibling abuse is highest in multiassaultive families.

These professionals conclude that the data cannot be used to establish a relation between sibling abuse and other forms of family violence. Additionally, no concrete data from these studies establish the fact that violence in families causes sibling abuse.

Gelles and Cornell's research confirmed another commonly held belief, namely, that as siblings grow older the abuse decreases.[14] A number of reasons have been advanced for this phenomenon. As a child ages, his or her verbal and coping skills increase. Also, as the child victim reaches adolescence, he or she becomes able to spend more time out of the home and away from the abusing sibling.

A great deal more research needs to be done in this, the most common form of family violence. As parents become more sensitive to aggressive behavior between siblings, its incidence may decrease. Another form of sibling abuse continues nevertheless to defy any effort to stop it or find a reason for its existence. The serial abuse of siblings within the family unit is examined in the next section.

FOCUS Difficult Choices

In 1986, a mother poisoned her first child with psychotropic drugs. The child died of poisoning from antidepressant and antipsychotic drugs that had been prescribed for the mother. The mother pled guilty to felony child neglect. In September 1988, the mother was again pregnant, and the judge who sentenced her to prison offered to reduce her sentence if she would agree to be sterilized, stating, "Here is a woman who should not be a mother, someone who has killed her child and pleaded guilty to neglect. I think she needs to recognize that the same thing can happen again and take steps to control that it doesn't.

Source: Tybor, J. R. "Does Sterilization Fit the Crime? Women Must Decide." *Chicago Tribune.* September 24, 1988, p. C4.

Serial Abuse of Siblings

The Focus "Difficult Choices" illustrates one of the dilemmas facing professionals in the area of sibling abuse. What should they do when they discover that one sibling has been abused? Should they remove any other siblings from the custody of the parents to prevent further abuse? Can or should they recommend birth control measures to abusing parents to prevent them from conceiving and abusing other children? This section examines these issues and offers some guidelines to consider when making decisions regarding intervention in child abuse cases involving siblings.

Overview

Social workers, probation officers, police, attorneys, and judges have all heard stories of the sibling who was left behind with the abusive family and suffered death or serious injury. This situation is a nightmare that haunts all professionals who work in the area of family violence. *Serial abuse of siblings occurs when the perpetrator who is a member of the family first abuses one child and then abuses another sibling.* The type of abuse inflicted on a sibling may be physical, emotional, sexual, or a combination of various types of abuse. Either or both parents or caretakers may participate in this form of family violence. This abuse may take place within a matter of months of abusing the first child, or the perpetrator may wait years until the younger sibling reaches a certain age before beginning the abuse.

As discussions in previous chapters have illustrated, professionals have been unable to agree on specific characteristics, forces, and factors that cause parents to abuse their children. With such disagreement, how can professionals attempt to predict with any accuracy that a parent or caretaker who has abused one child will abuse a sibling or siblings? When a person is accused of child abuse, professionals may assume that other children are also being abused or will be abused in the future. Additionally, many professionals will argue that proof of abuse of one child indicates that the parent or caretaker is unfit to care for the siblings.

The question of serial abuse of siblings has generated both controversy and continued research. In 1981, Farrell determined that 53 percent of female children whose siblings were infected with gonorrhea also contracted the disease.[15] In 1989, the Tennessee Department of Human Services conducted a study of all children who were closely associated with a victim of sexual assault and exposed to the perpetrator.[16] This study revealed that 58 percent of these girls also admitted to being victims of sexual abuse. In 1992, Gutman and her associates examined the sexual abuse of children exposed to offenders carrying the human immunodeficiency virus (HIV).[17] They determined that 50 percent of twenty-two cohabiting children were confirmed to have been sexually abused by the perpetrator. Of these children, two were determined to be HIV positive and thirteen HIV negative. These two children were thought to have acquired their infections through vertical transmission because their mothers were HIV positive. However, acquisition by sexual abuse could not be ruled out.

Sexual abuse of children is not the only form of serial abuse of siblings. Herrenkohl and his associates found that in 45 percent of all families studied, more than one child was abused.[18] Alexander and his associates studied babies who were seen at hospitals and clinics in Iowa with the diagnosis of shaken baby syndrome.[19] He concluded that the risk of abuse to siblings may be approximated by the findings that in 33 percent of families with more than one child, two or more siblings had experienced abuse or neglect. Because of the nature of the study, Alexander cautions that this figure was most likely an underestimate of the true extent of serial sibling abuse. Newlands and Emery found that names of families on the child abuse register in Derbyshire, England, were the same as the names of families who were reporting deaths of other siblings. She found that approximately 10 percent of the children whose deaths were reported as accidental also had siblings who had been abused by their families.[20]

Interventions

Removal of an abused child from the care and custody of the parents is a serious step for any professional to take. This form of intervention is discussed in detail in Chapter 7, which deals with responses to child abuse. This section examines other, more controversial forms of intervention—removal of children from a home based on abuse of a sibling and sterilization of the mother to prevent further births.

Removal of a sibling from the home of the abusing parents or caretaker is an obvious form of intervention. It is designed to protect both the abused child and her siblings from future injury. Many courts have upheld the removal of a child with a showing that another sibling has been abused. The District of Columbia Court of Appeals stated,

> *. . . a substantial number of decisions in other jurisdictions support the proposition that trial judge may legitimately find, on the basis of a parent's abusive conduct towards one child, that the child's siblings are also in danger of abuse and should be removed from the home for their own safety.*[21]

Removing a child from a home is one form of intervention. The child may be placed with another relative or in a foster home while the abusing parents seek counseling or other forms of assistance. However, sometimes the abuse is so serious that courts will consider another more serious form of intervention—terminating the parental rights of the abusing parent.

Some state statutes authorize removal from the home and termination of parental rights without a showing of abuse to a sibling. In 1991, the Florida Supreme Court upheld that state's statute authorizing such action. In *Padgett v Department of Health and Rehabilitative Service,* the department sought to terminate the parental rights of Mary and Tom Padgett to their child, identified as W. L. P.[22] On a previous occasion, Mary's parental rights to a newborn infant had been terminated on the basis of acts of physical child abuse. Tom's parental rights to five children from a previous marriage had also been terminated. Two days after W. L. P.'s birth, the department filed a petition asking the court to terminate the parents' rights. This petition was based on three grounds: another child had been removed from the parents' custody, Mary was mentally ill, and she had tried to perform an abortion on herself by using a pair of scissors to terminate the birth of W. L. P. In upholding the trial court's order terminating the parents' rights, the Florida Supreme Court stated that

> *to require a child to suffer abuse in those cases where mistreatment is virtually assured is illogical and directly adverse to society's fundamental policy of preserving the welfare of its youth.*[23]

Other jurisdictions have upheld the termination of parents' rights on the basis of their abuse of siblings. In the California case of *In re Luwanna,* an appeals court upheld the termination of the parental right of Luwanna's parents on the basis of evidence that her younger brother had been repeatedly beaten with a stick.[24] The appeals court affirmed the termination of parental rights of both children even though there was no evidence that Luwanna's father had beaten her. In Missouri, the state filed for termination of parental rights to a daughter, C. M. W., on the basis of the abuse of a sibling.[25] In *C. M. W. v P. W.,* the state had terminated the parental rights of C. M. W.'s older brother, C. C., on the basis of a showing of severe physical and sexual abuse by the father and the mother's uncle. The Missouri court upheld the termination of parental rights because the conditions that led to the abuse of the older brother still existed. Termination of parental rights is a harsh but sometimes necessary act if children are to be protected from abuse. A more controversial method of intervention is to request or demand that the abusing parent undergo sterilization to prevent giving birth to more children, who might then be abused.

Numerous courts have attempted to deal with the issue of parents who abuse their children and the issue of future births of siblings who might suffer the same or similar fates. The use of involuntary sterilization raises the specter of ethnic cleansing and Nazi Germany. Compulsory sterilization is a highly emotional and controversial subject. Additionally, the U.S. Supreme Court has ruled that parents have a "right to procreate."[26] However, that same court has ruled that in limited situations the state may involuntarily sterilize a person. In the still controversial decision of *Buck v Bell* in 1927, the Supreme Court upheld a Virginia statute allowing superintendents of various state mental institutions to order the sterilization of any patient if the sterilization served the best interests of the patient and of society.[27]

In 1991, Darlene Johnson, a pregnant twenty-seven-year-old mother of four children, was convicted of physically abusing her children.[28] Johnson had prior convictions for burglary, battery, and other theft-related crimes. California Superior Court Judge Broadman suspended Johnson's prison sentence on the condition that she use Norplant, a long-term form of birth control, as a condition of her probation. Johnson originally agreed but later recanted and filed an appeal. The appeal was rendered moot because she subsequently violated another condition of her probation and was sentenced to prison.[29]

In January 1993, Ronald and Barbara Gross were convicted of sexual abuse of their four children and were sentenced to ten years in prison.[30] Judge Lynn Brown of Washington County, Tennessee, offered to suspend the sentence and place the defendants on probation if they would agree to Barbara Gross's submitting to a tubal ligation. Judge Brown's order is just one of many judicial responses to child abuse.

All states provide for the termination of parental rights of parents of children who have been abused, and a number of these states authorize the termination of parental rights on the basis of sibling abuse. Termination of parental rights is one method of intervention that attempts to prevent further injury to siblings. Sterilization of abusing parents will continue to be a hotly debated topic.[31] Although many trial court judges have conditioned probation for abusing parents on acceptance of sterilization, no modern appellate court has approved such a remedy.

Summary

Sibling abuse is the most common form of family violence. Society often accepts violence between siblings as normal. Sibling abuse can have long-term consequences for its victims.

Two types of sibling abuse have been discussed: those acts perpetrated against another child in the family until by a sibling and abuse visited on a child by an adult who has abused that victim's sibling. Professionals must be aware of both types of sibling abuse. Sibling abuse may include physical, emotional, or sexual abuse by either male or female children. Like other forms of family violence, it crosses all socioeconomic lines and may be present in the homes of the rich and famous as well as those who live in abject poverty.

Serial abuse of siblings presents another aspect of sibling abuse. Professionals must determine how they are going to intervene to protect not only the abused child but also the welfare and best interests of other siblings. Many states authorize the termination of parental rights to siblings on the basis of the abuse of another child in the family. Another controversial alternative is the sterilization of women in order to prevent the conception and birth of other children who might be subjected to abuse.

Key Terms

sibling abuse—any form of physical, mental, or sexual abuse inflicted by one child in a family unit on another.

child—a person under the age of legal majority, which is typically stated to be eighteen.

child sexual abuse—sexual exploitation or sexual activities with a child under circumstances that indicate that the child's health or welfare is harmed or threatened.

intrafamilial sexual abuse—incest; refers to any type of exploitative sexual contact occurring between relatives.

serial abuse of siblings—occurs when the perpetrator who is a member of the family first abuses one child and then abuses another sibling.

Discussion Questions

1. How serious is sibling abuse? Do you believe it is more serious than rape? Why?
2. When does normal childhood curiosity become abuse?
3. What should we do with children who abuse their siblings? What if the perpetrator is eight years old and has sexually molested his five-year-old sister? What if he were twelve years old and molested his six-year-old sister?
4. If a father sexually abuses his ten-year-old daughter, should we remove his eight-year-old daughter? What about his five-year-old son?
5. Should certain people be sterilized? Who? Justify your answer.

Suggested Readings

Bard, M. "The Study and Modification of Intra-family Violence." In J. L. Singer, ed. *The Control of Aggression and Violence.* (Academic Press, New York) 1971.

Gelles, R. J. and C. P. Cornell. *Intimate Violence in Families.* 2d ed. (Sage, Newbury Park, California) 1990.

Hotaling, G. T., A. Strauss, and A. J. Lincoln. "Intrafamily Violence and Crime and Violence Outside the Family." In Straus and Gelles, eds. *Physical Violence in American Families.* (Transaction Publishers, New Brunswick, New Jersey) 1990.

Kempe, R. S., and C. H. Kempe. *The Common Secret: Sexual Abuse of Children and Adolescents.* (W. H. Freeman, New York) 1984.

Laredo, C. "Sibling Incest." In S. Sgroi, ed. *Handbook of Clinical Intervention in Child Sexual Abuse.* (Lexington Books, Lexington, Massachusetts) 1982.

Mott, S. R., S. R. James, and A. M. Sperhac. *Nursing Care of Children and Families.* (Addison-Wesley, Redwood City, California) 1990.

Steinmetz, S. K. *The Cycle of Violence: Assertive, Aggressive, and Abusive Family Interaction.* (Praeger, New York) 1971.

Straus, M., R. Gelles, and S. Steinmetz. *Behind Closed Doors: Violence in the American Family.* (Doubleday, New York) 1980.

Wiehe, V. R. *Sibling Abuse.* (Lexington Books, New York) 1990.

Wolfgand, M. *Patterns in Criminal Homicide.* (John Wiley, New York) 1958.

Endnotes

1. Gelles, R. J. and C. P. Cornell. *Intimate Violence in Families.* 2d ed. (Sage, Newbury Park, California) 1990, p. 85.
2. See Bard, M. "The Study and Modification of Intra-Family Violence." In J. L. Singer, ed. *The Control of Aggression and Violence.* (Academic Press, New York) 1971, for the study of homicides in Philadelphia and Wolfgand, M. *Patterns in Criminal Homicide.* (John Wiley, New York) 1958, for the study of homicides in New York.
3. Steinmetz, S. K. *The Cycle of Violence: Assertive, Aggressive, and Abusive Family Interaction.* (Praeger, New York) 1971.
4. Whipple, E. E. and S. E. Finton, "Psychological Maltreatment by Siblings: An Unrecognized Form of Abuse," 12(2) *Child and Adolescent Social Work Journal* (April 1995).
5. "Battered Families: A Growing Nightmare." *U.S. News & World Report.* 15 January 1979, pp. 60–61.
6. Straus, M., R. Gelles, and S. Steinmetz. *Behind Closed Doors: Violence in the American Family.* (Doubleday, New York) 1980.
7. Steinmetz, S. "A Cross-Cultural Comparison of Sibling Violence." *International Journal of Family Psychiatry* 2(3/4), 1981, pp. 337–351.
8. Wiehe, V. R. *Sibling Abuse.* (Lexington Books, New York) 1990.
9. Mott, S. R., S. R. James, and A. M. Sperhac. *Nursing Care of Children and Families.* (Addison-Wesley, Redwood City, California) 1990, pp. 224–225.
10. Kempe, R. S., and C. H. Kempe. *The Common Secret: Sexual Abuse of Children and Adolescents.* (W. H. Freeman, New York) 1984.
11. Laredo, C. "Sibling Incest." In S. Sgroi, ed. *Handbook of Clinical Intervention in Child Sexual Abuse.* (Lexington Books, Lexington, Massachusetts) 1982.
12. O'Brien J., *Characteristics of Male Adolescent Sibling Incest Offenders.* (The Safer Society Program, Orwell, Vermont) 1989.
13. Hotaling, G. T., M. A. Straus, and A. J. Lincoln. "Intrafamily Violence and Crime and Violence Outside the Family." In Straus and Gelles, eds. *Physical Violence in American Families.* (Transaction Publishers, New Brunswick, New Jersey) 1990.
14. Gelles, R. J., and C. P. Cornell. *Intimate Violence in Families,* 2d ed. (Sage, Newbury Park, California) 1990.
15. Farrell, M. K., M. E. Billmire, J. A. Shamroy, and J. G. Hammond. "Prepubertal Gonorrhea: A Multidisciplinary Approach." *Pediatrics* 67(151), 1981.
16. Muram, D., P. M. Speck, and S. S. Gold. "Genital Abnormalities in Female Siblings and Friends of Child Victims of Sexual Assault." *Child Abuse and Neglect* 15(105), 1991.
17. Gutman, L. T., K. K. St. Claire, C. Weedy, M. Herman-Giddens, and R. E. McKinney, Jr. "Sexual Abuse of Human Immunodeficiency Virus-Positive Children; Outcomes for Perpetrators and Evaluations of Other Household Children." *American Journal of Diseases of Children* 146(1185), October, 1992.
18. Herrenkohl, R. C., et al. "The Repetition of Child Abuse: How Frequently Does It Occur?" *Child Abuse and Neglect* 3(67), 1979.
19. Alexander, R., L. Crabbe, Y. Sato, W. Smith, and T. Bennett. "Serial Abuse in Children Who Are Shaken." *American Journal of Diseases of Children* 144(58), January, 1990.
20. Newlands, M., and J. L. Emery. "Child Abuse and Cot Deaths." *Child Abuse and Neglect* 15(275), 1991.
21. *In re S. G.,* 581 A.2d 771, 778 (D.C.Ct.App. 1990).
22. 577 So. 2d 565 (Fla. 1991).
23. Ibid., p. 570.
24. 107 Cal. Rptr. 62 (1973).
25. *C. M. W. v P. W.* 813 S.W. 2d 331 (Mo.Ct. App. 1991).
26. *Skinner v Oklahoma.* 316 U.S. 535 (1942).
27. 274 U.S. 200 (1927). In that decision, a highly regarded Justice, Oliver Wendell Holmes, uttered his now infamous statement that "three generations of imbeciles is enough."
28. Arthur, S. L. "The Norplant Prescription: Birth Control, Women Control, or Crime

Control." *University of California at Los Angeles Law Review* 40(1), 1992.

29. *People v Johnson.* No. 29290 Slip Opinion (Tulare County Superior Court) January 10, 1991.
30. Curriden, M. "Sterilization Ordered for Child Abuser." *American Bar Association Journal.* May 1993, p. 32.
31. Blum, E. T. "When Terminating Parental Rights Is Not Enough: A New Look at Compulsory Sterilization," 28 *Georgia Law Review* 977 (Summer 1994).

6

RITUALISTIC CHILD ABUSE

Chapter Outline

Learning Objectives

After reading this chapter, you should be able to discuss the following concepts:

- The development of satanic beliefs.
- The various symbols used by satanic cults.
- Satanic worship and ritualistic abuse.
- The various types of ritualistic abuse.
- Victims who have been physically or sexually abused and survivors of ritualistic abuse.
- The consequences of ritualistic abuse.

Introduction

Almost daily, the press releases stories of horror and disgust involving children being victimized in so-called satanic cults. Adults who were victims are coming forward and shedding light on this new form of family violence. Like the slow acceptance of the fact that fathers were molesting their young daughters, so society is hesitant to believe that many of the described practices of ritualistic abuse actually occur. Child abuse, neglect, and sexual molestation are difficult to accept, but satanic ritualistic abuse not only causes harm to children but strikes a chord in the collective consciousness as to the evil perpetrated by humanity. For all these reasons this controversial and highly emotional issue should be examined.

Professionals are just now beginning to treat survivors of ritualistic abuse.[1] However, a raging controversy exists as to the validity of many of the claims made by these survivors and to the extent of their abuse. Other scholarly works in the field are silent or only briefly touch on this new issue.[2] Even though this is a relatively new form of family violence and professionals are still researching its causes and consequences, it is included in this text to familiarize students with the general nature and types of ritualistic abuse.

During the 1970s, a movie entitled *Rosemary's Baby* became a smash hit. This tale involved a young couple who moved into an apartment next door to a supposedly friendly elderly couple who turned out to be followers of Satan. The young wife had intercourse with a beast like creature and eventually gave birth to a monster who was Satan's child. The moviegoers shivered in delight because they understood that this could never actually happen. Unfortunately, stories are beginning to surface that individuals, groups, or cults may in fact be engaging in ritualistic abuse. Although a great deal of controversy exists regarding the nature and extent of satanic worship and child abuse, there is sufficient evidence to support more study and research in this area. In order to understand this phenomenon, it is necessary to review the growth and development of the satanic movement.

Historical Background

Stories of Satan and satanic worship are interspersed throughout our history.[3] There is no simple definition of satanism. For purposes here, however, *satanism is the worship of Satan.* Satan's name is derived from early Egyptian theology where Set, the killer of Osiris, represented the forces of disharmony and disorder.[4] During the third and fourth centuries, a group identified as the Phibionites was discovered. They were promiscuous, consumed semen during the sacrament, andpracticed abortion. This early group had much in common with modern day cults in that the masses were held in secret, semen was used ritualistically, and they subscribed to other practices abhorred by modern religions.[5]

During the fourteenth century, nature itself aided in the development of the satanic movement. The climate began to change, crops failed, and the population began to starve—perfect conditions for the spread of the bubonic plague, which was also known as the Black Death. Beginning in 1348 and continuing until the start of the sixteenth century, the Black Death was responsible for the demise of more than one-third of the entire population of Europe, thereby decimating the labor force.[6]The ensuing labor shortage set the stage for workers to demand higher wages and more freedom. Both the church and the state responded brutally in an attempt to restore order. Governments attempted to set the prices of goods and services. The ensuing legislation of economics made large families an economic liability.[7] As a result, large families became an economic burden, and the population responded with a brutal form of contraception—infanticide.

As the populace struggled to survive with only death and poverty surrounding them, they began to search for explanations to the chaos that existed in their lives. The belief in powers that could be manipulated began to take hold. In this environment, magic and magical powers became an accepted alternative to traditional beliefs and religions. The populace began to view the Catholic Mass and its transformation of bread and water into the body and blood of Christ as another form of magic. Once the population had accepted the sacrament as simply a form of magic rather than a religious experience, the stage was set for the acceptance of other unnatural phenomenon. Thus, witches, warlocks, and magic were able to become a part of society.

In France during the 1680s, Catherine Deshayesa, also known as LaVoisin, practiced magic and astrology for the French aristocrats. She subsequently joined forces with Abbe Guibourg, and the two of them routinely sacrificed children to Astaroth and Asmodeus for the Black Mass.[8]

During the 1800s, Theosophy began to gain acceptance. Theosophy accepted Lucifer as a benign force and required believers to answer for their earthly actions. It was founded by Helena Blavatsky and borrowed from Hindu and Gnostic concepts. Theosophymade occultism more acceptable by portraying Lucifer as benign and was responsible for introducing the concept of *white magic.*

During the early twentieth century, one of the most important figures in the development of magic and mysticism appeared. Hisname was Aleister Crowley, and he authored the book *Magick in Theory and Practice.*[9] Crowley's book was a "how to" for neophytes who wanted to experiment with magic. It told them what to do, what to say, and how to feel. For those who were unable to achieve the desired psychological state, Crowley recommended the use of various drugs, including hashish, mescaline, and cocaine.

The 1960s and 1970s were decades of rebellion in the United States. The concept of mind-expanding drugs gained widespread acceptance. During this period of change, it was popular to question authority and beliefs. The advent of birth control, the first stirrings of the women's movement, and the breakdown of traditional roles all combined to force change in the United States. Magic, free love, and drugs were accepted tenets.

During this period, Anton LaVey established the Church of Satan and drafted *The Satanic Bible.* Although denounced as a fraud by some, LaVey had a far greater impact than most people were willing to admit. He took the position that individuals could make a conscious choice to live in a world without God, and then he thrust this idea on the general public.[10] It should be stressed that the Church of

FOCUS Day Care Centers—Sexual and Ritualistic Abuse

The nature and extent of allegations of sexual abuse of children in day care settings has posed difficult challenges to clinicians in recent years. Cases of sexual abuse in day care often involve numerous factors that differ from what clinicians are typically confronted with in cases of intrafamilial sexual abuse. These factors include the young ages of the children, the involvement of multiple victims and multiple perpetrators, females as perpetrators, the use of extreme threats, and in some cases ritualistic activities.

Day care cases involving multiple perpetrators had the largest number of victims. They were more likely to involve allegations of sexual penetration, pornography, and ritualistic abuse as well as forced sexual acts between children and women as perpetrators. These cases have appeared to have the most serious impact on victims.

Clinicians need to be knowledgeable about the spectrum of abuse reported by children victimized in day care centers. In addition to sexual abuse, they also report physical and psychological abuse. Therefore, a multidimensional approach to evaluating sexually abused children in day care is necessary.

Sexual Abuse

The types of sexually abusive acts committed in day care range from the fondling of genitals to vaginal and rectal intercourse. Insertion of foreign objects into children's vaginas and rectums is a sadistic type of abuse that has been commonly reported by children in day care abuse studies. Foreign objects used to penetrate children in day care center cases have included pencils, needles, knives, scissors, and crucifixes.

In some instances, perpetrators purposefully distort the child's perception of what is being inserted inside them. For example, in one case a large butcher's knife was shown to children who were told, "I'm going to put this knife up your bun."

The children were made to bend over and were therefore unable toview what was actually placed inside their rectums. Thus, when a finger was inserted instead of a large knife they were shown, the children continued to believe it was the large knife that was placed inside them. Thus, when children related to an investigator or therapist that a "big knife was put up my bun," their allegations were often treated as suspect, particularly in the absence of physical findings. Allegations of pornographic photographs and videos being taken of children in day care center cases sometimes surface. Unfortunately, in very few cases have law enforcement officials been able to locate the pornography after the case has come to light.

Psychological Abuse/Threats

The use of threats to silence young victims is an integral component of abuse in day care settings. Threats used by perpetrators in day care settings appear to be of a different nature than threats used by family members. Threats used in daycare center cases are more likely to involve talk of physical harm as opposed to the threats of loss of love or separation from family members that are often used in cases of intrafamilial abuse. Threats of physical harm to children and their family members is the most widely reported technique for silencing victims in day care centers.

Physical Abuse

Most reports of multiple perpetrator cases of sexual abuse in day care centers were also accompanied by disclosures of physical abuse. Although there were reports of children being-given drugs in day care center cases, it was difficult in most instances to determine which drugs were used. Children are often told that the drugs are "magic medicine." Drugs may be given to children for a variety of reasons, including an effort to make them less resistant to the abusive activities, to distort their percep-

continued

FOCUS *Continued*

tions and recall of events, and to make them fall asleep so that they can be photographed for pornographic purposes.

Ritualistic Abuse

A particularly disturbing type of reported day care center abuse is the ritualistic abuse of children. Children who have been ritualistically abused describe participation in group ceremonies; use of chants and songs; adults dressed in costumes and masks; threats with supernatural powers often involving Satan or demons; the sacrifice of animals; the ingestion of blood, feces, and urine; and murders.

Intensity of Abuse

Another troublesome finding in day care studies is that the children are subjected to a considerable number of different sexually abusive acts. Because of the young age of children at the time of the onset of abuse in day care and time of disclosure, it is difficult to accurately determine with any degree of certainty the number of times a child was abused or the duration of the abuse.

Source: Adapted from Kelly, S. J., R. Brant, and J. Waterman, "Sexual Abuse of Children in Day Care Centers." *Child Abuse & Neglect* (17), 1993, pp. 71–89. Reprinted with permission of Elsevier Science Ltd., Pergamon Imprint, Oxford, England.

Satan does not condone ritualistic child abuse. It is listed in the telephone directory and has its headquarters, or Grotto, in San Francisco, California.

In 1980, the reading public was shocked by a book that brought the specter of satanism and ritualistic abuse into grim reality. In *Michelle Remembers*, a book written by psychiatrist Lawrence Pazder, Michelle Smith recounts a tale of satanism and ritual abuse that occurred to Michelle as a child at the hands of a satanic cult in Victoria, Canada.[11] The book describes how Michelle recovered her memories during therapy. She claimed that she was to be a designated bride to Satan and was to be presented to him at a ceremony during the Year of the Beast, which occurs only every twenty-eight years. One of the most controversial portions of *Michelle Remembers* details how, with the help of the Virgin Mary, she resisted Satan's attempts to claim her.

In late 1980s, tales began to surface of massive sexual abuse at day care centers. Americans were angered and repulsed by allegations of ritualistic child abuse allegedly perpetrated on scores of preschool children by Peggy McMartin Buckey and her son, Raymond Buckey, at the Virginia McMartin Preschool in Manhattan Beach, California. Several children testified that they had been subjected to satanic rituals, including animal sacrifices and sexual abuse inside churches. After one of the longest and most expensive trials in the United States, all the defendants were acquitted. Although the defendants were found innocent, the trial raised awareness of this new form of child abuse. The issue of day care abuse is included in this chapterrather than in the chapter dealing with sexual abuse because of its specific nature.

On October 25, 1988, millions of people across the United States watched a prime-time Geraldo Rivera special on NBC entitled "Devil Worship: Exposing

Satan's Underground." It was one of the most widely watched documentaries of the season. By 1993, ritualistic child abuse had become such a common topic that *The New Yorker* magazine published a lengthy two-part series entitled "Remembering Satan," which detailed the accounts of a family in Olympia, Washington, accused of ritualistic child abuse.[12]

To explain satanism as the creation of a deranged mind would be easy. Doing so would permit researchers to dismiss it as something undeserving of serious consideration. That approach, however, would not allow for a complete understanding of this form of family violence. Although historians still dispute the historic nature and extent of satanism, and many present-day scholars continue to discount stories of ritualistic child abuse, more and more people are coming forward and claiming to be victims of this type of abuse. It is therefore imperative that professionals in the field have a general understanding of ritualistic abuse.

Definition

The definition of *ritualistic child abuse* is still evolving. One of the most cited definitions was established by the Los Angeles County Commission for Women in 1989. This commission set forth the following definition of ritual abuse:

> *A brutal form of abuse of children consisting of physical, sexual, and psychological abuse, and involving the use of rituals. Ritual does not necessarily mean satanic. However, most survivors state that they were ritually abused as part of satanic worship for the purpose of in doctrinating them into satanic beliefs and practices. Ritual abuse rarely consists of a single episode. It usually involves repeated abuse over an extended period of time.*[13]

As the definition states, ritualistic child abuse does not have to involve religion. However, most of the survivors claim the ritualistic abuse was definitely tied to satanic worship. All rituals are not evil. The word *ritual* is defined as the established form for a ceremony, a system of rites, or any formal and customarily repeated act or series of acts.[14] It is only when ritual is combined with abuse that society can intervene. As stated previously, ritualistic child abuse involves-long-term repeated abuse of the most severe form. These abuses may be inflicted (and believed justified) because of certain religious tenets held by the cult or organization.

Kahaner has developed a typology of three distinct types of satanic groups.[15] M. D. Langone and L. O. Blood have also developed a very similar typology. However, theirs includes individuals or psychopaths who act alone and adopt the more violent forms of satanism as a way of expressing their own beliefs and actions.[16] In dealing with groups that engage in ritualistic child abuse, Kahaner's definitions seem more appropriate. Kahaner's typology includes the following classifications of satanic groups:

1. *Publicly known cults.* These groups deny that they engage in any abusive conduct and are generally accepted as operating within the bounds of the law. The Church of Satan and the Temple of Set are examples of these groups.
2. *Self-styled satanists.* These are loosely knit groups of individuals who band together occasionally to dabble in magic and the occult. They include teenagers who are attracted to this behavior by heavy-metal music, easy-to-read books, and fantasy role-playing games.
3. *Formal satanists.* These groups are highly organized and secretive. They may have national or international connections with other similarly organized cults.

Although both law enforcement and scholars are skeptical regarding the extent of satanic cults and ritualistic child abuse, others accept their existence because of the similarity of stories related by survivors. However, it must be restated that the study of ritualistic child abuse is still in its infancy. As more is learned about this modern-day problem, professionals will begin to understand more about the structure, functioning, and beliefs of the satanic cults that practice this form of family violence. Additionally, fact will eventually separate from fantasy in dealing with actual survivors and those who only believe they were victims. Professionals in the field will gain the knowledge and the ability to evaluate and treat individualswho have been victims of ritualistic child abuse.

Types of Ritualistic Abuse

Professionals in the field must understand the different aspects of ritualistic abuse. This knowledge will aid in identifying victims, apprehending offenders, and treating survivors of this type of abuse. Ritualistic abuse can take manydifferent forms and variations. The following sections examine satanic beliefs and activities as they relate to ritualistic child abuse.

Satanic Beliefs and Practices

All cultures, societies, and religions have certain formalities that must be observed. In some fraternal organizations, there are candles, oaths of secrecy, and pledges of allegiance to the organization. Satanic cults follow this practice. One of the most commonly shared beliefs among these cults is the belief in magic. *Magic is a method of harnessing the secret powers of nature to influence events for one's own purpose.* It is believed that magic empowers all living entities with a source of power. Ancient civilizations called this power different names. The Chinese named it *qi,* the Hindus call it *prana,* and the Polynesians call it *mana.*

Satanism usually embraces the opposite of Christianity. The Bible prohibits incest, the worship of idols, magic, the sacrifice of children, and the drinking of blood. On the other hand, satanic cults adopt these practices as a method of gaining power and practicing magic. Other well-known reversals of Christianity include the use of an inverted cross, backward prayers, and of course the Black Mass, the purpose of which was and is to blaspheme the sacrament of Christ.[17]

The use of sacrifices is based on the theory that all livingthings contain energy. When the animal or human is killed, this energy is liberated. Aleister Crowley in *Magick in Theory and Practice* stated,

> *. . . it was the theory of the ancient Magicians, that any living being is a storehouse of energy varying in quantity according to the size and health of the animal, and in quality according to its mental and moral character. At the death of the animal this energy is liberated suddenly.*[18]

If the killing is done inside a certain type of circle, the energy is contained and concentrated within that circle for use by the magician. The animal or human should be healthy, young, and a virgin so that its internal energy and power is strong. The magician is then able to use this energy to make magic.[19]

A common prelude to the actual sacrifice is torture or sexual activities. Torture and sex is a common way to arouse the victim emotionally and thereby extract the greatest amount of life force at the time of death. One authority points out that during the practice of "White Magic," the witch engages in flogging the "victim" in order to overload the nervous system and thereby transcend normal consciousness, which the high priestess calls the ecstasy of magic.[20] Survivors of ritualistic child abuse have confirmed the use of torture and sex during satanic rituals.

Another common belief in satanic cults is the *theory of transmission. This is the belief that the qualities of objects or beings can be transmitted from them to another person.* Some ancient societies ate the hearts of their enemies, African tribesmen once ate the hearts of lions to obtain the animal's courage, and British Columbian Indians used to rub the body of a beaver on a young female baby to make her industrious. Black magic and voodoo rites include obtaining a portion of an enemy's body, such

FOCUS Black Magic, Voodoo, and Zombies

In Wade Davis's classic work *The Serpent and the Rainbow,* he exposed the existence of secret societies that practice black magic in Haiti. These groups worship an evil deity known as Samedi. Davis was able to show that truth may really be more scary than fiction.

Davis relates how these groups take criminals or persons who have violated certain norms, convince them that they have been turned into zombies, and sell them to plantation owners as slaves. The victim is given a drug that induces an almost trancelike state. The sorcerer then buries the victim, digs him up, and sells him into slavery.

Source: From Davis, W. *The Serpent and the Rainbow.* (Simon and Schuster, New York) 1985.

as nail clippings or hair, and using it to harm the intended victim. Being aware of these ancient beliefs, it is easy to understand how satanic cults could engage in cannibalism or the drinking of blood, semen, and other body fluids as a form of transmission.

Magic, witchcraft, sorcery, and the occult often employ symbols to represent certain forces (see Figure 6.1). Therapists treating survivors have reported various satanic or occult symbols that have been burned, cut, or tattooed on various portions of the victims' bodies. *Pentagrams and hexagrams are common symbols of the occult and satanism.* These figures are in the form of either a square or a five- or six-pointed star. These figures are believed to form the mystical system that links together all parts of the universe.[21] Colors are often used as symbols during cult ceremonies. Black represents death, darkness, and evil. White is the symbol of purity or truth. Red represents blood, vitality, and sexual potency.

Many of the rituals carried out in satanic cults are contained in handbooks or grimoires. These instruction manuals are guarded by the cult leader and passed down from one generation to another. To ensure secrecy, every *grimoire* will have a critical section in the rituals omitted or transposed. This is to ensure that the uninitiated do not accidentally come on the source of power of the cult.[22]

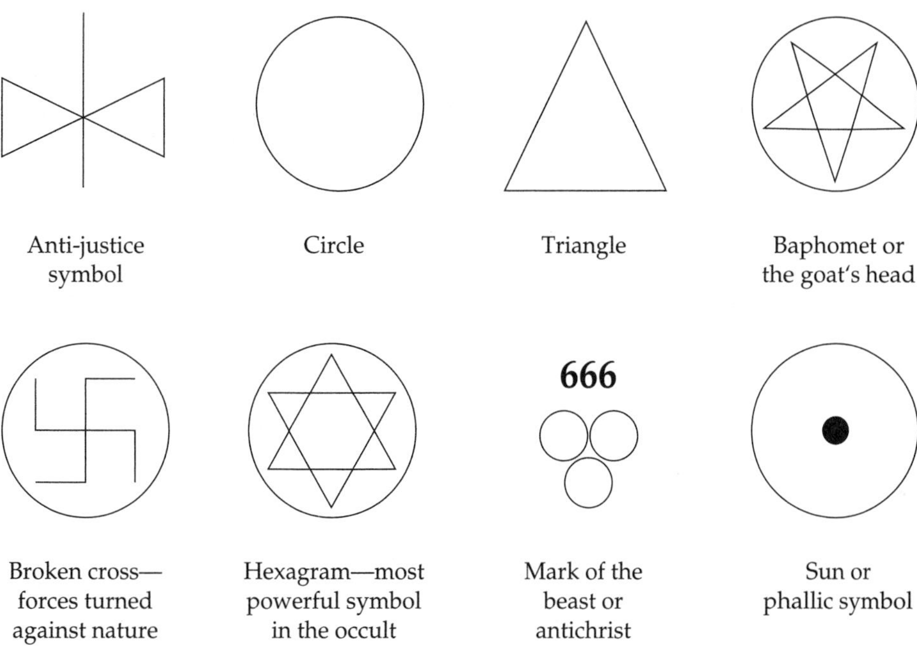

FIGURE 6.1 Some Occult Symbols

One final aspect of satanic practices needs to be examined. As mentioned earlier, all groups have certain rites or ceremonies for admission into the organization. They may be formal, as in the case of a professional or social fraternity or sorority, or informal, as occurs when joining a service organization.

Any former Marine will tell you that Marine Corps boot camp builds character and forms a sense of esprit or loyalty to the corps. This form of indoctrination is deemed necessary by senior Marine officers. They believe, on the basis of more than 200 years of experience, that Marines must be conditioned to react because they may not have time to think in combat. In many cases, they must blindly and faithfully follow the orders of their officers. This type of training has proven successful, and many former Marines believe that it kept them alive in combat. They would not view boot camp as a ritual or evil—they would argue that although it may have been abusive at the time, it was for their own good.

The same type of indoctrination occurs in law school. The experience of law school can be compared to a form of boot camp. Young students are taught to question and think in ways they have not experienced. Their minds are changed or conditioned to view a set of facts differently from other people. This is not a painless experience. Many law students are humiliated in front of their peers by professors intent on ensuring that they learn how to think on their feet logically.

The same type of conditioning that occurs at Marine boot camp or law school is used in satanic cults that engage in ritualistic abuse. However, the difference is the degree and the resulting injury to the survivors. The indoctrination goes beyond the bonds of the law and results in severe emotional trauma.

Many survivors describe rituals involving death and rebirth as a member of the cult. These ritualistic deaths may involve being buried and "born anew" into the cult. Various techniques include being physically and sexually abused and then placed in a coffin with a dead animal and brought forth as a new member of the cult community. One reported case involved a child being placed inside a dead or dying animal, sewing the animal closed, then reopening the carcass and telling the child that she is now reborn as evil and a member of the cult.

Another characteristic of cult indoctrination includes the use of guilt. Being forced to participate in killing animals and group sex with other children and adults impairs the child's self-worth. Adult cult members explain to the child that he is bad, evil, and no good. This constant downgrading of the child affects the child's ability to resist further demands from the cult.

As with other forms of abuse, isolation and the feeling of helplessness are also important characteristics of satanic cults and ritualistic abuse. Children are often threatened that members of the cult will find them and kill them, their parents, or any other loved one if the child ever tells anyone about the cult. Survivors are informed that their every move can be watched, which only adds to their paranoia. The cult members become all-powerful and invulnerable. The child is helpless to fight against them.

All these techniques involve modifying the victim's thinking and behavior. Many of the actions cause the victim to confront past or existing values. This in turn causes an extreme conflict within the personality of the victim. Because of the nature of the acts, the impact on the victim can be greater and more severe than that of a victim of incest or other forms of sexual or physical abuse. The next section examines satanic activity and the different types of ritualistic abuse.

Satanic Activity

The true extent of ritualistic child abuse is unknown. Intermingled with true accounts of abuse by survivors of past ritualistic abuse are accounts by persons suffering from mental illness and other mental problems. Some of the stories of survivors are so horrible and outlandish that many people have a great deal of difficulty accepting them as true. However, humanity is capable of incredible acts of savagery. A quick review of history, especially the Holocaust, indicates that we can kill, torture, and abuse millions of people only because of their religious belief. Some groups today still argue that the Holocaust did not really happen.

Satanic ritualistic abuse basically involves three distinct abuses: physical, sexual, and psychological. Each of these abuses is repeated over an extended period of time, and they are often intermingled so that the victim is exposed to psychological, sexual, and physical abuse simultaneously. The following is a brief summary of each of these forms of abuse.

Physical

Ritualistic physical abuse can take many different forms. Cutting, branding, or tattooing symbols into the victim's body is one clear example of this type of abuse. This establishes the cult's ownership of the victim and is a symbol that reinforces the image of ownership and loss of the victim's individual identity. Forcing the victim to drink contaminated water, urine, semen, or even eat feces are other forms of physical abuse. Ingesting raw meat and cannibalism have also been reported in ritualistic physical abuse cases. Burning portions of the body with branding irons, flames, or acid is another method of breaking down the victim's resistance. Deprivation of sleep, food, or water causes the child to become more confused and suggestible to cult demands and threats. Drugs and torture are common. All of these forms of physical abuse create instability in the victim's psyche. The addition of sexual abuse accelerates the destruction of the child's personality.

Sexual

Sexual abuse is more than simple intercourse. The victim may have to engage in group sex with other children of the same or different sex. Adult members of the cult may use the child sexually either in a group or individually. Pictures or videos of these acts may be taken and shown to the victim. Sex with animals has been reported by survivors of ritualistic abuse. Sexual abuse may continue for hours at a time, with the victim subjected to repeated sexual assaults by other children, adults, or animals, all within the period of a day. These acts may occur each day for days at a time. The use of urine, semen, blood, and other body fluids during sexual abuse is not uncommon. The child may be sexually stimulated while forced to watch the killing of animals, thus planting the thought in the child's mind that he enjoyed the killing. Some survivors have related being impregnated for the purpose of giving birth to a child who is to be sacrificed by the cult.

Psychological

Psychological abuse involves a destruction of the child's personality and the ability to resist. Sleep deprivation and isolation are two of the fastest ways to indoctrinate any person. Prisoners of war report that this method of torture is often the hardest to resist. Survivors have reported being bound and placed in coffins for long periods of time. Being enclosed in a dark box or other small space with insects, spiders, or snakes is another form of psychological torture that rapidly breaks down the will.

Forcing the child to engage in physical and sexual acts that run counter to his morality can cause a loss of identity. The victim is told that the cult always knows what she is doing and that, if she ever tells anyone, revenge will be swift and severe.

The victim may also have to participate in killing animals. This may cause guilt and shame, which is then used by the cult members to point out how bad and evil the victim has become. The child is then told that because she has now participated in, committed, or witnessed these unspeakable acts, only the cult will accept her as a person. A feeling of total dependency and despair overwhelms the child's psyche.

Each of these forms of abuse is severe by itself. Combining them places an incredible strain on the child and may lead to dissociation episodes. Some survivors develop multiple personalities or other forms of mental illness in an effort to cope with the ritualistic abuse. The consequences of this form of abuse are long-lasting and may require long-term therapy.

Responding to Ritualistic Abuse

As stated earlier, a great deal of controversy surrounds the existence and extent of ritualistic abuse.[23] Its very existence is questioned by a number of educated, well-intentioned professionals. Affirming the existence of ritualistic abuse means that there are groups of individuals who practice some of the most bizarre forms of abuse known. If this is the case, it would seem only reasonable that at least one satanic cult practicing ritualistic abuse would have been discovered and prosecuted by law enforcement agencies. That trial, like the McMartin day care center trial, would have made national and international news. But so far, no such trial has occurred. If these cults operate according to the survivors' statements, skeletal remains, remnants of clothing, or some other form of physical evidence should have been discovered.

Skeptics of ritualistic abuse abound. They argue that the survivors are not victims of satanic cults but instead have been victimized by sophisticated sex rings similar to the ones discussed in Chapter 3. Others allege that overzealous therapists put these ideas in the minds of their patients. And still others explain that these stories are simply the delusions of the mentally ill.

Jones sets forth three explanations that should be examined in assessing the validity of claims of ritualistic abuse: the events did in fact occur as described; the events did not occur, and children or adult survivors are mistaken or telling lies; and some of the events did in fact happen, and others did not.[24] He points out that the problem with the first alternative is the lack of physical evidence to support the victim's claims. A second problem deals with the dynamics of conspiracies. Law enforcement agencies know that the longer a conspiracy continues, the more likely one of the co-conspirators will break from the conspiracy and disclose the activity or crime. In terms of ritualistic abuse, no co-conspirator has come forward and testified. However, the counter to this argument is the depth of the cult's indoctrination of its members. This indoctrination and the nature of the activity that occurs during ritualistic abuse may make it very difficult for a co-conspirator or member to break away and discuss these acts with law enforcement officials. Also, the survivors may have been drugged, and their recollection of dates and places may be inaccurate; therefore, no evidence would be found at the location they specify.

The second possibility is that the allegations are false. This flies in the face of the belief that children do not normally fabricate stories of sexual or physical abuse. Jones points out that mechanisms such as mass hysteria, contamination from one source to another, leading and suggestive questions by interviewers, child fantasies that are fed by video and movies containing scenes of the occult, and horror movies may explain some of these stories.[25] However, all these explanations cannot account for all the statements made by all the various victims.

The final possibility is that some events did in fact occur and that others did not. The use of physical, sexual, and psychological abuse may be so overwhelming as to distort the child's memory and may account for some of the inaccuracies.

The controversy surrounding ritual abuse continues unabated. For example, in 1995, when this text was originally written, reviewed, and published, only a few references to ritualistic child abuse existed. In 1998, a search of the World Wide Web revealed a number of Web sites either dealing with the existence of ritual abuse or claiming that it did not exist. For example, a Web site listed as Witchhunt lists a number of cases of "false claims regarding ritual abuse."[26] Witchhunt has links to other sites that are skeptical of cases or incidents involving ritualistic child abuse. On the other hand, the Ritual Abuse Homepage site has a list support groups for survivors of ritualistic abuse.[27] This site also has compiled an impressive list of articles and journals on ritualistic abuse and ritual crime. This site listed 200 articles and journals that discuss a wide variety of topics in this area. Unlike some resources on the World Wide Web, this list is composed of articles written by a number of respected researchers.

No single theory explains all the variations of ritualistic abuse. More research is necessary before the nature and extent of ritualistic abuse can be determined. Yet, there are too many stories and statements by survivors of ritualistic abuse to completely deny the existence of this form of family violence.[28] This section is included in this text because of the special trauma suffered by survivors of ritualistic abuse. If ritualistic abuse does in fact exist, professionals must be able to recognize the symptoms and understand how to respond to victims of this type of abuse.

Recognition of Ritualistic Abuse

Recognition of ritualistic abuse is a critical aspect of this form of family violence. What may appear to be a rather simple form of child abuse or child sexual abuse may turn out to be just the tip of the iceberg. The emotional, behavioral, and medical indicators present in a child who has been sexually abused may also indicate that the child has been ritualistically victimized. The symptoms described in this section may be observed by law enforcement officers, social workers, medical personnel, or teachers. Each professional should be aware that the symptoms observed may indicate a need to evaluate the situation from the perspective of ritualistic abuse. At the same time, extreme care must be used not to plant ideas in the victim's mind or suggest factual situations that the victim may adopt as his own. This issue is still unresolved, and more research is being done on recall and ritualistic abuse. Caution should be exercised and professionals should not jump to the conclusion that every child is a victim of ritualistic abuse, nor should they turn away from that possibility.

One of the most extensive lists of symptoms of ritualistic abuse was written by Catherine Gould in "Diagnosis and Treatment of Ritually Abused Children," in Sakheim and Devine's *Out of Darkness*.[29] Although many of these symptoms are exhibited by children who have been sexually or physically abused, the extent and nature of these indicators should alert the professional to the possibility that the child may have been ritually abused. The following is a shortened version of Gould's analysis:

1. *Strange or unusual sexual behavior or beliefs.* A child may have knowledge of sexual activities far beyond his normal developmental stage. These activities may include unusual or bizarre sexual practices or activities. The child may act out sexually in an aggressive manner toward other children. The child may report that she is married. Discussions of group sex and of sex with children and adults or even with animals are indications of possible ritual abuse.
2. *Unusual distress regarding bowel movements or body wastes.* The child may speak of drinking urine or eating feces. Some children spread urine or feces on their body orconsume it. Whereas many children discuss toilet training, the ritualistically abused child is more compulsive and less innocent in discussing this body function.
3. *Belief in the supernational, rituals, occult symbols, and religion.* Many ritually abused children state that they have been married to Satan or are Satan's bride. They have been indoctrinated to believe the cult has spies everywhere and knows what they do. They will have an unusual knowledge of satanic symbols or methods. They may draw pentagrams, hexagrams, or other symbols and signs associated with ritualistic abuse.

4. *A fear of enclosed or small spaces.* As indicated above, many children are buried and reborn into the cult. The child may become tense or even hysterical at being enclosed in a confining space or location. They may also act out these fears by trying to confine a pet, sibling, or even the therapist.
5. *A preoccupation with death and dying.* The child may believe she has died or will die soon. Concern that the child's parents, siblings, or friends will die is sometimes present. The child may ask questions regarding death and have strange or bizarre beliefs about death and dying.
6. *Other strange or unusual beliefs or actions.* The child may have a preference for certain colors associated with satanic practices. Fear of police and other authority figures is not uncommon. Familiarity with cemeteries, mortuaries, and other locations that children normally do not visit is another indication of ritualistic child abuse.

If a professional has reason to believe a person is or has been a victim of ritualistic abuse, he or she must proceed very carefully. The consequences of this type of family violence are still being determined, researched, and studied. The next section briefly discusses this new form of abuse.

Consequences of Ritualistic Abuse

Extreme caution must be used in making a diagnosis of ritualistic abuse. Because the research in this area is still evolving, professionals must be careful not to jump to any unfounded conclusions simply because a person describes what is believed to be satanic abuse. As with any child abuse case, extreme care must be taken not to plant ideas in the mind of the victim. Not only would this be poor therapy, but it could destroy the credibility of the victim during any court proceedings.

If a professional comes to the conclusion that a child has been a victim of any form of abuse, including ritualistic abuse, this suspicion must be reported to the local authorities. This aspect of family violence is examined in detail in later chapters. Once the report is made, child protective services (CPS) and law enforcement agencies enter the picture. Their responsibility is not to treat the victim but to prove or disprove that criminal actions have occurred or, in the case of CPS, to determine whether the child is at risk and, if so, to remove him or her from that situation.

The investigation of ritual crimes is a specialty within law enforcement agencies.[30] These kinds of offenses are similar to serial murders or other complex and difficult crimes. Theyshould be handled with care and sensitivity. If the victim can identify individuals, caution must be used in interviewing potential witnesses or defendants. Compounding the problem of investigating this type of crime is the fact that the victim may have been drugged during the abusive acts. Persons, places, times, and dates may be hazy at best.

If the scene of the ritualistic abuse can be located, it must be carefully checked for evidence such as blood, semen, candle wax, fibers or hair from animals, and signs of fire. In the event the victim is able to identify a specific residence, business, or location, law enforcement officials should attempt to obtain a search warrant.

Any search warrants must be based on probable cause and should include lists of items that, although not directly tied to the abuse, may provide corroboration to the victim's testimony. The following is a list of some of the more common items that should be included on any search warrant dealing with ritualistic abuse: occult games, ashes from any fires, robes, stands that might have been used for altars, swords, knives, animal masks or trophies, gloves (especially right-handed gloves), incense, body paint (especially red or black), animal bones or remains, any books dealing with satanism or the occult, all drugs (prescription or not), any handwritten notes or diaries, and any videos on witchcraft, the occult, or devil worshipping.

The criminal justice process is one aspect of ritualistic child abuse. Another aspect concerns the impact of this form of family violence on the survivor. This is not a text in abnormal psychology. However, a brief discussion of some of the mental and emotional problems that survivors of this form of abuse face is considered necessary to fully inform professionals of the repercussions of these types of offenses.

Posttraumatic stress disorder (PTSD) came into the lexicon as a result of the Vietnam war. Returning veterans reported flashbacks, severe depression, and other symptoms. Posttraumatic stress disorder is now recognized as a mental disorder. The DSM-IV states that the essential feature of this disorder is the development of characteristic symptoms following a psychologically distressing event that is outside the range of usual human experience. The stressor is usually experienced with intense fear, terror, and helplessness. The characteristic symptoms involve flashbacks where the patient relives the experience, avoidance of stimuli associated with the event, and numbing of general responsiveness.[31] Some authorities have concluded that PTSD is a frequently observed symptom of sexually abused children.[32]

Dissociative disorders include several recognized mental illnesses. These disorders are characterized by changes in consciousness, identity, or memory so that the individual becomes impaired. These changes may be sudden or gradual. The impairment may be amnesia, affecting memory. Impairment of identity occurs when the patient's normal identity is replaced by an alter or satellite identity. There are four types of dissociative disorders: multiple personality disorder, depersonalization disorder, psychogenic amnesia, and psychogenic fugue. Depersonalization disorder occurs when a patient's feeling of reality is lost and is replaced with a feeling of unreality. Psychogenic amnesia involves a sudden loss of memory in which the person is unable to remember important personal information. Psychogenic fugue occurs with a sudden flight from one's workplace or home and the subsequent assumption of a new identity with no memory of the past identity. The one disorder currently receiving the most attention is the multiple personality disorder (MPD).

During the 1970s and 1980s, the diagnosis of MPD was considered quite rare and carried with it overtones of "another self."[33] It was considered an almost nonexistent mental illness. Today, it is one of the most talked about disorders. The cluster of symptoms was once known as multiple personalitydisorder (MPD), but the DSM-IV now describes it as dissociative identity disorder (DID).

Some professionals claim the number of DIDs to be exaggerated. Others believe that people are claiming to be DIDs to avoid responsibility for their actions. Similar to ritualistic abuse, the diagnosis of DID is a controversial subject.

Dissociative identity disorder is the existence within a person of two or more distinct personalities or personality states where at least two of these personalities recurrently take full control of the person's behavior.[34] Personality in this context is the relatively enduring pattern of perceiving, relating to, and thinking about the environment and one's self that is exhibited in a wide range of social and personal settings. The DSM-IV states that the predisposing factor included in nearly all cases is the fact that the disorder has been preceded by abuse (often sexual) or another form of severe emotional trauma in childhood.[35]

One of the most dramatic cases of MPD was reported in the book *Sybil*, which detailed the variety of interests and characters that may exist in this disorder.[36] Sybil was a young woman who was eventually diagnosed as having at least sixteen distinct personalities. Another popular book dealing with MPDs was *The Three Faces of Eve*, which chronicled the story of Mrs. Chris Sizemore.[37] Eve, as she was known in the book, had twenty-two personalities that always manifested themselves in sets of three. *The Three Faces of Eve* was published in 1957. In 1975 Mrs. Sizemore publicly revealed herself to be Eve and subsequently wrote an autobiography, *I'm Eve.*

Researchers are continually learning about ritualistic child abuse and the impact it has on its victims. More study and research needs to be done in this area.[38] At present, very little academic work is available that deals with the long-term effects of this type of abuse. Walter Young and his associates conducted an analysis of thirty-seven patients who claimed to be victims of ritualistic abuse. Although some criticism exists of their methodology and the conclusion reached by this group, the study does provide an overview of some of the possible or potential effects of ritualistic abuse.[39]

Young's group evaluated thirty-seven patients ranging in age from eighteen to forty-seven years over a two-year period. Each of these patients had been referred for treatment of a dissociative disorder. Both male and females participated in the group. However, most of the patients were female. These patients reported being abused as children during satanic rituals.

The patients reported ritualistic abuse involving sexual abuse, witnessing and receiving physical abuse, witnessing animal mutilation and killings, and death threats.

Table 6.1 indicates some of the most extreme forms of abuse inflicted on these patients. The results of these actions had long-term emotional and psychological consequences for the victims. The study group exhibited a series of symptoms that included unusual fears, guilt, indoctrinated beliefs, severe PTSD, and dissociative states with satanic overtones. Table 6.2 sets forth the psychiatric sequelae for these thirty-seven patients.

Wilson and his associates conclude that although no independent evidence supports the existence of satanic ritualistic abuse, professionals should listen to the survivors and make careful assessments when dealing with this type of abuse.

TABLE 6.1 Young's Study of Ritualistic Abuse

1. Sexual Abuse	37
2. Witnessing and receiving physical abuse or torture	37
3. Witnessing animal mutilation or killing	37
4. Death threats	37
5. Forced drug usage	36
6. Witnessing and forced participation in human adult and infant sacrifice	31
7. Forced cannibalism	30
8. Marriage to Satan	26
9. Buried alive in coffins or graves	27
10. Forced impregnation and sacrifice of own child	20

Source: Adapted from Young, W. C., R. G. Sachs, B. G. Braun, and R. T. Watkins, "Patients Reporting Ritual Abuse in Childhood: A Clinical Syndrome. Report of 37 Cases." *Child Abuse & Neglect* (15) 1991, pp. 181–183. Reprinted with permission from Elsevier Science Ltd., Pergamon Imprint, Oxford, England.

TABLE 6.2 Reporting Symptoms

1. Severe posttraumatic stress disorder	37
2. Dissociative states with satanic overtones	37
3. Survivor guilt	36
4. Indoctrinated beliefs	35
5. Unusual fears	34
6. Sexualization of sadistic impulses	32
7. Bizarre self-abuse	31
8. Substance abuse	23

Source: Adapted from Young, W. C., R. G. Sachs, B. G. Braun, and R. T. Watkins, "Patients Reporting Ritual Abuse in Childhood: A Clinical Syndrome. Report of 37 Cases." *Child Abuse & Neglect* (15) 1991, pp. 181–183. Reprinted with permission from Elsevier Science Ltd., Pergamon Imprint, Oxford, England.

Professionals must be aware of the possibility of ritualistic child abuse, familiar with its symptoms, and understanding of the consequences of this severe form of family violence.

Summary

Ritualistic child abuse is a complex and controversial form of family violence. It is a distinct form of child abuse that involves repeated, multifaceted forms of physical, sexual, and psychological violence over an extended period of time.

Some argue that the extent and nature of ritualistic abuse is exaggerated. These persons point to the fact that there has never been one successful prosecution of a satanic cult engaged in ritualistic abuse. However, the number of survivors who claim to be victims, their strikingly similar but independent statements, and the proven existence of individuals who have engaged in satanic crimes support the position that this type of abuse may exist. The exact nature and the extent of this form of family violence will continue to be discussed, researched, and debated for the foreseeable future.

Professionals must be able to recognize the symptoms of ritualistic abuse. They should be able to distinguish these indicators from the types observed in physical and sexual abuse. Care must be taken to ensure that ideas are not planted in the victim's mind. Law enforcement agencies must attempt to obtain evidence that will support a conviction in a court of law. Medical personnel must ensure that the child is no longer at risk and must begin the arduous process of long-term treatment in an attempt to bring the survivor back into society.

Key Terms

satanism—the worship of Satan.

ritualistic child abuse—a brutal form of abuse of children, adolescents, and adults, consisting of physical, sexual, and psychological abuse and involving the use of rituals. Ritual does not necessarily mean satanic. However, most survivors state that they were ritually abused as part of satanic worship for the purpose of indoctrinating them into satanic beliefs and practices. Ritual abuse rarely consists of a single episode. It usually involves repeated abuse over an extended period of time.

magic—a method of harnessing the secret powers of nature to influence events for one's own purpose.

transmission—the belief that the qualities of objects or beings can be transmitted from one person to another.

pentagrams and hexagrams—common symbols of satanism and the occult.

grimoires—instruction manuals setting forth the rituals of satanic cults.

Dissociative identity disorder—the existence within a person of two or more distinct personalities or personality states where at least two of these personalities recurrently take full control of the person's behavior.

Discussion Questions

1. Does ritualistic abuse exist?
2. Take a position on satanism and justify your answer.
3. How long has ritualistic child abuse existed?
4. Is a sex ring a form of ritualistic abuse? Why? Why not?
5. Should we enact special laws that enhance punishment for those convicted of ritualistic abuse?

6. What type of education or information should be supplied to children regarding ritualistic abuse? If we educate them regarding this form of family violence, are we programming or predisposing them to believe they have been ritually abused?
7. Do you believe in the diagnosis of multiple personality disorder?

Suggested Readings

Ammerman, R. T., and M. Hersen, eds. *Case Studies in Family Violence.* (Plenum Press, New York) 1991.

Cavendish, R. *The Black Arts.* (G. P. Putnam, New York) 1967.

Crowley, A. *Magick in Theory and Practice.* (Dover, New York) 1924, reprinted in 1976.

Davis, W. *The Serpent and the Rainbow.* (Simon and Schuster, New York) 1985.

Gallagher, B. J. *The Sociology of Mental Illness.* 2d ed. (Prentice Hall, Englewood Cliffs, New Jersey) 1987.

Gottfried, R. S. *The Black Death: Natural and Human Disaster in Medieval Europe.* (Free Press, New York) 1983.

Hill, D., and P. Williams. *The Supernatural.* (New American Library, New York) 1965.

Investigation of Ritualistic Abuse Allegations: Think Tank Report (The National Resource Center on Child Sexual Abuse, Huntsville, Alabama) 1989.

Kahaner, L. *Cults That Kill.* (Warner Books, New York) 1988.

King, F. *Sexuality, Magic, and Perversion.* (Citadel Press, Secaucus, New Jersey) 1971.

LaVey, A. *The Satanic Bible.* (Avon Books, New York) 1969.

Ofshe, R., and E. Watters. *Making Monsters: False Memories, Psychotherapy, and Sexual Hysteria.* (Charles Scribner's Sons, New York) 1994.

Rasche, G. *Painted Black: Satanic Crime in America.* (Harper and Row, San Francisco) 1990.

Rhodes, H. T. F. *The Satanic Mass.* (Citadel Press, Secaucus, New Jersey) 1954.

Ryder, D. *Breaking the Circle of Satanic Ritual Abuse.* (CompCare, Minneapolis) 1992.

Sakheim, D. K., and S. E. Devine. *Out of Darkness.* (Lexington Books, New York) 1992.

Schreiber, F. R. *Sybil.* (Warner, New York) 1973.

Smith, M., and L. Pazder. *Michelle Remembers.* (Congdon & Lattes, New York) 1980.

Thigpen, C., and H. Cleckley. *The Three Faces of Eve.* (McGraw Hill, New York) 1957).

Valiente, D. *An ABC of Witchcraft Past and Present.* (Phoenix Publishing, Custer, Washington) 1973.

Endnotes

1. Ireland, S. J., and M. J. Ireland. "A Case History of Family and Cult Abuse," *The Journal of Psychohistory* 21(4) Spring, 1994, pp. 417–428.
2. See Cicchetti, D., and Vicki Carlson, eds. *Child Maltreatment.* (Cambridge University Press, Cambridge, United Kingdom) 1989; Tower, C. C. *Understanding Child Abuse and Neglect,* 2d ed. (Allyn & Bacon, Boston) 1993; Ammerman, R. T. and M. Hersen. *Assessment of Family Violence.* (John Wiley, New York) 1992, which do not discuss ritual abuse; and compare Kent, C. C. "Ritual Abuse." In *Case Studies in Family Violence.* R. T. Ammerman, and M. Hersen, eds. (Plenum Press, New York) 1991; and Sakheim, D. K., and S. E.

Devine. *Out of Darkness.* (Lexington Books, New York) 1992, which covers the entire realm of ritualistic abuse.

3. Gail Feldman, "Satanic Ritual Abuse: A Chapter in the History of Human Cruelty," *Journal of Psychohistory,* 22(3) (Winter, 1995), p. 340.
4. Rasche, C. *Painted Black: Satanic Crime in America.* (Harper and Row, San Francisco) 1990, pp. 140–141.
5. Hill, S. and J. Goodwin. "Satanism: Similarities between Patient Accounts and Pre-Inquisition Historical Sources."*Dissociation* 2(1) 1989, pp. 39–43.
6. Gottfried, R. S. *The Black Death: Natural and Human Disaster in Medieval Europe.* (Free Press, New York) 1983, p. 100.
7. Ibid., p. 133.
8. Rhodes, H. T. F. *The Satanic Mass.* (Citadel Press, Secaucus, New Jersey) 1954, pp. 113–122.
9. Crowley, A. *Magick in Theory and Practice.* (Dover, New York) 1924, reprinted in 1976.
10. Raschke, C. *Painted Black: Satanic Crime in America.* (Harper and Row, San Francisco) 1990, p. 123.
11. Smith, M., and L. Pazder. *Michelle Remembers.* (Congdon & Lattes, New York) 1980.
12. Wright, L. "Remembering Satan." *The New Yorker,* May 17 and 24, 1993.
13. *Ritual Abuse: Definitions, Glossary, the Use of Mind Control.* (Ritual Abuse Task Force, Los Angeles County Commission for Women) September 15, 1989.
14. *Webster's Ninth New Collegiate Dictionary* (Merriam-Webster Inc., Springfield, Massachusetts) 1987, p. 1018.
15. Kahaner, L. *Cults That Kill.* (Warner Books, New York) 1988.
16. Langone, M. D., and L. O. Blood. *Satanism and Occult Related Violence: What You Should Know.* (American Family Foundation, Weston, Massachusetts) 1990.
17. Valiente, D. *An ABC of Witchcraft Past andPresent.* (Phoenix Publishing, Custer, Washington) 1973.
18. Crowley, A. *Magick in Theory and Practice.* (Dover, New York) 1924, pp. 94–95.
19. Cavendish, R. *The Black Arts.* (G. P. Putnam, New York) 1967, p. 272.
20. King, F. *Sexuality, Magic, and Perversion.* (Citadel Press, Secaucus, New Jersey) 1971, pp. 8 and 163.
21. Hill, D., and P. Williams. *The Supernatural.* (New American Library, New York) 1965, pp. 107–108.
22. Ibid., pp. 110–111.
23. Fine, J. "Seeking Evil," *California Lawyer* (July, 1994), pp. 50–55.
24. Jones, D. P. H. "Ritualism and Child Sexual-Abuse." *Child Abuse and Neglect* (15) 1991, pp. 163–170.
25. Ibid., p. 168.
26. See http://web.mit.edu/harris/www/witch hunt.html (January 13, 1998).
27. See http://www.xroads.com/rahome/rahome.html (January 13, 1998).
28. See Gonzalez, L. S., J. Waterman, R. J. Kelly, J. McCord, and M. K. Oliveri, "Children's Patterns of Disclosures and Recantations of Sexual and Ritualistic Abuse Allegations in Psychotherapy." *Child Abuse and Neglect* (17) 1993, p. 281, for an excellent discussion of how disclosure occurs with victims of abuse.
29. Sakheim, D. K., and S. E. Devine. *Out of Darkness.* (Lexington Books, New York) 1992, pp. 210–216.
30. Jenkins, P. "Investigating Occult and Ritual Crime: A Case for Caution," *Police Forum, Academy of Criminal Justice Sciences* 2/1 (January, 1992), pp. 1–7.
31. *Diagnostic and Statistical Manual of Mental Disorders* (Fourth Edition-Revised) [DSM-IV-R] (American Psychiatric Association, Washington D.C.) 1994, p. 424.
32. See Deblinger, E., S. V. McLeere, M. S. Atkins, D. Ralphe, and E. Fox, "Post-Traumatic Stress in Sexually Abused, Physically Abused, and Nonabused Children." *Child Abuse and Neglect* (13) 1993, p. 403.
33. Gallagher, III, B. J. *The Sociology of Mental Illness.* 2d ed. (Prentice Hall, Englewood Cliffs, New Jersey) 1987, pp. 117–119.

34. *Diagnostic and Statistical Manual of Mental Disorders* (Fourth Edition) [DSM-IV] (American Psychiatric Association, Washington, D.C.) 1987, pp. 484–487.
35. DSM-IV, p. 485.
36. Schreiber, F. R. *Sybil.* (Warner, New York) 1973.
37. Thigpen, C., and H. Cleckley. *The Three Faces of Eve.* (McGraw Hill, New York) 1957.
38. McMinn, M. R. and N. G. Wade, "Beliefs about the Prevalence of Dissociative Identity Disorder, Sexual Abuse, and Ritual Abuse among Religions and Nonreligious Therapists, "*Professional Research and Practice,* 26(3) (June, 1995), pp. 257–261.
39. Putnam, F. W. "The Satanic Ritual Abuse Controversy." *Child Abuse and Neglect* (15) 1991, p. 175.

7

PROFESSIONALS AND THEIR RESPONSE TO CHILD ABUSE

Chapter Outline

Learning Objectives

After reading this chapter, you should be able to discuss the following concepts:

- The objectives of child abuse reporting laws.
- The issues of confidentiality and when there are exceptions to this privilege.
- The techniques for proper interviewing of children.
- The basic evidentiary rules and procedures involved in a court hearing.
- The differences between a civil and a criminal hearing.
- The rights of children and parents in the legal process.

Introduction

The previous chapters have focused on specific incidents of family violence. Because children cannot speak for themselves when they are in an abusive situation, courts have determined that others must act on their behalfs. This chapter explains what must occur once child abuse has been discovered. Chapter 9 will examine the criminal justice response to spousal assault, and Chapter 14 will review victim's rights.

Once students graduate from a college or university and enter certain professions, their is a high probability that they will come into contact with a child who has been neglected or abused. Every state has passed laws that mandate certain actions on the part of any professional who has reason to believe a child is abused. Before these laws were passed, numerous children became victims of the system that was supposed to protect them.

Great strides have been made in protecting children since the incidents reported in the Focus "Failures in the System" occurred. Many states and counties in the United States have demanded that professionals who deal with abused children become more sensitive to children's special needs and requirements. In fact, all states in the United States have enacted statutes that have a specific goal of protecting abused children by mandating reporting of suspected child abuse cases to the authorities.

Reporting

No uniform reporting code has been adopted by all states in this area of the law. However, most states have passed legislation that contains similar characteristics that include when reporting is required, who must report, and the consequences of reporting.

FOCUS Failures in the System

When Joseph Bellamy's parents were reported for child neglect, social workers failed to follow the case. When his mother was turned in or beating Joseph two months later, onesocial worker figured it was a hoax. Joseph Bellamy, now sixteen months old, is brain damaged from a series of savage shakings.

Child abuse incidents tend to escalate in severity over time and early reporting can make the difference between life and death. In 1985, 1,000 children were killed in abusive or neglectful situations. Between 35 and 50 percent had been previously reported.

One child may experience thirty-six different interviews for one report of child abuse. One three-year-old child had fifty-two different contacts with the system before he died as a result of abuse.

Source: Adapted from *President's Child Safety Partnership, Final Report.* (Washington, D.C.) 1987, pp. 80–83.

Elements of Reporting Laws

State reporting laws have as their ultimate goal the protection of the child from violence or abuse within the home or family. To accomplish this, statutes require that certain classes of professionals who normally come into contact with children report cases of suspected child abuse. The theory is that a young child cannot speak for himself or herself and, therefore, intervention and protection from a dangerous situation is necessary.

Definition of Abuse

Most statutes define child abuse from a physical, neglectful, and sexual perspective. Some states include emotional abuse within this area. The professional need not prove the child was actually abused. A suspicion based on the professional's education and training is sufficient to trigger the reporting mandate.

Persons Covered

These statutes apply to most professionals who might have regular contact with young children. Physicians, nurses, social workers, teachers, psychologists, psychiatrists, and counselors are normally covered by these laws and are therefore required to report cases of suspected child abuse.

Filing of the Report

The report must be made to a specific agency named in the law. Normally a social service agency or department is tasked with conducting the initial investigation of the alleged child abuse.[1] Some jurisdictions require the report to go both to a social service agency such as child protective services (CPS) and the local law enforcement agency.[2] Many states have standardized forms that the professional must use in filing the report (see Figure 7.1). These forms may be a combination of fill-in boxes and a narrative summary of the facts surrounding the suspected abuse.

Waiver of Privilege

Many professional relationships establish a confidential relationship between the patient or client and the professional offering treatment. The reporting statutes require incidents of suspected child abuse to be reported even when this confidential relationship exists. In essence, this privilege is waived for purposes of reporting.

Timely Investigation

These statutes mandate that the professional who suspects or has reason to believe child abuse has or is occurring must report that information within a certain period of time from discovery of the abuse. Once the report has been made, an investigation must be commenced within a certain period of time, normally forty-eight hours, and concluded usually no later than six months after receipt of the report.

SUSPECTED CHILD ABUSE REPORT

To Be Completed by Reporting Party
Pursuant to Penal Code Section 11166

A. CASE IDENTI-FICATION	*TO BE COMPLETED BY INVESTIGATING CPA*
	VICTIM NAME
	REPORT NO./CASE NAME
	DATE OF REPORT

B. REPORTING PARTY

NAME/TITLE		
ADDRESS		
PHONE ( )	DATE OF REPORT	SIGNATURE OF REPORTING PARTY

C. REPORT SENT TO

☐ POLICE DEPARTMENT ☐ SHERIFF'S OFFICE ☐ COUNTY WELFARE ☐ COUNTY PROBATION

AGENCY	ADDRESS	
OFFICIAL CONTACTED	PHONE ( )	DATE/TIME

D. INVOLVED PARTIES

VICTIM

NAME (LAST, FIRST, MIDDLE)	ADDRESS	BIRTHDATE	SEX	RACE
PRESENT LOCATION OF CHILD		PHONE ( )		

SIBLINGS'

NAME	BIRTHDATE	SEX	RACE	NAME	BIRTHDATE	SEX	RACE
1.				4.			
2.				5.			
3.				6.			

PARENTS

NAME (LAST, FIRST, MIDDLE)	BIRTHDATE	SEX	RACE	NAME (LAST, FIRST, MIDDLE)	BIRTHDATE	SEX	RACE
ADDRESS				ADDRESS			
HOME PHONE ( )	BUSINESS PHONE ( )			HOME PHONE ( )	BUSINESS PHONE ( )		

E. INCIDENT INFORMATION

IF NECESSARY, ATTACH EXTRA SHEET OR OTHER FORM AND CHECK THIS BOX ☐

1. DATE/TIME OF INCIDENT	PLACE OF INCIDENT	*(CHECK ONE)* ☐ OCCURRED ☐ OBSERVED

IF CHILD WAS IN OUT-OF-HOME CARE AT THE TIME OF INCIDENT, CHECK TYPE OF CARE:
☐ FAMILY DAY CARE ☐ CHILD CARE CENTER ☐ FOSTER FAMILY HOME ☐ SMALL FAMILY HOME ☐ GROUP HOME OR INSTITUTION

2. TYPE OF ABUSE: *(CHECK ONE OR MORE)* ☐ PHYSICAL ☐ MENTAL ☐ SEXUAL ASSAULT ☐ NEGLECT ☐ OTHER

3. NARRATIVE DESCRIPTION:

4. SUMMARIZE WHAT THE ABUSED CHILD OR PERSON ACCOMPANYING THE CHILD SAID HAPPENED:

5. EXPLAIN KNOWN HISTORY OF SIMILAR INCIDENT(S) FOR THIS CHILD:

SS 8572 (REV.7/87) *INSTRUCTIONS AND DISTRIBUTION ON REVERSE*

DO NOT submit a copy of this form to the Department of Justice (DOJ). A CPA is required under Penal Code Section 11169 to submit to DOJ a Child Abuse Investigation Report Form SS-8583 if (1) and active investigation has been conducted and (2) the incident is not unfounded.

Police or Sheriff-WHITE Copy; County Welfare or Probation-BLUE Copy; District Attorney-GREEN Copy; Reporting Party-YELLOW Copy

FIGURE 7.1 Suspected Child Abuse Report

SUSPECTED CHILD ABUSE REPORT
DEPARTMENT OF JUSTICE FORM SS 8572
(REQUIRED UNDER PENAL CODE SECTIONS 11166 AND 11168)

I. REPORTING RESPONSIBILITIES

• No child care custodian or health practitioner reporting a suspected instance of child abuse shall be civilly or criminally liable for any report required or authorized by this article (California Penal Code Article 2.5). Any other person reporting a suspected instance of child abuse shall not incur civil or criminal liability as a result of any report authorized by this section unless it can be proved that a false report was made and the person knew or should have known that the report was false.

• Any child care custodian, health practioner, or employee of a child protective agency (CPA) who has knowledge of or observes a child in his or her professional capacity or within the scope of his or her employment whom he or she reasonably suspects has been the victim of child abuse shall report such suspected instance of child abuse to a child protective agency immediately or as soon as practically possible by telephone and shall prepare and send a written report thereof *within 36 hours* of receiving the information concerning the incident.

• Any child care custodian, health practitioner, or employee of a child protective agency who has knowledge of or who reasonably suspects that mental suffering has been inflicted on a child or its emotional well-being is endangered in any other way, may report such suspected instance of child abuse to a child protective agency. Infliction of willful and unjustifiable mental suffering must be reported.

II. DEFINITIONS

• "Child care custodian" means a teacher, administrative officer, supervisor of child welfare and attendance, or certificated pupil personnel employee of any public or private school; an administrator of public or private day camp; a licensee, an administrator, or an employee of a community care facility licensed to care for children; headstart teacher; a licensing worker or licensing evaluator; public assistance worker, an employee of a child care institution including, but not limited to, foster parents, group home personnel and personnel or residential care facilities; a social worker or a probation officer or any person who is an administrator or presenter of , or a counselor in, a child abuse presentation program in any public or private school.

• "Health practitioner" means a physician and surgeon, psychiatrist, psychylogist, dentist, resident, intern, podiatrist, chiropractor, licensed nurse, dental hygienist, marriage, family, and child counselor, or any other person who is currently licensed under Division 2 (commencing with Section 500) of the Business and Professions Code, and emergency medical technician I or II, paramedic, a person certified pursuant to Division 2.5 (commencing with Section 1797) of the Health and Safety code, a psychological assistant registerd pursuant to Section 2913 of the Business and Professions code, a marriage, family and child counselor trainee, as defined in subdivision (c) of Section 4980.03 of the Business and Professions Code, an unlicensed marriage, family and child counselor intern registered under section 4980.44 of the Business and Professions Code, a state or county public health employee who treats a minor for venereal disease or any other condition, a coroner, or a religious practitioner who diagnoses, examines, or treats children.

• "Child protective agency" (CPA) means a police or sheriff's department, a county probation department, or a country welfare department.

III. INSTRUCTIONS

(Section A to be completed by investigating child protective agency)
SECTION A - "CASE IDENTIFICATION": Enter the victim name, report number or case name, and date of report.

(Section B through E are to be completed by reporting party)
SECTION B - "REPORTING PARTY": Enter your name/title, address, phone number, date of report, and signature.

SECTION C - "REPORT SENT TO": (1) Check the appropriate box to indicate which CPA this report is being sent; (2) Enter the name and address of the CPA to which this report is being sent; and (3) Enter the name of the official contacted at the CPA, phone number, and the date/time contacted.

SECTION D - "INVOLVED PARTIES":

a. VICTIM: Enter the name, physical data, present location, and phone number where victim is located (attach additional sheets if multiple victims).
b. SIBLINGS: Enter the name and physical data of siblings living in the same household as the victim.
c. PARENTS: Enter the names, physical data, addresses, and phone numbers of father/stepfather and mother/stepmother.

SECTION E - "INCIDENT INFORMATION": (1) Enter the date/time and place the incident occured or was observed, and check the appropriate boxes; (2) Check the type of abuse; (3) Describe injury or sexual assault (where appropriate, attach Medical Report - Suspected Child Abuse Form DOJ 900 or any other form desired); (4) Summarize what the child or person accompanying the child said happened; and (5) Explain any known prior incidents involving the victim.

IV. DISTRIBUTION

A. Reporting party: Complete Suspected Child Abuse Report Form SS 8572. Retain yellow copy for your records and submit top three copies to a child protective agency.

B. Investigating Child Protective Agency: Upon receipt of Form SS 8572, *within 36 hours* send white copy to police or sheriff, blue copy to county welfare or probation, and green copy to district attorney.

FIGURE 7.1 *Continued*

Emergency Removal

Most of these reporting laws authorize agencies to remove the child from the custody of the parents if there is reason to believe the child is in imminent danger. Emergency removal is usually valid for up to forty-eight hours and must normally be based on specific evidence from a professional that the child is in a dangerous situation. At the end of this time period, there must be a judicial review of the agency's actions to continue the separation of the child from his parents.

Emergency Treatment

Most state statutes authorize emergency medical treatment of the child to protect his or her health. Once the child's condition is stabilized, however, any further medical treatment must be authorized by the court after notice to the parents and an opportunity for them to respond to the request for treatment.

Immunity

These laws establish immunity from civil lawsuits for any professional who acted in good faith. This provision is present to encourage professionals to report without fear of facing an expensive lawsuit by the parents after the incident is concluded. This immunity is a defense to any civil action and allows the professional to move for dismissal of the lawsuit at an early stage in the proceedings.

Penalties

Most statutes establish both civil and criminal penalties for failing to report suspected child abuse. Some statutes hold the professional liable for any damages or injuries that occur to the child as a result of the professional's failure to report. Most states authorize the filing of misdemeanor charges against the party who did not report. As a result, a professional may face fines or incarceration if found guilty of violating these statutes.

Reporting statutes provide a valuable tool in the fight against child abuse. They mandate that professionals who have reason to believe or suspect that a child is a victim of abuse report such information to agencies tasked with the responsibility of investigating child abuse. On occasion, a professional will have to disclose confidential information received from clients or patients in order to comply with these reporting mandates.

Confidentiality

A confidential communication is information that is made under circumstances in which the speaker intends that the statement be shared only with the recipient of the information.[3] This communication is protected by a privilege that prohibits the recipient from disclosing the communication to any unauthorized person. Normally, confidential communications are based on state statutes that establish certain categories of relationships that society has deemed require or need such confidentiality. Typical relationships include spouses, physician–patient, confessor–penitent, and others who are involved in a professional relationship with persons.

From early times, certain information relayed to a physician was considered confidential. The Hippocratic oath states that whatever a physician hears or sees in the course of his or her profession shall not be disclosed and that he or she will never divulge this information, holding such things to be holy secrets. Many professions have adopted ethical standards or codes that make communication between patients or clients confidential. For example the American Medical Association requires physicians (and psychiatrists) to safeguard patient's communications within the constraints of the law.[4]

In addition to ethical considerations, all states have adopted statutes that make certain information privileged if disclosed in a professional relationship that the law has established as being confidential. If a privileged communication has occurred, the law normally prevents the recipient from disclosing the content or substance of any information. This prohibition against disclosure includes all information obtained during the professional relationship. Many of these statutes prevent the professional from identifying the person who transmitted the information.

The person who communicates the information to the professional is the holder of the privilege and can bar disclosure or waive it as deemed necessary but cannot be forced to waive this privilege. The professional who has received the confidential information cannot, absent certain statutory exceptions, disclose this information to any other person. Most statutes authorize professionals to communicate with other professionals if necessary to treat or work with the client. For example, a medical doctor may be authorized to inform a nurse or specialist about a patient's conditions so as to provide the necessary treatment to the patient. Many states provide that professionals may or must disclose this information if they receive a duly executed court document such as a subpoena for records. Absent such a court-sanctioned process, the information cannot be divulged to unauthorized third parties.

This privilege, however, is not absolute. Under certain circumstances, state statutes hold that the privilege or communication is not confidential and may or must be disclosed without the necessity of service of court papers. This is the case when a professional encounters a situation where he has reason to believe or suspects that a child may be a victim of abuse. As discussed previously, certain professionals are mandated to report incidents of suspected child abuse. Although the statutes mandate reporting, this does not end the professional's duty and obligation to the child. They should attempt to obtain information regarding the incident, and to do so they have to interview the child. This process is critical and if improperly conducted may result in the child being returned to the abusive situation.

Sex Offender Community Notification (Megan's Law)

A large population of prison inmates are sexual offenders.[5] Although community programs and agencies exist that specialize in treating sex offenders, few incarcerated sex offenders receive any treatment. Additionally, the debate continues regarding the effectiveness of treatment for the various types of sex offenders.[6]

A series of highly publicized violent sex offenses committed on unsuspecting victims by newly released sex offenders heightened the general public's awareness of this type of offender.[7] One of the most famous cases concerned a recently released sex offender who raped and murdered seven-year-old Megan Kanka in 1994. Her family became one of the guiding forces behind the adoption of the sex offender notification law in New Jersey. The movement by victims and their families to prevent these types of offenders from committing new crimes gained momentum. As a result of these forces, by August 1995, forty-three states had adopted laws requiring offenders to register with a department or law enforcement agency. The 1994 Violent Crime Control and Law Enforcement Act may result in the enactment of registration laws by all states because failure to do so may result in loss of funding from the federal government.

By 1996, at least thirty-two states had adopted laws requiring notification to individuals and organizations. These so-called Megan's laws reflect a community perception that registration alone is inadequate to protect the public against these types of sexual predators. Those in favor of notification laws believe that such a process allows neighbors to take action to protect themselves from sex offenders by keeping themselves and their children out of harm's way.[8] Proponents of notification also believe that these statutes improve public safety because the community will be on alert for risky or suspicious behavior (loitering around school grounds, talking with children in the park, and so on) that might escalate to criminal acts if left unchecked.

The existing notification statutes vary in their scope and level of detail. However, four models have emerged that typify existing laws:

1. An agency is identified as determining the level of risk posed by the offender and then implements the notification plan on the basis of that level of risk. Frequently, the notification plan has three levels or requirements, depending on the offender risk:
   - The first level may involve notification of only selected organizations.
   - The second level adds community residents.
   - The third level includes the media.

2. Some state statutes stipulate which type of offender is subject to notification and what notification methods to use. Under this model, a state agency may carry out the notification but plays no role in how notification will be implemented.
3. The offenders must do the actual notification, although they may be supervised by a criminal justice agency.
4. The burden is on the community organizations and individuals to take the initiative to request information about whether a sex offender is living in their community.

A wide variety of registration and notification procedures are in place in existing state statutes.[9] At this time, no empirical evidence suggests that notification increases the public safety or assists law enforcement agencies in their investigations of sex offenses. However, many professionals believe that notification can serve as a basis to further educate the community about sex offending and offenders. Notification must be considered as only one of a number of techniques that must be employed in our quest for a community free from the threat of sexual violence.

Interviewing

Once any professional suspects that a child has been a victim of abuse, the interview process takes on an entirely different perspective. The questions asked, the environment in which the interview is conducted, and the motives of the interviewer could have a direct impact on any court intervention. All professionals must keep in mind that their actions will be reviewed and judged by others who have not had their training or expertise. This review or judgement of the professional and the interview of the child victim occurs in court and is conducted by both the prosecutor and the attorney representing the person accused of abusing the child.

The Interview Process

During the 1970s and 1980s, a common defense tactic was to attack the credibility of the child by inferring or stating that the child was lying about the incidents. When dealing with children under the age of seven, these attacks centered on the child's inability to remember specific facts, distinguish between truth and falsehoods, and the intermingling of fact and fantasy in the child's mind. Older children were accused of being spiteful and seeking revenge for real or imagined discipline by the parents. Soon, however, defense attorneys began to realize that jurors and judges were capable of evaluating the truthfulness of children, and for the most part there were very few cases in which children engaged in lying regarding incidents of physical or sexual abuse. As a result of this almost universal acceptance of the credibility and lack of bias on the part of children, the defense establishment moved from attacking the child directly to attacking those who interact with the victim before trial.

Today, one of the most commonly raised issues in child abuse cases is the validity of out-of-court interviews with the victim. Charges are levied against professionals that suggestions or memories have been planted in impressionable young minds. The interviewer is accused of being biased and unprofessional. Defense attorneys will further claim that the interviewer has brainwashed or tainted the recollection of the child and therefore that the victim's testimony should be considered untrustworthy.[10]

The fact that defense attorneys and others may second-guess an interviewer's professionalism should not deter those charged with safeguarding victims of abuse from carrying out their duties. However, all professionals must be aware of the possibility of these accusations being levied against them and conduct the interview in an unbiased manner. Interviews with victims of abuse should not be dreaded; rather, they must be approached with the understanding that the ultimate goal is safeguarding the child.

As any professional knows, children are not small adults. They have different perceptions, abilities, and needs than adults. Understanding how children react to events is critical in conducting a valid interview.

One of the most important aspects of interviewing child abuse victims is their ability to recall the incident or incidents. It is generally accepted by scholars and professionals that children have the ability to recall events and relate details concerning those events.[11] Although there is some debate whether stressful events promote or impair memory, most authorities agree that the child will remember the substance of the event, if not all the details.[12]

Children's memory can be classified into two types: recognition and free recall. *Recognition memory occurs when the child is cued or is able to perceive an object or event that was first perceived at an earlier time.* For example, showing a child a photographic lineup and having the child identify the perpetrator is a form of recognition memory.[13] *Recall memory occurs when the child can recollect the event without the aid of cues or other assistance.* This is the most complex form of memory.[14] This type of memory is used most often in court proceedings. As discussed in more detail later in this section, questions such as "What happened on this night?" would trigger recall memory. These types of questions do not prompt or cue the witness.

Researchers have determined that when children are asked questions that prompt free recall memory, they relate fewer details than adults.[15] Although the information they do recall is as accurate as that from adults, it is not as detailed.[16] And even though children may be as accurate as adults in recalling recent events, their memories fade faster on points of detail than those of adults. This is especially the case with young children.[17]

Most interviews are not conducted in a random manner. There is usually a reason for talking with the child. It may be part of a normal medical interview, a discussion at school regarding why the child is acting in a certain manner, or in response to a request for assistance from the child. Professionals conducting interviews should have as much information as possible prior to the interview.[18]

Simply having this information does not prejudice the interviewer. In fact, an argument can be made that, armed with this information, the person conducting the interview is able to ask questions in such a manner as to avoid suggestions or improperly influencing the child. The type of questions asked of child abuse victims is a critical aspect of the interview.

Depending on the dynamics of the interview, the professional may attempt to gain information from the victim in a variety of ways. This may require that questions be poised in different forms, and there are several types of questions that may be used in any interview of an abused child. These questions range from open-ended to coercive.

From a legal perspective, the most acceptable form of questioning of an abused child is using open-ended questions. *An open-ended question does not suggest or imply an answer.* Examples of open-ended questions are "Did anything happened to you?", "Were you doing anything?", and "Where was your daddy?"

After receiving certain information from the victim, the interviewer will need to obtain more specific facts. Often focused questions are used when this need arises. *A focused question narrows the scope of inquiry and requires the witness to answer within certain parameters.* Examples of focused questions are (after establishing that the father entered the child's bedroom) "When your Daddy walked into the room, what did he do?"; (after the child states that he was hurt at a particular time) "On the morning you were hurt, where was your mother?"; and (when the child has indicated that the father touched her genitals) "Did your daddy say anything before he touched you?"

A leading question is one that suggests the answer to the witness.[19] It is a question that includes the desired reply within it, or it may be a statement posed to the witness under the guise of being a question. The rationale behind prohibiting leading questions is to remove the ability of the interviewer to suggest answers to the victim. Examples of leading questions are "Your daddy touched your private parts, didn't he?"; "Did your mother hit you every day when she drank?", and "Is it true that you saw your brother being hit by your mother?"

The final form of questioning involves the use of coercive questions. *Coercive questions promise rewards or threaten punishment for certain answers.* Coercive questions should never be used when interviewing children. They are normally employed in court with a hostile witness. Examples of coercive questions are "Are you aware that telling a lie is considered perjury and subjects you to criminal sanctions?"

Once a professional interviews the child, the process has just begun. There will be other interviews and other persons who interact with the child along the way, but one of the most critical interviews is that conducted by the prosecuting attorney. This final prefiling interview will determine whether the prosecutor believes there is sufficient evidence to go forward with the case. This interview is conducted in the same manner as other interviews, and its goal is to allow the prosecutor to determine the competency and credibility of the victim and how the judge or jury will react to the child's testimony.

As the previous discussion illustrates, several different types of questions may be used when interviewing child abuse victims. No clear-cut rule exists as to when an open-ended question is more appropriate than a focused question. This will depend on the dynamics of the interview, the age of the child, the trauma of the incident, and the experience of the interviewer. What is clear is that all interviewers must guard against influencing or suggesting certain answers or stories to the child. They must be prepared to explain why they chose certain questions over others and what their purpose or intent was when they used those questions.

Evidentiary Issues

Knowledge of the rules of evidence and what courts consider important will assist the professional in conducting these interviews. Although this is not intended as a law school text, certain legal and procedural aspects of questioning witnesses and using their responses should be discussed.

FOCUS The Prosecution's Interview

The following are guidelines followed by prosecutors when interviewing children who have been sexually abused.

1. Be yourself.
2. Introduce yourself, tell the child your name, and ask the child his name and if he has a nickname.
3. Demonstrate a genuine interest in the child by inquiring about the child's interests, family and friends, school, pets, and so on.
4. Find out whether the child knows why she is there to see you. Explain who you are and what you do in simple terms. Let her know you have talked to other children who have had similar things happen to them.
5. Find out from the child what he thinks should happen to the suspect. Does the child love or hate the suspect? The child's feelings toward the suspect will enable you to better assess the case.
6. Determine the child's capacity for understanding "telling the truth."
   - **a.** "Do you know the difference between right and wrong?
   - **b.** "Do you know what it is to tell a lie?"
   - **c.** "If I said it was Christmas today, would that be a truth or lie?"
   - **d.** "What happens when you lie?"
   - **e.** "Do you promise to tell me only things that really happened?"
7. Use open-ended questions. Do not lead the child. Never confront the child. Instead, ask the child to explain her statement in more detail. Let the interview flow on the child's level.
   - **a.** "Can you tell me what happened?"
   - **b.** "Have you ever been touched in a way that made you feel funny or uncomfortable?"
   - **c.** "What kind of touching was it?"
   - **d.** "Who touched you?"
   - **e.** "How/when did it start?"
   - **f.** "What happened next?"
   - **g.** "What did he/she touch you with?"
   - **h.** "Where did he/she touch you?"
   - **i.** "How were you feeling?"
   - **j.** "What did he/she say?"
   - **k.** "Who was the first person you told?"
8. Do not use accusatory questions when interviewing the child.
   - **a.** "Why didn't you tell someone right away?"
   - **b.** "Why did you let this go on?"
   - **c.** "You should have told Mommy. Tell me why you didn't. Don't you trust her?"
9. Remember that children can be very literal and think in concrete terms.
10. If you sense that the child is fearful, confront her fears.
11. Remember that abused children are guilt-ridden and feel that they are somehow responsible for what happened to them. Relieve the guilt of the child. Tell the child that he did nothing wrong and won't get in trouble for telling. Tell them that it is not your job or their job to punish the defendant; that is the job of the judge.
12. Let the child draw pictures or play with dolls. [See the discussion of the use of anatomical dolls later in this chapter.] Some children find it easier to answer more difficult questions when it appears that they are occupied with other things.
13. Show the child the courtroom. Introduce him to the staff. Let him go up to the witness stand and play with the microphone if he wishes. Make him comfortable in this environment.
14. End the interview by thanking the child for helping you understand what happened. Do not mislead the child about the judicial process.

Source: Adapted from Susan Etezadi, "Interviewing and Preparing the Child Witness for Court." *Introduction to Sexual Assault Prosecution.* (California District Attorneys Association, Sacramento, California) 1991.

Hearsay is one of the simplest and most complex subjects in the area of evidence. Numerous texts, articles, and treatises have been written about the subject of hearsay.[20] These publications deal with the nuances and exceptions to the hearsay rule. Simply stated, *hearsay is any out-of-court statement that is offered in court for the truth of the matter stated.* This definition can be broken down further into three distinct areas:

1. Any out-of-court statement
2. Offered in court
3. For the truth of the matter stated

Any out-of-court statement: These may be statements made by the victim or the suspect. For example, the child may have told a nurse in a hospital emergency room, "My daddy hurt me." When the nurse attempts to repeat or testify to the statement in court, she is stating something that occurred outside the presence of the judge and jury. Thus, any statement that occurs outside of the courtroom agrees with this element of the hearsay rule.

Offered in court: The second element of the hearsay rule requires that the out-of-court statement be offered as testimony or evidence in a court proceeding. In the example above, if the nurse were to repeat the statement to a police officer who responded to the call for assistance at the emergency room, simply telling the officer what the child said is not hearsay because the repeating of the statement did not occur in court.

For the truth of the matter stated: The statement when offered in court must be offered as true. In other words, it is not offered for any other reason than to show that the child stated, "My Daddy hurt me." If it is offered for any other reason, the final element of the hearsay rule has not been satisfied. This might be the situation in which the statement is offered to show that the officer had probable cause to arrest the suspect and not to show that the child was in fact molested or abused.

For a statement to be objectionable on hearsay grounds, all three of the previously discussed elements must be present. Courts have traditionally been reluctant to admit out-of-court statements because they lacked reliability, and many times offering such as statement in court denied the defendant the opportunity to confront and cross-examine the person who made the statement. Additionally, because these statements were not made under oath, there was a judicial inclination not to accept them as trustworthy.

Some commentators argue that the hearsay rule has been consumed by the number of exceptions written into statutes by legislatures. These exceptions allow certain types of out-of-court statements to be admitted as truthful. The major exceptions to the hearsay rule that are of interest to professionals dealing with family violence are the following:

1. Excited utterance
2. Admissions
3. Declarations against interest

4. State of mind
5. Statements made to medical professionals
6. Statements made by victims of abuse

Excited utterance: Excited utterances are also known as spontaneous declarations. *An excited utterance is a statement made whenever a person is excited or under stress as a result of a traumatic event.* Many of us have hit our hand with a hammer and without any conscious effort uttered a cuss word or two. These cuss words were not planned or thought out, they just happened as a result of the pain we suffered when the hammer struck our hand. The theory behind admitting such statements is that the person making the statement has had no opportunity to fabricate a false story. Suspects or the victims of child abuse may make these same types of statements. For a statement to be classified as an excited utterance, it must meet the following criteria: There must have been some events startling enough to produce this excitement and render the statement spontaneous and unreflecting, the utterance must have been made before there was an opportunity to contrive and misrepresent any feelings, and the utterance must relate to the circumstances of the occurrence preceding it.[21]

Admissions: An admission is a statement or conduct of a party in the action that is offered against him in the trial. The theory behind admitting such evidence is that the party who made the statement is present in court and can testify and explain the comments or action. An admission may occur as a result of a person's actions. For example, a classic form of admission is flight from the scene of the crime. This flight shows a "consciousness of guilt" and can be introduced during trial to indicate that the party who fled had something to hide or was trying to get away and avoid apprehension.[22]

Declarations against interest: Declarations against interest are very similar to admissions except they are not made by a party to the action. *A declaration against interest is a statement by a nonparty that is against his or her own interest.* The theory behind admitting such statements is that a person will normally not speak against his or her own interest unless it is true. For the statement to be admitted, several conditions must be satisfied: the declarant, or person making the statement, must not be available as a witness, and the statement must be against the person's pecuniary or proprietary interest or subject him or her to civil or criminal liability as a result of the statement.

For the unavailability requirement to be met, the person making the statement must be insane, dead, or absent from the jurisdiction of the court. The declaration must be against the declarant's financial, property, civil, or criminal interests and of such a nature that a reasonable person would not have made the statement unless he or she believed it to be true.

State of mind: A state of mind statement relates a fact regarding the declarant's mental or emotional condition. The theory behind admitting these statements is that a person would not normally tell a falsehood about his or her state of mind. This area is one of the most complex areas in the exceptions to the hearsay rule. For these types of statements to be admissible as an exception to the hearsay rule, they must be offered to prove the declarant's state of mind at the time when it was an issue in the action or when the statement is offered to prove or explain conduct of the declarant. For example, a person's statement to a friend, "When I get home, I'm going to beat her blue for breaking that dish," would be admitted to show the declarant's state of mind or explain his subsequent conduct if he did batter his child. Some jurisdictions allow statements that pertain to previously existing as well as present states of mind to be admitted into evidence.

Statements made to medical professionals: Closely related to the state of mind exception are the statements made to medical professionals. The theory behind this exception is that spontaneous statements describing present pain or other physical conditions are likely to be true. *A statement made to medical professionals is information given for purposes of diagnosis or treatment of a medical condition.* The Federal Rules of Evidence allow statements made to medical professionals to be admitted as an exception to the hearsay rule when they are made for purposes of medical diagnosis or treatment and describe medical history, past or present symptoms, pain or sensations, or the general character of the medical problem.[23]

Statements made by victims of abuse: Some jurisdictions have amended their evidence code statutes to specifically provide for an exception to the hearsay rule for statements made by victims of abuse. The U.S. Supreme Court upheld the concept underlying this exception to the hearsay rule in *Idaho v Wright* when it stated that judges could consider the totality of the circumstances surrounding the making of the statement to determine whether it was reliable and therefore admissible under this type of exception.[24]

The previous discussion has briefly examined the hearsay rule and some of its more common exceptions. Professionals need to be familiar with these technical rules to understand the importance of information received from victims of child abuse. Clearly documenting the circumstances surrounding statements made to the professional may provide the necessary factual information that will allow these statements to be admitted as evidence in court proceedings.

Another aspect of the legal system professionals must understand deals with the concept of competency. For a witness to testify in a court of law, a determination must be made that the witness is competent. In most cases, the judge will make an initial ruling and allow the jury to give whatever weight it desires to that witnesses testimony. *Competency is the ability of the witness to accurately testify to events.* This requirement involves two distinct elements: Does the witness understand the nature of the proceedings, and can the witness accurately relate what transpired? Both these elements must be satisfied before a witness is considered competent. For adult victims or witnesses, these requirements are simple to meet: They understand that they are testifying under oath in a criminal proceeding, and they can describe what they saw or did not see.

The issue of competency is much more complex when dealing with children. The child must understand that he or she is swearing or affirming to tell the truth, and the child must be able to testify accurately as to the events in question.

The first element requires that the child understand that he or she must tell the truth. Depending on the age of the child, the concept of truthfulness becomes a

FOCUS Recovered Repressed Memories

One of the more controversial issues facing professionals in the field today is recovered repressed memories. This condition is known by a variety of names, including repressed memory, delayed recall memory, and false memory syndrome. It has resulted in families suing each other; claims of sexual abuse surfacing years, even decades, after the incidents; and lawsuits against therapists who treated survivors of abuse.

In a relatively short period of time since the 1992 founding of the False Memory Syndrome Foundation (FMSF), claims and counterclaims regarding the accuracy of recovered memory have reached new heights. A valid concern exists regarding the validity of recovered repressed memories and the damage that can result when false accusations of abuse are levied against-someone.

In order to interpret some of the dynamics in this area it is important to understand that long-term memory, rather than being a reliable tape recording, is a reconstruction that is subject to distortions based on later experience and influence. It has also been established that the accuracy of the memories cannot be established by the confidence of the subject in the reality of the memory. Otherwise, we would have to accept the reality of abduction and abuse of humans by aliens in UFOs—a claim, despite the popularity of the television show *The X-Files,* that has never been proven.* However, we can also accept the fact that incertain situations memory blockage does in fact occur. This process is better described as a continuum where people experience varying degrees of access to different parts of memory at different points of time. There are documented situations in which, because of a harrowing event, a person suffers trauma-induced amnesia. In certain combat situations, veterans suffered battle-induced amnesia that was later recovered during therapy.

A number of court cases have dealt with repressed memories that have been reported in the national media. These have ranged from reports of daughters witnessing the killing of playmates by their father to cases of long-term sexual molestation by family members. Additionally, courts have allowed those who have been accused of these incidents to sue the therapists.

A variety of claims have been made against the validity of recovered memories, including Holmes, who believes that there is a complete lack of research support for the concept of repression. On the other hand, widespread support exists for the theory of repressed memories by other scholars. For example, Briere and Conte, in a study of 450 adult victims of child sexualabuse, found that 59 percent of these survivors had at some point prior to their eighteenth birthdays been unable to recall the abuse.

In summary, evidence supports the existence of the repressed and false memories. At this time, no consensus exists among scholars and researchers regarding the prevalence of either type of memory. This will continue to be a controversy in the field, and professionals who work with victims of family violence must understand both sides of this debate.

Sources: Adapted from Pope, K. S. "Memory, Abuse,and Science, Questioning Claims About the False Memory Syndrome Epidemic," 51 *American Psychologist,* (51) (September,1996), p. 957; Reisner, A. D. "Repressed Memories: Trueor False?" 46 *The Psychological Record* 563 (1996); Bowman, C. G., and E. Mertz. "A Dangerous Direction: Legal Intervention in Sexual Abuse Survivor Therapy," 109 *Harvard Law Review* 551 (1996); Fisher, C. "Amnestic States in War Neurosis: The Psychogenesis of Fugues," 14 *The Psychoanalytic Quarterly* 437 (1945); See, e.g., *Sullivan v Cheshler,* 846 F. Supp. 654 (N.D. Ill. 1994); Holmes, D. S. "The Evidence for Repression: An Examination of Sixty Years of Research," in *Repression and Dissociation.* J. L.Singer, ed. (University of Chicago Press, Chicago) 1992, p. 85; and Briere, J. and J. Conte. "Self-Reported Amnesia for Abuse in Adults Molested as Children," 6 *Journal of Traumatic Stress* 21 (1993).

*A claim of abduction by aliens might be considered a psychotic disorder that is based on delusions rather than a repressed memory, depending on whether you believe in the existence of aliens.

critical issue in determining competency to testify. Many authorities have studied the ability of children to distinguish between truth and falsehood and have concluded that children under the age of seven are unlikely to be successful in telling a lie. However, by the time they reach fourth or fifth grade, they can tell lies.[25] Other scholars have concluded that although children and adults both engage in lying, there is no evidence to support the assumption that children lie more than adults.[26]

The second element requires that a child accurately testify as to what occurred. This requirement not only raises issues of memory but issues of fact versus fantasy. The world of make-believe and the normal fantasy play that all children engage in as they mature are normal functions of growing up. Many of us have seen children talking to an invisible friend. A common defense ploy is to argue that the child is testifying about an imaginary event. A tactic that many defense attorneys employ in sexual abuse cases is to say that the child is not bad or evil but cannot distinguish fact from normal childhood fantasy. Numerous scholars have established that children are able to tell the difference between imaginary and real-life events.[27]

Closely related to the concept of competency is the issue that someone may have implanted memories in the mind of the child. As was discussed earlier in this chapter, this is a favored defense tactic. If defense attorneys can convince the judge or jury that the treating professional or another party, such as a parent, has manipulated the child's memory and planted false memories in the child's mind, those accused of molesting or abusing the child may walk away free. Therefore, the manner and type of questions asked of child victims is important and should be framed to solicit what the child recalls, not what the professional expects the child to remember.

A number of different techniques are used in interviewing children who have been victims of abuse. Two of the most well-known methods involve the use of anatomical dolls and videotaping of the interview. One of the most highly debated techniques is the use of anatomical dolls during the interview process.

Anatomical dolls are used by CPS, law enforcement officers, and therapists during interviews with children who may have been victims of abuse.[28] These dolls assist professionals in a number of ways:

1. Dolls allow the child to explain what occurred by referring to the doll rather than themselves. By using the doll, the child does not have to identify his or her genital area but can instead point to the doll's genitals. This allows the interview to be less stressful from the child's perspective.
2. The child's interaction with the doll may provide clues for the interviewer as to what occurred during the molestation and therefore allow the professional to focus the questions that are asked of the child.
3. Anatomical dolls allow the child to communicate by using toylike objects that he or she is familiar with. This facilitates the communication process by placing the child in a familiar environment with familiar toys.

The use of anatomical dolls during the interview process has been both condemned and endorsed. Defense attorneys argue that the use of these dolls is suggestive and may lead the child to make untrue statements or act out in their play in sexually explicit ways. Researchers believe that there is no evidence to support this contention and that exposure to these dolls does not cause the child to fantasize or engage in sexual play.[29]

The use of anatomical dolls during the interview process should be documented. This documentation should include why the dolls were used, a clear description or picture of the dolls, and a detailed narrative summary of what the child did with the dolls. Although subject to criticism, the use of anatomical dolls may allow the interviewer to obtain information from a victim that might not otherwise be available. Perhaps the best use of dolls during the interview process is as an aid in allowing the child to communicate. If they are used in this manner, defense charges of fantasy or sexual play may be discounted.

The second interview technique involves videotaping the child's statements. Videotaping of child abuse victims' interviews involves recording the interview on videotape for future use in the courtroom. Similar to the use of anatomical dolls, this method of interviewing has both its supporters and critics. Supporters of video interviewing claim that is preserves evidence and rebuts charges of programming. Critics of videotaping claim that the process itself is subject to manipulation.

The use of videotaping varies from jurisdiction to jurisdiction. Some agencies require all sexual abuse cases to bee interviewed, whereas others do not engage in this practice at all. There are both advantages and disadvantages to videotaping child abuse victims.

The advantages include reducing the number of times a child has to repeat his or her story to different people within the criminal justice system. A videotape can be played for different parties without requiring the child to go through the trauma of telling the story over and over again. A second advantage is that it allows for an assessment of the credibility of the child by a number of people at one time as they view the videotape. A third advantage is that the tape can be replayed and critical statements reviewed and evaluated without having the child repeat portions of the story numerous times. A fourth advantage of videotaping is that it preserves the interaction between the interviewer and the child so that the defense cannot raise the issue of programming or leading the child to a certain result or statement. Fifth, interviews can be scheduled to accommodate the child witness and viewed later by prosecutors or other parties who may be involved in the decision-making process. Finally, interviewers can watch other videotapes and engage in peer reviews of techniques, thereby improving their own abilities to interview future victims of child abuse.

Significant disadvantages exist in videotaping interviews. First and most important, children seldom recount all the details of a molestation during a single interview. Therefore, if one interview is taped, all subsequent interviews must be taped. This may allow the defense to argue that the child was programmed off camera and that subsequent interviews are invalid because the child was simply repeating what he or she had been instructed to repeat. A second disadvantage is the cost of the video machine and equipment. Even with modestly inexpensive palm-sized recorders, the equipment is too expensive for many financially burdened agencies. Not only must the equipment be purchased, but someone must be trained to operate it, and the film must be cataloged and stored for future use. Third, videotaping interviews takes some of the feel of the interview away from the people who must assess the credibility of the child. In essence, they are watching a movie instead of evaluating a live victim. Finally, if the first recorded interview results in a denial of abuse by the child, it must be preserved and turned over to the defense. The initial interview will then be used in any subsequent court proceeding as proof that the child is lying or being untruthful.

Another critical aspect of the use of video cameras and recording equipment concerns the use of closed-circuit cameras during criminal proceedings. The U.S. Constitution has been interpreted to require that a defendant has a right to confront and cross-examine all witnesses against him. However, this right is not absolute. As the discussion of hearsay indicated, there are instances where statements of another person may be admitted against the defendant even though he or she does not have the opportunity to cross-examine the person making those statements. The Supreme Court addressed the issue of closed-circuit television in child abuse cases in *Maryland v Craig*.[30]

In October 1986, a Howard County grand jury charged Sandra Ann Craig with a number of child abuse offenses. The victim, Brooke, was a six-year-old girl who from August 1984 to June 1986 attended a kindergarten and prekindergarten center owned and operated by Craig. In March 1987, before the case went to trial, the state sought to invoke a Maryland statute that allowed the judge and jury to view the victim via closed-circuit television. The victim was to be located in a separate room outside the presence of the defendant. Although the defendant and her attorney could view the television and ask questions, they would not be allowed to physically confront the victim.

In support of its motion, the state presented expert testimony that Brooke, as well as a number of other children who were allegedly abused, would suffer serious emotional distress such that they could not reasonably communicate if required to testify in the courtroom and face the defendant. Another expert testified that Brooke would probably stop talking and would withdraw and curl up into a ball if she were in the same room with the defendant. The trial court ruled that because of the possible distress that the victims would suffer in seeing the suspect, the closed-circuit television would be authorized.

In upholding such a procedure, the Supreme Court held that a strict reading of the confrontation clause would do away with every hearsay exception and that this was too extreme a result. Therefore, the court held that the confrontation clause reflects a preference for face-to-face confrontations at trial but that that preference must occasionally give way to considerations of public policy and the necessities of the case. Thus, the holding in *Maryland v Craig* allows the use of closed-circuit television under certain circumstances in child abuse cases. Specifically, there must be a state statue that authorizes such a procedure, and the state must establish that the child is unable to face his or her molester in person.

Interviewing child victims is a critical aspect of any professional involvement in this area of family violence. It must be conducted in a fair and unbiased manner

FOCUS The Emotional Effects of Testifying on Sexually Abused Children

Child sexual abuse presents complicated issues of physical, emotional, and psychological trauma for its victims. This is especially true for child victims who are thrust into a process with adult rules and values. These victims are required to testify about intimate details that are embarrassing to them.

The National Institute of Justice (NIJ) and the Office of Juvenile Justice and Delinquency Prevention (OJJDP) awarded three grants to examine the emotional effects of the court process onsexually abused children. These studies occurred in North Carolina and Denver and as part of the Child Victim as Witness Research and Development Program (see Table 7.1). This research resulted in a variety of findings, points of similarity, and conclusions that are of interest to those who work with victimsof child sexual abuse.

The three studies appear to agree on three basic conclusions: (1) that at the initial testing, prior to their involvement in the court process, children score high on measures of stress and anxiety; (2) that most children tend to improve with time, regardless of their experience in court; and (3) that maternal support is associated with improvements in these children's mental health. Perhaps the most compelling difference among these studies is the context of the children's testimony. The children in North Carolina testified in CPS proceedings in a juvenile court setting, whereas the other studies occurred in a criminal court environment. The difference between the experience of testifying in a juvenile court proceeding is vastly different than the experience of testifying in criminal court. These findings indicate that we need to examine courtroom proceduresand, consistent with constitutional requirements, relax rules of evidence and procedure in criminal cases. Additionally, the number of hearings in which the child is required to testify in should be limited.

On the basis of these studies, it cannot be stated with any certainty that testifying is either harmful or beneficial to sexually abused children. One consistent and encouraging findingis that all children improved emotionally regardless of their experience in court. At worst, testifying may impede the improvement process for some children. Even if current research does not reveal substantial long-term negative effects on child witnesses in the criminal justice system, professionals must continue to be sensitive and supportive of these vulnerable victims.

Source: Adapted from Whitecomb, D. et al. "The Emotional Effects of Testifying on Sexually Abused Children," *Research in Brief,* (National Institute of Justice, Washington, D.C., April, 1994).

One hundred completed the first interview, seventy-six completed the second, and sixty-two completed the third interview.

with regard for the child's best interests. Many times, the initial interview forms the basis for intervention into the privacy of the family.

Intervention

The goal of intervention is to protect the child from abuse. The child's safety and health must be the overriding issue in any decision to intervene. The child's future safety and well-being must also be considered in evaluating the type of intervention. Finally, any decision to intervene should also consider that children

TABLE 7.1

	State of North Carolina	Denver, Colorado	Child Victim Witness Research and Development Program
Number of children examined	62–100	218	256
Ages	6–17	4–17	4–17
Characteristics of cases	Victims of intrafamilial abuse	Victims primarily of extrafamilial abuse	Victims primarily of extrafamilial abuse
Nature of proceedings	CPS hearing in juvenile court	Criminal court prosecutions	Criminal court prosecutions
Number of mental health assessments	After case accepted by CPS	After case accepted for prosecution	After case referred for prosecution
	5 months later	3 months after testifying	7–9 months later
	18 months later	7 months after testifying	
		After case disposition	

need positive parenting models after which they can bond and model their actions.

At a certain point, a professional will make a decision to inject him- or herself into the family to protect a child. This decision should not be made lightly, nor should professionals hesitate to do so if there is reason to believe that the child may be in danger. A delicate balance must be maintained between the parents' right to raise their children without interference and society's obligation to protect those who cannot speak for themselves. Because a professional may disagree with a certain type of lifestyle does not mean that the official can intrude into the family without facts that indicate that the child is in danger of neglect or physical or sexual abuse. The decision to intervene normally starts with an investigation.

Investigation

An investigation of child abuse does not occur in a vacuum.[32] It involves different parties and affects various interest. The child's family, medical, educational, and social services, as well as law enforcement agencies, are all involved and interact in a child abuse investigation.

Medical Professionals

The medical professionals have a number of roles to play in the investigative process. They must report suspected incidents of child abuse, they provide information on the nature and extent of physical injuries, and they are responsible for healing those injuries. As indicated in previous chapters, doctors were traditionally hesitant to invade the privacy of the home. However, individuals such as John Caffey and C. Henry Kempe brought startling evidence of the nature and extent of child abuse to the attention of physicians in the United States. This knowledge, coupled with continuing education and mandated reporting laws, has dramatically increased the "suspicion index" of the general medical community.[33]

Physicians are not the only members of the medical profession who are involved in the investigative process. Nurses are also required to report suspected cases of child abuse. Many statutes require them to report such cases even if the treating physician is reluctant to do so. Nurses have taken on an expanded role within the medical profession, and the advent and growing popularity of the nurse-practitioner will undoubtedly further expand the role of nurses in the area of child abuse reporting and investigation. Because nurse-practitioners receive special education and training that allows them to treat patients without the direct supervision of a physician, they may be the only person to have contact with the abused child.

Psychiatrists and mental health workers may also have an occasion to report suspected cases of child abuse. The information may come from an adult patient who is in therapy or from a child in treatment. As discussed earlier, many states classify emotional abuse as child abuse and therefore require the treating professional to report these cases to the appropriate agency.

Education Professionals

Teachers, principals, advisors, coaches, and school nurses are mandated to report suspected cases of child abuse. Unlike members of the medical professions, they may not be directly involved in the treatment of the victim but may discover evidence of abuse in a variety of ways. Discussions with the student or the student's classmates may lead them to conclude that the child is a victim of abuse. Teachers are in a unique position in our society because they are in close personal contact with children for several hours each day of the week. This contact allows them to observe the child over extended periods of time and note any changes in behavior or physical appearance that may be indicative of child abuse.

Unfortunately, many educational professionals do not feel comfortable in reporting suspected incidents of child abuse. Some believe in corporal punishment, and others have not received the proper training to allow them to recognize cases of child abuse. To correct this perception, many states require education professionals to undergo specialized training in child abuse or neglect prior to receiving their credentials that authorizes them to be employed in a school district.

As the investigation proceeds, educators may assist the law enforcement agency and CPS by reporting the academic progress or any marked changes in the child's behavior. This information may be critical in determining how the child is adapting to the situation and helpful in deciding where the child should be placed.

Social Services

Welfare departments, housing authorities, and other agencies that deliver social services may have the occasion to observe incidents of suspected child abuse. These situations can range from physical or sexual abuse to incidents of dirty homes. Once these situations are discovered, these professionals should not only report the incident to the appropriate agency but document the facts to support the case because they may be the only ones who have the authority to do so. Pictures or diagrams of dirty homes may be invaluable in assisting the prosecution in filing and proving the case.

Most reporting statues mandate that the information be forwarded either to the local law enforcement agency or to CPS, the latter of which in many jurisdictions is mandated to conduct the initial investigation. A trained social worker may contact the reporting party and develop additional information requiring emergency removal of the child from the home. In some jurisdictions CPS has this authority, although in other states CPS is required to contact a law enforcement officer and request that the officer remove the child from the home. In either event, social workers are an important part of the entire process, and their ability to assess a situation is critical to protecting the child from further harm. It is a heavy burden that CPS workers bear on a daily basis. They must evaluate the degree of risk a child faces if the child remains in the home. If the risk is low, treatment should be offered in a manner that protects the integrity of the family system. Services provided to the parents and child while they remain in their own home would be the treatment of choice. If the risk is high, the child must be removed, which causes an emotional scar on both the child and the family because involuntary separation can have drastic emotional consequences for all concerned. On the other hand, failure to remove the child in a hazardous situation could result in further abuse and possible death. Each case must be fully evaluated, and the final decision must always be weighted on the side of protecting the child from further injury.

Law Enforcement

These professionals are tasked with gathering evidence that will support a dependency petition or criminal charges. Many large jurisdictions have specialized teams of detectives who are assigned full-time to this area. Other jurisdictions require that the patrol officer carry out this function. Law enforcement officers may have to remove the child from the custody of her parents and interview the parents in an attempt to find out exactly what happened. In many cases, the investigating officer can compare statements made to her with information gained from other professionals and determine whether there are any inconsistencies. Once the law enforcement officer has finished the initial investigation, it will be forwarded to the prosecutor's office for a determination as to whether to file dependency or criminal charges.

Family

The child's family is an integral part of this process. As was discussed earlier, there may be occasions in which a spouse is incapable of leaving the abusive partner. The

FOCUS Child Development–Community Policing: A Different Type of Law Enforcement Intervention

The New Haven Department of Police Services and the Child Study Center at Yale University have developed a unique collaborative program to address the psychological impact of exposure to community violence on children. The Child Development–Community Policing (CD–CP) program brings police officers and mental health professionals together to provide each other with training, consultation, and support and to provide direct interdisciplinary intervention to children who are victims, witnesses, or perpetrators of violent crime.

The CD–CP program consists of interrelated training and consultative components that aim to share knowledge and develop ongoing collegial relationships between police officers and mental health professionals. It involves five distinct but interrelated programs: child development fellowships, police fellowships for clinicians, seminars on child development, consultation services and weekly program conferences. Child development fellowships help provide supervisory officers with the special psychological expertise they need to lead a cohesive team of community-based officers in a wide variety of crime prevention and relationship-building activities involving children, families, and community agencies in their individual neighborhoods. Police fellowships provide clinicians with opportunities to spend time with police colleagues in squad cars, in police stations, and in the streets observing and learning directly from the officers about their day-to-day activities. The CD–CP seminar on child development, human functioning, and policing strategies is a course for police officers, mental health professionals, and related professionals (others from the criminal justice system) that is co-led by a clinical faculty member and a police supervisor experienced in the CD–CP program. Consultation services allow police officers to make referrals and obtain immediate clinical guidance, especially when the child is in great distress, as often occurs following exposure to serious violence. Police officers and clinicians meet to discuss difficult cases at weekly program conferences. This innovative program aims to reduce the trauma suffered by child victims and has been so successful that it is being replicated in other cities throughout the United States.

Source: Adapted from Marans, S., and M. Berkman. "Child Development-Community Policing: Partnership in a Climate of Violence," *Juvenile Justice Bulletin* (OJJDP, Washington, D.C. March 1997).

intervention of certain professionals may provide this spouse with the resources to leave the abuser and begin a new lifestyle. The loss of custody of a child, even on a temporary basis, is a traumatic event for the family and affects not only the child but also the parents. The decision to remove should not be made lightly, but neither should it be stayed simply because the parents may be upset or hurt.

Understanding who the parties are in an investigation is merely the first step in the process. The investigative function in child abuse cases is a multifaceted process that involves various stages leading to the decision by the prosecutor whether to file a petition or criminal charges. The investigative process includes reporting, investigation by CPS and/or law enforcement agencies, and referral to the prosecutor or county attorney for filing of charges.

Once one of the professionals mandated to report suspected child abuse files a report, the investigative process begins. The professional who files this report

TABLE 7.2 Professional Recording Protocol

Statements made by:

- the child
- the caretaker at the time of injury
- family members
- other persons that may have knowledge of the incident

The exact type of injury:

- when noted
- who observed the injury
- who reported the injury
- approximate day the injury was inflicted
- medical tests conducted to rule out other causes

Professionals involved:

- physicians who treated the child
- paramedics or fire personnel who transported the child
- nurses and medical social workers who interacted with the child or family

Miscellaneous information:

- clothing worn by child when first observed
- attitude and actions by parents toward child
- any other information that may assist CPS or law enforcement

should be aware that his or her actions will be scrutinized by the prosecutor, defense attorney, and court. Therefore, it is incumbent on that professional to maintain accurate records of all events, conversations, and other pertinent data involving the decision and the status of the child. This information may be included in the standard medical protocol, school records, or other information maintained by the reporting party. No matter where it is maintained, the professional filing the report should be able to testify at a later date that it was accurate when recorded. Small details, such as the type of clothing worn by the child when admitted to the emergency room, may turn out to be important during any subsequent hearing. Table 7.2 is a list of items or data that professionals should record or note in their own organization's records in addition to filing the report.

The second phase of the investigative process involves the actual investigation by CPS or law enforcement. Once notified that a child has been abused, these workers will review the report and may conduct an initial investigation to determine whether the child is in immediate peril. This initial investigation may entail no more than reviewing the report and discussing the matter with the reporting professional. On the basis of information received from the initial report and the reporting official, CPS workers may decide to immediately remove the child from the custody of her parents. This is normally done in all cases of suspected sexual abuse and in those physical abuse cases where it is demonstrated that the child is in imminent danger in the existing home environment.

If CPS does not immediately remove the child from the care and custody of his or her parents, it begins an investigation to determine whether it is necessary to file a petition with the appropriate court. This investigation normally involves interviewing the parents to determine whether the situation can be corrected that placed the child in danger without the intervention of law enforcement or a court order. Many times, simply informing the parents of the resources available in the community is sufficient to alleviate a problem in the home. In more serious situations, the worker can develop a written service agreement with the parents identifying what needs to be corrected and who needs to do what to achieve the desired changes. Services would be provided to satisfy the conditions of the plan, and the progress of the family would be monitored. In the absence of progress, CPS may come to the conclusion that voluntary services have not worked and request that a petition be filed.

Filing a petition involves presenting evidence to either the prosecuting attorney or county attorney who appears in juvenile court. In some jurisdictions prosecuting attorneys or district attorneys make the decision as to whether to file dependency petitions, and in other jurisdictions county counsels or county attorneys represent CPS in these matters. These attorneys evaluate the facts to determine whether there is sufficient evidence to proceed and may request further information from the reporting professional, CPS worker, or law enforcement officers. Sometimes these attorneys are tasked with evaluating the case from both the civil and the dependency aspects as well as deciding whether to file criminal charges against the parents. Once the decision to file formal court documents is made, the next stage, the hearing process, begins.

The Hearing Process

If the investigation has resulted in removing the child from the home, the judicial process begins. Basically, two forums are used in child abuse cases. Civil proceedings may be filed in family or juvenile court, whose objectives are protecting the child from further injury. Criminal proceedings are filed in courts of general jurisdiction with the purpose of punishing the offender for committing a crime against the state (this process is explained in more detail in Chapter 9, which discusses law enforcement responses to spousal assault). On occasion, both civil and criminal processes will be initiated. These are completely separate hearings with different purposes and procedures.

Depending on the jurisdiction, a civil proceeding may be initiated in courts known as family or juvenile courts. These courts originated in the state of Massachusetts in 1870 with the passage of legislation that required separate hearings for juveniles.[34] However, it was not until 1899, when the state of Illinois passed the Illinois Juvenile Court Act, that the juvenile court system as known today came into existence.[35] This statute separated the juvenile court system from the adult criminal system. It labeled minors who violated the law as delinquents rather than criminals and required that juvenile court judges determine what "is in the best interest of the minor" in rendering their decisions.

The juvenile court system is guided by five basic principles:

1. The state is the ultimate parent of all children within its jurisdiction.
2. Children are worth saving, and the state should use nonpunitive measures to do so.
3. Children should be nurtured and not stigmatized by the court process.
4. Each child is different, and justice should be tailored to meet the individual needs and requirements of each child.
5. The use of noncriminal sanctions are necessary to give primary consideration to the needs of the child.[36]

Although these principles were originally adopted for delinquents or minors who committed criminal acts, they have been broadly applied to proceedings involving children who are victims of abuse. Juvenile courts have jurisdiction over three types of minors: delinquents, status offenders, and dependent children. *Delinquents are those minors who have committed criminal offenses. Status offenders are minors who are truant from school, have runaway from home, or are considered incorrigible. Dependant children are those who are in need of state intervention because of neglect or abuse by their caretakers.*

The juvenile court process is normally initiated by filing a petition with the court. *A petition is a formal pleading that alleges that the parents or custodians endangered the health or welfare of the child.* The petition may allege neglect or physical, emotional, or sexual abuse of the child and gives the juvenile court authority to act.

Once the petition is filed, many jurisdictions hold a show-cause, or detention, hearing. This hearing is usually conducted within twenty-four to forty-eight hours after filing the petition or the emergency removal of the child. The *detention hearing requires CPS or police to produce evidence justifying the emergency removal of the child or to present evidence that would allow the court to order the removal of the child if he or she is still in the custody of the parents.* The parents may also admit or deny the allegations contained in the petition at this hearing. If they admit the allegations, the court orders CPS to conduct an investigation to determine where the child should be placed as a result of the admissions by the parents. If the parents deny the allegations, the court sets a date for an adjudicatory or jurisdictional hearing. Pending this hearing, the court may order the child temporarily placed in a living arrangement outside the home.

An adjudicatory or jurisdictional hearing is used to determine whether there is sufficient evidence to find that the allegations in the petition are true. At the conclusion of this hearing, the court will render its decision. If the petition is upheld, the court sets a date for a dispositional hearing. If the petition is not upheld, the child is returned to the parents and the case dismissed.

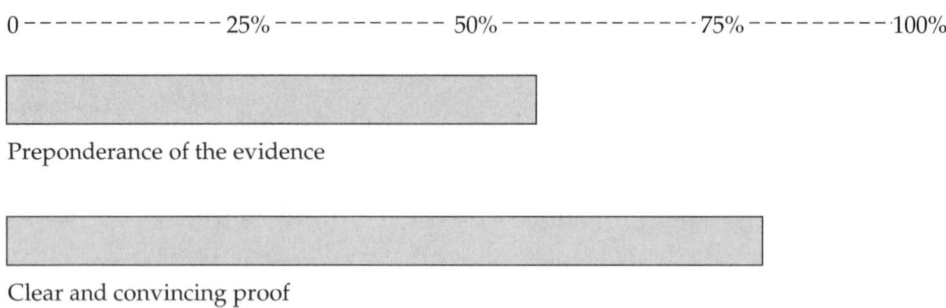

FIGURE 7.2 Levels of Proof

During the adjudicatory hearing, the state presents evidence to support its claim that the child has been abused. This may take the form of having the child testify to the incident, or experts employed by the state may render their opinions regarding the facts surrounding the case. The state is represented by a prosecutor, county counsel, or other government attorney. The parents have a right to cross-examine witnesses and present any evidence they desire in rebuttal to the state's evidence. At the end of the hearing, both parties may present arguments in favor of their positions.

The burden of proof to uphold the petition is the same as in civil cases. In civil trials, the plaintiff has the burden of proving the case by a preponderance of the evidence. This is normally defined as more than 50 percent. A criminal case requires proof beyond a reasonable doubt. This is not proof beyond all doubts but proof of the material facts to a moral certainty that they did occur. In juvenile dependency cases, in order to remove the child from the custody of his or her parents, some jurisdictions require proof by clear and convincing evidence. This is more than a preponderance of the evidence but less than beyond a reasonable doubt (see Figure 7.2).[37]

Once the adjudicatory or jurisdictional hearing concludes, the next hearing to occur is the *dispositional hearing. This hearing is to determine where the child should be placed.* The court will decide whether the child should be immediately returned to his parents or placed in an out-of-home environment for a period of time. The guiding principle in this hearing is the best interest of the child. If the court orders the child to be placed outside the home, it may schedule periodic reviews to determine whether or when the child will be reunited with the parents.

From the beginning of the intervention process until the final dispositional hearing and beyond, every party in the action has certain rights. Both the parents and the child have distinct rights that must be observed and protected. These rights involve notice, an opportunity to be heard, and effective representation by an attorney.

In a dependency hearing, the rights of a child include appointment of an attorney who will speak on behalf of the child. This attorney must represent what he or she believes is in the best interest of the child regardless of what CPS or the parents advocate. In some jurisdictions, this is a county attorney and in others a private attorney appointed by the court to represent the child. Depending on the case, the attorney may side with the parents and argue for return of the child to their care, or the attorney may take the position that it is in the best interest of the child to be removed from the custody of the parents. Even if the child is removed temporarily from the custody of his or her parents, the child has a right to reunification efforts after a reasonable time.

During dependency hearings, parents have a right to notice of the hearing and an opportunity to be present at that hearing and to be represented by an attorney. They may present any evidence they desire to rebut the charges. If the child is removed from their custody, they have the right in most jurisdictions to a reunification plan that will allow them to regain custody of the child once they have finished treatment or counseling.

In criminal proceedings, the child is normally not appointed an attorney but may be represented by a child advocate whose mission is to assist the child and represent his or her best interest. The parents have a right to any attorney and all other rights accorded those accused of committing crimes against society.

Summary

Child abuse is a serious form of family violence. It is an accepted fact that parents or caretakers do abuse children, and, as a result of efforts of concerned citizens and professionals, every state ha adopted mandatory reporting laws. These laws require certain individuals who come into contact with children to file reports with designated agencies if they have reason to believe a child is the victim of abuse.

These reporting laws require immediate reporting, waive any privilege that may have existed between the caretakers and the professionals, and mandate that CPS or law enforcement agencies conduct an investigation into the circumstances surrounding the abuse. These laws also authorize the emergency removal of the child if there is reason to believe that he or she is in imminent danger.

Interviewing a child is more an art than a science. Questions should be phrased in certain ways to avoid charges that the professional programmed or suggested the answer to the child. Understanding the basics of the hearsay rule will allow professionals to ask children and their caretakers the right types of questions.

The intervention process involves both an investigation and a court hearing. The purpose of both these activities is to protect the child. If the nature of the abuse is serious, civil and criminal actions may be initiated against the parents. In many jurisdictions, the juvenile court is tasked with the responsibility of conducting dependency hearings aimed at protecting the child from further abuse. These courts have the power to remove the child from the custody of his or her parents and order placement outside the home.

Key Terms

confidential communication—information that is made under circumstances in which the speaker intends that the statement be shared only with the recipient of the information.

recognition memory—occurs when the child is cued or is able to perceive an object or event that was first perceived at an earlier time.

recall memory—occurs when the child can recollect the event without the aid of cues or other assistance.

open-ended question—does not suggest or imply an answer.

focused question—narrows the scope of inquiry and requires the witness to answer within certain parameters.

leading questions—promise rewards or threaten punishment for certain answers.

hearsay—any out-of-court statement that is offered in court for the truth of the matter stated.

excited utterance—a statement made whenever a person is excited or under stress as a result of a traumatic event.

admission—a statement or conduct of a party in the action that is offered against him or her in the trial.

declaration against interest—a statement by a nonparty that is against his or her own interest.

state of mind—a statement that relates a fact regarding the declarant's mental or emotional condition.

statement made to medical professionals—information given for purposes of diagnosis or treatment of a medical condition.

delinquents—those minors who have committed criminal offenses.

status offenders—minors who are truant from school, runaway from home, or are considered incorrigible.

dependent children—those who are in need of state intervention because of neglect or abuse by their caretakers.

petition—a formal pleading that alleges that the parents or custodians endangered the health or welfare of the child.

detention hearing—requires child protective services or police to produce evidence justifying the emergency removal of the child or present evidence that would allow the court to order the removal of the child if still in the custody of the parents.

adjudicatory or jurisdictional hearing—used to determine whether there is sufficient evidence to find that the allegations in the petition are true.

dispositional hearing—used to determine where the child should be placed.

competency—the ability of the witness to accurately testify to events.

Discussion Questions

1. If you could revise the elements of the reporting laws discussed in this chapter, what would you add or delete? Why?
2. What is the single most important aspect of the existing reporting laws?
3. Can you list any other professionals who should be mandated to report suspected cases of child abuse? Who are they? Why should they be included?
4. Should we waive the privilege that many professionals have with their clients or patients? Why? Why not? If individuals know that whatever they tell certain professionals may end up in a police report, will they be truly candid?
5. Should all cases of child abuse be automatically referred to the district attorney for filing of criminal charges? What does this do to the family and the child?

Suggested Readings

Fox, S. *Modern Juvenile Justice: Cases and Materials* (West, St. Paul) 1972.

Johnson, T. A. *Introduction to the Juvenile Justice System.* (West, St. Paul) 1975.

McCloskey, P. L. and R. L. Schoenberg, eds. *Criminal Law Advocacy.* (Matthew Bender, New York) 1986.

Sagatum I. J., and L. P. Edwards, *Child Abuse and the Legal System.* (Nelson-Hall, Chicago) 1995.

Spencer, J. R., and R. Flin. *The Evidence of Children: The Law and Psychology.* (Blackstone, London) 1990.

Tower, C. C. *Understanding Child Abuse and Neglect.* (Allyn and Bacon, Boston) 1993.

Zaragoza, M. S., J. R. Graham, G. C. N. Hall, R. Hirschman, and Y. S. Ben-Porath, eds. *Memory and Testimony in the Child Witness.* (Sage, Thousand Oaks, California) 1995.

Endnotes

1. Approximately thirty states mandate that reports be filed with with local child protective agencies. For example, see Florida Statutes Annotated Section 415.504(2)(a) (West Supp. 1990) and New York Social Services Law Section 415 (McKinney supp. 1990).
2. See Iowa Code Annotated Section 232.70(2) (West 1985).
3. *Black's Law Dictionary.* 6th ed. (West, St. Paul) 1990, p. 298.
4. *Principles of Medical Ethics.* (American Medical Association, Washington D.C.) 1989.
5. This section has been adapted from Peter Fin. "Sex Offender Community Notification," *Research in Brief,* (National Institute of Justice, Washington, D.C., February 1997).
6. Prentky, R. A., R. A. Knight, and A. F. S. Lee. "Child Sexual Molestation" *Research Issues,* (National Institute of Justice, Washington D.C., March 1997).
7. Davis, P. "The Sex Offender Next Door." *The New York Times Magazine,* (June 28, 1996) pp. 20–43.
8. Petrucelli, P. L. "Megan's Law: Branding the Sex Offender or Benefitting the Community?" 5 *Seton Hall Constitutional Journal* 1127–1169 (1995).
9. Bedarf, A. R. "Examining Sex Offender Community Notification Laws," 83(3) *California Law Review* 885 (1995).
10. Weidlich, T. "False Memory, Big Award," *The National Law Journal* 17/19 (January 9, 1995), p. A6.
11. Flush, R. J. T. Grey, and F. A. Fromhoff. "Two-Year-Olds Talk about the Past." *Cognitive Development* (2) (1987), p. 393.
12. Goodman, G. S., J. E. Hirschman, D. Hepps, and L. Rudy. "Children's Memory for Stressful Events." *Merrill-Palmer Quarterly* 37, 1990, p. 109.
13. Perry, N. W. "Child and Adolescent Development: A Psycholegal Perspective." In J. E. B. Myers, ed. *Child Witness Law and Practice.* (Wiley, New York) 1987.
14. Ibid.
15. Saywitz, K. J., G. S. Goodman, E. Nicholas, and S. F. Moan. "Children's Memories of Physical Examinations Involving Genital Touch: Implications for Reports of Sexual Abuse." *Journal of Consulting and Clinical Psychology* (59) 1991, p. 682.
16. Spencer, J. R., and R. Flin. *The Evidence of Children: The Law and Psychology.* (Blackstone, London) 1990.
17. Ibid., p. 250.
18. Fieldings, N. G., and S. Conroy, "Interviewing Child Victims: Police and Social Work Investigations of Child Sexual Abuse," *Sociology* 16/1 (February, 1992) pp. 103–125.

19. McCloskey, P. L., and R. L. Schoenberg, eds. *Criminal Law Advocacy.* (Matthew Bender, New York) 1986, Vol. 4, pp. 3–5.
20. See Swift, E. "Abolishing the Hearsay Rule." *California Law Review* (75) 1987, p. 495.
21. See *Federal Rules of Evidence* 803(2), which requires the statement to relate to a startling event or conditions made while the declarant was under the stress of the excitement caused by the event.
22. Some states have statutes that provide for introduction of this form of admission. California Penal Code Section 1127c provides that the jury shall be instructed as follows: "The flight of a person immediately after the commission of a crime, or after he is accused of a crime that has been committed is not sufficient in itself to establish his guilt, but is a fact which if proved, the jury may consider in deciding his guilt or innocence. The weight to which such circumstance is entitled is a matter for the jury to determine."
23. *Federal Rules of Evidence* 803(4).
24. 110 S. Ct. 3139 (1990).
25. Quinn, K. M. "The Creditability of Children's Allegations of Sexual Abuse." *Behavioral Science and Law* (6) 1988, p. 181.
26. Spencer, J. R., and R. Flin. *The Evidence of Children: The Law and Psychology.* (Blackstone, London) 1990, p. 270.
27. Sivan, A. B. "Preschool Child Development: Implications for Investigation of Child Abuse Allegations," *Child Abuse and Neglect* (15) 1991, p. 485.
28. Conte, J. R., E. Sorenson, L. Fogarty, and J. Dalla Rosa. "Evaluating Children's Reports of Sexual Abuse: Results of a Survey of Professionals." *American Journal of Orthopsychiatry* (61) 1991, p. 428.
29. Everson, M. D., and B. W. Boat. "Sexualized Doll Play among Young Children: Implications for the Use of Anatomical Dolls in Sexual Abuse Evaluations," *Journal of the American Academy of Children and Adolescent Psychiatry* (29) 1990, p. 736.
30. 110 S. Ct. 3157 (1990).
31. Tower, C. C. *Understanding Child Abuse and Neglect.* (Allyn and Bacon, Boston) 1993.
32. For an excellent discussion of child abuse investigations see Pence, D., and C. Wilson, *The Role of Law Enforcement in Response to Child Abuse and Neglect* (U.S. Department of Health and Human Services, Washington, D.C.) 1992.
33. The term *suspicion index* was used by Dr. David Chatwick in conversations with the author.
34. Johnson, T. A. *Introduction to the Juvenile Justice System.* (West, St. Paul, Minnesota) 1975, p. 3.
35. Fox, S. *Modern Juvenile Justice: Cases and Materials* (West, St. Paul, Minnesota) 1972, p. 47.
36. See Cadwell, R. G. "The Juvenile Court: Its Development and Some Major Problems." In *Juvenile Delinquency: A Book of Readings.* (John Wiley, New York) 1966, p. 358.
37. See Otterson, D. V. "Dependency and Termination Proceedings in California—Standards of Proof." *Hasting Law Journal* (30) 1979, p. 1815.

8

SPOUSAL ABUSE

Chapter Outline

Learning Objectives

After reading this chapter, you should be able to discuss the following concepts:

- The nature and extent of spousal abuse.
- The different theories of spousal abuse.
- The different types of spousal abuse.
- Why battered spouses stay with their abusers.
- Self-defense as it applies to spousal homicide.
- Why it is necessary to use an expert witness in spousal homicide cases.

Introduction

Up to this point, this text has discussed violence against children. Children are younger and dependent on adults for food, clothing, shelter, and emotional support. Therefore, it is understandable why they do not flee an abusive situation. This chapter examines the dynamics of spousal abuse. Questions always arise in the beginning of any discussion of spousal abuse as to why the abused partner stays in the relationship. This issue, as well as other misconceptions and characteristics of this form of family violence is explored here.

The Focus "Acknowledging Domestic Violence" on page 178 indicates the turmoil that domestic violence is generating within the professions. If well-educated and knowledgeable individuals such as physicians are having difficulty with spousal abuse, it would stand to reason that many other profession-

FOCUS Violence against Women

- Females were more likely to be victimized by persons whom they know (62 percent), whereas males were more likely to be victimized by strangers (63 percent).
- In 1994, for every five violent victimizations of a female by an intimate, there was one of a male.
- For homicides in which the victim-offender relationship was known, an intimate killed 31 percent of female victims and 4 percent of male victims.
- Women separated from their spouses had a violent victimization rate over one and a half times that of separated men.

Source: Adapted from Diane Craven, *Sex Differences in Victim Victimization, 1994,* (Office of Justice Programs, U.S. Department of Justice, Washington,D.C. September, 1997)

als still harbor doubts, misconceptions, and half-truths about this form of family violence.

Throughout this chapter, the word *her* will generally be used to denote the victim or abused party. This is not to indicate that men are not victims of spousal abuse; they are, and, as will be seen, some studies indicate that this type of abuse is far more common than imagined. However, the abuse visited on women is more severe and long-lasting than the type of abuse men suffer. Additionally, research has shown that men have far greater opportunities to leave the abusive situation than women.

Both modern and ancient history is replete with a generalized domination of women by men. In early times, women were looked on as property and as a method of ensuring that a man's heritage and line continued. Husbands were allowed to beat, torture, and even kill their wives. In Rome, where the first laws of marriage were enacted, a husband was the absolute ruler who controlled all properties and persons in his household. The wife was required to obey her husband, and he was given the legal right to punish her for any misbehavior.[1] Even today, many marriage ceremonies still include instructions for the wife to love, honor, and obey her future husband.

In France, Napoleon Bonaparte enacted the Civil Code, which stated that women were property. They were first "owned" by their fathers, then in marriage that ownership transferred to their husbands.[2] Under English common law, wives and children were property of the husband.[3] The famous legal commentator Blackstone stated that husbands had a right and duty to "chastise" their wives like apprentices or children for "correctional" purposes.[4] Englishmen followed the "rule of thumb" law that restricted the size of the stick they could beat their wives with to no thicker than a man's thumb.[5]

It took a constitutional amendment in the United States to allow women the right to vote. Even after women were granted this *privilege,* they continued to be viewed as extensions of their husbands. It wasn't until the 1960s and 1970s with the explosive growth of the women's movement that women began to be viewed as equals. It was during this time that women began to seek help and protection from abusive spouses and that the first shelters for battered women opened. In 1974, a feminist organization known as Women's Advocates opened Women's House in St. Paul, Minnesota. This was the first unrestricted shelter for abused women in the United States.[6] From this humble beginning, women's shelters have sprung up in every major metropolitan center in the United States. This is not to imply that the establishment or maintenance of these shelters has been easy or painless. Traditionally, these shelters rely on contributions or grants from local, state, or federal sources. Today, these funds are in short supply, and many social programs for the establishment and maintenance of women's shelters are viewed as less of a priority than funding police and fire operations. Part of the reason for this cutback on funding is the general public's lack of understanding of the exact nature and extent of spousal abuse. The following sections examine these issues.

FOCUS Acknowledging Domestic Violence—Opening Pandora's Box

The impact of repetitive violence on an individual'shealth often brings domestic violence into the medical setting. In a nationwide random sample of couples, 28 percent were found to have experienced violence at some point in their history. When extrapolated to the general population, this represents 1.8 million women per year being battered; if divorced or separated women are included, this estimate rises to 3 to 4 million women per year.

Recently, concern about physicians' responsiveness to domestic violence has been expressed. Several studies have shown that even with knowledge of the underlying cause of the trauma, many physicians fail to respond to the battering. Repeatedly, the image of opening Pandora's box was used by physicians to describe their reactions to exploring domestic violence with patients. This metaphor suggests the fear of unleashing a myriad of evils. The close identification that physicians have with their patients may preclude them from considering the possibility of domestic violence in their differential diagnoses. Physicians who come from white, middle-class backgrounds with no experience of domestic violence often assume that their patients with similar characteristics would likewise not be at risk for violence. Although most physicians intellectually acknowledge that domestic violence cuts across all races, classes, and ethnic groups, the socioeconomic status of the patient was clearly used as a marker for determining whether abuse was likely.

Fear of offending the patient was one of the strongest concerns expressed by physicians. This discomfort often arose from areas that are culturally defined as private. Physicians felt that by broaching the subject of violence, the patient would take offense at the implications of the question. It appeared that to suggest the diagnosis of domestic violence was to accuse the partner of being a batterer.

Many physicians voiced frustration and feelings of inadequacy when discussing what would constitute appropriate interventions. Many pointed to the complexity of the problem and the fact that they had no tools to help. There was a strong sense of powerlessness when physicians described their inability to "fix it."

The physicians' greatest fear was that this is one more issue that will consume more of their scarce time. The majority of physicians felt that domestic violence was so rare in theirpatient population that pursuing it was not a good investment of time. Several physicians voiced frustration with the overwhelming role they were being asked to fill.

Source: Adapted from Sugg, N. K., and T. Inui."Primary Care Physicians' Response to Domestic Violence, Opening Pandora's Box." *Journal of American Medical Association.* Vol. 267, No. 23, June 17, 1992, pp. 3157–3160.

Definition

No clear definition of spousal abuse exists. Different authorities include different acts within their definitions, and some authorities have established levels of spousal abuse. They categorize spousal abuse into two forms of violence. The lesser forms include yelling and throwing things, and the more severe forms include striking and hitting.

Shades of grey exist in any situation, and reasonable people may disagree as to what constitutes spousal abuse. For purposes of this chapter, *spousal abuse is defined as any intentional act or series of acts that cause injury to the spouse. These acts may be physical, emotional, or sexual. Spouse is gender neutral, and therefore the abuse may occur to a male or female. The term includes those who are married, cohabitating, or involved in a serious relationship. It also encompasses individuals who are separated and*

PRACTICUM

Which of the following in your opinion would be considered spousal abuse?

- A boy is upset at his girlfriend who is late for a date. He calls her lazy and irresponsible.
- During a date, the male takes his date's arm and steers her to an entrance, commenting that she is stupid for not seeing that this is the fastest way to leave the theater.
- A couple who is living together while attending college get into a yelling match, each calling the other names.
- The same couple's argument escalates, and the female throws a textbook at her male friend. It misses and strikes the television.
- During a heated argument, the male grabs the female by the arms and shakes her.
- A husband slaps his wife after she overdraws the bank account, causing him to bounce a check.
- The husband does not allow his wife access to any funds after she bounced three checks and almost caused him to lose his job at the bank.
- The wife is tired and wants to sleep, but the husband forces her to engage in sex.

living apart from their former spouse. Although some disagreement exists regarding the exact definition of spousal abuse, all scholars and authorities agree it exists. The next section examines the extent of this form of family violence.

Extent of the Problem

Depending on which study is reviewed, the extent of spousal abuse varies. In their landmark study of 8,145 families, Straus and Gelles estimated that just over 16 percent, or one in six, American couples experienced an incident of physical assault during 1985. Projecting that number to the 54 million couples in the United States in that year leads to a startling figure of approximately 8.7 million couples who were involved in spousal abuse.[7] Other scholars point out that 20 percent of all women who go to emergency rooms for treatment have been battered.[8] These authorities cite figures that pertain to physical violence. As the definition presented previously indicates, spousal abuse includes psychological and sexual abuse as well. When a person is emotionally abused, she may not go to an emergency room or even report the acts because she may believe she deserved the treatment, and therefore it is not abuse. "After all, he didn't hit me" is a common refrain in some spousal abuse cases.

One of the more surprising results of some of these studies is the indication that spousal abuse may have declined by as much as 20 percent in recent years. Several explanations exist for this apparent decline. One is the existence of shelters for women who are abused. This escape valve allows them a way to leave an abusive relationship. Another is the widespread publicity that has occurred in recent years about spousal abuse. A third possible explanation is more effective punishment and better treatment for the assaultive partner.[9] Even though the incidence of spousal abuse may be declining, many scholars believe its severity is increasing. Even with a decline in the number of reported cases in recent years, this form of family violence is still prevalent and requires any professional to be familiar with the nature and dynamics of spousal abuse.

Theories of Spousal Abuse

If professionals knew the causes of spousal abuse, they could correct it. To date, no one has yet come forward with a definitive answer to this question. However, numerous scholars in different professions have studied this form of family violence and come up with a variety of reasons or causes for this type of abuse. These causes are specific to the phenomenon of spousal abuse and must be considered and evaluated in light of the earlier discussion in Chapter 1 that dealt with the general characteristics of family violence. Although there are many theories and studies in the area of spousal abuse, space dictates that only a few of the more well known theories be discussed.

Social Stress

The family system in the United States is a system of contradictions. Citizens retreat from the city streets to their homes and install bars on their windows to keep out the violence. Yet the family structure is one of the most violent settings a person is likely to encounter.

For purposes of this discussion, *a family is a group of persons who cohabit.* Marriage is not a requirement. Within this living arrangement, forces converge to cause stress. This increased level of stress in turn leads to a high rate of violence within the family. Many times this violence is directed at the spouse in the form of physical assaults. It should be pointed out that stress does not cause violence; it is one of the many responses available to persons who suffer from stress.

Family life has a different set of behaviors than other social settings. How the members within a family setting dress, talk, and act in their home is different from how they act when they attend social functions. Additionally, violence in the form of physical punishment is accepted by many as a characteristic of the family. Parents can and do slap infants' hands in order to teach them not to touch the hot coffee pot. This form of physical violence may be used on loved ones for their own benefit. Therefore, when stress occurs, there is already a preconditioned response or behavior that has been used and is easy to use when one is under pressure.

Power

Power is the ability to impose one's will on another and make life decisions. Couples who share power or are equals in the decision-making process have the lowest level of both conflict and violence.[10] When there is a conflict, these families display the greatest resistance to the use of violence.

As indicated in Chapter 1, one of the characteristics of family violence is the use and abuse of power. Additionally, battered women report a feeling of powerlessness as a result of the spousal abuse they have suffered. If the male desires power and control in the relationship, this represents one of the factors that may indicate a potential for violence (see Figure 8.1).

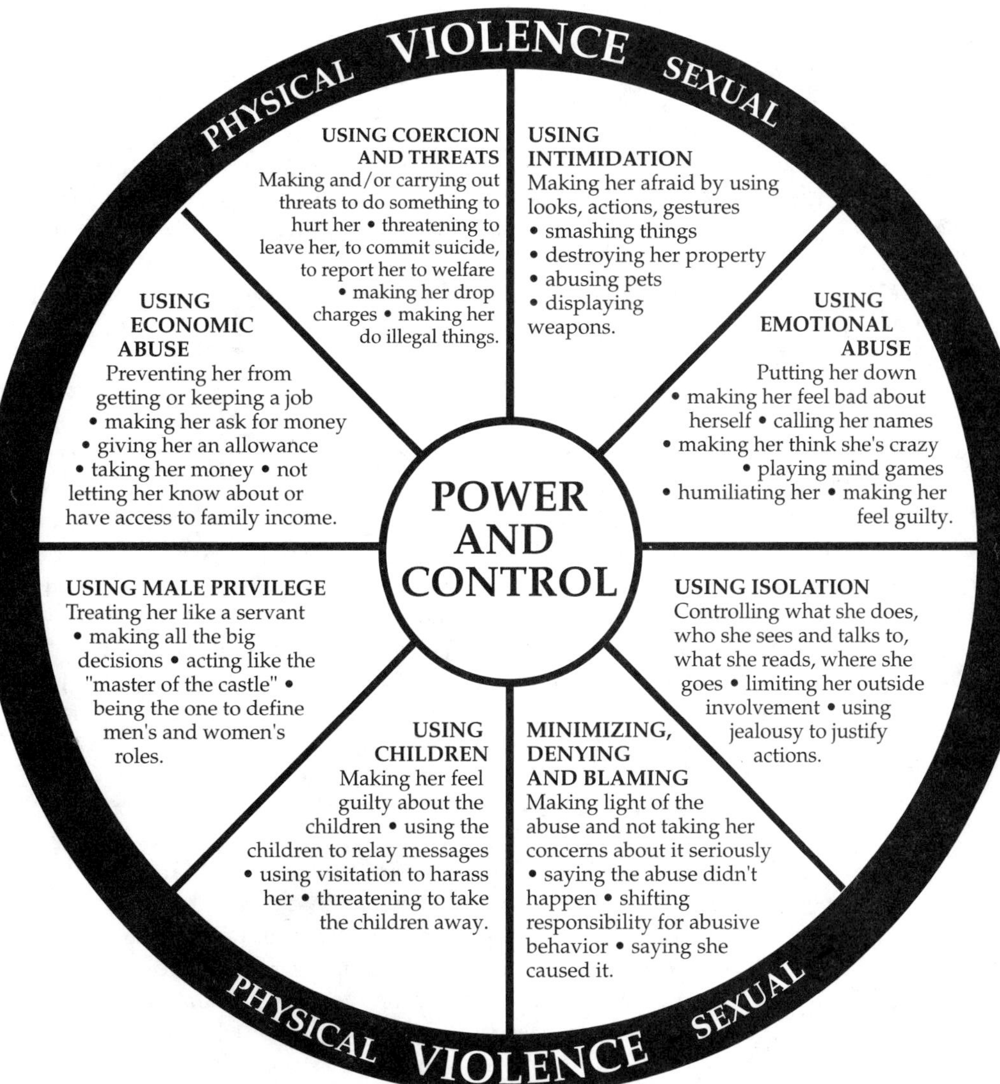

FIGURE 8.1 Power and Control Wheel

Source: Domestic Abuse Intervention Project. 206 West Fourth Street, Duluth, Minnesota 55806.

Dependency

As the introduction to this chapter indicated, our society has fostered women's dependency. Women's financial and social success in many instances has been dependent on the men they marry. Although this is beginning to change, the "glass ceiling" still remains for the most part an impenetrable barrier (this phenomenon is discussed in more detail later). A few examples bring home this point. There are only two female U.S. Supreme Court justices, only six women are U.S. senators, and only a small percentage of women are chief executive officers of major corporations.[11] Statistically, after a divorce a man's standard of living increases while a women's declines.[12]

The meaning of marital dependency is subject to debate, but the most common meaning includes economic dependency. The female spouse has little or no earning power and is therefore dependent on her male partner for the necessities of life.[13] A variation on this theme of economic dependency is the presence of children. Although a female may be able to leave an abusive relationship and make ends meet, the addition of children multiplies the difficulties inherent in any separation. A third factor in dependence is society's expectation of women as caregivers and the further hidden message that a woman is not whole until she is married.[14]

Thus, *marital dependency is a multifaced concept that involves economic, emotional, and societal forces that result in a woman being dependant on her spouse for support.* This dependency on a man and marriage for economic, emotional, and other support increases a woman's tolerance for physical abuse.

Straus and Gelles and their associates conducted an in-depth study of dependency and violence and reported that women whose dependency on marriage is high tend to suffer more physical violence than women whose dependency is low. Dependent wives have fewer alternatives to marriage and fewer resources within the marriage with which to cope or modify their husband's behavior.[15] This dependency is a pair of "golden handcuffs" that binds the spouse to the abusive partner.

Alcohol

A common perception is that males who drink alcohol beat their spouses. Therefore, so the reasoning goes, alcohol causes violence. Movies, books, and to some extent our own personal experiences support the concept that alcohol causes problems in relationships. The relationship between alcohol and abuse has been studied extensively, and several theories have been formed regarding alcohol and its relationship to violence. A few of the more common theories follow.

Disinhibition theory: This theory is based on the principle that alcohol releases inhibitions and alters judgment. Medical evidence regarding the effects of alcohol on the central nervous system supports this theory. However, recent research into disinhibition theory reveals that alcohol interacts with individuals, depending on varying individual expectancies, which is only one aspect of the alcohol–violence equation.[16]

Social learning and deviance disavowal theory: Coleman and Straus have argued that individuals learn violence by observing others who drink and become violent. This violent behavior is excused, pardoned, or justified because the individual was drunk and, therefore, not accountable for his actions.[17] Other scholars have suggested that individuals use alcohol to increase their sense of power and as an excuse for the exercise of unlawful force against others.[18]

Integrated theoretical models: Pernanem's research into alcohol and violence indicates numerous factors that interact in alcohol and violence. These factors may include the inherent conflict present in marriages.[19] A second factor is society's belief that drinking is an acceptable and expected form of male behavior.

All these theories and studies have attempted to determine whether alcohol causes spousal abuse. At this stage, there is no definitive answer, but there appears to be a link between alcohol and spousal abuse. However, there are persons who drink and do not abuse their spouses, so it would appear that alcohol by itself cannot be defined as the cause of spousal abuse.

Pregnancy

Pregnancy and spousal abuse is a controversial subject, and studies indicate that a relationship exists between the two.[20] Despite this linkage, the question remains of whether pregnancy causes domestic violence or whether it is just another factor to be considered. Most of the studies are based on small samples and have internal validity problems. However, the Straus and Gelles survey of violence, using the National Family Violence Survey, determined that the rates of violence were higher for households where the female partner was pregnant.[21] Subsequently, the authors concluded that previously reported associations between pregnancy and violence were not valid and that age is a more critical factor in determining violence than pregnancy. Young women have higher pregnancy rates and experience violence more often than older women. Females under the age of twenty-five appeared to be at the highest risk.

Marriage

"The marriage license as a hitting license" was adopted in the early 1970s by Gelles and Straus when they discovered that married couples suffered assault at a much greater rate than strangers.[22] They reasoned that the common-law tradition that allowed a husband to discipline his wife was alive and well. However, more recent studies indicate that the highest rate and greatest severity of assault is among cohabitating couples.[23]

Age may also be a factor because dating and cohabitating couples tend to be younger than married couples. However, other research indicates that age and marital status have no relationship to violence. Therefore, significant relationships, whether they involve dating, cohabitation, or marriage, place women at risk. As indicated previously, cohabitating couples may be at a higher risk than married couples. In a more recent evaluation of the National Family Violence Surveys, Straus and Gelles set forth the following factors as having more impact on the degree of risk a women faces in a cohabitating relationship.

> *Isolation:* Couples who are living together may be more isolated than married couples. Part of this isolation may be because of the stigma that society attaches to cohabitation before marriage. This isolation allows for spousal abuse because no supporting network of friends or family is available for the abused spouse.
>
> *Autonomy and control:* Some people prefer cohabitation over marriage with the thought that they can retain their independence. However, any living arrangement brings with it duties, obligations, tensions, and the resulting disagreements. Some authorities point out that when the issue of control arises, violence occurs.[24] As the relationship becomes more serious, the issue of control becomes more important and violence is more likely to occur.
>
> *Investment in the relationship:* Cohabiting couples may share some characteristics that trigger violence while lacking others shared by married couples that stop the conflict from escalating into physical violence.[25]

As with other theories of spousal abuse, more study and research needs to be done before researchers can understand whether women who enter into any significant relationship are at risk of spousal abuse. This section has discussed various theories of spousal abuse, and it is clear that professionals have not as of yet discovered a cure for this type of abuse. Because the cause of this type of violence may never be determined, professionals must understand some of the characteristics of spousal abuse.

Characteristics of Spousal Abuse

Various factors or characteristics may indicate a higher probability of spousal abuse. These characteristics may take the form of personality traits in men or women or present themselves as situations. Distinctions should be made between theories regarding spousal abuse and situations that may increase the likelihood of this form of family violence. In the previous section, various theories were set forth that attempted to explain why spousal abuse occurs; this section deals with factors or characteristics that are present when spousal abuse happens.

Anderson and her associates presented a series of factors that characterize abusive relationships. Although their study concerned psychological abuse of spouses, psychological and physical abuse are usually intertwined in spousal abuse. Therefore, these characteristics or situations are deemed applicable to all forms of spousal abuse. These factors include traumatic bonding, psychological entrapment, social isolation, economic stress, alcohol abuse, power imbalance, and intergenerational transmission.[26]

Traumatic bonding: In spousal abuse, many times the abuser will use violence as a means of gaining a power advantage over the abused partner. This is accomplished by control over the spouse's time, contacts, and perception of herself. The battering may be followed by periods of calm, which is then followed by another incident of violence. This intermittent reinforcement creates a traumatic bond in which the abused partner becomes progressively more attached to the abuser and intent on modifying him.

Psychological entrapment: This situation occurs when the woman begins the relationship with the intent of making it work. When incidents of abuse occur, she tries harder to maintain the relationship and thereby invests more of herself in it. Abusers seek out partners who are easily victimized, willing to take responsibility for the relationship, passive, and fit the self-sacrificing role.

Social isolation: The abuser isolates the spouse so that no family or support system is available to give her feedback on the acts of the abuser. Her entire world is limited to the values and actions of her spouse. This in turn leads to domination and control by the abuser.

Economic stress: Dependency is associated with economics. The abuser may cut off the spouse's financial support system. She may not have the financial ability to leave the relationship.

Alcohol abuse: Alcohol does not cause abuse but is present in many abusive relationships. The spouse may believe that if the abuser simply did not drink, the abuse would stop. This faulty logic may lead the spouse to believe that alcohol is the cause of the problem.

FOCUS Things to Look for and Avoid in an Intimate Relationship

1. Dating violence: continuation of intimate relationships in which any degree of courtship violence has occurred.
2. Youth: marriage or cohabitation at a young age, especially after a brief courtship period.
3. Premarital pregnancy: dependency is already established; a combination of youth and premarital pregnancy is extremely dangerous.
4. Stepchildren: entering a new relationship with a dependent child or children by another man.
5. Isolation: breaking off close contact and relationships with friends and family; lack of support systems.
6. Unknown history: lack of knowledge about the man's former intimate relationships whether they were with lovers, wives, or parents.
7. Dependence: lack of ability to function independently because of health, education, or occupational deficits.

Source: Adapted from Pagelow, M.D. *Family Violence.* (Praeger Publishers, New York). Copyright © 1984, p. 305. Reprinted with permission of Greenwood Publishing Group, Inc., Westport, CT.

Power imbalance: If the male or abuser is threatened by the other's achievements, this imbalance of power may lead to abuse. Traditionally, abusive partners want to maintain control over their victims.

Intergenerational transmission: The cycle of violence theory discussed in Chapter 3 may apply in spousal abuse. Some authorities believe that if the batterer witnessed violence as a child, there is an increased chance that violence will be present in his adult life.

Other authorities such as Pagelow have established a list of factors that may indicate the possibility of increased violence in an intimate relationship. These factors are danger signals or early warnings that women should examine when entering into or maintaining an intimate relationship.

Although individuals who abuse or are abused may suffer from mental disorders, mental classifications have not been established for those who abuse or are abused. Nor from a psychological point of view has a clear diagnosis been developed that deals with the dynamics involved in an abusive relationship. The following sections highlight some of the more common characteristics of each of the parties—the abuser and the abused.

The Abuser

Why does he hit her? Is the spousal abuser some sort of sadistic, overbearing bully? Is he a person who enjoys inflicting pain? Did she drive him over the edge and cause him to react in the only way he knows how? These and other questions are often asked by people when they first hear about spousal abuse. Unfortunately, no established physical characteristics of a spousal abuser exist. Causal scrutiny will not reveal who will become violent in an intimate relationship, nor will it explain why the abuse occurs. Scholars have conducted many studies and dedicated years of research in an effort to understand this phenomenon. Several different approaches have been developed as a consequence of this effect.

The feminist approach in evaluating spousal abuse is to view it as a reflection of the sexist culture and sexist institutions that perpetuate the oppression of women. The male abuser is sexist, dominating, and controlling in intimate relationships with women.[27] The systematic approach attempts to determine the patterns of anger arousal, problem-solving deficits, and miscommunication that occur between couples in an intimate relationship.[28] The psychopathological perspective examines potential mental disorders or processes and attempts to identify psychological sources of violence for the abuser.[29] As indicated previously, no clear diagnosis has been established for those who batter. They can be short, tall, fat, or slim. In reality, they can be anyone. However, researchers have attempted to define some general characteristics of the batterer. The following is a summary of some of the more popular profiles of batterers. As with all characterizations, caution should be used because batterers are not a homogeneous group.

Rosenbaum and Maiuro established the following common backgrounds and characteristics of those who batter:

Exposure to violence in the family of origin: This characteristic is consistently associated with spousal abuse. The batterers may have been subjected to corporal punishment or witnessed violence in their families as children. Although violence in the family of origin and spousal abuse are strongly related, there does not seem to be a requirement that a person be raised within a violent family for him to become a batterer.

Sex role and self-image: A lack of self-identity on the part of the male may be associated with spousal abuse. Those with defective self-images may exhibit more aggression than other males with positive self-images. One study pointed out that males with low self-esteem are more prone than others to interpret their spouses' actions as damaging to their self-images.

Verbal skills deficits: Abusers may have verbal skills that are inferior to those of their wives. They may resort to violence as a method of compensating for this deficit.

Psychopathology: As indicated earlier, research is still being conducted in this area. However, Rosenbaum believes that batterers may demonstrate more psychopathology than the general population.

Alcohol abuse: As with other forms of violence, alcohol has been identified as a common denominator in family violence. Several alternatives regarding alcohol and family violence need further study.[30]

Pagelow presented the following as some of the factors responsible for men abusing their spouses:

Violence in home of orientation: Where the father figure was violent toward his spouse or children.

Low self-esteem: Abusers believe they are losers. Although they gain a great deal of satisfaction from their spouses' achievements, this also causes them to feel threatened, and they respond with violence.

Alcohol dependency: Many abusers accept the use and consumption of alcohol.

Traditionalist: Abusers believe in male supremacy and the stereotyped role of males as the head of the family.

Emotionally inexpressive: Abusers are incapable of expressing certain emotions. They can and do express anger and jealousy and will resort to violence as a form of communication.

Lack of assertiveness: Individuals who are incapable of asserting themselves often resort to violence.

Social isolation: Abusers have difficulty in maintaining social relationships.

Employment problems: Abusers may be unemployed or underemployed. Job dissatisfaction adds stress to the relationship and may lead to violence.

Authoritarian personalities: These individuals defer to higher authority but will scapegoat others.

Moody: Abusers may have wide mood swings alternating between happy and sullen from moment to moment.

Wall-punchers: They may demonstrate frustration by punching walls, kicking chairs, or hitting animals.[31]

Anderson and her associates list the following characteristics of those who batter:

Personality disorder: Many batterers display antisocial personality disorders. Some studies have found that although a percentage of batterers have no evidence of personality disorders, the great majority have demonstrated personality types that involve aggressive behavior.

Easily threatened masculinity: Abusers have more traditional views of women. Some may resort to violence when they believe their masculinity is challenged.

Low self-esteem: Abusers may have low self-esteem and resort to violence to compensate for these feelings of inadequacy.

Lack of assertiveness: Abusers lack communications skills and may resort to violence as an alternate form of expression.

Excessive, hostile attachment to wife: Abusers may make strong demands on their spouses and respond with anger when these demands are not met.

Need for power and control: The abuser's fear of loss of control or power may trigger abusive behavior.

Pathological jealousy: The batterer may be extremely jealous and demand absolute loyalty from his spouse.

Alcohol or drug abuse: The abuser may have a drug or alcohol dependency.

Violence in his family of origin: This approach focuses on assaultive behavior that either attempts to control the spouse or is a method of harming her. In either case, these reactions may have been learned from experiences observed in the family of origin.

Coping by minimizing abusiveness: Abusive partners will minimize the seriousness and extent of their abusive behavior.[32]

A review of the above theories indicates that certain traits characterize an abuser, and many studies have revealed similar hallmarks of behavior. Table 8.1 illustrates these findings.

TABLE 8.1 Abuser Traits

Characteristic	Rosenbaum and Maiuro	Pagelow	Anderson and Associates
Violence in family of origin	x	x	x
Alcohol abuse	x	x	x
Low self-esteem	x	x	x
Verbal skills deficits	x		
Psychopathology	x		x (personality disorders)
Traditionalist		x	x (easily threatened masculinity)
Emotionally inexpressive		x	
Lack of assertiveness		x	x
Isolation		x	
Employment problems		x	
Authoritarian personalities		x	
Moody		x	
Wall punchers		x	
Excessive attachment to wife			x
Need for power or control			x
Coping by minimizing abusiveness			x

As the previous discussion indicates, no clear picture emerges of a person who abuses his spouse. However, a series of characteristics should alert professionals to the possibility of abuse. More research may help to clearly define the profile of the spousal abuser.[33]

The Abused

Just as no definite set of characteristics defines the abuser, little if any agreement exists concerning the personality traits of those who are abused. Additionally, the issue of men who may be abused adds confusion to this area of family violence.

In 1977, Suzanne Steinmetz presented a paper entitled "The Battered Husband Syndrome." This presentation was the basis for an article dealing with battered husbands.[34] Steinmetz' research, which was widely publicized in the media, claimed that men were abused at a far greater rate than previously believed.

Steinmetz went further and claimed that wives abused their husbands more often and more severely than vice versa. This claim was attacked by feminists, professionals, and scholars. In 1988, Steinmetz and Lucca published a follow-up article that discussed husband battering in more detail.[35] In this article, they continued to assert that husbands are battered and concluded that all forms of violence must be prevented by placing greater emphasis on changing the attitudes and values of a society that glorifies violence.

One of the results of Steinmetz's position is the acknowledgment that both parties in an abusive relationship need to be evaluated. Studies have indicated that there are higher levels of female aggression toward their spouses than previously thought.[36] However, most authorities agree that the type and severity of aggression is different from that experienced by women.[37]

Although it may be true that some men are abused by women in an intimate relationship, the majority of all abuse is inflicted by men. The abuse inflicted on women is more severe and life threatening than those instances of husband battering. The remainder of this section examines the abused from the perspective of women as the victims.

Dynamics of Battering

One of the most often asked questions is, Why does the victim stay in an abusive relationship? The reasons that women stay with abusive partners are complex and multifaceted, and a number of theories attempt to explain the dynamics involved in battering. This section briefly discusses some of the more well known concepts in this area.

Lenore E. Walker is one of the leading authorities in the area of spousal abuse.[38] She coined the term *cycle theory of violence* as a result of her research in the area of battered women. This concept does not attempt to explain the cause of spousal abuse; rather, it examines the dynamics of this form of family violence.

The cycle theory of violence sets forth the dynamics of battering in spousal abuse. Walker's theory has three distinct phases: the tension-building phase; the explosion, or acute battering, phase; and the calm, loving respite phase. These phases can vary in length and intensity, depending on the relationship.

The Tension-Building Phase

As the name of this phase implies, tension increases within the relationship, at which time the husband may engage in minor battering of his spouse. The wife attempts to calm him by agreeing to his demands, becoming more nurturing or simply attempting to stay out of his way during this phase. The victim may rationalize that perhaps she is really at fault and deserves the abuse, accepting the batterers faulty logic as her own. Women who have been in a battering relationship for any extended period of time know only too well that the minor battering will increase in time. She may try to withdraw more from the abuser in an attempt to avoid more conflict, but the tension in the relationship will continue to increase until the batterer explodes in a fit of rage.

The Explosion or Acute Battering Phase

During this phase, the abuser loses control and engages in major incidents of assaultive behavior. This intense violent aggression is what distinguishes this phase from the minor or occasional battering that takes place in the first phase. When the first serious attack is over, both parties may feel shock, disbelief, and denial. For example, the woman may attempt to minimize her injuries.

The Calm, Loving Respite Phase

This phase is characterized by contrite loving acts on the part of the abuser. The batterer may understand that he has gone too far during the previous phase and will beg forgiveness and promise never to let it happen again. The woman will want to accept the abuser's promises that he can change and that his loving behavior is an inducement for her to stay in the relationship.

Walker's theory is generally accepted in both academia and the legal system. Her explanation for the dynamics of battering has been cited in numerous court decisions that dealt with battered spouses.

Walker also presented the concept of the battered woman syndrome.[39] Some authorities prefer the term *battered women's experiences* because they believe (1) the former term implies that there is one syndrome that all battered women develop and (2) carries with it pathological connotations that suggest that battered women suffer from some sort of sickness; (3) expert testimony on domestic violence refers to more than women's psychological reactions to violence; and (4) the former term focuses attention on the battered woman rather than on the batterer's coercive behavior and (5) creates an image of battered women as suffering victims rather than active survivors.[40] However, because most court cases and most experts still refer to this experience as *battered woman syndrome,* that term will be used in this text. Walker theorized that *victims of spousal abuse gradually become immobilized by fear and believe they have no other options. As a result, these women stay in the abusive relationships, coping the best they can. The battered woman syndrome involves one who has been, on at least two occasions, the victim of physical, sexual, or serious psychological abuse by a man with whom she has an intimate relationship. It is a pattern of psychological symptoms that develop after someone has lived in a battering relationship.* This is a gradual process of conditioning in which the victim feels both helpless and hopeless and, according to Walker, is one of the main reasons that spouses stay in these situations longer than people would expect. The abuse tends to follow the three-stage cyclical pattern of tension building, acute explosion, and loving contrition. The following responses are typical of women suffering from battered woman syndrome: (1) traumatic effects of victimization induced by violence, (2) learned helplessness deficits, and (3) self-destructive coping responses to the violence.[41]

Very similar in dynamics to battered woman syndrome is a condition referred to as the *Stockholm syndrome. This phenomenon occurs when persons who are held as hostages, captives or prisoners of war begin to identify with their captors.*[42] These victims are isolated, mistreated, and in fear of their lives. They become helpless, confined to the area they are ordered to stay in, and dependent on their captors to supply everything they need to survive. They begin to develop positive feelings for their captors. The syndrome was named after an incident in Stockholm, Sweden, in which four bank employees were held hostage in the bank's vault for 131 hours by two perpetrators. When the victims were finally freed, they expressed gratitude toward the offenders for sparing their lives.

NiCarthy indicated that the dynamics of spousal abuse are very similar to techniques used to control or brainwash prisoners of war: "As stated in a report published by Amnesty International, these techniques induce 'dependency, dread and debility.' To the extent that a person is victimized by these techniques, she or he tends to become immobilized by the belief that she or he is trapped, cannot escape."[43] This heightening of fear, helplessness, dependency, and dread are all intertwined in the definition and dynamics of spousal abuse.

Dutton and Painter developed the *traumatic bonding theory* to explain why battered women stay in abusive relationships.[44] *This theory holds that when a women finally leaves an abusive partner, her immediate fears begin to diminish and her hidden attachment to her abuser begins to manifest itself. Emotionally drained and vulnerable, she becomes susceptible to her partner's loving contrite pressure to return. As her fears lessen and the needs previously provided by her partner increase, she may decide to give him another chance.*[45]

Dutton's theory is based on the concepts of power distribution and emotional bonding that focus on the dynamics of the abusive relationship rather than on any personality defect or socioeconomic status of the victim. Dutton states that these two features—the existence of a power imbalance and the intermittent nature of the abuse—can explain why abused women stay with their abusers or even return to the relationship.

Dutton theorized that when power imbalances exist in a relationship, the person of low power feels more negative in her self-appraisal and more incapable of fending for herself and thus in need of the person with more power. This cycle of dependency and lowered self-esteem repeats itself over and over and eventually creates a strong affective bond to the high-power person.[46]

The second factor in traumatic bonding is the intermittent nature of the abuse. This occurs when the abusive partner periodically abuses the submissive partner by threats or physical acts. The time between these incidents is normally characterized by normal, socially acceptable behavior. Thus, the victim is subjected to negative arousal and the relief or release associated with its removal. This situation of alternating negative and pleasant conditions is known in learning theory as partial, or intermittent, reinforcement. Dutton states that this situation is highly effective in producing persistent patterns of behavior that are associated with strong emotional attachment to the abuser that is hard to change or modify.[47]

Another theory is that women develop a distinct set of beliefs during the abusive process. These beliefs may be classified on the basis of the time of the abuse: preexisting beliefs, beliefs that develop during the abusive relationship, and beliefs that occur as a result of the violence experienced. Preexisting beliefs are formed as a result of early childhood experiences. The woman may have been raised in a violent household and believe that all women are abused, or she may confuse abuse with love. Beliefs developed during the abusive relationship may involve a sense of fear, low self-esteem, learned helplessness, or other dynamics that prevent the spouse from leaving the abuser. Beliefs that result because of the battering may include posttraumatic stress syndrome, depression, and other symptoms that affect women's ability to function normally in society. All these beliefs influence the abused spouse and contribute to her decision to stay in the relationship.[48]

One approach examines the subjective feelings of women and lists a series of factors that explain why women stay in these relationships. These factors include fear, helplessness, guilt and feelings of failure, and lack of resources:[49]

> *Fear:* The most commonly expressed feeling for staying in an abusive relationship is fear that the batterer will come after the victim if she leaves. The abuser may threaten not only the spouse but also her child and other family members. Because she has lived with his violence, she believes the threats and rightfully fears for her family's safety.
>
> *Helplessness:* Many abused women feel trapped and cannot envision a way out of their situations. A feeling of being completely alone with no one to turn to is common. The abuser takes on bigger-than-life proportions and becomes all-powerful.
>
> *Guilt and feelings of failure:* Many women have been raised to believe that it is their responsibility to make the marriage work and that leaving the abusive situation would be an admission of failure. Additionally, some women believe that they cause or deserved the punishment.
>
> *Lack of resources:* Battered spouses are isolated and have little if any ability to access funds or social support systems. Even if they would like to leave, they do not have the financial ability to do so.

Anderson and her associates listed a series of factors that are characteristic of battered spouses.[50] These characteristics also help explain why spouses stay in these relationships:

> *Traumatic bonding and entrapment:* Once the abuse starts, the woman may believe that the spouse will get through this rough time and return to normal behavior again. As the battering continues and increases in severity, the woman may believe she has too much invested in the relationship to leave. This leads her to deny the intensity or frequency of the abuse.
>
> *Fear and terror:* The battered spouse may respond with fear or terror to her husband's threats of punishment. She will always try to be alert and sense his feelings, dreading any action that may lead to aggressive behavior.
>
> *Learned helplessness:* The abused spouse may believe that there is no way for her to prevent the violence. Therefore, she simply gives up and accepts the abuse from the husband. Learned helplessness usually follows entrapment and is more likely as the violence increases and the isolation becomes more complete.

Guilt and self-blame: Many battered spouses develop a sense of self-blame, as do most victims of severe violence who cannot control it or the situation that causes it. They attempt to invest more in the relationship to make it work and blame themselves for its failure.

Low self-esteem: Increased violence is associated with low self-esteem among battered women. As the battering continues, the spouse's value of herself declines.

Violence in her family of origin: Some authorities have suggested that the battered spouse has learned to stay in the relationship by observing violence in her own family or by experiencing it during childhood.

Coping by minimizing her abuse: All the previously listed factors contribute to a battered spouse's resistance to leaving her husband. She has learned to cope with the abuse by minimizing its extent, severity, or the cause of it.

As the previous discussion indicates, women stay in battering relationships for a number of reasons. Although some might question some of these reasons or their validity, women living with men who kick, choke, beat, and rape them on a regular basis are totally invested with these factors. Because many women do stay in these relationships, professionals need to be able to recognize the symptoms of abuse so that assistance can be offered.

Pagelow developed a list of factors that professionals, friends, or family members may observe that might indicate that a spouse is involved in a battering relationship (see the following Focus). As with all checklists, care must be taken when evaluating the factors.

FOCUS Factors That May Indicate That a Woman Is in an Abusive Relationship

- She is not active in social activities or withdraws from them after having been an active participant.
- She has no close friends of her own. She seldominvites people to her home, or when she does, visitors get subtle clues that they must leave before her spouse returns.
- She appears nervous and will never accept an invitation or a responsibility without checking first withher spouse.
- She seldom has any cash and has "forgotten" her checkbook but may have a credit card with her.
- She wears heavy makeup or sunglasses, even indoors. Her wardrobe includes scarves, turtleneck sweaters, long sleeves, and slacks.
- She has many "accidents," and at her place of employment she receives and places many calls to her spouse.
- She and her spouse have frequent changes of residence that seem unrelated to employment requirements.

Source: Pagelow, M. D. *Family Violence.*(Praeger, New York). Copyright © 1984, pp. 320–321. Reprinted with permission of Greenwood Publishing Group, Inc., Westport, CT.

This section has examined the characteristics and personality traits of both those who abuse and those who are abused. Unfortunately, professionals cannot predict when spousal abuse will occur or who the parties to this violence will be. However, some factors may indicate that certain persons may be at risk of either abusing or being abused. Because researchers cannot explain why it occurs or who it will happen to, it is critical to understand the different types of spousal abuse.

Types of Spousal Abuse

As with other subjects in the area of spousal abuse, there is disagreement on the different types of spousal abuse. Many of the studies have focused solely on physical abuse, documenting the number of times a husband strikes his wife, whereas others have looked at sexual violence in a marriage. Still others examine the psychological or emotional abuse a spouse suffers at the hands of her tormenter. Finally, some classify abuse as a property form and discuss the financial dependence imposed by the abuser. No matter how many types or variations employed, it is important to realize that they all work together to form a net that completely encompasses the woman in a world of physical, sexual, or emotional violence.

For purposes of clarity, spousal abuse in this chapter is classified as physical, sexual, or emotional abuse. Within each area are degrees of severity and differences. A woman may suffer from one or all forms of spousal abuse.

Determining who has suffered what type of abuse is more of an art than a science. Two major types or techniques are relied on in assessing spousal abuse: self-reporting and interviews. Self-reports such as the Conflict Tactics Scale developed by Straus contain eighteen items that measure or assess reasoning and aggression during conflicts within a family. Another self-report is the Spouse Specific Aggression Scale, which measures psychological but not physical aspects of abuse. These inventories allow a quick and confidential screening of physical and verbal abuse. Additionally, they are checklists that provide answers or information that may not be obtained in a clinical setting. A disadvantage of these inventories is that they fail to provide information on how aggression is related to or interacts with control and power in the relationship.

Another form of gathering information is the clinical interview. For any interview to be successful, it requires the interviewer be knowledgeable in the various forms of spousal abuse. The interview process assesses the effects of abuse as well as the dynamics of power and control in the relationship. The main disadvantage to the interview process should be obvious—the spouse or spouses must agree to be interviewed. Because one of the characteristics of spousal abuse is isolation, the interview process is limited to those situations where one or both of the spouses have come forward and agreed to be interviewed.

Physical Abuse

Physical aggression may take the form of minor acts that escalate over time. It may begin with an arm being grabbed, a dish thrown, or a slap to the arm or face. This aggression increases in severity until the victim has no way out of the relationship. The following is a list of the more common forms of physical abuse suffered by spouses.

The abuser may engage in striking acts. He may strike the face, arms, body, or legs of the spouse. The violence may be delivered with an open or closed hand. These acts include punching with his fist.

Throwing or destruction of property. The abuser may throw dishes, small appliances, or other objects at the spouse, or he may go on a rampage and destroy household property.

Control or chocking acts. Choking is a common form of abuse. It sends a very clear message that the abuser is stronger and more powerful. Choking allows the batterer to control the spouse and have her beg for mercy.

Repeated beating using objects. The use of belts, sticks, or other objects during the assault is not uncommon. Using the same object allows the abuser to completely control the victim simply by laying his hand on the object.

Humiliation violence. Some abusers will require their victims to assume certain positions for the imposition of violence. Having the victim undress before yelling and beating her adds to the feeling of helplessness.

Physical violence takes many forms. The results of these acts will leave certain physical marks or injuries on the women. In the event that they require medical treatment, the physician should be alert to the possibility of abuse if an injury is not consistent with the medical history given by the spouse. The second form of spousal abuse is even harder to detect.

Sexual Abuse

Physical violence is often accompanied by sexual abuse. Sex on demand or after physical assaults is very common. Since the woman does not believe that she has any choice or free will, she will submit to the abuser's demands. Additionally, she may fear that a refusal to engage in sexual activity will cause the abuser to react violently.

Sexual acts that humiliate or degrade the wife are not uncommon. The husband may demand oral sex without any regard for his spouse's feelings or beliefs. Anal intercourse is a common form of sexual abuse. The abuser may say things to the spouse or require her to say things that are degrading to her. Some abusers may require their spouses to share sex with friends or co-workers.

Violence during the sexual act may occur. The abuser may engage in sexual activities in a violent and forceful manner intended to injure or hurt his spouse.

Sometimes, *sex will occur after a physical altercation.* This may be loving and caring and an attempt by the abuser to make up for the aggression. This offers false hope to the abused spouse and is intended to make her believe that the abuser is really sorry and that the physical acts will not occur again.

Sexual abuse may provoke intense emotional and physical reactions in the abused spouse. This intensity and humiliation may become addictive and be looked on as a form of release. It may on occasion take on a narcotic effect for the abused spouse.

At one time in our history, a man had a right to sex with his wife. There was no such thing as spousal rape. Today, laws prevent this form of assault. Sexual abuse may not leave physical scars visible to the naked eye, but it will certainly leave emotional scars that may be even longer lasting and more devastating.

Emotional Abuse

Emotional abuse is far more than a husband simply calling his wife degrading names. This form of spousal abuse has far-reaching consequences for the victim and leaves scars that require long-term treatment. Emotional abuse includes many different acts that all contribute to a feeling of helplessness and inability.

The batterer may engage in *verbal dominance.* At first, the spouse may believe this is simply ego or a strong person speaking. However, in time she learns her opinions, feelings, and thoughts carry no weight, and if she expresses herself at all, she is subject to verbal and possibly physical abuse.

Isolation is a common form of emotional abuse. The abuser may isolate the victim by limiting her access to money, use of the car, or other normal activities. He talks negatively about her family and friends, thereby making it uncomfortable for the spouse to maintain outside relationships. Isolation prevents feedback. The only feedback she receives is from the abusing partner who distorts both his and her realities, leaving her feeling dumb, lazy, and unattractive. After a period of time, the abused spouse comes to accept these statements as true.

Guilt is a common form of emotional abuse. The abuser usually blames the spouse for his assaultive behavior with the rationale that if she had only carried out her duties better he would not have had to hit her. After a period of time, the abused spouse begins to accept these pronouncements and blames herself for the battering.

Fear is a common form of emotional abuse. The abuser may threaten to reveal secrets or private information to family and friends, or the batterer may threaten the spouse with a beating when he gets home. The spouse then waits hours for the expected assault. The abuser may threaten to harm her or her family if she ever leaves him or does anything else he does not approve of.

Humiliation is another common form of emotional abuse. The spouse may be put down in front of friends, family, or children. In extreme cases, the abuser may require her to perform degrading acts in public such as having sex in front of friends or her children or requesting permission before leaving the room or going to the bathroom. This type of emotional abuse destroys the spouse's sense of self worth and ability to resist further acts of control by the abuser.

Using fear, guilt, and isolation, the abuser will promote a *feeling of helplessness* within the spouse. This further ties the victim to the abuser. She believes that there is no way to break the cycle and feels trapped.

One aspect of emotional abuse that deserves special attention is *financial dependence.* The abuser may require the spouse to work and turn her check over to him. He will control all finances and ensure she never has any funds that he does not approve. The abuser may control the funds in order to isolate the spouse, deny her opportunities to improve herself, or to demean her. This financial dependence adds to the spouse's feelings of helplessness and entrapment. Even if she wanted to leave, she would have no money to support herself or even rent a room for a night.

Emotional abuse is a serious form of spousal abuse. Although it leaves no physical scars, it can bind the abused spouse to the perpetrator far more effectively than chains or ropes. The next section examines a controversial aspect of spousal abuse—women who kill their abusers.

Spousal Homicide

As the Focus on spousal homicide illustrates, women do strike back and kill their abusers. As professionals become more knowledgeable about spousal abuse and battered woman syndrome, they will hear more about women who kill their abusive partners. The next section examines this topical aspect of spousal abuse.

Self-Defense

Self-defense is the right of a person to use reasonable force to defend herself from physical violence. Traditionally, a person could use deadly force to protect his home from an intruder. The common law and many statutes today do not require a person to retreat in his own home before using deadly force on an intruder. If

FOCUS 'Til Death Do Us Part

Rita Collins was a professional working in a high-level position for the Navy in Washington, D.C. Her husband was a military recruiter who threatened her with a knife, kicked her in the stomach, and slammed her against doors, resulting in bruises and black eyes. Rita tried to get out ofthe marriage by filing for divorce, obtaining a restrainingorder, and filing assault charges against her ex-husband. None of this stopped him from returning to the house, bangingagainst windows and doors, and trying to get in. She calledthe police, but they said there was nothing they could do andthat she should buy a gun. She did buy a gun and subsequentlyshot and killed her ex©husband. The prosecution portrayedRita as a scheming, jilted divorcee who lured the victim tothe house so that she could kill him and receive all theirassets. Despite testimony from friends, relatives, andseveral experts regarding the violence she suffered, a jury convicted her of second-degree murder, and her appeals weredenied. Rita is only one of several women who have resorted to killing their spouses in order to stay alive or protect themselves from further violence.

Source: Booth, C., J. McDowell, and J. C. Simpson. " 'Til Death Do Us Part." *Time.* January 18, 1993, pp. 38–45.

this is the law, why must a spouse who was in fear for her life kill her husband and claim self-defense? The problem exists because the self-defense plea also requires the victim to be placed in fear of immediate injury. A percentage of spouses who have killed their abusers testified that their abusers were not in the process of striking them or hurting them at that moment.

The two issues that cause problems with a self-defense plea are proof that the spouse reasonably believed that she was in danger of death or great bodily injury and that the injury or death was imminent. Both of these issues have been discussed by various courts that have considered cases of spousal homicide.

In *State v Gallegos,* Anita Gallegos was charged with the murder of her ex-husband and long-time companion George Gallegos by shooting him at close range while he was lying in bed, then stabbing him numerous times in the neck.[51] Mrs. Gallegos suffered a long history of physical and sexual abuse prior to meeting her husband. As a child, she had been sexually and physically abused by her brother and one of her mother's lovers. She met and married George Gallegos and began to be subjected to abuse in the marriage. George drank heavily and beat her, leaving scars on her nose, near her eyes, and on her forehead. At one time, he displayed a knife and threatened to cut off her breasts if they grew any larger. When she was pregnant with their second child, he picked her up and threw her against a wall, causing the premature birth of the child.

On the day of the killing, George sodomized the defendant against her will, causing rectal bleeding. When Mrs. Gallegos threatened to leave, George pulled out his gun and said that he would kill her if she left. After another argument later that day, the husband went into the bedroom and called for Mrs. Gallegos to come into the room. She testified that she didn't know whether she was going to be killed, raped, or beaten. Mrs. Gallegos picked up her husband's rifle, walked into the room, and shot him as he lay on the bed. She then grabbed a knife and stabbed him numerous times in the neck.

She was charged and convicted of voluntary manslaughter. The trial court refused to instruct the jury on the issue of self-defense or to allow testimony on battered woman syndrome. The New Mexico Court of Appeals reversed the conviction holding that, under these facts, the issue of self-defense was proper and that the trial court erred in refusing to allow testimony regarding the term *battered woman syndrome.*

One of the most notable cases involving a battered woman and self-defense was the case of *People v Aris.*[52] Brenda Denise Aris was married to her husband for ten years. During that time, he threatened and beat her numerous times. On the night of the killing, he beat her and threatened to kill her in the morning. Suffering from bruises, Mrs. Aris went next door to a neighbor's house to get some ice to ease the pain of the blows. While there, she saw a revolver and took it back with her to the bedroom. While her husband was asleep, she shot him five times in the back. She was charged and tried for the crime of murder.

During the trial, the defense called Dr. Lenore E. Walker, author of *The Battered Woman* and *Terrifying Love,* as an expert witness to testify about battered woman syndrome and Mrs. Aris's state of mind.[53] Although Dr. Walker was able to testify generally about battered women, she was precluded from stating her opinion that Mrs. Aris was suffering from battered woman syndrome at the time she shot her husband. Thus, the trial court allowed evidence that Mrs. Aris was battered and believed her life was in danger but refused to allow Dr. Walker to testify as to the *reasonableness* of that belief.

The trial court also instructed the jury on the issue of imminent danger of death or great bodily injury stating,

> Imminent peril *as used in these instructions, means that the peril must have existed or appeared to the defendant to exist at the very time the fatal shot was fired. In other words, the peril must appear to the defendant as immediate and present and not prospective or even in the near future. An imminent peril is one that, from appearances, must be instantly dealt with.*[54]

Several times the jury asked for clarification on the term *imminent.* After repeating the instructions to them, the jury found the defendant guilty of second-degree murder. The appeals court upheld the lower court decision, and Brenda Denise Aris was sentenced to state prison.

Fortunately, the case of Brenda Aris was not over. In 1993, California governor Pete Wilson reduced Aris's fifteen-years-to-life sentence to twelve years to life—a move that under California's complex sentencing laws made her eligible for parole in July 1994. Wilson, a strong law-and-order governor, stated, "The test of whether clemency should be considered in cases where the request is based upon battered women's syndrome must be: Did the petitioner have the option to leave her abuser, or was the homicide realistically her only chance?[55]

The case of *Bechtel v State* decided in 1992 gives some insight into the continuing lack of understanding of the issues of self-defense and battered woman syndrome by some trial judges.[56] Donna Lee Bechtel and Ken were married in 1982. From that date until the day of the killing in September 1984, Donna was battered twenty-three different times. These assaults occurred when her husband was drinking and included grabbing Donna by her ears or hair and pounding her head on the ground, wall, door, cabinet, or other available objects.

On the day of the killing, Ken returned home drunk, beat her, sexually assaulted her, and threatened to kill her. After a final assault in which he first choked her and then passed out, Donna obtained a gun and shot him. The trial court refused to admit testimony regarding battered woman syndrome and how it related to the requirement of imminence in self-defense. The jury convicted Mrs. Bechtel of first-degree murder, and she was sentenced to life imprisonment.

The Oklahoma Court of Criminal Appeals reversed the conviction stating that expert opinion regarding battered woman syndrome and how it related to the issue of imminence of death or danger should have been admitted. The court held that thirty-one states and the District of Columbia allowed use of expert testimony on the subject of the battered woman syndrome. It went further and stated that battered woman syndrome is a substantial, scientifically accepted theory.

Although not dealing specifically with spousal homicide, another court opinion illustrates how far courts are now willing to extend the concept of battered woman syndrome. In *People v Romero,* Debra Romero was charged with one count of second-degree robbery and four counts of attempted robbery.[57] Debra met, and began living with, Terrance Romero in March 1989. They were both cocaine addicts, and Terrance soon began hitting Debra if she didn't somehow get the money for his habit. From the day she moved in, Debra testified that he hit her almost every day. He would get angry and rip screens off the windows, throw things out the windows, and threaten to kill her if she left.

From May 28 until July 23, 1989, Terrance and Debra engaged in one actual and several attempted robberies. They were caught and convicted on all counts, and Debra was sentenced to state prison for five years. During the trial, Debra testified that she was afraid of Terrance and committed the crimes under duress. Duress is very similar to self-defense in that it requires the party committing the crime to prove that they acted out of an immediate or imminent fear of injury. The defense attorney did not call any experts to testify regarding battered women syndrome.

Debra appealed her conviction and claimed that she was denied effective counsel because her attorney did not raise the issue of battered woman syndrome to support her claim of duress. The appeals court reviewed the history of battered woman syndrome and its growing acceptance in homicide trials. The court reversed the conviction, stating that the defense attorney should have presented evidence to corroborate Debra's testimony and informed the jury of the dynamics of her mental state. Failure to do so, the appeals court reasoned, denied Debra her right to effective counsel.

In 1996, the California Supreme Court addressed the issue of battered woman syndrome and self-defense in *People v Humphrey.*[58] Evelyn Humphrey was forcefully molested by her father from the time she was seven until she was fifteen. She had three previous abusive relationships before she met Albert Hampton. Her relationship with Hampton involved frequent arguments and beatings. Hampton once broke her nose by throwing a beer can at her face. He hit her in the back of the head because he told her that it won't leave bruises. On March 27, 1992, the evening before the killing, he grabbed his gun and fired one round at her, which missed. The next day they continued to argue, and in the evening he hit her and stated that this time when he shot at her, he wouldn't miss. She grabbed the gun and backed him into the kitchen. As he was reaching for her hand, she shot him in the chest. The police arrived, and she admitted shooting Hampton. He died in the hospital, and Evelyn was charged with murder and with use of a firearm during the commission of a crime.

In 1991, the California legislature adopted Evidence Code 1107 which provides that expert testimony is admissible regarding the battered woman syndrome in criminal cases. Relying on this statute and other case law, Humphrey's attorney presented both expert and lay witness evidence regarding her experiences. The expert testified that Evelyn was suffering from battered woman syndrome and believed that she was in mortal danger from Hampton. Evelyn also testified about her experiences with Hampton. The prosecutor argued that she could have left the victim on the evening before the killing when he shot and missed her. At the end of the trial, the court dismissed the charge of first-degree murder but allowed the second-degree charge and the manslaughter charge to remain. Although the court allowed evidence regarding battered woman syndrome, it refused to allow the jury to consider whether a reasonable person in the defendant's circumstances would have perceived a threat of imminent injury or death. The jury convicted Evelyn of voluntary manslaughter. The Supreme Court reversed, holding that expert testimony that Evelyn was suffering from battered woman syndrome was generally admissible in homicide cases, not only on the question of whether the defendant actually believed that it was necessary to kill in self-defense but also on the question of reasonableness of that belief.[59]

In 1997, in *State v Thomas,* the Ohio Supreme Court reaffirmed its position on self-defense and battered woman syndrome.[60] On September 15, 1993, Teresa Thomas shot and killed Jerry Flowers, her live-in boyfriend. They had lived together two years prior to the shooting. Flowers continually abused Teresa, including hitting, pushing, and choking her. He would purposefully soil his clothes and demand she clean them. Two days before the shooting, he forcibly sodomized her. On the day of the killing, Flowers returned home and advanced toward Teresa. She ran into the bedroom, grabbed Flowers's gun, and shot him six times. The jury convicted her of murder with a firearm specification.

The Ohio Supreme Court upheld the jury instruction dealing with self-defense, stating that it combines both an objective and a subjective test. The jury must first consider the defendant's situation objectively to determine whether a reasonable person would believe she was in imminent danger and then consider subjectively whether this particular defendant had an honest belief that she was in danger. The court reversed the decision on other grounds.

In 1997, in *People v Morgman,* a California appellate court upheld using battered woman syndrome to impeach the victim's recantation of her previous statements to police.[61] Julie Parker and David Morgman were dating for approximately three years. On February 5, 1995, neighbors called regarding screams coming from Julie's apartment. When the police arrived, Julie ran naked from her apartment and stated that Morgman had hit her and punched her in the face. Morgman was arrested and Julie taken to the hospital. An examination at the emergency room revealed multiple blunt injuries to her face, wrist, and shoulder. Three days later, Julie reaffirmed the abuse to a police detective. By the time of the trial, Julie and Morgman were back together, and she recanted her testimony on the stand. Julie testified that the injuries occurred as a result of hallucinating from drugs and alcohol and Morgman was simply trying to restrain her and prevent more serious injuries.

The prosecutor then called an expert witness to testify about battered woman syndrome and why some victims stay with the abuser. The defense objected, but the trial court allowed the testimony. The jury convicted Morgman on five counts. The appellate court upheld this use of battered woman syndrome, stating that such testimony assisted the jury in understanding Julie's motive to recant her previous testimony. This evidence allowed the jury to evaluate Julie's credibility in light of her conflicting stories and the dynamics of battered woman syndrome.

Thus, courts are now accepting testimony of experts regarding battered woman syndrome. This testimony allows the jury to understand the dynamics involved in these situations. Additionally, it allows them to find that, as far as the abused spouse was concerned, she was in imminent danger and was therefore justified in striking back at her abuser, even to the point of killing him in his sleep.

Use of Experts

If a woman kills her abusing partner, she may be charged with homicide. As the previous discussion indicates, it is necessary to present evidence during the trial to prove that a woman suffered from battered woman syndrome. Simply having her testify that she was beaten and afraid of her partner does not educate the jury to the dynamics of the situation.[62]

The first hurdle in admitting expert testimony is to prove to the court that the testimony is relevant to the facts in the case. This is normally accomplished by showing that the expert will testify regarding the battered spouse's belief that she was in immediate or imminent peril. This raises the issue of self-defense, and the expert's testimony becomes relevant.

The next obstacle to overcome is proof that the expert use of methodology has gained general acceptance within the scientific community and permits a reasonable opinion to be expressed by the expert. In *People v Torres,* the court held that

> *the theory underlying the battered woman's syndrome has indeed passed beyond the experimental stage and gained a substantial enough scientific acceptance to warrant admissibility. [N]umerous articles and books have been published about the battered woman's syndrome; and recent findings of researchers in the field have confirmed its presence and thereby indicated that the scientific community accepts its underlying premises.*[63]

The court must only be satisfied that the methodology used is accepted by the scientific community, not the individual opinion based on that methodology. Therefore, once the expert has satisfied the court that her research is sound, any opinion is admissible.

As indicated in earlier chapters, an expert is someone with special training or education that enables her to assist the jury on issues that are beyond the range of normal understanding. A doctor, psychiatrist, or psychologist would naturally qualify as an expert in her field. However, in order to testify regarding battered woman syndrome, they should have some special education or experience dealing with family violence in general and battered spouses specifically. Even those without advanced degrees may qualify as experts in this area if they have special training or knowledge in the area. In *Commonwealth v Craig,* the director of a women's shelter with a masters degree in counseling, five years experience working with battered women, and previous experience as an expert witness in this area was deemed qualified to testify regarding the defendant and battered woman syndrome.[64]

Although one study has indicated that jurors may have more knowledge about spousal abuse than previously believed, an expert witness can ensure that they understand the dynamics of spousal abuse.[65] The witness should be able to dispel myths, stereotypes, and misconceptions regarding spousal abuse. The witness can use the courtroom to educate the judge, jury, and even the prosecutor as to why the spouse did not leave the relationship and believed killing her partner was the only way out of the situation. Most important, the expert witness can answer the unasked question, Why didn't she simply leave or call the police?

When a battered woman kills her spouse, the battle has just begun. The justice system may decide that she could have left the abuser and charge her with homicide. If this occurs, it is essential that an expert witness testify regarding battered woman syndrome. Such testimony will assist in educating the jury regarding why the woman acted the way she did instead of pursuing other alternatives.

Summary

Although spousal abuse has been intensely researched in the past years, it is still one of the most commonly misunderstood issues within the study of family violence. Society has placed women in inferior and subordinate positions throughout history, and even today the glass ceiling exists both public in and private institutions. These factors contribute to the interpersonal dynamics that result in violence against women. The nature and extent of spousal abuse is staggering. Current figures indicate that women today are being brutalized in alarming numbers.

Numerous theories try to explain why men batter women. In fact, there are so many theories that entire textbooks are devoted to explaining them. Yet, no theory is accepted by all scholars, practitioners, or professionals in the field as the only theory that explains spousal abuse. Even though no theory prevails, professionals should be aware of the more common and well-known studies of spousal abuse. They include social stress, power, dependency, alcohol, pregnancy, and marriage.

The characteristics of those who abuse and those who are abused have been researched by well-known and respected scholars. Unfortunately, no set of personality traits can be listed that automatically indicate who will be an abuser or who will be abused. Although no agreement exists regarding the theories or characteristics of spousal abuse, all professionals acknowledge that there are three basic types of spousal abuse—physical, sexual, and emotional.

When a spouse who has been abused finally reacts, she may kill her abuser. When this occurs, the secret of abuse comes out into the open and enters the judicial arena. The most common defense used in these cases is self-defense. Expert witnesses are necessary to educate the jury regarding battered woman syndrome and to explain why the spouse did not leave her abuser. Even today that question is being asked by those who should know better.

Key Terms

spousal abuse—any intentional act or series of acts that cause injury to the spouse. These acts may be physical, emotional, or sexual. The term spouse is gender neutral, and therefore the abuse may occur to a male or female. The term includes those who are married, cohabitating, or involved in a serious relationship. It also encompasses individuals who are separated and living apart from their former spouses.

Battered woman syndrome—one who has been, on at least two occasions, the victim of physical, sexual, or serious psychological abuse by a man with whom she has an intimate relationship. It is a pattern of psychological symptoms that develop after a woman has lived in a battering relationship.

Stockholm syndrome—a phenomenon that occurs when persons who are held as hostages, captives, or prisoners of war begin to identify with their captors.

power—the ability to impose one's will on another and make life decisions for that person.

family—a group of persons who cohabit.

marital dependency—a multifaceted concept that involves economic, emotional, and societal forces that results in a woman's being dependent on her spouse for support.

Discussion Questions

1. Should we call this form of family violence spousal abuse or wife abuse? Justify your answer.
2. Is it important to understand the different theories regarding why spousal abuse occurs?
3. List what you think are the most important aspects of our society that cause spousal abuse or allow it to happen.
4. If your spouse grabs your arm during an argument and squeezes it very tightly, would you leave him or her? Why or why not?
5. Which, in your opinion, is the most severe form of abuse—physical, sexual, or emotional? Why?
6. Have you ever known a friend that you had reason to believe may have been or is now being abused? What were the characteristics you observed?
7. Should the justice system charge women who kill their abusers with homicide? Why? Why not?

Suggested Readings

Ammerman, R. T., and M. Hersen, eds. *Treatment of Family Violence.* (John Wiley, New York) 1990.

Ammerman, R. T., and M. Hersen, eds. *Case Studies in Family Violence.* (Plenum, New York) 1991.

Collins, Jr., J. J. ed. *Drinking and Crime: Perspectives on the Relationships between Alcohol Consumption and Criminal Behavior.* (Guilford Press, New York) 1981.

Costanzo, M., and S. Oskamp, eds. *Violence and the Law.* (Sage, Thousand Oaks, California) 1994.

Dobash, R. E., and R. P. Dobash. *Violence against Wives: A Case against the Patriarchy.* (Free Press, New York) 1979.

Gottheil, E., K. A. Druley, T. E. Skoloda, and H. M. Waxman, eds. *Alcohol, Drug Abuse and Aggression.* (Charles C. Thomas, Springfield, Illinois) 1983.

Hasselt, V. B., R. L. Morrison, A. S. Bellack, and W. Frazier, eds. *Handbook of Family Violence.* (Plenum, New York) 1988.

Hotaling, G. T., D. Finkelhor, J. T. Kirkpatrick, and M. A. Straus, eds. *New Directions in Family Violence Research,* (Sage, Beverly Hills, California) 1988.

Jaggar, A. M., and P. S. Rothenberg, eds. *Feminist Frameworks.* 3d ed. (McGraw Hill, New York) 1993.

Martin, D. *Battered Wives.* (Glide, San Francisco) 1976.

McClelland, D. C., W. N. Davis, R. Kalin, and E. Wanner. *The Drinking Man.* (Free Press, New York) 1972.

Merlo, A. V., and J. M. Pollock. *Women, Law, and Social Control* (Allyn and Bacon, Boston) 1995.

NiCarthy, G. *Getting Free: A Handbook for Women in Abusive Relationships.* (Seal Press, New York) 1986.

Pagelow, M. D. *Family Violence.* (Praeger, New York) 1984.

Roy, M. ed. *Battered Women: A Psychosociological Study of Domestic Violence.* (Van Nostrand Reinhold, New York) 1977.

Roy, M., ed. *A Psychological Study of Domestic Violence.* (Van Nostrand Reinhold, New York) 1977.

Sonkin, D. J., ed. *Domestic Violence on Trial.* (Springer, New York) 1982.

Stone, L. *The Family, Sex and Marriage in England 1500–1800.* (Harper & Row, New York) 1977.

Straus, M. A., and R. J. Gelles. *Physical Violence in American Families.* (Transaction Publishers, New Brunswick, New Jersey) 1990.

Walker, L. E. *The Battered Women.* (Harper & Row, New York) 1979.

Walker, L. E. *Terrifying Love.* (Harper & Row, New York) 1987.

Endnotes

1. Dobash, R. E., and R. P. Dobash. "Wives: The 'Appropriate' Victims of Marital Violence." *Victimology* 2 (3/4) 1978. p. 426.
2. Davidson, T. "Wifebeating: A Recurring Phenomenon Throughout History." M. Roy, ed. *Battered Women: A Psychosociological Study of Domestic Violence.* (Van Nostrand Reinhold, New York) 1977.
3. For an excellent historical overview of this area, see Stone, L. *The Family, Sex, and Marriage in England 1500–1800.* (Harper & Row, New York) 1977.
4. Davidson, T. "Wifebeating: A Recurring Phenomenon Throughout History." In M. Roy, ed. *Battered Women: A Psychosociological Study of Domestic Violence.* (Van Nostrand Reinhold, New York) 1977.
5. Gondolf, E. W., and E. R. Fisher. "Wife Battering." In R. T. Ammerman and M. Hersen, eds. *Case Studies in Family Violence.* (Plenum, New York) 1991, p. 274.
6. Martin, D. *Battered Wives.* (Glide, San Francisco) 1976, pp. 197–198.
7. Straus, M. A., and R. J. Gelles. *Physical Violence in American Families.* (Transaction Publishers, New Brunswick, New Jersey) 1990, pp. 96–98.
8. Stark, E., and A. Flitcraft. "Violence among Intimates: An Epidemiological Review." In V. B. Hasselt, R. L. Morrison, A. S. Bellack, and W. Frazier, eds. *Handbook of Family Violence.* (Plenum, New York) 1988, pp. 293–317.
9. Gondolf, E. W., and E. R. Fisher. "Wife Battering." In R. T. Ammerman, and M. Hersen, ed. *Case Studies in Family Violence.* (Plenum, New York) 1991, pp. 273–274.
10. Kurz, D. "Battering and the Criminal Justice System: A Feminist View." In E. S. Buzawa,

and C. G. Buzawa, eds. *Domestic Violence: The Changing Criminal Justice Response.* (Auburn House, Westport, Connecticut) 1992.

11. For an excellent discussion of these issues, see Spiller, K. "The Feminist Majority Report: Corporate Women and the Mommy Track." In A. M. Jaggar, and P. S. Rothenberg, eds. *Feminist Frameworks,* 3d ed. (McGraw Hill, New York) 1993, pp. 316–318.
12. See Newman, K. "Middle-Class Women in Trouble." In A. M. Jaggar, and P. S. Rothenberg, eds. *Feminist Frameworks,* 3d ed. (McGraw Hill, New York) 1993, pp. 319–323.
13. This does not imply that middle-class women are not abused. See Johnson, H., and F. G. Hermelin. "The Truth about White-Collar Domestic Violence," *Working Woman* (20/3) March, 1995, pp. 54–62.
14. Roy, M. "A Current Study of 150 Cases." In M. Roy, ed. *A Psychological Study of Domestic Violence.* (Van Nostrand Reinhold, New York) 1977.
15. Kalmuss, D. S., and M. A. Straus. "Wife's Marital Dependency and Wife Abuse." In M. A. Straus, and R. J. Gelles, eds. *Physical Violence in American Families.* (Transaction Publishers, New Brunswick, New Jersey) 1990, pp. 379–380.
16. Sher, K. J. "Subjective Effects of Alcohol: The Influence of Setting and Individual Differences in Alcohol Expectancies." *Journal of Studies on Alcohol* (46) 1985, pp. 137–146.
17. Coleman, D. H., and M. A. Straus. "Alcohol Abuse and Family Violence." In E. Gottheil, K. A. Druley, T. E. Skoloda, and H. M. Waxman, eds. *Alcohol, Drug Abuse, and Aggression.* (Charles C. Thomas, Springfield, Illinois) 1983, pp. 104–124.
18. McClelland, D. C., W. N. Davis, R. Kalin, and E. Wanner. *The Drinking Man.* (Free Press, New York) 1972.
19. Pernanem, K. "Theoretical Aspects of the Relationship between Alcohol Use and Crime." In J. J. Collins, Jr., ed. *Drinking and Crime: Perspectives on the Relationships between Alcohol Consumption and Criminal Behavior.* (Guilford Press, New York) 1981.
20. Helton, A. "Battering during Pregnancy." *American Journal of Nursing* (86) 1986, pp. 910–913.
21. Gelles, R. J. "Violence and Pregnancy: Are Pregnant Women at Greater Risk of Abuse?" In M. A. Straus, and R. J. Gelles. *Physical Violence in American Families.* (Transaction Publishers, New Brunswick, New Jersey) 1990, p. 282.
22. Straus, M. A., and R. J. Gelles. "How Violent Are American Families? Estimates from the National Family Violence Survey and Other Studies." In G. T. Hotaling, D. Finkelhor, John T. Kirkpatrick, and M. A. Straus, eds. *New Directions in Family Violence Research,* (Sage, Beverly Hills, California) 1988.
23. Sets, J. E., and M. A. Straus. "The Marriage License: A Comparison of Assaults in Dating, Cohabitating, and Married Couples." In M. A. Straus, and R. J. Gelles, eds. *Physical Violence in American Families.* (Transaction Publishers, New Brunswick, New Jersey) 1990, pp. 227–244, published earlier in *Journal of Family Violence* (4) 1989, pp. 161–180.
24. Sets, J. E., and M. A. Pirog-Good. "Violence in Dating Relationships." *Social Psychology Quarterly* (50) 1987, pp. 237–246.
25. See Sets, J. E., and M. A. Straus. "The Marriage License: A Comparison of Assaults in Dating, Cohabitating, and Married Couples." In M. A. Straus, and R. J. Gelles. *Physical Violence in American Families.* (Transaction Publishers, New Brunswick, New Jersey) 1990, pp. 227–244.
26. Anderson, S. M., T. R. Boulette, and A. H. Schwartz. "Psychological Maltreatment." In R. T. Ammerman, and M. Hersen, eds. *Case Studies in Family Violence.* (Plenum, New York) 1991, pp. 304–308.
27. Dobash, R. E., and R. P. Dobash. *Violence against Wives: A Case against the Patriarchy.* (Free Press, New York) 1979.
28. Everstein, D., and L. Everstein. *People in Crisis: Strategic Therapeutic Interventions.* (Brunner/Mazel, New York) 1983.
29. B. M. Quigley, and Ken E. Leonard, "Desistance of Husband Aggression in the Early Years of Marriage." *Violence and Victims,* 11(4), Winter 1996, p. 355.
30. Rosenbaum, A., and R. Maiuro. "Perpetrators of Spouse Abuse." In R. T. Ammerman, and M. Hersen, eds. *Treatment of Family Violence.* (John Wiley, New York) 1990, pp. 280–309.

31. Pagelow, M. D. *Family Violence.* (Praeger, New York) 1984.
32. Anderson, S. M., T. R. Boulette, and A. H. Schwartz. "Psychological Maltreatment of Spouses." In R. T. Ammerman, and M. Hersen, eds. *Case Studies in Family Violence.* (Plenum, New York) 1991.
33. See Bersani, C. A., H. T. Chen, B. F. Pendleton, and Robert Denton. "Personality Traits of Convicted Male Batterers." *Journal of Family Violence* (7) 1992, p. 123 for a study regarding personality traits of abusers and an acknowledgement that further study needs to occur in this area.
34. Steinmetz, S. "The Battered Husband Syndrome." *Victimology* 2 (3/4) 1978, pp. 499–509.
35. Steinmetz, S. K., and J. S. Lucca. "Husband Battering." In V. B. Van Hasselt, R. L. Morrison, A. S. Bellack, and M. Hersen, eds. *Handbook of Family Violence.* (Plenum, New York) 1988.
36. O'Leary, K. D., J. Barling, I. Arias, A Rosenbaum, J. Malone, and A. Tyree. "Prevalence and Stability of Physical Aggression between Spouses: A Longitudinal Analysis." *Journal of Consulting and Clinical Psychology* (57) 1989, pp. 263–268.
37. Kevin Hamberger, et al., "An Empirical Classification of Motivations for Domestic Violence," *Violence Against Women,* 3(4), pp: 401–423 (August 1997)
38. Walker, L. E. *The Battered Women.* (Harper & Row, New York) 1979.
39. Walker, L. E. *The Battered Woman Syndrome.* (Springer, New York 1984).
40. See *People v Humphrey,* 96 Daily Journal D.A.R. 10609 at 10612, where the California Supreme Court addressed this issue.
41. Douglas, M. A. "The Battered Women Syndrome." In D. J. Sonkin, ed., *Domestic Violence on Trial.* (Springer, New York, 1982)
42. Pagelow, M. D. *Family Violence.* (Praeger, New York, 1984) p. 308.
43. NiCarthy, G. *Getting Free: A Handbook for Women in Abusive Relationships.* (Seal Press, New York, 1986) pp. 117–118.
44. Dutton, D. G., and S. L. Painter. "Traumatic Bonding: The Development of Emotional Attachments in Battered Women and Other Relationships of Intermittent Abuse," 6 *Victimology* 139 (1981).
45. Dutton, D. G. *The Domestic Assault of Women.* (UBC Press, Vancouver, British Columbia)1995.
46. Ibid., p. 190.
47. Ibid., p. 191.
48. Webb, W. "Treatment Issues and Cognitive Behavior Techniques with Battered Women." *Journal of Family Violence* (7) 1992, p. 205.
49. Pagelow, M. D. *Family Violence.* (Praeger, New York) 1984.
50. Anderson, S. M., T. R. Boulette, and A. H. Schwartz. "Psychological Maltreatment of Spouses." In R. T. Ammerman, and M. Hersen, eds. *Case Studies in Family Violence.* (Plenum, New York) 1991.
51. 719 P. 2d 1268 (1986).
52. 215 Cal. App. 3d 1178 (1989).
53. Walker, L. E. *The Battered Women.* (Harper & Row, New York) 1979, and *Terrifying Love.* (Harper & Row, New York) 1987.
54. 215 Cal. App. 3d 1187.
55. Ellis, V. "Battered Wives Granted Clemency." *The Fresno Bee.* May 29, 1993, A–1 at A–18.
56. 840 P. 2d 1 (Okl.Cr. 1992). The delay between the time of the killing in 1982 and the appellate court decision was a result of an earlier murder trial that required the state to retry the defendant.
57. 13 Cal. Rptr 2d 332 (1992).
58. 13 Cal. 4th 1073, 56 Cal. Rept. 2d 142 (1996)
59. The court noted that some experts do not advocate using the phrase "battered woman syndrome" for a variety of reasons, including the fact that it implies that this is only a syndrome battered women develop. However, the court pointed out that others continue to use the term, and the California legislature adopted a statute in 1991 using the term.
60. 673 N.E.2d 1339 (1997).
61. 97 *Daily Journal D.A.R.* 13497 (October 31, 1997).
62. Schuller, R. "Juror's Decisions in Trials of Battered Women Who Kill: The Role of Prior Beliefs and Expert Testimony," *Journal of Applied Psychology* (24) 1994, p. 316.
63. 128 Misc. 2d 129 at 134–135, 488 N.Y.S. 2d 358 at 363 (1985).
64. 783 S.W. 2d 387 (Ky 1990).
65. Greene, E. A. Raitz, and H. Lindblad. "Jurors' Knowledge of Battered Women." *Journal of Family Violence* (4/2) 1989, p. 105.

9

THE CRIMINAL JUSTICE RESPONSE TO SPOUSAL ABUSE

Chapter Outline

Learning Objectives

After reading this chapter, you should be able to discuss the following concepts:

- The risk factors associated with individuals who commit spousal assault.
- Saunder's typology of aggressors.

- The social forces that affected traditional police response to spousal assault.
- The theories that were tested in the Minneapolis experiment and other replications involving arrest of offenders.
- The advantages and disadvantages of the existing and proposed alternatives to arresting the perpetrator of spousal abuse.
- The advantages and disadvantages of temporary restraining orders.
- The process of prosecuting spousal assault cases.

Introduction

Chapter 7 examined professionals and their responses to domestic violence, specifically child abuse. This chapter explores law enforcement and criminal justice responses to spousal assault. Excellent texts and research material can be found that discuss police and domestic violence.[1] That material provides an in-depth scholarly examination of the causes, effects, and police responses in this area. The purpose of this chapter is to acquaint readers with an overview of policing and prosecution of spousal assault cases. This will facilitate an understanding of some of the existing controversies in this highly debated area of domestic violence.

The term *spousal assault* is used to distinguish this form of family violence from spousal abuse. From a legal perspective, the term *spousal assault* is inaccurate. An assault does not involve any physical injury to the victim. However, in order to be consistent with other professionals and writers in the field of family violence, *spousal assault* is used and defined as *the act of intentionally inflicting physical injury on a spouse or other person who is cohabitating with the abuser.* It is distinct and yet a part of spousal abuse in that all the dynamics that cause spousal abuse may be present in spousal assault. However, this form of assault may occur without the existence of the other forms of abuse such as emotional or psychological injury, which typically accompany spousal abuse.

Similar to many other areas of domestic violence, police response to spousal assault is still being researched and studied. Like so much of domestic violence and other criminal acts, professionals simply do not have the answers to the problems. Scholars such as Cynthia Bowman would argue that they do not even know which questions to ask.[2]

If spousal assault were like any other crime, the police response would be fairly simple: investigate, arrest, charge, and cooperate with the district attorney in the prosecution of the perpetrator. Unfortunately, spousal assault involves certain factors that make it a special problem. These factors are explored in detail in this chapter. These forces interact to cause law enforcement agencies to respond differently to spousal assault than they would to robberies, rapes, and other crimes of violence.

Spousal assault can have serious consequences for both the victim and any professionals who are involved with either the abuser or the victim. Spousal assault is one of the crimes society ha+s ignored. Part of the reason for society's delayed reaction to this form of domestic violence is the perceived difficulty in responding to

FOCUS A Case of Indifference

Starting in October 1982 and continuing until June 1983, Tracey Thurman repeatedly contacted the Torrington Connecticut Police Department begging for protection from her estranged husband, Buck. Tracey signed several sworn complaints against Buck; however, the police department considered the incidents a family matter and did not respond to them in the same manner as they did to "stranger assaults."

On the day of the final beating, Buck stabbed Tracey repeatedly. A police officer arrived and asked Buck for the knife but did not arrest or restrain him in any manner. Buck gave the officer the knife and then proceeded to stomp on Tracey's head in front of the officer. He then went inside the house, returned with their son, and cursed and kicked Tracey in the head. This series of blows left her partially paralyzed. Other officers arrived, and they did not arrest Buck until he tried to assault Tracey as she lay on the ambulance stretcher.

Tracey filed suit in federal court against the City of Torrington, its police department, and all twenty-four officers who she had contacted over the years about Buck's assaultive acts. She alleged that the police department and its officers had been negligent in responding to her and, further, that they had violated her constitutional right to equal protection under the law by treating her differently than they would persons who were assaulted by strangers.

The jury awarded Tracey $2.3 million[3] in damages, and although the city's insurance company paid the judgment, it indicated that it might not pay any future awards against any police department that refused or failed to educate its officers about domestic violence.

Sources: From Buddy, M., and K. Taylor. "Please Somebody Help Me." 20/20 News, January 23, 1986; and *Thurman v City of Torrington.* 595 F.Suppl 1521 (Conn. 1984).

physical assaults between adult family members. Another factor is the apparent inability to classify those who assault their spouses into any identifiable category. Finally, as with other forms of family violence, professionals cannot predict with any certainty who will be the aggressor or who will be the victim in a spousal assault. The following sections examine a risk profile that attempts to identify potential abusers and briefly discuss a new typology of husbands who assault their spouses.

Extent of the Problem

Spousal assault is one of the most common forms of violence in the United States.[4] Sherman estimates that 2 to 8 million incidents come to the attention of police each year where a victim has been beaten by a spouse or lover.[5] Using Straus's figures, Sherman speculates the actual rate of spousal assault may be as high as 18 million incidents per year.[6]

As difficult as it is to accurately predict the rate of spousal assault in the United States, it is equally difficult to establish a profile of individuals who assault their spouses. Saunders has established a profile that is specific to spousal assault.[7] This "risk profile" includes childhood violence, low socioeconomic status, and alcohol use. Although no causal relationship has been established on the basis of these factors, their presence distinguishes husbands who assault their spouses from those who do not engage in this type of aggressive behavior.

Childhood violence: The cycle of violence theory has been discussed in Chapter 2. Saunders utilizes this concept and indicates that a consistent risk factor for those who engage in spousal assault is a history of witnessing parental violence or being physically assaulted as a child.

Low socioeconomic status: Although spousal assault can occur in all economic groups, the rate of spousal battering was five times higher in lower-income families than in the higher-income brackets. The stresses of unemployment, poverty, and intercity living conditions appear to increase the risk of spousal assault.

Alcohol use: Similar to other forms of domestic violence, alcohol use is present in a high percentage of spousal assault cases.

Saunders lists other factors that increase the risk of spousal assault. These factors include youth, behavioral deficits, personality disorders, anger, stress, depression, and low self-esteem.[8] Saunders has also explored the characteristics of those who assault their spouses and has established a typology of three types of males who engage in spousal assault. This typology, although tentative, may be the starting point for further research in this area.

Generalized aggressor: This type of abuser has long-term chronic mental problems. He may be invested in holding on to his aggression and use alcohol as a method of keeping his childhood abuse covered. This type of aggressor has rigid sex-role beliefs. He is unable to empathize with his victim and thus shows little or no remorse for his actions.

Family-only type: This aggressor lacks communication skills and is unable to express his anger in an appropriate manner. He therefore turns to assaultive behavior as a means of expressing his frustration. This type of aggressor also abuses alcohol.

Emotionally volatile: This type of abuser reaction is clouded by anger. He has rigid sex-role expectations and little self-control.

As the preceding discussion indicates, researchers are still learning about the extent of spousal assault and its characteristics. However, spousal assault is not a new form of aggression. It has existed for years, and society has turned away from it. The following section examines some of the social forces that affected law enforcement's response to spousal abuse.

Factors Affecting Police Response

Law enforcement's acknowledgement and response to spousal assault has been slow in coming. Even today, there are police officers who would rather not get involved in a "family matter." This should not be surprising because the battering of women has existed for thousands of years. As indicated in Chapter 8, women were once considered chattel, and it was perfectly proper to discipline spouses as long as no permanent injury was inflicted on the wife.[9] Clear evidence exists that numerous early laws accorded men rights and power over women.[10] The privacy that families enjoyed behind closed doors of the home continued into modern times.

The *Journal of Marriage and the Family* did not even discuss spousal assault until 1971.[11] Slowly, however, scientific data emerged that indicated criminal violence occurred in the home.[12] By the mid-1970s, numerous other studies began to elevate spousal abuse to the status of a national social problem.

Feminist groups, scholars, and other raised the hue and cry in response to this form of criminal conduct. Between 1975 and 1980, forty-four states passed some sort of legislation on domestic violence. Despite the existence of laws regarding spousal abuse, studies have indicated that police have been reluctant to enforce violations of this type of criminal conduct.[13]

No single factor has resulted in this hesitation or reluctance to enforce spousal assault laws.[14] Scholars have examined this phenomenon in detail and have noted a series of influences that have affected police agencies' enforcement of spousal assault. These factors include call screening, beliefs regarding financial hardship on the family in the event of an arrest, the family argument theory, the classification of spousal assault as a misdemeanor, the victim's preference not to arrest, and perceived danger to the police in domestic violence situations.

Numerous police departments have engaged in *call screening. This is downgrading by the law enforcement agency of the service priority assigned to domestic violence calls.* Call screening results in a slower response time by the police officer than for other calls of the same or similar seriousness. This dynamic allows the abuser to beat the victim and leave the scene of the crime before the arrival of the officers. In addition, the failure of police to respond in a timely manner may increase the power of the abuser over the victim and lead the victim to believe that she is truly alone and helpless.

Police officers are reluctant to arrest the abuser in the mistaken belief that an arrest would pose a financial hardship on the family. *An arrest is the taking of a person into custody in the manner prescribed by law.* In addition, many law enforcement officers believe arrest is a futile act in view of the lack of prosecution and lenient sentences imposed by the courts.

Many officers would make an arrest only if the injury to the victim were severe in their estimation. This is clearly not the law. It does, however, illustrate the thinking and reluctance of police to intervene in a "family argument."[15]

Until recently, another factor affecting the decision to arrest was the statutory limit on arrests for certain types of crimes. Traditionally, criminal violations are divided into two major classifications: felonies and misdemeanors. In the United States, this distinction is spelled out by statute or state constitution.[16] *A felony is considered the most serious type of crime and usually punished by imprisonment in state prison.* Many statutes provide that all other crimes are misdemeanors. *A misdemeanor is considered a less serious type of crime and punished by incarceration in local jails not to exceed one year.* Normally, police may arrest persons who have committed felonies on the basis of reasonable grounds or probable cause. *Probable cause is that set of facts that would lead a reasonable person to believe a crime has been committed by the suspect.* A felony arrest may occur even if the officers did not personally witness the offense. Misdemeanor arrests, on the other hand, require the officers to witness the crime. If they did not see the offense committed, they could request the victim to make a citizen's arrest and then on behalf of the citizen would take the perpetrator into custody.

This distinction in the nature and classification of crimes had a direct impact on the ability of police officers to make arrests for domestic violence assaults.

Many domestic violence disputes involve a battery. Most statutes define a *battery as the unlawful application of force to a person.*[17] Battery is the unlawful touching of another; assault, conversely, does not require any physical touching of the other person.[18] Absent serious injury, many state laws define battery as a misdemeanor. Thus, until recently officers could not make an arrest for spousal assault unless they witnessed the act or the victim was willing to make a citizen's arrest.

The victim's preference not to file charges also affect the police's decision not to arrest the offender.[19] Several studies have indicated that victims of spousal assault often do not want the police to make an arrest.[20] This results in the officers merely admonishing the offender and then leaving the scene of the crime.

Many police officers perceive family disputes as potentially dangerous situations where both the abuser and the victim may turn on the officer. Although there are conflicting studies as to whether family disputes are more dangerous to police officers, the fact that many officers believe this to be the case often results in a delayed response to these types of calls.[21] This perception may also cause officers to delay responding to spousal assault calls until they have a backup unit.

In the past several years, many states have passed mandatory arrest statutes that require the officer to arrest the suspect. These laws allow police to make arrests for misdemeanors not committed in their presence. The passage of these laws and their effectiveness is a subject of debate within the field of criminal justice. The following section discusses the factors that resulted in the passage of these statutes.

Arrest and Other Alternatives

In recent years, victims of spousal abuse have turned to the courts in an attempt to force police departments to arrest the perpetrators of this form of family violence. Increasingly, courts have begun to listen to and rule in favor of the abused on both constitutional and tort grounds. However, lawsuits and personal liability did not result in the amendment of various state statutes mandating arrest of abusers. This development started in 1984 with a federally funded experiment in Minneapolis.

The Minneapolis Experiment

In the area of policing and domestic violence, probably no more controversial study has been conducted than the Minneapolis experiment, which dealt with the effect of arrest on those who batter their spouses. The Dean of Policing and Domestic Violence, Lawrence Sherman, was the architect of the 1984 Minneapolis Domestic Violence Experiment. This study was the first controlled evaluation of the effect of arrest on individuals who commit assaultive types of crimes against their spouses.[22]

The Police Foundation and the Minneapolis Police Department joined forces to conduct a controlled experiment to test the effectiveness of arrest on prevention or deterrence of domestic violence. Funded in part by the National Institute of Justice, the experiment used a lottery system of three possible actions by police when dealing with domestic violence.

FOCUS The Use of Courts as a Last Resort

In recent years, victims of family violence have turned to the courts in an attempt to require law enforcement departments to provide effective intervention and protection against spousal assault.

In *Raucci v Town of Rotterdam,* a federal court ruled that the municipality owed a battered woman a special duty to protect her from her estranged husband because of actions by the police department that had assured her of protection.* In spite of these assurances, the husband killed their six-year-old son and-wounded the wife. The court upheld a verdict awarding the wife damages.

In *Watson v City of Kansas City,* a federal court ruled that the victim could proceed with her suit against the police department.† Nancy Watson was married to a Kansas City police officer who abused her and her son on numerous occasions. When she requested assistance from the police, they refused to help and threatened to take her child away and arrest her. After being raped and battered by her husband, she escaped and he committed suicide. She sued the police department for a denial of equal protection.[24]

In *Calloway v Kinkelaar,* the Supreme Court of Illinois discussed municipalities' liability for willful and wanton conduct on the part of its agents.‡ The victim had obtained a restraining order that had been served on her husband. He violated the order by calling her and threatening her and her child. She notified the sheriffs department of the threats and his location, but they failed to take the abuser into custody. He subsequently kidnapped the victim, but she was able to escape when state troopers stopped the perpetrator at a roadblock. She sued the county and the county sheriff, alleging willful and wanton conduct for failing to protect her from being abducted by her husband. The Supreme Court of Illinois allowed the action, stating that the state's Domestic Violence Act allowed such an action for civil damages.

In *Campbell v Campbell,* the plaintiff sued her former husband, certain police officers, and the City of Plainfield.§ The victim brought a negligence suit against the city and its police officers after they responded to a disturbance call and failed to arrest the estranged husband. The police told the abuser to leave and he did, but a short time later he returned and shot the victim. There was a restraining order on file, and a copy had been served on the husband and the police department. The New Jersey court held that the city and police had constructive notice of the existence of the restraining order and that they were negligent in failing to arrest the perpetrator.

Simpson v City of Miami involved a wrongful death lawsuit filed against the City of Miami and its police department.‖ The victim called the police department to complain that the perpetrator was violating a restraining order. A Miami police officer showed up and arrested the abuser but later released him after he promised not to contact the victim. The next day, the perpetrator shot and killed the victim. The heir filed suit, claiming that the City of Miami had violated a duty of care owed to the victim. The Florida Supreme Court agreed, holding that once an officer had taken the perpetrator into custody because of a violation of a domestic abuse restraining order, a special relationship was formed that required the officer to act in a manner to protect the victim from injury by that perpetrator.

* 902 F. 2d 1050 (1990);

† 520 N.Y. S. 2d 352 (1987);

‡ 659 N. E. 2nd 1322 (1995);

§ 682 A. 2d 272 (1996); and

‖ 22 *Florida L. Weekly* D2313 (Fla. App. 3rd Dist. October 1, 1997).

Police officers responding to a domestic disturbance were required to use one of the following options:

1. Arrest with at least one night incarceration,
2. Sending the offender away from the scene of the disturbance or arresting him if he refused to leave,
3. Or giving the couple some form of advice including mediation.

The officers were not allowed to select which opinion would be used; rather, they carried a pad of forms that listed the available options. Whenever they encountered a situation that met the experiment's criteria, they were required to use the option listed on the top form.

The experiment involved only misdemeanor batteries where both the victim and the suspect were present when the officers arrived at the scene of the disturbance. Cases involving serious threats or danger to the victim were excluded, as were situations in which the victim demanded that the officers arrest the suspect.

After the officers finished their assignments, they turned in a brief report to the researchers for follow-up. The research staff used two measures to determine the amount of repeated violence by the offenders: official police reports and victim interviews. Official police reports were monitored to determine whether the suspect committed another similar offense within a specified time period. In addition, the research staff contacted the victims and conducted a detailed interview and subsequent interviews for a period of twenty-four weeks after the initial offense.

The experiment produced a sample of 314 cases that met all the criteria. The results indicated that the arrest option produced the lowest percentage of repeated violence of all the alternatives. Official police reports revealed that 10 percent of the arrested suspects committed a subsequent offense, 24 percent of those suspects who were sent from the home repeated acts of violence against their spouses, and 19 percent of the suspects who were advised by the officers committed another offense. Interviews with victims produced even more dramatic percentages: 19 percent of the arrest suspects, 33 percent of those suspects sent from the home, and 37 percent of those advised by the officers committed another offense.

On the basis of the results of the study, Sherman and his colleagues made three recommendations. The first and probably the least controversial of these alternatives was to change existing laws to allow the police to make warrantless arrests for misdemeanor spousal assaults not committed in their presence. The second recommendation implied that mandatory arrest was the preferred option in most cases of domestic violence. The final recommendation suggested that additional experiments be conducted in other cities to validate the results of the Minneapolis study.

The Minneapolis experiment acted as an agent for change within the criminal justice system. Armed with its results, advocates of mandatory arrest and other sanctions were able to find support in various state legislatures for long overdue reform of criminal statutes dealing with domestic violence. Eleven states adopted legislation that authorized warrantless arrest in misdemeanor domestic violence cases, and another sixteen states enacted mandatory arrest laws in family violence situations.[23]

Prior to the experiment, only 10 percent of police departments serving cities over 100,000 in population encouraged their officers to make arrests in domestic violence situations. Within five years of the announcement of the results of the experiment, 84 percent of all major police departments in the United States had adopted a policy that stated arrest was the preferred option in domestic violence situations.[24]

The Minneapolis experiment was hailed as a breakthrough study of domestic violence as well as criticized by a number of prominent scholars as inadequate and flawed.[25] In retrospect, it may not matter whether the results of the study were accurate. Its greatest contribution may be that it generated an incredible amount of debate within academia and the law enforcement profession as to how to respond to domestic violence.

Other Replications

One of the direct results of the Minneapolis experiment was the funding of additional replications by the National Institute of Justice. Five additional studies were undertaken in the following locations: Metro-Dade (Miami), Colorado Springs, Milwaukee, Omaha, and Charlotte. What was consistent about these additional studies was the finding of inconsistency in the deterrent effect of arrest.

The Metro-Dade experiment established two major categories with two subgroups under each of these categories. The two major subdivisions were those suspects who were arrested and those who were not arrested. Each of these groups was further divided into subgroups that did or did not receive follow-up counseling by specially trained police officers.[26] The Metro-Dade experiment clearly supports the theory that arrest is a deterrent to future domestic violence.

The Colorado Springs experiment employed four options in its replication: arrest and issuance of a restraining order, counseling for the offender and issuance of a restraining order, issuance of a restraining order, and restoring order at the scene of the crime without arrest or use of a restraining order. The Colorado Springs study supports the hypothesis that arrest in some situations does in fact act as a deterrent to future violence.[27]

The Milwaukee experiment was carried out in a city that in May 1986 had adopted a citywide policy of mandatory arrest for domestic violence cases.[28] However, the study did not involve arrests of all offenders. Rather, it utilized three options: full arrest, short arrest, and warning. The full arrest involved taking the suspect into custody pursuant to existing policy and allowing him bail in the amount of $250. The short arrest required officers to arrest the suspect but allowed him to be released on his own recognizances, preferably within two hours after arrest. The last option used a standard warning of arrest, being that if the officers had to return to the location anytime during the same day, an arrest would be made.

The results were obtained by a review of police records and follow-up interviews with the victims. The researchers found a clear initial deterrent in both the full-arrest and the short-arrest situations. However, this deterrence did not last, and there appeared to be no long-term difference between the arrest options and the warning option.

The original Minneapolis study and the three replications might lead one to conclude that arrest does in fact deter either short-term or long-term spousal assault. Unfortunately, the Omaha and Charlotte replications came to the opposite conclusion. These studies were conducted in the same manner as the other replications but indicated that arrest does not deter future violence.

The Omaha experiment randomly assigned eligible police calls regarding domestic violence into three categories when both the suspect and the victim were present.[29] These classifications were arrest, separation, or mediation. In those cases in which the suspect had already left the scene of the crime when the police arrived, the police randomly assigned him to a warrant group or a no warrant group.

The results of the experiment were measured in two ways: review of police reports and victim interviews. Contrary to the Minneapolis experiment, the Omaha study concluded that arrest of a suspect at the scene of the domestic assault was not a greater deterrent than the other two options.[30] However, the issuance of a warrant for an offender who was absent from the scene of the crime at the time the officers arrived did appear to significantly extend the time frame in which the victim was free from further violence.

The Charlotte experiment tested three distinct alternatives to domestic violence.[31] Police responses included advising the couple, issuing a citation to the offender, or arresting the offender. Excluded from the study were situations in which the victim insisted on the arrest of the suspect, the suspect threatened or assaulted the officer, or the officer believed the victim to be in imminent danger. Similar to the other replications, the Charlotte study evaluated the effect of these alternatives using only two methods: police reports and victim interviews. The results indicated that no significant difference existed between advising, citing, or arresting the offender.

All these replications indicate that there is no clear answer as to whether arrest deters those who commit spousal assault. Scholars have found different interpretations in the data collected by these studies. Some authorities suggest that arrest may have a harmful effect on the victim because statistics support the position that arrest may lead to future violence rather than deter spousal assault. Others have hypothesized that arrest will deter certain types of suspects such as those who are employed or have something to lose as a result of arrest. What is needed is more study in this area of domestic violence. If arresting the offender does not prevent spousal assault, other alternatives must be sought in order to determine whether other mechanisms can stop this form of family violence.

Alternatives to Arrest

Most people know someone who has "talked their way out of a speeding ticket." This doesn't mean that the individual did not violate a law or that he or she is especially glib. Rather, it means that, for whatever reason, the police officer decided to exercise discretion not to give the offender a ticket. This exercise of discretion is an integral part of police work.

In the area of spousal assault, at least one authority has examined the use of police discretion and mediation as an alternative solution to family violence.[32]

Mediation is a private, informal dispute resolution process where a neutral third person, the mediator, helps disputing parties reach an agreement. Prior to the Minneapolis study, Lerman points out that most law enforcement agencies used mediation in an attempt to deal with spousal abuse. Law enforcement agencies across the United States trained their officer in dispute resolution techniques specifically in the area of domestic violence. Officers attempted to use crisis intervention techniques to solve the problem in the home rather than take any formal action.

Although mediation is an excellent dispute resolution for business and labor, it was doomed to failure in domestic violence situations. Mediation assumes that each party is equal or nearly equal in power, status, or need. Further, mediation requires that parties negotiate as equals and reach an agreement that will serve their own best interests. Informal mediation does not result in an enforceable agreement. Therefore, either party, specifically the abuser, can break this agreement without facing any sanctions.

Thus, informal mediation does not work as an alternative to decreasing or ending spousal assault. However, a variation of the mediation concept is now employed in some jurisdictions that does establish accountability and attempts to place the parties in a more equal bargaining position. Using the court system, law enforcement officials and prosecutors are able to require counseling of both the abuser and the victim. This concept will be discussed in more detail later in this chapter.

Goolkasian in *Confronting Domestic Violence* recommends a series of steps that all police officers can take on arrival at the scene of the crime.[33] These steps may be used whether or not the suspect is arrested. They provide the victim of the crime with support and encouragement that are critical to her.

Medical care: Often, the officer will be able to observe that the victim needs medical attention. On other occasions, the victim may claim that she needs medical attention although no injuries are visible. Many abusers are adept at inflicting injuries that are not visible to the naked eye. Officers should always inquire whether the victim needs medical attention, and, if the answer is yes, they should arrange for transportation of the victim to an emergency room.

Transportation: In addition to transporting the victim for medical assistance, officers can provide for transportation of the victim to a battered women's shelter. Officers may either personally transport the victim to these shelters or make arrangements to meet staff from the shelter and turn the victim over to their care.

Requiring the suspect to leave the residence: In the event that the suspect cannot be arrested, officers should as a minimum request that the offender leave the premises. If he refuses to leave and the victim, rather than the offender, is entitled to possession of the residence, officers can then arrest the suspect on trespassing charges.

Ensuring the victim's safety if she leave the residence: If the victim desires to leave the premises, officers should stand by to ensure that she can leave with her personal property without interference from the suspect.

Advising the victim on her legal options and community resources: Many departments have developed handbooks, brochures, and other materials that officers can give to victims of spousal assault. This information provides a list of resources that specialize in assisting battered spouses. Caution must be used when adopting this alternative because many victims will be highly emotional and incapable of reading material.

Case follow-up information: In addition to advising the victim of community support resources, officers should leave their cards and other information with the victim so that she can request follow-up information.

None of these options will stop or deter future spousal abuse. However, they do provide support to the victim and offer her alternatives to staying in an environment that places her at risk.

Another alternative to arresting the abusive spouse is the concept Sherman calls "Smart Policing."[34] This approach is based on his analysis of arrest and its effect on future violence. Sherman would have legislatures and police take the following steps:

1. Authorize police to make warrantless arrests in domestic violence situations. Although most states now allow police to make such arrests, several states have not enacted this type of legislation. Because some evidence suggests that arrest deters spousal assault, police should be empowered to take this step if they believe it is necessary.
2. State statutes that mandate arrest should be amended to require mandatory action from a list of alternatives. Sherman argues that there is evidence that in some cases arrest may cause more harm to the victim. He would repeal mandatory arrest policies and substitute a list of actions that allow the officers more discretion.
3. The range of options in domestic assault cases should include the following:

    a. Offering to transport the victim to a shelter.
    b. Transporting the victim or the suspect to a detoxication treatment center.
    c. Allowing the victim to decide whether arrest should be made.
    d. Mobilizing the victim's own social network to provide short-term protection.

4. Police and prosecutors should develop offender-absent warrant procedures. Although Sherman urges caution in this approach, he points out that many domestic violence calls involve situations where the suspect has already left the scene of the crime by the time the police arrive. In view of the results, though tentative, of the Omaha replication, offender-absent arrest warrant procedures should be pursued by police and prosecutors.
5. Police should not be held civilly liable for failure to prevent domestic homicide or serious injury because of failure to make arrests in spousal assault situations. Sherman cites statistics to support his position that not one of the victims in the Minneapolis experiment was murdered.
6. Police should continue to examine various alternatives in an effort to identify chronically violent couples and their residences. Sherman argues that this is an area that needs special attention by the police and suggests that every large department detail at least one officer to identify chronically violent couples and work with them.

7. Police should advise victims that restraining orders may have limited value and not provide the victim with any substantial protection. Sherman states that the administration of restraining orders is still experiencing major problems and that officers should not offer false hope to victims by suggesting that a restraining order will solve their problems or keep the suspect at bay.
8. Police and victim-rights advocates should continue to lobby Congress for additional funds to continue research in this area.

Although Sherman's approach has it supporters, several of its steps seem to ignore basic constitutional principles and other accepted research about family violence. For instance, the idea of using the victim's own social network may not be feasible because many abusers isolate their victims, and thus the victim has nowhere or no one to turn to in times of crisis. Additionally, the granting of immunity from civil action to police for failure to respond in certain situations goes against existing U.S. Supreme Court decisions that cannot be changed by merely amending certain statutes. The Supreme Court has found that citizens have certain constitutional rights, and these rights cannot be abridged by legislative or other action.[35]

There are alternatives other than arrest of the offender. These include social support systems that may provide either short-term or long-term relief to the victim. Police officers should be aware of these resources in order that they can properly advise the victim regarding these support systems.

Many cities and agencies have established telephone hotlines for battered spouses. These hotlines are often operated by shelters and provide the victim with information on alternative housing, employment, financial aid, legal aid, counseling, and other forms of emotional support. Hotlines are often a spouse's first attempt at reaching out from her isolation in an effort to save herself from further battering.

Shelters provide a safe haven for victims of spousal assault. These shelters are operated by charities or other private groups. They may offer counseling, child care, or even have a victim's rights advocate on staff. The victim may find the support in these shelters necessary to make the final break with the abuser.

Numerous other community groups provide support for victims of spousal assault. These groups may work with shelters to provide counseling and advocacy for victims of spousal assault.

The San Diego Police and Phoenix police departments are examples of law enforcement agencies that are taking a holistic approach to spousal abuse. These agencies involve social workers and prosecutors who work with law enforcement officers from the start of the case. Services are housed in a central location, and some cities include child protection services (CPS) workers, physicians, sexual assault experts, and various victim service providers.[36]

It should be obvious that none of the alternatives to arrest will completely stop or deter future spousal assault. Sufficient information is not available at this stage in research to propose a single approach to this problem. However, recent changes in the law do offer victims other options.

Federal Legislation

In 1994, Congress enacted the Violent Crime Control and Law Enforcement Act, Title IV of which is called the Violence Against Women Act (VAWA). Congress mandated that various professions form partnerships and work together to respond to all forms of violence against women.

The U.S. attorney general is required to make a report to Congress annually on the grants that are awarded under the act and ensure that research examining violence against women is encouraged. The report must include the number of grants, funds distributed, and other statistical information. Additionally, the report must assess the effectiveness of any programs that are funded under VAWA.

The act provides funding for a variety of research-based studies. It also requires that federal agencies engage in research regarding violence against women. For example, the National Institute of Justice is mandated to conduct four important projects: the development of a research agenda that will address violence with particular emphasis on underserved populations, the assessment of establishing state databases to record the number of sexual and domestic violence incidents, a study to determine how abusive partners obtain addresses of their victims, and examination with other agencies of battered woman syndrome.[37]

The National Domestic Violence Hotline (800-799-SAFE) was established in 1996 under the authority set forth in VAWA. The hotline was cited by President Bill Clinton in his 1997 National Crime Victims' Rights Week proclamation as having already responded to 73,000 calls for assistance from across the United States.

It is now a federal crime to enter or leave Native American reservations or cross state lines to injure and intimidate partner. The injury must be physical, and the abuser must have intended to commit the crime when he or she crossed the state line.[38] It is also a federal crime to cross a state line or to enter or leave Native American reservations and violate a restraining order. This law also requires that the perpetrator intended to violate the order when crossing the state line.[39] One of the most far-reaching and controversial laws makes it a federal crime to possess a firearm after conviction of a qualifying misdemeanor crime of domestic violence. The controversial aspect of this law is that it applies to law enforcement officers.[40] In some jurisdictions, police officers have been placed on light duty or terminated because they had a prior conviction and now cannot carry a weapon.

Although not a federal statute, model codes have affected the practice of law for many years. The Model Domestic Violence Code, drafted by the National Council of Juvenile and Family Court Judges, was presented to the National Conference of State Legislatures in 1994.[41] Several portions of the model code have been enacted into law in some jurisdictions.

Restraining Orders

Restraining orders (protective orders) are court orders that prohibit the offender from having any contact with the victim.[42] They are civil versus criminal and require a judge to rule that sufficient evidence supports the issuance of such an order. These orders are now available in forty-eight states and the District of Columbia. They offer the option of preventing contact such as harassment or threats that might ordinarily lead to an escalation of emotions and future violence. As the following discussion indicates, research is inconclusive regarding the effectiveness of this unique tool in preventing spousal abuse.

Background and Use of Restraining Orders

In the past, problems with the use of restraining orders stemmed from lack of clarity in the law and police unfamiliarity with this civil sanction. In 1983, only seventeen states provided protection against abuse from individuals who were living together but not married. However, by 1988, twenty-two states had added such protection to their statutes authorizing restraining orders.

The use and nature of restraining orders vary from state to state. Most states now authorize persons who are married, related by blood, or cohabitants to request the issuance of such an order. Six types of behavior may be prohibited by a restraining order:

1. Protection against physical assault
2. Threatened physical abuse
3. Attempted physical abuse
4. Sexual assault of an adult
5. Sexual assault of a child
6. Damage to personal property of the victim

As this list indicates, restraining orders may be issued for a wide variety of acts committed by the offender. However, simply having the order issued does not solve the problem. Due process requires that the offender be served with a copy of the order for it to be effective.

Most states provide for the issuance of temporary or emergency restraining orders. These orders are issued by a judge and usually require the threat of immediate injury to the victim. The U.S. Supreme Court has upheld the issuance of these ex parte type of orders if the request includes specific facts that justify the relief, the notice and opportunity for a full hearing are given as soon as practicable, and the order is issued by a judge.[43]

In most jurisdictions, police officers or process servers are responsible for serving restraining orders. There are five basic methods of service of a temporary or emergency restraining order: personal service, informing the offender of the existence of the order, leaving a copy with the victim so that she can serve the offender, posting of the notice and order at the residence of the victim, and mailing a copy of the order via certified mail to the offender.

Some police departments have established procedures where officers can contact judges while they are at the scene of a domestic dispute and have the judge authorize the issuance of such an order by way of telephone. The officer then serves the suspect at the scene and requires him to leave the premises. Once a temporary order is issued, it becomes effective immediately and is valid until a formal hearing can be held, at which time the abuser has a right to contest the allegations made by the victim. However, the issuance of the temporary order prevents the offender from having any contact with the victim until the formal hearing.

Restraining orders may provide different forms of relief for the victim of spousal assault. The traditional and most common form of relief is a no-contact order that prevents the offender from having any form of contact with the victim at her residence, work, or anywhere else. This no-contact order includes telephonic, written, and physical contacts. Many orders will set forth specific conditions regarding the visitation of any children that may be involved in the situation. Some will designate certain locations for the visit, and others will require that the offender not consume any alcohol or drugs prior to the visit. Most statutes authorize the court to require counseling for both parties. Even if the counseling does not solve the immediate problem, it is a very visible sign of the authority of the court and should serve as a constant reminder to the offender of the power that the court now has over his existence.

In the event that the abuser violates the restraining order, many statutes authorize charging the offender with civil contempt, criminal contempt, or a misdemeanor violation of a court order. Although police officers cannot normally arrest a person charged with civil contempt, the court may order that the offender pay a fine and serve a period of incarceration. Criminal contempt, if authorized by state statute, would allow officers to arrest the offender if they found him in violation of the order. Criminal contempt in many jurisdictions is treated as a misdemeanor. However, many restraining order statutes allow officers to make warrantless arrests in these situations. If the violation of the order is considered a misdemeanor, many statutes also authorize the warrantless arrest of the offender.

Temporary restraining orders do not solve spousal abuse. As the next section discusses, problems continue to exist with the use of this form of sanction.

Advantages and Disadvantages

Restraining orders provide the victim with another option in lieu of arrest. The use of restraining orders has several advantages.[44] Most arrests result in the offender being released in a matter of hours or within a few days at the most. A restraining order can be valid for an extended period of time, up to a year in most cases.

Arrests may result in the loss of employment, which might increase the tension that already exists in the relationship.Restraining orders do not preclude the offender from continuing his employment but do prevent him from living with the victim.

Restraining orders carry the weight and gravity of a judicial edict, and some offenders may think twice before violating a court order. Although some offenders may have had numerous contacts with police and the judicial system, most have not been involved with a direct order from a judge banning certain conduct. The specter of facing a judge after violating a judicial order may act as a deterrent for some abusers.

Just as there are advantages in this form of protection, so are there serious potential disadvantages in relying solely on the use of restraining orders in this area of family violence. The most obvious and threatening is that the offender may simply ignore the order, with injury to the victim resulting. A restraining order is merely a piece of paper that carries only as much force and effect as the offender attaches to it. If he chooses to ignore it, there is no protection for the victim unless she can contact the police and they can arrive and intercede before the abuser attacks and harms her.

There are additional disadvantages to the use of restraining orders. Many of these weaknesses are written into the very statutes that were enacted to protect the victim. Some statutes require the payment of a filing fee prior to issuance of a restraining order. Although most jurisdictions allow for the waiver of the fee if the victim cannot afford to pay it, some include the income of the abuser in determining if the fee can be waived. The cost of such fees act as a deterrent to requesting a restraining order.

Some statutes require court or county clerks to assist the victim in filling out the forms requesting the restraining order. However, no state provides funds or mandates special training for these clerks in this sensitive function. Most spousal assault occurs in the evening or on the weekend after the courts are closed. Only twenty-three states provide for the issuance of emergency orders after normal working hours. Thus, during the victim's greatest time of need, no alternative is available to obtain restraining orders.

Most states require personal service of the order for them to become effective. However, many offenders are difficult to locate, and therefore the victim is not protected until the abuser has been served. There is a lack of monitoring of compliance with restraining orders. If the offender can convince or threaten the victim to remain silent, neither law enforcement officers nor the court will be aware if he violates the order. Although there are serious problems with restraining orders, they do provide some victims of spousal assault with an option that may protect them.

Effectiveness of Restraining Orders

The effectiveness of restraining orders depends on a variety of factors, including how specific and comprehensive the orders are and how well they are enforced. In an effort to understand how effective restraining orders are from the victim's perspective, scholars studied the restraining order process in three jurisdictions.[45] These jurisdictions were the District of Columbia superior court, the family court in Wilmington, Delaware, and the county court in Denver. The researchers contacted 285 women who had filed for restraining orders. They used telephone interviews, follow-up interviews, records from the civil case, and criminal records of the men named in the orders.

In most cases, victims felt that restraining orders protected them against repeated incidents of physical and psychological abuse and were valuable in assisting them in regaining a sense of well-being. However, a restraining order against an abuser with a history of violent offenses was not as likely to be effective. Before receiving a restraining order, victims experienced abuse ranging from intimidation to injury with a weapon. Researchers found that 37 percent of the women had been threatened or injured with a weapon; more than half had been beaten or choked, and 99 percent had suffered other forms of intimidation, including threats, stalking, and harassment.

Seventy-two percent of the victims in the initial interviews stated that the restraining order was effective and reported no continuing problems. However, in several instances, a small percentage of the victims experienced continuing acts of abuse ranging from continuing calls at work or home, stalking of the victim, repeated physical abuse, and continuing psychological abuse. As this research indicates, in many instances, restraining orders may prove effective; however, there are situations in which the abuser will simply ignore the order and continue or escalate the abuse.

Courts and Spousal Assault

Spousal assault does not end with an arrest or with the issuance of a restraining order. A necessary part of this process is the court's and prosecutor's responses to this form of family violence. It is appropriate that the prosecution of spousal assault be examined in this chapter because law enforcement and the criminal justice system are closely tied together. This section examines the judicial system's reactions to spousal assault and how cases are processed, from the screening of reports to the presentation of evidence in a trial.

Introduction

Spousal assault is a crime. In almost every jurisdiction, the striking of another person is a misdemeanor and may be a felony if there is serious physical injury. However, making an act a crime does not mean that it will be prosecuted. Sherman and Beck pointed out in the Minneapolis experiment that only 3 of the 136 suspects who were arrested were ever fined or incarcerated.[46] This is not the type of statistic that promotes confidence in the ability of police to protect the victim from further injury.

The face very few spousal assault cases are prosecuted is not a newly discovered fact. The judicial system's apparent indifference to victims of family violence is well known. This indifference resulted in the U.S. Attorney General's Task Force on Family Violence recommending that prosecutors establish special units to prosecute family violence cases.[47] The report states:

> *Staffed with both attorneys and victim assistance professionals or volunteers, the unit should review all law enforcement reports involving incidents of family violence whenever possible. . . . The attorneys of the unit develop an expertise in dealing with family violence that results in more accurate case evaluation and more effective prosecution. The creation of a special unit also fosters the development of an individual bond of trust and concern between the victim and a prosecutor sensitive to the complexities of family violence.*[48]

Many prosecutors' offices in major cities have adopted the attorney general's recommendation. The office of the district attorney in San Francisco, for example, has established filing and charging policies that recognize the unique nature of domestic violence.[49] This policy states:

> *Special care will be taken to insure that [domestic violence] cases are treated as crimes against the state and prosecuted to the fullest extent in order to avoid continuation and escalation of the violence.*[50]

The prosecution of spousal assault cases requires that prosecutors understand the dynamics involved in this form of family violence and be willing to approach them in a sensitive manner. Spousal assault is a crime against the state. However, the close relationship between the victim and the offender presents unique victim/witness problems.

Prosecution of Spousal Assault

Prosecution *can be defined as a proceeding instituted and carried on by due course of law before a competent tribunal for the purpose of determining the guilt or innocence of a person charged with a crime.*[51] All criminal cases are prosecuted by an authorized agent of the state. Normally, this person is called the district attorney or prosecuting attorney. Some jurisdictions have highly trained career civil servants who are attorneys admitted to practice law and whose full-time job is to prosecute cases. Other jurisdictions use attorneys who practice civil law on the side and hold office as the prosecutor on a part-time basis. Many of these smaller offices are not automated and have not had the luxury of specializing in any particular area of criminal law. These prosecutors are truly jacks-of-all-trades and prosecute any criminal violation that occurs within their jurisdictions.

The prosecution of any criminal offense including a spousal assault case starts with a *case screening* by the prosecutor. A case may arrive at the district attorney's office in one of two ways: A private citizen, in some cases the victim, may file a complaint, or the police may bring a case to the prosecutor. In either situation, the prosecutor assigned to screen the case *will review the facts and evaluate those facts to determine whether the defendant has violated a criminal statute.*

Once the police forward a case to the prosecutor's office or a citizen's complaint is received, a decision must be made whether to file the case and what type of charges, felony or misdemeanor, should be filed. That decision is a crucial one in a prosecutor's office. In deciding whether to issue the case as a felony or misdemeanor, the prosecutor should review the following facts:

1. The extent of any injuries
2. Whether the defendant intended to inflict serious bodily injury
3. The use of a deadly weapon
4. Threats made to the victim, children, family, or friends of the victim
5. Prior incidents of violence on the part of the defendant
6. The defendant's use of drugs or alcohol
7. The defendant's present and past mental state
8. Any other facts that concern possible danger to the victim or others[52]

Although some of these factors may not be admissible as evidence during the criminal trial, they are important for a prosecutor to consider in exercising his or her discretion as it elates to the type or seriousness of the charge to be filed.

Filing of Criminal Charges

The case may be filed as either a misdemeanor or a felony, depending on the state statute and seriousness of the offense. The defendant may be in custody or surrender to the police at this time. An arrest warrant may be issued for his apprehension at this time.

↓

Arraignment

This is the first formal appearance of the defendant in the criminal justice system. It is at this hearing that he will enter a plea to the charges. The defendant may enter a plea of not guilty, guilty, or nolo contendre.[55] At this hearing, an attorney will be appointed to represent him if he cannot afford to hire an attorney.

↓

Bail Hearing

In many jurisdictions, this hearing occurs at the same tine as the formal arraignment. At this hearing, the court will establish bail to ensure the future appearances of the defendant.[56]

↓

Trial

This may be a trial in front of a judge or a jury, depending on the desires of the defendant. After the prosecution has presented its evidence, the defendant may present any evidence he desires.

↓

Verdict: Guilt or Not Guilty

After considering the evidence, the trier of fact, being either the judge or the jury, will render a verdict of guilty or not guilty.

↓

Sentencing

If the defendant is found not guilty, this ends the process. If he is found guilty, the judge may ask for a presentencing report from the probation department. After receiving this report, the court will impose whatever it considers an appropriate sentence.

FIGURE 9.1 The Criminal Justice Process

One factor that is conspicuously absent from this list is the desires of the victim. Some jurisdictions take the position that if the act is a crime, the victim is merely a witness to the crime and the state is the victim. Others believe the victim should have input into the charging process and be involved in all stages of the prosecution.[53]

Once the decision has been made to file criminal charges, the normal criminal justice process begins. It is not necessary to explain in detail how the criminal justice system functions. There are several excellent introductory texts available that go into great detail regarding this facet of the legal system.[54] However, in order to place spousal abuse in its proper perspective in this ungainly and often slow-moving bureaucracy, Figure 9.1 presents a simplified overview of this process.

During this process, the offender may have an opportunity to avoid prosecution by agreeing to counseling regarding family violence. Many jurisdictions offer a person accused of spousal assault the opportunity to obtain counseling and avoid a criminal trial. This process in many jurisdictions is known as diversion. *Diversion allows the offender to attend an education or counseling program rather than being processed in the criminal justice system.* Some programs require that the defendant first plead guilty. After he successfully completes that program, the guilty plea is withdrawn and the case dismissed. Other jurisdictions allow the defendant to waive his right to a speedy trial and attend counseling, and the case is then dismissed after the offender has completed the program. Several variations on the diversion process are implemented throughout the United States. Its purpose is to afford individuals the opportunity to receive education or counseling regarding their problems and to keep them out of the criminal justice system.[57]

It is not uncommon for victims of spousal assault to be reluctant to testify against their spouses. Some of the more common reasons include fear of the offender, shame for being a victim in a close personal relationship with the assailant, distrust of the police and the court process, a desire to put the entire episode behind them and forget it occurred, and a belief that somehow their own behavior caused the attack.[58]

Almost all victims of violent crimes have a fear of the court and the perpetrator. However, victims of spousal assault have other valid reasons for fearing possible retribution by the defendant. He knows her residence and work address, professional habits, friends, and family. And she knows by experience his violent nature and the possible injuries that this person is capable of inflicting.

Therefore, some prosecutors' offices have established guidelines for questioning reluctant victims. These guidelines serve several purposes: They are a checklist that allows the prosecutor to establish the facts of the assault by asking certain questions; if the victim has changed her story, these questions may explain why that has occurred; and, finally, they inform the judge or jury of the victim's feelings and fears. The following is a series of questions or guidelines that prosecutors might use in questioning a victim of spousal abuse:

- Would you prefer to talk with the judge privately in his chambers?
- Are you aware that you are under oath to tell the truth?
- Are you aware that the People of the State of California are bringing these charges and that the decision to prosecute the defendant is up to the prosecutor rather than you?
- (If the victim is subpoenaed) You don't want to be here do you? Why are you here: ("Because I was subpoenaed by you"—this helps protect the victim from the defendant).
- Are you aware that the fact that you have been subpoenaed means that you have been called as a witness, that you must testify, and that you may be held in contempt if you do not do so?
- Why do you feel reluctant to (or refuse to) testify?

- When did you become reluctant (or decide to refuse) to testify?
- Were you living with the defendant when the incident happened?
- Are you now living with the defendant or with the defendant's family?
- (If not,) does the defendant know where you are staying?
- Are you financially dependent on the defendant?
- Do you and the defendant have children together?
- Have you discussed the case with the defendant?
- Has the defendant made any promises to do something for you if you do not testify?
- Is that promise to do something the reason you do not wish to proceed or testify?
- Has the defendant or anyone else threatened you or told you not to testify or told you to tell us a different version of what really happened?
- Has the defendant or anyone else threatened your children, family, or close friends?
- Is there some other reason why you are afraid of the defendant?
- Are you aware that this court can issue an order telling the defendant to stay away from you and have no contact with you or your family?
- Are you aware that if the case is prosecuted, the defendant can be required to get counseling, pay for your damages, and stay away from you and your family?
- (If injuries are alleged or visible) How did you receive the injuries (allude to police reports, medical reports, photos, injuries still visible in court, and so on)?
- Have you talked about your desire not to testify or to change your version of what happened with the victim/witness staff or staff of the local domestic violence agency?
- If not, would you be willing to talk with them now?
- Would you like the bailiff or officer to escort you when you leave court today?[59]

As with any checklist, discretion must be used when employing it. However, the items do establish guidelines that allow the prosecutor to present the evidence of the assault in a logical manner. If victims are concerned or express fear about the criminal justice system to police or other professionals, consideration should be given to referring them to victim advocates.

The use of family violence victim advocates is absolutely critical to the effective prosecution of spousal abuse cases. These individuals, whether employed by a public agency or private social services organization, offer a personal support system for the victim. Some state statutes require prosecutors' offices to use victim advocates in this role.[60]

Victim advocates provide invaluable services to spousal assault victims. The advocate can work with the victim by accompanying her to any interview, informing her of court procedures, and explaining the criminal justice operation. The advocate can also provide a source of emotional support to the victim. The advocate in effect becomes a human link between the victim and an impersonal legal system. The advocate may also assist the victim by preparing her for court. The advocate might, for example, accompany the victim to a pretrial visit to the courtroom and explain the functions of the various parties. Finally, and perhaps most important, the victim advocate can supply the victim with information on community and criminal justice support providers. This information may range from the names and locations of support groups to the victim's right to file claims for compensation from the state for injuries.

Family Violence Courts

Some jurisdictions have created specialized courts to process family violence cases and intensive systemic reforms designed to revise the components of the criminal and civil systems to ensure that proper sanctions and other relief is accorded to victims of family violence.[61] Programs such as the Dade County, Florida, Domestic Violence Court (DCDVC) embed legal protections in a web of social control that reinforces the message of treatment and the threat of criminal punishment. The DCDVC is a criminal court with a civil component designed by a team of representatives from every segment of the criminal justice system to serve as a coordinated, systemic response to the treatment of family violence cases in the courts. The DCDVC represents an innovative, interdisciplinary, and integrated systemwide approach, consisting of a team of criminal justice system professionals, to the treatment of misdemeanor cases, civil protection orders, and the violation of those orders.

The members of the court, led by the judiciary, work together as a team toward the shared goal of reducing family violence. From arrest to the completion of a sentence, only judges who are specially trained in family violence handle these cases. The founders of DCDVC believe that the combination of intensive victim services, treatment for the abusers, and an active informed judiciary can improve the control of misdemeanor family violence cases. The court is based on the following principles:

- The administration of justice should expand the traditional role of the criminal justice system, which has traditionally been concerned with punishment but which has failed to consider the role of treatment in family violence cases.
- There is an emphasis on the needs of children who live in violent homes. Parents are educated about the effects of family violence on their children.
- The members of the court acknowledge and accept the responsibility to educate the general public about family violence and the fact that it is a crime.
- The court serves as a catalyst for change as a community leader by coordinating a community-wide approach to combat family violence.
- Judicial education and training in family violence is mandatory for all judges and prosecutors and some public defenders assigned to the DCDVC.

Although the DCDVC represents a giant step forward, much more needs to be accomplished with the court system. For example, the DCDVC deals only with misdemeanors and leaves felonies to the regular criminal court system. Additionally, some judges and prosecutors still do not understand the dynamics of family violence. The court system, by its nature, is tradition bound and slow to change. We must continue to educate our judges, prosecutors, public defenders, and the general public regarding spousal abuse.

Summary

Law enforcement's responsibilities to victims of spousal assault are continually evolving. In the past and in many police departments today, officers are reluctant to become involved in "family disputes."

Several experiments have attempted to gauge the effectiveness of arrest in deterring future spousal assault. Although these experiments often raise more questions than they answer, it is clear that spousal assault is a crime and that professionals must come to some sort of resolution on how to respond to it.

The judicial system is closely linked to law enforcement. In recent years, most states have passed laws in an attempt to protect victims of spousal assault. These laws have ranged from mandatory arrest to the use of restraining orders.

Restraining orders are intended to protect the victim from future injury by the offender. However, some serious shortcomings remain with their operation and effectiveness. These problems can be addressed only by changes in state laws.

Arrest of the defendant in a spousal abuse case is only the first step in the judicial system. Occasionally, victims are reluctant to testify against the defendant. These fears are normal and in most situations justified and valid. Prosecutors must be sensitive to these issues and, if necessary, frame questions in such a manner as to educate the judge or jury of these fears. The case must be issue and tried and the defendant convicted of a crime if the criminal justice system is to fulfill its responsibilities to the victim.

Key Terms

spousal assault—the act of intentionally inflicting physical injury on a spouse or other person who is cohabiting with the abuser.

call screening—downgrading by police departments of the service priority assigned to domestic violence calls.

arrest—the taking of a person into custody in the manner prescribed by law.

felony—considered the most serious type of crime and usually punished by imprisonment in state prison.

misdemeanor—considered a less serious type of crime and punished by incarceration in local jails not to exceed one year.

probable cause—that set of facts that would lead a reasonable person to believe a crime has been committed by the suspect.

battery—the unlawful application of force to a person.

mediation—a private, informal dispute resolution process where a neutral third person, the mediator, helps disputing parties reach an agreement.

restraining orders or protective orders—court orders that prohibit the offender from having any contact with the victim.

prosecution—a proceeding instituted and carried on by due course of law before a competent tribunal for the purpose of determining the guilt or innocence of a person charged with a crime.

case screening—a review and evaluation of facts to determine whether the defendant has violated a criminal statute.

diversion—allows the offender to attend an education or counseling program rather than being processed in the criminal justice system.

Discussion Questions

1. What is the best indicator of the potential for spousal assault? Why do you believe this is more important than any other factor?
2. Do you believe arrest deters future spousal assault? Explain your reasons.
3. Is the use of human subjects without their consent in an experiment ethical? The suspects in the policing and spousal assault experiments were unaware that they were part of the experiment. Would it change your answer if they had been informed of this fact? As a practical matter, how would you inform them?
4. Does your community have victim's advocates? How do they operate? Do you believe they serve a purpose?
5. Should individuals who assault their spouses be subjected to mandatory imprisonment? Why?
6. Do you believe that diversion works?

Practical Application

A professor in your university has received a grant to do a follow-up study on the effects of arrest and prosecution on deterring future spousal assault in your community. Assume that the local police chief and prosecuting attorney have agreed to cooperate in this study.

Your community has a population of 300,000 residents, 1,000 sworn police officers, and 80 deputy district attorneys. Your professor has asked for your input in the following areas of the experiment:

1. How many arrest categories would you recommend? Why?
2. How would the police officers select one of the alternatives?
3. Would you request that the prosecuting attorney participate in the study by not filing charges on some offenders? What are the advantages of this course of action? What are some of the disadvantages.
4. Certain members of the medical profession have objected to this study on ethical grounds. List possible objections and your responses to them.

Suggested Readings

Domestic Violence: The Law and Criminal Prosecution. 2d ed. (The Family Violence Project, San Francisco) 1990.

Black, D. *The Manners and Customs of Police.* (Academic Press, New York) 1980.

Bolton, F. G., and S. R. Bolton. *Working with Violent Families.* (Sage, Newbury Park, California) 1987.

Buzawa, E. S., and C. G. Buzawa. *Domestic Violence: The Criminal Justice Response.* (Sage, Newbury Park, California) 1990.

Buzawa, E. S., and C. G. Buzawa, eds. *Domestic Violence: The Changing Criminal Justice Response.* (Auburn House, Westport, Connecticut) 1992.

Hilton, N. Z., ed. *Legal Responses to Wife Assault.* (Sage, Newbury Park, California) 1993.

LaFave, W. R., and A. W. Scott, Jr. *Criminal Law.* 2d ed. (West, St. Paul) 1986.

Merlo, A. V., J. M. Pollock. *Woman, Law, and Social Control* (Allyn and Bacon, Boston) 1995.

Ohlin, L. and M. Tonry, eds. *Family Violence.* (University of Chicago Press, Chicago) 1989.

Perkins, R. M., and R. N. Boyce. *Criminal Law.* 3d ed. (Foundation Press, New York) 1982.

Schmalleger, F. *Criminal Justice Today.* 2d ed. (Prentice Hall, Englewood Cliffs, New Jersey) 1993.

Sherman, L. W. *Policing Domestic Violence.* (Free Press, New York) 1992.

Siegel, L. J. *Criminology.* 3d ed. (West, St. Paul, Minnesota) 1989.

Steinman, M., ed. *Women Battering: Policy Responses.* (Anderson, Cincinnati) 1991.

Straus, M. A., R. J. Gelles, and S. K. Steinmetz. *Behind Closed Doors: Violence in the American Family.* (Anchor Books, New York) 1980.

Endnotes

1. See, e.g., Sherman, L. W. *Policing Domestic Violence.* (Free Press, New York) 1992; Bolton, F. G., and S. R. Bolton. *Working with Violent Families.* (Sage, Newbury Park, California) 1987; and Buzawa, E. S. and C. G. Buzawa, eds., *Domestic Violence, The Changing Criminal Justice Response.* (Auburn House, Westport, Connecticut) 1992.
2. See Bowman, C. G. "The Arrest Experiments: A Feminist Critique." Vol. 83, No. 1 *The Journal of Criminal Law and Criminology,* (1992) pp. 201–208, where Bowman argues that current research in the area of spousal assault is flawed because it is usually conducted from the abusers perspective, ignores feminist thinking, and does not consider various social factors.
3. The judgement was later reduced to $1.9 million.
4. *Violence between Intimates* (Bureau of Justice Statistics, Selected Findings, Washington, D.C.) November 1994.
5. Sherman, L. W. *Policing Domestic Violence,* (Free Press, New York) 1992, p. 6.
6. Straus, M. A., R. J. Gelles, and S. K. Steinmetz. *Behind Closed Doors: Violence in the American Family.* (Anchor Books, New York) 1980, p. 32.
7. Saunders, D. G. "Husbands Who Assault, Multiple Profiles Requiring Multiple Responses." In N. Z. Hilton, ed. *Legal Responses to Wife Assault.* (Sage, Newbury Park, California) 1993, pp. 9–34.
8. Ibid., pp. 11–16.
9. Frisch, L. A. "Research That Succeeds, Policies That Fail." Vol. 83, No. 1. *The Journal of Criminal Law & Criminology* 1992, p. 209.
10. For an excellent discussion of these laws, see Binder, A., and J. Meeker." The Development of Social Attitudes toward Spousal Abuse." In E. S. Buzawa, and C. G. Buzawa, eds. *Domestic Violence, The Changing Criminal Justice Response.* (Auburn House, Westport, Connecticut) 1992.
11. O'Brien, J. E. "Women Abuse: Facts Replacing Myths." *Journal of Marriage and the Family.* Vol. 33 1971, pp. 362–398.

12. One of the earliest studies in this area was the breakthrough discussion of child abuse by Kempe discussed in Chapter 5.
13. Erez, E. "Intimacy, Violence, and the Police," *Human Relations* (39) 1986. pp. 265–281.
14. Sherrie Bourg and Harley V. Stock, "A Review of Domestic Violence Arrest Statistics in a Police Department Using a Pro-Arrest Policy: Are Pro-Arrest Policies Enough?" *Journal of Family Violence.* (9) No. 2 June 1994, p. 177.
15. Buzawa, E. S., and C. G. Buzawa. *Domestic Violence: The Criminal Justice Response.* (Sage, Newbury Park, California) 1990, p. 44.
16. LaFave, W. R., and A. W. Scott Jr. *Criminal Law,* 2d ed. (West, St. Paul, Minnesota) 1986, p. 30.
17. Perkins, R. M., and R. N. Boyce. *Criminal Law,* 3d ed. (Foundation Press, New York) 1982, p. 152.
18. LaFave, W. R., and A. W. Scott Jr. *Criminal Law,* 2d ed. (West, St. Paul, Minnesota) 1986, p. 684.
19. Buzawa, E. S., and T. Austin. "Determining Police Response to Domestic Violence Victims: The Role of Victim Preference," *American Behavioral Scientist.* (36) No. 5 May–June 1993, p. 610.
20. See Black, D. *The Manners and Customs of Police.* (Academic Press, New York) 1980, p. 189.
21. For an excellent discussion of this area, see Sherman, L. W. *Policing Domestic Violence.* (Free Press, New York) 1992, pp. 30–31.
22. Sherman, L. W., and R. A. Berk. "The Specific Deterrent Effects of Arrest for Domestic Assault." *American Sociological Review* (49) 1984, p. 261.
23. Clark, J. R. "The Minneapolis Study: Policy Gets Made Despite Cautions." *Law Enforcement News,* March 31, 1993, p. 9.
24. Hirschel, J. D., and I. Hutchinson. "Police-Preferred Arrest Policies." In M. Steinman, ed. *Women Battering: Policy Responses* (Anderson, Cincinnati) 1991, p. 59.
25. See Elliot, D. S. "Criminal Justice Procedures in Family Violence Crimes." In L. Ohlin, and M. Tonry, eds. *Family Violence.* (University of Chicago Press, Chicago) 1989, p. 458, which cites the study as a landmark study on the effectiveness of alternative police responses to family violence, and compare that position with Richard Lempert, "Humility is a Virtue." *Law and Society Review* (23) 1989, p. 146, which argues that the experiment lacked a scientific basis.
26. Pate, A., E. E. Hamilton, and A. Sampson. *Metro-Dade Spouse Abuse Replication Project, Draft Final Report.* (National Institute of Justice, Washington, D.C.) 1991.
27. Berk, R. A., A. Campbell, R. Klap, and B. Western. "A Bayesian Analysis of the Colorado Springs Spouse Abuse Experiment." *The Journal of Criminal Law and Criminology* Vol. 83, No. 1 (1992), p. 170.
28. Sherman, L. W., J. D. Schmidt, D. P. Rogan, D. A. Smith, P. R. Gartin, E. G. Cohn, D. J. Collins, and A. R. Bacich. "The Variable Effects of Arrest on Criminal Careers: The Milwaukee Domestic Violence Experiment." *The Journal of Criminal Law and Criminology.* Vol. 83, No. 1 1992, p. 137.
29. Dunford, F. W., D. Huizinga, and D. S. Elliot. *The Omaha Domestic Violence Police Experiment: Final Report to the National Institute of Justice.* (National Institute of Justice, Washington, D.C.) 1989.
30. Ibid., p. 34.
31. Hirchel, J. D., W. Hutchison III, C. W. I. Dean, J. J. Kelly, and C. E. Pesackis. *Charlotte Spouse Assault Replication Project, Final Report to the National Institute of Justice.* (National Institute of Justice, Washington, D.C.) 1991.
32. Lerman, L. G. "Mediation of Wife Abuse Cases: The Adverse Impact of Informal Dispute Resolution on Women." *Harvard Women's Law Journal* (7) 1984, p. 57.
33. Goolkasian, G. A. *Confronting Domestic Violence: A Guide for Criminal Justice Agencies.* (National Institute of Justice, Washington, D.C.) 1986, pp. 41–51.
34. Sherman, L. W. *Policing Domestic Violence.* (Free Press, New York) 1992, pp. 253–260.
35. See, e.g., the cases discussed in Chapter 12 in which some of the decisions reflect the constitutional requirement that all persons be granted equal protection under the law.

36. See "Message to Batterers: If You Hit, We'll Arrest." *Law Enforcement News,* September 15, 1997, p. 7.
37. Travis, J. "Violence against Women: Reflections on NIJ's Research Agenda," *National Institute of Justice Journal,* February 1996.
38. 18 U.S.C. 2261 (a) (1) and (2) (1996).
39. 18 U.S.C. 2262 (a) (1) and (2) (1996).
40. 18 U.S.C. 992 (g) (9) (1996).
41. See *Family Violence: A Model State Code* (The National Council of Juvenile and Family Court Judges, Reno, Nevada, January, 1994).
42. This section has been adapted from Finn, P. and S. Colson. *Civil Protection Orders: Legislation, Current Court Practice and Enforcement.* (National Institute of Justice, Washington, D.C.) March 1990.
43. *Mitchell v W. T. Grant Co.,* 416 U.S. 600 (1974).
44. For an excellent discussion of the advantages to using restraining orders, see Topliffe, E. "Why Civil Protection Orders Are Effective Remedies for Domestic Violence but Mutual Protective Orders Are Not." *Indiana Law Journal* (67) Fall, 1992, p. 1039.
45. This section has been adapted from Keillitz, S. L., C. Davis, H. S. Efkeman, C. Flango, and P. L. Hannaford. "Civil Protection Orders: Victim's View on Effectiveness," *National Institute of Justice Journal* (September, 1997), pp. 23–24.
46. Sherman, L. W. and R. A. Berk. "The Specific Deterrent Effects of Arrest for Domestic Assault." *American Sociological Review* (49) 1984, p. 261.
47. *Attorney General's Task Force on Family Violence.* (U.S. Department of Justice, Washington D.C.) 1984.
48. Ibid., p. 29.
49. See *Domestic Violence: The Law and Criminal Prosecution.* 2d ed. (The Family Violence Project, San Francisco) 1990, p. 12.
50. San Francisco Office of the District Attorney Protocol for the Handling of Domestic Violence. (undated)
51. *U.S. v Reisinger,* 128 U.S. 398, 9 S. Ct. 99, 32 L. Ed 489 (1888).
52. *Domestic Violence: The Law and Criminal Prosecution.* 2d ed. (The Family Violence Project, San Francisco) 1990, p. 13.
53. Ibid., pp. 13–14 which states, "The case should be file when a provable case exists regardless of the victim's stated wishes. Victims should not be asked if they want the case prosecuted. Nor should they be told the DA will prosecute only if requested, or only if the victim signs the complaint.
54. Schmalleger, F. *Criminal Justice Today.* 2d ed. (Prentice Hall, Englewood Cliffs, New Jersey) 1993.
55. Nolo contendre is a Latin phrase that means "I will not contest it." It has the same force and effect as pleading guilty. The principle difference between a guilty plea and one of nolo contendre is that the latter pleas may not be used against the defendant in any subsequent civil trial. *Hudson v U.S.* 272 U.S. 451, 47 S.Ct. 127, 71 L. Ed. 347 (1926).
56. See *Domestic Violence: The Law and Criminal Prosecution.* 2d ed. (The Family Violence Project, San Francisco) 1990, pp. 20–26, which has an excellent discussion of bail and domestic violence.
57. See Siegel, L. J. *Criminology,* 3d ed. (West, St. Paul) 1989, p. 214.
58. Goolkasian, G. A. *Confronting Domestic Violence: A Guide for Criminal Justice Agencies.* (National Institute of Justice, Washington, D.C.) 1986, footnote 31.
59. Adapted from *Domestic Violence: The Law and Criminal Prosecution.* 2d ed. (The Family Violence Prevention Fund, San Francisco, California) 1990, pp. 79–80. Co-authored by Nancy K. D. Lemon and M. Kandel. Production was funded in part by the Office of Criminal Justice Planning.
60. See for example, California Penal Code Section 273.82(a)(2). Unfortunately, the legislature never provided funds to implement this requirement.
61. This section has been adapted from J. Fagan, *The Criminalization of Domestic Violence: Promise and Limits* (National Institute of Justice, Washington, D.C. January, 1996).

10

ELDER ABUSE

Chapter Outline

Introduction
- *Extent of the Problem*
- *Definition*
- *Types of Elder Abuse*

Theories of Elder Abuse
- *Cycle of Violence*
- *Psychopathology*
- *Social Exchange Theory*
- *Family Stress Theory*
- *Neutralization Theory*

Reporting and Intervention
- *Reporting Laws*
- *Interested Parties*
- *Guardians and Conservators*
- *Other Intervention Strategies*

Summary

Learning Objectives

After reading this chapter, you should be able to discuss the following concepts:

- The nature and extent of elder abuse in the United States.
- Some of the definitional issues that affect the validity of examining the problem of elder abuse.
- The distinction between the different types of elder abuse.

- The different causation theories of elder abuse.
- The various intervention strategies for elder abuse.

Introduction

Elder abuse can, if left untreated, have serious and often times deadly consequences for victims. Although the public became aware of certain forms of family violence in the 1960s and 1970s, it wasn't until the 1980s that elder abuse came to widespread public attention. This chapter examines various aspects of this complex form of family violence.

One of the first studies of elder abuse was published in 1979. Block and Sinnott entitled their work "The Battered Elder Syndrome: An Exploratory Study." They contacted twenty-four agencies in Maryland and surveyed 427 professionals and 443 elders. They found twenty-six cases of elder abuse. Unfortunately, the study went no further, but it was the first step in the long process of recognizing that elders can be victims of family violence.[1] By 1988, scholars had identified over 200 research papers examining elder abuse.[2] Today, that number continues to expand rapidly. Although there are several problems in the study of elder abuse, defining the term itself and determining its extent are two of the most controversial.

FOCUS Elder Abuse—A National Tragedy

Several years ago, officers of the Austin, Texas, Police Department discovered the partially clothed body of a sixty-eight-year-old woman in an apartment shared by her son. The woman wore a diaper fashioned from a vacuum cleaner bag and was found lying on the kitchen floor in the fetal position. Police later discovered that the victim did not die of any aggressive action—she died of starvation.

Elder abuse is increasingly being recognized as a national tragedy in the United States. In 1989, hearings before the Subcommittee on Aging indicated that one out of every twenty-five U.S. citizens over the age of sixty-five suffers from some form of abuse, neglect, or exploitation.

Furthermore, the elder population is increasing. In 1989, persons sixty-five years of age or older numbered 31 million, representing 12.5 percent of the total population. By the year 2030, an estimated 66 million persons will be over the age sixty-five, representing 21.8 percent of the total population.

Although incidents of elder abuse in domestic settings are estimated at 1.5 million cases per year, only one out of eight cases comes to the attention of the authorities. Because many older people wish to maintain their privacy, they do not report the abuse or neglect, or they tell practitioners that they do not wish to take any action against their abusers.

Source: Adapted from Weith, M. E. "Elder Abuse A National Tragedy." *FBI Law Enforcement Bulletin.* February, 1994, pp. 24–25.

Extent of the Problem

How pervasive is elder abuse? Domestic elder abuse, like other forms of family violence, occurs behind closed doors in the privacy of the home. One of the breakthrough studies of elder abuse that was published in 1988 by Pillemer and Finkelhor involved 2,020 Boston elders. The authors found a rate of thirty-two abused elders per 1,000. This study selected persons sixty-five and older living by themselves or with their families. The results of this survey would translate into over a million abused elders in the United States in 1988.[3]

Estimates on the nature, type, and prevalence of elder abuse continue to vary widely. In 1989, one congressional committee estimated that 1.5 million cases of elder abuse occur each year.[4] What is more shocking is the fact that this figure has steadily increased by a half million each year since 1980.[5] Callahan claims that between 4 and 10 percent of all elders suffer abuse.[6] Other researchers believe that the figure is higher, contending that only one in six incidents of elder abuse is ever reported to the authorities.[7]

The National Center on Elder Abuse estimates that elders suffered the following types of abuse: physical abuse (15.7 percent), sexual abuse (.04 percent), emotional abuse (7.3 percent), neglect (58.5 percent), financial exploitation (12.3 percent), all other types (5.1 percent), and unknown (.06 percent).[8] Nationally, about 70 percent of the annual caseloads of adult protective services agencies involve elder abuse.[9] Among murder victims over the age sixty, their offspring were the killers in 42 percent of the homicides.[10]

The Administration on Aging (AoA), an agency of the U.S. Department of Health and Human Services, estimates that in the future America's elder population will change and grow rapidly.[11] By the year 2030, those age sixty and older will more than double to 85 million, whereas the number of elders over the age of eighty-five will triple to 8 million. At the same time, the number of minority elderly will increase dramatically, and it will do so more rapidly than the general population. Whereas the number of Angelo elders will increase by 97 percent, elderly black Americans will increase by 265 percent and Hispanic Americans by 530 percent. The minority elderly may face more serious problems than the white elderly because they are sometimes less able to advocate for themselves because of cultural, language, or educational barriers. This graying of America greatly increases the risk of elder abuse and the necessity of understanding its dynamics.

Controversy continues regarding who is abused and who is the abuser—are they family members, the wife, or the husband? This confusion is illustrated by the fact that some authorities believe that elder victims are females over the age of seventy-five,[12] whereas others believe that the wife is the one who perpetrates the abuse.[13] Other scholars argue that adult children inflict abuse on their parents. The Boston survey indicated that elders were abused more by their spouses than by their children. This result is to be expected once it is understood that elders live with spouses more than with adult children, and therefore the chance of being abused by a spouse is greater than by that of an adult child. Although both males and females may be victims of elder abuse, the abuse inflicted by husbands is more severe than that inflicted by wives. More research is necessary to determine the extent and nature of elder abuse, but the central issue is that abuse is likely to be inflicted by the people with whom the elder is living.

There is a continuing failure to report and act on elder abuse, and Decalmer lists two major factors that may contribute to this failure:

1. There is failure to understand the size, severity, and nature of the problem because of the conflicting definitions of elder abuse.
2. The number of controlled studies and the case reporting methods that are used in most of the research in this area have produced difficulties in estimating the true extent of the various acts of abuse and neglect.[14]

In addition, methodology and sampling procedures differ from study to study. Some research focuses on the elderly population, and other studies examine agency records. Still other investigations poll professionals. As a result, no clear-cut figures exist that are accepted by all scholars and researchers.

Definition

The term *elder abuse* was first used during congressional hearings in the late 1970s. The House Select Committee on Aging, chaired by Representative Claude Pepper (The Pepper Commission), examined the mistreatment of the elderly and introduced the term *elder abuse* to the United States.[15] Simply coining a term, however, does not make it clear or acceptable to all scholars or professionals.

Some scholars examined elder abuse and included persons under the age of sixty in their research, whereas others classified elders as those over the age of sixty.[16] Well-respected authorities defined elder abuse as occurring only between those who share a residence with the victim, whereas in other studies out-of-home caretakers were included.[17] Because of the problems inherent in defining elder abuse, as well as what is to be studied or how a study is to be conducted, it is easy to understand the confusion and debate that encompasses the term.

In an effort to end this confusion, some authorities have developed a list of definitions by establishing typologies involving elder abuse. Unfortunately, these typologies lacked uniformity and resulted in more confusion. Hudson and Johnson pointed out that some typologies differed considerably in defining neglect, whereas others classified withholding of personal care as physical abuse and/or psychological abuse.[18] As a result of this continuing confusion, other researchers began to frame the definition of elder abuse from a conceptional perspective. For example, some scholars attempted to place the issue of elder abuse within the broad category of inadequate care.[19] However, the same problems that were faced in attempting to establish an acceptable typology were present in the effort to conceptualize elder abuse.[20]

Several prominent scholars, including Wolf, Pillemer, and Godkin, distilled these various definitions down to a multifaceted definition that classifies elder abuse into five areas:

1. Physical abuse includes the infliction of physical pain or injury, physical coercion, sexual molestation, or physical restraint.
2. Psychological abuse includes the infliction of mental anguish.
3. Material abuse includes the illegal or improper exploitation and/or use of funds or resources.
4. Active neglect includes the refusal or failure to undertake a caretaking obligation.
5. Passive neglect includes the refusal or failure to fulfill a caretaking obligation.[21]

The previous discussion clearly illustrates that simply attempting to define the term *elder abuse* has generated scholarly debate and controversy. Based on this confusion and conflict, a simple, clear-cut definition of elder abuse may not be possible. However, for purposes of consistency with other definitions contained in this text, *elder abuse is defined as conduct that results in the physical, psychological, or material neglect, harm, or injury to an elder.* This definition applies both to domestic as well as institutional abuse. All the terms used in this definition have been clarified and explained in previous chapters with the exception of the word *material. Material in the context of elder abuse refers to the exploitation or use of resources. An elder is a person sixty-five years or older.* The initial age determination of sixty-five is based on common acceptance of that age by most authorities, scholars, and professionals.[22] This age-group may be further subdivided into those between sixty-five and seventy-five, the young–old, and those above seventy-five, the old–old.[23]

Elder abuse can occur in a domestic or institutional setting. Pillemer and Moore point out that despite two decades of state and federal regulation of nursing homes, abuse of the elderly continues to occur on a regular basis.[24] The focus of this chapter is on domestic abuse because it is related to the concept of family violence. However, abuse of the elderly in nursing homes and long-term care institutions is a fact of modern life and should not be forgotten or overlooked when considering the overall plight of the elderly in society.

Types of Elder Abuse

Previous chapters have already discussed the different types of abuse that are inflicted on children, women, and even strangers. Elder abuse is very similar to these other forms of family violence, but the age, mental condition, and perspective of the victim make this form of abuse distinct from other forms of family violence. As discussed earlier, elder abuse may involve physical, psychological, material, or neglect that results in injury to the victim.

Physical Abuse

This form of elder abuse may include any of the following signs, symptoms, or classifications. In many instances, the victim may deny abuse or may not even remember the acts that resulted in the injury. It is therefore important that any professional carefully examine any unexplained or suspicious physical injury to an elder.

Bruises: Any unexplained bruise or bruising that forms a pattern or shape of another object such as cords, belts, or hands should be carefully investigated.

Bruising that occurs after visits by relatives should be carefully examined. Bite and teeth marks should immediately raise suspicion in any professional.

Burns: Cigarette burns, burns with distinctive shapes or patterns, immersion burns, or burns from ropes or other restraints should be carefully evaluated.

Fractures: The aged have fragile bones. Unlike the young child whose bones are limber, the elderly's bones and skeleton are stiffer and more apt to break. However, injuries to the head, multiple breaks, or spiral fractures should be carefully noted, and a specific inquiry regarding the circumstances surrounding these injuries should be made by any professional who observes them.

Lacerations, abrasions, or hair loss: Injuries to the lips, ears, face, or extremities should be examined and documented. Loss of hair may be simply a natural occurrence of increasing age or may indicate that the abuser has grabbed the victim by the hair.

Sexual activity: Any evidence of forced sexual activity should be examined. This includes genital or rectal bleeding, difficulty in walking or sitting, pain or itching in the genital area, and evidence of any newly acquired sexually transmitted disease.

Psychological Abuse

This type of elder abuse is more difficult to identify than physical abuse. The injury to the victim may not leave marks that can be documented. However, as with psychological abuse to women and children, the effects of this type of abuse can be long-lasting and in some cases more severe than physical abuse. The victim may feel deprived of family support, may be fearful of further continued rejection by the caretaking relative, and may believe that there is no further purpose in continuing to live or function.[25]

Depression: Many of the elderly may display symptoms of depression. However, extreme depression in the absence of other factors should prompt an inquiry into the area of abuse.

Overly anxious or fearful of adults: An elder who shrinks from contact with adults or is withdrawn may have been ridiculed by a family member or caretaker in the past. This experience can make the victim fearful of any contact with other adults. The victim may also have been threatened with harm if the abuser is disclosed and therefore avoids contact with others.[26]

Neurotic traits: Sleep disorders, speech disorders, and other activities not associated with a physical cause should be carefully evaluated.

Psychoneurotic behavior. Hysteria or obsession or hoarding food or other material items may indicate that the elder is being denied certain essentials such as food, water, toilet paper, and other common amenities. This type of abuse, closely associated with neglect, is discussed later in this section.

Material Abuse

This is a common form of elder abuse. It involves the exploitation of the elder's finances and resources. It may be as obvious as taking money from the elder's bank account or as subtle as unduly influencing the elder in the disposition of her property. This undue influence may pressure the elder to transfer property to the abuser or change her will to leave that property to the perpetrator when the elder dies.

Lack of clothing: The elder's clothing may have been sold or appropriated by the caretakers for their own use. Lack of proper clothing for a particular season may mean the elder's resources have been depleted by a caretaker.

Lack of food: The caretaker may be using the elder's normal food allowance for other purposes and thereby starving the elder. The victim may be losing weight or constantly snacking or eating when away from the caretaker.

Loss of residence: The sudden unexplained transfer of ownership of the elder's home or apartment to the caretaker should prompt an immediate inquiry regarding the reasons for the transfer.

Lack of funds: The elder's social security or retirement checks may be converted to the caretaker's own use without approval or knowledge of the elder. The elder's savings or checking account should be checked to determine whether any unusual withdrawals have occurred in the recent past.

Loss of personal property: The elder may claim to have lost jewelry or other personal items. The unexplained loss of expensive jewelry should be investigated.

Neglect

Most scholars distinguish between active and passive abuse of the elderly.[27] Neglect may be an action or a failure to act on the part of the caretaking relative.

FOCUS Alzheimer's Disease—A Case of Abuse Waiting to Happen

Alzheimer's disease is a relatively new form of disability that affects persons as early as the age of forty. The disease has three major facets: intellectual deficits, personality deficits, and stress-tolerance deficits.[28] Intellectual deficits are characterized by inattention to time, difficulty in making decisions, inability to make decisions or plan activities (such as dressing, bathing, or eating), and, most commonly, the loss of memory. Personality deficits include inappropriate affection, lack of inhibitions, delusions, paranoia, hallucinations, and social withdrawal. Stress-tolerance deficits commonly include confusion, nighttime awakening, pacing and wandering, fatigue, anxiety, and violence.

In the final stage of Alzheimer's disease, the patient no longer recognizes himself, relatives, or close friends. He becomes bedridden, and any activity may consist of random movements. Verbal communications cease. However, he may cry out or scream without reason. He will have lost control of his bowel movements and will require feeding, changing, and constant care.

It is easy to see how a person suffering from Alzheimer's disease can become the victim of elder abuse. They may not remember acts of abuse, they are very easy to manipulate, and because of their wandering need to be restrained for their own protection. These elders may be subjected to all forms of abuse and never even be aware that it has occurred. The stress that is generated in‹j‹caring for an Alzheimer's patient may lead a caretaker to engage in acts that are considered abusive. Tying the patient down at night, sedating the patient so that he or she does not require constant attention, or slapping the patient to vent frustration are common forms of abuse.

Failure to care for the elder: Neglect includes failure to feed, clothe, or bathe the elder. Improper diet, lack of supervision of the elder, and other acts that expose the elder to possible injury fall within this classification.

Misuse of medication: Some caretakers will not provide or administer necessary medications to the elders. Others use medication as a form of restraint and overmedicate the elder so that he or she becomes less of a caretaking problem.

Failure to seek medical care: Many caretakers will not take the time or effort to transport the elder to a physician's office or outpatient clinic even when there are clear signs of injury or other symptoms that require medical intervention.

Not all injuries to an elderly person indicate abuse, but professionals who come into contact with the elderly must be aware of that very real possibility and be prepared to pursue any signs of abuse. Social workers, physicians, therapists, and nurses may all come into contact with elderly persons who have been victims of abuse. Because of the confusion regarding a definition of elder abuse, no clear-cut protocol exists on exactly what to look for or how to diagnose elder abuse. However, T. F. Johnson, in her book *Elder Mistreatment: Deciding Who Is at Risk,* has prepared an excellent table that lists certain indicators of possible elder abuse (see Table 10.1).

The table listing the various types of elder abuse should be taken with caution. All activities undertaken by relatives or caretakers should not be automatically categorized as elder abuse. Elders may have valid tax reasons for transferring ownership of property to family members. Elderly persons are, in fact, injured more easily than middle-aged adults. In addition, they may be used to wearing certain types of clothing and resistant to change, even with the coaxing of relatives. However, professionals cannot afford to ignore the possibility of elder abuse and need to take reasonable actions to assure themselves of the physical and emotional well-being of the elderly client or patient.

Theories of Elder Abuse

Although authorities may disagree as to the exact cause of elder abuse, there is general agreement that it is similar to other forms of family violence and that it crosses all social and economic lines. Most researchers agree that elder abuse is not an isolated event; rather, it is a repetitive pattern of acts by the abuser toward the victim.

Cycle of Violence

The cycle of violence or intergenerational transmission of violence theory has been discussed in detail in Chapter 1. Galbraith argues that it has proven ineffective in predicting elder abuse.[29] Wolf and Pillemer also point out that those who abuse elders did not necessarily grow up in families characterized by violence.[30]

Psychopathology

This theory is based on the premise that abusers have mental disorders that cause them to be abusive. Douglas indicated that the flawed development of the abuser is one of the causes of elder abuse. Wolf found a high prevalence of mental illness among

TABLE 10.1 Elder Abuse Risk Indicators

I Physical	II Psychological	III Sociological	IV Legal
A. Medication misuse	A. Humiliation	A. Isolation	A.Material misuse
1. Absence	1. Shame	1. Involuntary withdrawal	1. Property mismanagement
2. Improper use	2. Blame	2. Inadequate supervision	2. Contract mismanagement
3. Adverse interaction	3. Ridicule	3. Improper supervision	3. Blocked access to property
4. Unnecessary use	4. Rejection		4. Blocked access to contract
B. Bodily impairment	B. Harassment	B. Role confusion	B. Theft
1. Unmet medical needs	1. Insult	1. Competition	1. Stealing property
2. Poor hygiene	2. Intimidation	2. Overload	2. Stealing contracts
3. Ingestion problems	3. Fearfulness	3. Inversion	3. Extorting property
4. Rest disturbance	4. Agitation	4. Dissolution	4. Extorting contracts
C. Bodily assaults	C. Manipulation	C. Misuse of living arrangements	C. Misuse of rights
1. External injuries	1. Information withheld	1. Household disorganized	1. Denied contracts
2. Internal injuries	2. Information falsified	2. Lack of privacy	2. Involuntary servitude
3. Sexual assaults	3. Unreasonable emotional deprivation	3.Unfit environment	3. Unnecessary guardianship
4. Suicidal/homicidal act	4. Interference with decisions	4. Abandonment	4. Misuse of professional authority

Source: Johnson, T. F. *Elder Mistreatment: Deciding Who Is at Risk.* (Greenwood Press, Westport, Connecticut). Copyright © 1991. Reprinted with permission of Greenwood Publishing Group, Inc., Westport, CT.

elder abusers.[31] This approach seems to have greater validity in explaining elder abuse than in explaining either child or spousal abuse. Researchers have found psychopathology present in cases of physical and verbal abuse of elders.[32] Other scholars indicate that a number of abusers have previous hospitalizations for serious psychiatric disorders such as schizophrenia and other psychoses.[33]

Social Exchange Theory

The social exchange theory assumes that dependency in relationships contributes to elder abuse. One social exchange theory proposes that the increased dependency of the victim on the abuser results in acts of abuse. Several scholars have found support for this theory in their studies.[34] Financial dependency of the abuser on the victim also has been found to be present in a number of studies of elder abuse.[35]

When there is a loss of mutual sharing of resources between the elder and the caretaker, the quality of the relationship degenerates. This results in the caretaker's perceiving the relationship as unfair with a subsequent increase in hostility toward the elder. This imbalance results in some caretakers abusing elders.[36]

A second social exchange theory assumes that the dependency of the abuser on the elder causes abuse. This concept focuses on adult children who are dependent on the elder for material rewards such as housing and finances. Because these children perceive themselves as weaker and less powerful than the elder, abusing the elder is a way to equalize the balance of power and gain control over the relationship.[37]

Family Stress Theory

This is one of the most accepted theories of elder abuse.[38] *The family stress theory is based on the premise that providing care for an elder induces stress within the family.* This stress may take many forms, including economic hardship, loss of sleep, and intrusions into normal family privacy routines and other activities, that may cause the caregiver to feel resentment toward the elder. Adult children may have to give up economic security to provide care for an aged parent or other close relative. In addition, the physical toll of caring for an ill elderly person can sometimes overwhelm the adult child, resulting in a loss of control and abuse.[39] This theory is also subject to controversy. Phillips suggests that stress levels may not be as important a factor as previously believed in causing elder abuse.[40]

Neutralization Theory

The neutralization theory was originally developed by Sykes and Matza to explain juvenile delinquency in society.[41] This theory *views the delinquent as being affected by the norms and values of a larger social system rather than a counterculture. This concept holds that delinquents show guilt and shame for their antisocial behavior.*[42] In order to commit criminal or antisocial acts, people develop techniques of neutralization. These techniques are rationalizations or justifications for their behavior. Matza established five techniques that allow a person to justify his or her acts:

1. *Denial of responsibility:* The person may claim that something else, such as alcohol, made him commit the criminal act.
2. *Denial of injury:* Juveniles may believe that even though they violated the law, no one was really hurt. For example, theft of an automobile is acceptable because the owner's insurance company will replace it with a new model anyway.
3. *Denial of victim:* Delinquents may claim that the victim had it coming and therefore that their acts were justified under the circumstances.
4. *Condemnation of the condemners:* Juveniles may shift the blame to others, calling them corrupt or incompetent.

5. *Appeal to higher loyalty:* Some offenders will claim they violated the law in order to satisfy a higher authority or goal.

Tomita has applied the neutralization theory to elder abuse and suggests that, although it cannot be used to establish a direct cause, it may be viewed as methods employed by abusers to justify their acts.[43] She examines each of the techniques of neutralization and explains that they may be used by the perpetrators to justify their abuse of elders.

1. *Denial of responsibility:* In these situations, the abuser claims the mistreatment was caused by forces beyond her control such as poverty, bad parents, and so on.
2. *Denial of injury:* The abuser will rationalize that the injury was not really that serious because the victim did not have to go to the emergency room. In material abuse situations, the abuser will justify her actions by stating that the parent can afford to give away property or assets.
3. *Denial of the victim:* Abusers may state that the victim doesn't need help or that she is just attempting to gain attention. For example, the abuser may refuse to dress the victim, claiming that the victim just wants attention, when in reality the victim cannot dress herself.
4. *Condemnation of the condemners:* In these situations, the abuser condemns protective services or other agencies for interfering with the family.
5. *Appeal to higher loyalty:* The abuser may believe that he must act a certain way to satisfy her spouse.

As the previous discussion illustrates, several theories attempt to explain why persons abuse the elderly. Just as with other causes of family violence, no single theory is accepted by all scholars. More research needs to be done in this area to determine whether a cause can be established for this type of abuse. In the absence of definite answers, elder abuse will continue to be a problem. This type of behavior necessitates the reporting of abuse and the intervention by authorities.

Reporting and Intervention

Even with programs such as the Triads Program, elder abuse will continue. When professionals have reason to suspect that an elder is the victim of abuse, they must take certain actions not only to protect the elder but also to notify specified authorities of the incident. These actions are normally defined in the various reporting statutes adopted by each state.

Reporting Laws

As indicated earlier, elder abuse came to public consciousness during the 1980s. As a result of congressional hearings, such as the Pepper Commission, as well as

FOCUS Triads—Community Involvement in Fighting Elder Abuse

A new concept that emphasizes community cooperation in combating elder victimization is succeeding in a number of areas throughout the United States. This innovative concept is called the Triad Program.

Triads are formed when the local police and sheriff's departments agree to work cooperatively with senior citizens to prevent the victimization of the elderly in the community. The three groups share ideas and resources to provide programs and training for vulnerable and often fearful elderly citizens.

A triad usually begins when a police chief, a sheriff, or a leader in the senior citizen community contacts the other two essential participants to discuss a combined effort. Although each entity may already have programs in place to reduce victimization among the elderly, the three-way involvement of triads adds strength, resources, and greater credibility.

Most triads include representatives from agencies that serve older persons, such as the Agency on Aging, senior centers, and adult protective services. Law enforcement leaders then invite seniors and those working with them to serve on an advisory council, often called Seniors and Lawmen Together (SALT).

Some triads establish programs to prevent elder abuse through education and to address the plight of seniors in personal care homes. For example, in Columbus, Georgia, the plight of some seniors in such facilities came to the attention of a very active SALT council. Learning that older residents were suffering from abuse and neglect, the SALT council devised a strategy to investigate specific situations.

To begin, the council enlisted the assistance of the sheriff's office and the police and health departments. Through these agencies, a search warrant of the homes was obtained, proper lodging and care was arranged for those seniors living in unhealthy and unsafe conditions, and a plan for more careful monitoring of such homes was initiated.

The essence of the triad is cooperation. This program allows the service providers (law enforcement) to work together with the consumers (senior citizens). Through positive programs that enhance safety and quality of life, mutual respect and appreciation evolves between the law enforcement community and citizens.

Source: Adapted from Cantrell, B. "Triad, Reducing Criminal Victimization of the Elderly." FBI *Law Enforcement Bulletin.* February 1994, pp. 19–23.

scientific publications and media attention, state legislatures passed a series of laws aimed at this aspect of family violence. Although they differ in content, all states have laws relating to elder abuse.[44] Forty-two states have specific statutes that mandate reporting of suspected abuse by certain professionals.[45] Many of these reporting statutes were modeled after existing child abuse reporting laws. The major problem with elder abuse mandatory reporting laws is the lack of research comparing the needs of the elderly to the needs of abused children. These laws and their effect on child abuse and the professionals that come into contact with abused children are discussed in detail in Chapter 7. For purposes of understanding elder abuse and reporting, this section provides a brief introductory overview of these laws.

Most reporting laws require certain designated professionals to report to a specific agency if they have reason to believe an elder has been the victim of abuse. The professionals that are included in these laws are medical personnel, educators, and others who might come into contact with elder clients on a regular basis. These laws are mandatory in nature, meaning that the professional does not have discretion in deciding whether to report the suspicious activity. The person who suspects abuse must file the report or face civil or criminal sanctions by the state. Many of these statutes provide immunity from lawsuit for the professional who reports suspected abuse.

Ehrlich and Anetzberger conducted a nationwide survey in the United States of all fifty state health departments on procedures for reporting elder abuse.[46] They found that although there is an awareness of elder abuse reporting laws, none of the fifty state agencies had developed a protocol to further their implementation. Sixty-four percent of these departments did not conduct in-service training for health care providers in the area of elder abuse. Part of the reason for the failure of these state agencies to act aggressively in this area of abuse may be due to the confusion and widespread diffusion of responsibility within a number of distinct agencies.

Elder abuse reporting laws authorize various local or county organizations such as human services, welfare departments, and law enforcement agencies to act rather than state health departments. Health professionals list the following problems in reporting elder abuse: limited knowledge of the reporting requirements, difficulty in understanding the definition of elder abuse, apprehension in reporting based on denial of abuse by the victim, and a lack of a high suspicion index of this type of family violence.[47]

In a study conducted by Blakely and his associates regarding physicians' responses to elder abuse and neglect, they found a low incidence of reporting to the appropriate agencies.[48] Instead, many physicians attempted to deal with the problem themselves or recommended counseling to the parties involved.

The reasons for the lack of appropriate physician response may be attributed in part to inadequate training received in medical schools. A number of researchers have suggested that medical schools have not devoted sufficient study to the problems of the elderly. Blakely found the following:

1. Medical schools presented limited training to physicians in preparation for treating the elderly.
2. Medical schools did not provide students with basic medical and sociological information about elders.
3. Few medical students expressed an interest in working with elderly patients.
4. Although there are several recent studies regarding the attitudes of the young toward the elderly, medical schools have failed to alter students' attitudes toward the elderly.[49]

Reporting suspected incidents of elder abuse is just the beginning. Once a report is filed, other agencies become involved with all parties: the elder, the abuser, and the reporting party. Understanding the roles of these interested parties is critical to understanding elder abuse.

Interested Parties

One of the most important parties to interact with the elder is the health care professional.[50] This person is not only tasked with reporting the abuse but also obligated to evaluate the injuries and offer alterative courses of action. Breckman and Adelman suggest that health care professionals use the following assessment guidelines when evaluating elder abuse:

1. *Access to the victim:* There may be a reluctance to allow the professional to have contact with either the victim or the abuser. Abusers will keep their actions hidden and threaten the victim against disclosure. Elders may feel ashamed that they allowed themselves to be victims and deny that anything is wrong.
2. *Health status:* Victims may tend to dismiss injuries as accidental, or abusers may prevent victims from receiving necessary medical care in order to avoid discovery. Professionals should distinguish between nonaccidental injuries and those normally associated with advancing age.
3. *Functional status:* Abusers who care for functionally dependent elders may appear overwhelmed and frustrated. Abusers and victims may have unrealistically high expectations of each other, resulting in frustration and abuse.
4. *Financial status and living arrangement:* Victims and abusers may be financially dependent on each other and forced to live in the same household. Victims may have given the abuser control over their finances.
5. *Social support:* Victims are often isolated and have limited contact with friends, social groups, other family members, or support systems within the community.
6. *Emotional support:* Effects of abuse may include depression, fear, and withdrawal.
7. *Stress:* External factors, such as loss of employment, death, retirement, or other incidents, may lead to stress that may result in abuse.
8. *Nature of abuse:*k Abuse often increases over time. Several types of maltreatment may be inflicted on the victim simultaneously, and denial of abuse is common.

In addition to health care professionals, various agencies, departments, or units are charged with enforcing statutes enacted to protect the elderly.[51] Each of these organizations carries out a needed mission to fulfill the stated goal of insuring that aged persons are not injured by family members or strangers. Although all these organizations serve valid purposes, this maze of interlocking and competing organizations can lead to confusion and a lack of coordination in attempts to combat elder abuse.

Various state statutes have established so-called Medicaid fraud units. These units are often located within the state attorney general's office and are charged with investigating and prosecuting violations of the state's Medicaid laws. These organizations may file criminal or civil actions against those who violate the rights of others who are entitled to receive medicaid.

Many states have licensing divisions located in their state health departments. These divisions are authorized by statute to supervise health care providers, including nursing homes, board and care homes, and home health services. These divisions investigate allegations of violations of state and federal regulations relating to the care of the elderly.

Local legal service organizations under the umbrella of the federally established Legal Services Corporation receive state and federal funding to provide legal advice and advocacy for elders who have civil problems. These local agencies can file civil actions against those who defraud or take advantage of elders.

In addition to these widely diverse organizations, adult protective services (APS) is actively involved in caring for the elderly and is usually tasked with responding to reports of elder abuse. In response to the growing awareness of elder abuse, many states enacted laws establishing adult protective services. These services are typically found in a local public social service agency, such as the welfare department.

The goal of APS is to coordinate the delivery of social services to those over eighteen years of age.[52] Most states that have enacted this type of legislation authorize APS to intervene on behalf of the state even if the client refuses assistance.[53] These statutes often authorize special court proceedings in family or probate court and provide for the imposition of guardianships or conservatorships of the adult who is incapacitated or incapable of caring for herself.

Guardians and Conservators

The power of the state to intervene and care for those who cannot care for themselves is a recognized principle of the sovereignty of the state. In the case of elders, the state acts by means of establishing either a guardianship or conservatorship.

Traditionally, *a conservator is a person appointed by a court to manage the estate of one who is unable to manage his or her own affairs.*[54] *A guardian is a person appointed by a court to take care of another person who for reasons of age, lack of understanding, or self-control is unable to care for him-or herself.*[55] Depending on the jurisdiction, these terms are interchangeable. For example, in California a conservatorship may be established for both the person and the property of an incompetent adult. Other states use the term *guardian* for matters affecting the person and *conservatorship* for matters affecting the property.

The initiation of a guardianship or conservatorship proceeding requires filing a petition in a court of competent jurisdiction. This petition is a formal pleading alleging that the elder is in need of the care of other persons. These pleadings usually take place in superior courts of the state and are often specialized courts such as probate or family courts that have been designated to handle these types of cases. The normal procedure requires notice to the affected elder and often his or her family. Once the notice has been served to the parties, the court holds a formal hearing on the issue of competency.

The alleged incompetent has a right to be represented by an attorney and be present at the hearing. Normally, APS or the person filing the petition presents evidence to support the allegations contained in the petition. This evidence may be an expert witness, such as a psychiatrist who can testify that the elder is incompetent or otherwise unable to care for him- or herself. Other witnesses may be called to testify as to any abuse that they may have observed.

The elder, through his or her attorney, has a right to cross-examine witnesses and present evidence in rebuttal to the charges. After hearing all the evidence, the judge or jury may find that the elder, as a result of a mental disease or defect, is incapable of providing for food, clothing, or shelter or otherwise caring for him- or herself.[56] Once the court renders this finding, it may appoint a guardian or conservator. This person may be authorized to assume total control over the fiscal and personal matters of the elder, including placement, finances, and in some cases the use of medication. The purpose of this type of action is to care for and protect the elder from abuse by others.

Other Intervention Strategies

Florida is considered a very desirable retirement state by many elders. A large portion of Florida's elderly population are retirees who moved there from different states. Many of these elderly now face isolation because of the death of a spouse and the fact that they live far away from their extended families. In an effort to address elder abuse issues, the governor of Florida appointed a task force that held public hearings and made a series of recommendations to combat elder abuse.[57] These recommendations included the following:

1. Changes to state law aimed at improving the coordination of elder abuse investigations among agencies in the criminal justice system
2. More formalized training for public guardians
3. The establishment of elder courts with specialized training for court personnel and others in the criminal justice system.

Florida is not the only state that is attempting to improve its response to elder abuse. The State of Massachusetts adopted an elder abuse reporting law in 1983. However, because of mistrust and lack of coordination among APS and the district attorney's office, very few elder abuse cases were being prosecuted. In 1988, the state and the district attorney for Middlesex County drafted a series of guidelines that established interagency protocols to increase communication and increase cross-agency referrals.[58] Both APS and the district attorney's offices agreed on common language, terms, and concepts. Protocols were also established to educate mandated reporters and make it clear that the decision to report was not discretionary. Cross-training between APS workers and the deputy district attorney resulted in more understanding of regarding each professional's roles and responsibilities. This collaboration has resulted in cases being identified earlier and critical support services for the elderly victim better coordinated. Many other states are attempting to address the problems of elder abuse. As the U.S. population ages, it is critical that we respond to this form of family violence.

Summary

Elder abuse has become yet another form of family violence. Authorities cannot agree on a definition, and, as a result, the outcome of different studies varies widely regarding its nature, cause, and extent. What can be agreed on is that it does exist and that more research is needed in this area.

Elder abuse, like other forms of family violence, is not an isolated event. Rather, it is a pattern of behavior that increases in both intensity and frequency over time. The rich, poor, college educated, and uneducated suffer from elder abuse. The dynamics and etiology of this type of abuse continue to spawn theories, some which seem to hold more promise than others. Continued research is of paramount important if professionals are to understand and treat the cause of elder abuse.

Professionals must be aware of possible instances of elder abuse and understand how to respond. Depending on the jurisdiction, a report of suspected elder abuse may have to be filed with a designated agency. The state may be required to intervene and place the elder under a guardianship or conservatorship of his or her own protection.

Key Terms

elder abuse—conduct that results in the physical, psychological, or material neglect, harm, or injury to an elder.

material abuse—the exploitation or use of resources of an elder.

elder—a person sixty-five years old or older.

psychopathology theory—based on the premise that abusers have mental disorders that cause them to be abusive.

social exchange theory—assumes that dependency in relationships contributes to elder abuse.

family stress theory—based on the premise that providing care for an elder induces stress within the family.

neutralization theory—views the delinquent as being affected by the norms and values of a larger social system rather than a counterculture. This concept holds that delinquents show guilt and shame for their antisocial behavior.

conservator—a person appointed by a court to manage the estate of one who is unable to manage his or her own affairs.

guardian—a person appointed by a court to take care of anotherperson who for reasons of age, lack of understanding, or self-control is unable to care of him- or herself.

Discussion Questions

1. Is elder abuse more or less serious than child abuse? Why?
2. Do you agree with the definition of elder abuse contained in the text? Draft another definition that you believe is more appropriate and justify your answer.

3. What is the most serious form or type of elder abuse?

4. Should elders have the right to accept abuse from a caretaker if they are competent?

5. Which of the theories discussing elder abuse do you favor? Why?

6. Are guardianships and conservatorships the best way to protect elders from abuse? What are some other alternatives?

Suggested Readings

Ammerman, R. T., and M. Hersen, eds. *Assessment of Family Violence, A Clinical and Legal Sourcebook.* (Wiley, New York) 1992.

Anetzberger, G. J. *The Etiology of Elder Abuse by Adult Offspring.* (Charles C. Thomas, Springfield Park, Illinois) 1987.

Block, M. R., and J. D. Sinnott, eds. *The Battered Elder Syndrome: An Exploratory Study.* (University of Maryland Center on Aging, College Park, Maryland) 1979.

Brubaker, T. H., ed. *Family Relationships in Later Life.* (Sage, Beverly Hills, California) 1983.

Decalmer, P. and F. Glendenning, eds. *The Mistreatment of Elder People.* (Sage, London, England) 1993.

Filenson, R., and S. R. Ingman, eds. *Elder Abuse: Practice and Policy.* (Human Sciences Press, New York) 1989.

Finkelhor, D., G. Hotaling, R. Gelles, and M. Straus, eds. *The Dark Side of Families: Current Family Violence Research.* (Sage, Beverly Hills, California) 1983.

Kosberg, J. I., ed. *Abuse and Maltreatment of the Elderly: Causes and Interventions.* (John Wright PSG, Boston) 1983.

Pagelow, M. D. *Family Violence.* (Praegar, New York) 1984.

Pillemer, K., and R. Wolf, eds. *Elder Abuse: Conflict in the Family.* (Auburn House, Dover, Massachusetts) 1986.

Schlesinger, B., and R. Schlesinger, eds. *Abuse of the Elderly: Issues and Annotated Bibliography.* (University of Toronto Press, Toronto) 1988.

Short, J. F. Jr., and F. Strodtbeck. *Group Process and Gang Delinquency.* (University of Chicago Press, Chicago) 1965.

Sloan, I. J. *The Law and Legislation of Elderly Abuse.* (Oceana Publications, Dobbs Ferry, New York) 1983.

Steinmetz, S. K. *Duty Bound: Elder Abuse and Family Care.* (Sage, Newbury Park, California) 1988.

Van Hasselt, V. B., et al. eds. *Handbook of Family Violence.* (Plenum Press, New York) 1988.

Wolf, R., M. Godkin, and K. A. Pillemer. *Elder Abuse and Neglect: Report from the Model Projects.* (University of Massachusetts Medical Center, University Center on Aging, Worcester, Massachusetts) 1984.

Wolf, R. S., and K. A. Pillemer. *Helping Elderly Victims: The Reality of Elder Abuse.* (Columbia University Press, New York) 1989.

Endnotes

1. Block, M. R., and J. D. Sinnott. "The Battered Elder Syndrome: An Exploratory Study." (Center on Aging, University of Maryland) 1979.

2. Schlesinger, B., and R. Schlesinger, eds., *Abuse of the Elderly: Issues and Annotated Bibliography.* (University of Toronto Press, Toronto) 1988.

3. Pillemer, K. A., and D. Finkelhor. "The Prevalence of Elder Abuse: A Random Sample Survey," *The Gerontologist* 28 (1) 1988, p. 51.
4. U.S. House of Representative, Select Committee on Aging, "Elder Abuse: Curbing a National Epidemic" (Hearings) (Washington D.C. GPO) December 10, 1990.
5. Ibid.
6. Callahan, J. J. "Elder Abuse: Some Questions for Policymakers." *The Gerontologist* (28) 1988, pp. 453–458.
7. Kosberg, J. I. "Preventing Elder Abuse: Identification of High Risk Factors Prior to Placement Decisions." *The Gerontologist* (28) 1988, pp. 43–50.
8. Toshio, T. "Elder Abuse in Domestic Settings," *Elder Abuse Information Series #1.* (National Center for Elder Abuse, Washington, D.C., May 1996) p. 8.
9. Ibid., p. 19.
10. Dawson and Larson. *Murder in Families.* (Bureau of Justice Statistics, Washington, D.C. 1994).
11. See *The Administration on Aging and the Older Americans Act* at http://www.aoa.dhhs.gov/aoa/pages/aoafact.html (November 1997).
12. U.S. House of Representative, Select Committee on Aging, "Elder Abuse: A Decade of Shame and Inaction" (Hearings) (Washington D.C. GPO) May 1, 1990.
13. Pillemer, K. A. and D. Finkelhor. "The Prevalence of Elder Abuse: A Random Sample Survey." *The Gerontologist* 28 (1) 1988, p. 51.
14. Peter Decalmer, and Frank Glendenning, eds. *The Mistreatment of Elder People.* (Sage, London, England) 1993, p. 35.
15. "Elder Abuse." Infolink 1 (17). (National Victim Center, Washington D.C.) 1992.
16. Pillemer, K., and J. J. Suitor. "Elder Abuse. V. B. Van Hasselt, et al. eds. *Handbook of Family Violence.* (Plenum Press, New York) 1988.
17. Compare Block, M. R., and J. D. Sinnott. "The Battered Elder Syndrome: An Exploratory Study." Center on Aging, University of Maryland (1979) with Steinmetz, S., and D. J. Amsden. "Dependent Elders, Family Stress and Abuse," T. H. Brubaker, ed. *Family Relationships in Later Life* (Sage, Beverly Hills, California) 1983.
18. Hudson, M. F., and T. F. Johnson. "Elder Abuse and Neglect: A Review of the Literature." In C. Eisdorfer, et al. eds. *Annual Review of Gerontology and Geriatrics* 6 (Springer, New York) 1986.
19. O'Malley, T. A., H. C. O'Malley, D. E. Everitt, and D. Sarson. "Categories of Family-Mediated Abuse and Neglect of Elderly Persons." *Journal of the American Geriatrics Society* 32(5) 1984, pp. 362–369.
20. Ibid.
21. See Wolf, R. S., and K. A. Pillemer. *Helping Elderly Victims: The Reality of Elder Abuse* (Columbia University Press, New York) 1989 and M. A. Godkin, R. S. Wolf, and K. A. Pillemer. "A Case-Comparison Analysis of Elder Abuse and Neglect." *International Journal of Aging and Human Development* 28(3) 1989, pp. 207–225.
22. Bachman, R. "Elderly Victim." *Special Report, Bureau of Justice Statistics.* (U.S. Department of Justice, Washington D.C.) 1992.
23. Pagelow, M. D. *Family Violence.* (Praegar, New York) 1984, p. 359.
24. Pillemer, K. A., and D. W. Moore. "Abuse of Patients in Nursing Homes: Findings from a Survey of Staff." *The Gerontologist* 29(3) 1989, p. 314.
25. Taler, G., and E. F. Ansello. "Elder Abuse." *Associations of Family Physicians* 32(2) 1985, p. 107.
26. Bloom, J. S., P. Ansell, and M. N. Bloom. "Detecting Elder Abuse: A Guide for Physicians." *Geriatrics* 44(6) 1989, p. 44.
27. Hall, P. A. "Elder Maltreatment Patterns: Items, Sub-Groups and Types, Policy and Practical Implications." *International Journal of Aging and Human Development* 28 (3) 1989, pp. 196–205.
28. Tackenberg, J. "Teaching Caregivers About Alzheimer's Disease." *Nursing* 92, May 1992.
29. Galbraith, M. W. "A Critical Examination of the Definitional, Methodological and Theoretical Problems of Elder Abuse." In R. Filenson, and S. R. Ingman, eds. *Elder Abuse: Practice and Policy.* (Human Sciences Press, New York) 1989, pp. 34–42.

30. Wolf, R. S., and K. A. Pillemer. *Helping elderly Victims: The Reality of Elder Abuse.* (Columbia University Press, New York) 1989.
31. Wolf, R., C. Strugnell, and M. Godkin. *Preliminary Findings from Three Model Projects on Elder Abuse.* (University of Massachusetts Medical Center, Worcester, Massachusetts) 1982.
32. Hickey, T., and R. L. Douglas. "Mistreatment of the Elderly in the Domestic Setting: An Exploratory Study." *American Journal of Public Health* (71) 1981, pp. 500–517.
33. Beckman, R. S., and R. D. Adelman. "Elder Abuse and Neglect." In R. T. Ammerman, and M. Hersen, eds. *Assessment of Family Violence, A Clinical and Legal Sourcebook.* (Wiley, New York) 1992, p. 238.
34. Davidson, J. L. "Elder Abuse." In M. R. Block, and J. D. Sinnott, eds. *The Battered Elder Syndrome: An Exploratory Study.* (University of Maryland Center on Aging, College Park, Maryland) 1979, pp. 49–55.
35. Wolf, R., M. Godkin, and K. A. Pillemer. *Elder Abuse and Neglect: Report from the Model Projects.* (University of Massachusetts Medical Center, University Center on Aging, Worcester, Massachusetts) 1984.
36. Steinmetz, S. K. *Duty Bound: Elder Abuse and Family Care.* (Sage Publications, Newbury Park, California) 1988.
37. Anetzberger, G. J. *The Etiology of Elder Abuse by Adult Offspring.* (Charles C. Thomas, Springfield Park, Illinois) 1987.
38. Steinmetz, S. K. *Duty Bound: Elder Abuse and Family Care.* (Sage Publications, Newbury Park, California) 1988.
39. Gelles, R. "An Exchange/Social Control Theory." In D. Finkelhor, G. Hotaling, R. Gelles, and M. Straus, eds. *The Dark Side of Families: Current Family Violence Research.* (Sage, Beverly Hill, California) 1983.
40. Phillips. L. "Theoretical Explanations of Elder Abuse: Competing Hypotheses and Unresolved Issues." In K. Pillemer, and R. Wolf, eds. *Elder Abuse: Conflict in the Family.* (Auburn House, Dover, Massachusetts) 1986.
41. Sykes, G. M. and D. Matza. "Techniques of Neutralization: A Theory of Delinquency." *American Sociological Review* (22) 1978, pp. 664–670.
42. Short, J. F. Jr., and Fred Strodtbeck. *Group Process and Gang Delinquency.* (University of Chicago Press, Chicago) 1965.
43. Tomita, S. K. "The Denial of Elder Mistreatment by victims and Abusers: The Application of Neutralization Theory." *Violence and Victims* 5(3) 1990, p. 171.
44. "Geriatrics: Responding to Elder Abuse," *Nursing* (24) No. 9 Sept. 1994, p. 76.
45. Fredriksen, H. I. "Adult Protective Services: Changes with the Introduction of Mandatory Reporting." *Journal of Elder Abuse and Neglect* (1) 1989, pp. 59–70.
46. Ehrlich, P. and G. Anetzberger. "Survey of State Public Health Departments on Procedures for Reporting Elder Abuse." *Public Health Report No. 106.* (U.S. Department of Health and Human Services, Washington D.C.) (March–April 1991) pp. 151–154.
47. Lachs, M. S., and K. Pillemer. "Abuse and Neglect of Elderly Persons." *The New England Journal of Medicine,* (332) No. 7 Feb. 16, 1995, p. 437.
48. Blakely, B. E., R. Dolon, and D. D. May. "Improving the Responses of Physicians to Elder Abuse and Neglect: Contributions of a Model Program." *Journal of Gerontological Social Work* 19(3) 1993, p. 35.
49. Ibid., p. 39.
50. Matlaw, J. R., and D. M. Spence. "The Hospital Elder Assessment Team: A Protocol for Suspected Cases of Elder Abuse and Neglect." *Journal of Elder Abuse & Neglect,* (6) No. 2 Summer 1994, p. 23.
51. Wolf, R. S., and K. Pillemer. "What's New in Elder Abuse Programming? Four Bright Ideas," *The Gerontologist,* (34) No. 1 1994, p. 126.
52. Regan, J. J. "Protective Services for the Elderly: Benefits or Threat?" J. I. Kosberg, ed. *Abuse and Maltreatment of the Elderly: Causes and Interventions.* (John Wright PSG, Boston) 1983.
53. Sloan, I. J. *The Law and Legislation of Elderly Abuse.* (Oceana Publications, Dobbs Ferry, New York) 1983.

54. See for example, the Uniform Probate Code Section 1-201(6) and 5-401(2).
55. *Blacks Law Dictionary,* 6th edition. (West, St. Paul) p. 706.
56. Regan, J. J. "Protective Services for the Elderly: Benefits or Threat?" J. I. Kosberg, ed. *Abuse and Maltreatment of the Elderly: Causes and Interventions.* (John Wright PSG, Boston) 1983.
57. *Report to the Governor and Legislature on the Activities of the Governor's Elder Abuse Prevention Task Force.* (Florida Department of Elder Affairs, Miami, Florida, April 1997).
58. Reulbach, D. M., and J. Tewksbury. "Collaboration between Protective Services and Law Enforcement: The Massachusetts Model" *Journal of Elder Abuse* 6 (2) (1994) p. 9.

11

GAY AND LESBIAN ABUSE

Chapter Outline

Learning Objectives

After reading this chapter, you should be able to discuss the following concepts:

- The definition of gay and lesbian abuse.
- The nature and extent of gay and lesbian abuse.
- The reasons for lack of study and reporting of gay and lesbian abuse by same-sex victims.
- How the courts and legal system have responded to gay and lesbian abuse.
- What professionals should do when confronted with a situation that involves gay or lesbian abuse.

Introduction

This chapter is included in this text because gay and lesbian abuse of partners does occur. Similar to Chapter 6, which dealt with ritualistic child abuse, there will be those who will respond negatively to the discussion of this type of aggression. Some would argue that including a discussion of gays and lesbians in a text dealing with "family violence" degrades the term *family.* To accept that premise is to deny reality and fail to anticipate issues that affect many professionals who work in the area of family violence. The fact of the matter is that gays and lesbians do live with, work with, and love same-sex partners. These living arrangements sometimes result in one of the members becoming a victim of violence by the other partner. Many of these individuals simply live together, and others have formalized an arrangement by declaring themselves to be domestic partners.

As explained in more detail later in this chapter, gays or lesbians who are victims of abuse by their partners fall within the definition of family violence used in this text. As more and more gays and lesbians acknowledge this form of violence, it will be incumbent on professionals to understand the dynamics that are involved and to offer support and treatment to the victims.

Gay couples can face the same kind of violence that sometimes occurs in heterosexual relationships. *When gays or lesbians live together as a family, some authorities refer to this as a nontraditional family.* By some estimates, there are several million nontraditional families in the United States.[1] Many of these families include children from previous marriages, adoptions, or artificial insemination of a lesbian

FOCUS Gay Love and Betrayal

Duane Rath at the age of fifty-one retired from the family business as a millionaire. For fourteen years he shared his life and love with his male partner, Ted Hurdman. They lived the life of the rich and famous, traveling across the country to posh resorts, attending opening ceremonies of AIDS clinics, being acknowledged by movie stars such as Elizabeth Taylor, and donating large sums of money to political campaigns.

On October 6, 1994, a groundskeeper at Rath's thirteen-acre estate in Janesville, Wisconsin, found his half-clothed body covered with blood in the master bedroom of his tudor-style mansion. Rath had been stabbed at least twelve times. One wound had punctured the main artery in his chest, causing him to bleed to death in a matter of seconds. Hurdman's body was discovered in the three-car garage where he had evidently turned on the engines of both a Mercedes Sports Coupe and a Toyota Land Rover, causing him to asphyxiate on the exhaust fumes of the cars.

No police reports of domestic violence between the couple were on file with the local police department. However, some locals and other knowledgeable friends suspect that increase tension in the relationship may have led to the fight that escalated into a murder/suicide.

Source: From Morales, J. "Sleeping with the Enemy," *The Advocate.* November 24, 1994, p. 41.

partner. These are family units in every aspect except for the issuance by the state of a marriage license. Polikoff proposes that these nontraditional families are defined by their sharing of emotions and their financial interdependence in the relationship.[2]

History and Attitudes

The history of the gay and lesbian struggle for equal treatment does not necessarily belong in a text on family violence. However, society's reactions to same-sex living arrangements does need to be explored so that professionals can understand some of the dynamics involved in a gay or lesbian relationship. Understanding these relationships will allow professionals to react properly when faced with a situation that involves gay or lesbian abuse.

Historically, homosexual behavior can be traced back to ancient Greece, where homosexuality was viewed as natural in many segments of Greek society. Plato's *Symposium* extolled the virtues of homosexual behavior and indicated that homosexual lovers would make the best soldiers.[3] One scholar indicates that homosexuality was not considered socially deviate behavior until Thomas Aquinas and St. Augustine argued that it was unnatural because it did not lead to conception.[4] In 1980, the DSM-III-R reclassified homosexual behavior as an alternative sexual lifestyle rather than deviant behavior. This view is not accepted by all members in society. Even in the medical community, there remains a core of opinion that homosexuality is unnatural sexual behavior.

Gay and lesbian couples have struggled for years to be accepted in society and accorded the same rights as heterosexual couples.

There is a continuing controversy surrounding the issue of marriage between gay and lesbian couples. However, this does not stop the formation or continuation of these relationships. The U.S. Census Bureau's annual survey in 1990 revealed 4.47 million households of unmarried adults with 1.6 million of this number composed of members of the same sex.[5] One of the most complex issues facing these couples is gay and lesbian abuse.

Definitions

Homosexual, gay, or *lesbian.* These terms standing by themselves evoke strong emotional responses from certain segments of society. However, in order to accurately discuss gay and lesbian abuse, one must start with a clear understanding of what these terms mean.

- *Homosexuality* is defined as the manifestation of sexual desire toward a member of one's own sex.
- *Gay* is defined as a male homosexual or a socially integrated group oriented toward and concerned with the welfare of homosexuals.

- *Lesbian* is defined as a female homosexual.[6] Lesbianism is believed to have been named for the Isle of Lesbos, where the practice of lesbianism was reputed to have been the norm in ancient days.

These terms are subject to debate and interpretation especially among members of the gay and lesbian community. If the gay and lesbian community cannot agree on what certain terms mean, and the heterosexual community cannot agree on what the term *family violence* means, it becomes very difficult to define abuse within the gay and lesbian communities.

In comparison to other forms of family violence, very little research has been done in the area of lesbian and gay abuse. However, some leaders within the profession have set forth definitions of gender-specific abuse. For example, Hart defines lesbian battering *as that pattern of violent and coercive behaviors whereby a lesbian seeks to control the thoughts, beliefs, or conduct of her intimate partner or to punish the intimate for resisting the perpetrator's control over her.*[7] Island and Letellier have published one of the first studies on gay abuse, and they define gay domestic violence *as any unwanted physical force, psychological abuse, material, or property damage inflicted on one gay man by another.*[8] Both of these definitions involve dynamics that have been discussed in other chapters dealing with spousal abuse. Some authorities might argue that gay and lesbian abuse should have its own definition because of the nature of the relationship. However, if one accepts that position, then heterosexual couples who live together but are not married should have their own definition of abuse. To approach this topic thusly would be to splinter all relationships into separate groups and lose sight of the overall dynamics that are involved in an abusive relationship. The definition of *family violence* established in Chapter 1 does not require that the parties be married or

FOCUS Some Myths and Facts about Gay and Lesbian Abuse

Myth: Battering and abuse do not exist in the lesbian community as only men abuse women.
Fact: Domestic violence does exist in the lesbian community. This is not a problem limited to heterosexual relationships.
Myth: Domestic violence affects only certain groups of lesbians.
Fact: Violence and abuse are found in all parts of the Lesbian community.
Myth: The problem in lesbian relationships is really fighting or mutual battering and not domestic violence.
Fact: The issue in domestic violence is control.
Myth: Domestic violence is not a problem for gay men.
Fact: Because men traditionally have been encouraged to use violence and power to control others, it is different for gay men to identify violence in their lives.
Myth: Domestic violence affects only certain groups of gay men.
Fact: Violence and abuse are found in all parts of the gay community.

Source: Adapted from New York City Gay and Lesbian Anti-Violence Project. "Behind Closed Doors, Battering and Abuse in Lesbian Relationships," and "Behind Closed Doors, Battering and Abuse in Relationships for Gay Men."

even of different sexes. Family violence was defined *as any act or omission by persons who are cohabitating that results in serious injury to other members of the family.* Because this term covers gay and lesbian abuse, it will be used to promote the fact that this type of aggression is in fact a form of family violence.

Nature and Scope of the Problem

To acknowledge that lesbian and gay couples face many of the same problems as heterosexual couples is to accord a legitimacy to their status. Some refuse to accept same-sex relationships as a legitimate expression of society's values. This viewpoint is only one of the reasons that very little research has been done in this area of family violence. There are other reasons for the failure to explore this type of aggression. Many of these reasons are unique to the lesbian and gay community and are discussed later in this chapter.

Extent of the Problem

The true extent of lesbian and gay family violence has never been accurately determined. Some researchers argue that battering within same-sex relationships is the same as it is for heterosexual couples, approximately 25 to 35 percent.[9] Other authorities have stated that domestic violence is the third most severe health problem facing gay men.[10]

The lesbian and gay communities themselves have contributed in some instances to a lack of hard scientific evidence concerning this form of family violence.[11] Lesbian communities may be reluctant for ideological reasons to admit that one woman can batter another. To do so is contrary to the idea of a peaceful, women-centered world. However, more discussion occurs in the lesbian community regarding battering than in the gay community. Gays may be reluctant to discuss gay abuse because, as one scholar put it, "The gay community would rather not know."[12]

When Yale University conducted a study dealing with battered women and the effectiveness of restraining orders, researchers discovered that gay and lesbian abuse was so extensive that they needed to include this segment of the population in the study.[13] A great deal of conflict exists among authorities as to whether gay men or lesbians are the more violent of the two groups. Some researchers claim that lesbians seem to be more aggressive than gay men or heterosexual women.[14] Other authors state that there is some evidence that violence may occur more frequently between gay men than between lesbians.[15] However, all parties to this debate agree that these conclusions are tentative at best and that more empirical research needs to be conducted in this area.

Types of Abuse

Lesbian and gay abusers typically use the same or similar types of violence on their victims. This includes techniques of physical and psychological terror such as rape, beatings, strangulation, humiliation, economic deprivation, and isolation. Hart established the following list of violent and coercive behaviors that are used in lesbian battering.

- *Physical:* Assaults with weapons; assaults with the abuser's own body such as biting, scratching, and so on; and deprivation of sleep, heat, or food
- *Sexual:* Rape, sex on demand, forced sex with others, physical assaults during sexual encounters, and sexually degrading language
- *Property:* Arson, slashing of belongings, pet abuse or destruction, and breaking household items
- Threats: Threats against the victim or her family or friends; stalking; and harassment
- *Economic control:* Control over income and assets of the partner and not working and requiring the victim to support the abuser
- *Psychological or emotional abuse:* Humiliation, lying, isolation, bursts of fury, pouting, and mind manipulation
- *Homophobic control:* Threatening to tell friends or family that the victim is a lesbian, telling the victim she deserves all she gets because she is lesbian, and reminding her she has no options because the homophobic world will not help her.[16]

Although no definitive study has been done on the different types of abuse suffered by gay couples, there is support for the proposition that they suffer the same types of abuse as lesbian couples do. There is an additional aspect to gay abuse that deals with forced sex.[17] In the past thirty years, a considerable body of knowledge and research has accumulated on sexual coercion in heterosexual relationships. Marital rape is discussed in depth in this text in Chapter 12. However, there is very little research into the area of gay men as victims of nonconsensual or forced sex.[18] Waterman and her associates conducted one of the first studies of sexual coercion in gay male and lesbian relationships.[19] The results of their research indicate that forced sex is a considerable problem for gay men. Hickson and his associates reviewed incidents of nonconsensual sexual activity among 930 gay men living in England and Wales.[20] Hickson points out that most research dealing with sexual assault on males has focused on prison populations. The presumed sexual orientation of men who rape other men has been subject to some debate. Hickson correctly states that men rape other men for the same reasons that they rape women and that male rape is rarely, if ever, a homosexual problem. Of the 930 men interviewed, 257, or 27 percent, stated that they had been subjected to nonconsensual sex at some point in their lives. After deleting ten of the men who were assaulted by women and twenty-eight respondents who declined to discuss the event or could not remember the details, the remaining 219 subjects' sexual histories were examined.

Hickson's research discloses a broad range of different types of sexual assaults on gay males. These assaults included older men touching younger boys, sexual assault of the victim by a heterosexual male after the victim had identified himself as gay, and a large number of assaults that occurred between gay males.

Legal and Judicial Responses

This section examines some of the legal aspects and other responses that are specific to lesbian and gay abuse within the context of family violence. Other chapters in this text have discussed the professionals's responsibility as well as law enforcement activities as they relate to child abuse and spousal abuse. This section points out that victims of gay and lesbian abuse face additional obstacles in reporting these crimes.

Reporting of Abuse

Just as female victims of male battering are reluctant or incapable of reporting or leaving the abusing spouse, so are same-sex victims.[21] However, gay and lesbian victims face additional problems when it comes to disclosure or detachment from the abuser. Many of these problems are unique to the lesbian or gay community and in the past have contributed to a lack of academic research in this area of family violence.

A great deal of misinformation exists regarding AIDS, its effects, and how it may be acquired. Gay or lesbian victims who are HIV positive may feel that they do not have any support system available to them other than the abusing partner. Also, if the abuser has AIDS or is HIV positive, the victim may feel a great deal of remorse at the thought of reporting their partners to law enforcement agencies or otherwise abandoning them.[22]

The abuser may also prevent the victim from disclosing the abuse or leaving the relationship by threatening to "out" the victim. *Outing is disclosure of the victim's sexual preference.* The abuser may threaten to tell the victim's friends, family, or others unless the victim agrees to conceal the abuse. Even if the victim is open about his or her sexual preference, the batterer may exploit fears of sexist and heterosexual stereotypes to convince the victim that reporting the incident is useless.[23]

Lesbian and gay victims face additional pressure from their peers within the gay community. Some authorities point out that the gay community's failure to acknowledge family violence within its ranks is based on a far that acknowledgment of such behavior will lead to increased derision from the heterosexual community because it will add credence to the homophobic attitude that gay men and lesbians are deviates.[24]

Another problem facing lesbian and gay victims is the critical shortage of support services and organizations that offer support for same-sex victims of family violence.[25] Specialized counseling services for gay and lesbian victims of family violence are available in only a few cities: New York, San Francisco, Seattle, and Minneapolis.[26] No city has established an emergency shelter specifically for gay men or lesbian victims of family violence.[27] Although some lesbian victims may be able to use battered women's services or shelters, this option is not available to gay men.

Legal Aspects of Gay and Lesbian Abuse

Gay and lesbian victims face additional hurdles when they attempt to prevent further abuse by their partners. These obstacles include outdated and, in many cases, homophobic attitudes by law enforcement officers, attorneys, and members of the judiciary. Simply reporting the incident may cause the victims to suffer more humiliation and pain from a system that is ill-equipped to deal with this form of family violence.

Law enforcement officers and members of the judicial system have historically been reluctant to acknowledge gay and lesbian abuse. In many instances, this leaves the victims without assistance from the legal system. Therefore, abused gays and lesbians are generally less likely to report incidents of domestic violence to the police.

There are reported cases where members of the judiciary have made comments reflecting their negative feelings toward gay and lesbian couples. In *Constant A. v Paul C. A.*, the court awarded custody of the children to the father stating, ". . . once the father established the mother's lesbian relationship and his own legitimate and stable heterosexual relationship, a presumption arose favoring the preferability of the traditional relationship."[28]

Although many professionals in the criminal justice system are aware of the dynamics involved in male battering of women, they may be unwilling to accept the fact that these same kinds of dynamics are operating in same-sex battery. This lack of knowledge on the part of police and the judicial system works to the advantage of the abuser; it is not uncommon for the abuser to claim that he is in fact the victim. Because many gay and lesbian couples may be the same size physically, the stereotypical view that the larger person is always the aggressor in a relationship may prevent professionals from seeing the facts as they are. Assuming professionals within the criminal justice system are willing to act on allegations of same-sex battering, the laws in sixteen states do not cover same-sex, nonrelated cohabitants.

Some states make certain sex acts criminal even when they occur between consenting adults. In *Bowers v Hardwick*, the U.S. Supreme Court has upheld the right of states to impose criminal sanctions on acts that occur in the privacy of the bedroom.[29] Although sodomy statutes among consenting adults are criminal in only six states, misinformation and fear may allow the perpetrator to threaten the victim with disclosure of certain sex acts that might be considered criminal. As stated in *Baker v Wade*, "the existence of these criminal laws, even if they are not enforced . . . does result in stigma, emotional stress and other adverse affects. The anxieties caused to homosexuals—fear of arrest, loss of jobs, discovery, etc.—can cause severe mental health problems."[30]

Intervention Issues

Professionals can support victims of lesbian and gay family violence in a variety of ways. Friman suggests the following intervention techniques for these types of survivors:

- *Acknowledge the violence:* Violence can occur in same-sex relationships. Additionally, same-sex victims may not receive the same type of support from their own communities as heterosexual victims of family violence.
- *Encourage the victim to report the violence:* Many victims have not come out and fear the repercussions of reporting the incident. Additionally, many victims believe that efforts to get assistance from law enforcement is futile.
- *Acknowledge the effects of religious oppression:* Some members of the gay and lesbian community have been told that the life they lead is immoral because it violates traditional religious tenets. Those victims may believe that family violence is part of the punishment meted out against them for their lifestyle.
- *Focus on empowerment:* Many same-sex partners already feel disempowered because of their lifestyle. Attempt to explain the power imbalances may also exist in heterosexual family violence.
- *Become part of a support network and act as a referral resource:* Many gays and lesbians live in isolation and do not have any support system or knowledge of where to turn for help and assistance. Professionals in this field should be aware of same-sex support groups or agencies that will assist these victims.
- *Don't blame and shame:* Many lesbians and gays have a heightened fear of abandonment. It is never appropriate to blame an individual for staying in an abusive relationship, even if you or others would terminate it.
- *Gain cultural sensitivity:* Professionals should seek out opportunities to educate themselves about gay and lesbian cultures and issues. Without such insight, it is almost impossible to provide support activities.[31]

Therapists are beginning to discuss gay and lesbian relationships more often.[32] Those in academia continue researching issues of gay and lesbian abuse.[33] An example of a local program that provides support for victims of gay and lesbian abuse is the New York City Gay & Lesbian Anti-Violence Project. It provides a number of services for victims of this type of family violence, including the following:

- Telephone counseling and crisis intervention
- Short-term in-person counseling
- Assistance in obtaining orders of protection
- Police advocacy and precinct accompaniment
- Crime victims' compensation filing and advocacy
- Court advocacy, monitoring, and accompaniment

- Information and referrals
- Community education and outreach
- Volunteer training
- Hospital accompaniment
- Advocacy with other service agencies

These services are very similar to those offered to heterosexual victims of family violence by a number of social service agencies. As more gays and lesbians accept the fact that it is all right to come out of another closet and admit that they have been victims of abuse, the sooner society will accept this form of aggression as a part of the totality of the circumstances that are involved in family violence.

Summary

Gay and lesbian abuse is slowly being recognized as a form of family violence. Although the true nature and extent of this type of aggression is unknown, more research is being conducted in this area. Some studies place the incidents of same-sex abuse at the same level of abuse experienced by heterosexual couples. Gay and lesbian victims of family violence face special problems that heterosexual victims do not. One of these is the lack of services for parties to this type of domestic violence.

Professionals in the field of family violence are just now awakening to the fact that gay and lesbian victims need assistance and support. Law enforcement officers and some members of the judiciary may still reflect homophobic attitudes when dealing with victims of gay and lesbian abuse. However, the fact that it is now being discussed in professional journals, conferences, and college texts indicates a new awareness and openness to deal with this last covert form of family violence.

Key Terms

nontraditional family—when gays or lesbians live together as a family.

lesbian battering—that pattern of violent and coercive behaviors in which a lesbian seeks to control the thoughts, beliefs, or conduct of her intimate partners or to punish the partner for resisting the perpetrator's control over her.

gay domestic violence—any unwanted physical force, psychological abuse, material, or property damage inflicted on one gay man by another.

outing—the disclosure of the victim's sexual preference.

family violence—any act or omission by persons who are cohabitating that results in serious injury to other members of the family.

homosexuality—the manifestation of sexual desire toward a member of one's own sex.

gay—a male homosexual or a socially integrated group oriented toward and concerned with the welfare of homosexuals.

lesbian—a female homosexual. Lesbianism is believed to have been named for the Isle of Lesbos, where the practice of lesbianism was reputed to have been the norm in ancient days.

Discussion Questions

1. Should there be a separate definition for gay abuse and lesbian abuse?
2. Are the dynamics involved in abuse of same-sex partners different from those that occur within heterosexual relationships? Justify your answer.
3. List the various stereotypes regarding gay and lesbian couples. Why do you think these stereotypes exist?
4. What can we do to limit or decrease the stereotypes that exist regarding gay and lesbian relationships?
5. Should lesbians be admitted to battered women's shelters? What alternatives would you recommend for gay victims of family violence?

Suggested Readings

Berrill, K. T., and G. M. Herek, ed. *Hate Crimes: Confronting Violence against Lesbians and Gay Men.* (Sage, Newbury Park, California) 1992.

Boswell, J. *Christianity, Social Tolerance, and Homosexuality.* (University of Chicago Press, Chicago) 1980.

Gonsiorek, J. C., ed. *Breach of Trust.* (Sage, Thousand Oaks, California) 1995.

Island, D., and P. Letellier. *Men Who Beat the Men Who Love Them.* (Harrington Park Press, New York) 1991.

Lobel, K., ed. *Naming the Violence: Speaking Out about Lesbian Battering.* (Seal Press, Seattle) 1986.

Masters, W., V. Johnson, and R. Kolodny. *Masters and Johnson on Sex and Human Loving.* (Little Brown, Boston) 1968.

Renzetti, C. M. *Violent Betrayal, Partner Abuse in Lesbian Relationships.* (Sage, Newbury Park, California) 1992.

Endnotes

1. Hunter, N. D., and N. D. Polikoff. "Custody Rights of Lesbian Mothers: Legal Theory and Litigation Strategy." *Buffalo Law Rev.* (25) 1976, p. 691.
2. Polikoff, N. "This Child Does Have Two Mothers: Redefining Parenthood to Meet the Needs of Children in Lesbian-Mother and Other Nontraditional Families." *Georgia Law Rev.* (78) 1990, p. 459.
3. Masters, W., V. Johnson, and R. Kolodny. *Masters and Johnson on Sex and Human Loving.* (Little Brown, Boston) 1968.
4. Boswell, J. *Christianity, Social Tolerance, and Homosexuality.* (University of Chicago Press, Chicago) 1980.
5. Saluter, A. F. "Marital Status and Living Arrangements: March 1990." *U.S. Bureau of the Census, Series P-20,* No. 450 (May 1991), p. 73.
6. *Webster's New Collegiate Dictionary.* (G & C Merriam Co., Springfield, Massachusetts) 1981.
7. Hart, B. "Lesbian Battering: An Examination." Kerry Lobel, ed. *Naming the Violence:*

Speaking Out about Lesbian Battering. (Seal Press, Seattle, Washington) 1986, p. 173.
8. Island, D., and Patrick Letellier. *Men Who Beat the Men Who Love Them.* (Harrington Park Press, New York) 1991, p. 27.
9. Renzetti, C. M. *Violent Betrayal, Partner Abuse in Lesbian Relationships.* (Sage, Newbury Park, California) 1992, pp. 17–18.
10. Island, D. and P. Letellier. *Men Who Beat the Men Who Love Them.* p. 14.
11. Jenness, V. "Social Movement Growth, Domain Expansion, and Framing Processes: The Gay/Lesbian Movement and Violence against Gays and Lesbians as a Social Problem," *Social Problems.* (42) No. 1 February 1995, p. 145.
12. Island, D., and P. Letellier. *Men Who Beat the Men Who Love Them.* pp. 10 and 36.
13. Brown, G., et al. "Starting a TRO Project: Student Representation of Battered Women." *Yale Law Rev.* (96) 1987, p. 1985.
14. Hunter, M. D. "Homosexuals as a New Class of Domestic Violence Subjects Under the New Jersey Prevention of Domestic Violence Act of 1991." *University of Louisville Journal of Family Law* (31) 1992/93, p. 557.
15. Bricker, D. "Fatal Defense: An Analysis of Battered Women's Syndrome, Expert Testimony for Gay Men and Lesbians Who Kill Abusive Partners." *Brooklyn Law Rev.* (58) Winter 1993, p. 1379.
16. Hart, B. "Lesbian Battering: An Examination." In *Naming the Violence.* pp. 188–189.
17. Coxwell, A. W., and M. B. King." Male Victims of Rape and Sexual Abuse," *Sexual and Marital Therapy* 11(3) August 1996, p. 297.
18. Waldner-Haugrud, L. K., and L. Vaden-Gratch. "Sexual Coercion in Gay/Lesbian Relationships: Descriptives and Gender Differences." 12(1) *Violence and Victims* (Spring 1997).
19. Waterman, C. K., L. J. Dawson, and M. J. Bologna, "Sexual Coercion in Gay Male and Lesbian Relationships: Predictors and Implications for Support Services." *The Journal of Sex Research* 26/1 (February, 1989), p. 118.
20. Hickson, F. C. I., P. M. Davies, A. J. Hunt, P. Weatherburn, T. J. McManus, and A. P. M. Coxon. "Gay Men as Victims of Nonconsensual Sex." *Archives of Sexual Behavior* (23/3) 1994, p. 281.
21. Snow, K. "The Violence at Home," *The Advocate.* June 2, 1992, p. 60.
22. "Violence against People with HIV/AIDS." Pamphlet prepared by the New York City Gay & Lesbian Anti-Violence Project. (New York) 1991.
23. Savin-Williams, R. C. "Verbal and Physical Abuse as Stressors in the Lives of Lesbian, Gay Male and Bisexual Youths: Associations with School Problems, Running Away, Substance Abuse, Prostitution, and Suicide." *Journal of Consulting and Clinical Psychology* (62) No. 2 April 1994, p. 261.
24. Benowitz, M. "How Homophobia Affects Lesbians' Response to Violence in Lesbian Relationships." In *Naming the Violence,* p. 200.
25. Margolies, L. and E. Leeder. "Violence at the Door: Treating Lesbian Batterers," *Violence Against Women* 1(2) June 1995, p. 139.
26. Winfield, P. "Rare Program Aids Battered Lesbians, Gays:Violence Mirrors Heterosexual Incidents." *Seattle Times.* September 24, 1990 at E3.
27. Mann, J. "A Grant in Trouble." *Washington Post.* July 5, 1995 at C3.
28. 496 A.2d 1 at 7 (1985).
29. 478 U.S. 186, (1986).
30. 553 F.Supp. 1121 (N.D. Tex. 1982), appeal dismissed, 743 F.2d 236 (5th Cir. 1984), Cert. denied 478 U.S. 1022 (1986).
31. Friman, K. "Intimate Partner Violence in Same Sex Relationships: Implications for Community Response," paper presented at the Twenty-Third North American Victim Assistance Conference (Houston, August 17–22, 1977).
32. See for example a special section entitled, "Gay and Lesbians Are Out of the Closet." In *The Family Therapy Networker.* January/February 1991.
33. Gwat-Yong Lie, and S. Gentlewarrier. "Intimate Violence in Lesbian Relationships: Discussion of Survey Findings and Practice Implications." *Journal of Social Service Research* 15 (1/2) 1991, p. 41

12

SPECIAL POPULATIONS AND FAMILY VIOLENCE

Chapter Outline

Learning Objectives

After reading this chapter, you should be able to discuss the following concepts:

- The HIV/AIDS disease.
- How the HIV/AIDS disease affects victims of crimes.

- The differences among the various victim populations that are affected by the HIV/AIDS disease.
- The victimization of disabled persons.
- The cultural issues of family violence.
- The issues facing rural family violence victims.

HIV/AIDS Victims[1]

HIV/AIDS is the black plague of the 1990s. It causes normally rational professionals to become emotional at the thought that they may have been exposed to AIDS. We are still learning the consequences of this disease, but one factor remains constant: Persons with AIDS die because of the infection, and at present there is no known cure. It is therefore critical that professionals in this area understand how to respond to victims who have been exposed to this disease.

Medical and Psychological Aspects of HIV/AIDS

AIDS is the acronym for the medical term *acquired immune deficiency syndrome.* The "acquired" portion of the term means that the condition is not a birth defect but was acquired after birth from another person. The "immune deficiency" portion of the term means that the immune system is repeatedly attacked by infections and diseases until it becomes so weak that it cannot perform its job. The "syndrome" portion of the term means that a series of signs or symptoms occur together and characterize this particular abnormality. The term *AIDS* should normally be used only when the person has become seriously ill and fulfilled the Center for Disease Control's criteria for a formal diagnosis of AIDS. Otherwise, the more correct description is "HIV+," or "HIV positive," for persons who have the HIV disease or infection.[2]

The abbreviation HIV stands for the *human immunodeficiency virus,* which takes over and destroys the body's natural immune system. As the immune system deteriorates, the person's body is unable to protect itself from infections and diseases. The person dies from a disease or an infection. The person does not die from AIDS or HIV; rather, death results from one or more of the infections that overcome the person's weakened immune system.

Two primary types of HIV are HIV-1, which is the most common and deadly, and HIV-2, which acts in the same way as HIV-1 but reproduces more slowly. Almost all infected persons in the United States suffer from HIV-1. Once a person is infected with HIV, there is no known cure. The progression of the disease can be slowed with medication but cannot be stopped. Most cases result in death, but some persons, known as "nonprogressive long-term survivors," have the virus, but it does not destroy their immune systems and they do not become sick and die from the disease. Researchers continue to study these individuals in an attempt to learn why the virus affects them differently than most of the infected population.[3]

The HIV disease is a spectrum disease; that is, it has various phases that run along a spectrum, from wellness to illness.[4] Normally, the virus replicates itself in the lymph glands and then begins to dump copious amounts of itself into the bloodstream, setting the stage for progression of the disease. There are five phases in the HIV Infection.

Phase 1. The *asymptomatic incubation period* lasts from four to six weeks. Phase 1 is often called the *window period* because the infected person has HIV present and replicating in the blood but generally no detectable symptoms. This is a dangerous period because the infected person has no idea that he or she is contagious. At some point during this phase, the first antibody is produced, and the person converts from HIV negative to HIV positive. This conversion is called the *seroconversion.*

Phase 2. The *acute primary infection* lasts from one to two weeks. During phase 2, the person will experience some symptoms of early infection but may not recognize the cause of the symptoms. For example, the person may attribute aches, pains, and swollen glands to the flu. The infected person has sufficient antibodies in his or her system to detect the HIV virus during this phase.

Phase 3. The *asymptomatic phase* lasts three to fifteen years. This phase is characterized by seeming good health while the HIV continues to replicate in the blood and certain tissues and begins to slowly erode the body's immune system. The length of this phase will vary from person to person, depending on a number of factors, including the person's overall general health, the way the person cares for him- or herself, and the medical treatment received.

Phase 4. The *symptomatic phase with persistent generalized lymphadenopathy* lasts one to three years. Serious symptoms signal the beginning of phase 4. Infections that a normal healthy person would fight off will make an HIV-positive person ill. The symptoms for this phase include fever, night sweats, diarrhea, enlargement of the lymph glands, weight loss, oral lesions, fatigue, rashes, and cognitive slowing.

Phase 5. The *AIDS case* lasts from one to three years. This condition meets the Center for Disease Control's criteria for the definition of AIDS. As the person approaches death (end-stage AIDS), it is common for him or her to have multiple symptoms. The person dies as a result of infections and disease.[5]

The HIV disease is not transmitted by animals or insects or by using swimming pools or hot tubs. It cannot be transmitted after contact with an infected person's clothes or by using the same toilet seat, eating utensils, drinking glasses, or telephone. There has never been a case in which HIV was transmitted by kissing or cardiopulmonary resuscitation. For HIV to be passed from one person to another, there must be an infected party, an uninfected party, and a route of entry to get particles of the virus from the donor to the recipient. The fact that HIV has been found in blood, semen, saliva, serum, urine, tears, breast milk, vaginal secretions, lung fluid, and cerebrospinal fluid, does not mean that it is transmissible through those fluids. The three most common routes of HIV transmission are sexual transmission, blood-to-blood transmission, and mother-to-child transmission.

Most cases of HIV transmission occur as a result of sexual activities. Anal intercourse carries the highest risk of transmission because the fragile tissues of the anus and rectum may tear as a result of the friction of intercourse. Vaginal intercourse is also a high-risk practice with an infection person. Oral sex with a man or a woman, although lower in risk than anal or vaginal intercourse, may also transmit the virus. Because of the violent nature of most sex crimes, there is much concern that victims may be exposed to HIV.

Blood-to-blood transmission can also occur in a variety of ways. Using infected needles can transmit the disease. This method of transmission is common among drug users and is of concern to health workers who receive needle sticks during their work with patients. The virus may be transmitted with contaminated blood or body fluids that come into contact with open wounds. This is an area of concern in domestic violence cases in which one party may get infected blood in an open wound of another person.

Mother-to-child transmission occurs when the virus is transmitted to the fetus of a pregnant women. This is the most common form of pediatric transmission. A newborn child may also become infected as a result of breast feeding from his or her HIV-positive mother.

Both AIDS and HIV present social, psychological, and medical problems. AIDS has changed our view of public health and affected how we judge others. People with HIV disease respond like all others in a crisis situation. Learning that one has HIV is a severe stressor because of the inevitable result: death. Service providers must understand that there is no right or wrong way to respond to this life-threatening disease.

When a person learns that he or she is infected with HIV, he or she may react with a wide range of emotions similar to those experienced by victims of crime. After passing through these emotions, he or she must face the physical, social, and psychological aspects of living and dying with this disease. As death becomes more imminent, AIDS victims began to plan for death. This process becomes difficult and sometimes impossible because the victim may be coping with HIV-related dementia.

The major characteristic of dementia as a result of HIV is the presence of a dementia that is judged to be the direct pathophysiological consequence of the HIV disease. The major features of this type of dementia are forgetfulness, slowness, poor concentration, and difficulties with problem solving. The infected person may exhibit apathy and social withdrawal and occasionally experience delirium, delusions, or hallucinations.[6]

Professionals must remember that AIDS is a medical disease that has additional social and psychological aspects. Because some victims of crimes may become infected with the virus, professionals must be knowledgeable regarding the disease and be prepared to address sensitive issues. The next section examines some of these issues.

Service Issues

Once society acknowledged the existence and impact of the HIV disease, victim service providers have attempted to deal with the impact of this disease on the victims they serve. Most service providers focused solely on victims of rape. However, with the passage of time and the expansion of knowledge regarding the disease, victim service professionals now must understand how the HIV disease affects victims of child sexual abuse and other forms of family violence. Service providers must also be ready to deal with persons who are infected with the disease and who are victimized. Additionally, they must respond to family members, friends, and colleagues of these victims who all bring their own concerns, biases, and feelings to their interactions with victim service providers.

The HIV/AIDS disease is a medical condition and is therefore considered confidential information. Victim service providers must always remember that they cannot disseminate the medical status of a victim suffering from this disease without their express permission. Victim professionals must be capable of explaining the consequences to victims of disclosing or not disclosing their condition to others.

A critical first step in responding to these victim's special needs is to create a safe and open environment in which a victim, family member, friend, or colleague will feel secure enough in raising the HIV/AIDS issue. By creating this safe environment, the victim will receive a message that he or she is with someone who has some knowledge of the disease and is open to discussing it. Victims must be reassured that the professional is not sitting in judgment of them or their lifestyle.

The displaying of AIDS-awareness posters in the office may assist in establishing this open environment. These posters can be obtained from local AIDS service organizations, county health departments, and the Center for Disease Control. Information regarding the disease should be made available in brochures. Many victims have found lists of local AIDS service organizations very helpful.[7]

Raising the issue of HIV/AIDS with a victim who may be at risk may be one of the most difficult tasks undertaken by a victim service provider. This topic may be made easier by the open and safe office environment. Victims may not want to discuss this topic for a variety of reasons: They may not realize that they are at risk, the victim may understand that he or she is at risk but fearful of discussing the risk with anyone, or the victim may already know that they are infected and decide not to disclose that fact.

Victim assistance professionals should take the time to review the victim's risk of infection and motivation for being tested. They should explain the testing process, including the various test results. They may need to consider a collaborative response to a victim's inquiry by using a local AIDS service provider. Victim service providers should never deliver the victim's HIV/AIDS test results. This would possibly introduce an uncomfortable aspect to an already existing relationship as the victim professional might become a constant reminder of the moment the positive results were delivered to the victim.[8]

PRACTICUM Who Should Undergo Mandatory Testing for HIV/AIDS Disease?

Sexual predators	Professional athletes
Physicians, dentists, nurses	Law enforcement personnel
Members of the military	All persons over the age of fifteen

One of the most controversial issues in the criminal justice field today involves involuntary testing of offenders. In recent years, several states have passed laws that give victims of sexual assault access to information about the HIV status of their offender.[9] These laws apply to those arrested or convicted or who have plead guilty to crimes involving sexual penetration or other exposure to an offender's bodily fluids. At the federal level, sexual assault victims can request an order requiring the HIV testing of the defendant if the court finds probable cause that the defendant committed the offense, that the victim has received appropriate counseling, and that the information is necessary for the health of the victim.

If the offender is positive, it does not mean that the victim will have contacted the virus, but simply learning of the offender's status may cause the victim unnecessary emotional upheaval. The victim must also be tested to be absolutely sure that the virus was or was not transmitted. Other professionals fear that imposing mandatory testing on offenders will lead to mandatory testing of other groups or professions. This continues to be a hotly debated topic.[10] The above *Practicum* lists distinct classes of persons in our society. Discuss the advantages and disadvantages of mandatory testing of these persons.

If we adopt mandatory testing of offenders and other groups for the HIV/AIDS disease, isn't it also reasonable to test those groups for additional diseases, such as all other sexually transmitted diseases?[11]

Professionals in this field normally work with persons who have already experience the trauma of victimization. Most victim assistance providers do not encounter a person who has a life-threatening illness such as the HIV/AIDS virus. When they work with these victims, it is with the knowledge that the victim will surely die as a result of this disease. It is therefore critical that everyone in the criminal justice system understand the effect and consequences of victims infected with the HIV/AIDS disease.

Specific Victim Populations

Victim service providers must not only understand the HIV/AIDS disease but also be able to relate to specific victim populations that might be exposed to the disease. This section focuses on those victims for which HIV/AIDS is a concern.

The victim populations include victims of rape, child victims, family violence victims, and HIV-positive persons who are victimized.

Victims of Rape

Many rape victims are concerned regarding possible exposure to HIV. There is a continuing controversy surrounding the transmission of HIV during a rape. This is not to say that such a transmission has not occurred only, that at present the Center for Disease Control, which officially tracks AIDS cases, does not classify cases by consensual or nonconsensual sex. Additionally, given the nature of the disease, it is difficult to link exposure to the virus to a rape. However, the concern about the disease and exposure to it is a very real concern for victims of rape and their consensual sexual partners.[12]

Even as enlightened as we like to think our society is about crime and victimization, victims of rape are still reluctant to report such assaults. Whereas many victims have experienced difficulty disclosing their rapes to their significant partners, the additional factor of possible exposure to the HIV virus may make disclosure even more difficult. The grieving process that normally occurs after a rape may now be extended and deepened because of the added fear regarding the HIV virus.[13] All these issues will continue to confront victim service providers as they work with victims of rape until we find a cure for the HIV/AIDS disease.[14]

Child Victims

The Center for Disease Control reports that there were 6,209 pediatric cases of AIDS in the United States as of the end of 1994. Children who are sexually assaulted are considered to be at higher risk than adult victims of sexual assault. This increased risk is based on two factors: (1) child victims may be repeatedly assaulted over a long period of time by the same perpetrator and (2) children are at a greater risk of injury during penetration and as a result there is a higher likelihood of transmission of the virus during the sexual act.

Victim service professionals must assist parents in making informed decisions regarding how much information to give to a young child who has been sexually assaulted by an HIV-positive perpetrator. The victim service professional should work closely with the AIDS service provider regarding counseling and other support techniques for both the child and the parents.[15]

Family Violence Victims

Family violence occurs every day, from the mansions of Brentwood to the slums of New York. This type of violence crosses all ethnic, social, and sexual boundaries and its victims include blacks, Hispanics, Asians, and homosexuals. Some family violence victims are forced to participate in drug usage with the abuser and his friends. Additionally, the abuser may be using drugs or engaging in sexual acts with multiple partners that exposes him to the disease. He then can pass the virus along to his partner during "consensual" sexual relations. The victim's request for use of a condom or other device may be met with violence by the abuser.

Shelters for battered women have traditionally been places of sanctuary for these victims. The spread of HIV/AIDS disease has added another complication to the heavy burden carried by these shelters. Victim service providers must ensure that staff working in the shelters understand the medical and legal aspects of the disease so as not to further traumatize those residents who are HIV positive.

HIV-Positive Persons Who Are Victimized

Persons who are HIV positive are no different from the rest of society as it relates to becoming a victim of a violent crime. What is different is that some persons have been victimized merely because of their real or perceived HIV status. Other HIV-positive victims must decide whether they are going to disclose their status to authorities when reporting crimes of violence.

Violence related to HIV covers a wide spectrum of acts, including simple verbal abuse, harassment, job discrimination, and actual physical attacks. The person's appearance may suggest that they are at risk of carrying the HIV virus. Certain groups, such as homosexuals, drug users, and those wearing AIDS support ribbons and other symbols, have suffered HIV-related violence.

A person who is living with the HIV virus must expend a great deal of energy on day-to-day survival, including taking medications, attending medical appointments and treatment sessions, and going to support groups. Suffering criminal victimization with its attendant responsibilities of reporting the crime, interviews with law enforcement officers, attending court, and facing the perpetrator can add a tremendous amount of stress to the victim's life. This increased stress can dramatically affect his or her health. For this and other reasons, HIV-positive victims may decide not to pursue reporting victimization. Still others may report, but as the burdens of appearing in court increase they may opt to drop the charges. Victim service providers must be aware of the dynamics of this form of victimization and respond accordingly by supporting the victim.

Disabled Victims

Introduction

Disabled victims have the same rights as any other victim, but they remain one of the largest categories of victims to be neglected by our criminal justice system.[16] This is because they are not afforded the same type of access, legitimacy, or respect as other victims. For example, as the previous *Practicum* shows, although some material in the criminal justice system is in several different languages, very few agencies may have information in braille. This section examines disabled victims and some forms of family violence.

Crimes against persons with developmental and other severe disabilities is a problem similar to other forms of violence.[17] Some research indicates that the level

PRACTICUM Disability and Crime

It was late in the evening when Jane was returning home from the local convenience store with a cartom of milk and some other groceries. It was cold and rainy, and Jane was hurrying as fast as she could to reach her apartment when two persons grabbed her from behind and pulled her into an alley.

They took her purse, trashed her bag of groceries, and proceeded to rape her. Several other people walked by the alley but did nothing to render assistance. The perpetrators fled only when they heard a police siren. Jane was taken to the local emergency room and after a medical examination gave a report to the police and was informed by the investigating officer of her right to contact the local victim/witness office. Several days later, Jane went downtown to the office. She had to ride ten stories in a crowded elevator and was late for the scheduled appointment. Once inside the office, she was asked to have a seat, then waited about thirty minutes before she finally was interviewed regarding her victimization. After the interview with a victim service volunteer, Jane wanted to take some of the information home so she could study her rights as a victim more closely, unfortunately, the office did not have any pamphlets in her language—Jane was blind.

1. What are the issues faced by a victim service provider in this situation?

2. What problems did Jane encounter? How would you attempt to solve those problems? Assume that you have no additional funds in your agency.

of violence against children and adults with developmental and other severe disabilities is as much as five times higher than against the general public, that such crimes are reported at a much lower rate, and that there are indications of lower rates of prosecution and conviction.[18]

One of the first issues confronting victim service providers is how to respond to victims of family violence who also have a disability.[19] Each type of disability may require a different response on the part of the victim service provider. For example, a victim with a hearing impairment will have different needs than a victim with a sight impairment. However, there are certain rules that apply to all family violence victims who are disabled:

- Do look directly at the victim when addressing him or her. Deliberately averting your eyes is impolite and can be uncomfortable.
- Do feel free to ask a disabled victim how you should act or communicate most effectively with him or her if you have any doubts about correctness in the situation.
- Do address and speak directly to the disabled person, even if he or she is accompanied or assisted by a third party nondisabled person.
- Do feel free to offer physical assistance to a disabled person, such as offering your arm if the need arises, but do not assume that he or she will need it or accept it.

- Do ask a disabled victim whether he or she has any needs that will require special services or arrangements and then attempt to make arrangements to meet those needs.
- Don't stare, and avoid looking at a visible disability or deformity or expressing sympathy to the disabled victim.
- Don't tell the disabled victim that you admire his or her courage or determination for living with the disability. The disabled person doesn't want to be thought of as a hero.
- Don't avoid humorous situations that occur as a result of a disability. Take your cue from the victim.[20]

These do's and don'ts should be used as guidelines when working with disabled persons. Victim service professionals must understand that the disabled person, just like all other victims, is an individual, and each must be approached and interacted with as an individual. For years, people with disabilities tolerated discrimination and hardship as a result of society's reaction to their disability. Congress finally addressed this issue when it enacted the Civil Rights Act of 1964 and the Americans With Disabilities Act of 1990 (ADA).

Legal Issues

About 43 million Americans have one or more disabilities, be they mental, physical, or both. They may be congenital (occurring at birth) or adventitious (occurring after birth). As indicated earlier in this chapter, a disabled person is one who has a physical or mental impairment that substantially limits one or more of the major life activities of that individual, one who has a record of such impairment, or one who is regarded as having such an impairment. This definition is founded on the language contained in ADA, which is one of the most comprehensive pieces of civil rights legislation ever passed by Congress since the Civil Rights Act of 1964. The ADA was enacted by Congress to protect the employment and accessibility rights of persons suffering from disabilities. Any agency receiving any type of government funding (federal, state, or local) must comply with the provisions contained in the ADA.

Some authorities state that persons with developmental and other severe disabilities represent about 10 percent of the U.S. population (1.8 percent developmental disabilities, 5 percent adult-onset brain impairment, and 2.8 percent severe major mental disorders). As many as 30 to 40 percent of all families may have loved ones or close friends with developmental or other severe disabilities. These numbers may increase as the U.S. population ages. Fifteen percent of Americans over the age of fifty-five have cognitive disabilities, and 25 percent of those over the age of seventy-five suffer from this form of disability.[21]

Disabilities covered by the law include physical and mental impairments. Physical disabilities include physiological disorders or conditions, disfigurement, or loss of the use of any body system. Specific examples include cerebral palsy, epilepsy, multiple sclerosis, AIDS/HIV infections, cancer, heart disease, and diabetes. Mental

FOCUS Memory and Disabled Victims

Children who are victims of sexual assault have been accused of fabricating the events. Others claim that these child victims have been programmed or had false memories implanted in their minds by social workers, counselors, law enforcement officers or others in the criminal justice system. (This topic is addressed in more detail in Chapter 3.) Whereas interviewing children takes a special kind of expertise, interviewing disabled victims takes the same skills plus a great deal of empathy.

Ann Craft has pointed out that professionals who work with disabled victims are becoming more aware of their lack of skills in assisting these victims to give accounts of what happened to them. In an early study, Pear and Wyatt studied the reliability of testimony from disabled child victims. They found that the disabled children's unprompted recall was reliable and that prompted recall was much less reliable than recall from children with normal intelligence.

Dent found that interviewing disabled children poses a real dilemma for professionals in this field: On one hand, disabled child victims are in need of prompts to access their memory. On the other hand, their recall may be influenced by the nature of the prompts used. She examined the effects on disabled children of three types of questions: free recall, specific, and general. Free recall questions consisted of a request for an unprompted narration where any cues contained in the instructions were given in all conditions. Specific questions took the form of "What color was the man's hair?" whereas general questions took the form of "What did the man look like?" Dent found that specific questions were the least accurate, free recall questions were higher in reliability than specific questions, and general questions were the most accurate. However, other scholars have questioned Dent's conclusion regarding the validity of specific questions. Bull argues that specific questions are not necessarily more suggestive than general questions. What all authorities agree on is that more research needs to be conducted in this newly emerging area of family violence.

Sources: Craft, A. "NAPSAC in Context," in *Newsletter of the National Association for the Protection from Sexual Abuse of Adults and Children with Learning Disabilities.* (Nottingham, England 1981); Pear, T., and S. Wyatt. "The Testimony of Normal and Mentally Defective Children," 3 *Journal of Psychology* 3 (1914), p. 388; Dent, H. R. "Experimental Study of the Effectiveness of Different Techniques of Questioning Mentally Handicapped Child Witnesses," *British Journal of Clinical Psychology* 27 (1986), pp. 13–17; and Bull, R. "Innovative Techniques for the Questioning of Child Witnesses, Especially Those Who Are Young and Those with Learning Disability," in M. S. Zaragoza, et. al., eds., *Memory and Testimony in the Child Witness.* (Sage Publications, Thousand Oaks, California 1995).

impairments include any mental or psychological disorder such as mental retardation, organic brain syndrome, emotional or mental illness, and specific learning disorders.

Victim service providers must anticipate serving disabled victims. They must work with local government agencies and be prepared to provide a wide variety of services to those disabled persons in need of their help. They should become familiar with the ADA and be spokespersons for disabled victims within the criminal justice system.

Types of Victimization

Disabled persons can be victimized in the same way as other persons are, but their response to crime is different than other victims. Crimes against disabled persons are underreported for a number of reasons: There may be communication and mobility barriers, the disabled person may be unable to report the crime because of a mental or developmental reason or he or she depend on others to do so, and some reporting agencies fail to record the fact that the victim was disabled.[22]

One researcher reported that 60 percent of all persons who have mental disabilities become victims of crime sometime during their lives and that 60 percent of all hearing-impaired women will be the victim of sexual assault.[23] Another source indicates that many disabled people do not receive any form of sex education and that some of them are socialized to obey others without question. Consequently, they do not complain or report acts of sexual maltreatment.[24] Disabled individuals in institutions are twice as likely as those in the community to be abused.[25]

Although the data are extremely limited, there is some reason to believe that substantial numbers of disabled persons are victims of domestic abuse. These studies also indicate that hearing-impaired females have a high probability of becoming victims of domestic violence.[26] For years professionals have acknowledged that there is a higher risk of child abuse if the child is suffering from a disability.[27]

Emerging Issues

The realization that disabled victims present unique challenges to those in the criminal justice system is just now being acknowledged in local, state, and federal jurisdictions. California has assembled a task force to study these issues, and this group has formulated a series of recommendations regarding the treatment of disabled crime victims.[28] These recommendations still need study and revision, but they represent an important first step in this newly emerging area of victimization of the disabled. The following is a brief summary of these recommendations.

The Legal Process

Each service provider should have a criminal justice coordinator. Knowledgeable service professionals and disability advocates should be available to assist the police, prosecutors, and courts. Each developmental disabilities regional center and other primary care or case management service agencies should have a twenty-four-hour phone number to respond to requests for information on an emergency basis. Criminal justice organizations should have specialized staff for cases involving persons with disabilities. This will allow for the gathering of information and building of expertise by those in the system. It will also provide a single point of contact for service organizations. There should be sentence enhancements when disabled persons are victims to protect those who cannot protect themselves. Regular and relatively comprehensive training on disabled victims should occur for police, prosecutors, judges, defense attorneys, probation officers, victim witness offices, and others in the criminal justice system.

Reporting laws should be amended to require mandatory reporting of possible crimes against disabled victims. Persons that deal with the disabled on a regular basis should receive training in recognizing criminal acts against these victims and how to report them. Multidisciplinary teams that include disabled victims should be formed in all local jurisdictions. These teams should meet on a regular basis to address various problems encountered by disabled victims. They should also review sudden unexpected deaths or major traumatic injuries to the disabled when the death or injury occurs in an institution, residence or other service facility.

Victim Support

Each community should develop multidisciplinary teams to cooperatively provide victim support. As a minimum, each team should include victim service providers, sexual assault advocates, and service providers who work with the disabled. All case management agencies should have a designated staffperson to serve as an advocate for disabled victims. There should be a coordinated public relations campaign to encourage disabled victims to report all crimes committed against them.

Risk Reduction/Prevention

Modify curricula and required training for residential programs, vocational training, day programs, recreational programs, and special education to include personal safety training skills for disabled persons. This training should include self-defense skills, individual rights, assertiveness training, social skills, and training about the criminal justice system. All education and service plans for disabled clients should include a personal safety plan as a component. Crime prevention should involve the client, service providers, family, and friends. Special training should be conducted for family members on how to overcome isolation, facilitate attachments, support family relationships, and increase and improve communication skills of the client and family members. Safer living environments are necessary to prevent victimization of the disabled. The more connected and integrated these persons are with their community, the lower the risk of victimization. Steps should be taken to break down the traditional barriers that exist between the disabled and the community. Adult protective service agencies should have adequate resources to investigate reported abuse of the disabled.

Institutional Abuse

There is a critical need to improve standards for screening and hiring of staff in institutions that serve the disabled. Staff training in institutions needs to be improved and updated. Use of the "buddy system" for mentoring new and problem employees should be implemented. Support and create advocacy systems that are independent of any institutional provider are needed. Ombudsperson programs need to be expanded to address these concerns. Administrators and professional staff must be actively present in all institutions to monitor and supervise staff and the clients. Management staff must be held accountable for abuse that occurs in their institutions, yet they must be encouraged to report such abuse. They must look beyond individual cases and accept their moral and professional responsibility to care for these individuals.

FOCUS The Exorcist—Guilty or Innocent?

On April 16, 1997, Los Angeles Superior Court Judge James Albright found two Korean Christian ministers guilty of involuntary manslaughter (the commission of an act, ordinarily lawful, which involved a high degree of risk of death or great bodily injury, without due caution and circumspection) for beating to death one of their wives during an exorcism. The prosecution had asked for second-degree murder and the defense had argued for an acquittal for the two defendants: Jae-Whoa Chung and Sung Soo Choi.

The defendants decided to go forward with the exorcism because Chung's wife had become spiritually arrogant and at times had refused to obey her husband. These acts supported their beliefs that she was possessed by a demon named Gundae.

The exorcism involved both defendants slapping the woman's face, holding her down, and pushing on her abdomen with their fingers, knuckles, and feet. She died as a result of blunt force trauma, and her injuries included sixteen broken ribs and crushed internal organs. It was conceded that the husband loved his wife.

The judge stated that the case involved a collision of California law with honestly held Christian beliefs influenced by Korean shamanist practices.

Source: Havies, M. D. "Priests Found Guilty in the Exorcist Case," *The Los Angeles Daily Journal,* Thursday, April 17, 1997, p. 1.

Cultural Issues

The United States has traditionally been a melting pot of different peoples who have come to its shores and taken their unique place in our society. We pride ourselves on our diversity and multiculturalism. New refugees, recent immigrants, and other minority groups often face misunderstanding and confusion when our traditional values conflict with their beliefs and customs. These groups may encounter an almost overwhelming task when attempting to understand the expectations regarding family behavior in the criminal or civil justice system. Victim service providers need to be aware of these issues when dealing with these individuals.

Introduction

Simply saying to those who work in the criminal justice system that a victim comes from a different culture and is different from the rest of us does not automatically guarantee sympathetic treatment and/or an understanding response to that person's special needs. Stereotyping must be guarded against, and relying on third-hand information when responding to the needs of minority populations should be avoided. Different cultures may not be as homogeneous as they appear on the surface, and care should be taken not to attribute characteristics to special populations on the basis of conversations or interactions with one member of the group. The person being interviewed may be advocating his or her personal beliefs, which may not represent the feelings of other members of that particular culture. It is essential that professionals working in the criminal justice profession be both culturally sensitive and careful to validate their information if possible.

Culture awareness can be defined as the understanding that an individual has regarding different cultures. The term *culture* includes different races, religions, genders, ages, and physical disabilities as well as gay or lesbian issues. Therefore, culture awareness encompasses a wide range of issues, any of which may confront those working in this field.

Hmong Culture

One of the most recent immigrants to our shores are the Hmong from southern China and Southeast Asia. Their history is unknown as they have no written language before the middle of the twentieth century. However, their presence has been recorded in Chinese literature as early as 2300 B.C.[29] One authority indicates that the Hmong lived along the Yellow River and were the first known enemy of the Chinese.[30] According to one source, five million Hmong still live in China today.[31] Some of them migrated to Southeast Asia sometime during the middle or last part of the nineteenth century. The migrating Hmong settled in Vietnam, Laos, and Thailand.

Hmong society is formed into groups rather than individual relationship. The family, clan, and ancestors are the three fundamental pillars of Hmong society. The basic unit of Hmong society is the family, with the father the head of the household. He makes all the major decisions regarding family matters, such as lifestyle, monetary issues, and community involvement. The women's primary role is to provide clothing and meals for the family members. Traditionally, child rearing is gender specific, with the father responsible for disciplining and raising the sons and the mother responsible for the daughters.[32] The children are taught that the needs of the family come before those of the individual.

The Hmong settled in the mountains in Laos, far from cities, the influence of other cultures, and modern technology. However, this tranquil environment was to be replaced with a series of wars and conflicts. During the 1960s and 1970s, many Hmong became involved in what they call the "Secret War." Funded and supported by the Central Intelligence Agency, the Hmong were one of the United States' most loyal allies during the Vietnam War. After the war, many Hmong fled to America to avoid retaliation by the victorious North Vietnamese. The Hmong continued to practice their traditional healing arts while learning about American customs, traditions, and laws.

As the Hmong resettled in the United States, many of them experienced severe cultural conflicts regarding the raising of children. Issues such as discipline, education, social activities, and health care that were not problems in their homeland now presented conflicts when measured against American ideals and culture. In Southeast Asia, Hmong parents could discipline their children by shaming, scolding, spanking, or even whipping them for failure to do well in school or misbehaving in public. Additionally, many Hmong still cling to the use of certain health practices that might be considered child abuse by some authorities.[33]

Coining, or rubbing (Kav), is one of the most practiced remedies in the Hmong community. The purpose of coining is to release pain and bad air out of the patient. It is administered to patients who have a long-lasting illness and high temperature and who cannot urinate or have a bowel movement. There are two methods: one leaves marks, and the other leaves no marks or bruises. The first type of coining involves the use of chicken fat, tiger balm, or Chinese medicated ointment and a ceramic spoon or small bowl. The ointment is applied to the body of the patient, and the spoon or bowl is rubbed back and forth gently until the area being coined is bruised. The coining usually occurs on the chest, the spine, the shoulders, or the neck muscles. The Hmong do not consider coining and the resulting bruising as abuse; rather, they look at it as a way to heal a sick person.

Air suctioning is a popular remedy used by the Hmong to cure headaches or pain in muscles or the chest. Several types of air suctioning are practiced by the Hmong. One method involves the use of tiny jars or glasses, candles, and copper coins. The candle is lit, then glued to the copper coin. The coin is placed on the area exhibiting pain, and the candle is covered with a tiny jar or glass. The candle burns off the oxygen in the glass, and a suctioning occurs, leaving bruises or marks on the patient's body. The deeper the suction, the darker the marks or bruising.

Many Hmong also believe that shamen not American doctors, should treat them. Some Hmong may take a sick child from one shaman to the next in search of a cure while the child gets sicker and sicker. The fact that one shaman could not cure their child does not shake their faith in this traditional method of healing.

As this discussion indicates, some Hmong practices could be considered child abuse. When the Hmong first arrived in the United States and continued to engage in these activities, they were reported to child protective services. As we have become more acquainted with their culture and they with ours, more understanding and communication is occurring. The plight and assimilation of the Hmong into our culture and the problems they experienced are representative of the types of issues that will confront professionals anytime a primitive culture arrives in the United States. By understanding the dynamics and cultures of these new citizens, we can work with them to preserve their culture and introduce them to ours.

Other Cultures

The Hmong are not the only culture to face family violence issues. Many other cultures have adopted a male-oriented perspective regarding the distribution of power in families. The Commonwealth of Puerto Rico illustrates another culture's views and reactions to some forms of family violence. Puerto Rico became a colony of Spain in 1493. In 1989, it became a colony of the United States, and in 1952 its citizens voted to become a Commonwealth. Its residents are U.S. citizens with the same rights and privileges as any other U.S. citizen. Many Puerto Ricans in the United States maintain close contact with the island communities.[34]

The colonization experience has created a feeling of powerlessness in Puerto Ricans. It also has induced a feeling of helplessness and feelings of inadequacy in many Puerto Ricans.[35] Colonized peoples suffer a variety of effects: During colonization males are killed or imprisoned and females are raped, enslaved, and otherwise sexually abused. Sexual abuse may therefore be seen by many Puerto Ricans as a familiar expected behavior by those with power (males) against those without power (females).

In the traditional Puerto Rican community, members beyond the nuclear family are considered part of the family. This cultural norm is reinforced by the concept of familism (*familismo*) which is the tendency to extend kinship beyond the nuclear family. Familism emphasizes family loyalty by emphasizing affiliation over confrontation and cooperation over competitiveness. It also fosters conformity and dependency. The well-being of the family is therefore more important than the needs of any individual. The sexual abuser uses this ingrained philosophy of familism as leverage to prevent the victim from disclosing the abuse. By telling the victim that the family will suffer and be disrupted if there is any disclosure, the abuser can carry out the sexual assault with immunity because of familism. It is true that this tactic is used by many abusers in various cultures, but it is very effective on Puerto Ricans because of their acceptance of familism.[36]

Respect (respeto) is another cultural value that can contribute to sexual abuse. Puerto Ricans are taught to respect all relationships and to display appropriate deferential behavior to others on the basis of their age, social position, sex, and authority status. This concept of respect may play a role in sexual abuse because a child may fear telling others out of respect for the abuser.[37]

Both machoism (*machismo*), or male virility, and *marianismo,* or female spiritual superiority, contribute to an atmosphere that allows for sexual abuse. Males are expected to be sexually active outside the family, and females are taught to endure all suffering inflicted by men. As with other societies, in Puerto Rico male power affords opportunities for dominance and sexual violence.[38]

As this discussion indicates, different peoples hold different values and beliefs. These differences can cause unfounded concerns or portray serious incidents of family violence. Those who work in this field must attempt to become more familiar with the various cultures that they interact with on a continuing basis.

Rural Victims[39]

Introduction

Although rural crime rates have traditionally been lower than urban crime rates, patterns of rural crime now indicate both the exporting of urban problems to rural areas and problems that are unique to rural areas. Although far less research has been conducted on rural than on urban family violence, the National Institute of Justice, in its publication *Rural Crime and Rural Policing,* indicates the following characteristics and dimensions of rural versus urban family violence:

- Recent studies indicate that children in rural communities are as likely, and possibly more likely, to be abused or neglected than children in cities.
- Crimes such as homicide, rape, and assault are more likely to occur among acquaintances in rural areas than in urban areas.

- Although a limited number of surveys of the level of rural domestic violence have been conducted, an Ohio study found that the highest rates for domestic violence disputes were in the least populated jurisdictions.
- Although rural families face the same drug, alcohol, poverty, and stress problems as families living in a metropolitan area do, rural communities typically have fewer resources.[40]

Many rural counties have very low populations. Currently, one out of three rural counties (850) have fewer than ten thousand residents. This presents a challenge to establishing even basic services for crime victims, such as counseling for child abuse victims and shelters for battered women. Many rural domestic violence victims face the additional problem of not only having to leave their homes but also their communities to find safety. Often, the nearest shelter may be several communities and many miles away. Not only are these victims forced to leave whatever support network was available, but their children must be taken out of school in order to reach safety.

Problems and Issues

Federal victims of family violence who reside in rural areas face serious problems. Many victims must travel long distances to a U.S. courthouse. Often, these victims face similar attitudinal problems that other victims face, such as a lack of understanding of the impact of distance and a lack of support services. In addition, rural federal crime victims are skeptical about seeking assistance from the U.S. attorney general, feeling that the federal official is really not "one of the locals." This feeling may arise because the U.S. attorney general is not elected by the populace, as are most county attorneys.

Violence on Native American tribal lands is one of the most pressing issues in modern society. Feelings of alienation and rage are common among members of various tribes. Victims of family violence on tribal lands face unique problems that are not duplicated elsewhere in the United States. In addition, confusing jurisdictional boundaries between state, federal, and tribal law is nowhere more evident than in victim's rights. For example, in a statewide survey of Wyoming's victim services, domestic violence victims who received orders of protection on the reservation had to file for similar protection orders in the local county in order to be protected from their abusers when they left the reservation. Often, their batterers would wait until the victims left the reservation to shop at the grocery store to intimidate, threaten, and harm them.

Although there is a tremendous amount of research being funded and conducted in this area and excellent support from the Office for Victims of Crime to local tribal victim assistance programs, very few of these projects have adopted a multisystems approach to researching and understanding issues of tribal victims of crime.

Economic problems facing rural areas increasingly affect the nature and extent of crime. The impact on the resources available to communities to respond to crime and to assist victims cannot be underestimated. In sentencing offenders, often the only option for judges to select is jail because few community sentencing programs exist in rural areas.

The effects of geography also pose serious problems for rural family violence victims. Distance affects the response time and the speed with which law enforcement and emergency services respond to victims' calls for assistance. Whereas urban areas judge emergency response time in minutes, access to medical treatment in rural areas takes longer, resulting in higher death rates for rural victims suffering the same injuries as those living in urban environments. In addition, rural law enforcement waits longer for backup, forcing decisions of responding to dangerous situations alone or the delay of critical emergency responses, such as on domestic violence reports.

For many rural family violence victims, simply traveling to the local police station to make a report takes on special significance because of the distance, lack of transportation, and time involved in making such a trip. Transportation issues are especially critical for elderly victims and children going to therapy sessions. Travel to criminal justice agencies is exacerbated for tribal crime victims that participate in the federal justice system. Many tribal crime victims have to travel hundreds of miles to participate in the criminal justice process. One crime victim from the Wind River Reservation in Wyoming had to travel over five hundred miles to present a victim impact statement at the federal courthouse—and was told of the sentencing hearing the day before!

In addition, aspects of the rural culture may affect the willingness of family violence victims to report this violence and to participate in the criminal justice system. One study found that shoplifting and employee theft were rarely reported to the police; rather, the cases were handled informally. One criminal justice official said, "I simply can't get people to tell me things. I hear about them two or three weeks later, and when I ask them why they didn't come to see me about it, they say, 'Oh, I took care of it myself.' We simply can't get people to take advantage of the services of this office."

Overall, the issues of rural family violence and rural justice have not received national attention in the development of policies and protocol for law enforcement or other areas of the criminal justice system. For example, in the 447-page book *Local Government Police Management*, considered by most law enforcement officers to be the definitive reference on municipal police administration, the distinction between rural and urban policing is covered in a brief one-page section.[41] Moreover, this one-page overview does not even appear in updated editions. Family violence in rural areas is an important topic that warrants further study. We must provide services in these areas if we are ever going to stop this form of violence.

Summary

This chapter is a general overview of a serious issue within the criminal justice system. Family violence within special populations continues to increase. Because the United States is becoming more diverse with the passage of each year, victim service professionals need to become aware of and sensitive to the needs of these special family violence victims. More important, they need to act as the spokespersons for these victims to individuals and agencies within the criminal justice system.

Both HIV and AIDS are terrible diseases with deadly consequences for any infected person. Victims of crimes may suffer a second trauma if there is the possibility that they were exposed to the virus during the commission of the crime. Victim service providers must be sensitive to these special needs.

Disabled victims are only one example of the many special populations that exist in the United States. However, their victimization carries special problems and issues that must be addressed by those within the criminal justice system. Because of their status, these victims may not report incidents of family violence. Additionally, they may be victimized a second time during the criminal justice process. The Hmong are representative of some of the new immigrants and the problems such immigrants face when attempting to adapt to the customs, regulations, and laws of the United States. Understanding these new cultures can assist those who work with victims of family violence. Other cultures, such as Puerto Rican, have their own system of beliefs and culture that can contribute to a continuing of family violence, including sexual abuse. By understanding some of these beliefs, those who work in this field will be better prepared to interact with victims of family violence from different cultures. Rural victims of family violence also face special problems when interacting with the criminal justice system. Something as important as filing a protective order may become an overwhelming task simply because of the distance between the victim's home and the courthouse. Victim professionals must be aware of these potential problems when dealing with these special populations.

Key Terms

Disabled person—one who has a physical or mental impairment that substantially limits one or more of the major life activities of that individual, who has a record of such impairment, or who is regarded as having such an impairment.

Family violence—any act or omission by persons who are cohabitating that results in serious injury to other members of the family.

Culture awareness—the understanding that an individual has regarding different cultures.

Discussion Questions

1. Should victims who are HIV positive be treated any differently than other victims? Why?
2. Should a person suffering from the HIV/AIDS disease be required to disclose that fact to family members? To sexual partners? To workplace associates? To friends?
3. Should there be stiffer criminal penalties for perpetrators who commit crimes while HIV positive? What if they were unaware of their infection?

4. Explain how you would work with a sight-impaired victim, a hearing-impaired victim, and a victim confined to a wheelchair. What problems or issues do you see that they will face in the criminal justice system?
5. Should a Hmong parent who coins his daughter be charged with child abuse?
6. If you were interviewing a Puerto Rican female child, how would you overcome the concept of familism?
7. Compare the problems facing rural and urban family violence victims. What is the most striking difference?

Suggested Readings

Fontes, L. A., ed. *Sexual Abuse in Nine North American Cultures.* (Sage Publications, Thousand Oaks, California) 1995.

Levin, J., and J. McDevitt. *The Rising Tide of Bigotry and Bloodshed.* (Plenum, New York) 1993.

Randel, W. P. *The Ku Klux Klan: A Century of Infamy.* (Chilton Books, New York) 1965.

Weisheit, R. A. et al. "Rural Crime and Rural Policing" *Research in Brief.* (National Institute of Justice, Washington, D.C.) October, 1994.

Zaragoza, M. S., et al., eds. *Memory and Testimony in the Child Witness.* (Sage Publications, Thousand Oaks, California) 1995.

Endnotes

1. This section has been adapted from *HIV/AIDS and Victim Services: A Critical Concern of the 90s,* sponsored by a grant from the Office for Victims of Crime (National Victim Center, Arlington, Virginia, February 1996), chapters 2, 3, and 4 (hereinafter cited as *HIV/AIDS and Victim Services*).
2. *HIV/AIDS and Victim Services,* pp. II-1–11-2.
3. *HIV/AIDS and Victim Services,* pp. II-3–II-4.
4. *HIV/AIDS and Victim Services,* p. II-5.
5. *HIV/AIDS and Victim Services,* pp. II-5–II-8.
6. *HIV/AIDS and Victim Services,* pp. II-30–II-32.
7. *HIV/AIDS and Victim Services,* p. III-3.
8. *HIV/AIDS and Victim Services,* p. III-5.
9. See, e.g., Florida Code Section 960.003 (1) (1994).
10. *HIV/AIDS and Victim Services,* p. III-18.
11. See *People v Adams,* 97 Daily Journal D.A.R. 4854 (April 16, 1995), in which a California appellate court held that transmitting genital herpes is an aggravating sentencing factor and that AIDS testing is not unconstitutional.
12. *HIV/AIDS and Victim Services,* pp. IV-1–IV-2.
13. *HIV/AIDS and Victim Services,* p. IV-7.
14. *HIV/AIDS and Victim Services,* pp. IV-21–IV-30.
15. *HIV/AIDS and Victim Services,* pp. IV-31–IV-33.
16. Much of the material in this section has been adapted from *Focus on the Future: A Systems Approach to Prosecution and Victim Assistance,* sponsored by a grant from the Office for Victims of Crimes, U.S. Department of Justice, Washington, D.C. (National Victim Center, Arlington, Virginia 1992).
17. Wolfe, K. "Bashing the Disabled: The New Hate Crime," *The Progressive* 9 (11) November 1995, p. 24.
18. This paragraph was adapted from the *Draft Report, Criminal Justice Task Force for Persons with Developmental Disabilities, Victim of Crime Section* (Office of Criminal Justice Planning, Sacramento, California October 1, 1996), p. 1 (hereinafter cited as *Task Force for Persons with Developmental Disabilities*).
19. Merkin, L., and M. J. Smith. "A Community Based Model Providing Services for the Deaf and Deaf–Blind Victims of Sexual Assault

and Domestic Violence," *Sexuality and Disability* 13(2) 1995, pp. 97–106.

20. "Eight Do's and Don'ts in Working with Disabled Victims of Crimes," *Focus on the Future: A Systems Approach to Prosecution and Victim Assistance,* (National Victim Center, sponsored by a grant from the Office for Victims of Crimes, U.S. Department of Justice, Washington, D.C.) 1992, p. C-13.
21. Adapted from *Task Force for Persons with Developmental Disabilities*, p. 1.
22. Tyiska, C. G. "Responding to Disabled Victims of Crime," *NOVA Network Information Bulletin,* no. 8–12 (NOVA, Washington, D.C.) 1990, p. 10.
23. Worthington, G. M. "Sexual Exploitation and Abuse of People with Disabilities," *Response to Violence in the Family and Sexual Assault* 7 (2) 1994, p. 43.
24. *Sexual Exploitation of Handicapped Students: Teachers Training Manual.* (Seattle Rape Relief Disabilities Project, Seattle, Washington) 1981.
25. McPherson, C. "Bringing Redress to Abused Disabled Persons," *NOVA Network Information Bulletin,* no. 8–12 (NOVA, Washington, D.C.) 1990, p. 14.
26. Melling, L. "Wife Abuse in the Deaf Community," *Response to Violence in the Family and Sexual Assault* 7 (1) 1984, p. 12.
27. Aiello, D. and L. Capkin. "Services for Disabled Victims: Elements and Standards," *Response to Violence in the Family and Sexual Assault* 7 (5) 1984, p. 14.
28. Adapted from *Task Force for Persons with Developmental Disabilities,* pp. 11–22.
29. Bliatout, B. *Hmong Sudden Unexpected Nocturnal Death Syndrome: A Cultural Study.* (Sparkle Enterprises, Portland, Oregon) 1982.
30. Quincy, K. *Hmong: History of a People.* (Eastern Washington University Press, Washington, D.C.) 1995.
31. Wong, How-Man. "Peoples of China's Far West Provinces," *National Geographic* (March 1984), p. 308.
32. McInnes, K. "The Hmong Family," in K. McInnes, et al., eds., *The Hmong in America: Providing Ethnic-Sensitive Health, Education, and Human Services.* (Kendall/Hunt, Dubuque, Iowa) 1990.
33. Yang, K., and K. K. Moua. "Some Traditional Healing Practice Arts of the Hmong," unpublished manuscript (Indochinese Family Maintenance Project, Fresno, California) May, 1987.
34. Comas-Diaz, L. "Feminist Therapy with Puerto Rican Women," *Psychology of Women Quarterly* 11(4) (1987), p. 461.
35. Lewis, G. "Notes on the Puerto Rican Revolution: An Essay on American Dominance and Caribbean Resistance," *New York Monthly Press Review* (1974).
36. Comas-Diaz, L. "Puerto Ricans and Sexual Child Abuse." In Lisa A. Fontes, ed., *Sexual Abuse in Nine North American Cultures.* (Sage Publications, Thousand Oaks, California) 1995.
37. Ibid.
38. Ibid.
39. This section has been adapted from H. Wallace and Chris Edmunds, *America's Forgotten Crime Victims,* a federal grant proposal to the Office for Victims of Crimes, Department of Justice, Washington, D.C., July 1, 1995.
40. Weisheit, R. A., et. al. "Rural Crime and Rural Policing," *Research in Brief.* (National Institute of Justice, Washington, D.C.) October, 1994.
41. Ibid.

13

WOMEN AND SEXUAL VIOLENCE

Chapter Outline

Learning Objectives

After reading this chapter, you should be able to discuss the following concepts:

- Why women continue to be sexually abused.
- Why rape is not a sexual crime.

- The distinction between stranger, marital, and acquaintance rape.
- Why sexual harassment is a form of sexual violence.
- What actions may constitute sexual harassment.

Introduction

This is a text on family violence; however, there are certain types of acts or actions that are specific to women and contribute to violence against women both within and outside the family. Some of these acts could have been examined in earlier chapters. They are so distinctive and important, however, that they have been placed in a separate chapter for emphasis and expanded discussion.

Many of the previous acts of violence involved husbands, lovers, or other significant individuals in a family situation. This chapter examines abusive actions that are perpetrated by those persons as well as strangers or persons with whom women have professional rather than personal relationships. Some of these acts are allowed by a society that permits certain forms of expression to continue that are degrading to women. Others involve coworkers and supervisors who treat women as inferiors or sexual playthings. Still others involve forced sexual activities either by a stranger or a person known to the woman. All these actions or situations are sexually abusive in nature.

FOCUS Sexual Violence in America

State of Florida v William Kennedy Smith involved allegations of rape brought against a member of the Kennedy family. The victim alleged that Willie Smith picked her up and took her to a beach house where he raped her against her will. The nation watched on live television as defense attorneys questioned the virtues and motives of the victim. While Mr. Smith was acquitted on all charges, the specter of something called "date rape" became a common topic throughout the United States.

State of Indiana v Mike Tyson involved a Black beauty contestant and the former heavyweight champion of the world. She claimed that he raped her in his hotel room. Mr. Tyson was convicted and sentenced to prison even though he maintained that the sexual acts were consensual.

Tailhook has become a word synonymous with sexual harassment. A Navy professional organization consisting of Marine and Navy flyers gathered at a Las Vegas hotel for a convention. Afterward, several women came forward and claimed that they were grabbed, fondled, or undressed while trying to walk down the hotel hallway. The resulting investigation exposed the existence of widespread sexual harassment in the Navy.

Anita Hill was a tenured law school professor when she head that a former employer of hers, Clarence Thomas, had been nominated for the U.S. Supreme Court. She appeared before a subcommittee of the Senate and testified to certain sexually oppressive acts that she alleged Mr. Thomas committed when she worked for him. Ms. Hill was accused of being psychotic and lying. Mr. Thomas was subsequently appointed to the Supreme Court.

It's little wonder that sexual violence is still present in today's society, considering Western history. Sigmund Freud, the father of psychoanalysis who invented the concept of primacy of the penis, declined to explore the concept of rape.[1] Marx and Engels, who developed the theory of economic determinism of crime, were silent concerning the exploitation of women by the act of rape.[2]

Three works by feminist authors and researchers set the stage for advancing the awareness of sexual violence against women. Millett's *Sexual Politics,* Griffin's "Rape: The All American Crime," and Brownmiller's *Against Our Will* each raised the collective consciousness regarding the domination of women by men.[3]

Sexual Politics examines the concept of patriarchy, which Millett claims is a social and political system used by men to control women. She argues that patriarchy is a feature of all past and present societies and exists across cultures and socioeconomic systems today. Millett concludes that power and coercion are central features of patriarchy and are used to control women's sexuality.

Griffin's short article "Rape, The All American Crime" contains numerous themes. One of the most important concerned the nature of the crime of rape. She argued that rape is not a sexual act; rather it is a violent, political act. Griffin concluded that the threat of rape is used as a method of social control that affects all women.

Brownmiller discussed the history of rape. She maintained that rape is an act used by men to maintain their dominance over women by the use of force. She expanded on both Millett's and Griffin's work and concluded that the threat of rape creates a climate of fear, and this fear acts as a form of social control that benefits men.

Kelly, in her book *Surviving Sexual Violence,* reviewed these early feminist approaches to sexual abuse and concluded that sexual violence is based on three concepts: power, sexuality, and social control.[4]

Power in the feminist analysis is not police or political power; rather, power is defined in terms of a relationship that structures the interactions between men and women. Power, therefore, is not a property right but a personal force that establishes male control and dominance over females. This power is multifaceted and complex. It is present not only in interpersonal relationships but extends to society's social structure and beliefs.

Sexuality has two aspects. First, male control of women's sexuality is a key factor in women's oppression. Second, sexuality is defined by men's experiences, which legitimatize the use of force or coercion in intimate relationships. Some conflict exists among feminists regarding the issue of sexuality and whether it has the same significance for women in all cultures.

Social control is the outcome of power and sexuality. The mere threat of sexual violence may result in women developing strategies for self-protection that will limit their mobility, work, or advancement. The reality of sexual violence not only impacts women in intimate relationships but spills over to the campus setting. Numerous colleges and universities provide "escort services" for females who attend evening classes. This speaks volumes for the fear that exists regarding sexual violence, even on campuses in the United States.

FOCUS Some Startling Facts about Rape

- Ninety-eight percent of rape victims will never see their attackers apprehended, convicted, or incarcerated.
- Over half (54 percent) of all rape prosecutions result in either a dismissal or an acquittal.
- A rape prosecution is more than twice as likely as a murder prosecution to be dismissed and 30 percent more likely to be dismissed than a robbery.
- Approximately one in ten rapes reported to the police results in time served in prison; one in one hundred rapes (including those that go unreported) is sentenced to more than one year in prison.
- Almost one-quarter of convicted rapists are not sentenced to prison but are instead released on probation.
- Nearly one-quarter of convicted rapists receive a sentence to a local jail for only eleven months (according to national estimates).
- Adding together the convicted rapists sentenced to probation and those sentenced to local jails, almost half of all convicted rapists are sentenced to less than one year behind bars.

Source: Violence against Women: The Response to Rape: Detours on the Road to Equal Justice. Prepared by the Majority Staff of the Senate Judiciary Committee, May 1993, p. 11.

These feminists laid the foundation that allows a greater understanding of the concept of sexual violence and women. The following sections examine this type of violence and explore some of the more common theories regarding its causes and consequences.

The Problem

How many women are raped each year? Exactly what is involved in the act of rape? Is sexual assault the same as rape? Should statisticians determine whether a women has been raped once in a lifetime or only attempt to determine how many rapes occur each year? These are legitimate questions that surface anytime the study and research of sexual violence is undertaken. Determining the exact nature and extent of sexual violence is a complex and difficult process.

One of the major problems in the area of women and sexual violence is the lack of agreement among scholars, researchers, and professionals on definitions and research methodology. Depending on which article, paper, or text one reads, the estimates regarding the incident of rape will vary. This disparity has caused problems and confusion within the professions from the outset. There are a number of reasons for the different figures and definitions within this area of family violence. The FOCUS "Some Startling Facts About Rape" provides a summary of some of the more common problems encountered when this phenomenon is studied.

Definitional issues: Some scholars use the term *rape,* others use *sexual assault,* and still others define each of the foregoing terms differently. For example, one researcher may define rape as vaginal intercourse accomplished by use of force or fear, whereas other researchers may define rape as vaginal, oral, or rectal intercourse accomplished by force or fear. The simple addition of two terms changes the entire results of any study.

Professional issues: Various professionals approach rape from different perspectives. Attorneys view rape in a certain legalistic way, physicians treat it as a medical problem, and psychologists approach it from a mental health point of view.

Gathering of information: Problems in the screening techniques, formation of questions, context of questioning, and issues of confidentiality all impact the validity and type of response that the researcher will receive.[5]

Koss compiled many of the various studies on rape, and her work illustrates the different approaches various researchers have used when attempting to determine the incidence of sexual violence against women in the United States.[6]

Sexual Violence and Women

Table 13.1 indicates that a wide discrepancy exists between the various studies as to the type and prevalence of sexual violence committed in the United States.

One of the most recent studies was conducted by the National Victim Center entitled *Rape in America: A Report to the Nation,* and it caused an uproar across the United States when it was released in April 1992.[16] The National Victim Center relied on a comprehensive study entitled "The National Women's Study" to

TABLE 13.1 Statistical Data on Sexual Assault

Study	Sample	Collection Method	Measured Phenomena and Prevalence Rate
Burt[7]	328	Interview	Completed rape 24 percent lifetime
Essock-Vitlae and McGuire[8]	300	Interview	Rape 8 percent since age eighteen
Kilpatrick and associates[9]	2,004	Telephone	Forcible rape including attempts 8.8 percent lifetime
Riger and Gordon[10]	693	Telephone	Rape or sexual assault 2 percent of telephone sample
National Victim Center[11]	4,008	Telephone	Rape 14 percent lifetime
Russell[12]	930	Interview	Completed rape 24 percent
Sorenson and associates[13]	1,444	Interview	Sexual assault 13.5 percent
Winfield and associates[14]	1,157	Interview	Sexual assault 5.9 percent lifetime
Wyatt[15]	248	Interview	Completed rape 25 percent for blacks and 20 percent for whites

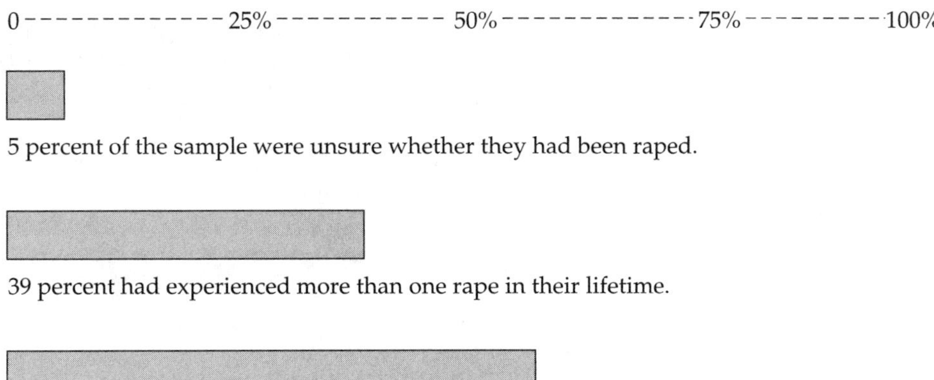

FIGURE 13.1 Percentages of Rape

gather its information. This report was based on a national sample of 4,008 women who were interviewed regarding their experience with rape. The report indicated that rape occurred at a much higher incidence than previously thought.

Using the 1990 U.S. Census figures that indicate there are approximately 96.8 million women in the United States, the National Victim Center estimates that one in every eight women has been raped at sometime in her life. This translates to an incredible 12.1 million women in the United States who have been raped. In reviewing the figures and percentages of those women, Figure 13.1 illustrates the number of times women have been raped.

In 1997, the U.S. Department of Justice released one of the most comprehensive studies of sexual violence in the United States.[17] This report, entitled *Sex Offenses and Offenders,* draws on more than two dozen data sets maintained by the U.S. Department of Justice in an effort to provide a comprehensive overview about the incidence of sexual assault, the response by the criminal justice system to such crimes, and the characteristics of both the offenders and the victims. The report drew on the National Crime Victimization Survey (NCVS), the Uniform Crime Reporting Program, the National Incident Based Reporting System, the National Judicial Reporting Program, and the Supplemental Homicide Reporting Program.

Review of the NCVS indicates that victims reported approximately 1 rape/sexual assault of a female for every 270 females in the general population, whereas males reported 1 rape/sexual assault for every 5,000 males in the population.[18] Overall, about 91 percent of all victims of rape or sexual assault were female. About two-thirds of all the offenses were found to occur between 6 P.M. and 6 A.M. About 60 percent of all the incidents occurred in the victim's own home or at the home of a friend, neighbor, or relative. More than half of all the rapes and/or sexual assaults occurred within one mile of the victim's home or at their home (see Figure 13.2). About 90 percent of all incidents involved a single offender. About 75 percent of the single offenders had a prior relationship as a

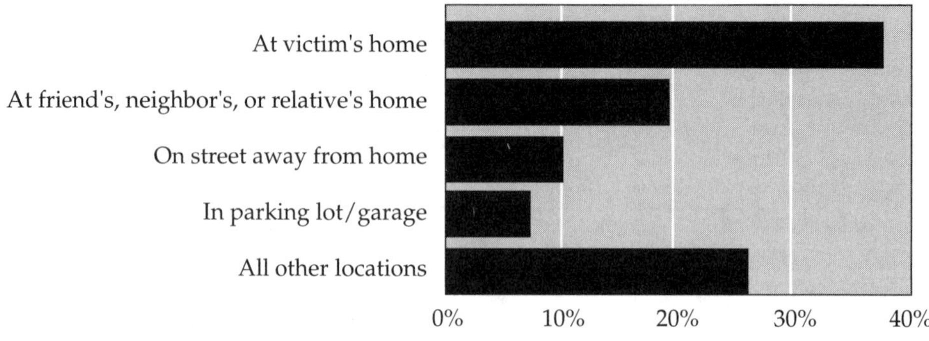

FIGURE 13.2 Victims' Reports of Where Rapes and Sexual Assaults Took Place, 1993

family member, intimate, or acquaintance. When multiple offenders engaged in rape or sexual assaults, about 76 percent of the victims were unknown to these offenders.

About 70 percent of all victims reported that they took some form of self-protective action during the crime. The most common form involved resisting the attack or attempting to chase and capture the offender (see Figure 13.3). Among those victims who took some form of self-protective action, over half felt that actions helped the situation.

In addition to the NCVS, the Department of Justice obtains data from law enforcement agencies that report crimes under the Uniform Crime Reporting (UCR) Program. Unlike in the NCVS, forcible rape in this program is limited to female victims. The UCR figures indicate that over the last ten years, there has been a substantial decline in rapes in metropolitan areas, whereas rapes in other areas, such as cities outside major metropolitan areas and rural areas, have increased. The highest rate of rapes are reported in August and the fewest in December. The UCR reports indicate that the racial distribution of persons arrested for rape are similar to the racial distribution for all other violent crimes (56 percent white, 42 percent black, and 2 percent other races).

Every other year, the Bureau of Justice Statistics obtains information on felony defendants from the nation's seventy-five most populous counties. Information from this survey indicates that 48 percent of all defendants charged with rape were released from detention prior to the adjucation of their cases. The most common method used by those charged with rape for obtaining their release was to post a bond. About two-thirds of all defendants convicted of the crime of rape received a prison sentence. Nineteen percent served their sentence in jail, and the remaining 13 percent received a sentence of probation. For those defendants sentenced to state prison, the average term was 146 months, or just under fourteen years. The average term for those defen-

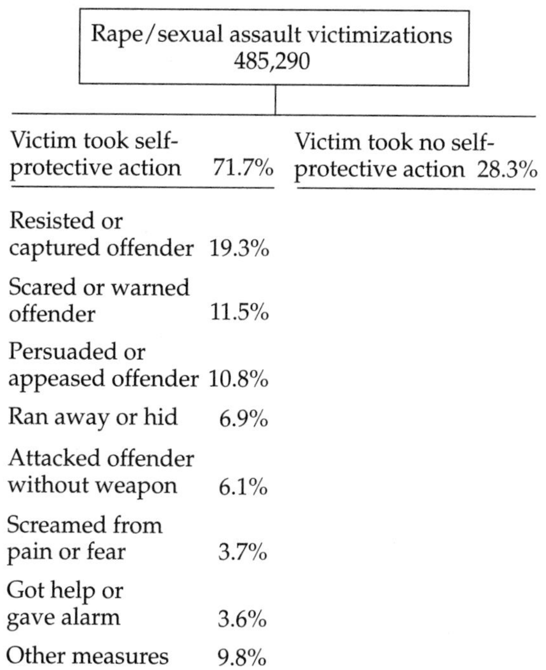

FIGURE 13.3 Self-Protective Measures Taken by Victims of Rape or Sexual Assault, 1993

dants sentenced to jail was eight months, and the average probationary period was six years.

The average age at time of arrest for rapists was thirty-one years, with sex offenders being slightly older, at age thirty-four. About one in four rapists and sexual assault offenders had a prior conviction for violent crimes. Ten percent of those incarcerated for rape had prior convictions for rape or sexual assault. Violent sex offenders reported that two-thirds of their victims were under the age of eighteen. Table 13.2 supports the proposition that rape occurs much more often between those who know each other than between strangers. About 30 percent of the rapists and less than 15 percent of the sexual offenders reported that their victims had been strangers.

The FBI collects additional information about murder in its annual Supplemental Homicide Reporting (SHR) Program. In this program, local law enforcement agencies provide a monthly report that includes a wide variety of information regarding homicides in their jurisdictions. Murder that was classified as involving rape or other sexual offenses accounted for 1.5 percent of all reported homicides where the circumstances of the crime were known to investigators. Sexual assault murder victims differ from other murder victims in that they were substantially more likely to be female and white than other murder victims. The weapon of choice in sexual homicides was a knife.

TABLE 13.2 Relationship to Offender

Family	12.9%	20.3%	37.7%
Spouse	2.5	1.2	.6
Child/stepchild	6.1	14.0	25.9
Other relative	4.3	5.1	11.2
Intimate	5.5	9.1	6.2
Boyfriend/girlfriend	5.0	8.8	5.4
Ex-spouse	.5	.3	.8
Acquaintance	34.7	40.8	41.2
Stranger	46.9	29.8	14.9

The previous figures indicate that rape in the United States is more common than previously thought, and rape is only one form of sexual violence that is perpetrated against women. The next section discusses the issues and forces that affect the definition of various terms in this area of family violence.

Definition

Exactly what do the terms *rape, marital rape, acquaintance rape,* and *sexual violence* mean? Should they be defined strictly from a legal perspective, a medical view, a psychological point of view, or a combination of all the foregoing? Each discipline has valid reasons for defining sexual violence in a certain manner.

A review of history indicates that the use of aggression and violence against women has existed for eons. Sexual violence against women traditionally has been viewed as stranger rape, a violent forceful sexual assault on a female. Only recently has society turned to acknowledge other forms of sexual violence. It is now acknowledged that spouses may be raped, and *acquaintance rape* has become a common term. In addition, other forms of sexual violence are more subtle but just as damaging; sexual harassment and sexual discrimination are still rampant in the United States. To define sexual violence by any one of these acts is to do injustice to the whole concept that women are equal to men. A legal definition of sexual violence focuses on certain conduct that is prohibited and strictly defined. A medical definition views sexual violence as injury to the body. A psychological evaluation of sexual violence examines the effect on the mind and the emotions of the victim. Each of these approaches has certain strengths and weaknesses.

Sexual violence can take the form of a single act or a long and protracted series of incidents. It can also involve aggression and/or discrimination against women. For purposes of this discussion, *sexual violence is any intentional act or omission that results in physical, emotional, or financial injury to another person.* The term *financial injury* is included to cover sexual harassment situations in which women have been terminated from employment for refusing to engage in sexual acts with their supervisors. Sexual violence does not include the termination of a romantic relationship. The ritual of courting, dating, and marriage in the United States commonly results in one person being hurt or heartbroken when the relationship ends. Although painful, it does not rise to the level of sexual violence. Some might argue that this definition is too comprehensive, but to narrow it would be to exclude certain types of acts that result in harm to women.

Sexual violence can happen to any person, at any time, and in any place. No one is completely secure from this type of assault. The following sections examine different aspects of this form of sexual violence.

Theories on Sexual Violence

As with other forms of family violence, a number of theories exist regarding this form of aggression, but the exact cause of sexual violence is undetermined. The following section examines some of the theories regarding the possible etiology of this violent act of aggression.

Causes of Rape

No single factor can be highlighted as the cause of rape. Just as there are many forms of sexual violence, so there are a multitude of theories on causes of sexual aggression toward women. Some of the more common theories on the causes of rape include the following: sexual motivation, socialization, machoism, biological factors, psychological forces, and the culture of violence.

Sexual motivation: Most current research dismisses this theory of rape. It is not viewed as a sexual act; rather, it is an act of violence, aggression, and power by the male.

Socialization: This concept holds that in society young boys are taught to be aggressive, forceful, tough, and a winner in any sport or activity. This socialization creates aggressors and can spill over into the sexual arena, where men are taught to sexually conquer as many women as possible. This aggressive attitude encourages and gives consent to men to engage in rape.[19]

Machoism: This theory holds that men who believe in male machoism will be more aggressive toward women. Machoism is a set of beliefs that include a view of women as objects simply to be added to a numerical list of sexual conquests. These conquests may include the act of rape.[20]

Biological factors: This view argues that rape is a male instinctive reaction that is a drive to perpetuate the species. Symons believes that men still have a genetic holdover that impels them to have sex with as many women as possible, and he argues that rape is closely linked to sexuality and violence.[21] Other scholars discount this position.[22]

Psychological forces: This theory purports that men rape because they suffer from some sort of personalty disorder or mental illness. Studies have attempted to define the dynamics of convicted sex offenders and exactly what mental condition causes them to rape. To date, there is no conclusive profile of a rapist.

FOCUS Movies, Books, Celebrities, and Sexual Violence

Is it any wonder that sexual violence is accepted in American culture? *Gone with the Wind* is famous for the scene in which Rhett Butler sweeps a protesting Scarlet off her feet and carries her up the stairs to the bedroom. The next morning finds Scarlet happy and fulfilled with her darling husband.

The classic play, *A Streetcar Name Desire,* involves Stanley raping his sister-in-law while his wife is in the hospital giving birth to their child.

The matinee hero of the 1940s and 1950s, Errol Flynn, was constantly overpowering resisting women who halfway through the first kiss gave up and responded just as passionately. People have been raised on a diet of male machoism and women who give in after a brief but half-hearted struggle. This has led to a certain mind-set toward sex and women.

Culture of violence: The culture of violence theory states that society is a violent environment that encourages some men to use violence to obtain sex. The use of violence and aggression is expected, and these individuals view women as legitimate targets of sexual aggression. These men believe that women want to be dominated and overpowered by an aggressive male.[23]

Types of Rape

Although there are many causes of rape and sexual violence, studies in the past have failed to clearly define or predict who will rape. Researchers have now developed different typologies of rapists in an effort to streamline and define this type of personality. One authority states that there are over fifty different types of rapists.[24]

Groth and his associates conducted a study in Massachusetts of 133 convicted rapists and 92 victims. This classic study, "Rape: Power, Anger and Sexuality," established that issues of power, anger, and sexuality are important concepts in understanding the various types of rape. Additionally, this was one of the first research efforts to recognize that rape is a crime of violence and not a sexual act.[25] Groth and his associates classified rape types into two major categories: power and anger.

Power rapes involve the offender seeking power and control over his victim by the use of force or threats. The sexual assault is evidence of conquest and domination. The perpetrator will plan and fantasize about the rape, believing that the victim will respond to his advances after initially resisting. Power rapes may be further classified as power-assertive rapes or power-reassurance rapes. The power-assertive rapist views the assault as an expression of his virility, mastery, and dominance. The power-reassurance rapist, on the other hand, commits rapes to resolve doubts about his masculinity and sexual adequacy.

Anger rapes involve the expression of anger, rage, contempt, or hatred toward the victim. The objective of this type of rapist is to vent his rage on the victim and retaliate for rejections or perceived wrongs that he has suffered in the past by other women. Anger rapes may be categorized as anger-retaliation or anger-excitation rapes. In anger-retaliation rapes, the rape is an expression of hostility and rage toward women. Anger-excitation rape occurs as a result of the offender's desire to obtain pleasure, thrills, and arousal secondary to the suffering of the victim during the assault.

Two years after their initial publication, Groth and Birnbaum established a more refined version of the original typology. In *Men Who Rape,* they established three categories of rapists and determined that there were three types of rape offenses: anger rapes, power rapes, and sadism rapes.[26]

The new definitions of anger and power rapes are very similar to those in the earlier study, and the sadistic rapist is obsessed with ritual during the rape. He may tie up his victim, torture her, or humiliate her, becoming intensely excited during the act. This type of rape is very traumatic, and Groth found that victims of this type of rate needed long-term psychiatric counseling.

Sexual violence continues to be researched, and perhaps one day rapists will be identified by a series of tests or events. However, until that time arrives, sexual violence continues to be a serious problem that must be evaluated and treated.

Consequences of Rape

Although this section deals specifically with the consequences of rape, it should be noted that it does not cover the entire range of possible consequences and treatment for all forms of sexual violence. This discussion instead focuses on the psychological damage that is a result of this act of aggression.

One of the first longitudinal studies of rape victims' reactions indicated that certain fears are more severe than those suffered by nonvictims.[27] However, fear is not the only symptom suffered by rape victims. Resick reports that rape victims suffer a variety of reactions, including the following: fear and anxiety, post-traumatic stress disorder, depression, social maladjustment, decreased self-esteem, impaired sexual functioning, and other reactions.[28]

Fear and anxiety: These are the most common reactions to the crime of rape. Burnam conducted a survey of 3,132 households and found that rape victims reported significantly higher levels of phobias and panic disorders than nonvictims.[29] Rape victims suffer a higher level of anxiety than other victims of violent crimes such as robbery.[30]

Posttraumatic stress disorder: This mental disorder has already been touched on when the consequences of ritual abuse on children were discussed. *Posttraumatic stress disorder is defined as the development of characteristic symptoms following a psychologically distressing event that is outside the range of usual human experience.* The characteristic symptoms involve reexperiencing the traumatic event, avoidance of stimuli associated with the event or numbing of general responsiveness, and increased agitation.[31] Victims of rape also have reported or been diagnosed as suffering from posttraumatic stress disorder (PTSD). Rothbaum's study found that 94 percent of rape victims displayed classic symptoms of PTSD one week after the assault. This figure dropped to 47 percent twelve weeks after the incident.[32] Kilpatrick's study, *Rape in America,* reported that 11 percent of all women raped still suffer from PTSD, and the authors estimated that 1.3 million women in the United States are currently suffering from PTSD as a result of a rape or multiple rapes.[33]

Rape crisis syndrome is very similar to PTSD. *Rape crisis syndrome occurs when the victim experiences feelings of shame, humiliation, disjointedness, anger, inability to concentrate, and withdrawal.*[34]

Depression: A number of studies have found that rape victims suffer from depression as a result of their experiences, with classifications ranging from moderate to severely depressed. Kilpatrick's *Rape in America* found that 33 percent of all rape victims thought seriously about suicide compared to 8 percent of nonvictims.[35]

Self-esteem: The issue of self-blame on the part of rape victims has been commented on by a number of authorities. However, no conclusive study indicates that rape victims as a class suffer from lower self-esteem than other victims or nonvictims. Although Resick and her associates found that there were long-term problems with self-esteem in rape victims, it is also clear that this is an area that needs further study.[36]

Social adjustment: Victims of rape often suffer from economic, social, and leisure adjustment. Studies indicate that marital and family adjustments may be more difficult for rape victims than for nonvictims.[37]

Sexual functioning: Although it is clear that rape is now accepted as a physical assault in which sex is used to dominate or control the victim, women who have been raped report continuing problems in sexual functioning. Sexual dysfunctions are one of the most long-lasting effects of rape with the most common reaction by rape victims being the avoidance of sex.

Other psychological reactions to rape: Other psychological problems may arise as a result of a rape. These include but are not limited to obsessive-compulsive disorders, anger, hostility, fatigue, and confusion.

Although the physical act of rape may last minutes, hours, or, in some cases, days, the effects and consequences to the victims may linger for months, years, or a lifetime. The rape is only the beginning of the suffering that the victim will endure. During the criminal justice system's response to this act of aggression, the victim will relive the trauma several times as she testifies in court.

Stranger Rape

There are still a number of myths regarding the crime of rape. These myths apply to stranger, marital, or acquaintance rape situations.

Definition

Carnal knowledge of a female was one of the first terms used to connote sexual violence. It was defined as *penile–vaginal penetration.*[39] *Black's Law Dictionary* defines carnal knowledge as "Coitus; copulation; the act of a man having sexual bodily connections with a woman; sexual intercourse."[39]

FOCUS Some Myths about Rape

1. They want it and enjoy it. It wasn't rape but "rough sex." Women say "no" when they mean "yes." Some women enjoy rape.
2. They ask for it and deserve it. Women provoke men by the way they dress, "leading men on." They take risks by going out alone or accepting lifts.
3. Rape only happens to a certain kind of woman or in certain kinds of families: women who live in poor areas; women who are sexually active; women who take risks; women who have previously been abused.
4. They tell lies or exaggerate. Women make false reports for revenge or to protect their "reputation."
5. If they would have resisted, they could have prevented it. An unwilling woman cannot be raped. If thee are no bruises, she must have consented.
6. The men who do it are sick, ill, or out of control. Abuse of alcohol or drugs, mental instability, or childhood experiences cause men to act violently.

Source: Adapted from Kelly, L. *Surviving Sexual Violence,* (University of Minnesota Press, Minneapolis) 1988, pp. 35–36. Copyright © Liz Kelly 1988.

Traditional penal codes reflected this bias and misunderstanding of the crime of rape. Criminal codes are enacted by each state and the federal government and set forth various definitions of crime. This has resulted in a patchwork of different definitions applied to basically the same act. In an effort to establish uniformity within the area of criminal law, a distinguished group of scholars and attorneys worked together for several years in drafting a Model Penal Code (MPC). The purpose of this code was to set forth the most reasoned thinking on various crimes and encourage states to adopt these definitions so that uniformity would be established throughout the United States. The MPC defines rape as follows:

A male who has sexual intercourse with a female not his wife, is guilty of rape if:

a. he compels her to submit by force or by threat of imminent death, serious bodily injury, extreme pain, or kidnapping to be inflicted on anyone or
b. he has substantially impaired her power to appraise or control her conduct by administrating or employing without her knowledge drugs, intoxicants, or other means for the purpose of preventing resistance, or
c. the female is unconscious, or
d. the female is less than 10 years old.

Rape is a felony of the second degree unless (i) in the course thereof the actor inflicts serious bodily injury on anyone, or (ii) the victim was not a voluntary social companion of the actor on the occasion of the crime and had not previously permitted him sexual liberties, in which case the offense is a felony of the first degree.[40]

The drafters of the MPC were not purposefully discriminating against women. However, it is clear that the MPC perpetuated the bias of the times. First, a reading of the MPC reveals several flaws: The statute is gender biased, does not punish acquaintance rape as seriously as stranger rape, and does not provide for marital rape. The MPC prohibits only males from raping women. It makes no provision for female rape of a male. Second, although it "allows" that an acquaintance might rape his companion, this form of rape is not as serious as stranger rape; therefore, it will not be punished as harshly. Finally, it would not be a crime for a husband to rape his wife under the code. Some states adopted the provisions of the code, and others have modernized their criminal statutes relating to the crime of rape. Many statutes now provide that the crime of rape is defined as *an unlawful act of sexual intercourse with another person against that person's will by force, fear, or trick.*[41]

First, this statute is gender neutral; either a male or a female may commit the crime. Second, the very definition allows for the charging and prosecution of marital rape. Finally, a person may be prosecuted for acquaintance rape under this statute. The only area that is not covered by this statute is insertion of an object into the vagina during the assault.

Some authorities define rape as the penetration by a penis or other object into the mouth, vagina, or anal openings by force or fear.[42] There is a small but growing movement among the states to adopt this more modern definition of rape. Part of the rationale for the expanded definition is that rape is not a sexual crime; rather, it is a violent assault on the victim, and any type of forced penetration should be punished. This definition attempts to punish all forms of sexual assault. Additionally, it attempts to provide uniformity in an area where each state has adopted differing statutes regarding sexual violence. Other authorities suggest doing away with the term *rape* and using instead *sexual assault* or *sexual battery* and prohibiting oral, vaginal, or anal penetration by force or fear.[43]

Someday the law may move toward a more comprehensive definition of this type of sexual violence, but at present most statutes define rape in a manner similar to that discussed previously. This definition in turn triggers reporting requirements by professionals in certain instances. Therefore, the definition set forth earlier will be used for purposes of clarity and conformity with existing statutes. This should not given the impression that forcible anal intercourse or oral copulation is not a crime in most states. Under most statutes, these are considered separate offenses that are distinct from the crime of rape.

Victim Selection

As with so many other aspects of sexual assault, we are not certain why certain rapists select certain victims. This is one of the many subjects in this area that needs further research. One study did attempt to answer this question by interviewing convicted sexual predators. Stevens used other convicted felons to conduct a survey of sixty-one sexual offenders incarcerated in a maximum-security prison.[44] Stevens trained thirteen incarcerated violent offenders enrolled in his class at a maximum-security prison as student-interviewers. They conducted interviews with convicted sexual predators and ended up with sixty-one valid interviews.

The average respondent was thirty-two years old and had served seven years in prison at the time of the interview. The average rapist had attended eighth grade and was employed in a menial type of job before his arrest. The subjects averaged 3.4 prior adult arrests. Fifty-six percent of the sample was black, 42 percent white and 2 percent Hispanic.

The author cautions against accepting the word of criminals. However, the data do show some interesting results: The most common characteristic for selecting victims was that the victims were perceived as "easy prey," meaning that the victims were thought to be vulnerable. In other words, these predators selected victims who they thought could not or would not resist an attack, or an opportunity presented itself that allowed them to attack the victim.

Some of the predators viewed young females as easy prey. Another predator talked about attacking sixty or seventy victims by scouting financial districts and looking for middle-class working females. Still other predators found that female shoppers were easy prey. They identified them by their demeanor. One predator stated, "If she's not watching what's happening all around her, then [she] doesn't know how to handle herself, how to use the things around her to hurt me, or get me caught." Finally, other predators wait for situations to develop in which the victim puts herself in a vulnerable position. For example, one predator attacked a female in the parking lot by threatening to harm her young child unless she cooperated. More study and research is needed in this area so that we may identify "risk patterns" that will allow us to avoid this type of violence.

Legal Aspects

Rape carries with it certain physical, mental, and legal consequences. Many times during a rape the offender will perform or attempt to perform a variety of acts, including vaginal, oral, and anal sex. As mentioned earlier, each of these acts is considered a separate and distinct crime.

The crime of rape requires penetration of the penis into the vagina. The offense is complete on the slightest entry into the victim; therefore, it is possible for a women to be raped and still retain her hymen. There is no requirement that the offender ejaculate for the crime to be complete.

As indicated previously, rape may be committed by force, fear, or trick. Forcible rape involves the offender using brute force to overpower the victim. He may use his fists, clubs, or other objects to strike the victim prior to raping her. The second situation occurs when the offender threatens the victim and she submits out of fear for her safety. This type of rape may not leave any physical scars, torn clothing, or other signs of physical violence. The third type of rape occurs when the offender tricks the victim. This is a broad category that includes sex with incompetents as well as the use of drugs and alcohol to render the victim incapable of consenting.

Sodomy or forcible and intercourse is defined as the unlawful sexual penetration of the penis of one person into the anus of another committed by use of force or fear.[45] Similar to the crime of rape, no emission or ejaculation is required. The offense is complete on the slightest penetration of the victim's anus.

FOCUS Did She Consent When She Asked Him to Wear a Condom?

One of the most common defenses in rape cases is that the victim consented. This is especially true in fear or trick rapes in which the victim suffers no outward physical injuries.

In Texas, a recent rape trial caught the attention of the media. The victim was single and lived alone. One evening after she returned from a friend's party, she looked up and saw the defendant with a knife in his hand who had entered through a sliding glass door. He approached her and demanded sex. The victim, fearing for her life, consented and asked the offender to wear a condom, which she supplied. The defendant was later arrested and tried for the crime of rape. He claimed that the act was consensual in nature and pointed to the victim's supplying him with a condom as proof of his assertion. The jury did not believe his story and convicted him of rape.

Oral copulation is the unlawful act of copulating the mouth of one person with the sexual organs or anus of another by use of force or fear.[46] Oral copulation does not require emission or ejaculation for the act to be completed. Penetration is not required for this crime. If the victim is forced to place her mouth on any part of the penis, the crime is complete. She does not have to place the penis in her mouth for this crime to occur.

Once the crime is complete and if the victim reports the offense to the authorities, the criminal justice system begins its slow and methodological prosecution of the offender. The rape victim will have to testify in open court about the incident. As late as the early 1960s, rape victims were treated as the criminals in sexual assault cases, and defense attorneys were allowed to ask questions regarding the victims' previous sexual experiences.[47] A variety of theories allowed for admission of this type of evidence. Two of the more common theories involved the victim's reputation: Because she had intercourse with other persons, she was therefore likely to have consented during this act, and this was proof that she was a person of loose morals and meant that she was willing to have sex with anyone, including this defendant. These antiquated and biased rules are no longer accepted in the judicial system. All fifty states and the federal government have adopted *rape shield laws. These statutes prohibit the defendant or his attorney from questioning the rape victim regarding her previous sexual history or introducing any other evidence concerning her past sexual practices.*[48]

Stranger rape is a violent physical assault on women. However, it is not the most common form of sexual assault. Recent studies have indicated that more women are raped by persons they know rather than by strangers. The next section examines two forms of this sexual violence: marital rape and acquaintance rape.

Marital and Acquaintance Rape

The article in the **Focus** "Marital Rape and the Medical Community's Response" goes on to discuss various forms of family violence with subsequent recommendations from the Council on Scientific Affairs that the American Medical Associa-

FOCUS Marital Rape and the Medical Community's Response

The medical community along with the criminal justice system is the most likely to see women victims and as such constitutes a frontline of identification and intervention. However, physicians and other medical staff are rarely provided with training or specific protocols to aid in dealing with these cases. The cost of the failure to identify and intervene in violence is incalculable, particularly in violence by intimates because assaults tend to be repeated over time, produce more injuries than assaults by strangers, and have complicated sequelae with implications for further violence.

Although a neglected topic in the areas of both family violence and medicine, empirical research has shown that marital rape is an integral part of marital violence. Sexual abuse is a serious form of marital violence. It is possible to inflict an intense level of physical pain over a long period and cause a wide range of injuries, from superficial bruises and tearing to internal injuries and scarring. The psychological impact of assault by an intimate can also be extreme. Yet, except for child sexual molestation, this type of violence is least likely to be reported by victims. An awareness of the potential for forcible sexual assault in marriage, particularly in cases in which other types of physical abuse have been identified, will enable the clinician to sensitively assess the cause of observed symptoms.

Source: Adapted from Council of Scientific Affairs. "Violence against Women," *Journal of the American Medical Association* (267/23) June 17, 1992, pp. 3184–3185.

tion undertake a campaign to sensitize its members to family violence. The recommendation includes training and dissemination of protocols on identifying and treating victims of family violence. The medical community is slowly becoming aware of the need to respond to intimate sexual violence. Although there is now more awareness of marital and acquaintance rape primarily because of the media, many people, including professionals, have difficulty with the concept that a man can be accused and convicted of raping his wife or that a date who "consented" the evening before can not raise the specter of rape the next day. Although the perception is slowly changing, those remain who believe that sex is a matter of right in marriage and in other intimate relationships.

The Problem

Intimate sexual violence includes marital and acquaintance rape. These forms of assault are not isolated incidents that occur to only a few women. *Rape in America* reported that only 22 percent of all women raped were sexually assaulted by someone they had never seen before or did not know.[49] Nine percent of all victims were raped by their husbands or ex-husbands, 10 percent by boyfriends or ex-boyfriends, and 21 percent by other nonrelatives such as friends or neighbors. The remaining percentages were made up of fathers, stepfathers, other relatives, and a not-sure category of 3 percent. This report indicates that approximately 683,000 women were raped in a one-year period. Using the figures provided in this report, that means that in one year 61,470 women were raped by their husbands or ex-husbands, 68,300 women were raped by their boyfriends or ex-boyfriends, and 143,430 women were raped by other known acquaintances.

Marital Rape

For centuries society has believed that a man is entitled to having sex with his wife. A man could not be charged or convicted of raping his wife in eighteenth-century England. Wives were considered chattel and clearly subordinate to the husband.[50] Fathers had a property right or interest in their daughters' virginity and husbands in their wives' fidelity. The rape of an unmarried women destroyed her value as a suitable bride and sexual mate. The rape of a married woman was an infringement on the property rights of her spouse and a disgrace to her husband.

The marital exemption for rape can be traced to Sir Matthew Hale, a seventeen-century English jurist. Sir Hale was the Chief Justice of King's Bench from 1671 to 1675. A book based on his writing was published after his death in 1736.[51] Geis in his review of early English common law indicates that Sir Matthew Hale's statement on rape helped establish a precedent for spousal immunity from rape when he held that "The husband cannot be guilty of rape committed by himself upon his lawful wife, for by their mutual matrimonial consent and contract the wife hath given up herself in this kind unto the husband which she cannot retract."[58]

Blackstone, the great English legal scholar, helped to perpetuate this reasoning. He stated that the legal existence of a woman is suspended during marriage or at the very least incorporated into that of her husband. Blackstone's argument served to continue the legal fiction of unity of the person on marriage. Therefore, a wife was deemed to have irrevocably consented to sex whenever and wherever her husband wished.[53] This philosophy continued in England and elsewhere into modern times. Martin points out that Winston Churchill's mother could not refuse her husband's sexual advances even though he was suffering from incurable syphilis.[54]

The feminist movement in the 1970s sought to change the laws to allow for charges to be brought against a husband who raped his wife. It was not an easy victory. State and congressional elected officials made comments like, "But if you can't rape your wife, who can you rape?" and "[T]he Bible doesn't give the state permission anywhere in the Book for the state to be in your bedroom. . . ."[55] Unbelievable as it may seem now, there was a great deal of resistance to passage of any laws that would delete spousal immunity from the books and thus allow a wife to charge her husband with rape. Through the efforts of several dedicated groups and individuals, laws began to be amended to define marital rape as a specific crime.

As mentioned earlier, many rape statutes now allow for the prosecution of a husband who rapes his wife. Therefore, there is no separate legal definition of marital rape. However, for purposes of explaining and distinguishing this form of sexual violence from stranger rape, *marital rape is defined as the unlawful sexual intercourse with a spouse or ex-spouse against her will by means of force or fear.*

Finkelhor and Yllo conducted extensive research in the area of marital rape and classified marital rapes into three categories: force-only rapes, battering rapes, and obsessive rapes. Force-only rapes occur when the husband attempts to gain control over the type and frequency of sexual activity within the marriage. Finkelhor and Yllo compare this type of rape to Groth and Birnbaum's power rapes. Battering rapes involve the husband attempting to humiliate and degrade his spouse. These type of marital rapes are very similar to Groth and Birnbaum's anger rapes. The last type of marital rape is the obsessive rape. These rapes involve sexual sadism, fetishes, and forcible anal intercourse. This type of rape is similar to Groth and Birnbaum's classification of sadistic rapes.[56]

Just as there are a number of theories as to why spousal abuse and stranger rape occur, so there are a variety of theories dealing with factors that encourage or promote marital rape. Previous chapters have discussed factors that increase the risk of family violence, including child physical and sexual abuse, spousal abuse, and marital rape. The following discussion focuses on factors and forces within society that specifically encourage or contribute to marital rape. These factors include the historical perspective toward the family, spousal immunity, economics, and Western culture's preoccupation with violence.

Historical perspective toward the family: For generations the family has been viewed as the last stronghold of absolute privacy. What happened in the wedding bed was believed to be no one else's business. This concept of family privacy has caused delays and problems in researching issues such as marital rape. Additionally, women were raised with beliefs that they had to submit to their husband's sexual advances. Only recently have we begun to study the dynamics within the family bedroom, and women now understand that they do not owe sex on demand to their spouses.

Spousal immunity: As mentioned earlier, early common law established the proposition that a husband could not be accused of raping his wife. Rape of a stranger was considered a violent and unspeakable act; however, rape of a wife was unknown. The wife was considered to be part of the husband, and he was therefore immuned from any charges of rape brought by his spouse. Only recently have spouses been able to bring charges of rape against their husbands.

Economics: Similar to other causes of family violence, economics and dependency play a role in promoting marital rape. Both spouses are aware of the wife's economic dependency. Some men argue that they provide the paycheck, so the wife must take care of the home. This "taking care of the home" includes, in the male's mind, sex on demand—any kind of sex.

Preoccupation with violence: Violence and its effect on family violence has been discussed in detail earlier in this text. Because some films, books, and television devalue women, it is easier for males to use violence as an acceptable form of sexual expression.

Although none of these factors may be the single cause of marital rape, they contribute along with other factors to a general climate of violence in the United States that promotes sexual violence against women.

Acquaintance Rape

Some males and defense attorneys would argue that situations 1 and 3 were clearly not rape and that a male should not be responsible for getting inside the mind of his date. Depending on what further facts are added, situation 1 may

FOCUS When Is It Rape?

1. A couple attending college decides to break up. They have been intimate for three years, engaging in oral, anal, and vaginal sexual activities. One week after they separate, the male arrives at the female's apartment intoxicated and states that they are going to have sex. The female insists that the relationship is over; however, the male gets angry, punches the wall, and demands sex. The female knows that he will not hit her and is therefore not frightened for her own safety but gives in, and they engage in sexual relations.

2. On a third date, the male double shots his date's drinks. She is not an experienced drinker and passes out while they are engaged in heavy petting. The male proceeds to have intercourse with her.

3. A couple has been dating for three weeks. They both have had several drinks and are intoxicated. They engage in heavy petting and the girl responds physically but says, "Please darling, no." The male continues his sexual advances, and the girl continues to respond physically but also continues to say, "No." They finally engage in intercourse.

Are any of the above acquaintance rape? Why? Who is responsible in these situations? Are both parties at fault?

Source: David W. Murray, "Poor Suffering Bastards: An Anthropologist Looks at Illegitimacy," *Policy Review, 68,* Spring 1994, 13.

have involved the use of force and therefore qualify as a sexual assault and rape. Situation 2 is clearly a rape-by-trick situation in which the victim was unable to give consent. Situation 3 may be classified as rape because many authorities argue that when a female says no the advances by the male must stop. Others argue that it may or may not be rape, depending on the victim's state of mind.[57]

Sexual violence in dating relationships is not a new topic to social scientists and other professionals. As early as 1957, Eugene Kanin studied college students' sexual aggression. He found that over half of all college women (50 to 60 percent) reported being the target of sexual aggression, whereas only 20 to 30 percent of college men admitted to such aggressive behavior.[58] This indicates a serious lack of empathy on the part of male college students as to what is appropriate behavior. Although most women found the acts aggressive, only 20 to 30 percent of the males found them to meet their definition of sexual aggression. Other researchers have confirmed these percentages and come to the conclusion that the double standard still exists in the United States.[59] This attitude in turn leads to situations where date rape can and does occur.

Although sexual aggression in dating relationships has been studied for over thirty years, U.S. citizens still have problems in accepting the concept of rape by a person known to the victim.[60] Some individuals want to believe that rape is committed only in some dark alley by a sadistic monster and that only "nice girls" who resist and whose resistance was overcome by physical force can be raped.

Stranger rape, at one time, was thought to be the most common form of sexual violence. However, we now understand that intimate violence is more fre-

FOCUS Rohypnol—The Date Rape Pill

Rohypnol is the trade name for the drug Flunitrazepam. It is a central nervous system depressant like Valium but ten times more potent. It is now banned in the United States but can be purchased cheaply on the streets.

Rohypnol abuse and distribution was first reported in the late 1980s in Florida, Texas, and California. By the end of 1995, the Drug Enforcement Agency (DEA) reported that Rohypnol abuse was present in at least thirty-two states. Its use appears to be spreading throughout the United States among high school and college youth. College students report mixing it with beer to enhance the feeling of drunkenness. It is also known as a "club drug" because it is being used by young adults at bars and nightclubs.

It is dropped in a drink to incapacitate an unsuspecting victim. The victim becomes dizzy, disoriented, has trouble moving the arms or legs, and finally passes out. This leaves her with no memory of a sexual assault. Hoffmann-LaRoche, the maker of Rohypnol, has produced and televised an ad campaign to fight its abuse and is converting the drug to a smaller dose that will not dissolve as easily in a drink.

Source: Adapted from "Fact Sheet: Rohypnol," *Drug Policy Information Clearinghouse* (Washington, D.C. September 1996).

quent than suspected. One survey reported that on a midwestern campus, 100 percent of all the rapists knew their victims.[61]

Similar to marital rape, date or acquaintance rape situations are covered by the general definition of rape set forth earlier. However, for purposes of explaining this special type of sexual violence, *acquaintance rape is defined as unlawful sexual intercourse accomplished by force or fear with a person known to the victim who is not related by blood or marriage.*

The following actual cases illustrate the continuing problems facing victims of acquaintance rape.

- A young woman reports to the police that she was kidnapped and raped by a former boyfriend. He had beaten her in the past, leading to his arrest on at least one occasion. The prosecutor resists bringing rape charges because of the victim's prior relationship with her assailant and offers the man a plea to reduced charges—a misdemeanor assault for which the attacker receives a six-month sentence and eighteen months' probation. Less than a year later, the attacker brutally rapes and almost kills another woman.
- A group of young men meet a woman in a bar at night; they surreptitiously slip a tablet of LSD in her drink on leaving the bar. At the home of one of the young men, they slip her four more doses of LSD. The woman is then repeatedly raped with objects as a group cheers and takes pictures, which are later destroyed. One of the assailants stops the attack when someone suggests raping the woman with a statue of Christ. Three of the attackers are given immunity for providing statements helpful to the prosecution; one defendant pleads guilty to evidence tampering and delivery of illegal drugs; he serves

three months of an eight-month sentence in jail with eight years probation. Not one of the defendants is convicted of sexual assault.

- A woman breaks off her engagement with a man. Several weeks later, he goes to her house and they get into an argument in his car. She tells the police that he dragged her into the back seat of the car and raped her. After the attack, she goes to the hospital and files a police report. The prosecutor in the case accepts the defendant's plea to unlawful restraint—a fourth-degree felony with a two-year sentence—saying, "It's not like she didn't have sex with him before." The attacker serves six months and one day in jail.[62]

Acquaintance rape will continue to be a serious problem in the United States as long as we socialize males to view women as inferior members of society who really want to be chased, conquered, and dominated.

Sexual Harassment

Sexual harassment is the overall umbrella under which specific forms of sexual violence take place. Although it is true that men have been targets of sexual harassment, most victims are women.[63] Because sexual harassment is form of violence against women, it is included in this chapter to allow for comparison between sexual violence within the family and sexual violence in the workplace. Only by understanding the full spectrum of sexual violence can professionals begin to respond appropriately to it.

Discrimination has existed in the United States since its founding. President Lincoln began the process of doing away with discrimination when he freed the slaves, and for decades U.S. courts have held that one citizen should not discriminate against another because of his skin color. However, that battle goes on today in coffeeshops that refuse to serve people of color, in banks that decline to make home loans to persons living in certain locations, and in many service-related businesses, such as automobile dealers that simply ignore persons of different races. Discrimination against women because of their sex is one bias that is also gaining attention. One of the most offensive forms of this discrimination is sexual harassment. Employment-based sexual harassment is dehumanizing, and it changes the focus of employment from the woman's work performance to her sex. Additionally, it degrades women by reinforcing their traditionally inferior role in the workplace. The following sections provide a brief overview of sexual harassment.

Introduction

Sexual harassment is a widespread phenomenon. One of the first work-related surveys of 9,000 women found that nine out of ten women reported instances of sexual harassment.[64] Probably the most comprehensive survey of sexual harassment ever done was conducted by the U.S. Merit System Protection Board in 1980.

The board surveyed 23,000 federal employees and reported that 42 percent of all women reported being the subject of some form of sexual harassment.[65]

The demands for sexual favors in exchange for continuing employment have long been a common abuse of personal power in the workplace. The clandestine squeeze on the factory floor, the stolen kiss in the copy room, or they lewd suggestion regarding sex have been commonplace in U.S. businesses for years. Until recently, the victim of such sexual violence has had two choices: agree to the demands or lose her job. Additionally, she was led to believe that the activities that she found offensive were in reality common practice in the workplace. There was no legal recourse for victims of sexual harassment until the 1980s.

In 1964, the United States began the long process of outlawing all forms of discrimination. Congress passed Title VII of the Civil Rights Act of 1964, which prohibited employment discrimination based on race, color, religion, sex, pregnancy, or national origin.[66] Title VII provides the following:

It shall be an unlawful employment practice for an employer—

1. *to fail or refuse to hire or to discharge any individual, or otherwise to discriminate against any individual with respect to his compensation, terms, conditions, or privileges of employment, because of such individual's race, color, religion, sex, or national origin; or*
2. *to limit, segregate, or classify his employees or applicants for employment in any way which would deprive or tend to deprive any individual of employment opportunities or otherwise adversely affect his status as an employee, because of such individual's race, color, religion, sex, or national origin.*[67]

Even though the language of the statute was clear, women continued to be exposed to discrimination either because they were pregnant at the time or because they might become pregnant in the future. This continuing discrimination caused Congress to pass the Pregnancy Discrimination Act of 1978, which prohibited discrimination based on pregnancy, childbirth, or other related medical conditions.[68]

Many scholars believe the Civil Rights Act of 1964 was the basis for the current prohibition against sexual harassment. However, Congress never directly addressed that issue when it passed the Civil Rights Act. In fact, sex was added as a prohibited classification in a last-minute attempt to block passage of the legislation.[69] Rather, courts and administrative agencies have used the Civil Rights Act as the foundation on which to base their rulings regarding sexual harassment.[70]

Definitions

A number of definitions of sexual harassment exist. From a traditional perspective, sexual harassment is a demand that a subordinate, usually a woman, grant sexual favors to retain a job benefit.[71] A more encompassing definition defines *sexual harassment as the imposition of any unwanted condition on any person's employment*

FOCUS Attitudes Regarding Sexual Harassment

In October 1997, NBC released the results of a poll it conducted regarding equity in the workplace. The network polled 1,019 adults in September in an effort to determine their views regarding whether society is doing enough to promote equality, especially in the workplace.

The pollsters found confusion among men and women about what is considered appropriate or offensive behavior in the workplace. This confusion occurred not as much by gender as by age. Younger women were less offended than older women regarding compliments about their appearance from male coworkers. This was especially true if the younger women had worked outside the home for a period of time.

This poll also pointed out that sexual harassment is still a major problem in the workplace. One in every five working women reported incidents of sexual harassment within the last two years. Both men and women reported making comments that were inappropriate and "crossed the line" to a coworker of the opposite sex within the last five years.

Source: Associated Press. "Men, Women Divided on Equality," *The Fresno Bee*, October 20, 1997, p. A-4.

because of that person's sex. Under this definition, harassment includes jokes, direct taunting, disruption of work, vandalism or destruction of property, and physical attacks.[72] Sexual harassment occurs in a wide variety of forms including rape, pressure for sexual favors, sexual touching, suggestive looks or gestures, sexual joking or teasing, and the display of unwanted sexual material.

Sexual harassment may occur in either of two forms: "quid pro quo harassment" or "hostile environment harassment." These are not mutually exclusive situations. Many times they will overlap, and both forms may be present in the workplace.

Quid pro quo harassment occurs when an agent or supervisor of the employer uses his position to induce a female employee to grant him sexual favors. The exchange of continued employment or job benefits for sex suggests the name "quid pro quo." The essence of a quid pro quo harassment is that the victim must choose between suffering economic disadvantage or enduring sexual advances.[73]

Hostile environment harassment occurs when unwelcome conduct of a sexual nature creates a hostile working environment. The conduct usually involves a series of incidents rather than a single episode of harassment. The essence of a hostile working environment form of harassment is that an individual is forced to work in an environment that, although not causing direct economic detriment, results in psychological or emotional harm or humiliation.

Barnes v Costle established the principle that sex-based assignments or sexual advances in which the employer enforces the demand by threat of discharge or other adverse economic consequences violates Title VII of the Civil Rights Act.[74] In this case, the plaintiff alleged that she was hired as an administrative assistant to the director of the agency's Equal Employment Opportunity Division at the Environmental Protection Agency. Shortly after commencing employment, the director solicited her to join him after hours at social functions and stated that if she cooperated with him in a sexual affair her employment status would be enhanced. She refused these advances, and her position was abolished. The appellate court held such actions to be a clear violation of Title VII of the Civil Rights Act.

In 1980, the Equal Employment Opportunity Commission (EEOC) adopted regulations in the form of guidelines that prohibited discrimination based on sex. These guidelines specifically state that an individual's response to unwelcome conduct of a sexual nature may not be made the basis of any adverse employment decision.[75] Although the EEOC guidelines are not binding, they have been held to constitute a body of experience and informed judgments to which courts and litigants may properly resort for guidance.[76]

It wasn't until 1986 that a case of sexual harassment based on a hostile working environment was decided. In *Meritor Savings Bank v Vinson,* the U.S. Supreme Court held that a working environment that is hostile to women may violate Title VII of the Civil Rights Act even without any question of economic detriment.[77] In this case, the victim was hired by the bank as a teller and eventually advanced to the position of assistant branch manager. She alleged that a supervisor subjected her to sexual harassment in excess of four years. This harassment included sexual intercourse, fondling her in front of other employees, exposing himself to her, and even following her into the ladies restroom. The Supreme Court upheld the victim's claim of sexual harassment based on the basis of the theory that the actions of the aggressor established a hostile working environment.

In 1993, the Supreme Court further clarified the meaning of sexual harassment when it decided *Harris v Forklift Systems, Inc.*[78] Teresa Harris worked as a manager at Forklift Systems, Inc., an equipment rental company, from April 1985 to October 1987. Charles Hardy, Forklift's president, often insulted Teresa because of her gender and made unwelcome sexual innuendos. Hardy told Harris several times in front of other employees that she was a women, didn't know anything, and what the company needed was a male manager. He also suggested that they go to the local hotel and negotiate Harris's salary. On other occasions, he threw objects on the ground and asked Harris to pick them up. Hardy also asked Harris and other female employees to get coins from his front pants pocket.

Harris finally complained to Hardy, who claimed he was only joking and apologized. He further promised not to engage in that behavior again. However, several weeks later he asked Harris whether she had slept with a customer to get that customer to sign a contract. Harris quit and filed a lawsuit, alleging violations of Title VII.

The Supreme Court ruled that there was no requirement that the conduct be so severe as to cause the victim to become physically ill or psychologically distressed. The court stated that victims of sexual harassment had met their burden if they proved that the environment was perceived as hostile or abusive. An environment is hostile or abusive by looking at all the circumstances. These circumstances include the frequency of the conduct, whether it is physically threatening, humiliating, or a mere offensive remark and whether it unreasonably interferes with an employee's work performance.

Tangri, Burt, and Johnson established three models or types of sexual harassment: the natural/biological model, the organizational model, and the sociocultural model.[79] Using data from the initial Merit Systems Protection Board 1980 survey, they partially tested these models.

The *natural/biological model* assumes that sexual behavior in the workplace is an extension of human sexuality. It is assumed that men and women possess strong sex drive, but the man whose sex drive is stronger takes the role of the aggressor. From this perspective, sexual harassment is not discriminatory in nature; it is simply the result of natural biological mating urges. This model presupposes that all sexual advances are mutual in nature and part of courtship or mating behavior. Researchers now understand that all advances are not in fact part of courtship, and therefore this model fails to explain sexual harassment.

The *organizational model* is a result of a workplace environment that provides opportunities for sexual aggression. From this perspective, sexual harassment becomes an issue of power, not sex. This power is derived from the formal roles in an organizational context. For this model to be valid, only those women in positions of low hierarchical power would be targets of sexual harassment. Women who hold a variety of positions have been harassed, some of whom were considered high on the organizational scheme. Therefore, this model does not adequately explain sexual harassment.

The *sociocultural model* views sexual harassment as reflecting the more dominant position of men in Western culture where they are the source of economic and political power. This model suggests that sexual harassment is the result of a patriarchal power system in which men rule society. From this perspective, sexual harassment is based on the personal power of gender where men are dominant. Power is an important factor in sexual harassment. The male aggressor may control advancement, benefits, and continued employment.

Sexual harassment does not exist only in the workplace. It has been called one of the best kept secrets on college campuses, and some feminists are concerned that some professors have used their positions of power to obtain sexual favors from students. Dziech and Weiner list the following actions that they consider as inappropriate behavior by professors:

Staring, leering, or ogling. These behaviors may be surreptitious or obvious. Professors who by the very nature of their occupation must look at and observe students should not cross over the boundaries of reason.

Frequently commenting on the personal appearance of the student. In an academic setting, professors should refrain from discussing apparel and physical characteristics of female students.

Touching out of context. Touching of students should be minimal and only to the extent necessary to carry out certain types of instruction.

Excessive flattery and praise for the student. This behavior, coupled with others listed here, is especially seductive to female students with low self-esteems or high expectations. By convincing the student that she is exceptional, the professor gains psychological access to her.

Injecting a "male versus female" tone into discussions with the student. This type of disparaging remark about women and their abilities is a clear signal of a bias or negative perception on the part of the professor.

Persistently emphasizing sexuality in all contexts. Pervasive emphasis on sex in or outside the classroom is inappropriate.[80]

The previous discussions should not be construed as labeling every professor as a potential sexual harasser. However, even in academia the controversy over professor–student relationships continues to be debated. In April 1993, the University of Virginia Faculty Senate was considering a policy that would prohibit faculty members from dating students. Representatives of the American Civil Liberties Union (ACLU) questioned the appropriateness of the actions, remarking that the university might be infringing on privacy and associational rights of teachers. The ACLU recommended that the university enhance its sexual harassment codes instead. The faculty senate proceeded to approve the no-dating policy. Many universities have sexual harassment codes, and some are beginning to adopt a no-dating policy among students and faculty members. The relationship between students and faculty members is one of power. When a professor uses his position to extract sexual favors from a student, this becomes a serious quid pro quo form of sexual harassment.

Simply having agencies and courts establish procedures and processes to handle sexual harassment cases does not do away with this behavior. The perception of women must be changed, and they should be viewed as equals instead of sex objects. Only when women are approached as partners and equals will sexual harassment stop.

Summary

Sexual violence is a complex and far-ranging topic. The study of sexual violence has been and will continue to be hindered by a lack of agreement among the different professions on terminology and research methodology. All professionals agree that sexual violence continues to be a serious problem. Recent studies have indicated that women are more at risk from someone they know than from the stranger lurking in the darkness. Also, the consequences of any type of sexual violence are severe and in many instances long-lasting.

Professionals are slowly advancing in their perception of rape victims. No longer can only "nice" girls be raped, and professionals have accepted that rape is a violent physical assault that has very little if anything to do with sexual gratification. Legislatures have passed rape shield laws that now provide some protection to rape victims. These laws bar questions to the victim that require her to explain her previous sexual experiences to the judge and jury. As long as men rape women, consent will be raised as a defense. However, as society becomes more educated, that rationalization will stop bearing credibility. Sexual harassment continues to be a form of sexual violence in the United States and will continue as long as men view women as sexual trophies or playthings instead of equals. Only by continuing education of the horrors of rape can this form of sexual violence be put to an end.

Key Terms

sexual violence—any intentional act or omission that results in physical, emotional, or financial injury to a women. Sexual violence does not include the termination of a romantic relationship.

carnal knowledge of a female—penile–vaginal penetration.

rape—An unlawful act of sexual intercourse with another person against that person's will by force, fear, or trick.

oral copulation—the unlawful act of copulating the mouth of one person with the sexual organs or anus of another by use of force or fear.

sodomy—the unlawful sexual penetration of the penis of one person into the anus of another committed by use of force or fear.

rape crisis syndrome—occurs when the victim experiences feelings of shame, humiliation, disjointedness, anger, inability to concentrate, and withdrawal.

posttraumatic stress disorder—the development of characteristic symptoms following a psychologically distressing event that is outside the range of usual human experience. The characteristic symptoms involve reexperiencing the traumatic event, avoidance of stimuli associated with the event or numbing of general responsiveness, and increased arousal.

rape shield law—prohibits the defendant or his attorney from questioning the rape victim regarding her previous sexual history or introducing any other evidence concerning her past sexual practices.

marital rape—the unlawful sexual intercourse with a spouse or ex-spouse against her will by means of force or fear.

acquaintance rape—unlawful sexual intercourse accomplished by force or fear with a person known to the victim who is not related by blood or marriage.

sexual harassment—the imposition of any unwanted condition on any person's employment because of that person's sex.

Discussion Questions

1. Based on your reading of this chapter, draft a definition of rape. Justify why your definition is better than the one given in the text.
2. Which of the causes of rape is the most important? Why? Can we do anything as a society to diminish the chances of a woman being raped? What?
3. Which of the most severe type of rape—stranger, marital, or acquaintance rape? Why? Should all forms of rape be punished the same, or should we have more harsh penalties for certain forms? Why?
4. How would you respond if a married friend of yours informed you that her husband had raped her last night? The husband is a good friend of yours. What are the options available to you?
5. Is the male always at fault in acquaintance rape situations? Why? Why not?
6. List at least ten types of sexual harassment. Explain why you think they qualify as sexual violence.

Suggested Readings

Brownmiller, S. *Against Our Will: Men, Women, and Rape.* (Penguin Books, New York) 1975.

deKoster, K. *Rape on Campus.* (Greenhaven Press, Inc., San Diego) 1995.

Epstein, J., and S. Langenbahn. *The Criminal Justice and Community Response to Rape.* (National Institute of Justice, U.S. Department of Justice, Washington, D.C.) May 1994.

Finkelhor, D., and K. Yllo. *License to Rape.* (Holt, Rinehart & Winston, New York) 1985.

Freud, S. *New Introductory Lectures on Psychoanalysis.* J. Strachey, ed. (W. W. Norton & Company, Inc., New York) 1965.

Groth, A. N., and J. Birnbaum. *Men Who Rape.* (Plenum Press, New York) 1979.

Jaggar, A. M., and P. S. Rothenberg, eds. *Feminist Frameworks.* 3rd ed., (McGraw-Hill, New York) 1993.

Kelly, L. *Surviving Sexual Violence.* (University of Minnesota Press, Minneapolis) 1988.

Lindemann, B., and D. D. Kadue. *Sexual Harassment in Employment Law.* (Bureau of National Affairs, Washington, D.C.) 1992.

Martin, R. E. *The Life of Lady Randolph Churchill.* (New York American Library, New York 1969).

McCaghy, C. *Deviant Behavior, Crime, Conflict and Interest Groups.* (Macmillian, New York) 1976.

Millett, K. *Sexual Politics.* (Abacus, London) 1972.

Phillips, P. *Marx and Engels on Law and Laws.* (Barnes and Noble, Totowa, New Jersey) 1980.

Russell, D. *The Politics of Rape.* (Stein and Day, New York) 1975.

Russell, D. E. H. *Sexual Exploitation.* (Sage, Beverly Hills, California) 1984.

Swisher, K. L. *What Is Sexual Harassment?* (Greenhaven Press, Inc., San Diego) 1995.

Symons, D. *The Evolution of Human Sexuality.* (Oxford University Press, Oxford) 1979.

Wallace, H., and C. Roberson. *Principles of Criminal Law.* (Longman, White Plains, New York) 1969.

Endnotes

1. Freud, S. *New Introductory Lectures on Psychoanalysis.* J. Strachey, ed. (W. W. Norton, New York) 1965.
2. Phillips, P. *Marx and Engels on Law and Laws.* (Barnes and Noble, Totowa, New Jersey) 1980.
3. Millett, K. *Sexual Politics.* (Abacus, London) 1972; Griffin, S. "Rape: The All-American Crime." *Ramparts* 10(3) 1971, pp. 26–35, and Brownmiller, S. *Against Our Will: Men, Women, and Rape.* (Penguin Books, New York) 1975.
4. Kelly, L. *Surviving Sexual Violence.* (University of Minnesota Press, Minneapolis) 1988.
5. For an excellent in-depth discussion of these issues, see Koss, M. P. "Detecting the Scope of Rape." *Journal of Interpersonal Violence* (8/2) June 1993, pp. 198–222.
6. Koss, M. P. "Detecting the Scope of Rape." *Journal of Interpersonal Violence* (8/2) June 1993, pp. 200–203.
7. Burt, M. R. "Attitudes Supportive of Rape in American Culture (Final Report, Grant #ROIMH29023). (National Institute of Mental Health, National Center for the Prevention and Control of Rape, Washington, D.C.) 1979.
8. Essock-Vitale, S. M., and M. T. McGurie, "Women's Lives Viewed from an Evolutionary Perspective." I. Sexual Histories, Reproductive Success, and Demographic Characteristics of a Random Sample of American Women. *Ethnology and Sociobiology* (6) 1985, pp. 137–154.
9. Kilpatrick, D. G., C. L. Best, L. J. Veronen, A. E. Amick, L. A. Villeponteaux, and G. A. Ruff. "Mental Health Correlates of Criminal Victimization: A Random Community Survey." *Journal of Consulting and Clinical Psychology* (53) 1985, pp. 866–873.
10. Riger, S. and M. T. Gordon. "The Fear of Rape: A Study in Social Control." *Journal of Social Issues* (37) 1981, pp. 71–92.
11. Kilpatrick, D. G., C. N. Edmunds, and A. K. Seymour. *Rape in America: A Report to the Nation.* (National Victim Center, Arlington, Virginia) 1992.

12. Russell, D. E. H. *Sexual Exploitation.* (Sage, Beverly Hills, California) 1984.
13. Sorenson, S. B., J. A. Stein, J. M. Siegel, J. M. Golding, and M. A. Burnam. "Prevalence of Adult Sexual Assault: The Los Angeles Epidemiologic Catchment Area Study." *American Journal of Epidemiology* (126) 1987, pp. 1154–1164.
14. Winfield, I., L. K. George, M. Swartz, and D. G. Blazer. "Sexual Assault and Psychiatric Disorders among a Community Sample of Women." *American Journal of Psychiatry* (147) 1990, pp. 335–341.
15. Wyatt, G. E. "The Sociocultural Context of African American and White American Women's Rape." *Journal of Social Issues* (48) 1992, pp. 77–92.
16. Personal communication with Christine N. Edmunds, co-author and Project Director, National Victim Center, Washington, D.C.
17. This section has been adapted from Lawrence A. Greenfield, *Sex Offenses and Offenders, An Analysis of Date on Rape and Sexual Assault,* (U.S. Department of Justice, Office of Justice Programs, Bureau of Justice Statistics, Washington, D.C.) February, 1997.
18. The extent of sex offenses was based on an analysis of the NCVS, which defines *rape* as forced sexual intercourse where the victim may be either male or female and the offender may be of the same sex or a different sex than the victim. Sexual assault includes a wide range of offenses, including attacks in which unwanted sexual contact occurs. Threats and attempts to commit both rape and sexual assault were included in the counts. This definition is different than the one contained in the UCR, which limits rape to female victims. However, similar to the NCVS, the UCR's definition of forcible rape and sex offenses did include attempts.
19. Russell, D. *The Politics of Rape.* (Stein and Day, New York) 1975.
20. Mosher, D., and R. Anderson. "Macho Personality, Sexual Aggression, and Reactions to Guided Imagery of Realistic Rape." *Journal of Research in Personality* (20) 1987, pp. 77–94.
21. Symons, D. *The Evolution of Human Sexuality.* (Oxford University Press, Oxford) 1979.
22. Personal correspondence from Owen D. Jones, Professor of Law, Arizona State University, Tempe, Arizona, dated August 27, 1994.
23. McCaghy, C. *Deviant Behavior: Crime, Conflict and Interest Groups.* (Macmillian, New York) 1976.
24. Rabkin, J. "Epideminology of Forcible Rape." *American Journal of Orthospychiatry* (49/4) 1979, pp. 634–647.
25. Groth, A. N., A. W. Burgess, and L. L. Holmstrom. "Rape: Power, Anger, and Sexuality." *American Journal of Psychiatry* (134:11) November 1977, p. 1239.
26. Groth, A. N., and J. Birnbaum. *Men Who Rape.* (Plenum Press, New York) 1979.
27. Kilpatrick, D. G., L. J. Veronen, and P. A. Resick. "Assessment of the Aftermath of Rape: Changing Patterns of Fear." *Journal of Behavioral Assessment* (1/2) 1979, p. 133.
28. Resick, P. A. "The Psychological Impact of Rape." *Journal of Interpersonal Violence* (8/2) June 1993, pp. 223–255.
29. Burnam, M. A., J. A. Stein, J. M. Siegel, S. B. Sorenson, A. B. Forsythe, and C. A. Telles. "Sexual Assault and Mental Disorders in a Community Population." *Journal of Consulting and Clinical Psychology* (56) 1988, pp. 843–850.
30. Resick, P. A. "Reactions of Female and Male Victims of Rape or Robbery." Final Report, Grant #85-IJ-CX-0042. (National Institute of Justice, Washington, D.C.) 1988.
31. DSM-IV, p. 424.
32. Rothbaum, B. O., E. B. Foa, T. Murdock, D. S. Riggs, and W. Walsh. "A Prospective Examination of Post-Traumatic Stress Disorder in Rape Victims." *Journal of Traumatic Stress* (5) 1992, pp. 455–475.
33. Kilpatrick, D. G., C. N. Edmunds, and A. K. Seymour. *Rape in America: A Report to the Nation.* (National Victim Center, Arlington, Virginia) 1992.
34. Bard, M., and K. Ellison. "Crisis Intervention and Investigation of Forcible Rape." In L. Brodyaga, M. Gates, S. Singer, M. Tucker, and R. White, eds. *Rape and its Victims: A Report for Citizens, Health Facilities, and Criminal Justice Agencies.* (Department of Justice, Washington, D.C.) 1974, pp. 165–171.
35. Kilpatrick, D. G., C. N. Edmunds, and A. K. Seymour. *Rape in America: A Report to the*

Nation. (National Victim Center, Arlington, Virginia) 1992.

36. Resick, P. A., G. G. Jordan, S. A. Girelli, C. K. Hutter, and S. Marhoefer-Dvorak. "A Comparative Outcome Study of Behavioral Group Therapy for Sexual Assault Victims." *Behavior Therapy* (19) 1988, pp. 385–401.
37. Thelen, M. H., M. D. Sherman, and T. S. Borst. "Fear of Intimacy and Attachment among Rape Survivors." *Behavior Modification* 22(1) January 1988.
38. Bienen, L. B. "Rape III—National Developments in Rape Reform Legislation." *Women's Rights Law Reporter.* (6) 1981, pp. 171–213.
39. Black, H. C. *Black's Law Dictionary.* (West, St. Paul) 1990, p. 213.
40. Model Penal Code Section 213.1 (American Law Institute, Chicago) 1985.
41. Wallace, H., and C. Roberson. *Principles of Criminal Law.* (Longman, White Plains, New York) 1994.
42. Kilpatrick, D. G., C. L. Best, B. E. Saunders, and L. J. Veronen. "Rape in Marriage and in Dating Relationships: How Bad Is It for Mental Health?" *Annals of the New York Academy of Sciences* (528) 1988, pp. 335–344.
43. Koss, M. P. "Detecting the Scope of Rape." *Journal of Interpersonal Violence* (8/2) June 1993, p. 198.
44. Stevens, D. J. "Predatory Rapist and Victim Selection Techniques," *The Social Science Journal* 31(4) 1994, p. 421.
45. Wallace, H., and C. Roberson. *Principles of Criminal Law.* (Longman, White Plains, New York) 1996.
46. Ibid.
47. For an excellent discussion of legal, ethical and professional issues in printing the name of a rape victim, see Cooper, C., and V. Whitehouse. "Rape: To Name or Not to Name," *St. Louis Journalism Review.* (24) No. 174 March 1995, pp. 10–12.
48. See *Michigan v. Lucas,* 111 S.Ct. 1743 (1991) where the United States Supreme Court upheld the constitutionality of these statutes. See also, *Vermont Statute,* Title 13, Chapter 72, Section 3255 (3)(A)(B) for an example of a rape shield law.
49. Kilpatrick, D. G., C. N. Edmunds, and A. K. Seymour. *Rape in America: A Report to the Nation.* (National Victim Center, Arlington, Virginia) 1992.
50. See Comment. "Abolishing the Marital Exemption to Rape: A Statutory Proposal." *University of Illinois Law Review* 201 (1983).
51. Hale, M. *The History of the Pleas of the Crown.* (1736). The first American edition of the book was published in 1874. See Comment, "Sexual Assault: The Case for Removing the Spousal Exemption from Texas Law." *Baylor Law Review* (38) 1986, p. 1941.
52. Geis, G. "Rape and Marrige: Historical and Cross-Cultural Considerations." Paper presented at the annual meeting of the American Sociological Association, New York, 1980. See also Hale, M. *The History of the Pleas of the Crown,* 1736, p. 629.
53. Waggoner, L. D. "New Mexico Joins the Twentieth Century: The Repeal of the Marital Rape Exemption." 22 *New Mexico Law Review* 1992, p. 551.
54. Martin, R. E. *The Life of Lady Randolph Churchill.* (New York American Library, New York) 1969.
55. Schulman, J. "The Marital Rape Exemption in the Criminal Law." *Clearinghouse Review* (13/6) 1980.
56. Finkelhor, D., and K. Yllo. *License to Rape.* (Holt, Rinehart, & Winston, New York) 1985.
57. Shotland, R. L., and B. A. Hunter. "Women's 'Token Resistant' and Compliant Sexual Behaviors Are Related to Uncertain Sexual Intentions and Rape," *Personality and Social Psychological Bulletin,* (21) No. 3 March 1995, pp. 226–237.
58. Kanin, E. "Male Aggression in Dating-Courtship Relationships." *American Journal of Sociology* (63) 1957, pp. 197–204.
59. Koss, M. P., and S. L. Cook. "Date and Acquaintance Rape Are Significant Problems for Women." In R. J. Gelles and D. R. Loseke, *Current Controversies on Family Violence.* (Sage, Newbury Park, California) 1993.
60. Pollard, P. "Rape Reporting as a Function of Victim–Offender Relationships: A Critique of the Lack of Effect Reported by Bachman," *Criminal Justice and Behavior.* (22) No. 1 March 1995, pp. 74–80.

61. Meyer, T. "Date Rape: A Serious Campus Problem That Few Talk About." *Chronicle of Higher Education.* December 5, 1990, p. A 15.
62. *The Response to Rape: Detours on the Road to Equal Justice.* Majority Staff of the Senate Judiciary Committee. May 1993, pp. 18–19.
63. Berdahl, J. L. et al. "The Harassment of Men: Exploring the Concept with Theory and Data," *Psychology of Women Quarterly* 20(4) December 1996, p. 527.
64. Safran. "What Men Do to Women on the Job: A Shocking Look at Sexual Harassment." *Redbook.* November 1976, p. 149. Redbook received over 9,000 responses to their questionnaire regarding sexual harassment.
65. "Sexual Harassment in the Federal Workplace—Is It a Problem?" (Merit Systems Protection Board) 1981; see also Pollack, W. "Sexual Harassment: Women's Experience vs. Legal Definitions." *Harvard Women's Law Journal* (13) Spring 1990, p. 35 for a discussion of this and other surveys.
66. 42 U.S.C. ss 2000e to 2000e-17 (1964).
67. 42 U.S.C. s 2000e-2(a) (1982).
68. 42 U.S.C. s 2000e(k) (1982).
69. *Wilson v Southwest Airlines Co.,* 517 F.Supp. 292, at 297 fn. 12 (N.D. Tex.) 1981.
70. *Meritor Saving Bank v Vinson,* 106 S.Ct. 2399, 2404 (1986).
71. Lindemann, B., and D. D. Kadue. *Sexual Harassment in Employment Law.* (Bureau of National Affairs, Washington, D.C.) 1992.
72. See Note. "The Dehumanizing Puzzle of Sexual Harassment: A Survey of the Law Concerning Harassment of Women in the Workplace." *Washburn Law Journal* (24) 1985, p. 574.
73. See *Barnes v Castle,* 561 F.2d 983 (D.C. Cir. 1977).
74. 561 F.2d 983 (D.C. Cir. 1977).
75. 29 C.F.R. ss 1604.11(a).
76. *Meritor Saving Bank v Vinson,* 106 S.Ct. 2399, (1986).
77. Ibid.
78. 510 U.S. 17 (1993).
79. Tangri, S., M. Burt, and L. Johnson. "Sexual Harassment at Work: Three Explanatory Models." *Journal of Social Issues* (38) 1982, pp. 33–54.
80. Dziech, B. W., and L.Weiner. "The Lecherous Professor." In A. M. Jaggar, and P. S. Rothenberg, eds. *Feminist Frameworks.* 3d ed. (McGraw-Hill, New York) 1993, pp. 323–327.

14

STALKING

Chapter Outline

Introduction
Definition
Types
Myths and Assessment of Stalking

Stalking Laws
Types of Stalking Laws
Constitutional Issues
Sanctions

Antistalking Measures
Physical Security Measures
Total Systems Approach

Summary

Learning Objectives

After reading this chapter, you should be able to discuss the following concepts:

- The various definitions and elements in the crime of stalking.
- The different types of stalkers and their motivations.
- The various types of stalking laws in comparison with a proposed model stalking law.
- The constitutional issues that are raised when dealing with stalking laws.
- The various civil and criminal sanctions available to victims of stalking.
- The different types of preventive measures a victim of stalking should take.
- Other antistalking measures that may prevent future stalking.

Introduction

Stalking is a crime that can happen to anyone at any time. It is included in this text because many spouses are stalked by their former husbands, live-in partners, or boyfriends. Any professional dealing with family violence must therefore be familiar with this newly emerging course of conduct and know how to respond to victims of this crime.

The term *stalking* has become a buzzword for the media. If someone is killed and evidence shows the killer followed the victim on the day of the killing, the media immediately labels the offender as a stalker. However, the act of stalking is much more complex than simply following an intended victim before committing a crime. It involves psychological, physical, and legal issues that all converge to form a course of conduct. Celebrities are often the victims of stalkers. Stalkers can also prey on strangers that they identify, or they can pursue former spouses. Additionally, the study of the dynamics of stalking is still in its infancy. A lack of academic research in this area makes it critical to include a brief overview of stalking in a text dealing with family violence.

In November 1997, the Department of Justice published research regarding the extent of stalking.[1] The National Violence Against Women Survey collected data from 8,000 men and women on a broad range of issues involving violence. Of those surveyed, 8 percent of the women and 2 percent of the men responded that they had been stalked sometime during their life. Using the 1995 estimates of adult population, this translates into 8.2 million women and 2 million men as stalking victims. Researchers estimate that 1 million women and 400,000 men are stalked each year. Most victims knew their stalker. Women tended to be stalked by one perpetrator, whereas in 50 percent of the male victimizations, the stalker had an accomplice.

Anyone can become a victim of a stalker at any time or in any place. However, researchers are not fully certain exactly who is or may become a stalker. Professionals are still researching this area, and like so many areas of family violence, they have yet to agree on a single definition of the term *stalker.*

Definition

Stalking involves more than simply following another person before committing a crime. If this action were considered stalking, then most street muggings would involve stalking. Stalking also does not have to result in death or injury to another person. Telephone calls, letters, or following the victim are acts that can cause a reasonable person to feel threatened or terrorized. The victim can be a celebrity, an average citizen related to the stalker by marriage, or a complete stranger.

As indicated previously, stalking involves a complex series of acts that, taken by themselves, might be normal everyday occurrences. Stalking has been examined from a psychological perspective, a physical security point of view, and a legal basis. By combining all of these disciplines the crime of stalking can be distilled down to the following definition: *stalking is a knowing, purposeful course of*

FOCUS Stalking and the Stars

In July 1989, an obsessed fan, John Bardo, finally met his celebrity. After sending numerous letters and making several long-distance telephone calls to actress Rebecca Schaeffer, costar of the television sitcom "My Sister Sam," he traveled to Los Angeles. After being turned away at the studio, he hired a private detective who supplied him with her home address. Bardo went to her apartment, and after seeing her the first time, he returned with a .357 magnum and shot her at point-blank range, killing her. Her method and manner of death shocked the entire United States. At the same time, no one had little if any understanding of the reasons behind this tragedy.

O. J. Simpson and his wife, Nicole Brown Simpson, were part of the beautiful people that everyone expects to see at Hollywood parties. He was an American dream come true; a poor kid who rose from the ghetto and a troubled childhood to sports, television, movies, fame, and fortune. Few persons could believe that O. J. had beaten his wife so badly that she sustained a black eye, a swollen cheek, a bruise to her forehead, and scratch marks on her neck. Nor could we accept that he would stalk her again and again to the point that she had to repeatedly call the police for assistance. Her death was yet another shock to the public.

conduct directed at a specific person that would cause a reasonable person to fear bodily injury or death to his- or herself or a member of his or her immediate family. Although the definition may appear simple, it is composed of six distinct elements that must be met before the crime of stalking has occurred.

1. *Knowing:* This requires knowledge that the victim will be placed in fear of injury. Acts that occur without knowledge of the victim's fear do not meet this criterion. However, this knowledge may be inferred from the perpetrator's actions. If a reasonable person perceives that his acts are placing another in fear, the requirement is satisfied.
2. *Purposeful:* The acts must be done in a conscious course of conduct that a reasonable person would know places another in fear.
3. *Course of conduct:* This element requires more than a single act. Thus, the mugger who follows a victim and then robs her has not engaged in the conduct necessary to be classified as a stalker. However, if an estranged husband followed his former spouse on more than one occasion, and if the other elements are satisfied, he may be guilty of stalking.
4. *Reasonable person:* The victim is judged by what a reasonable person would feel, not what the victim may experience. This poses a problem in the area of family violence because battered spouses are very sensitive to the potential injury from their abuser and jurors may not understand the victim's level of fear. However, if this standard is interpreted to mean what a reasonable person would feel having undergone what the victim has experienced, then jurors would be exposed to the feelings of a spouse who has been battered and can then place themselves in her position.

5. *Fear of injury or death:* The conduct must be more than simply an annoying series of acts. The victim must fear that she will be injured as the end result of the perpetrator's actions.
6. *Herself or immediate family:* The actions may be directed at the victim or her family. Immediate family is normally considered to be spouses, children, or parents.

Understanding stalking requires more than simply setting forth a definition of the act. Stalking is a course of conduct that may occur in a wide variety of situations. This characteristic makes it difficult to establish a clear typology of stalkers.

Types

The study of stalking is still in its infancy. However, several authorities have begun to attempt to classify stalkers according to certain characteristics.[2]

Zona, Sharma, and Lane have conducted an in-depth review of stalkers in the Los Angeles area.[3] Zona and his associates used the files of the Threat Management Unit (TMU) of the Los Angeles Police Department. This unit is the only one of its kind in the United States. During late 1989, the Los Angeles Police Department became aware of an increase in unsolicited contacts between mentally ill persons and Hollywood celebrities. After a meeting with various entertainment personal managers, the Threat Management Unit was formed.[4] Los Angeles Police Department Special Order Number 4 sets forth the background and purpose of this unit as follows:

> *Obsessed individuals with abnormal fixations on celebrities have recently received a great deal of media attention. However, becoming a victim of harassment, threats, or being stalked could happen to any member of society. Often these situations begin without any specific crime having been committed. If such a case is allowed to escalate, it could end in a tragedy to which law enforcement can only react after the fact. In response to the rapid increase of threats and harassment against a variety of public figures and other community members, the Department has developed the Threat Management Unit. This Order establishes the Threat Management Unit within Detective headquarters Division.*[5]

Zona was able to establish a data base of seventy-four subjects who had engaged in stalking behavior. Only cases that were officially opened and investigated by the TMU were considered. Unfortunately, none of the cases involved domestic violence situations. However, situations where the couple had physically separated and were living apart were included. All the cases were reviewed by a psychiatrist and a profile was established. This profile classified stalkers as erotomania, love obsessional, and simple obsessional.

Erotomania: This type of stalker has a *delusional disorder in which the predominant theme of the delusion is that a person, usually of higher status, is in love with the subject.* The victim does not know the stalker and many times will be a public figure or celebrity. The stalker is convinced that the victim, usually of the opposite sex, loves him and would return the affection if not for some external influence. The stalker rejects any contrary evidence and will remain delusional for years.

Love obsessional: The love obsessional stalker *is similar to the erotomanic in many ways.* The subject *does not know his or her victim except through the media. This stalker may also suffer from delusions. However, the subject has a primary psychiatric diagnosis.* These individuals often believe that if the victim would simply acknowledge their existence, then the victim would fall in love with the stalker. These subjects usually engage in a campaign to make their existence known to the victim by writing, telephoning, or otherwise attempting to contact the victim.

Simple obsessional: Unlike the two previous categories, *a prior relationship existed between the stalker and his or her intended victim. This relationship may have been a former spouse, employer, or neighbor, and in all cases the stalking begins after the relationship had soured or when there was a perception by the subject of mistreatment.* The stalking is an attempt to rectify the problem or seek revenge.

False victimization syndrome: This is the rarest category of stalkers. These are individuals with a desire to be placed in the victim's role. By insisting that someone is stalking them—they become the victim. There appears to be a similarity between this classification and Munchausen syndrome by proxy (discussed earlier in this text). Although this is not truly a "stalker," Zona and his associates included it for purposes of comparison and understanding of the stalking process.

The length of time of stalking varied with the type of stalker studied. The duration for erotomanics was 124 months and that of love obsessional slightly more, averaging 146 months. The simple obsessional stalker maintained contact for 5.1 months. The contact between the stalker and the victim ranged from visits to the subject's home or other locations to mailing letters or making phone calls. In addition, all categories of stalkers made threats to the victim.

Myths and Assessment of Stalking

Sharma has studied the profile of stalkers and established several myths regarding both stalking and the stalker.[6] Dr. Kausal Sharma, a well-respected psychiatrist at the Institute of Psychiatry, Law, and Behavioral Science of the University of Southern California School of Medicine's Psychiatric Hospital, based his conclusions on the evaluation and study of numerous referrals of stalkers by mental health professionals and law enforcement officials.

Myth #1: Most stalkers are mentally ill. Some stalkers are mentally ill, but most do not fall within the various DSM-IV classifications. Simply being strange is not considered a mental illness.

Myth #2: Most stalkers are dangerous. Less than five percent of stalkers commit dangerous acts against their victims.

Myth #3: Psychiatry can help stalkers discontinue their acts. Only a small percentage of stalkers respond to psychiatric treatment.

Myth #4: Most stalkers continue their stalking behavior. Most stalkers will eventually stop their stalking. Most of the individuals who come to our attention are long-term stalkers, but many will stalk their victims for only a short period of time.

Myth #5: Most stalkers look like sleezeballs and have beady eyes. Stalkers can be anyone including policemen, doctors, judges, and even psychiatrists.

Myth #6: Stalkers are just into stalking. Stalkers commit related and unrelated crimes.

Myth #7: Victims must do something to attract stalking. Anybody can be a victim of stalking.

Myth #8: Stalking is a crime of the young and restless. Stalking is many times a crime of the old and calm.

Myth #9: Stalking is bad for you. Stalking is bad for the stalker and the victim but has become a big business for government, security firms, movies, and authors.

Dispelling the myths surrounding this form of family violence allows professionals to offer support and advice to victims of stalking. In addition to understanding the myths surrounding stalking, family violence practitioners should be aware of the various factors that can be used in assessing a stalking case. Michael Zona, M.D., is one of the first experts in this area to develop such an assessment protocol. He established ten factors that should be considered in assessing a stalking case.[7]

The first factor is the history of violence exhibited by the stalker. This, according to Zona, is the single most reliable factor in assessing the danger and propensity for future violent acts. The professional should review criminal records, review school and work histories, and interview family and friends of the stalker.

The second factor is the presence of physical abuse or domestic violence. Domestic violence is often a pattern of behavior and represents poor coping strategies on the part of the stalker. He is less likely to express feelings or frustrations with words and has found that physical violence meets his needs.

The third factor is the presence or absence of threats. Verbal or written threats very frequently precede acts of violence by the stalker. Threats also allow the professional an opportunity to understand the suspect by analyzing the content and nature of the threat.

The fourth factor is determining whether the suspect is stalking the same or a similar victim over a period of time. If the stalker is obsessed with a particular victim or a certain type of victim, this represents the greatest risk of harm for the victim. This also provides insight into the nature of the stalking pattern and provides an opportunity to understand the suspect.

The destruction of property is the fifth factor. Those who destroy property represent a greater percentage of stalkers who go on to commit further acts of interpersonal violence. The destruction of property represents increasing frustration and desperation on the part of the stalker and is usually a series of acts of vandalism.

The sixty factor involves access and approach behaviors of the stalker. These behaviors include telephone contact, letter writing, faxing, visits by the stalker to the work or home of the victim, physical stalking, and face-to-face contacts. Careful assessment of access and approach behaviors can assist in evaluating the risk of danger to the victim. Letter writing is seen as posing less risk of harm to the victim, but a transition into more personal forms of contact increases the risk of violence.

The seventh factor involves the sex and sexual orientation of the stalker. In general, men are more dangerous than women and represent 80 percent of all stalking cases. Both men and women stalkers will commit dangerous acts.

The eighth factor is an evaluation of psychiatric disorders affecting the stalkers. Mood disorders, psychotic disorders, personality disorders, and alcohol or substance abuse are found to be present in many stalkers. Understanding the mental status of a stalker allows treatment plans to be crafted to fit that particular individual.

Investment in the object of the stalking is the ninth factor. The meaning or value the stalker places on the victim is an important assessment tool. This allows for an evaluation of the effectiveness of legal restraints such as temporary restraining orders.

The tenth and last assessment factor is the stalker's insight into the relationship between himself and the victim. This factor may give an indication to the stalkers amenability to treatment. All of the factors will allow professionals to more fully understand the dynamics of stalking.

Experts in the field continue to attempt to establish an accepted typology of stalkers. Disagreement exists among various researchers and other authorities regarding the dynamics of stalking and the categories that should be used when examining this type of individual.[8] However, from a family violence perspective it is important that professionals understand that stalking does in fact occur and be prepared to offer assistance to victims of this type of family violence.

Stalking Laws

Stalking laws are a relatively recent phenomenon. As a result of the 1989 stalking murder of actress Rebecca Schaeffer and other reports of stalking of high-profile celebrities, California enacted the United States' first stalking legislation in 1990. In retrospect, it is hard to believe that any sane person could oppose legislation that would protect persons from possible danger and harassment. However, proponents of California's stalking law have indicated that there was a great deal of resistance within the legislature to passage of the proposed law.[9] The statute as finally adopted was very narrow and required the prosecution to prove a creditable threat to kill or commit great bodily injury against the victim. Fortunately, California and other states have since adopted a more comprehensive series of stalking laws, which in many instances offer victims of family violence protection where none existed before.

Types of Stalking Laws

Forty-eight states and the District of Columbia have adopted stalking laws. The remaining two states, Arizona and Maine, use their harassment and terrorizing statutes to combat stalking. States continue to amend their statutes to provide more protection to victims of stalking. Depending on the jurisdiction, various acts are prohibited. For example, a suspect may not be present, approach, pursue or follow, trespass onto property, lay in wait, intimidate, vandalize, conduct surveillance, harass, show a weapon, restrain, or commit bodily injury against the victim. Because of this varied patchwork of statutes, in 1993 the National Institute of Justice was tasked by Congress to develop a model stalking act.[10]

In October 1993, the National Institute of Justice published its findings and recommended a Model Stalking Code for consideration by states when they amend their existing statutes. This model is a well-reasoned approach to stalking and considers the rights of individuals as well as the rights of victims.[11] The Model Code Provides that any person who

> a. *purposefully engages in a course of conduct directed at a specific person that would cause a reasonable person to fear bodily injury to himself or a member of his or her immediate family or to fear the death of himself or herself or a member of his or her immediate family; and*
>
> b. *has knowledge or should have knowledge that the specific person will be placed in reasonable fear of bodily injury to himself or herself or a member of his or her immediate family or will be placed in reasonable fear of death of himself or a member of his or her immediate family; and*
>
> c. *whose acts induce fear in the specific person of bodily injury to himself or herself or a member of his or her immediate family or induce fear in the specific person of the death of himself or herself or a member of his or her immediate family; is guilty of stalking.*[12]

The drafters of the code preferred not to list specific acts of stalking and instead inserted the more encompassing term *course of conduct*. They believed that this would provide for more effective coverage than listing a series of acts and finding out later that another specific act had not been included. Further, the course of conduct provision requires two or more occasions of maintaining visual or physical proximity to the victim or repeatedly conveying threats by words or conduct toward the victim. Part of the problem in enacting any legislation that criminalizes certain types of conduct involving expression of thoughts and ideas is the inevitable confrontation with the rights guaranteed under the Constitution.

Constitutional Issues

Any law that attempts to regulate the exercise of speech is subject to scrutiny by the courts.[13] The First Amendment to the U.S. Constitution states, "Congress shall make no law . . . abiding the freedom of speech."[14] Some scholars argue that the First Amendment is the most important protection within the Constitution.

Stalking laws by their very nature regulate the expression of ideas and thoughts. The stalker may engage in conduct that is intended to express his or her feelings of love or hate toward the victim. This conduct may involve following the victim, sending the victim objects such as flowers, and other conduct that at first glance is clearly protected by the First Amendment. Stalkers may also engage in pure speech activities such as sending letters or phoning the victim proclaiming their underlying love for that person. All of these acts raise constitutional issues that must be addressed.

The U.S. Supreme Court has held that certain conduct that is intended as a form of communication is protected by the First Amendment. Demonstrations protesting governmental decisions are examples of such speech-related conduct. However, the courts have held that even First Amendment rights can be regulated. The Supreme Court decision in *Madsen v Women's Health Center, Inc.*, illustrates this position.[15] In *Madsen*, the court stated that abortion protestors were exercising their First Amendment rights; however, other considerations, such as safety of individuals who worked at the clinics and those who desired to use the services of the clinics, were proper factors that the legislature could consider in setting up a zone of protection that the protestors could not enter. Thus, stalking laws may be drafted so as to regulate conduct that otherwise might be protected by the First Amendment.

Another aspect of stalking laws involves punishment for sending letters or making telephone calls. These activities by the stalker are clearly forms of expression. However, the Supreme Court has held that the First Amendment does not prevent the government from regulating speech that contains threats. Threats of violence are outside the protection of the Constitution because they protect victims from a fear of violence and the disruption that such a fear causes.[16] In *Thorne v Bailey*, the 4th Circuit Court of Appeals upheld the constitutionality of a statute prohibiting telephone harassment that included a provision against using the phone to make threats against persons or property.[19] The appellate court held that harassment was not protected even though it took the form of speech and involved the use of a telephone.[18]

For stalking laws to withstand a constitutional challenge, they must prohibit specific, clearly defined activity. In the legal profession, this requires that the stalking statute not be overbroad or vague. Each of these requirements involves shades of gray within the realm of constitutional law.

A statute is overbroad if it prohibits both activities that are not constitutionally protected as well as activities that are protected. The Supreme Court has stated several justifications for voiding overbroad statutes. First in the fear that if a statute is overbroad, individuals may refrain from carrying out protected activities as well as regulated activity. The second rationale for voiding overbroad statutes is the fear that an overbroad statute will allow law enforcement agencies to selectively enforce it against unpopular groups or activities. This danger is avoided if the statute is narrowly drafted.

A vague statute fails to provide explicit grounds for enforcement. A statute is vague if a person of common intelligence cannot ascertain the limits of lawful behavior.[19] If a statute is vague, it will be struck down or declared void. This void-for-vagueness doctrine is based on the due-process requirements of the Fifth and Fourteenth Amendments.[20] This doctrine requires that all criminal legislation satisfy a two-pronged test. The first prong requires notice and clarity such that ordinary persons can understand what conduct is prohibited. The second prong requires all criminal laws to provide explicit standards to prevent arbitrary and discriminatory enforcement.[21] Similar to overbroad statutes, the danger with a vague statute is the fear that individuals will fail to exercise their right to free speech because of a belief that they will be prosecuted under the statute that regulates unprotected activities. However, the Supreme Court does not require that words in a statute reach mathematical or scientific precision to be valid and enforceable.[22]

The drafters of the Model Code considered these issues when they proposed their version of a stalking statute. It is drafted to ensure that specific activities are clearly prohibited. Further, it does not attempt to regulate protected speech. Simply drafting or adopting a stalking law, however, does not prevent stalking. Since 1990 to the present, courts consistently upheld the constitutionality of these laws.

Sanctions

For any statute to be effective, it must provide for sanctions when it is violated. Sanctions for stalking are as different as the statutes that define stalking in the various states. However, most sanctions can be classified into three distinction areas: pretrial release or bail provisions, types of punishment, and civil remedies.

Most state constitutions include provisions that allow for bail of persons awaiting trial or pending appeal of a conviction.[23] The practice of granting bail to accused persons developed in England, where accused persons were otherwise held in disease-infected jails. The right to bail in England was established because of numerous instances where those accused of crimes were not released or the bail was set at such a high level that they could not afford to post it. As a result, when the founding fathers adopted the Constitution, special provisions were included regarding bail. The Eighth Amendment to the U.S. Constitution provides that "[e]xcessive bail shall not be required."[24] In analyzing this amendment, the Supreme Court concluded that there is no absolute right to bail, only that it will not be excessive in those cases where it is proper to grant bail.[25]

Concern for the safety of victims, witnesses, and others prompted Congress to pass the Federal Bail Reform Act of 1984.[26] This act specifically provided for preventive detention of dangerous individuals. As a result, federal courts imposed preventive detention of dangerous offenders in excess of 1,600 times during a one-year period.[27] This provision was challenged in *United States v Salerno,* in which two defendants were charged with twenty-nine counts alleging various organized crime activities, including mail fraud, extortion, and criminal gambling violations.[28] These defendants were detained pending trial under the dangerous offenders provision of the Federal Bail Act. However, the Supreme Court upheld the provisions of the act, holding that it did not violate the provisions of the Eighth Amendment. Thus, preventive detention is permissible in appropriate situations.

Unfortunately, most state statutes or constitutions dealing with bail mandate reasonable bail for those charged with crimes with the exception of persons charged with capital offenses. Approximately half the states allow the court to detain a suspect pending trial if the offense was violent or a felony and the accused met other requirements such as a history of prior violence or other factors that definitely indicate his dangerousness.[29] The National Institute of Justice recommends amendment to these statutes or constitutions to allow for pretrial bail in stalking cases.[30] Pending such modifications, courts should include conditions that the suspect stay away from the victim pending the trial. A violation of this condition would then allow the courts to confine the stalker until the trial.

The second category of sanctions deals with the classification of the crime of stalking. Traditionally, crimes are classified as either felonies or misdemeanors. Felonies are punishable by imprisonment in state prison, and misdemeanors are punishable by incarceration in local jails for no longer than one year. Until recently, most stalking statutes were classified as misdemeanors. The rationale for this appears to be that no physical injury is required for the crime to be complete, and felonies should be reserved for the more serious property or personal crimes. Unfortunately, in numerous instances the stalker seriously wounded or killed his victim.

California has made stalking a felony under certain conditions.[31] In addition, the California statute mandates state prison for a stalker if a temporary restraining order, injunction, or any other court order is in effect at the time of the offense. California was the first state to adopt a stalking law, and other states may follow its lead and revise their statutes to make stalking a felony.

The final category of sanctions involves the use of various civil remedies to prevent stalking. These alternatives include the issuance of temporary retraining orders, injunctions, mental evaluations, and civil commitments. All these options, although available for use by professionals and the courts, are surrounded in controversy.

One of the most controversial civil tools available to victims of stalking is the use of a temporary restraining order. *Restraining orders or protective orders are court orders that prohibit the offender from having any contact with the victim.* Numerous articles have commented on the availability and use of restraining orders in stalking situations.[32] Additionally, there are many instances where issuance of the restraining order may have been a factor in assaultive behavior that ended in serious injury or death to the victim.

Law enforcement officials believe in the use of restraining orders. In California for example, if the stalking occurs when a restraining order is in effect, the offense is a felony subjecting the suspect to state prison. Other authorities believe that restraining orders may enrage the stalker and cause him to react in a violent and sometimes fatal manner. It is clear that more study needs to be done on the relationship between restraining orders and subsequent violence. However, continuous debate in this area should not stop professionals from recommending that victims of stalking obtain a restraining order. In the proper situation, a restraining order may be effective in deterring or stopping the stalker.

Mental evaluations are another civil alternative that should be considered. Most states have established procedures that allow for involuntary commitments of short duration for the purpose of evaluating the mental status of those who are a danger to themselves or others. If mental health professionals come to the conclusion that the stalker falls within this classification, they can institute proceedings to have him civilly committed to a mental institution for treatment.

Many states provide for civil commitments of individuals who are a danger to themselves or others. These commitments are normally for a specified period of time, at the end of which the patient must be reevaluated or released. If a stalker is suffering from a mental disease or defect that renders him a danger to himself or others, a civil commitment allows for placement in a mental hospital where he could receive the type of treatment that might cure the disorder. Civil commitments of this type require less proof than criminal convictions and thereby offer professionals another option with which to respond to a stalking situation.

Antistalking Measures

Physical Security Measures

A stalking victim can employ many different types of physical security measures.[33] Many of these are commonsense approaches that many people already use to protect their own homes. Some of these measures, such as training household staff, are obviously directed at celebrities and the wealthy. Victims of stalking are often so emotionally distraught that they do not think to employ preventive physical security measures. Therefore, this aspect of stalking is included within this text. Professionals in the field not only must understand how to assist with the legal and emotional problems but also should be able to offer concrete advice on how the victim can physically protect herself. However, it must be stressed that these are only guidelines, and professionals should ensure that the victim of a stalker does not gain a false sense of physical security simply by using some or all these techniques. The following series of physical security tactics have been adapted from material provided by the Threat Management Unit of the Los Angeles Police Department.

Residence Security

1. Be alert for any suspicious persons.
2. Positively identify callers before opening doors.
3. Install a porch light that cannot be easily removed.
4. Install deadbolts on all outside doors.
5. Keep garage doors locked at all times.
6. Install adequate outside lighting.
7. Trim shrubbery.

8. Keep the fuse box locked.
9. Install a loud exterior alarm bell that can be manually activated in more than one location from within the house.
10. Maintain an unlisted phone number.
11. Any written or telephone threats should be treated as legitimate and should be referred to the appropriate law enforcement agency.
12. Household staff should have a security check prior to employment and be thoroughly briefed on security precautions. Strictly enforce a policy that the staff not discuss family matters or movements with anyone.
13. Be alert for any unusual packages, boxes, or devices on the premises. Do not disturb such objects. Call the local law enforcement agency immediately.
14. Install a smoke detector system.
15. Tape emergency numbers on all phones.
16. When away from the residence for an evening, place a light and a radio on a timer.
17. Intruders will attempt to enter unlocked doors and windows without causing a disturbance. Keep all doors and windows locked.
18. Prepare an evacuation plan and ensure that all members of the household are aware of it.
19. A family dog is one of the least expensive but most effective alarm systems.
20. Know the whereabouts of all family members at all times.
21. Children should accompanied to school or bus stops.
22. Vary all routes and times spent exercising outdoors.
23. Require identification of all repairmen before permitting them entry into the residence.
24. Always park in a secured garage if available.
25. Inform a trusted neighbor regarding the situation. Provide the neighbor with a photograph or description of the suspect and any possible vehicle.

Personal Security

1. Remove your home address from personal checks and business cards.
2. Place real estate in a trust and list the utilities under the name of the trust.
3. Utilize a private mailbox service to receive all personal mail.
4. File for confidential voter status or register to vote utilizing a mailbox address.
5. Destroy discarded mail.
6. Phone lines can be installed in a location other than the person's residence and call-forwarded to the residence.
7. Place residence rental agreements in another person's name.
8. Do not obtain a mailbox with the U.S. Post Office.
9. All current creditors should be given a change of address card using a mailbox as the new address. Some credit reporting agencies will remove past addresses from credit histories if requested.
10. File a change of address with the Department of Motor Vehicles to reflect the new mailbox address. Obtain a new driver's license with the new address on it.

Vehicle Security

1. Park vehicles in well-lit areas. Do not patronize parking lots where car doors must be left unlocked and keys surrendered. Allow items to be placed in or removed from the trunk only in your presence.
2. When parked in the residence garage, turn the garage light on and lock the vehicle and the garage door.
3. Equip the gas tank with a locking gas cap.
4. Visually check the front and rear passenger compartments before entering the vehicle.
5. Select a reliable service station for vehicle service.
6. Keep doors locked while the vehicle is in use.
7. Be alert for vehicles that appear to be following you.
8. When traveling by vehicle, plan ahead. Know locations of police stations, fire departments, and busy shopping centers.
9. Use a different schedule and route of travel each day. If followed, drive to a police station, fire department, or busy shopping center and sound your horn to attract attention.
10. Do not stop to assist a stranded motorist (phone in).

These recommendations do not stop the stalker. They merely prevent the stalker from approaching and possibly harming the victim. Other techniques must be employed in an attempt to permanently remove the threat of the stalking. The total systems approach to stalking is one method that professionals should consider when dealing with a stalking situation.

Total Systems Approach

The previous discussion set forth a number of physical security measures or tactics that a victim can take to protect herself from attack or harassment by the stalker. However, all the experts in this field, including Lieutenant John Lane, Doctor Kaushal Sharma, Doctor Michael Zona, and Gavin de Becker, agree that each case of stalking must be individually evaluated. The actions taken by the victim must be tailored to the tactics and type of stalker that is involved. To be successful, professionals should recommend a total systems approach to stalking.

A total systems approach does not rely solely on law enforcement, medical or psychiatric professionals, or the courts to ensure the safety of the victim. The total systems approach is a combination of all professional knowledge to craft an individualized response to stalking for a particular victim. Depending on the dynamics involved in the specific stalking situation, the total systems approach may increase physical protection measures and rely less on psychiatric intervention. On the other hand, a particular stalker may respond very favorably to mental health treatment but become angry if a restraining order is filed. Thus, each case must be evaluated and treated according to the type of stalker as well as the desires and needs of the victim.

Consideration should be given to forming multidisciplinary committees composed of law enforcement, medical personnel, and prosecutors. Much like existing child abuse coordination councils, these committees could address the stalking issue from an informed total systems approach. By evaluating individual cases of stalking, the best possible intervention strategy could then be implemented.

Professionals involved in stalking situations should use all available resources. By using law enforcement, medical, and other assistance, there is a better chance of success. The principle objective of intervention is to prevent the victim from being injured or killed. Law enforcement officials should coordinate their activities with the victim and mental health professionals. Occasionally, stalkers may agree to mental health counseling, and that may end the problem. More serious cases may involve the decision to obtain a restraining order. Finally, the stalker may be charged criminally for his acts. Treatment programs should be evaluated and modified as more is learned about the dynamics of stalking. No single approach will stop stalking or cure those who engage in this form of family violence.

Summary

Stalking is a complex crime that affects many victims of family violence. Professionals are just beginning to react to this type of activity, and it is imperative that they understand both the dynamics of stalking and the possible alternatives that are available to the victim.

Stalking may occur in a domestic situation, or it may involve a stranger. In either situation, it can be a terrorizing experience for the victim, sometimes resulting in serious injury or death. Numerous typologies of stalkers are beginning to emerge as researchers analyze this type of behavior. To date, no single classification of stalking is accepted as standard by all scholars or authorities in the field of domestic violence.

Stalking laws have been passed that allow law enforcement to act before there is physical injury to the victim, but these statutes need revision in several important areas. Unfortunately, many states continue to allow stalkers to be released prior to trial. Few states treat stalking as a felony, which would subject the stalker to long-term incarceration.

Although there is continuing debate in this area, it may be positive in that it signals an increased awareness of the seriousness of this problem. As long as a spouse can be terrorized by a phone call in the middle of the night by her former spouse, more work has to done in this area of family violence. Only by understanding stalking can future injury to its victims be prevented.

Key Terms

stalking—a knowing, purposeful course of conduct directed at a specific person that would cause a reasonable person to fear bodily injury or death to herself or a member of her immediate family.

erotomania—a delusional disorder in which the predominant theme of the delusion is that a person, usually of higher status, is in love with the subject.

love obsessional stalker—does not know his victim except through the media. This stalker may also suffer from delusions; however, the subject has a primary psychiatric diagnosis.

simple obsessional stalker—there existed a prior relationship between the stalker and his intended victim. This relationship may have been a former spouse, employer, or neighbor, and in all cases the stalking began after the relationship had soured or when there was a perception by the subject of mistreatment.

threat—any offer to do harm, however implausible.

restraining orders or protective orders—court orders that prohibit the offender from having any contact with the victim.

Discussion Questions

1. What is stalking? What if the victim is unaware that she is being watched and followed? Has the perpetrator committed the crime of stalking? Is it stalking if someone uses a telescope and repeatedly observes the victim from a distance? Has a former spouse committed the crime of stalking if he writes a letter expressing his frustration at the breakup of his marriage? What if he continues to write letters every week demanding that he and his spouse reunite?
2. Based on your reading of this chapter, which typology best explains the categories of stalkers? Why?
3. How can we help dispel the various myths that surround stalking?
4. Do you believe existing stalking laws are effective in preventing stalking? What else should we do?
5. Are temporary restraining orders an effective legal tool in stalking cases?
6. How does the use of temporary restraining orders in stalking compare with their use in cases of domestic violence?
7. What is the most effective preventive measure that a victim of stalking can use?
8. Should stalkers be treated, punished, or both?

Suggested Readings

Gross, L. *To Have or to Harm.* (Warner Books, New York) 1994.

Hickey, E. W. *Serial Killers and Their Victims.* (Brooks/Cole, Pacific Grove, California) 1991.

LaFave, W. R., and A. W. Scott Jr. *Criminal Law.* 2d ed. (West, St. Paul) 1986.

Whitebread, C. H., and C. Slobogin. *Criminal Procedure.* 3d ed. (Foundation Press, Westbury, New York) 1993.

Endnotes

1. This information had been adapted from Tjaden, P. "The Crime of Stalking: How Big Is the Problem?" *Research Preview.* (National Institute of Justice, Washington, D.C. November 1997).
2. Holmes reviewed some of the current literature in the area and established six distinct types of stalkers based on their victims. Holmes, R. M. "Stalking in America." *Law and Order.* May 1994, pp. 89–92). This classification included celebrity, lust, hit, love-scorned, domestic, and political stalkers.

   Celebrity stalker: The victim of this type of stalker is usually in the entertainment field. Although the victim may be extremely well known, the stalker normally has not had any personal contact with the object of his obsession.

   Lust stalker: This type of stalker is motivated by sex and will stalk one victim after another in a serial fashion. The victim is pursued for sexual gratification. This type of stalker may escalate from a sexual pursuit to more violence, including murder of the victim.

   Hit stalker: This stalker is the paid, professional killer who follows his victim to establish the target's habits and then kills for profit. There is no passion or feeling with this type of stalker, nor is he obsessed with his victim.

   Love-scorned: This stalker intends to frighten or injure the object of his hunt. Although this stalker intends violence, it is not normally fatal. He may be a rejected boyfriend, husband, or even a casual acquaintance. The stalker has a deep, abiding love for the victim and believes that if she would just realize how much he cares, then she would return his love.

   Domestic: This stalker is the former husband or boyfriend of the victim. The stalking may take place over an extended period of time, and the motive for the stalking is to get even with the victim. There is no sexual or fatal violence involved in this type of stalking, but the stalker may engage in violent acts to terrorize his intended victim.

   Political stalker: The victim of this stalker is an appointed or elected official. The stalker carefully selects his victim, and political ideology usually precipitates the stalking. There is no sexual motivation in this type of stalker.

   Holmes's classification covers all conceivable situations and includes individuals such as the hit stalker, who is a paid assassin and is not motivated by emotion or desire. The victim of a hit stalker is usually not even aware of the stalking until the assassin strikes. Because of a lack of knowledge on the part of the victim, it appears that Holmes's categories, although providing a useful starting point for an overview of stalking, need to be compared with other profiles.

   Geberth established a typology of stalkers based on their mental status. (Gerberth, V. "Stalkers." *Law and Order.* October 1992, p. 138). This approach focuses on the state of mind of the stalker rather than the object of the stalking. Geberth has classified stalkers into two areas: the psychopathic personality stalker and the psychotic personality stalker.

   Psychopathic personality stalker: This stalker has lost control over the subject and intends violence to the victim. This type of stalker is a male offender and represents the largest percentage of stalkers. The object of the stalker is normally a former girlfriend or spouse. According to Geberth, this type of stalker insists on male dominance and exhibits a macho image in order to hide feelings of inferiority.

   Psychotic personality stalker: This stalker becomes obsessed with an unobtainable love object such as a movie star. This stalker may be either male or female. This stalker has the delusion that the victim also loves the stalker and would respond to his advances except for outside factors. This stalker is a stranger to the victim but has become obsessed with her. He mounts a campaign of harassment to make the victim aware of his existence.

Various experts in the field of serial killers have established stalking patterns as it relates to stalking and killing. Hickey, in *Serial Murders and Their Victims,* examines the dynamics of stalking and serial killers (Hickey, E. W. *Serial Killers and Their Victims.* (Brooks/Cole, Pacific Grove, California) 1991, p. 17). He established one category of serial killers based on mobility. These individuals were classified as traveling, local, or fixed serial killers. Traveling serial killers often cover thousands of miles each year as they stalk and kill their victims. Local serial killers never leave the state they live in when searching for victims. Fixed serial killers never leave their homes or places of employment. This last category of killers includes nurses and others who are self-employed who prefer to stay at home and kill rather than go hunting.

Although the body of research in the area of serial killing is growing, many of these incidents involve victims who were not aware that they were the intended prey of the killer, and therefore many serial killers will not fall within the definition of stalking that is being used in this text. However, more study is needed in this area to determine whether the dynamics involved in serial killing are the same or similar to the dynamics involved during a stalking.

Dietz and his associates have examined stalkers of celebrities and political officials. They examined threatening letters and other inappropriate material sent to these high-profile people (Dietz, P. E., et al. "Threatening and Otherwise Inappropriate Letters to Hollywood Celebrities." *Journal of Forensic Sciences* (36) January 1991, p. 185). Dietz's database for celebrities was drawn from material maintained by Gavin de Becker, Inc., a Los Angeles–based security agency. This firm has amassed data on 143,000 items of correspondence, from individuals to entertainment celebrities. Dietz and his associates analyzed the content of 107 stalkers drawn from this sample. In the study of stalking of public figures, the data were drawn from the files of the U.S. Capital Police in Washington, D.C. (Dietz, P. E. "Threatening and Otherwise Inappropriate Letters to Members of the United States Congress." *Journal of Forensic Sciences* (36) September 1991, p. 1445.) Dietz studied eighty-six stalking cases of members of Congress.

Dietz developed a concept of patronage that classified the level of attachment the stalker had for the victim. This level of attachment was called either minimal, moderate, or maximal.

Minimal patronage: This level of patronage appears normal. The stalker does what all other persons do—he attends movies, speeches, buys books, or votes in elections for the person he is stalking. The critical difference is that normal persons do this out of a feeling of obligation or attraction for a particular celebrity or public official. Stalkers carry out these acts in an effort to be close to or noticed by the subject.

Moderate patronage: This level of patronage is slightly excessive. The stalker creates an extensive collection of the victim's works, may engage in extensive travel to see the public figure, or may engage in fund-raising or in circulating petitions for the public figure. Similar to the minimal patronage category, normal persons engage in these functions for healthy reasons or ideals, but stalkers engage in these acts out of an overpowering desire or obsession to become close to the victim.

Maximal patronage: This level of patronage is clearly extraordinary in that the stalker may have devoted a room to collecting information, pictures, or other paraphernalia about the victim. In essence, this room may resemble a shrine to the public figure. The stalker is obsessed with the public figure and devotes a significant amount of his daily activities to behavior that is directly related to the public figure.

Dietz and his associates also analyzed the threatening content of the letters sent to celebrities and public figures. *A threat was defined as any offer to do harm, however implausible.* Threats were classified as direct, veiled, or conditional. Direct threats were straightforward, explicit statement with an intent to commit harm such as "I'm going to kill you." Veiled threats were indirect or subtle statements suggesting potential harm such as "There's no saying what might happen." Conditional threats portrayed harm and specify that certain conditions must be met in order to avert the harm.

Gavin de Becker, an expert in security consultations in Los Angeles, established four categories of stalkers based on the relationship between the pursuer and the victim (de Becker, G. "Intervention Decisions—The Value of Flexibility." Paper presented at the 4th Annual Threat Management Conference. (Disneyland Hotel, Anaheim, California) June 29, 1994). Gavin de Becker's firm has been involved in more than 16,000 cases involving persons who inappropriately pursue other individuals. Gavin de Becker's classifications include the pursuit of public figures by the mentally ill with no prior relationship, pursuit of public figures by healthy persons with no prior relationship, pursuit of regular citizens with no prior relationship, and pursuit of regular citizens with some prior interpersonal relationship.

Pursuit of public figures by the mentally ill with no prior relationship: These are individuals who are suffering from a mental disorder or defect who write letters, attempt to telephone, or otherwise contact public figures even though no prior relationship exists between the stalker and the victim.

Pursuit of public figures by healthy persons with no prior relationship: These individuals may write letters, telephone, or otherwise attempt to contact the public figure. These stalkers may be obsessed with the public figure but do not suffer from a mental illness.

Pursuit of regular citizens with no prior relationship: These victims are not public figures and have no previous relationship with the stalker. The stalker will have selected them for his own reasons. The stalker may either be healthy or suffering from a mental disorder.

Pursuit of regular citizens with some prior interpersonal relationship: In these stalking situations, there was some prior relationship such as romantic, employment, or litigants. The stalker may be seeking revenge for an actual or perceived wrong. He may either be healthy or suffering from a mental disorder.

3. Zona, M. A., K. K. Sharma, and J. Lane. "A Comparative Study of Erotomanic and Obsessional Subjects in a Forensic Sample." *Journal of Forensic Sciences* (38) July 1993, p. 894.
4. Lane, J. C. "Threat Management Fills Void in Police Services." *The Police Chief.* August 1992, p. 27.
5. Special Order No. 4, Office of the Chief of Police, February 12, 1992.
6. Presentation at the 4th Annual Treat Management Conference, Disneyland Hotel, Anaheim, California, June 29, 1994.
7. Zona, M. A. "Psychiatric Factors Involved in the Assessment of Stalking Cases." Paper presented at the 4th Annual Threat Management Conference, Disneyland Hotel, Anaheim, California, June 29, 1994. The factors set forth in this paragraph are taken from an outline and accompanying speech made by Doctor Zona at the conference.
8. Coleman, F. L. "Stalking Behavior and the Cycle of Domestic Violence," 12(3) *Journal of Interpersonal Violence* 12(3) June 1997, p. 420.
9. Rhonda Saunders, Los Angeles Deputy District Attorney, "Legal Tools for Case Management." Paper presented at the 4th Annual Threat Management Conference, Disneyland Hotel, Anaheim, California, June 29, 1994.

10. U.S. Departments of Commerce, Justice, and State, and the Judiciary and Related Appropriations Act for Fiscal Year 1993, Public Law 103–395, Section 109(b).
11. *Project to Develop a Model Anti-Stalking Code for States,* National Institute of Justice, U.S. Department of Justice (Washington, D.C.) October 1993.
12. Ibid., pp. 43–44.
13. Wallace, H. "Stalkers, the Constitution, and Victims' Remedies," *Criminal Justice.* (10) No. 1 Spring 1995, p. 16.
14. U.S. Constitution, Amendment I.
15. 1994 U.S. LEXIS 5087 (June 30, 1994).
16. *R.A.V. v City of St. Paul, Minnesota,* 112 S.Ct. 2538, 2546 (1992).
17. 846 F. 2d 241 (4th Cir. 1988), cert. denied, 448 U.S. 984 (1976).
18. Ibid., p. 243.
19. *Winters v New York,* 333 U.S. 507 (1948).
20. LaFave, W. R., and A. W. Scott Jr., *Criminal Law.* 2d ed. (West, St. Paul) 1986. Section 2.3, pp. 90–91.
21. *Kolender v Lawson,* 461 U.S. 352 (1983).
22. *Grayned v City of Rockford,* 408 U.S. 104 (1972).
23. See Whitebread, C. H., and C. Slobogin. *Criminal Procedure,* 3d ed. (Foundation Press, Westbury, New York) 1993, pp. 487–508.
24. U.S. Constitution, Amendment XIII.
25. *Carlson v Landon,* 342 U.S. 524 (1952).
26. 18 U.S.C. Section 3141-3150 (1984).
27. Kurtz, "Detention Law, Further Crowds Prison." *The Washington Post.* January 9, 1986, A4.
28. 418 U.S. 739 (1987).
29. *Project to Develop a Model Anti-Stalking Code for States.* National Institute of Justice, U.S. Department of Justice (Washington, D.C.) October 1993, pp. 55–67.
30. Ibid.
31. California Penal Code Section 646.9 as amended on September 29, 1993.
32. See Thomas, K. R. "How to Stope the Stalker: State Antistalking Laws." *Criminal Law Bulletin* (29/2) March–April 1993, p. 124, and Karen S. Morin, "The Phenomenon of Stalking: Do Existing State Statutes Provide Adequate Protection?" *San Diego Justice Journal* (1) 1993, p. 123.
33. Wallace, H. "A Prosecutor's Guide to Stalking" *The Prosecutor.* (29) No. 1 January/February 1995, p. 26.

15

THE CONSEQUENCES OF FAMILY VIOLENCE

Chapter Outline

Learning Objectives

After reading this chapter, you should be able to discuss the following concepts:

- The types of physical injuries suffered by family violence victims.
- From a medical perspective, the extent and nature of the various physical injuries inflicted on victims of crime.
- The three stages of crisis.
- The effects on victims suffering from posttraumatic stress disorder.

- The symptoms of acute stress disorder.
- The difference between posttraumatic stress disorder and long-term crisis reaction.
- The other types of mental consequences suffered by family violence victims.
- The financial consequences of family violence.

The effects of the different types of family violence have been addressed in each of the chapters that discuss these acts. However, it is also important to take a global view on the consequences of family violence. Therefore, this chapter is presented to allow professionals in the field to understand the far-reaching impact that family violence has on its victims and society. The term *family violence* was defined in Chapter 1 as "any act or omission by persons who are cohabitating that results in serious injury to other members of the family." This text also discusses sexual violence and women, so, for purposes of understanding the consequences of this form of victimization, sexual violence visited on women is included within the definition of family violence as used in this chapter.

Physical Consequences

One of the most obvious consequences of family violence is the physical injuries suffered by victims. These injuries are easy to observe and treat. They are also the

PRACTICUM What is a Crime Worth?

Stephanie is a thirty-five-year-old school teacher who lives by herself in a modern condominum project in an upper-middle-class section of her city. One night at approximately 1:00 A.M., she heard a sound of breaking glass. Before she could reach her phone to dial 911, a male dressed in black entered the bedroom and shoved a knife against her chest. The perpetrator wore a ski mask and latex gloves. He said, "You do what I want and I won't cut you." He proceeded to rape and sodomize her over the next hour.

Afterward, as he was preparing to leave, he saw a cameo broach laying on Stephanie's night stand. As he picked it up and placed it in his pocket, Stephanie pleaded with him not to take it because it had belonged to her deceased mother. The perpetrator merely laughed and struck her on the side of her head with the butt of his knife, stating that it would remind him of her.

The perpetrator, who was a wealthy playboy, was eventually arrested, charged with a number of similar sexual assaults, and convicted on all counts by a jury. At sentencing, Stephanie asked to speak regarding her losses. She asked the court to order the defendant to pay for her counseling ($5,000), the time she lost at her job ($2,000), her medical expenses ($3,000), pain and suffering ($10,000), and the fair market value of her broach, which was never recovered ($750).

What should the perpetrator pay? Supposing that he didn't have enough money to pay all the victim's claims, which one is the most important? The least important?

ones we are the most knowledgeable about because most us know someone who has suffered a broken arm or leg or other injury.

Types of Injuries

There are four general classifications of physical injuries inflicted on victims of family violence: immediate injuries that heal leaving no trace, injuries that leave visible scars, unknown long-term physical injuries, and long-term catastrophic injuries.

Immediate injuries include bruises, contusions, cuts, and broken bones. These injuries generally heal quickly and are not perceived as serious by most people. In fact, many of us have suffered these same types of injuries on a vacation trip. However, some family violence victims face more serious consequences as a result of these types of injuries. As Chapter 2 pointed out, certain types of bruises represent a serious form of child abuse. An elderly person who suffers a broken hip as a result of a shove by a caretaker may have significant complications during the healing process that could lead to death. A diabetic suffering from a stab wound inflicted during a domestic dispute may take two to three times as long to heal as another person.

Injuries that leave visible scars include those that result in facial scars; loss of teeth, fingers, or toes; scars on the neck, arms, or legs; and loss of mobility due to incomplete healing. The injuries are not considered catastrophic but can cause changes in life activities. For example, a stalker might inflict scars on the face of his victim that may result in a model being unable to pursue her career.

Unknown long-term physical injuries can include a potential exposure to HIV and AIDS. These types of diseases can result in loss of life or a complete change in life activities. Other sexually transmitted diseases may occur as a result of a sexual attack, including, but not limited to, gonorrhea, syphilis, and the herpes simplex viruses.

Long-term catastrophic injuries include those that restrict a victim's physical movements. For example, a person struck by a drunk driver may become a paraplegic or may lose an arm or a leg. Some victims of spousal abuse have suffered loss of liver function as a result of repeated beatings by their abuser. These severe injuries often result in family members having to alter their lifestyles in order to care for the victim, whereas others may result in a reduction in the life span of the victim, a change in identity, and change in the quality of life.

Medical Aspects

The types of physical injuries suffered by victims of family violence can cover the entire spectrum of illness, from simple bruises to deadly gunshot wounds to the head. Although professionals in this area are not expected to be physicians, they should have a basic understanding of the various types of injuries that family violence victims may suffer. The next section briefly examines the medical aspects of some of the more common traumatic injuries.[1]

Gunshot Wounds

The civilian population in the United States is the most heavily armed in history.[2] More than 850,000 civilians have been killed by bullets in the twentieth century.[3] The science of ballistics is complex, but a few basic rules will assist in understanding the nature of injuries that result from gunshot wounds. The magnitude of the injury is proportional to the amount of kinetic energy impacted by the bullet striking the victim. This kinetic energy is determined by a variety of factors, including the distance between the assailant and the victim, the muzzle velocity, and the various characteristics of the bullet. At medium velocity, the missile has an explosive impact and creates a temporary passage in the tissue along its course. Bone and tissue may be fractured and torn without being directly struck by the missile. High-velocity missiles cause additional problems, including the possibility of fragmentation, which will cause additional multiple trajectories and injuries. Medical personnel are interested in obtaining information regarding the type of weapon used, the distance from the assailant when the victim was shot, the suspected number of shots, the blood lost at the scene, and any type of fluids administered prior to arrival at the hospital.

Shotgun wounds present special types of problems. The shotgun was designed to strike a small, fast-moving target at close range. Because of the design of the pebbles inside the round, the shotgun is not an effective weapon at long range. However, when used at close range, a shotgun is extremely lethal. Shotgun wounds have been classified into three groups according to the range, the pattern of the pellets, and the depth of penetration. Type I wounds involve long range (greater than seven yards) and basically result in a penetration of subcutaneous tissue and deep fascia only. Type II wounds involve medium range (between three and four yards) and may create a large number of perforated wounds. Type III wounds involve short or point-blank range (less than three yards) and involve a massive destruction of tissue. Type III wounds are very lethal, carrying a mortality rate of 39 to 65 percent.

Stabbing Wounds

Knives are not the only instrument used in stabbings. Ice picks, pens, coat hangers, screwdrivers, broken bottles, and other sharp objects have all been used as weapons by assailants. Stabbing wounds usually result in lacerations or punctures. These injuries may be only a minor inconvenience, or they may be life threatening, depending on the location and depth of the wound. Frequently, more than one stab wound is sustained. Medical personnel are interested in obtaining information regarding the type and size of the weapon, the estimated blood loss at the scene of the crime, the time of injury, and whether the victim had ingested any drugs or alcohol.

Burns

As discussed in Chapter 2, burns are one of the most painful and devastating types of physical injury. They are classified into first, second or third degree, according to the depth of the burned area. First-degree burns involve the epidermal tissue and may exhibit red or pink skin accompanied by hyperesthesia and tingling. The more common causes of first-degree burns are sunburn and brief contact with hot liquids. Second-degree burns involve the epidermal and dermal tissues and may exhibit red or mottled skin with blisters, considerable swelling, wet surfaces, pain, and sensitivity to cold air. The most frequent cause includes scalds and flash flames. Third-degree burns involve dermal or deeper tissues and may exhibit a pale white or charred appearance with a dry surface. Body fat may be exposed, and systemic symptoms include shock, hematuria, and hemolysis. The most common causes include fire, contact with hot objects, and electrical and chemical burns.

The severity of burns is based on both the extent and the type of burn. The American Burn Association classifies burns as major, moderate, and minor. Major burns include second-degree burns over more than 25 percent of an adult's body and 20 percent of a child's body; third-degree burns involving 10 percent of the body surface; all burns involving hands, eyes, face, ears, and feet; and all inhalation injuries and all burns complicated by other injuries. Moderate burns include second-degree burns over 15 to 25 percent of an adult's body and 10 to 20 percent of a child's body and all third-degree burns of 2 to 10 percent not involving eyes, ears, face, hands, or feet. Minor burns include second-degree burns less than 15 percent of an adult's body and less than 10 percent of a child's body and third-degree burns of 2 percent or less and not involving eyes, ears, face, hands, or feet.

Trauma to the Head

A significant portion of all emergency department work involves the care of people suffering from trauma to the head. Vehicle accidents, including drunk driving incidents, account for a significant percentage of this form of injury. Other acts, such as child abuse and spousal abuse, also constitute another important cause of head trauma. Often, people who sustain head injuries also have other associated major traumatic injuries that they received at the same time.

One of the effects of trauma to the head may be the inducement of a coma. Comas may be a result of a subdural hematoma, epidural hematoma, traumatic intracerebral hemorrhage, contusion, or concussion. Defining a coma is difficult, but for the purposes here it is an altered state that exists in a person manifesting inappropriate responses to external stimuli and who maintains eye closure throughout the stimuli.

The victim's ability to relate the course of events leading to the injury may be compromised by injury, alcohol, drugs, hysteria, or any number of factors. Medical personnel will want to know whether the victim was struck on the head by the assailant and, if so, what the object was. Police and firefighters will be questioned about whether the victim was awake on their arrival. Any changes in consciousness between the incident and arrival at the emergency room should be noted.

Other Medical Concerns

In addition to the different types of physical injuries suffered by victims of violent crimes, victims of sexual assault endure a specific trauma that results in specialized medical issues. Rape victims will undergo a very particular type of examination intended to assist in the prosecution of the perpetrator. In the recent past, these medical examinations were conducted by hospital staff with little or no specialized training regarding the effects of rape on the victim. Additionally, there were times when a male police officer remained in the examination room to conduct questioning of the victim during the exam. Fortunately, we have progressed in our medical treatment of sexual assault victims, and in many jurisdictions rape crisis counselors are available and present during this examination. They have been trained to provide support to the victim during this and other phases of the criminal justice process.

The rape victim should discuss the issue of pregnancy with hospital staff. If she was pregnant prior to the assault, the possible effects on the fetus should be discussed. If she was not pregnant, the possibility that the assailant impregnated her should be evaluated. The victim should discuss all aspects of this issue at the earliest possible time with the medical staff at the hospital or her own physician.

The possibility of contracting a sexually transmitted disease (STD) must be evaluated. Many of these diseases can be successfully avoided if treated immediately after the assault; however, many STDs will not show up during the physical examination, so rape victims should be tested for several weeks after the attack. It is therefore critical that victims discuss this possibility with medical personnel.

With the threat of the AIDS/HIV virus so much a part of our lives today, the possibility of contracting the disease is perhaps one of the most frightening aspects of sexual assaults. Human immunodeficiency virus (HIV) causes acquired immunodeficiency syndrome (AIDS), which is a disease that attacks the body's immune system, rendering the person vulnerable to infections and diseases and ultimately resulting in death. A victim may contract the HIV virus in a variety of ways. Victims should be tested immediately for the HIV virus and request appropriate periodic follow-up testing.

Mental Consequences

Crisis

Eric Lindemann is considered by many scholars to be one of the leading pioneers in the study of the effects of crisis on the mental health or emotional being of humans.[4] Lindemann offered both a new understanding of the dynamics of crisis and a systematic approach to treating those suffering from it.[5] His study dealing with the grieving process of the survivors in the Coconut Grove fire in Boston in 1942 has become the foundation on which much of the knowledge concerning the grief process has been built. Lindemann believed that acute grief was a natural and necessary reaction to significant loss. Another scholar, Gerald Caplin, extended Lindemann's theories to include all human reactions to traumatic events, not just the grieving process as a result of loss.[6]

Individuals react differently to different situations, and what may be a crisis to one person may only be a minor annoyance to another. As a result, the term *crisis* has many valid meanings. In medicine, *crisis* has one meaning, whereas in psychiatry it is used in a different context. A number of scholars have defined the term. Rather than adopt a sociological, medical, psychological, or legal definition of *crisis,* it will be viewed from the perspective of a family violence victim's reactions to violence. *Crisis,* therefore, is defined as a specific set of temporary circumstances that results in state of upset and disequilibrium, characterized by an individual's inability to cope with a particular situation using customary methods of problem solving.[7]

Although some authorities may differ regarding the number of steps in the crisis reaction, one of the most common approaches describes this process as involving three stages: impact, recoil, and reorganization.

The Impact Stage

This phase occurs immediately after the violence. Victims feel as if they are in shock. Some victims cannot eat or sleep, whereas others may express disbelief that the violence actually occurred. Statements such as "I can't believe this happened to me!" are common during this stage. Many victims feel exposed and vulnerable or express feelings of helplessness.

The impact phase may last for several hours to several days after the crime and is often punctuated by episodes of severe mood swings. One moment the victim may appear to be in control and the next moment exhibit disorganized and uncontrolled emotions. A family violence victim is especially vulnerable at this time and suspectable to the influence of others. What may appear to be innocent statements offered by friends may be interpreted by the victim as blame for being the victim.

The Recoil Stage

During this phase, victims attempt to accept or adapt to the violence and begin to reintegrate their personalities. Victims commonly experience a wide variety of emotions, including guilt, fear, anger, self-pity, and sadness. Some victims struggle to accept the painful feelings caused by the violence; at other times will they deny experiencing any of these feelings at all. Caplin explained this process as involving victims who need opportunities to rest from wrestling with their situations, but who must eventually awake and return to consider the problem.[8] In essence, after trying to cope with their feelings regarding the violence, victims become emotionally exhausted and put these feelings aside so that they can rest, recover, and begin the healing process. Later, they are able to examine their feelings regarding the violence with renewed emotional resources.

Many victims will be in denial during this phase. This emotional detachment can be an extension of the shock of the impact phase. Such detachment allows victims to develop a gradual immunity to the feelings that would overwhelm them if they faced them all at once. Victims may believe that they must seal off any feelings in order to get on with their lives. Some victims defend against any feeling during this phase by emerging themselves in work or other projects. Other victims accomplish the same objective by becoming almost obsessional with the criminal justice system, learning about the procedures, criminal laws, parties, and so on.

During this phase, victims begin to deal with their feelings about the violence. Some victims will reexamine every detail of the crime in their minds and may want to talk about it endlessly. Others will dream about the violence. As victims confront the reality of the violent act, they may reexperience the fear. Some victims allow themselves to feel the full intensity of emotions only after the immediate threat of the violence has passed. This feeling of fear can be immobilizing. Victims must verbalize their fears and other intense emotions associated with the violent act in order to begin the healing process. With time, most of the traumatic impact associated with these feelings will lessen.

Another common feeling during the recoil stage is anger toward the perpetrator. Victims may experience rage but be unable to vent this feeling. Some victims may spend hours thinking about revenge, especially those who have suffered from a violent attack. Victims must understand that the desire for revenge is a natural and normal part of the healing process. Many victims want to construct a reason for their victimization. These victims will search for the answer to the question, "Why me?"

The Reorganization Stage

After a period of time, the recoil stage will give way to the reorganization stage. The victim becomes more normal as feelings of fear and rage diminish in intensity and the victim has energy left over to confront life's daily activities. The victim becomes more normalized as the need to deny the victimization lessens and gradually is able to put the experience in perspective and commit energy to the task of living in the present.

Victims will never forget the experience, and, as indicated earlier, they will respond in a variety of ways. The above discussion has focused on one method or approach to victimization. Other victims may experience different feelings. Acute stress disorder is another reaction that family violence victims may experience.

Acute Stress Disorder

Acute stress disorder (ASD) is acute stress that is experienced in the immediate aftermath of a traumatic event. This is a newly categorized disorder that was first listed in the *Diagnostic and Statistical Manual of Disorders,* fourth edition (DSM-IV), in 1994.[9] The characteristic feature of ASD is the development of anxiety, dissociative symptoms, and other manifestations that occur within one month after exposure to the traumatic event. In order to receive a diagnosis of ASD, the victim must have experienced, have witnessed, or have been confronted with an event that involved actual or threatened death, serious injury, or a threat to the physical safety of the victim or others. Additionally, the victim's response to such a condition must involve intense fear, helplessness, or horror. This diagnosis requires that the victim experience several of the symptoms of posttraumatic stress disorder

(PTSD) and that he or she must experience three of five PTSD dissociative symptoms during or immediately after the traumatic incident. These symptoms must persist for at least two days but last no more than thirty days. The dissociative symptoms are derealization, depersonalization, dissociative amnesia, subjective sense of numbing, and reduction in awareness of surrounding. In the event these symptoms last longer than thirty days, the victim may be suffering from PTSD.

Posttraumatic Stress Disorder

Posttraumatic stress disorder was first identified when some Viet Nam Veterans began experiencing flashbacks of events that occurred during combat. *Posttraumatic stress disorder* is defined as the development of characteristic symptoms following a psychologically distressing event that is outside the range of usual human experience.[10] Traumatic events include, but are not limited to, military combat, violent personal assault, being kidnaped, being taken hostage, terrorist attack, torture, incarceration as a prisoner of war, natural or manmade disasters, severe automobile accidents, or being diagnosed with a life-threatening illness. The characteristic symptoms involved require that the person experience, witness, or be confronted with an event or events that involved actual or threatened death or serious injury or a threat to the physical integrity of self or others and the person's response involved intense fear, helplessness, or horror. The symptoms the victim may experience include reexperiencing the traumatic event, avoiding stimuli associated with the event, or numbing of general responsiveness and increased agitation.[11]

Victims of many forms of family violence can experience PTSD. However, several scholars have carried out research regarding the effect of rape on victims.[12] Victims of rape have reported or been diagnosed as suffering from PTSD. Rothbaum's study found that 94 percent of rape victims displayed classic symptoms of PTSD one week after the assault. This figure dropped to 47 percent twelve weeks after the incident.[13] Kilpatrick's study *Rape in America* reported that 11 percent of all women raped still suffer from PTSD, and the authors estimated that 1.3 million women in the United States are currently suffering from PTSD as a result of a rape or multiple rapes.[14]

Long-Term Crisis Reaction

Long-term crisis reaction is the name of a condition identified by the National Organization for Victim Assistance (NOVA), which is considered one of the early leaders in the victim's rights movement. They have responded to a number of crises throughout the world. Professionals from NOVA working with crisis victims have observed this reaction on a number of occasions. Long-term crisis reaction is a condition that occurs when victims do not suffer from PTSD but may reexperience feelings of the crisis reaction when certain events trigger the recollection of the trauma in their lives.[15] The trigger event may be a number of situations, including the anniversaries of the crisis, birthdays, or holidays of loved ones lost during the trauma; significant life events such as marriage, divorces, births, and graduations; media events that broadcast similar types of incidents; and involvement in the criminal justice system.

The intensity and frequency of long-term crisis reactions usually diminish with the passage of time. As the victim develops coping mechanisms to deal with the trauma, these resources may lessen the victim's reaction to triggering events. The victim must learn to continue to function despite these reactions.

Other Mental Disorders

Victims of family violence may suffer a wide variety of mental disorders as a result of their victimization. They are going through a process of attempting to regain their mental equilibrium that is off center as a result of the traumatic event. The following is a brief discussion of two of the more common mental problems faced by victims of crime.

Depression

Depression consists of a major depressive episode lasting at least two weeks, during which there is either a depressed mood or the loss of interest or pleasure in nearly all activities. Possible symptoms include changes in appetite, weight, sleep, and psychomotor activity; decreased energy; feelings of worthlessness or guilt; difficulty thinking, concentrating, or making decisions; and recurrent thoughts of death or suicide. The victim must experience clinically significant distress or impairment in social, occupational, or other important areas of functioning.

Substance Abuse

The essential feature of this disorder is a maladaptive pattern of substance use leading to significant adverse consequences related to the repeated uses of substances. Normally, these substances are drugs or alcohol. The victim may suffer repeated failure in fulfilling major role obligations, repeated use of substances in situations in which it is physically dangerous, legal problems related to the use of the substance, and social and interpersonal problems.

Other Effects

Different victims of family violence suffer different reactions to that event, and, conversely, victims of different forms of family violence may suffer similar reactions. There is no "clear bright line" that professionals can look to and determine which symptoms victims will suffer. However, researchers have attempted to establish broad general categories of problems suffered by victims of certain crimes. Susman and Vittert's text *Building a Solution: A Practical Guide for Establishing Crime Victim Service Agencies* lists certain crimes and typical reactions.[16] Although individual crime victim's reactions vary, depending on a number of factors, these findings can be summarized (see Table 15.1).

TABLE 15.1 Problems Suffered by Victims of Crime

Battered Women	Homicide–Survivor Victims	Child Victims	Elderly Victims	Assualt	Sexual Assault
Decision to stay	Acceptance of death	Parents' reaction	Fear of crime	Anger and/or bitterness	Embarrassment
Decision to leave	Funeral arrangements	Signs of emotional distress	Acute financial loss	Realization of mortality	Difficulty in describing the incident
Financial worries	Financial problems when breadwinner is killed	Guilt	Change in lifestyle	Physical injury	Concern about STD/pregnancy
Decision to prosecute	Delayed emotional reaction	Parents' unconcern	Loneliness	Medical bills	Bills for the medical exam
Desire counseling for batterer and/or themselves	Reaction of children	Difficulty in describing incident	Family reactions	Time lost from work	Fear of telling family members
For separated couples, visiation offers opportunities for further attacks	Need for information on the criminal case	Fears about testifying	Reluctance to get involved in the criminal justice system	Fear of reprisals	Fear the neighbors will find out
Isolation	Media publicity	Incest-decision about family future		If assailant is a family member, feelings of betrayal	Fear of media publicity
Helplessness	Feelings of powerlessness in the criminal justice system	Incest-mixed reaction by mother		If a result of a traffic incident, fear of driving	Recurring nightmares, changes in sleeping patters, loss of appetite
Pyschological dependence	Ordeal during trial	Reaction of other children		If a result of jealousy, feeling of vulnerability	Decision to prosecute
Fear of reoccurrence	Loneliness	Fear of intimidation		For male victims, shame at losing a "fight"	Fear that they will have to testify about prior sexual history
Feeling of personal failure	Can't stop ruminating				Bitterness against the offender
Fear for safety of any children	Desire for revenge				Sexual dysfunction

With the passage of time and other intervention techniques, the mental and/or emotional consequences associated with the trauma of a criminal act may lessen or be alleviated, but the victim may never be the same person he or she was before the crime. In addition to the mental effects that victims endure as a result of the crime, they also suffer fiscal consequences.

Financial Consequences

In 1996, the National Institute of Justice released *Victim Costs and Consequences: A New Look,* an in-depth study of the costs of victimization.[17] This study raises serious questions regarding previous estimates of the cost of crime. Using the data from the Bureau of Justice Statistics and including "quality of life" or intangible losses, this study concludes that the cost of crime is higher than previously suggested. This study is important to professionals who deal with family violence in that it points out the cost of this form of violence. The following sections examine the results of this study.

Introduction

It is fairly easy to establish the tangible costs of crime. These include a number of fairly easy-to-measure items, such as medical care, police services, and other items that have a specific monetary value. However, it not so easy to value the loss of quality-of-life or intangible losses suffered by victims of family violence. How much is a murder spouse's life worth? What is the cost for the pain and suffering experienced by a rape victim? Additionally, costs associated with society's response to crime are difficult if not impossible to measure. Table 15.2 lists society's costs associated with crime. As the figure indicates, society's response to

TABLE 15.2 Society's Costs Associated with Crime

Cost of Crime	Cost of Society's Response to Crime
Medical and mental health care	Fear of crime
Victim services	Criminal justice system
Lost workdays	Victim service organizations andvolunteer time
Lost school days	Other non-criminal programs
Lost housework	Incarcerated offender costs
Pain and suffering/quality of life	Overdeterrence costs
Loss of affection/enjoyment	Justice costs
Death	
Legal costs associated with tort claims	
Second generation costs	

crime includes a variety of items that are not normally considered when discussing costs of crime. Measuring our actions and resulting costs on the basis of our fear of crime is difficult.[18] On the other hand, measuring items (e.g., filing fees paid for a protective order are typical of the precautionary expenditures associated with protecting ourselves from an abusive partner) is relatively easy. Additionally, everyone understands the costs associated with running the criminal justice system and keeping offenders incarcerated. Thus, it can be observed that society's response to crime includes both tangible and intangible costs. The cost-of-crime section also includes tangible and intangible losses suffered as a result of family violence. These costs include tangible items such as medical and mental health treatment cost. The intangible costs include quality of life and loss of companionship. Table 15.3 examines both tangible and intangible costs of this form of violence. This figure indicates that costs of family violence show that quality-of-life losses generally exceed tangible losses. The next section examines the tangible costs of family violence.

Tangible Losses

Family violence costs taxpayers, businesses, and victims in medical costs, lost earnings, and public programs related to family violence prevention or assistance. These tangible losses do not account for the full impact of crime on victims of family violence because they ignore pain and suffering and the reduced quality of life that many victims suffer as a result of the violence.

Victims of family violence usually suffer three types of losses: out of pocket expenses such as medical costs and property loss, reduced productivity at work because of sick days and so on, and nonmonetary losses such as pain and suffering and loss of quality of life. Although some of these losses are easily quantified, even the intangible losses may be valued in dollars. Tangible losses include property damage and loss, medical care, mental health care, police and fire services, victim services, and productivity. Each of these losses is explained below.

Property damage and loss. This includes the value of the property damaged during a violent act. It also includes insurance claims administration costs that arise as a result of compensating the victim under an insurance policy.

Medical care. This includes payments for hospital and physician care, emergency medical transportation, rehabilitation, prescriptions, allied health services, medical devices, and related insurance claim processing costs. Managed care systems are

TABLE 15.3 Tangible and Intangible Costs of Violence

Crime	Tangible Costs	Intangible Costs	Total Costs
Murder of a spouse	$ 1,000,000	$ 1,910,000	$ 2,940,000
Rape/sexual assault	5,100	81,400	86,500
Assualt or attempt	1,500	7,800	9,350

changing health care payments and are not reflected in these costs. More study is necessary in this area as medical costs adapt to changing circumstances.

Mental health care. This provides funding for services to family violence victims by psychiatrists, psychologists, social workers, and counselors. This cost has been one of the least researched areas in crime victimization.

Police and fire services. This includes initial police and fire responses as well as follow-up investigations. The costs of other components of the criminal justice system are not included in this element. Generally speaking, police and fire costs are a relatively small portion of the cost of family violence, averaging $100 per case.

Victim services. Costs include victim service agencies and child protective services agencies as well as foster care for maltreated children removed from their homes.

Productivity. Costs include lost wages, fringe benefits, housework, and lost school days suffered by victims and their families. This category includes lost productivity of coworkers and supervisors recruiting and training victims who are disabled as a result of a violent act. It also includes processing costs for insurance claims.

Intangible Losses

Intangible losses are hard to quantify, but scholars have begun to place monetary values on certain aspects of a victim's quality of life. Researchers such as Ted R. Miller and others have divided intangible losses into two categories: fatal and nonfatal injuries. The monetary value for fatalities is based on the amount people routinely spend to reduce their risk of death. For example, this amount would include the cost of smoke detectors, alarm systems, and bars on house windows.

The intangible value for nonfatal injuries was established by analyzing jury verdicts for pain, suffering, fear, and loss of quality of life. As discussed in other chapters of this text, violent perpetrators rarely have sufficient funds to pay these awards, but third-party codefendants, such as insurance companies or businesses that were negligent, can be held liable for injuries to the victim.

There is no doubt that attempting to establish a monetary value on intangible aspects of victimization is a relatively recent development in the field of victimology. For example, in 1994, a Bureau of Justice Statistics publication, *The Costs of Crime to the Victim,* specifically did not examine the intangible costs of crime or family violence.[19] Because this is a new aspect of victimization, it will continue to be controversial. However, we cannot truly appreciate the consequences of family violence and victimization until we begin to accept that there are intangible costs to victims and their families. This is an area of family violence that will continue to generate more study and debate in the future.

Summary

We have known for years that victims of family violence suffer from specific types of physical injuries as a result of their victimization. These are, for the most part, easy to recognize and treat. The broken arm or jaw may be repaired, and it is hoped that the victim will regain full use of his or her physical faculties.

More recently, society has acknowledged that victims of family violence may also suffer mental problems as a consequence of their victimization. They may experience a wide variety of mental problems, including acute stress disorder, posttraumatic stress disorder, long-term crisis reaction, or other mental disorders. These reactions do not mean that family violence victims are insane or crazy; rather, these are normal reactions to an abnormal event. Victim service providers and professionals who deal with family violence victims must understand these dynamics in order to work with and assist victims of crimes.

In addition to the physical and mental injuries suffered by victims are the financial consequences. Recent studies have begun to address this long-overlooked aspect of victimization. The consequences of family violence are multifaceted and, like a stone dropped in a calm pool of water, move out in ever-widening circles, affecting victims, their families and society as a whole. Professionals in the field must understand all the consequences of family violence victimization in order to function effectively.

Key Terms

crisis—a specific set of temporary circumstances that result in a state of upset and disequilibrium, characterized by an individual's inability to cope with a particular situation using customary methods of problem solving.

long-term crisis reaction—a condition that occurs when victims do not suffer from posttraumatic stress disorder but may reexperience feelings of the crisis reaction when certain events trigger the recollection of the trauma in their lives.

posttraumatic stress disorder—the development of characteristic symptoms following a psychologically distressing event that is outside the range of usual human experience.

acute stress disorder—acute stress that is experienced in the immediate aftermath of a traumatic event.

Discussion Questions

1. What are the four stages of physical injury? How do they differ from one another?
2. Describe the various types of physical injuries that family violence victims may suffer.
3. List and discuss the three stages of crisis. In your opinion, which is the most critical for the victim? Justify your answer.
4. What is acute stress disorder? How is it different from a crisis reaction?
5. Explain the symptoms of posttraumatic stress disorder.
6. Define *long-term crisis reaction* and explain what a trigger event is.
7. Compare and contrast posttraumatic stress disorder with long-term crisis reaction.
8. List other mental effects of family violence on victims. In your opinion, which effect is the most serious? Justify your answer.

Suggested Readings

Reiss, A. J., Jr., and J. A. Roth, eds. *Understanding and Preventing Violence.* (National Academy Press, Washington, D.C. 1993).

Roberts, A. R., ed. *Crisis Intervention and Time-Limited Cognitive Treatment.* (Sage, Thousand Oaks, California 1995).

Wing, C. P. *Crisis Intervention as Psychotherapy.* (Oxford, New York 1978).

Caplin, G. *Principles of Preventive Psychiatry.* (Basic Books, New York 1964).

Bard, M., and D. Sangrey *The Crime Victim's Book,* 2d ed. (Brunner/Mazel, New York 1986).

Endnotes

1. Much of this information was gathered from interviewing members of the Fresno Valley Medical Center emergency room staff. Barbara Miller, R.N., was of significant assistance in providing guidance for material in this section.
2. Wright, J. D. "The Demography of Gun Control," *The Nation,* September 20, 1976, p. 241.
3. Adelson, L. "The Gun and the Sanctity of Human Life: or the Bullet as a Pathogen," *The Phasos* (Summer 1980), p. 15.
4. Roberts, A. R., and S. F. Dziegielewski. "Foundation Skills and Applications of Crisis Intervention and Cognitive Therapy," in *Crisis Intervention and Time-Limited Cognitive Treatment.* Albert R. Roberts, ed. (Sage, Thousand Oaks, California 1995).
5. Lindemann, E. "Symptomatology and Management of Acute Grief," *American Journal of Psychiatry* 101 (1994), pp. 141–148.
6. Wing, C. P. *Crisis Intervention as Psychotherapy.* (Oxford, New York 1978), and Gerald Caplin, *Principles of Preventive Psychiatry.* (Basic Books, New York 1964).
7. See Roberts, A. R. *Crisis Intervention Handbook: Assessment, Treatment and Research.* (Wadsworth, Belmont, California 1990), and Bard, M. and D. Sangrey. *The Crime Victim's Book,* 2d ed. (Brunner/Mazel, New York 1986).
8. Caplin, p. 46.
9. *Diagnostic and Statistical Manual of Mental Disorders,* 4th ed. (American Psychiatric Association, Washington, D.C. 1994).
10. Ibid., pp. 427–429.
11. Ibid., pp. 427–249.
12. For an excellent discussion of the effects of rape on victims, see Bruce Taylor, "The Role of Significant Others in a Rape Victim's Recovery: People Who Are More Likely to Be Harmful Than Helpful," paper presented at the 1996 ACJS Annual Meeting, Law Vegas, Nevada, March 1996.
13. Rothbaum, B. O., E. B. Foa, T. Murdock, D. S. Riggs, and W. Walsh. "A Prospective Examination of Post-Traumatic Stress Disorder in Rape Victims," *Journal of Traumatic Stresss* (1992), pp. 455–475.
14. Kilpatrick, D. G., C. N. Edmunds, and A. K. Seymour. *Rape in America: A Report to the Nation,* (National Victim Center, Arlington, Virginia 1992).
15. Young, M. A. "Crisis Response Teams in the Aftermath of Disasters," in *Crisis Intervention and Time-Limited Cognitive Treatment,* Albert R. Roberts, ed. (Sage, Thousand Oaks, California 1995).
16. Susman, J., and C. H. Vittert. *Building a Solution: A Practical Guide for Establishing Crime Victim Service Agencies.* (National Council of Jewish Women, St. Louis Section, 1980).
17. Miller, T. R., M. A. Cohen, and Brian Wiersema. *Victim Costs and Consequences: A New Look.* (National Institute of Justice, U.S. Department of Justice, Washington, D.C. February 1996). This section is adapted from the material presented in this study.
18. Cohen, M. A., and T. R. Miller. "The Cost of Mental Health Care for Victims of Crime." *Journal of Interpersonal Violence* 13(1) (February 1998) p. 93.
19. Klaus, P. A. "The Cost of Crime to Victims," *Crime Data Brief.* (Bureau of Justice Statistics, Washington, D.C. February 1994).

16

VICTIM'S RIGHTS

Chapter Outline

Learning Objectives

After reading this chapter, you should be able to discuss the following concepts:

- The forces that shaped the victim's movement in the United States.
- Why both criminal and civil remedies are important to victims.
- The historical development of victim impact statements.
- How a victim of family violence can receive financial assistance from the state and the abuser.

Introduction

Although all authorities acknowledge that those who are abused in an intimate relationship are victims, many researchers tend to focus on the medical or psychological treatment of these victims. However, another aspect to victimization occurs in family violence situations. Many victims of family violence suffer both psychological and physical injuries as well as financial loss. In the fairly recent past, these injuries were forgotten in the rush to punish the perpetrator or treat the victim. Professionals are beginning to realize that victims should be made whole not only emotionally but financially as well. Victims of all crimes are now accorded certain rights. Understanding these rights will assist in treating victims and allowing them to progress toward complete recovery. The study of family violence in many ways parallels the development of the victim's rights movement in the United States.

Historical Perspective

The victim of a crime has not always been the forgotten voice in the courtroom. Early civilizations accorded victims many more rights than did modern states until the birth of the victim's rights movement in the United States. Early laws were known as *primitive law, which was a system of rules in preliterate societies.* These rules or regulations represent the foundation on which the modern legal system is built. Primitive laws usually contained three characteristics: Acts that injured others were considered private wrongs, the injured party was entitled to take action against the wrongdoer, and this action usually amounted to in-kind retaliation. These types of laws encouraged blood feuds and revenge as the preferred method of making the victim whole.

As society matured, people learned the art of reading and writing. One result of this evolution was the development of written codes of conduct. The Code of Ur-Nammu dates to the twenty-first century B.C. Other early written codes include the Twelve Tables of Rome, the laws of Greece, and the Mosaic Code. Many of these codes treated certain wrongs such as theft or assault as private wrongs with the injured party being the victim rather than the state.[1]

One of the most comprehensive criminal codes was the Code of Hammurabi, which was adopted in 1750 B.C. Although this code was still based on revenge, it required the victim's family and, if necessary, the entire community to take responsibility for making restitution to the victim if the perpetrator escaped or was unable to be found.[2] As the feudal system developed in England, the right to seek redress from a wrongdoer passed from the hands of the victim of his or her family to the state. The state was more concerned about bringing the perpetrator to justice than compensating the victim for any injuries, and this philosophy has continued to modern times.[3]

Previous chapters discussed the slow but growing awareness of family violence. At the same time that society was beginning to acknowledge family violence, so were people beginning to understand that victims of all crimes, including those who suffered abuse in an intimate relationship, should have their day in court. A number of forces have contributed to the development of victim's rights. The major contributors to the rights of victims were the feminist movement, the development of civil rights laws, and a growing conservatism regarding crime.[4]

The feminist movement made plain the plethora of discrimination and violence against women. By speaking out, feminists engendered the realization that women were victims, not only by violent crime on the streets of cities but also from sexual harassment within the work environment and family violence in the home. The types of crimes suffered by women are distinct from those suffered by men.

As was discussed in previous chapters, many of these crimes, though sexual in nature, are in fact nothing more than aggressive assaults that have very little to do with sex. Sexual assaults are, in reality, a way for the perpetrator to control, dominate, and humiliate the victim.

The first coordinated effort by feminists groups in the United States to help women who were victims of crimes was the establishment of rape crisis centers in Berkeley, California, and in Washington, D.C., in 1972. These centers spread rapidly and are now an accepted part of the criminal justice system. In 1976, the federal government established a research center, the National Center for the Prevention and Control of Rape, within the Department of Health, Education, and Welfare (this agency is now called Health and Human Services). A National Coalition against sexual assault was established and began the process of improving communication between victims of sexual aggression, rape crisis centers, and victim's advocates.[5]

The feminist movement not only attacked society's perceptions regarding victims of sexual assault but also focused its efforts on educating the public regarding domestic violence. Although their efforts have been discussed previously, it is important to note that at the same time battered women's shelters were being established, there was a growing awareness that victims of crimes, as a class of citizens, were being treated unfairly by the criminal justice system. This awareness coincided with changes within the judicial system.

During the 1960s and 1970s, a series of U.S. Supreme Court decisions established certain principles regarding the constitutional rights of individuals. These decisions were in the area of both criminal procedure and civil rights. The Supreme Court established constitutional safeguards for those accused of crimes. By interpreting the U.S. Constitution as applying to each and every individual, the Court required that society afford those accused of crimes certain procedural and substantive rights. These rights embraced the entire spectrum of liberties, including freedom from unreasonable search and seizures, the right to an attorney, and fundamental fairness during a criminal trial. By adopting a philosophy that individuals carried with them certain inalienable rights, the Court was posed to expand this concept in the area of civil rights.

The Supreme Court acted to enforce both statutory and constitutional provisions during the 1960s and 1970s in the area of civil rights. These decisions allowed a black man to attend a previously all-white university, held that police officers could be held liable for use of excessive force, and required that all persons be treated equally under the law. As a result of these and other decisions, cases such as *Thurman v City of Torrington*[6] were decided in favor of victims of family violence.

Another factor that contributed to the awareness of the plight of victims arose as a result of a change in attitude in the United States. In the 1980s and 1990s, citizens became more conservative and concerned about crime in general. This law-and-order movement resulted from citizens becoming more fearful of violent crime, with many groups consequently calling for more stringent punishment of those who violated the law. In addition, the victim's rights movement was gaining momentum, and imprisoning offenders was viewed as a way of vindicating victims of crimes. National organizations composed of victims began lobbying for changes in the criminal justice system. These changes were aimed at making the system more victim oriented. The rights of victims of family violence began to grow and expand as society became more concerned about crime in general.

In what may become one of the most critical dates in the history of victim rights, on June 25, 1996, President Bill Clinton proposed the Victims' Rights Constitutional Amendment to the Constitution. In a speech made in the Rose Garden announcing the amendment, President Clinton stated,

> *Having carefully studied all of the alternatives, I am now convinced that the only way to fully safeguard the rights of victims in America is to amend our Constitution and guarantee these basic rights—to be told about public court proceedings and to attend them; to make a statement to the court about bail, about sentencing, about accepting a plea if the victim is present, to be told about parole hearings to attend and to speak; notice when the defendant or convict escapes or is released, restitution from the defendant, reasonable protection from the defendant and notice of these rights.*[7]

The Victims' Rights Constitutional Amendment faces a long and complex process before it becomes law. It must be approved by Congress and then adopted by three-quarters of the states to become part of the Constitution. It is not something that will happen in a few weeks or months, and already some claim that the proposed amendment is too detailed and should be broadened. No matter what the outcome, the simple fact that such an amendment has actually been proposed is a significant acknowledgment of the plight of victims of crimes.

All these combined forces focused an awareness on the plights of crime victims and the dilemma of victims of family violence.[8] As a result, victims began to realize that they could have an effect on sentencing in criminal cases and could pursue civil litigation to recover for damages they suffered as a result of the perpetrator's actions. This twofold approach to making victims whole is the topic of the next section.

Victims and Civil Litigation

Restoring the victim's emotional and financial status by using the judicial system cannot occur in a single court hearing. It is a multifaceted process that involves

Victims' Rights Constitutional Amendment

Section 1. To ensure that the victim is treated with fairness, dignity, and respect, from the occurrence of a crime of violence and other crimes as may be defined by law pursuant to section two of this article, and throughout the criminal, military, and juvenile justice process, as a matter of fundamental rights to liberty, justice and due process, the victim shall have the following rights: to be informed of and given the opportunity to be present at every proceeding in which those rights are extended to the accused or convicted offender; to be heard at any proceeding involving sentencing, including the right to object to a previously negotiated plea, or to a release from custody; to be informed of any release or escape; and to a speedy trial, a final conclusion free from unreasonable delay, full restitution from the convicted offender, reasonable measures to protect the victim from violence or intimidation by the accused or convicted offender, and notice of the victim's rights.

Section 2. The several States, with respect to a proceeding in a State forum, and the Congress with respect to a proceeding in a United States forum, shall have the power to implement further the rights established in this article by appropriate legislation.

Source: OVC, U.S. Department of Justice, Washington D.C. 1996.

prosecutors, judges, court personnel, and private attorneys.[9] However, before discussing civil and criminal actions against perpetrators of family violence, it is important to understand the development of the discipline that studies victims.

The term *victimology* was coined by Benjamin Mendelsohn.[10] The modern definition of victimology states *it is the study of the victim, the offender, and society.* From its inception in the 1940s to the present day, victimology, like family violence, has been an interdisciplinary approach to violence and its effect on victims. Mendelsohn developed a typology of victims and their contribution to the criminal act.[11] This classification ranged from the completely innocent victim to the imaginary victim. Mendelsohn classified victims into six distinct categories:

1. *The completely innocent victim.* This victim may be a child or completely unconscious person.
2. *The victim with minor guilt.* This victim might be a woman who induces a miscarriage and dies as a result.
3. *The victim who is as guilty as the offender.* Those who assist others in suicide or euthanasia fall within this classification.
4. *The victim more guilty than the offender.* These are persons who provoke others to commit a crime.
5. *The most guilty victim.* This victim acts aggressively and kills in self-defense.
6. *The imaginary victim.* These are persons suffering from mental disorders such as paranoia who believe they are victims.

Other scholars have studied the dynamics of victim participation. In an early classic text, von Hentig explored the relationship between the "doer," or criminal, and the "sufferer," or victim. He theorized that a large percentage of victims, because of their acts or behavior, were responsible for their victimization.[12] This concept has been repudiated by modern research and studies that have more closely examined the relationship between the victim and the offender.

From 1948 to 1952 in Philadelphia, Wolfgang conducted the first major study of victim precipitation.[13] He focused on homicides and studied both the victim and the offender as separate entities and as "mutual participants in the homicide."[14] Wolfgang evaluated 588 homicides and found that 26 percent (150) of all the homicides studied in Philadelphia involved situations in which the victim was a direct, positive precipitator in the crime—the first to use force during the acts leading to the homicide.[15]

Victimology continued to grow in popularity. Scholars expanded their scope of inquiry and began exploring other aspects of the victim's role in society. Karmen discussed the development of victimology and pointed out that this relatively new discipline has three main areas of concentration:

1. Victimologists study the reasons (if any) of why or how the victim placed herself in a dangerous situation. This study does not attempt to fix blame on the victim; rather, it examines the dynamics that resulted in the victim being in the risky situation.
2. Victimology evaluates how police, prosecutors, courts, and related agencies interact with the victim. How was the victim treated at each stage in the criminal justice system?
3. Victimologists evaluate the effectiveness of efforts to reimburse victims for their losses and meet victims' personal and emotional needs.[16]

Researchers are still learning about the dynamics of victims' interaction with the judicial system, and victims are learning that they can make a difference within the system. Some jurisdictions have victim's rights advocates who appear with or on behalf of the victim at the sentencing of the offender. These victim advocates also offer advice regarding filing of civil lawsuits against the perpetrator or against other third parties.

As was discussed in previous chapters, in a criminal case the prosecutor represents the people and not the victim. Civil law, however, focuses on the private rights of individuals. Therefore, civil law allows an injured person to file a lawsuit against the injuring party. If successful, the injured party may recover monetary damages from the wrongdoer. Additionally, civil law allows for the imposition of certain types of orders regulating conduct such as the temporary restraining orders.

There are numerous types of civil litigation; however, one that is of particular importance to victims of domestic violence is called a tort. *A tort has been defined as a legal wrong committed on the person or property of another independent of contract.* A tort may occur either as the result of the negligence of another or as the consequence of another's intentional act.[17] Torts include actions that result in physical injury or death and damage to one's reputation. The same act that may be punished under a criminal code may also give rise to a civil cause of action in tort. For example, the rape of a female is a criminal offense but is also a civil wrong of battery. Battery is an intentional tort that would allow the victim to sue the perpetrator for monetary damages.

Negligence is a civil law concept that holds persons liable for injuries that result from their acts or actions. Negligence is a complex legal theory that gives first-year law students headaches. However, it is necessary to understand this concept in order to grasp the nature of various rights available to victims. Negligence consists of the existence of a legal duty owed by one party to another, the breaching or breaking of that duty, a proximate cause or relationship between the breaching of the duty, and the injuries suffered by the injured party and damages. Actions for negligence may be filed against parties such as businesses or government agencies that violated a duty that resulted in injuries to the victim.

Previous chapters examined the criminal process and briefly touched on certain aspects of civil procedures such as dependency or conservatorship hearings. The civil process used to bring an action against a perpetrator for a tort in many ways parallels the criminal process; however, there are significant differences. The following is a brief summary of a trial that a victim would use in pursuing civil damages from the perpetrator.

Determination That a Civil Action Is Available

The victim of a crime will talk with the prosecutor and testify in court. However, the prosecutor is not her personal attorney, nor will the prosecutor give the victim legal advice regarding her civil remedies. Therefore, the victim may have to consult with a private attorney or a victim's rights organization to determine whether filing a civil lawsuit is advisable. Numerous factors should or will be considered in this determination: the expense and time involved in a civil case, the emotions or mental condition of the victim, the chances of obtaining a verdict in favor of the victim, and the availability of collecting any judgment from the perpetrator. These are critical factors that will be evaluated by any attorney in advising a victim on whether to proceed with a civil action.

Filing of a Pleading

The person filing the complaint is known as the plaintiff, and the person who is alleged to have committed the acts that resulted in injury to the plaintiff or victim is called the defendant. Filing a civil complaint is the first formal step in the litigation process. *The complaint is a formal written document stating certain causes of actions that the plaintiff alleges to entitle her to recover damages from the perpetrator.* Once the plaintiff has filed the complaint in court and served a copy to the defendant, the defendant must reply or file an answer to the complaint. *An answer is a formal written document that either admits or denies the allegations contained in the complaint and raises defenses to the charges.*

Many times plaintiffs will allege several different theories of recovery on the basis of the same set of facts. This is a common practice that allows plaintiffs to file lawsuits early before all the facts are known to them. For example, the plaintiff may allege that the defendant intentionally struck her or, in the alternative, that the defendant acted recklessly in striking her, or she may allege that the defendant was negligent and that this resulted in her injury. Once all the facts surrounding the incident are known to the plaintiff, she has the option of dismissing the other causes of action and concentrating on the allegation that most closely fits the facts.

Discovery

The facts surrounding the incident are determined during the process known as *discovery*. This is a *formal method of learning the facts, theories, and positions of opposing parties by means of written or oral questioning*. Depositions are a form of discovery in which the sworn oral testimony of a person is taken prior to the trial. Interrogatories are written questions posed to the other party who must reply in writing and under oath to each of the questions. Discovery is a method to perpetuate or fix the testimony of another party so that they cannot later change their story or testimony. Unlike some television shows, in real life civil attorneys know the answer to almost every question before it is asked, and there are few if any surprises because each side has engaged in extensive and costly discovery prior to trial.

Motions

Once all the facts have been made available by use of the various discovery techniques, each side may engage in a series of motions designed to either have the case decided or limit the scope of the case. For example, if both sides have engaged in discovery and there is no dispute as to the facts surrounding the incident, the only issue left to be decided is the application of the law to the facts. When this is the case, the parties may submit what is called a *summary judgment motion*. This motion is used when the facts are not in dispute and the parties are asking the judge to apply the law to this set of facts and rule in favor of one party.

Trial

Similar to a criminal case, a civil case may be adjudicated by either a jury or a judge. The trial is conducted in the same manner as a criminal case but with one significant difference. The standard of proof in a civil case is a preponderance of the evidence rather than the much higher criminal standard of beyond a reasonable doubt to a moral certainty.

The perpetrator may be liable to the victim because of intentional or negligent acts. Many criminal acts have counterparts in the civil law that allow a victim to recover independent of the criminal process. Therefore, the same acts that give rise to a criminal complaint may be used in the civil action.

During the trial, responsibility for the injury to the plaintiff will be decided, as will an apportionment of fault if there is more than one defendant. Many times trials are divided, or bifurcated, into two phases: liability and damages. During the first phase, the issue before the judge or jury is whether the defendant caused the injuries to the plaintiff. If there is a determination that the defendant did not cause the injuries, the trial is over at that stage. However, if there is determination that

FOCUS Crimes and Torts

Murder or manslaughter	Assault
Criminal assault	Battery
Criminal battery	Assault, battery, and emotional distress
Rape, sodomy, or oral copulation	Same as rape
Child sexual abuse	Intentional torts and negligence
Child neglect	All of the above plus fraud (if the caretaker appropriated the victim's money or property)
Elder abuse	
Wrongful death	

the defendant did cause or contribute to the injuries of the plaintiff, the second stage or phase will examine how much money the defendant should pay the plaintiff for his injuries. *When the plaintiff asks to be made whole or reimbursed for expenses incurred as a result of an injury, this is known as compensatory damages. Punitive damages are asked for or awarded to punish the defendant for conduct that is considered outrageous.* Punitive damages are also a method of sending a message to others that certain acts will not be tolerated and, if engaged in, will result in financial punishment above and beyond the injury that resulted from the questionable conduct.

Recovery

Simply receiving a favorable verdict does not automatically mean the plaintiff will receive the amount of money set forth in the verdict. Motions for new trials and appeals are likely to occur before any judgment is final. In addition, the perpetrator may not have the financial resources available to pay the judgment.

Prevailing in a civil suit is only half the battle; the plaintiff must also be able to obtain the money awarded by the judge or jury. Even if it can be proved that the perpetrator is at fault, he may not have any funds available to compensate or make the victim whole financially. In an effort to gain compensation for victims of family violence, attorneys have explored different alternatives when filing lawsuits against wrongdoers. For example, civil actions may be brought against the perpetrator, third parties that may have contributed to the victim's injuries such as private businesses or government agencies, the offender's insurance company, and even the victim's insurance company.

Third parties are those individuals or entities that have intentionally or negligently contributed to the injury suffered by the victim. Typical third parties may be businesses that failed to provide a safe working environment for their employees, government agencies or employees that had a duty to protect or serve the victim and failed to do so, and insurance companies that provided insurance coverage to either the perpetrator or the victim. In many jurisdictions, worker compensation statutes are considered the sole source of recovery for workers injuried on the job; however, court decisions sometimes allow workers to bring civil lawsuits for job-related injuries.

Businesses may fail to provide adequate protection for their workers. For example, a business may fail to light the parking lot where its employees park. If a female is leaving work late and is assaulted in the parking lot, she may have a civil cause of action against the business for failing to provide proper lighting. She could sue both the perpetrator and the business. The causes of action against the perpetrator might include assault, battery, and intentional infliction of emotional distress, and the causes of action against the business might be based on negligence for failing to fulfill its duty to employees by providing a safe working environment. One of the more famous third-party lawsuits involved the singer Connie Francis. She was in her hotel room at a Howard Johnson's Motor Lodge when an assailant entered through a sliding glass door that was known by the hotel management to be defective. The perpetrator sexually assaulted Ms. Francis, escaped, and was never apprehended. She filed a civil action and in 1976 was awarded $2.5 million against the hotel for failing to provide adequate security.[18]

Victims have successfully sued third-party businesses using a variety of legal theories: landlords who have failed to provide adequate security similar to the causes of action alleged in the Connie Francis case, customers against stores,[19] students against private schools, and patients against hospitals.[20] The common thread running though all these actions is the existence of a duty owed by the business to protect the victim and failure to do so that resulted in the victim's being injured by the perpetrator.

Government agencies or their employees have been sued as third parties in situations in which their actions or failure to act contributed to injuries suffered by victims as a result of acts by perpetrators. Several cases involved police officers who stopped to render aid to stranded motorists and then left the victims on the side of the road without protection. When that person was subsequently assaulted, courts have allowed civil lawsuits against both the perpetrator and the government agencies. In these situations, courts have stated that when the officer initially stopped to render aid, a duty to protect the motorist from foreseeable harm was established and the officer breached that duty when the motorist was left alone.

In addition, government agencies may be responsible as third parties for the actions of their employees. If an employee assaults the victim, she may have a cause of action against the government agencies that employed the perpetrator. For example, if the agency knew or should have known that an employee might assault a citizen, it should have taken appropriate steps to prevent those acts or terminate the employee.

However, not all assaults against victims occur as a result of a breach of duty by businesses or government agencies. In these instances, the victim must look elsewhere in her quest to recover finances that would compensate her for injuries. The first and most obvious source of funds are those held by the perpetrator. The victim may attempt to obtain a judgment and levy against the defendant's income or other assets. Many perpetrators may not have sufficient funds available to compensate the victim for all the injuries inflicted. However, they may have automobile or homeowner's insurance. The victim may have a right to recover from these insurance companies for the actions of the perpetrator.

Homeowners policies are written to protect the owner from injuries that occur on his or her property as a result of an accident or an unintended occurrence. The term *homeowner's insurance* is really misleading because most of these policies provide coverage for accidents or injuries away from the home. Most litigation involves the nature of the acts that resulted in injuries, not the location of where the injuries occurred. Automobile policies are very similar to homeowner's insurance in that they are designed to provide coverage for accidental or unintended events.

Both types of insurance have exclusions for intentional acts committed by the insured. For example, if a homeowner murdered his spouse, insurance policies exclude this type of act from coverage. In many jurisdictions, statutes prevent insuring against criminal conduct of the insured. However, simply because there are exemptions or exclusions for most intentional or criminal acts should not deter the victim from examining the various insurance policies. If it can be proved that the insured owed the victim a duty and that duty was breached, the victim may be able to recover under a theory of negligence.

There is a long-standing judicial and statutory public policy that holds that a person should not be able to obtain homeowner's insurance against his or her own intentional wrongdoing. Courts have struggled with this policy and the desire to compensate victims of crimes by turning to the deep pockets of insurance policies. Some courts have found creative ways to get around the intentional act exclusion by holding that insanity negates the intentional aspect of any offense, and if the perpetrator is insane, the criminal act exclusion does not apply.

In the area of automobile insurance, the issue of coverage is complicated by the fact that there are many different types of insurance, and some states require all owners of cars to maintain certain levels of insurance. Many jurisdictions require drivers to purchase two types of insurance: uninsured motorist and underinsured motorist insurance. Uninsured motorist policies pay for any injuries suffered by the driver or their passengers that are caused by other motorists who have no insurance. Underinsured motorist insurance policies apply when the driver who caused injuries is insured but does not carry enough insurance to cover all the injuries that were inflicted.

Similar to homeowner's policies, automobile insurance applies to accidental injuries and excludes from coverage intentional acts by the insured. In homeowner's insurance, courts look to the perpetrator's state of mind to determine whether the act was intentional and therefore excluded from coverage. However, in automobile insurance cases, many jurisdictions determine whether the incident was an accident from the victim's point of view. This perspective is a more favorable position to crime victims who are attempting to recover from the perpetrator's automobile insurance company. Courts have allowed victims or their families to recover from automobile insurance companies after the victim was kidnapped, sexually assaulted, and died when the perpetrator fled with the victim in an automobile;[21] where the perpetrator used his automobile as a battering ram to strike the victim's car;[22] and where the accused kidnapped and killed the victim while driving around in a car.[23]

Most of the litigation regarding whether automobile insurance applies is centered around the question of whether the injury arose out of the use, ownership, or maintenance of the car. In several cases, victims left their cars during arguments with other drivers and were attacked by the other driver. Courts have held that the injuries did not arise out of the use of the victim's automobile, and therefore the insurance company was not liable.

Financial rehabilitation of the victim is an often overlooked area of family violence. Victims, professionals, and others must be educated regarding this important aspect of making the victim whole. Insurance, both homeowner's and automobile, is one method of providing victims of family violence with the possibility of recovering financially for the inflicted injuries. Civil lawsuits against the perpetrator or his insurance company is an expensive, complex, and drawn out affair. Many victims do not have the financial ability or emotional stability to endure months and years of protracted litigation. However, civil action against the perpetrator or his insurance company is not the only avenue available to those who have suffered injuries as a result of family violence. All states now allow victims to be compensated from state-supported funds, and most states allow courts to order restitution during sentencing in criminal cases.

Compensation and Restitution

Introduction

The growth of victim compensation statutes and restitution of victims in the United States is a relatively recent phenomenon. Much of this slowness to react to the victim's plight was based on our concept of the criminal justice system. As discussed earlier, the victim was viewed as merely one more witness, and the state was the party that was injured when perpetrators committed crimes.

Both compensation and restitution are aimed at making the victim financially whole; however, they are separate and distinct concepts. Victim compensation funds are provided by the state, whereas restitution comes from the perpetrator. Understanding how they operate will assist any professional in advising victims of family violence.

Compensation

Compensation can be defined as public funds that are paid to victims or their families to recover out-of-pocket expenses for injuries suffered as a result of another's criminal act. Victim compensation laws allow those who have suffered economic loss to partially recover funds from a state-supported fund established for that purpose. Eligible expenses include medical expenses, including the costs of counseling; burial expenses; special services to the victim; and rehabilitation expenses.

In 1965, California became the first state to establish compensation funds for victims of crimes. In 1966, New York followed California's lead by setting up a special board to allocate funds to victims. In 1967, Massachusetts organized a procedure whereby the state attorney general grants compensation to victims. Today, all states have a mechanism in place that allows victims of crimes to be compensated for their losses.

Although victim compensation programs vary from state to state, they generally have certain common characteristics:

- All programs grant aid to innocent victims. Perpetrators who were injured during the commission of the crime are not eligible for compensation under these statutes.
- Many states have boards or commissions that investigate victim's claims and eliminate or reduce any award if the victim contributed to his or her injury by participating in or provoking the offender.
- Most of these programs compensate only the more serious offenses. They do not pay for property that was damaged or stolen in burglaries or robberies.
- All the states prevent "double dipping," or recovering from more than one source for the same injury. When the victim receives funds from other state agencies, insurance companies, or the perpetrator in the form of a civil judgment or an order for restitution, that amount is deducted from any award.
- Most states require the victim to report the crime to the police and cooperate with them in any investigation and court proceeding.

From a family violence perspective, one of the most troubling aspects of some early victim compensation statutes was the prohibition against awarding any funds to victims if they were related to the offender. Under these programs, battered spouses and abused children were deemed ineligible for compensation. The rationale for this male-oriented rule was that the offender should not be indirectly rewarded by granting money to the family. Other arguments included the fear that families will conspire to defraud the state by claiming injuries where none exist. Amendments to the Victims of Crime Act required states to provide compensation to victims of family violence.

Although at first glance victim compensation programs appear to provide a long-needed solution to the financial problems faced by victims of family violence, several problems still exist within most programs. As indicated earlier, many of these statutes apply only to victims of violent criminal acts, and as such the financial crimes committed against elders would not be covered. Additionally, some of these statutes reimburse the victim only above a certain minimum level and do not provide compensation above a stated limit. State compensation is not the only method of making crime victims financially whole. The use of restitution in criminal cases is becoming more common.

Restitution

Restitution is part of a criminal sentence that requires the offender to pay for injuries suffered by the victim. The original rationale for restitution was to require the party that injured the victim to pay for her injuries. The ability of courts to order restitution has been a part of the common law in the United States. The increased awareness of the victim's plight resulted in the passage of the Victim Witness Protection Act of 1982. This federal statute specifically authorizes the imposition of an order of restitution in addition to or in lieu of any other sentence in a criminal proceeding. Every state has restitution statutes that allow courts to order the perpetrator to pay the victim for any injuries suffered as a result of the offender's criminal act or acts.

Restitution statutes, like compensation laws, provide the victims of family violence with some financial relief. However, many of these restitution statutes have shortcomings: Some statutes prohibit restitution for certain types of injuries, such as emotional distress. Other statutes allow the sentencing court not to order restitution if to do so would overly burden the criminal justice system. Still others do not address future costs such as continuing medical expenses.

Restitution and compensation laws provide the victims of family violence with some financial assistance. They are not perfect, but they are a beginning, and an acknowledgement that the plight of the victim in the criminal justice system must be considered. One of the most dramatic examples of including the victim in the criminal process is the use of victim impact evidence at sentencing.

Victim Impact Statements

Introduction

A new series of rights are emerging in the judicial system. These rights confer on the victim or the relatives of decreased victims the opportunity to speak out or be heard during various phases of the criminal justice process. As with many rights when they converge on a single point, there is an actual or potential conflict. This section reviews the history of these various rights and examines the rationale behind the current status of the law as it relates to victim impact statements.

Purpose and Procedure

One of the most controversial rights bestowed on victims is known as *victim impact statements. In essence, these statements present the victim's point of view to the sentencing authority.* Providing the sentencing authority with all relevant information is not a new phenomenon in the criminal justice system. For many years, courts have received information regarding the defendant prior to imposition of sentence.

Traditionally, presentence reports have been used by judges to determine the proper punishment for criminal defendants. The report, which is normally prepared by a probation officer, details the defendant's background, education, and prior criminal record. Many of these reports have included information concerning the victim of the crime.[24]

Victim impact evidence is now admitted in sentencing for a wide variety of criminal acts, including those that fall within the realm of family violence. However, the law on admissibility and use of victim impact statements is based on use of this evidence during death penalty cases. To understand the nature of victim impact statements, it is necessary to review how this evidence is used in the most serious type of criminal case—those involving capital punishment.

The use of victim impact evidence during the sentencing phase of a criminal crime raises serious constitutional issues. The right to confront witnesses comes against the right to have all relevant evidence placed before the sentencing authority. As will be seen, the use of victim impact statements has aroused intense feelings in the Supreme Court when it addressed this issue.

Content

In *Booth v Maryland,* the Supreme Court initially addressed the issue of the use of victim impact statements in a sentencing jury's determination.[25] In 1983, John Booth and Willie Reed bound and gagged an elderly couple. Believing the couple might be able to identify them, Booth stabbed them numerous times with a kitchen knife. The trial judge in this case allowed the jury to consider a victim impact statement that detailed the family and community's respect and admiration for the victims as well as the impact of the murder on the victims' family.[26]

The Supreme Court, in reversing the death sentence, held that it was impermissible to allow the jury access to such evidence in the sentencing phase of a death penalty proceeding.[27]

In summing up the Court's holding that introduction of the victim impact statement violates the Eighth Amendment's prohibition against cruel and unusual punishment, Justice Powell commented,

> *One can understand the grief and anger of the family caused by the brutal murders in this case, and there is no doubt that jurors generally are aware of these feelings. But the formal presentation of this information by the State can serve no other purpose than to inflame the jury and divert it from deciding the case on the relevant evidence concerning the crimes and the defendant. As we have noted, any decision to impose the death sentence must "be, and appear to be, based on reason rather than caprice or emotion." The admission of these emotionally-charged opinions as to what conclusions the jury should draw from the evidence clearly is inconsistent with the reasoned decision making we require in capital cases.*[28]

As may be apparent at the time of the decision in *Booth v Maryland,* the relevant considerations at the sentencing phase of a murder trial were those aspects of a defendant's background or character or those circumstances that extenuate or mitigate the defendant's culpability.

South Carolina v Gathers followed the rationale of *Booth* and held unconstitutional the imposition of a death penalty based on prosecutorial remarks that were considered inflammatory.[29] Demetrius Gather and three companions sexually assaulted and killed Richard Haynes, a man they encountered in a park. During the incident, the perpetrators ransacked a bag the victim was carrying. The bag contained several articles pertaining to religion, including a religious tract entitled "Game Guy's Prayer." During the sentencing phase of the trial, the prosecutor's argument included references to Haynes's personal qualities and included a reading of "Game Guy's Prayer." The Supreme Court reversed the sentence, stating that such references to the qualities of the victim were similar to the *Booth* holding that prohibited victim impact statements. The court determined that such evidence was likely to inflame the jury and thus violated the defendant's Eighth Amendment rights. In a well-reasoned and logical dissent, Justice O'Conner stated, "Nothing in the Eighth Amendment precludes the community from considering its loss in assessing punishment nor requires that the victim remain a faceless stranger at the penalty phase of a capital case." The dissent by Justice O'Conner was a signal that the winds of judicial temperament might be changing.

In *Payne v Tennessee,* the court completely reversed itself and allowed to stand the imposition of a death sentence that was based in part on evidence contained in a victim impact statement. In 1987, Pervis Tyrone Payne entered the apartment of Charisse Christopher and her two children. Payne stabbed Charisse and her two children numerous times with a butcher knife. Charisse and her daughter died; however, three-year-old Nicholas survived.

Payne was caught and convicted for the murders. During the penalty phase, four witnesses testified regarding the defendant's background, reputation, and mental state. All these witnesses urged the jury not to impose the death penalty. In rebuttal, the prosecution called the maternal grandmother who was caring for Nicholas. She was allowed to testify, over the defendant's objection, that Nicholas continued to cry out calling for his dead mother and sister. The witness was also allowed to testify regarding her personal grief over the loss of her loved ones.

During closing argument, the prosecutor hammered on the pain and suffering that Nicholas and his deceased family had endured, stating,

> *But we do know that Nicholas was alive. And Nicholas was in the same room. Nicholas was still conscious. His eyes were open. He responded to the paramedics. He was able to follow their directions. He was able to hold his intestines in as he was carried to the ambulance. So he knew what happened to his mother and baby sister.*
>
> *There is nothing you can do to ease the pain of any of the families involved in this case. There is nothing you can do to ease the pain of any of the families involved in this case. There is nothing you can do to ease the pain of Bernice or Carl Payne, and that's a tragedy. There is nothing you can do basically to ease the pain of Mr. and Mrs. Zvolanek, and that's a tragedy. They will have to live with it for the rest of their lives. There is obviously nothing you can do for Charisse and Lacie Jo. But there is something you can do for Nicholas.*

Some where down the road Nicholas is going to grow up, hopefully. He's going to want to know what happened. And he is going to know what happened to his baby sister and his mother. He is going to want to know what kind of justice was done. He is going to want to know what happened. Wit your verdict, you will provide the answer.[30]

The jury sentenced Payne to death and the case was appealed to the Supreme Court. Payne contended that the trial court erred when it allowed the maternal grandmother to testify. Relying on *Booth* and *Gathers,* Payne argued that such evidence was a violation of his Eighth Amendment rights.

After reviewing the principles that have guided criminal sentencing over the ages, the Court stated that the consideration of the harm caused by the crime has been an important factor in the existence of the exercise of judicial discretion. The majority opinion went on to state that neither *Booth* nor *Gathers* even suggested that a defendant, entitled as he is to individualized consideration, is to receive that consideration wholly apart from the crime that he had committed.

In setting forth the groundwork for overruling *Booth* and *Gathers,* the Court stated,

Under our constitutional system, the primary responsibility for defining crimes against state law, fixing punishments for the commission of these crimes, and establishing procedures for criminal trials rests with the States. The state law respecting crimes, punishments, and criminal procedures are of course subject to the overriding provisions of the United States Constitution. Where the State imposes the death penalty for a particular crime, we have held that the Eighth Amendment imposes special limitations upon that process. . . .

The States remain free, in capital cases, as well as others, to devise new procedures and new remedies to meet felt needs. Victim impact evidence is simply another form or method of informing the sentencing authority about the specific harm caused by the crime in question, evidence of a general type long considered by sentencing authorities. We think the Booth Court was wrong in stating that this kind of evidence leads to the arbitrary imposition of the death penalty. In the majority of cases, and in this case, victim impact evidence serves entirely legitimate purposes.[31]

Thus, the Supreme Court overruled *Booth* and *Gathers* to the extent that they prohibited introduction of evidence or argument regarding the impact of the crime on the victim, families, and the community. In addition, the Court's decision clearly stated that the decision regarding the admission of such evidence was the prerogative of the individual states. The Court ruled it would not intervene unless the evidence introduced was so unduly prejudicial to render the trial fundamentally unfair.[32] If this occurred, the Court reasoned, the due process clause of the Fourteenth Amendment provides a mechanism for relief.

The decision was not without heated dissent. In a dissenting opinion, Justices Marshall and Blackmun uttered a quote that will continue to be heard in the halls of justice and law school classrooms: "Power, not reason, is the new currency of this Court's decisionmaking."[33] Justice Marshall and Blackmun went on to point out that the court was disregarding the accepted judicial principle of stare decisis. In a well-reasoned but emotional conclusion, the justices states,

> *Today's decision charts an unmistakable course. If the majority's radical reconstruction of the rules for overturning this Court's decisions is to be taken at face value—and the majority offers us no reason why it should not—then the overruling of Booth and Gathers is but a preview of an even broader and more far-reaching assault upon this Court's precedents. Cast aside today are those condemned to face society's ultimate penalty. Tomorrow's victims may be minorities, women, or the indigent. Inevitably, this campaign to resurrect yesterday's "spirited dissents" will squander the authority and the legitimacy of this Court as a protector of the powerless.*[34]

The decision has also generated controversy in the academic world with a series of articles condemning the court for both allowing victim impact evidence and appearing to repudiate its acceptance of stare decisis.[35] Although the dissent and certain individuals with the academic community may condemn the majority's opinion, it is now clearly the law of the land. In addition, the Supreme Court's decision enhanced the victim's rights movement in the United States. It allowed individual states to determine what is relevant evidence in the death penalty phase of a capital crime.

Some would argue that the decision in *Payne* Leaves prosecutors and defense attorneys scrambling to determine what type of evidence is admissible under the guise of victim impact statements. The answer is evidence that does not result in rendering a trial fundamentally unfair. This concept of fundamental fairness is not a new, untested, or ill-defined doctrine.

There is a long history defining acts that establish the parameters of fundamental fairness. The doctrine has its roots in two early cases. In *Powell v Alabama,* several black youths were accused of repeatedly raping two young white girls. They were caught, tried, and convicted. Their conviction was overturned on the ground that the failure of the trial court to appoint counsel until the day of the trial was a violation of the defendants' due process.[36] In *Brown v Mississippi,* a sheriff

FOCUS Feelings Regarding Victim Impact Statements

"My victim impact statement was the last opportunity I had to let anyone know about my daughter."—A victim

"I want you to go over each victim impact statement. . . . You have to live with the stupidity of your behavior for the rest of your life, but you also have to understand what these families have to live with as well."—Judge to a defendant at the time of sentencing

Source: From Alexander, E. K., and J. H. Lord. *Impact Statements: A Victim's Right to Speak—A Nation's Responsibility to Listen.* (National Victim Center, Arlington, Virginia) 1992, pp. 10, 17.

hung the defendant from a tree and whipped him until he confessed to the murder of a white man. The Supreme Court held that such actions are revolting to the sense of justice, and the confession was suppressed.[37]

The doctrine of fundamental fairness accepts the concept that due process is a generalized command that requires states to provide the defendant with a fair trial. If the admission of the victim impact evidence "revolts the sense of justice" or "shocks the conscience" of the court, such admission would be error under the due process clause.

Effect of Victim Impact Statements

Victim Satisfaction

The effect of victim impact statements is still being studied and debated. One area being looked at very carefully is victim satisfaction with victim impact statements. Some authorities believe that impact statements help the victim emotionally deal with the consequences of the crime. Others believe victims are more satisfied with the criminal justice system if they participate by being allowed to express their feelings in a victim impact statement. This section briefly examines these and other aspects of victim satisfaction and victim impact statements.

In 1981, a National Institute of Justice study revealed that victims' satisfaction with the criminal justice system increased if they believed that they had influenced the process, regardless of whether they really had. For example, victims who had been able to speak to prosecutors and judges were more satisfied with the system than those who believed that they were not able to do so.[38] In 1982, another study indicated that a sense of participation was more critical to victims' satisfaction with the criminal justice process than how severely the defendant was published.[39] In 1984, another study revealed that victims wanted more information about their cases and the opportunity to tell the prosecutor and judge how the case affected them.[40]

In 1989, Dean Kilpatrick reported the results of his research, which indicated that victim participation not only affected potential cooperation within the criminal justice system but also was critical in promoting victims' recovery from the aftermath of crime by helping them reassert a sense of control over their lives.[41] Kilpatrick stated that a criminal justice system that denies victims a chance to participate fosters a sense of helplessness and lack of control. He pointed out that there is a great danger in promising victims participation in the system and then failing to follow through with that promise because it results in further victimization.

Robert Wells, another noted authority, stated that victim impact statements may promote the psychological recovery of victims. Just as talking about what happened promotes healing, writing about it may also assist victims to emotionally deal with the crime. Allowing victims to tell how they were affected by the crime sends a supportive message that the criminal justice system cares about what happened.[42]

However, other experts claim that the mental and emotional benefits of victim impact statements and victim participation are overrated. In a 1985 study carried out in Brooklyn, New York, Davis compared the outcome of two court experiments in which victims gave impact statements in one court and no statements were allowed in another court. He found no evidence that victims in the court that mandated impact statements felt a greater sense of participation or increased satisfaction.[43] Davis followed up this research with a 1989 study in the Bronx Supreme Court in New York.[44] The study analyzed 293 victims of robbery, nonsexual assault, and burglary. Each victim was assigned to one of three classifications: some victims were interviewed and a victim impact statement written and distributed; other victims were interviewed but no impact statement was prepared; or only the name and address of the victim was recorded. A series of interviews was conducted with each victim. The results of this study indicate that victim impact statements are not an effective means of promoting victim satisfaction within the criminal justice system. No data support the theory that victim impact statements led to greater feelings of involvement, greater satisfaction with the criminal justice system, or greater satisfaction with the sentences imposed on the offenders. Davis concluded that more research is necessary regarding the effect of impact statements on victim satisfaction with the system.

As the above discussion indicates, a controversy continues over the effect of victim impact statements on victim satisfaction. However, there is sufficient individual and anecdotal evidence of victim approval of the use of impact statements that we should continue using them until definitive studies can be conducted. The next section examines whether victim impact statements affect the outcome of sentencing.

Sentencing

Limited research exists on the effect that victim impact statements have on judges. On the surface it would appear that such evidence can only assist the court in rendering its decision and therefore should be readily accepted and consistently used by the judicial system. However, judges, like every other member of the criminal justice system, are understaffed and overworked. Does additional information really help, or does the process simply take more time? Are judges swayed by the emotional appeal of a citizen, or are they bound to render impartial justice to the defendant?

Early research indicates that state trial court judges found financial information contained in a victim impact statement very useful in determining appropriate sentences and restitution orders.[45] Seventy percent of those judges interviewed found the information very useful and another 20 percent found it useful in terms of restitution orders. Although this research indicates that victim impact evidence is "very useful" to judges, this "usefulness" appears limited to the area of restitution and financial issues, not to other aspects of sentencing the defendant.

In 1990, Erez and Tontodonato produced an important study involving five hundred Ohio felony cases and found that the cases in which victim impact statements were taken were more likely than those without statements to result in prison rather than probation.[46] This research has been cited by a number of victim impact statement proponents as authority for the position that such statements have an effect on sentencing. Although this was a significant study, it had several flaws, including a wide disparity in the seriousness of offense among cases that had impact statements. Additionally, the authors acknowledged that further research needed to be conducted in this area.

Davis and Smith also researched the effect of impact statements on sentencing. In the same 1989 study that examined victim satisfaction, Davis and Smith evaluated the significance of impact statements on judicial sentencing.[47] They concluded that victim impact statements do not produce sentences that reflect the effects of crime on the victims, nor did they find that sentencing decisions were affected by impact statements once the charge and the defendant's prior record were taken into consideration by the court. They did find that the severity of the charges is a high predictor of sentences. Although judges professed to be interested in impact statements, prosecutors believed that judges only occasionally considered this information when imposing sentences. Conversely, prosecutors claimed that victims should be consulted on a regular basis, but judges stated that prosecutors rarely related impact evidence to them.

Clearly, more research is also needed in this area. Additionally, such research must find a way to get around the "political correctness" of advocating the use of victim impact statements. As Davis and Smith's study points out, judges claim that they endorse impact statements, but prosecutors don't believe them. On the other hand, the same prosecutors claim that they use impact statements, but the judges don't see them. Realistically, very few elected or appointed officials in today's climate within the criminal justice system will admit to anything less than wholehearted endorsement of victim impact statements. What is needed is an in-depth study to determine the impact of such evidence outside the realm of political correctness. Until such research is done, we can only speculate on its real effect.

Victim impact evidence is now an accepted part of the judicial process. The ability of a victim of family violence to inform the court of the impact of the offender's acts on her life can only benefit the victim and continue to educate the public regarding the dynamics of family violence.[48]

Summary

Victim's rights are an important aspect of family violence. Professionals not only must understand the dynamics of family violence but also must be prepared to offer support and guidance to victims as they move through the judicial system. Repairing the body and spirit is only half the battle; society must be able to make the victims of family violence completely whole. This effort has to include financial reimbursement from the offender.

Victims must be aware of the various alternatives available to them to make them financially whole. These alternatives include actions against the perpetrator and his insurance companies. Statutes exist that allow victims of family violence to be compensated by the state for certain types of injuries suffered at the hands of an abuser. Additionally, courts routinely order restitution as a part of criminal sentencing. All these mechanisms allow victims to gain greater financial independence.

Society is beginning to accept the fact that victims of crimes in general, and victims of family violence in particular, have rights and need to be active participants in the criminal justice system. This includes giving their input during sentencing of the offender. The use of victim impact statements is a giant step forward for victims of family violence.

Key Terms

primitive law—a system of rules in preliterate societies.

victimology—the study of the relationship between the criminal and the victim.

tort—a legal wrong committed on the person or property of another independent of contract.

plaintiff—the person filing the civil complaint.

defendant—the person who is alleged to have committed the acts that resulted in injury to the plaintiff or victim.

complaint—a formal written document stating certain causes of actions that the plaintiff alleges entitles him or her to recover damages from the perpetrator.

answer—a formal written document that either admits or denies the allegations.

discovery—the formal method of learning the facts, theories, and positions of opposing parties by means of written or oral questioning.

compensatory damages—when the plaintiff asks to be made whole or reimbursed for expenses incurred as a result of an injury.

punitive damages—asked for or awarded to punish the defendant for conduct that is considered outrageous.

third parties—those individuals or entitles that have intentionally or negligently contributed to the injury suffered by the victim.

compensation—public funds that are paid to victims or their families to recover out-of-pocket expenses for injuries suffered as a result of another's criminal act.

victim impact statements—presents the victim's point of view to the sentencing authority.

Discussion Questions

1. What is the most important development in the area of victim's rights?
2. What are the advantages and disadvantages of compensation statutes?
3. Is it reasonable to expect a victim of family violence will sue the perpetrator? Why? Why not?
4. What new rights do you believe victims of family violence will acquire in the near future? Why?
5. Are victim impact statements of any real use in sentencing? Why? Why not?

Suggested Readings

Costanzo, M., and S. Oskamp, eds. *Violence and the Law.* (Sage, Thousand Oaks, California) 1994.

Drapkin, I., and E. Viano, eds. *Victimology: A New Focus.* Vol. 2 (D. C. Heath, Lexington, Massachusetts) 1974.

Karmen, A. *Crime Victims, An Introduction to Victimology.* (Brooks/Cole, Pacific Grove, California) 1984.

Maine, Sir H. S. *Ancient Law.* 10th ed. (John Murray, London) 1905.

Miethe, T. D., and R. F. Meier. *Crime and its Social Content.* (Suny, New York) 1994.

Schafer, S. *The Victim and His Criminal.* (Random House, New York) 1968.

von Hentig, H. *The Criminal and His Victim.* (Yale University Press, New Haven, Connecticut) 1948.

Weiner, N. A., and M. E. Wolfgang, eds. *Pathways to Criminal Violence.* (Sage, Newbury Park, California) 1989.

Wolfgang, M. E. *Patterns of Criminal Homicide.* (University of Pennsylvania Press, Philadelphia) 1958.

Endnotes

1. Maine, Sir H. S. Ancient Law. 10th ed. (John Murray, London) 1905.
2. Schafer, S. *The Victim and His Criminal.* (Random House, New York) 1968.
3. Mueller, G. O., and H. A. Cooper. "Society and the Victim: Alternative Responses." In I. Drapkin, and E. Viano, eds. *Victimology: A New Focus.* Vol. 2 (D. C. Heath, Lexington, Massachusetts) 1974, pp. 85–102.
4. Karmen, A. *Crime Victims: An Introduction to Victimology* 2nd (Wadeworth, Belmont, California) 1996.
5. Largen, M. "Grassroots Centers and National Task Forces: A History of the Anti-Rape Movement." *Aegis* (32) Autumn 1981, pp. 46–52.
6. 595 F.Supp. 1521 (Conn. 1984).
7. "Remarks by the President at Announcement of Victims, Constitutional Amendment," *Press Release.* (The White House, Office of the Press Secretary, Washington, D.C. June 25, 1996), p. 2.
8. Gottfredson, G. D. "The Experiences of Violent and Serious Victimization." In N. A. Weiner, and M. E. Wolfgang, eds. *Pathways to Criminal Violence.* (Sage, Newbury Park, California) 1989, pp. 202–234.
9. An excellent source of cases dealing with victims is the National Victim Center's, *Crime Victims' Litigation Quarterly.* (National Victim Center, Arlington, Virginia) 1995.
10. Mendelsohn, B. "Rape in Criminology". *Giustizia Penale,* 1940.
11. Mendelsohn, B. "The Origin and Doctrine of Victimology." *Excerpta Criminologica* (3) June 1963, pp. 239–244.
12. von Hentig, H. *The Criminal and His Victim.* (Yale University Press, New Haven, Connecticut) 1948.
13. Wolfgang, M. E. *Patterns of Criminal Homicide.* (University of Pennsylvania Press, Philadelphia) 1958.
14. Wolfgang, M. E. *Analytical Categories for Research in Victimization.* (Kriminologische Wegzeichen, Munich, Germany) 1967, p. 17.
15. Ibid., pp. 24 and 72.
16. Karmen, A. *Crime Victims, An Introduction to Victimology.*
17. *Black's Law Dictionary.* 6th ed. (West, St. Paul) 1990, p. 1489.
18. *Garzilli v Howard Johnsons Motor Lodge, Inc.* 419 F.Supp. 1210 (E.D. N.Y. 1976).
19. *Jardel Co. v Hughes,* 523 A. 2d 518 (Del. 1987).
20. *Small v McKennan Hospital,* 403 N.W. 2d 410 (S.D. 1987).
21. *Harrinton v New England Mutual Life Insurance Co.,* 873 F 2d 166 (7th Cir. 1989).
22. *State Farm Fire and Casualty Co. v Tringali,* 686F 2d 821 (9th Cir. 1982).
23. *Alabama Farm Bur. Mutual Casualty Insurance Co. v Mitchell,* 373 So. 2d 1129 (1979).
24. See Talbert, P. A. "The Relevance of Victim Impact Statements to the Criminal Sentencing Decision." *UCLA Law Review* (36) 1988, pp. 199, 202–211 and Maureen McLeod, Victim Participation at Sentencing, 22 *Criminal Law Bulletin* 501, 5055–11 (1986).
25. *Booth v Maryland,* 482 U.S. 496 (1987).
26. Ibid., pp. 500–501.
27. Ibid., p. 509. The Court did, however, carefully note that information typically contained in a victim's statement is generally admissible in noncapital cases and may be considered in capital cases if directly related to the circumstances of the crime. Ibid., p. 508 n. 10. For example, the Court noted that the prosecution may produce evidence as to the

characteristics of the victim to rebut an argument made by the defendant (e.g., victim's peaceable nature to rebut claim of self-defense).

28. Ibid.
29. 490 U.S. 805 (1989).
30. 115 L.Ed. 728–729.
31. 115 L.Ed.734–735.
32. 115 L.Ed. 2d 735.
33. 115 L.Ed. 748.
34. 115 L.Ed. 756.
35. See Jimmie O. Clements Jr. *Casenote, Criminal Law—Victim Impact Evidence—The Scope of the Eighth Amendment Does Not Include a Per Se Bar to the Use of Victim Impact Evidence in the Sentencing Phase of a Capital Trial Payne v. Tennessee.* 23 St. Mary's L. J. 517 (1991), Aida Alaka, *Note, Victim Impact Evidence, Arbitrariness and the Death Penalty: The Supreme Court Flipflops in Payne v Tennessee,* 23 Loy. U. Chi. L.J. 581 (1992), K. Elizabeth Whitehead, *Case Note, Mourning Becomes Electric: Payne v. Tennessee's Allowance of Victim Impact Statements during Capital Proceedings,* 45 Ark. L. Rev. 531 (1992).
36. *Powell v Alabama,* 287 U.S. 45, 53 S.C. 55, 77 L.Ed. 158 (1932).
37. 297 U.S. 278, 56 S.Ct. 461, 80 L.Ed. 682 (1936).
38. Smith, B., and S. Hillanbrand. *Non-Stranger Violence: The Criminal Courts Responses.* (National Institute of Justice, Washington, D.C. 1981).
39. Kelly, D. P. "Delivering Legal Services to Victims: An Evaluation and Prescription," *Justice System Journal* 9 (1982), p. 62.
40. Hernon, J., and B. Forst. "The Criminal Justice Response to Victim Harm," *Research Report.* (National Institute of Justice, Washington, D.C. 1984).
41. Kilpatrick, D., and R. K. Otto. "Constitutionally Guaranteed Participation in Criminal Proceedings for Victims: Potential Effects on Psychological Functioning," *The Wayne State Law Review* 34 (1989), p. 17.
42. Wells, R. "Victim Impact: How Much Consideration Is It Really Given?" *The Police Chief,* February 1991, p. 44.
43. Davis, R. C. *First Year Evaluation of the Victim Impact Demonstration Project.* (Victim Services Agency, New York, 1985).
44. Davis, R. C., and B. E. Smith. "Victim Impact Statements and Victim Satisfaction: An Unfulfilled Promise," *Journal of Criminal Justice* 22 (1994), p. 1.
45. Hillenbrand, S. *Victim Rights Legislation: An Assessment of its Impact on the Criminal Justice System,* (American Bar Association, Chicago, Ill. 1987)
46. Erez, E., and P. Tontodonato. "The Effect of Victim Participation in Sentencing on Sentence Outcomes," 28 *Criminology* 28 (1990), p. 451.
47. Davis, R. C., and B. E. Smith. "The Effects of Victim Impact Statements on Sentencing Decisions: A Test in an Urban Setting," *Justice Quarterly* 11(3) September 1994, p. 453.
48. For a contrary position, see Davis, R. C., and B. E. Smith. "The Effects of Victim Impact Statements on Sentencing Decisions: A Test in an Urban Setting," *Justice Quarterly* 11 (3) September 1994, which points out that victim impact statements neither increased officials' consideration of harm to victims nor resulted in generally harsher sentencing decisions.

INDEX